ECONOMIC AND BUSINESS MANAGEMENT

SIXTH INTERNATIONAL CONFERENCE ON ECONOMIC AND BUSINESS MANAGEMENT (FEBM 2021), OCTOBER 16–17, 2021 (HELD ONLINE)

Economic and Business Management

Edited by

Xiaoxia Huang
School of Economics and Management, University of Science and Technology Beijing, China

Feng Zhang
The Pennsylvania State University Abington, USA

CRC Press is an imprint of the
Taylor & Francis Group, an **informa** business

A BALKEMA BOOK

CRC Press/Balkema is an imprint of the Taylor & Francis Group, an informa business

© 2022 selection and editorial matter, Xiaoxia Huang & Feng Zhang; individual chapters, the contributors

Typeset by MPS Limited, Chennai, India

The right of Xiaoxia Huang & Feng Zhang to be identified as the authors of the editorial material, and of the authors for their individual chapters, has been asserted in accordance with sections 77 and 78 of the Copyright, Designs and Patents Act 1988.

All rights reserved. No part of this book may be reprinted or reproduced or utilised in any form or by any electronic, mechanical, or other means, now known or hereafter invented, including photocopying and recording, or in any information storage or retrieval system, without permission in writing from the publishers.

Although all care is taken to ensure integrity and the quality of this publication and the information herein, no responsibility is assumed by the publishers nor the author for any damage to the property or persons as a result of operation or use of this publication and/ or the information contained herein.

Library of Congress Cataloging-in-Publication Data
A catalog record has been requested for this book

First published 2022
Published by: CRC Press/Balkema
 Schipholweg 107C, 2316 XC Leiden, The Netherlands
 e-mail: enquiries@taylorandfrancis.com
 www.routledge.com – www.taylorandfrancis.com

ISBN: 978-1-032-06754-4 (HBk)
ISBN: 978-1-032-06755-1 (Pbk)
ISBN: 978-1-003-20370-4 (eBook)
DOI: 10.1201/9781003203704

Economic and Business Management – Huang & Zhang (Eds)
© 2022 Copyright the Editor(s), ISBN: 978-1-032-06754-4

Table of contents

Preface	ix
Technical Program Committee	xi

A content analysis of online reviews to identify hotel attributes across different platforms
Z. Zhao & V.T.P. Cheng — 1

Research on the brand building strategy of small- and medium-sized enterprises in the
Digital Economy Era
X. Zhang — 9

Stock forecast model based on random forest
X. Li — 13

β-Convergence analysis in the European Union
R. Kožiak & D. Benčiková — 17

Research on the influence of R&D on firm performance from the perspective of executive
equity incentive
C. Lyu, K. Guo & H. Wang — 21

Analyst attention and earning management
J. Chen & H. Liang — 25

Labor market analysis within the Slovak healthcare sector
M. Kordoš — 34

Real options, firm valuation, and corporate information environment
Y. Bao & C. Lyu — 39

An empirical analysis of the E-commerce impact on social consumption
G. Tang & H. Zeng — 44

Study on the trade effects of China's outward foreign direct investment—data from the
countries along the Belt and Road
K. Sun & X. Zhang — 49

The comparative studies of Great Divergence from 1850 to 1914
Y. Liu — 55

The analysis of inter-industry VaR on China stock markets—based on the GARCH-EVT-copula model
F. Jiang & Y. Liu — 61

The effect of managerial ownership on corporate value
Y. Zhang & Y. Liu — 66

The analysis of the impact of Shenzhen-Hong Kong stock connect on the stock market
co-movement between the mainland and Hong Kong—based on the GARCH-copula model
X. Zhang & Y. Liu — 73

The impact of logistics performance on China's cross-border e-commerce trade
H. Li & Y. Xia — 77

Research on the optimization path of catastrophe insurance business development from the
perspective of the Guangdong-Hong Kong-Macao Greater Bay Area linkage
X. Dang — 82

Financing difficulties and solutions in the development of rural tourism 88
X. Hu

Analyst coverage, corporate governance, and firms' innovation output: Evidence from China 93
Y. Yang

The impact of green finance on the value of Chinese photovolatic enterprises in the context of
COVID-19—based on the research of listed photovoltaic enterprises 106
F. Wang

Study on the relationship between capacity regulation, internal control and economic
benefits in China's iron and steel industry 111
Y. Chen & X. Zhu

Political economic capacity traps on the development of Indonesia's international hub ports 121
Z. Salim

Hospitality and tourism under COVID-19: A bibliometric analysis 126
S. Wang & J.W.C. Wong

The effect of video attributes on memorable short video experience and intention to visit:
The case of tiktok 130
X. Bai & F. Hong

An economic theoretical analysis of collusive behavior: Based on the international iron ore
industry as an example 134
Y. Zhang

Research on the construction of brand stories of a regional brand of agricultural products
under the background of the internet 138
C. Chen, S. Pei, X. Jiang & W. Lu

Research on the influence of leverage ratio on the credit risk of commercial banks based on
entropy weight method 143
Y. Tao

Research on two-stage price volatility of Beijing carbon market 149
J. Cai

Differential game research on fresh food supply chain based on fresh-keeping efforts 153
L. Deng & C. Peng

Research on the effect of RCEP on China's manufacturing trade—based on the dynamic
recursive GTAP model 158
N. Zhu, L. Lv, S. Huang & K. Gong

Cost leadership strategy, diagnostic control style and firm performance 165
W. Sun & C. Li

Digital transformation of agricultural enterprises during COVID-19: The design of a
recommendation technology 172
L. Hu

An empirical study of skewness on stock returns forecast 176
C. Yang & Y. Liu

Moderating role of marketization process in the analyst tracking and corporate social responsibility 180
Z. Zhang, J. Song & Y. Song

Research on the co-agglomeration and spatial similarity of producer services and
manufacturing industries in Jiangxi 186
S. Huang

Financial flexibility, R&D investment and corporate value: Evidence from new energy
companies in China 192
J. Li, Y. Fan, H. Jin & C. Deng

Study on supply chain logistics ecosystem under the background of big data 198
X. He, Y. Sun & F. Chen

Consumer empowerment, enterprise life cycle, and R&D 204
C. Lyu, Z. Yang & Y. Huang

Survival of self-employment under COVID-19—evidence from Slovakia 208
M. Knapková

Research on the development of rural credit bank's e-commerce platform in China 212
B. Ma, Y. Wang, D. Zhao & K. Ma

The impact of consumer perceived value on purchase intention under Blockchain Technology 216
D. Fu, C. Wang & Y. Deng

The impact of policy risk perception in media information on stock markets during epidemic events 222
T. Li, H. Yu, G. Yu & Y. Yu

The offsetting role of diversification for negative impact of COVID-19 on firm performance:
Evidence from China 228
F. Guan & T. Wang

The influence of family on the development of family business 232
W. Zhang & B. Feng

A two-stage model of tacit knowledge updating in family business 237
Y. Liu & X. Sun

A review on crisis management for small and medium-sized travel companies under COVID-19 242
Y. Feng, X. Chen & Z. Huang

Construction and analysis of green logistics service supply chain operation model 246
Q. Ding & H. Li

When is "free" a bad choice? An empirical approach of promotional effects on "free trials" reviews 252
X. Sun, Y. Li & Y. Pan

The empirical study of trust and behavioral intention to use the smart healthcare system
based on structural equation modeling 257
J. Ling, N. Sheng, W. Ling & H. Huang

Impacts of job insecurity on burnout: Examining the mediating role of job stress among
Thai bank tellers 262
B. Peng & W. Potipiroon

Research on the impact of corporate social responsibility fulfillment on ambidextrous
innovation performance of high-tech enterprises 267
Y. Hu & J. Huang

The success of salesforce.com: From the perspective of social capital 275
Z. Dai & W. Chiu

Author index 281

Economic and Business Management – Huang & Zhang (Eds)
© 2022 Copyright the Editor(s), ISBN: 978-1-032-06754-4

Preface

The Sixth International Conference on Economic and Business Management (FEBM2021) was successfully held online on October 16–17, 2021. The conference was an annual forum for researchers and application developers in the area of Economic and Business Management.

This conference proceeding includes 51 accepted articles selected from 94 submissions.

We would like to express our gratitude to the reviewers of these manuscripts, who provided constructive criticism and stimulating comments and suggestions to the authors. We are extremely grateful as organizers, technical program committee and editors and extend our most sincere thanks to all the authors for their excellent contributions and work. Our sincere gratitude also goes to the CRC Press/ Balkema (Taylor & Francis Group) editors and managers for their helpful cooperation during the preparation of the proceeding.

On behalf of the Organizing Committees of FEBM2021,

Xiaoxia Huang
Editor, Proceedings of the Sixth International Conference on Economic and Business Management
Professor, School of Economics and Management, University of Science and Technology Beijing, China.

Feng Zhang
Co-Editor, Proceedings of the Sixth International Conference on Economic and Business Management
Associate Professor of Management, The Pennsylvania State University Abington, USA.

Economic and Business Management – Huang & Zhang (Eds)
© 2022 Copyright the Editor(s), ISBN: 978-1-032-06754-4

Technical Program Committee

Conference Chair
Xiaoxia Huang, *School of Economics and Management, University of Science and Technology Beijing, China*

Conference Co-Chair
Qiang Wu, *Lally School of Management, Rensselaer Polytechnic Institute, USA*

Technical Program Committee Chair
Feng Zhang, *The Pennsylvania State University Abington, USA*

Technical Program Committee
Changzheng Zhang, *School of Economics and Management, Xi'an University of Technology, China*
Sang-Bing Tsai, *Nankai University & University of Electronic Science and Technology of China, China*
Gordon Huang, *University of Regina, Regina, Canada*
Virginia Barba Sánchez, *University of Castilla-La Mancha (UCLM), Spain*
Fernando Merino de Lucas, *Facultad de Economía y Empresa, Universidad de Murcia, Spain*
Haoxun Chen, *University of Technology of Troyes, France*
Yushan Zhao, *Department of Marketing, University of Wisconsin, USA*
Huchang Liao, *Business School, Sichuan University, China*
Félix J. García Clemente, *Department of Computer Engineering, University of Murcia, Spain*
Carlos Pinho, *Department of Economics, Management and Industrial Engineering and Tourism, University of Aveiro, Portugal*
Libiao Bai, *Green Engineering and Sustainable Development Research Center, Chang'an University, China*
Hedayat Omidvar, *Communication Affairs with Science & Research Centers, Research & Technology Department, National Iranian Gas Company, Iran*
Dewan Ahsan, *Department of Environmental and Business Economics, University of Southern Denmark, Denmark*
Jalel EUCHI, *Sfax University, Tunisia*
Maria Cristina Longo, *Department of Economics and Business, University of Catania, Italy*
Zaheer Anwer, *Department of Business and Economics, University of Management and Technology Lahore, Pakistan*
LiWei Lin, *Department of Electronic Commerce, Zhejiang University of Finance & Economics Dongfang College, China*
Dhouha Jaziri Bouagina, *Faculty of economic and management science of Sousse, University of Sousse, Tunisia*

Economic and Business Management – Huang & Zhang (Eds)
© 2022 Copyright the Author(s), ISBN: 978-1-032-06754-4

A content analysis of online reviews to identify hotel attributes across different platforms

Zhongqi Zhao & Vincent T.P. Cheng
Faculty of Hospitality and Tourism Management, Macau University of Science and Technology, Taipa, China

ABSTRACT: This study analyzes the similarities and differences of hotel attributes' consumer preferences in online reviews between different platforms through content analysis. A text-mining software, CATPACII, with a self-organizing artificial neural network was employed to analyze the online review content. Examining the word frequency tables and each platform's dendogram outputs reveals that the most influential consumer hotel satisfaction attributes are hotel, room, stay, staff, and location in all three selected platforms. Consumers who comment on different platforms do have their various concerns. While some attributes show small statistical values, the online review platforms can use the findings to understand the diversity of consumer preferences and each platform's characteristics.

1 INTRODUCTION

Online reviews nowadays become an essential reference material for consumers (Lee & Youn, 2009) to decide whether to purchase the goods and services. Online reviews often serve as an evaluation index, while the service and experience can be figured in feedback and turn into the reference of travel products selection. Sparks and Browning (2011) confirmed that for many consumers who plan to participate in travel activities and purchase hotel products, online reviews constitute their information collection process. In contrast to the information provided by hotel operators or service providers, comments updated by other tourists are more enjoyable and more reliable (Gretzel & Yoo, 2008). Online reviews generated by customers provide comparative insights about customer satisfaction (Zhou, Ye, Pearce, & Wu, 2014), having an impact on hotel popularity (Xie, Chen, & Wu, 2016), which then influence customers' expectations and hotel booking intention (Chang, Rhodes, & Lok, 2013; Mauri & Minazzi, 2013), and ultimately affect hotel booking transactions and business performance (Torres, Singh, & Robertson-Ring, 2015; Vermeulen & Seegers, 2009; Ye, Law, Gu, & Chen, 2011). Empirical and theoretical evidence have both proven that the more online reviews a hotel receives, the better the quality of reservation it will obtain (Blal & Sturman, 2014; Xie et al., 2016).

Although there are many review platforms, few studies have compared them to each other, especially whether online review content has significant discrepancy on different review platforms. And with ample quantity of positive or negative online reviews, limited studies have focused on consumer preferences for hotel attributes revealed by the reviews. This study aims to compare and analyze the similarities and differences of consumer preferences of hotel attributes in online reviews between different platforms through content analysis. The online reviews of three tourism-related review platforms are analyzed, using content analysis to understand the differences expressed by other platforms' consumers in online reviews, as well as the comparison of platforms. In particular, through online reviews generated by the customer, it is explored which hotel attributes focus on consumer attention and is there any connection between those attributes.

2 THEORETICAL BACKGROUNDS

2.1 *Online reviews*

Chen and Xie (2008) defined online reviews as product information created by consumers based on their personal user experience. Online reviews have built a new communication bridge of product and service directly to the customer that replace the traditional way of getting information only from the producer and service provider, and they are very influential in purchasing decisions (Doh & Hwang, 2009; Ladhari & Michaud, 2015; Lee & Youn, 2009). Moreover, online reviews have an increasingly significant reference value in traveling decision-making. Online reviews can help potential tourists to decrease uncertainty and enhance the exchange utility in choosing travel products like vacation destinations, hotels, and restaurants (Jalilvand & Samiei, 2012; Manes & Tchetchik, 2018; Simpson & Siguaw, 2008). Extant research had already explored various aspects of online reviews and how it influences purchase intention. In most

DOI 10.1201/9781003203704-1

studies on online reviews, empirical research methods are used to establish hypotheses and demonstrate hypotheses.

2.2 Content analysis of online reviews

Online reviews contain comments contributed by consumers to express their experiences, perceive product performance and emotions. Lockie, Waiguny, and Grabner-Kräuter (2015) indicated that readers of online reviews pay more attention to the entire content. Other consumers' content appears to show a high degree of integrity and highly trustworthy (Dickinger, 2011). Mak (2017) also confirms the quality of content is more attractive than purchasing. Analysis of online review content can better understand consumers' authentic thoughts and sentiments. Content analysis is gradually gaining popularity in online review research (Marine-Roig & Clavé, 2015). Neuman (2011) pointed out that content analysis is a technique for collecting and analyzing text content to determine each content category's frequency of occurrence. By employing content analysis, Liu, Kim and Pennington-Gray (2015) reveal hotel response behavior is related to hotel popularity and average rating, and Wang and Hung (2015) identify seven major success factors of a hotel. Scholars continue to use content analysis to study a topic like destination choice (Mak, 2017; Marine-Roig & Clavé, 2015), hotel booking intention (Xiang, Du, Ma, & Fan, 2017; Zhang & Cole, 2016), review trustworthy, and helpfulness (Lockie et al., 2015), as well as consumer decision-making (Kou et al., 2020; Marcolin, Becker, Wild, Behr, & Schiavi, 2021).

2.3 Hotel selection attributes

Hotel attributes are the performance of a hotel, the service, and the operator's facilities. Alpert (1971) believes that the perception of hotel attributes can be defined as the extent to which visitors evaluate various hotel services and facilities as meeting their needs. Attributes like room quality and location directly affect hotel room pricing (Zhang, Ye, & Law, 2011). Xie et al. (2016) regard purchase value, location, and cleanliness to influence a hotel's performance. Suppose a hotel wants to maintain its competitiveness in the market by evaluating the customer's experience, it is essential to understand the customer preference for the relevant attributes in the customer's selection decision (Roman & Martin, 2016). Yen and Tang (2015) confirmed hotel attributes are affiliated with customer affect-related motivations. The hotel attributes mentioned in online reviews can help understand customer preferences and their emphasis on different hotel amenities and service levels.

A hotel's attributes can be roughly divided into two categories: hotel's attributes and experiential attributes (Cheng, Pai, & Chen, 2017). The hotel's attributes include the hotel's tangible attributes and facilities such as hotel location, the hotel decoration, the room quality, amenities in the room, and whether there is a swimming pool or a business center. Experiential attributes are intangible attributes, mainly the customers' feelings after staying, such as good, great, and nice. Those feelings usually come from the hotel's overall facilities and the services provided by staff, followed by other factors like hotel safety and security, atmosphere, and price issue (Huertas-Garcia, García, & Consolación, 2014).

3 RESEARCH METHODOLOGY

The online reviews analyzed are genuine consumer evaluations collected from three famous platforms: Tripadvisor.com, Expedia.com, and Booking.com. Penaflorida (2018) reported that Tripadvisor, Expedia, and Booking are the three most popular review websites that focus on hotel-related reviews. The three platforms have distinctly different coverage of travel products and business nature. Booking is the largest hotel only booking portal, Expedia offers a comprehensive range of travel products, for instance, hotel, flight, and car rental, and Tripadvisor is a site for the travel fraternity that lets tourists write reviews on anything related to travel, such as destinations, restaurants, airlines, and hotels. The online reviews collected for content analysis came from hotels in Hong Kong. Hong Kong is an international metropolis, a well-developed and popular destination. As Hong Kong has a prodigious number of tourists with different backgrounds and different tourism purposes, choosing online reviews of Hong Kong hotels for research is reasonable.

Positive, neutral, and negative online reviews are selected as analytical text. Rhee and Yang (2015) mentioned that the overall rating from the customer (high rating and low rating) is a critical factor in the differences in hotel attributes. Park and Nicolau (2015) indicate that consumers usually regard reviews with extreme ratings (positive and negative) as more enjoyable and useful than moderate ones (Park & Nicolau, 2015). Tang, Fang, and Wang (2014) verified the moderating effect of neutral online reviews and confirmed that neglecting neutral ones can result in underestimating or overestimating the positive and negative online review effects. The convenience sampling approach has been used to collect online reviews among three different levels of hotel reviews. The online reviews were collected within the time frame of 2014 to 2017. Ten reviews are selected from each hotel's positive (5 stars in Expedia, 5 diamonds in Booking, and 5 bubbles in Tripadvisor), neutral (3 stars/diamonds/bubbles), and negative (1 stars/diamonds/bubbles) reviews in each platform. Any hotel with less than ten reviews would jump directly to the next category or the next hotel until the number of each rating category reaches 300. The summary of collected reviews shows that a total of 2,700 total reviews with a total number of 237,131 words were collected, as shown in Table 1.

Table 1. Summary of online reviews.

Platform	Rating	No. of hotel	Total No. of hotel	No. of Online review	Word count
Expedia	1	48		300	23080
	3	34	48	300	19271
	5	31		300	15602
Booking	1	47		300	15641
	3	30	49	300	48456
	5	31		300	11686
Tripadvisor	1	32		300	54749
	3	30	32	300	14015
	5	30		300	34637
Total			129	2700	237131

Table 2. Words appearing in all three platforms.

	Booking	Expedia	TripAdvisor
ROOM	783	1082	2057
HOTEL	474	1230	2168
LOCATION	397	389	393
STAFF	343	395	629
GOOD	332	342	551
STAY	249	436	1037
BED	164	141	164
GREAT	155	301	429
CLEAN	143	148	177
BOOKING	129	126	327
NICE	113	198	276
SERVICE	94	227	554
CHECKIN	88	152	315
TIME	87	130	328

4 DATA ANALYSIS

The software CATPACII was employed to analyze the online review content. CATPACII is a text-mining software (Woelfel, 1993) with a self-organizing artificial neural network that can identify the most important words in the text and determine the similarity pattern depending on how they are used in the text (Woelfel, 1998). Neural networks can find connection weights between nodes to reveal relationships among keywords in text. CATPACII can read any text and assemble its main ideas (Tang, Choi, Morrison, & Lehto, 2007). Before the analysis, the text was cleaned during the pre-processing process to ensure the results' accuracy. First, exclude some grammatical terms and words that are not analytical, such as "a," "and," "the," "Hong Kong," and so on. Second, combine synonyms to ensure that only a single word appears in the same sense. For example, "rooms" is changed to "room"; "stayed," "stays" and "staying" are unified as "stay"; "front desk" and "front-desk" are adjusted to "frontdesk." And the adjectives such as "amazing," "perfect," and "wonderful" of the feeling class are unified into "exceptional." The CATPAC II program was run repeatedly until the output is a list of high-frequency words with analytical significance. CATPAC II generates frequency tables and dendogram (neighboring matrices) for the most commonly used words in reviews of three different platforms.

5 FINDINGS

5.1 Word frequency table

Appendix 1 shows the word, and the word frequency appears in each platform. The most frequently used words in the reviews reveal the relative importance of the customers' attributes.

The chosen words were classified into two categories to compare the homogeneity and heterogeneity among the three platforms. Table 2 shows the word appear on all plat-forms.

The same most frequent word "hotel," "room," "stay," "location," "service," and "staff" occupied the top 10 rankings among 25 frequency words of all three platforms. The following service is provided to the customer, including "booking," "checking", and "breakfast," which combine into the customer's service. On the other side, experiential attributes are emotional words such as "great," "nice," and "good" which also show on the top 10 rankings of all, but only a few portions of a negative word like "poor" were shown. Since the data was collected from three platforms, including positive, neutral, and negative online reviews in the same proportion, the positive experiential attribute words and the negative ones do not balance. This finding might show that people tend to express positive feelings by using direct words like "good," "nice" and "great," but express negative emotions by describing the detail.

Appendix 2 shows the filtered words to display words that have only appeared in one of those platforms. This table is a clue to the characteristic differences or the primary user cluster differences among the three platforms. Booking.com, "place" and "bathroom" are unique words that show more concern about hotel facilities. Unique words like "price" and "money" describe the user characteristics of price-sensitivity. Also, words that describe service like "helpful," "pleasure" show that Booking's user is more focused on focused facilities, price, and compare than the other two platforms. On the other hand, Expedia users focus more on location-related words such as "MTR," "bus," and "close," which are all related to hotel location and convenient transportation, which they value more. Tripadvisor users, in contrast, prefer more entertainment facilities. Unique words are "experience," "airport," "pool," and "club," which most likely de-scribe the extra facilities.

5.2 Dendogram

Cluster analysis is often used to determine which of the most commonly used words appear or are expressed together to explore the attributes' relationships further. The dendrograms of Booking, Expedia, and Tripadvisor are shown in Appendix 3. The dendogram contains the 25 high-frequency words, and the proximity height of each word is the indicator of corresponding word clusters (Woelfel, 1998).

In the dendogram of Booking, it is evident that "room" "location" are the two highest and most tightly clusters, illustrating that the neural net believes those two words have the most substantial relationship. Soon the word "exceptional" also joined the highest cluster. In summary, the most frequent mentions of the hotel's attributes are "room," "hotel" "place," and "bed," which means Booking guests have more requirements on the hotel's hardware and facilities, and positive comments are more likely to come from meeting their expectations. In the dendogram of Expedia, the words "hotel" and "room" show the most substantial relationship by neural net output. The words "stay" and "staff" join the cluster, followed by "nice" and "good." Next come "great" and "location," followed by "excellent." The cluster shows Expedia customers are concerned with the room of a hotel most. The attribute room is the most potent reason to make them feel good. In summary, the positive comments of Expedia consumers are usually achieved from a hotel with a good room, nice staff, and great location with convenient traffic, like close to MTR or a hotel's free shuttle bus. In Tripadvisor's dendrogram, the most substantial relationship is first "hotel" and "room." Then the word "stay" joins in the cluster, soon followed by "exceptional" and "service," as well as "great" and "staff." The next joined words are "experience," "location," "view," "breakfast," and "good." The composition of the cluster indicates customers of Tripadvisor pay most attention to the hotel room, and regard the room as the most critical attribute of a hotel. In summary, Tripadvisor consumers care about attributes that provide an excellent stay experience. These come first from the hotel room and staff's service, then good location and view plus breakfast, including the free airport bus, reasonable check-in time, clean food, and excellent bar.

6 CONCLUSIONS

The content analysis of online reviews reveals that the most influential consumer hotel satisfaction attributes are hotel, room, stay, staff, and location. These attributes have top-ranking and similar weights in the three selected platforms. Most consistent with previous research (e.g., Zhang & Mao, 2012), room, service, and location are essential elements that tourists will consider when evaluating hotels. From the analysis results, the room is undoubtedly the most critical attribute of a hotel, consistent with earlier literature that tourists consider the room to be the most important determinant of customer satisfaction (Choi & Chu, 2001; Liu, Teichert, Rossi, Li, & Hu, 2017). However, previous research, such as Liu et al. (2017) regards service to be more important than the room in each segment. Guests also are concerned about the stay experience in addition to the hotel room. Although less literature mentions the word "stay," many hotel attributes are aimed to serve the staying experience of hotel guests.

Moreover, the result confirms that the staff is still an essential part of the hotel, which is consistent with Han, Mankad, Gavirneni, and Verma's (2016) findings that staff and service are the most influential aspects to consumers. Technology development enables the hotel industry to use more advanced technology such as the check-in/out machine, service robot, and even the no-staff hotel. But for now, most consumers still believe that the service provided by hotel staff is irreplaceable.

Consumers who comment on different platforms do have other concerns. Some attributes that show small statistical values can be used to understand the diversity of consumer preferences and each platform's characteristics. Through the content of online reviews, the users of Booking are more concerned about the accommodation properties of hotels than the users of the other two platforms, having higher requirements for hotel facilities, and being more price-sensitive. Besides, they are more accustomed to using some written words like "pleasure" and "helpful" when posting. Hence, users who post on Booking have a considerable number of business travelers. Guests who post on Expedia place greater value to transportation convenience and hotel rating, suggesting that Expedia users pay more attention to the journey and have specific travel quality requirements. Tripadvisor's guests are different from the other two platforms. The total word number in comments is the largest among the three platforms, showing they are more willing to share. Tripadvisor's guests emphasize more the hotel's attributes, especially entertainment facilities, indicating they are more likely to take leisure travel. All three platform users present a significant number of positive words in the online reviews like "exceptional," "good," and "nice"; "poor" is the only negative word that appears in the high-frequency words list of Booking. This finding indicates that customers tend to express positive feelings and comments directly by words but describe dissatisfied aspects in detail, which extends the result of Sweeney et al. (2005) that emotional feelings strongly drive negative reviews.

The implications for the platforms are mainly in the context of marketing. For Booking customers who pay more attention to hotel facilities and are price-sensitive, the platform can first show hotels with special prices and good facilities. Expedia can present hotels with more convenient transportation and better locations in higher ranking order for consumers who are more concerned about location. Hotels with more entertainment facilities can be ranked on the first Tripadvisor page. Second, a focus on the different attributes in advertising highlights the differences between platforms. Although Booking, Expedia, and Tripadvisor have a separate business scope, all three platforms have built themselves into a comprehensive travel website through cooperation and other means; thus differentiated advertising is vital. Advertisements of Tripadvisor can highlight helping tourists to find hotels in good locations. Advertisements that express not just selling for profit are more effective in persuading customers to make purchase decisions.

There are some limitations and areas that deserve further research. First, the extraction of online tourist reviews was conveniently collected according to the ratings (positive, neutral, and negative) and did not distinguish the hotel category. Whether different hotel star ratings or other types of hotels (such as independent hotels and hotel chains) would affect content analysis results is a topic worth discussing in future research. Second, only 2700 online reviews were selected. A more considerable amount of content data might yield more comprehensive coverage. Future research may consider using software to extract more reviews from these platforms, leading to more accurate theoretical and practical contributions. Third, only one city Hong Kong was chosen for online review content analysis. Future research on cross-culture comparison can be made by selecting online reviews of different representative cities from various platforms.

REFERENCES

Ahmad, W., &Sun, J. (2018). Modeling consumer distrust of online hotel reviews. *International Journal of Hospitality Management*, 71, 77–90.

Alpert, M. I. (1971). Identification of determinant attributes: A comparison of models. *Journal of Marketing Research*, 8, 184–191.

Baber, A., Thurasamy, R., Malik, M. I., Sadiq, B., Islam, S., & Sajjad, M. (2016). Online word-of-mouth antecedents, attitude and intention-to-purchase electronic products in Paki-stan. *Telematics and Informatics*, 33(2), 388–400.

Blal, I., & Sturman, M. C. (2014). The Differential Effects of the Quality and Quantity of Online Reviews on Hotel Room Sales. *Cornell Hospitality Quarterly*, 55(4), 365–375.

Chang, T. P. V., Rhodes, J., & Lok, P. (2013). The Mediating Effect of Brand Trust Between Online Customer Reviews and Willingness to Buy. *Journal of Electronic Commerce in Organizations*, 11(1), 22–42.

Cheng, T. P. V., & Pai, C., Chen, Y. (2017). An investigation of the differences in the content of online hotel reviews on different platforms, The 2017 (Tourism Sciences Society of Korea) *International Tourism Conference*, 5–7 Jul Ulsan Korea.

Cheung, M. K., & Thadani, D. R. (2012). The impact of electronic word-of-mouth communication: a literature analysis and integrative model. *Decision Support Systems*, 54(1), 461–470.

Choi, T.Y., & Chu, R. (2001). Determinants of hotel guests' satisfaction and repeat patronage in the Hong Kong hotel industry. *International Journal of Hospitality Management*, 20(3), 277–297.

Dickinger, A. (2011). The trustworthiness of online channels for experience and goal- directed search tasks. *Journal of Travel Research*, 50 (4), 378–391.

Doh, S. J., & Hwang, J. S. (2009). How Consumers Evaluate eWOM (Electronic Word-of-Mouth) Messages. *Cyberpsychology & behavior*,12(2), 193–197.

Filieri, R., & McLeay, F. (2013). eWOM and accommodation: an analysis of the factors that influence travelers' adoption of information from online reviews. *Journal of Travel Research*, 53(1), 44–57.

Gretzel, U.& Yoo, K. (2008). Use and impact of online travel reviews. In: O'Connor, P., Hopken, W., Gretzel, U. (Eds.), In-formation and communication technologies in tourism (pp. 35–46). *New York: Springer-Verlag.*

Han, H. J., Mankad, S., Gavirneni, N., & Verma, R. (2016). What guests really think of your hotel: Text analytics of online customer reviews. *Cornell Hospitality Report*, 16(2), 3–17.

Hsu, C., Yu, L., & Chang, K. (2017). Exploring the effects of online customer reviews, regulatory focus, and product type on purchase intention: Perceived justice as a moderator. *Computers in Human Behavior*, 69, 335–346. https://www.reviewtrackers.com/hotel-review-sites/

Huertas-Garcia, B., García, M. L., & Consolación, C. (2014). Conjoint Analysis of Tourist Choice of Hotel Attributes Presented in Travel Agent Brochures. *The International Journal of Tourism Research*, 16(1), 65–73.

Hussain, S., Wang, G., Jafar, R. M. S., Ilyas, Z., Mustafa, G., & Yang, J. (2018). Consumers' online information adoption behavior: Motives and antecedents of electronic word of mouth communications. *Computers in Human Behavior*, 80, 22–32.

Jacobsen, G. D. (2015). Consumers, experts, and online prod-uct evaluations: Evidence from the brewing industry. *Jour-nal of Public Economics*, 126, 114–123.

Jalilvand, M. R., &Samiei, N. (2012). The impact of electronic word of mouth on a tourism destination choice: Testing the theory of planned behavior (TPB). *Internet Research*, 22(5), 591–612.

Kima, W. G., Limb, H., & Brymer, R. A. (2015). The effective-ness of managing social media on hotel performance. *International Journal of Hospitality Management*, 44, 165–171.

Kou, G., Yang, P., Peng, Y., Xiao, F., Chen, Y., & Alsaadi, F. E. (2020). Evaluation of feature selection methods for text classification with small datasets using multiple criteria decision-making methods. *Applied Soft Computing*, 105836.

Ladhari, R., & Michaud, M. (2015). eWOM effects on hotel booking intentions, attitudes, trust, and website perceptions. *International Journal of Hospitality Management*, 46, 36–45.

Lee, M., & Youn, S. (2009). Electronic word of mouth (eWOM) How eWOM platforms influence consumer product judgement. *International Journal of Advertising*, 28(3), 473–499.

Levy, S.E., Duan, W., & Boo, S. (2013). An analysis of one-star online reviews and responses in the Washington, DC, lodging market. *Cornell Hospitality Quarterly*, 54(1), 49–63.

Liu, B., Kim, H., & Pennington-Gray, L. (2015). Responding to the bed bug crisis in social media. *International Journal of Hospitality Management*, 47, 76–84.

Liu, Y., Teichert, T., Rossi, M., Li, H., & Hu, F. (2017). Big data for big insights: Investigating language-specific drivers of hotel satisfaction with 412,784 user-generated reviews. *Tourism Management*, 59, 554–563.

Lockie, M., Waiguny, M., & Grabner-Kräuter, S. (2015). How style, information depth and textual characteristics influence the usefulness of general practitioners' reviews. *Australasian Marketing Journal*, 23, 168–178.

Mak, A. (2017). Online destination image: Comparing nation-al tourism organisation's and tourists' perspectives. *Tourism Management*, 60, 280–297.

Manes, E., & Tchetchik, A. (2018). The role of electronic word of mouth in reducing information asymmetry: An empirical investigation of online hotel booking. *Journal of Business Research*, 85, 185–196.

Marcolin, C. B., Becker, J. L., Wild, F., Behr, A., & Schiavi, G. (2021). Listening to the voice of the guest: A framework to improve decision-making processes with text data. *International Journal of Hospitality Management*, 94, 102853.

Marine-Roig, E. & Clavé, S. (2015). Tourism analytics with massive user-generated content: A case study of Barcelona. *Journal of Destination Marketing & Management*, 4(3), 162–172.

Mauri, A. G., & Minazzi, R. (2013). Web reviews influence on expectations and purchasing intentions of hotel potential customers. *International Journal of Hospitality Manage-ment*, 34, 99–107.

Munzel, A. (2016). Assisting consumers in detecting fake re-views: The role of identity information disclosure and con-sensus. *Journal of Retailing and Consumer Services*, 32, 96–108.

Nath, P., Devlin, J., & Reid, V. (2018). The effects of online re-views on service expectations: Do cultural value orientations matter? *Journal of Business Research*, 90, 123–133.

Neuman, W.L. (2011). Social Research Methods: Qualitative and Quantitative Approaches. *Allyn & Bacon: Boston*.

Nieto, J., Hernández-Maestro, R. M., & Muñoz-Gallego, P. A. (2014). Marketing decisions, customer reviews, and business performance: The use of the Toprural web-site by Spanish rural lodging establishments. *Tourism Management*, 45, 115–123.

Noone, B., & Robson, S. K. A. (2014). Using eye tracking to obtain a deeper understanding of what drives online hotel choice. *Cornell Hospitality Report*, 14(18), 6–16.

Parasuraman, A., Zeithaml, V. A., & Berry, L. L. (1985). A conceptual model of service quality and its implications for future research. *Journal of Marketing*, 49(4), 41–50.

Park, S., & Nicolau, J. L. (2015). Asymmetric effects of online consumer reviews. *Annals of Tourism Research*, 50, 67–83.

Penaflorida, R. (2018). The 22 Hotel Review Sites You Should Monitor. Retrieved from

Rhee, H. T., & Yang, S. (2015). Does hotel attribute importance differ by hotel? Focusing on hotel star-classifications and customers' overall ratings. *Computers in Human Behavior*, 50, 576–587.

Roman, C., & Martin, J. C. (2016). Hotel attributes: Asymmetries in guest payments and gains e A stated preference approach. *Tourism Management*, 52, 488–497.

Simpson, P. M. & Siguaw, J. A. (2008). Destination Word of Mouth: The Role of Traveler Type, Residents, and Identity Salience. *Journal of Travel Research*, 47(2), 167–182.

Sparks, B. A. & Browning, V. (2011). The impact of online re-views on hotel booking intentions and perception of trust. *Tourism Management*, 32, 1310–1323.

Sparks, B. A., So, K. K., & Bradley, G. L. (2016). Responding to negative online reviews: The effects of hotel responses on customer inferences of trust and concern. *Tourism Management*, 53, 74–85.

Sweeney, J. C., Soutar, G. N., & Mazzarol, T. (2005). The Differences Between Positive And Negative Word-Of-Mouth –Emotion As A Differentiator? ANZMAC 2005 Conference: *Consumer Behaviour*, 331–337.

Tang, L., Choi, S., Morrison, A. M., & Lehto, X. Y. (2007). The many faces of Macau: A correspondence analysis of the images communicated by online tourism information sources in English and Chinese. *Journal of Vacation Marketing*, 15(1), 79–94.

Tang, T. Y., Fang, E. E., & Wang, F. (2014). Is neutrual really neutrual? The effects of neutral user-generated content on product sales. *Journal of Marketing*, 78, 41–58.

Teso, E., Olmedilla, M., Martínez-Torres, M. R., & Toral, S. L. (2018). Application of text mining techniques to the analysis of discourse in eWOM communications from a gender perspective. *Technological Forecasting and Social Change*, 129, 131–142.

Torres, E. N., Singh, D., & Robertson-Ring, A. (2015). Consumer reviews and the creation of booking transaction value: Lessons from the hotel industry. *International Journal of Hospitality Management*, 20, 77–83.

Vermeulen, I. E., & Seegers, D. (2009). Tried and tested: the impact of online hotel reviews on consumer consideration. *Tourism Management*, 30, 123–127.

Wang, S., & Hung, K. (2015). Customer perceptions of critical success factors for guest houses. *International Journal of Hospitality Management*, 48, 92–101.

Woelfel, J. (1993). Artificial neural networks in policy research: A current assessment. *Journal of Communication*, 43(1), 63–80.

Woelfel, J. (1998). CATPAC: User's guide. *New York: RAH Press*.

Xiang, Z., Du, Q., Ma, Y., & Fan, W. (2017). A comparative analysis of major online review platforms: Implications for social media analytics in hospitality and tourism. *Tourism Management*, 58, 51–65.

Xie, K. L., Chen, C., & Wu, S. (2015). Online Consumer Review Factors Affecting Offline Hotel Popularity: Evidence from Tripadvisor. *Journal of Travel & Tourism Marketing*, 1–13.

Xu, Q. (2014). Should I trust him? The effects of reviewer pro-file characteristics on eWOM credibility. *Computers in Human Behavior*, 33, 136–144.

Yang, J., Kim, W., Amblee, N., & Jeong, J. (2012). The heterogeneous effect of WOM on product sales: why the effect of WOM valence is mixed? *European Journal of Marketing*, 46(11/12), 1523–1538.

Ye, Q., Law, R., Gu, B., & Chen, W. (2011). The influence of user-generated content on traveler behavior: An empirical investigation on the effects of e-word-of-mouth to hotel online bookings. *Computers in Human Behavior*, 27(2), 634–639.

Yen, C., & Tang, C. (2015). Hotel attribute performance, eWOM motivations, and media choice. *International Journal of Hospitality Management*, 46, 79–88.

Zhang, J., & Mao, Z. (2012). Image of all hotel scales on travel blogs: its impact on customer loyalty. *Journal of Hospitality Marketing & Management*, 21(2), 1–19.

Zhang, Y., & Cole, S. T. (2016). Dimensions of lodging guest satisfaction among guests with mobility challenges: A mixed-method analysis of web-based texts. *Tourism Management*, 53, 13–27.

Zhang, Y., & Vásquez, V. (2014). Hotels' responses to online reviews: Managing consumer dissatisfaction. *Discourse, Context and Media*, 6, 54–64.

Zhang, Z., Ye, Q., & Law, R. (2011). Determinants of hotel room price. *International Journal of Contemporary Hospitality Management*, 23(7), 972–981.

Zheng, X., Gretzel, U., & Fesenmaier, D. R. (2009). Semantic representation of tourism on the internet. *Journal of Travel Research*, 47(4), 440–453.

Zhou, L., Ye, S., Pearce, P. L., & Wu, M. (2014). Refreshing hotel satisfaction studies by reconfiguring customer review data. *International Journal of Hospitality Management*, 38, 1–10.

Appendix 1. Words frequency of three different platforms.

Booking		Expedia		Tripadvisor	
Words	Frequency	Words	Frequency	Words	Frequency
ROOM	783 (16.20%)	HOTEL	1230 (18.60%)	HOTEL	2168 (18.20%)
HOTEL	474 (9.80%)	ROOM	1082 (16.30%)	ROOM	2057 (17.30%)
LOCATION	397 (8.20%)	STAY	436 (6.60%)	STAY	1037 (8.70%)
STAFF	343 (7.10%)	STAFF	395 (6.00%)	STAFF	629 (5.30%)
GOOD	332 (6.90%)	LOCATION	389 (5.90%)	SERVICE	554 (4.70%)
STAY	249 (5.10%)	GOOD	342 (5.20%)	G0OD	551 (4.60%)
SMALL	194 (4.00%)	GREAT	301 (4.50%)	GREAT	429 (3.60%)
BED	164 (3.40%)	SERVICE	227 (3.40%)	LOCATION	393 (3.30%)
GREAT	155 (3.20%)	NICE	198 (3.00%)	VIEW	342 (2.90%)
EXCEPTIONAL	154 (3.20%)	SMALL	166 (2.50%)	TIME	328 (2.80%)
CLEAN	143 (3.00%)	CHECKIN	152 (2.30%)	BOOKING	327 (2.80%)
POOR	142 (2.90%)	EXCELLENT	149 (2.20%)	CHECKIN	315 (2.70%)
BOOKING	129 (2.70%)	CLEAN	148 (2.20%)	BREAKFAST	307 (2.60%)
PLACE	128 (2.60%)	BED	141 (2.10%)	NICE	276 (2.30%)
NICE	113 (2.30%)	VIEW	136 (2.10%)	EXCEPTIONAL	265 (2.20%)
PLEASANT	108 (2.20%)	TIME	130 (2.00%)	FLOOR	264 (2.20%)
PRICE	100 (2.10%)	BOOKING	126 (1.90%)	AIRPORT	201 (1.70%)
BATHROOM	98 (2.00%)	MTR	120 (1.80%)	EXPERIENCE	199 (1.70%)
FLOOR	96 (2.00%)	CLOSE	119 (1.80%)	FOOD	197 (1.70%)
SERVICE	94 (1.90%)	FREE	118 (1.80%)	POOL	184 (1.50%)
FRIENDLY	91 (1.90%)	BREAKFAST	109 (1.60%)	CLUB	179 (1.50%)
HELPFUL	90 (1.90%)	FOOD	108 (1.60%)	CLEAN	177 (1.50%)
MONEY	89 (1.80%)	STAR	105 (1.60%)	EXCELLENT	171 (1.40%)
CHECKIN	88 (1.80%)	FRIENDLY	102 (1.50%)	FREE	171 (1.40%)
TIME	87 (1.80%)	BUS	101 (1.50%)	BED	164 (1.40%)

Appendix 2. Words appear only in one platform.

Booking		Expedia		Tripadvisor	
POOR	142 (2.90%)	MTR	120 (1.80%)	AIRPORT	201 (1.70%)
PLACE	128 (2.60%)	CLOSE	119 (1.80%)	EXPERIENCE	199 (1.70%)
PLEASANT	108 (2.20%)	STAR	105 (1.60%)	POOL	184 (1.50%)
PRICE	100 (2.10%)	BUS	101 (1.50%)	CLUB	179 (1.50%)
BATHROOM	98 (2.00%)				
HELPFUL	90 (1.90%)				
MONEY	89 (1.80%)				

Appendix 3. Dendograms of each platform.

Booking

Expedia

Tripadvisor

Economic and Business Management – Huang & Zhang (Eds)
© 2022 Copyright the Author(s), ISBN: 978-1-032-06754-4

Research on the brand building strategy of small- and medium-sized enterprises in the Digital Economy Era

Xiaohong Zhang
Shandong Institute of Commerce and Technology, Jinan, Shandong, China

ABSTRACT: This paper discusses the impact of digital economy on the brand building of enterprises, as well as the significance, existing problems and countermeasures of brand building of small- and medium-sized micro-enterprises under the digital economy. Small- and medium-sized enterprises need to re-recognize the ways and methods of brand building, carry out personalized brand positioning and image system construction, make full use of network platform and digital technology for brand communication and promotion, so as to establish their own brand influence and competitive advantage.

Keywords: Digital economy; Small and medium-sized micro-enterprises; Brand building

1 INTRODUCTION

Digital economy is an economic model that uses digital technology to drive the whole process of economic activities and create benefits. Digital technology mainly includes three aspects: data related technology, network related technology and computing related technology. These technologies have penetrated into all aspects of the three industries, triggered profound changes in industrial structure, industrial organization, industrial resource allocation and industrial layout, and promoted the emergence of new formats, new models and new norms. The development of digital economy and the advancement of digital technology have changed the environment of brand building, accelerated the speed of brand communication, and reduced the cost of brand communication. These changes have brought new opportunities for the brand building of small and medium-sized enterprises.

2 THE INFLUENCE OF DIGITAL ECONOMY ON ENTERPRISE BRAND BUILDING

The digital economy is a key force to continuously promote China's economic growth in recent years, which has penetrated into all fields of production and life. The digital economy makes consumption demand personalized, consumption scenarios diversified, information channels diversified, products and services integrated, and brand communication real-time. Changes in business models and brand values have made the market competitive environment more complicated. Crossover, integration, sharing and

ecology have become the main factors to be considered in the operation of enterprises in the digital economy environment, and digitalization has become the key measure of enterprise development. Today's enterprises need to think about their strategic decisions, product development, production and operation, human resources, financial management, and other work with new ideas. Similarly, brand building of enterprises also needs new ways of thinking. and thinking to guide when considering brand building.

Digital technology has changed the environment of enterprise brand building, brand communication speed and communication ability. On the one hand, digital technology broadens the cognitive channels of brands, expands the communication scenarios between brands and consumers, increases the connection between brands and consumers, and greatly reduces the time required for people to establish brand awareness. Compared with the traditional means of brand communication, enterprises can now use low-cost product information and brand core value to accurately spread to the target consumers and can get real-time feedback from consumers. But, on the other hand, the shortcomings and negative information of a brand will be magnified infinitely, and a bad comment from consumers may destroy a brand in an instant. Therefore, in the era of the digital economy, the brand building of enterprises has changed from the one-way communication mode in the past to the interactive communication mode nowadays. The methods and means used in each link of enterprise brand building need to be changed, which is both an opportunity and a challenge for small, medium and micro-enterprises.

DOI 10.1201/9781003203704-2

9

3 THE SIGNIFICANCE OF BRAND BUILDING OF SMALL- AND MEDIUM-SIZED ENTERPRISES

Small and medium-sized enterprises play a vital role in the economic growth of any country. They are the main channel for increasing employment, the main platform for entrepreneurs' entrepreneurial growth They are the strong support to meet the diversified needs of the people, and the important foundation to increase national income. China's reform and opening up make the scale of small and medium-sized enterprises continue to expand. In recent years, China has put forward the policy of 'mass entrepreneurship and innovation', which makes newly established enterprises springing up and playing an increasingly important role in national economic and social development According to statistics, more than 90% of China's market players are small and medium-sized enterprises. They have solved 80% of China's employment, created about 70% of patent invention rights, and contributed more than 60% of GDP and more than 50% of tax revenue (Fan 2019). Therefore, the Chinese government attaches great importance to the healthy development of SMEs. Various provinces and autonomous regions have introduced a series of supporting policies, such as simplifying administrative examination and approval, financial tax incentives, financial subsidies for entrepreneurship, and talent skills training. The purpose is to encourage and support mass entrepreneurship and innovation.

Even so, in the fiercely competitive market environment, many small and medium-sized enterprises still have problems such as insufficient financial strength, limited technical level, and talent bottleneck, so they can only maintain their survival through OEM production and have no spare capacity for brand building. In the OEM mode, passive production, low added value, meagre profits, poor bargaining power and irregular management have led to slow growth of enterprises and insufficient development potential. This is the main reason for the short average life span of small enterprises in China. In the long run, the brand is the core competitiveness of an enterprise, and only a brand can solve the problem of sustainable development of small and medium-sized enterprises.

4 THE STATUS QUO AND PROBLEMS OF BRAND BUILDING IN SMALL AND MEDIUM-SIZED ENTERPRISES

4.1 *Weak awareness of brand building*

Many small and medium-sized enterprises are unaware of the importance of brand building, and they are unaware of the huge promotion that brands will bring to their sustainable development. Because brand building needs a lot of time, energy, and cost, it is difficult to bring direct economic benefits in the short term, especially in the initial stage of enterprises, brand building often means the increase of enterprise expenditure. Therefore, many small and medium-sized enterprises will not invest a lot of manpower and material resources in brand building under the situation of tight corporate funds.

4.2 *Lack of brand planning ability*

Only by endowing products with excellent brand planning genes can we go further in the competitive market. Clear brand positioning, shape brand personality, create core values, design brand image and other work, is an enterprise's products to the market before the need to do important planning work. Excellent brand planning requires more professional knowledge and wisdom. For small- and medium-sized enterprises, due to their own limited ability, it is difficult to carry out high-quality brand planning according to the market situation, competitors' situation and consumer demand, and quite a lot of brand planning is made by managers relying on their own feelings and personal preferences. Such decisions can hardly stand the test of the market and consumers.

4.3 *Weak brand promotion*

Brand promotion is the process of transforming the brand and product image completed by brand planning into brand equity, that is, the process of building brand awareness, reputation and loyalty. Brand promotion is an effective support for product sales, but in reality, many small- and medium-sized enterprises, due to financial problems, tend to pay more attention to immediate interests, focus on the product itself rather than the value of the product, focus on how to sell the product rather than how to promote the brand. Some small- and medium-sized enterprises have initially established their own brand, but how to make the brand realize enterprise benefit increment is unknown.

4.4 *Lack of brand management talents*

Small- and medium-sized enterprises are not as perfect as large enterprises in department setting and personnel segmentation. Large enterprises have huge marketing departments, including the sales department, marketing department, customer service department, etc. the staff of these departments have a clear division of labor and perform their duties. However, it is very common for many small- and medium-sized microenterprises to set up only one sales department. The employees are mainly engaged in sales functions, supplemented by marketing and planning functions. Therefore, many small- and medium-sized enterprises do not have a special person responsible for brand management, but the sales department staff to take care of brand management. People in these departments often equate brand management with trademark management or advertising management. In the recruitment of talents, only focus on sales and publicity, leading to the lack of real brand management talents.

5 BRAND BUILDING STRATEGY OF SMALL, MEDIUM AND MICRO-ENTERPRISES IN THE DIGITAL ECONOMY

5.1 *A new understanding of brand building*

In the digital economy environment, the rapid development of new-generation technology has transformed the brand-building concepts of many companies from taking products as the core to taking customer value as the core, and the past brand-building methods have become obsolete. Small- and medium-sized enterprises should let innovative thinking replace the traditional view, make full use of the characteristics of the digital economy and the advantages of digital technology, to build and promote brand value from multiple dimensions such as cross-border, integration, sharing and ecology. The new media network communication trend of interconnection has brought challenges to the brand building of small- and medium-sized enterprises, as well as opportunities.

5.2 *Personalized brand positioning*

For the newly established small and microenterprises, the most urgent work to be done is brand system positioning and image building. Among them, brand positioning is the core. Brand positioning is to find a suitable label, find the brand meaning of 'investment value', and then spread the label repeatedly to form consumer psychological inertia: 'if I buy a certain type of product, I must first consider a certain brand, which has done a very good job in this respect'.

Under normal circumstances, the brands of small and medium-sized enterprises usually belong to the follower position in the market competition, but blindly following and imitating big brands will make their own brands lose their personality. In today's serious competition of product homogeneity, it is difficult to leave a mark in the hearts of consumers. Therefore, in brand positioning, small- and medium-sized enterprises must carefully analyze the market and fully consider the consumer demand, competitive environment and their own characteristics. In order to find out their own leading advantages which are urgently needed by consumers and which are not satisfied or possessed by competitive enterprises, so as to define their own brand positioning.

In brand positioning, small- and medium-sized enterprises should pay attention to clearly expressing core values. From these two dimensions, we can see that what is not or rare in competitive products becomes 'the first or the only' through market segmentation, which can better meet the needs of consumers than competitors, so as to become the preferred choice of consumers. In this way, we can avoid the competition The edge of the hand, to find their own place.

5.3 *Design brand image according to brand positioning*

Brand positioning and brand image are two sharp swords to attack consumers' minds. If a brand is compared to a person, the brand positioning is like a person's thought and knowledge, and it is the inner core, while the brand image is the external display of a person's appearance, figure, dress, hairstyle, etc. The brand image includes brand naming, brand logo design, IP image design, advertising film design, terminal image design, etc. Brand image should have a good fit with its own brand positioning so that the connotation of brand positioning can be effectively extended. If creative design is carried out in a wild way, the brand image will become a 'beautiful waste paper', but not a 'marketing weapon'.

Many young entrepreneurs act quickly. Maybe they just have a good idea to set up a company quickly. In terms of quality and speed, most entrepreneurs may choose speed. Indeed, many business opportunities are fleeting, so they may ignore the brand building. But what needs special attention of small, medium and microenterprises is that in modern business competition, brand name (trademark) is one of the most core intellectual property rights of enterprises, which is the carrier and concentrated embodiment of an enterprise's resources. Therefore, at the beginning of the establishment of the enterprise, we should pay attention to the brand naming and upgrade it to the top-level design of the enterprise, because the cost of changing the brand name is huge, especially for the intangible assets in the market. Therefore, it is one of the basic principles that a brand name can be registered as a trademark. No matter how good a name is, if it cannot be registered and protected by law, it will not really belong to its own brand.

Brand logo design, IP image design, advertising film design and terminal image design are the carrier of brand vision and communication, the way to show brand positioning and values, and the communication tool between brand and consumers. Therefore, matching design should be carried out according to the brand positioning, and a unified brand visual style and tonality should be formed. Once the tonality of brand visual style is determined, all links of the brand can be referred to for application, such as the development of product appearance, the image of the sales terminal, all the communication advertisements of the brand, the website/online store of the brand, the brand press conference, and the product promotion site, for the future uniform brand communication and promotion to lay the foundation.

However, based on the importance of brand image work, small- and medium-sized enterprises should seriously design their own brand image, and can also complete this work by choosing a third-party service company.

5.4 *Using network platform and digital technology to promote brand communication*

Small- and medium-sized microenterprises in the initial stage, whether personnel or communication funds, cannot be surplus, so it will be difficult to really carry out the brand integrated marketing communication work. Traditional media is not suitable for small and medium-sized enterprises because of its huge investment. The emerging network platform has the advantages of less investment, rapid communication, accurate positioning, and effective docking. The core difference between new media and traditional media lies in interactivity. The new generation of young people are Internet natives, and they are better at discovering 'circles' with common interests and hobbies. Therefore, mobile Internet technology has boosted various new media applications. In addition to specialized social app applications (such as WeChat), various platforms (Taobao) and businesses (microblog) are designing interactive interfaces to facilitate the development of new media They interact with consumers, listen to their voices, and push back the transformation of enterprises' products and services. Micro-blog Tik-Tok, WeChat, jitter, Kwai and other network platforms expand the contact between brands and consumers, providing more ways and means for brand promotion.

Small- and medium-sized enterprises need to realize that under the influence of the digital economy, the brand is no longer just the communication of concept and vision, but the feeling, experience, sharing, and co-construction of consumers. Therefore, small- and medium-sized enterprises should flexibly use the Internet to build enterprise official website, online shop, and we media matrix and operate effectively to reach consumers in multiple scenarios. At the same time, with the help of digital technology, we can track consumer behavior, analyze consumer demand, link with consumers, improve the accuracy of brand promotion and conversion efficiency, and achieve win-win value between brands and consumers.

5.5 *Cultivate professional brand management team*

In the era of digital economy, the main responsibility of brand managers is to enhance the core competitiveness and overall, the strength of enterprises through the establishment of brand building and marketing systems. They need to complete the tasks of developing the market, promoting brand building, taking customers as the center, realizing the continuous improvement of enterprise value through Omnichannel promotion and other ways. In addition, we should also carry out the protection of brand intellectual property rights, brand image management, brand crisis public relations, and other work. When enterprises gradually grow from small and microenterprises to medium-sized enterprises, they need to start the work such as a brand extension.

Small and microenterprises or newly established companies, under the pressure of operating costs, generally do not set up special departments and can carry out centralized brand planning services through the external brain, such as VI design and product packaging. Later through a variety of service providers for point-to-point services, such as exhibition building design, album design, etc. If a small and micro-enterprise has a copy or design position, it can be established in the office or sales department.

For medium-sized enterprises, brand management has become indispensable. At this stage, enterprises need professionals with strong practical abilities. Even if there is no separate brand management department, it is also necessary to recruit or cultivate a talent who has the knowledge of brand planning and management and is good at new media operation as soon as possible, so as to quickly accumulate the brand reputation of the enterprise.

6 CONCLUSIONS

The brand is the soul of an enterprise. Precise positioning, shaping image, skillful communication, and good management are the quintessence of brand building. The digital economy and digital technology have created a lot of opportunities for the brand building of small- and medium-sized enterprises. As long as small- and medium-sized enterprises can comply with the development of the times, take advantage of Internet communication, and actively use new thinking, new technology, and new means, they will be able to establish their own brand influence and competitive advantage.

REFERENCES

Bai Jinfu. 2017. Brand building in the Internet era. *Chinese business*: 61–63.

Fan Shi. 2019. Research on the income tax preferential policies of small low profit enterprises from the perspective of policy implementation–a case study of Heyuan City. *South China University of Technology*: 1

Ma Zhiping. 2020. Research on brand building of small and medium-sized enterprises in the era of all media marketing. *Management and technology of small and medium-sized enterprises*: 156–157.

Shi Yumei. 2017. Brand building of small, medium and micro enterprises in the Internet era. *Jiangsu business theory*: 39–42.

Zhang Xiaohong. 2020. Brand planning and promotion practice. *Beijing: Posts & Telecom Press Co., LTD.*

Economic and Business Management – Huang & Zhang (Eds)
© 2022 Copyright the Author(s), ISBN: 978-1-032-06754-4

Stock forecast model based on random forest

Xintao Li
School of Business and Management, Shanghai International Studies University, Shanghai, China

ABSTRACT: With the rapid development of artificial intelligence, more and more people combine it with stock prediction. Stock analysis is divided into technical analysis and fundamental analysis. This paper forecasts the rise and fall of stocks through technical indicators and machine-learning algorithms. And eight technical indicators (EMA, MACD, LINREG, MOMENTUM, RSI, VAR, CYCLE, and ATR) were adopted to predict the rise and fall of a stock. We find that RSI has the largest weight among the eight technical indicators, and the final model prediction accuracy is 75%.

1 INTRODUCTION

Artificial intelligence has always been the focus of people's attention, such as Tesla's self-driving technology, smart home, Google Alfa dog, and artificial intelligence chip. The concept of artificial intelligence (McCarthy, Minsky, Rochester, & Shannon, 1955) was first proposed in the 1950s, but at the time, researchers thought that by giving machines the ability to reason logically, they would be intelligent. Until the 1980s, with the development of artificial intelligence reached a certain stage, machine learning began to rise (Boden, 1980). Machine learning is to "train" by using large amounts of data, from which to induct, parse the data, and then test events.

As artificial intelligence (AI) is the rapid development of information processing applications, AI has been applied to business industry, engineering, management, science, military, financial, and other different fields (Pannu, 2015). Machine learning is widely used in financial time series forecasts. As machine-learning techniques can imitate fluctuations and predict the trends in stock market, they can produce better prediction results than traditional approach. Machine-learning algorithms for financial time series prediction include support vector machine (SVM) (Xintao, 2017), artificial neural network (ANN) (Xintao, 2017), decision tree (Kamble, 2017), etc.

In recent years, along with the heat of machine learning research increasing, machine learning in the field of financial time series is widely used (Krollner, Vanstone, & Finnie, 2010). Li, Fong, and Chong (2017) use a neural network approach to predict the REITs and stock indices. Li et al. (2020) find a method to predict housing prices through autoML. Because the artificial neural network has an outstanding ability to deal with nonlinear problems and strong fitting ability, it has obtained more accurate prediction results in other fields. And because it has good predictability and

practicability, so more and more researchers combined them with financial time series for application in the stock trend prediction. Random forest is a set of decision trees. It is a newly emerging and highly flexible machine learning algorithm because it builds multiple trees randomly and votes the classification results of all decision trees. The minority is the majority, and it has the ability of strong anti-interference, to process huge data fastly, and to predict results accurately. Therefore, the random forest provides a new possibility for financial time series prediction and has great development potential.

2 RANDOM FOREST AND BAGGING ALGORITHM

The decision tree is a popular method for various machine learning tasks (Myles, Feudale, Liu, Woody, & Brown, 2004). In particular, deep trees tend to learn highly irregular patterns: they overtrain training sets, that is, the deviation is small, but the variance is large. Random forest is a method of averaging multiple depth decision trees, training in different parts of the same training set, aiming at reducing variance. This is at the cost of a small increase in deviation and some interpretable losses, but it usually greatly improves the performance of the final model.

Random forest is an integrated learning method for regression, classification, and other tasks, which is operated by constructing a large number of decision trees during training and outputting the categories as category patterns or average prediction of individual trees. Random decision forest corrects the habit of decision tree over-adapting to the training set. The first random forest algorithm was created by Tian Jinhao (1995) using the random subspace method. Breiman

DOI 10.1201/9781003203704-3

and Cutler (1994) developed the extension of this algorithm, and "Random Forest" is their trademark. The extension combines Breiman's bagging idea (Breiman, 1996) and random selection of features, which was first introduced by Ho (1998) and then independently introduced by Amit and Geman (1999) to construct a decision tree set with controlled variance. Because of the stability of the bagging algorithm, this paper applies the bagging algorithm to the random forest model.

The random forest algorithm is an evolutionary version of the bagging algorithm. In other words, its idea is still bagging, but some improvements have been made. In machine learning, the random forest algorithm is a classifier with multiple decision trees, and its output type is determined by the number of single output trees.

Random forest is a statistical learning theory. Its randomness has two aspects. First, in each round of training, each sample is taken from the original sample set. After k rounds of value taking, we can get k different sample sets. Secondly, for the establishment of each decision tree, a certain number of attributes are randomly selected from the total attributes as split attribute sets, which makes the K-tree classifiers different. Random forest is composed of randomly generated K decision trees.

There are two genres of integrated learning, one is the boosting faction, which is characterized by the dependency between each weak learning device. Another is the bagging faction, which has no dependency between each weak learning device and can be fitted in parallel. In this paper, the bagging algorithm was used for the random forest. Random forest is an important algorithm, which can compare with GBDT (Gradient Boosting Decision Tree) algorithm, especially its convenient parallel training mode. It has a large temptation in this era of big data.

In Figure 1, there is no relationship between weak learner devices of the bagging algorithm like boosting algorithm. It is characterized by random sampling. Random sampling is to extract several samples from the sample set, but after each extraction, the extracted samples will return to the sample set. That is to say, the previous sample that has been collected can be collected continuously in the next sampling.

3 EXPERIMENTS

Feature selection usually has the greatest influence on the accuracy of machine learning models. In this study, we use eight characteristics (MACD, ATR, LINREG, VAR, MOMENTUM, RSI, CYCLE, and EMA) to predict the direction of stock price movement. The stock closing price is compared; if today's closing price is greater than yesterday's closing price, then set the value 1 for the label selection classifier. Otherwise, set the value −1 as the label selection classifier. Examples are shown in Table 1.

We use the data of a stock in a certain year and label them as shown in Table 1. We also get the data of a stock open price, close price, high price, and low price. The part of stock price data that is used in python is shown in Table 2.

Table 2. Stock price data.

	Open	Close	High	Low
2018-01-02	725.8561	469.0662	726.2446	468.9485
2018-01-03	382.1769	478.7797	518.2170	377.2799
2018-01-04	482.4064	539.8082	543.7394	468.4666
2018-01-05	481.1499	294.3839	481.1499	284.7374

One year's stock price data are used in python and one year's feature data which have already been discussed above are used in python for training the model. The part of the feature data is shown in Table 3.

After getting the feature data, we need to calculate the daily rise and fall value, that is, the prediction of stock up or down. Then make the classification of label selection classifier. The label one is defined to tell us the stock price is rising. The label two is defined to tell us the stock price is falling. Through the label

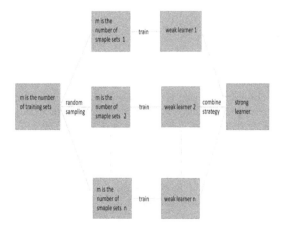

Figure 1. Bagging algorithm working principle.

Table 1. The label of stock up or down.

Date	2020/02/03	2020/02/04	2020/02/05	2020/02/06	2020/02/07	2020/02/10	2020/02/11	2020/02/12
Direction	up	down	up	down	down	down	down	up
Label	1	−1	1	−1	−1	−1	−1	1

selection classifier, an array of the stock price data will be created. Finally, we get the prediction of a stock.

Table 3. Feature data.

	EMA	MACD	LINREG	MOMENTUM
1	77.867530	−72.551032	5.560171	−69.2400
2	68.372444	−72.223805	7.213880	−106.3416
3	67.273106	−61.520744	5.561929	−11.9872
4	66.702060	−51.868543	0.835060	4.7234

	RSI	VAR	CYCLE	ATR
1	36.069329	731.304947	19.732060	91.197608
2	40.253178	366.226885	20.798451	90.905871
3	48.482451	353.998150	21.582273	93.271881
4	48.927622	994.531713	22.133418	89.337989

In this paper, 90% of the sample data are used for training, and the rest of the 10% sample data are used for testing. Predict if the number of the stock price will rise up or go down and the number of prediction will be calculated. The result is shown in Table 4.

Table 4. Report of classification.

	Precision	Recall	Support
−1	0.82	0.88	64
1	0.67	0.73	36
Avg	0.75	0.81	100

In Table 4, the precision of the stock trend prediction is close to 75%. After training, the precision of the backtracking test stock trend prediction is close to 81%. It shows us that more training can give us a good performance for stock trend prediction. In addition, it is important to learn the proportion of features from classifiers. Choose one kind of classification model,

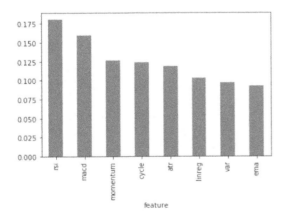

Figure 2. The weight of features.

and train the classifier under this feature individually, and count the accuracy from the test sample set. The feature weight result is shown in Figure 2. Through Figure 2, the value of the RSI indicator is the highest among the eight values.

4 CONCLUSION

For the existing problems of the inaccurate estimation of stock prices, this paper proposes a stock trend forecasting model. By analyzing the importance of input features with the random forest model, we can find the more important input features in the appearance stage. In addition, in order to get a better performance of this model, we can change different technical indicators and different characteristics to get different weights in the random forest model. In this paper, the accuracy of the model is 75% which is still not perfect. In the future, we will try to combine more artificial intelligence models to predict. Therefore, we give a good direction for future research through this model.

ACKNOWLEDGMENT

We gratefully acknowledge the Tutor Academic Leadership Program of Shanghai International Studies Universities [2020114224]. The ideas, methodology, and findings expressed in this paper remain our sole responsibility.

REFERENCES

Amit, Y., & Geman, D. (1999). A computational model for visual selection. *Neural computation*, 11(7), 1691–1715.
Boden, M. (1980). *Artificial intelligence and natural man*.
Breiman, L. (1996). Bagging predictors. *Machine learning*, 24(2), 123–140.
Cutler, A., & Breiman, L. (1994). Archetypal analysis. *Technometrics*, 36(4), 338–347.
Ho, T. K. (1995, August). *Random decision forests*. In Proceedings of 3rd international conference on document analysis and recognition (Vol. 1, pp. 278–282). IEEE.
Ho, T. K. (1998). The random subspace method for constructing decision forests. *IEEE transactions on pattern analysis and machine intelligence*, 20(8), 832–844.
Kamble, R. A. (2017, June). Short and long term stock trend prediction using decision tree. *In 2017 International Conference on Intelligent Computing and Control Systems (ICICCS)* (pp. 1371–1375). IEEE.
Krollner, B., Vanstone, B. J., & Finnie, G. R. (2010, April). Financial time series forecasting with machine learning techniques: a survey. *In ESANN*.
Li, R. Y. M., Fong, S., & Chong, K. W. S. (2017). Forecasting the REITs and stock indices: group method of data handling neural network approach. *Pacific Rim Property Research Journal*, 23(2), 123–160.
Li, R. Y. M., Chau, K. W., Li, H. C. Y., Zeng, F., Tang, B., & Ding, M. (2020, July). Remote Sensing, Heat Island Effect and Housing Price Prediction via AutoML. *In International Conference on Applied Human Factors and Ergonomics* (pp. 113–118). Springer, Cham.

McCarthy, J., Minsky, M. L., Rochester, N., & Shannon, C. E. (2006). A proposal for the dartmouth summer research project on artificial intelligence, august 31, 1955. *AI magazine*, 27(4), 12–12.

Myles, A. J., Feudale, R. N., Liu, Y., Woody, N. A., & Brown, S. D. (2004). An introduction to decision tree modeling. Journal of Chemometrics: *A Journal of the Chemometrics Society*, 18(6), 275–285.

Pannu, A. (2015). Artificial intelligence and its application in different areas. *Artificial Intelligence*, 4(10), 79–84.

Xintao, L., & Lee, S. U. J. (2017). Support Vector Machine for Predicting Stock Price Based on RBF Kernel. *한국정보과학회 학술발표논문집*, 856–858.

Xintao, L., Siddiqui, M. J., Abbas, A., & Lee, S. U. J. (2017). A Feed-forward Neural Network Model for Predicting Stock Price. *한국정보과학회 학술발표논문집*, 1018–1020.

Economic and Business Management – Huang & Zhang (Eds)
© 2022 Copyright the Author(s), ISBN: 978-1-032-06754-4

β-Convergence analysis in the European Union

Radoslav Kožiak*
Faculty of Economics, Matej Bel University, Banská Bystrica, Slovakia
College of Polytechnics Jihlava, Jihlava, Czech Republic

Dana Benčiková
College of Polytechnics Jihlava, Jihlava, Czech Republic

ABSTRACT: Regional disparities are considered a complex, not just an economic, issue outside of Europe, too. This is the main reason for the EU to invest billions of Euros into a regional (cohesion) policy annually. This policy has accompanied the EU member states since the mid-20th century. This brings up the question of its demonstration in economic practice examination. As the aim of the common regional policy is to reduce the differences in social-economic development of its regions, we decided to analyze the β-convergence of the gross domestic product (GDP) per capita in purchasing power parity (PPP) during the statistically maximum available period of 20 years. The concept of β-convergence represents a regression analysis. In our case, it is 262 NUTS2 regions of the EU that will reveal convergence/divergence of the examined regions from the analysis indicator's point of view. The result of this analysis will indicate how appropriately the common regional policy is being implemented.

Keywords: disparities, β-convergence, regional policy, regression analysis

1 INTRODUCTION AND PAPER STRUCTURE

Inter-regional disparities – the term used to refer to differences among regions, is a rather common in multiple areas of scientific research. The word derives from Latin "disparitas," meaning inequality, and is frequently used in several forms, adjectives being closely related to the field of its contemporary use. Originally, the term disparity means difference, dissimilarity, inequality, diversity, disproportion, or imbalance. "Disparities are generally understood as imbalances, discrepancies, heterogeneities, or differences." (Viturka, 2010)

We agree with the approach of the team Tvrdoň et al. (1995) who define two primary reasons of inter-regional disparities. The first reason is the fact that in a specific time period, regions tend to be unequally equipped with growth factors, and the second one refers to different intensity and character of these factors and their utilization. This definition summarizes the key elements of the majority of definitions regarding inter-regional disparities in both domestic and foreign literary sources, and we feel the way it grasps the causes of existence of the phenomenon is highly appropriate to our research.

The motivation of our research is to find out if the NUTS 2 regions in the EU converge or diverge and to indicate how appropriately the common regional policy is being implemented.

This paper presents the basic theoretical and practical aspects of a research involving inter-regional disparities, that being within the regions of the European Union member states. Its primary focus it to point out the research of β-convergence at a regional level NUTS 2 (Nomenclature of territorial units for statistics), which is a unified system of the EURSTAT classification.

The structure of our paper beyond this part should be viewed as follows. In the third part, the authors provide a theoretical discourse to research into inter-regional disparities, by means of the concept of convergence/divergence. The following section specifies the methodology of research into β-convergence, while in the final fifth part, we pursue a detailed empirical analysis of convergence in the conditions of 262 NUTS 2 regions of the EU, that being within the time period between the years 2000–2019, while taking account of the availability of the statistical data.

2 THE CURRENT RESEARCH ON THE TOPIC

One of the methods that are frequently used in regional statistics is the method of convergence. It is a method of analyzing the directions in which the inter-regional disparities are developing. The results of convergence

---

*Corresponding Author

DOI 10.1201/9781003203704-4

analysis show as disparity development trends, i.e., the convergence (=joining, coming closer) or divergence (=separating, parting) of the levels of observed indicators. This method and its variances, namely the analysis of β-convergence of the selected parameters, appears most appropriate to serve our purposes, while its proportion within the results plays the key role.

The term convergence is generally understood as a process approaching a certain level, or, in other words, reducing the disparity among the values of two or more variables in time, up to a level when the difference between the values approaches zero, i.e., it becomes insignificant. As to convergence, economics understands the term as a "process of balancing the differences of various economic indicators within a group of countries, which means it also refers to balancing the living standard in the individual countries" (Baraněok et al., 2006). According to Green (2003), convergence occurs between time periods t and t+1. For the observed economic indicators in two difference economies (countries, or regions) x, y, it stands that:

$$|x_{t+1} - y_{t+1}| < |x_t - y_t| \tag{1}$$

Based on the aforementioned, it can be concluded that certain common features may be observed between the process of convergence, understood through the Solow Growth Model, and the neoclassical approach to regional development, which is based on a belief that inter-regional disparities are balancing automatically due to the movement of capital and migration of the labor force. If inter-regional disparities occur, the more developed regions tend to accumulate capital more rapidly, which leads to a decrease in the marginal product of capital, and is consequently followed by the decreasing capital revenue. Capital then flows into regions which experience its deficiency, and is further appreciated in its value. The capital is pulled by higher interest rates in peripheral regions with sufficient available labor force, and by low wages (assuming the existence of flexible wages and prices). The production factor – labor force, on the other hand, migrates from the peripherals into more developed regions, where the income rate is higher. Thus the mechanism of balancing the disparities among the production factors triggers the process of convergence of regions at the level of production per capita (Sloboda, 2006).

According to Eurostat, the definition of the indicator we are monitoring is as follows: Gross Domestic Product at market prices is the final result of the production activity of resident producer units, created during the current accounting period. "Regional GDP is calculated as a sum of values added by industries for each single region, and taxes on products less subsidies on products. For international comparison, the Regional Gross domestic product is expressed through parity of purchasing power. The purchasing power parity is calculated on the basis of prices and sales volumes of goods that are comparable and representative

for the countries which are included in comparison. The purchasing power parity eliminates the effects of different price levels between countries. GDP cannot be mistaken for the household income indicator" (Sloboda, 2012).

It is with no doubt that we fully realize the possible deficiencies of this indicator, e.g., the fact that it cannot grasp the processes of grey and black economies, or the fact that it is dependent on prices, which may be significantly distorted due to bureaucracy or by lack of competition. Despite this, we do consider this indicator to be appropriate for the evaluation and analysis of inter-regional disparities, referring to its high acceptance by academic authorities, analysts, as well as the professional public.

3 METHODOLOGY AND RESEARCH OF THE β-CONVERGENCE

Despite the majority empirical studies of regional convergence drawing theoretical background from the neoclassical theory of growth, the individual studies differ in the concepts of convergence that they apply, as well as in the methodology of its assessment. The following three concepts of regional convergence are commonly used: σ-convergence, ß-convergence, and the convergence clubs. (Kováč et al., 2011) Within our research, we focus primarily on explaining and expressing the ß-convergence.

The neoclassical approach to investigating the presence or absence of convergence at the empirical level uses and tests so-called σ-convergence and ß-convergence hypotheses. The hypothesis of σ-convergence assumes a decrease in dispersion of real income per capita throughout the regions in time. The hypothesis of ß-convergence identifies a negative relation between the growth rate in income per capita in time, and the initial level of income per capita throughout regions. (Soukiazis, 2000)

β-Convergence is understood as a process in which the growth rate of a poorer region is higher than the growth rate of a more affluent region, i.e., the poorer region "catches up" with the more affluent one in the income level parameter, or the GDP, per capita. It expresses a negative relation between the growth rate of GDP per capita in time and the initial level of GDP per capita throughout economies. The concept of β-convergence is directly related to the neoclassical theory of growth, which states that one of the key prerequisites is the production factors, mainly capital, which are subject to the law of diminishing returns. With regard to the above, the process of growth should lead the economies into a long-term stabilized state, characterized by the growth rate that is only dependable on the (exogenous) rate of technological development and growth rate of the labor force. Diminishing return suggests that the growth rate in poorer economies should be higher, and the GDP per capita should balance up with the GDP per capita of more affluent economies (Monfort & Nicolini, 2008). The methodology used to assess the β-convergence was introduced by Barro and Sala-i-Martin.

In our analysis, we will use the GDP per capita indicators expressed through parity of purchasing power. The presence (occurrence) of β-convergence is verified by regression analysis that estimates the growth of a selected indicator (in our case it is GPD per capita) within a specific time period in relation to the initial level (value) of this indicator. Within the neoclassical model, a temporary growth may be approximated by applying the following formula:

$$\frac{1}{T} \cdot \ln\left(\frac{y_{it}}{y_{i,t-T}}\right) = x_i^* + \frac{1}{T} \cdot \ln\left(\frac{\hat{y}_i^*}{\hat{y}_{i,t-T}}\right) \cdot \left(1 - e^{-\beta T}\right) + u_{it} \quad (2)$$

where i indexes the economy (country, region); t indexes time; y_{it} is GDP per capita in economy i in time t; $y_{i,t-T}$ is GPD per capita in economy i in time t–T; T is the period through which the data is observed; x_i^* is the value of steady-state growth rate per capita (corresponding to exogenous, labor-augmenting technological progress in the standard model); y_{it} refers to GDP adjusted for the effect of technological progress; y_i^* is the value of steady-state GDP adjusted for effect of technological progress; the coefficient β is a rate of convergence; and u_{it} expresses a random component (error term).

The coefficient of convergence β indicates the rate at which y_{it} approaches y_i^*, i.e., at which the economies approach the steady state. (Barro & Sala-i-Martin, 1991)

Where all economies converge to the same steady state, e.g., by achieving the same GDP per capita or the same growth rate in the long term, it stands that β-convergence is absolute. Convergence to the same steady state requires that economies do not differ in technological development levels, investment rates, savings rates, tax rate, or other structures. It can thus be concluded that unconditional (absolute) convergence occurs more between the regions of the same country, which tend to have a higher mutual level of homogeneity, higher mobility factor, similar technologies, as well as similar administrative and legal systems.

The main difference between β-convergence and σ-convergence can be illustrated in using them to search for answers to two different questions. If we are interested in how fast and at which rate the GDP per capita of a certain economy has a chance to catch up with the average GDP per capita throughout economies in a researched sample, then it is highly appropriate to use the concept of β-convergence. If, however, we wish to investigate the behavior of GDP per capita distribution in the past, or how it will develop in the future, the σ-convergence appears to be a more relevant concept. (Barro & Sala-i-Martin, 1991)

4 THE ANALYSIS OF β-CONVERGENCE ON AN EXAMPLE OF NUTS2 REGIONS OF THE EU

The data related to GDP per capita, expressed as a parity of purchasing power, were obtained from a web application of EUROSTAT – the European Statistical Office. The data that were available for us to process and analyze concerned the given the macro-economic aggregate formed by the individual regions of the EU member states, and were for the years 2000–2019. Therefore, in our research, we focused on this particular 20-year time period. The source statistical data are available at the EUROSTAT website.

The inability to obtain data regarding the selected indicator from France in the time period between 2000 and 2014 forced us to disregard this member country, since the data of the 2015–2019 period would not be considered sufficient for the purposes of our analysis. With regard to the economic development rate of France and its regions, we presume to state that in case the given data had been available, including this member country to the analysis would have undoubtedly contributed to a significantly stronger divergence than the one we calculated without them.

After disregarding France, the remaining statistical data were subjected to β-convergence. For a more thorough understanding, the outcomes of the regression analysis are presented in Graph 1.

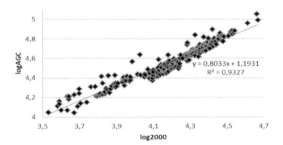

Graph 1. Graphical interpretation of β-convergence in the time period between 2000–2019.
Source: https://ec.europa.eu/eurostat/web/main/data/database. [NAMA_10R_2GDP__custom_667100]
Log2000 = logarithm of the GDP in the year 2000
LogAGC = logarithm of the GDP average growth coefficient

Graph 1 presents 262 points, which represent 262 analyzed regions of the EU member states at the end of 2019, while it expresses statistical dependence of two variables. The x-axis shows logarithmic data regarding the level of GDP per capita in the individual regions, in the baseline year 2000. The y-axis shows logarithmic data of the average growth coefficient for the years 2000–2019, the same for all analyzed EU regions.

We also equipped the graph with a trend line, as well as its equation, and the R^2 value. The equation of the trend line suggests a positive value k = 0.8033, while at the same time, the growing tendency of the line is obvious from the graph. This proves divergence, i.e., a year-on-year deepening of inter-regional disparities among the individual regions in the years 2000–2019 considering the GDP per capita expressed in the parity of purchasing power. The steeper the trend line grows, the more significant the divergence is, and vice versa.

In order to explain the value of the R^2 equation, we wish to point out here that this data conveys how "accurately" the trend line intersects the individual points of Graph 1, or, how reliable the given trend line is. In an ideal (theoretical) case, the maximum value R^2 may reach 1. However, from the statistical point of view, all values approximating the value 1 are considered relevant. Since in our case the value $R^2 = 0.9327$, or 93.27%, respectively, the trend line, and analogically, the development of inter-regional disparities, may be considered statistically significant and reliable. We may, therefore, claim that trend of development of inter-regional disparities from the GDP per capita point of view is 93% reliable (in parity or purchasing power). The economies of the individual NUTS 2 regions of the EU member states in the analyzed time period diverge from each other, i.e., they grow apart from each other in time, and in a relatively dynamic manner (with regard to the trend line development).

5 CONCLUSION

Despite the fact that the concept of β-convergence is based on a relatively simple regression analysis, it is generally accepted and considered to be relevant, that being not only from the regional science point of view.

In the limited space of our paper, we have attempted to point out two significant facts, the former being the non-optimal functioning of the common regional (cohesive) policy of the European Union, the latter being the fact that the individual regions of the NUTS 2 level economically diverge from each other despite the existence and the implementation of the common regional policy that was applied as early as in the middle of the 20th century.

Regions are, that is to say, the priority of the EU and those member states which the cohesive assistance is aiming at. We are aware that convergence (and divergence, respectively) are affected by multiple factors, not only the regional policy itself. Even though the available data and their development prove that the mechanisms are not optimally set, the development standards of the individual member states and their regions cannot be simplified by prioritizing one

single indicator (GDP per capita), but should rather be viewed in the context of inter-regional disparities while considering different aspects, that is not only the economic ones, but also the social, environmental, and other factors.

REFERENCES

Barro, R.J., & Sala-I-Martin, X. 1991. *Economic Growth and Convergence across the United States.* Cambridge, Mass.: National Bureau of Economic Research, Brookings Papers on Economic Activity, no. 1: 107–182. Retrieved on 12.02.2021 from http://www.nber.org/papers/w3419

Barančok, M. et al. 2006. Convergence of the Slovak economy to advanced economies – status, risks and scenarios. *Bratislava (Slovakia): Institute of Financial Policy, Ministry of Finance*: 42 p. Retrieved on 10.01.2021 from http://www.finance.gov.sk/Default.aspx?CatID=5589

Retrieved on 10.02.2021 from https://ec.europa.eu/eurostat/web/main/data/database. [NAMA_10R_2GDP__custom_667100]

Greene, W. 2003. *Econometric Analysis.* 5th Edition, Prentice Hall.

Kováč, U. et al. 2011. Methodological approaches to measuring convergence. *Forecasting Papers*, 3 (5): 395–407. Retrieved on 26.02.2021 from http://www.aae.wisc.edu/coxhead/courses/731/pdf/DurlaufJohnson%20XC%20growth%201995.pdf

Monfort, P. & Nicolini, R. 2000. Regional convergence and international integration. *Journal of Urban Economics*, 48 (2): 286–306. Retrieved on 24.02.2021 from https://dx.doi.org/10.1006/juec.1999.2167

Sloboda. D. 2006. Slovakia and regional differences: Theories, regions, indicators, methods. *Bratislava: M. R. Štefánik Conservative Institute*. Retrieved on 26.01.2021 from http://www.konzervativizmus.sk/upload/pdf/Slovensko_a_regionalne_rozdiely.pdf

Sloboda, D. 2012. Eurofunds and regional disparities in the European Union. *Bratislava: M. R. Štefánik Conservative Institute*. Retrieved on 06.01.2021 from http://www.konzervativizmus.sk/article.php?4721

Soukiazis, E. 2000. What we have learnt about convergence in Europe? Some theoretical and empirical considerations. In Discussion paper no. 2. *CEUNEU-ROP, Faculty of Economics, University of Coimbra, Portugal 2000*. Retrieved on 12.01.2021 from http://www4.fe.uc.pt/ceue/working_papers/iconv.pdf

Tvrdoň, J. et al 1995. *Regional development.* Bratislava: Economist.

Viturka, M. 2010. Regional disparities and their evaluation in the context of regional policy. *Geography-proceedings of the Czech Geographical Society*. 115 (2): 131–143. Retrieved on 15.12.2020 from http://geography.cz/sbornik/wp-content/uploads/2009/03/gcgs022010_viturka.pdf

Economic and Business Management – Huang & Zhang (Eds)
© 2022 Copyright the Author(s), ISBN: 978-1-032-06754-4

Research on the influence of R&D on firm performance from the perspective of executive equity incentive

Chan Lyu, Kangde Guo & Hongyan Wang
School of Business, Macau University of Science and Technology, Macau, China

ABSTRACT: By analyzing the data of all listed companies with A shares in China from 2007 to 2019, this paper discusses the relationship between R&D investment and enterprise performance by establishing a research model. This paper also adds the executive equity incentive as one of the factors affecting its relationship. According to the data of this paper, the greater the R&D investment, the better the enterprise performance. As for the influence factor of executive equity incentive, its influence on enterprises is a positive regulatory effect. It can help enterprises to improve the impact of R&D investment on corporate performance.

1 INTRODUCTION

At present, China is carrying out the policy of "innovative country." The current development strategy of the country is mainly to ensure the stable growth of the economy to adjust the national industrial structure chain at the same time, and through various means to promote the rapid development of the economy, to achieve the rapid recovery of our economy and continue to improve. According to the data published on the China Science and Technology Statistics Network and the website of the National Bureau of Statistics, the growth rate of investment in scientific research and innovation funds in the whole country began to increase greatly from 2013, reflecting the great importance that the country attaches to technology research and development, and China has also been promoted to the second largest R&D investment country in the world, and maintained the growth rate of R&D investment at about 10%. (China Science and Technology Statistics Network and website of National Bureau of Statistics). Thus, more and more enterprises realize the importance of technological innovation to the development of enterprises. R&D is an important way to realize the technological development of enterprises. Solow (1957) established a basic research method of the impact of R&D activities on economic growth. He believes that R&D activities affect economic growth in two ways. The first way is called embodied technological progress, and the second way is called non-embodimental technological progress.

In the study of improving the relationship between R&D investment and performance, scholars focus on the supervision mechanism, and rarely discuss the relationship between them from the perspective of executive mechanism, so the research in this area is not very deep. On the basis of exploring the influence of R&D investment on enterprise performance, this paper introduces executive equity incentive as a regulatory variable and puts it into a structural framework. The aim is to improve the research content of innovation on enterprise performance, expand the theoretical scope, and provide new empirical verification and support.

It is more helpful for managers to clearly realize the influence of R&D activities on performance in different periods, so as to allocate resources more reasonably and to promote the improvement of enterprise performance.

2 LITERATURE REVIEW AND HYPOTHESIS DEVELOPMENT

R&D investment is becoming more and more important to maintain the competitive advantage of enterprises. At the same time, R&D investment is the key and effective way for enterprises to reduce production costs and introduce new products. It can help enterprises to seek longer-term development in fierce market competition. R&D investment can not only produce new knowledge and expand the basic cognitive scope of enterprises, but also effectively improve the ability of enterprises to absorb and integrate existing knowledge, both of which will enhance the performance level of enterprises. Qi et al. (2016) and Wang and Zhu (2018) believe that through the development of innovative activities, enterprises can make better use of the results formed by R&D investment, thus becoming leaders in the field of technology.

However, R&D needs a long period and has high risk. It is also affected by technological development and market development. At the same time, the ability and level of R&D technicians, the effectiveness and technical expectation of R&D organization, and the

DOI 10.1201/9781003203704-5

investment and schedule of R&D planning affect the efficiency of R&D activities to some extent, which makes the economic benefits of R&D activities take a certain time to attain. Hu and Jefferson (2004), Li and Zhang (2013), and Xue and Li (2015) believe that from the initial R&D funds to develop new products and new processes onto the market, and bring profits to enterprises takes time.

H1: R&D investment has a positive lag effect on enterprise performance.

O'Sullivan and Torrens (2001) put forward the first organizational control theory. They state that the effective integration and allocation of enterprise resources can support the internal innovation of enterprises, and the rational allocation of control resources is also an important means to realize the high efficiency governance of enterprises. By designing reasonable management agreements, especially for executives with innovative investment strategies, the goal of more rational and effective allocation of resources can be achieved. Bushee (1998) thinks executives have actual control in business activities. As an agent, the attitude to the investment activities of enterprises is very critical. Therefore, equity incentive can not only restrain management from taking decisions that are contrary to the interests of shareholders, but also can actively mobilize the enthusiasm of executives, and even arouse the "master" consciousness of executives. The interests and goals of executives and shareholders are tied together. At the same time, because R&D activities have the characteristics of uncertain return, large amount of resource input, long period and so on, the attitude of executives towards them will also tend to be conservative, thus reducing the capital investment of enterprises and seeking lowrisk performance development level. At this time, a reasonable and effective equity incentive mechanism can urge executives to make more R&D investment plans, allocate more innovative resources and improve the efficiency of innovative investment in order to obtain greater and longer-term benefits and thus improve the relationship between R&D investment and corporate performance. Based on the above analysis, the following assumptions are proposed:

H2: executive equity incentive plays a positive role in the impact of R&D investment on corporate performance.

3 RESEARCH DESIGN

3.1 Measurement of variables

ROA is a wider definition, including the operation and profitability of all assets, and no distinction between the sources of funds. Hence, by considering the stability and comprehensiveness of the measurement index, this paper selects ROA as the defining index of enterprise performance by citing Dai and Li as (2013), Wang and Zhu (2018), etc.

The explanatory variable of this paper is R&D investment. Because different enterprise size will have an impact on the R&D investment of the enterprise, the amount of R&D investment will be different, so the direct use of R&D investment amount will lead to a lack of comparability. Accordingly, in order to meet the comparable needs among enterprises, this paper uses the R&D investment of enterprises through the index of R&D input/total assets (RD), etc.

This paper mainly takes the equity incentive of senior executives as the adjustment variable of this paper. Through this long-term incentive mechanism, it is used to investigate the incentive mode of executives and the relationship between R&D investment and enterprise performance. The equity incentive mode of enterprises mainly considers the share of open executive ownership (SP).

To better test the hypothesis, referred to by Alam et al. (2019) and Böckel et al. (2020), that corporate performance is affected by many factors, this paper uses company size (Size), operating income growth rate (Growth), asset-liability ratio (Lev), total asset turnover rate (TAT), top ten shareholder shareholding ratio (Top), and enterprise age (Age) as control variables.

3.2 Empirical model

Design model for validation assumptions:

$$\begin{aligned} ROA_{i,t} = {} & \beta_0 + \beta_1 RD_{i,t-j} + \beta_2 Size_{i,t} \\ & + \beta_3 Growth_{i,t} + \beta_4 Lev_{i,t} + \beta_5 TAT_{i,t} \\ & + \beta_6 Top_{i,t} + \beta_7 Age_{i,t} + \Sigma Industry \\ & + \Sigma Year + \varepsilon_{i,t} \end{aligned}$$

$$\begin{aligned} ROA_{i,t} = {} & \beta_0 + \beta_1 RD_{i,t-j} + \beta_2 SP_{i,t} + \beta_3 SP_{i,t} \\ & \times RD_{i,t-j} + \beta_4 Size_{i,t} + \beta_5 Growth_{i,t} \\ & + \beta_6 Lev_{i,t} + \beta_7 TAT_{i,t} + \beta_8 Top_{i,t} \\ & + \beta_9 Age_{i,t} + \Sigma Industry \\ & + \Sigma Year + \varepsilon_{i,t} \end{aligned}$$

4 SAMPLE SELECTION AND DESCRIPTIVE STATISTICS

4.1 Sample selection

Financial data of A stock listed companies from 2007 to 2019 are used as the research sample. Before 2007, China's listed companies rarely disclosed data on R&D investment. Through the revision of the Enterprise Accounting Standards in 2007, China's listed companies began to disclose relevant data. At the same time, Cathay Pacific R&D investment data from 2007 began to be gathered. In this paper, the relevant enterprise data collected have been effectively screened: (1) all ST enterprise data in the data were deleted to avoid the influence of extreme values on the result; (2) all financial enterprise data were removed from the data; (3) other enterprises with incomplete data were excluded from the sample; (4) enterprises that do not carry out R&D investment and enterprises that do not publicly disclose R&D investment were deleted; (5) considering the stability of the whole sample, the sample data were treated with bilateral 1% tail shrinkage. After lagging screening, 15116 sample data were selected. With the exception of enterprise age (Age) data, the other variables were collected from the CSMAR database (https://www.gtarsc.com) and Wind databases (https://www.wind.com.cn).

4.2 Descriptive statistical

Table 1 shows the analytical results of descriptive statistics in this paper. From Table 1, the average return on total assets is 0.045, Relative to the maximum of 0.214, the difference between the two is obvious. From the overall R&D investment, the maximum value is 0.098 and the minimum value tends to be 0. This shows that the gap between different enterprises is very large. The average R&D investment of 0.022 is far from the maximum of 0.098. The overall level of R&D investment needs to be further improved. But the standard deviation is 0.018, which reflects that the level of R&D investment of listed companies is in a relatively stable state. In the context of executive equity incentives, the minimum value of executive equity incentive is 0, the maximum is 0.631, which shows that the degree of equity incentive of listed companies is small.

Table 1. The analytical results of descriptive statistics.

	N	Mean	Std. Dev.	Min	Max
ROA	15116	0.045	0.060	−0.218	0.214
RD	15116	0.022	0.018	0	0.098
SP	15116	0.087	0.148	0	0.621
Size	15116	22.119	1.242	20.009	26.063
Growth	15116	0.166	0.318	−0.447	1.711
Lev	15116	0.397	0.194	0.052	0.853
TAT	15116	0.613	0.368	0.113	2.283
Top	15116	0.591	0.143	0.254	0.901

4.3 Correlation

In this paper, before the regression analysis, person correlation analysis is used to test the correlation between the variables, and investigate the possible multicollinearity problems, so as to provide a guarantee for the accuracy and reliability of the next regression analysis results.

5 MULTIPLE REGRESSION RESULTS

5.1 Regression results

The results shown in Table 2 are as follows: the model (1) used in this paper is to discuss the impact of the change of R&D investment (RD) on the performance level (ROA) of enterprises. The results show, the impact of lagging R&D investment on corporate

Table 2. Regression results.

	ROA	ROA
RDi,t-1	0.423***	0.413***
	(16.630)	(16.190)
SP		0.009***
		(2.787)
RDi,t-1*SP		0.367**
		(2.479)
Size	0.014***	0.014***
	(29.414)	(29.576)
Growth	0.045***	0.045***
	(35.058)	(34.848)
Lev	−0.155***	−0.155***
	(−58.971)	(−58.908)
TAT	0.028***	0.028***
	(23.040)	(23.258)
Top	0.042***	0.041***
	(12.574)	(12.308)
Age	−0.006***	−0.005***
	(−7.501)	(−6.501)
Constant	−0.238***	−0.241***
	(−21.767)	(−21.945)
Year	Yes	Yes
Industry	Yes	Yes
Observations	15116	15116
R-squared	0.327	0.328

t-statistics in parentheses
*** p < 0.01, ** p < 0.05, * p < 0.1

performance is 1%, and the correlation coefficient between the two is 0.423. This coefficient indicates that, by increasing R&D investment in innovation activities, it can effectively improve the performance level of enterprises. As a result, the assumptions made in this paper are that H1 is valid. Compared to model (1), model (2) mainly discusses whether executive equity incentive can positively improve the influence of R&D investment on enterprise performance. The empirical data show that, at a 5% level, the coefficient is 0.367, which is significant. This coefficient indicates that executive equity incentives can improve the impact of R&D investment on performance. As a result, the assumptions made in this paper are that H2 is valid.

5.2 Robustness test

In this paper, considering the influence of R&D investment on enterprise performance, there is usually lag, so this paper brings the data of R&D investment in the second phase into two models to test. In model (1), the influence of R&D investment in the second phase of lag on enterprise performance is consistent with the previous significant level, which is 1%, and the hypothesis H1 is tested. According to model (2), the interaction between R&D investment and equity incentive is significant at the level of positive 5%, and the coefficients are 0.401 respectively. The hypothesis H2 is tested.

6 CONCLUSIONS

Based on the research sample of A stock listed companies from 2007 to 2019, this paper focuses on how executive equity incentive affects the relationship between R&D investment and enterprise performance. Through regression analysis, the following conclusions are obtained:

China's A stock listed companies' R&D investment for corporate performance has a lagging impact. This paper uses R&D investment/final total assets (RD) as the index to define R&D investment, and uses total asset return (ROA) as the measure of enterprise performance level. An empirical test shows that lagging R&D investment can effectively promote the improvement of enterprise performance. Empirical research shows that executive equity incentive can effectively improve the impact of R&D investment on corporate performance.

REFERENCES

Böckel A, Hörisch J, Tenner I (2020) A systematic literature review of crowdfunding and sustainability: highlighting what really matters.

Bushee, B. J. (1998). The influence of institutional investors on myopic R&D investment behavior. *Accounting review*, 305–333.

Dai Xiaoyong, Cheng Liwei (2013) Research on the Threshold Effect of R&D Investment Intensity on Corporate Performance Research in Science of Science, (11): 1708–1716 (In Chinese).

Hu, A. G., & Jefferson, G. H. (2004). Returns to research and development in Chinese industry: Evidence from state-owned enterprises in Beijing. *China economic review*, 15(1), 86–107.

Li Lu, Zhang Wanting (2013) Research on the impact of R&D investment on the performance of Chinese manufacturing enterprises. *Technological progress and countermeasures*, 30(24): 80–85 (In Chinese).

M.S. Alam, M. Atif, C. Chien-Chi, U. Soytaş, Does corporate R&D investment affect firm environmental performance? *Evidence from G-6 countries Energy Economics*, 78(2019), pp.401–411.

O'sullivan, D., & Torrens, P. M. (2001). Cellular models of urban systems. Theory and practical issues on cellular automata, 108–116. *Springer, London.*

Wang Hanyu, Zhu Heping (2018) Research on the Relationship between R&D Investment and Manufacturing Enterprise Performance – Based on the Moderating Effect of Executive Incentives Finance and Accounting Communications, (17): 28–33 (In Chinese).

Xue Qiao, Li Gang (2015) The Impact of Growth Enterprise Market R&D Investment on Financial Performance: The Moderating Effect of Executive Incentives. *Finance and Accounting Monthly*, (32): 123–128 (In Chinese).

Economic and Business Management – Huang & Zhang (Eds)
© 2022 Copyright the Author(s), ISBN: 978-1-032-06754-4

Analyst attention and earning management

Jiamin Chen
School of Business, Macau University of Science and Technology, Macau, China

Huaxian Liang
School of Economics and Management, Hubei Polytechnic University, Wuchang, China

ABSTRACT: Under the continuous improvement of the governance environment, will the management really reduce earnings management? We selected Chinese A-share listed companies from 2010 to 2019 as the research samples. This paper explores the relationship between analyst attention and earnings management from the perspective of long-term equilibrium relationship. The empirical results show that when security analysts pay more attention to listed companies, enterprise managers will reduce the accrual earnings management. When the accrual earnings management loses its manipulable space under the analyst attention, the enterprise managers will manipulate profits through the way of real earnings management. This paper reveals the evolution mechanism between accrual earnings management and real earnings management under the influence of analysts' attention, which helps shareholders and potential investors identify the earnings management methods that managers may use.

Keywords: Long-term equilibrium relationship, Analyst attention, Accrual earnings management, Real earnings management

1 INTRODUCTION

Financial scandals have never been interrupted. Therefore, corporate governance and earnings management have always been one of the hot topics in the academia and business. As for earnings management research, there have been many literatures related to the definition, motivation, approach, and influencing factors of earnings management. However, a lot of scholars discuss the influencing factors of earnings management in the research literature from the perspective of governance environment, such as executive compensation, equity incentive, internal control mechanism, information transparency, and accounting information quality. This paper studies how analyst attention affects firms' earnings management behavior from the perspective of long-term equilibrium relationship. In recent years, security analysts have become an important role in the capital market. As an information intermediary, analyst is an important supervisory force in the capital market. Most scholars only focus on the relationship between analyst attention and accrual earnings management. It is generally believed that the more analysts pay attention to an enterprise, the more managers pay attention to the earning quality, which reduces the whitewash of operating profits. There is a lack of literature on the influence of analyst attention on real earnings management and on the influence of analyst

attention on the intrinsic relationship between accrual earnings management and real earnings management. Compared with accrual earnings management, real earnings management is more flexible and concealed. When an enterprise concerns about its operating conditions by analysts, its managers may not try to fundamentally improve the internal governance of the enterprise, but seek more hidden methods to replace accrual earnings management, such as the accounting policy selection, accounting method change, and accounting error correction. Therefore, this paper will elaborate on the influence path between analyst attention and earnings management in detail, aiming to solve two problems. The first problem is whether enterprises will reduce accrual earnings management when analysts' attention to enterprises increases. The second question is that if accrual earnings management is too easy to be found, will the managers of enterprises turn to real earnings management, which is a more covert means compared with accrual earnings management, to achieve its purpose?

This paper mainly studies the influence path of analyst attention on earnings management. The full text is divided into six sections. The first section is the introduction; the second section is the literature review; the third section is the research hypothesis; the fourth section is the research design; the fifth section is the empirical analysis; the sixth section is the conclusion.

DOI 10.1201/9781003203704-6

2 LITERATURE REVIEW

2.1 Research on analyst attention and accrual earnings management

As an information intermediary and an important external supervisor between enterprises, shareholders, and small- and medium investors from the capital market, analysts obtain relevant information about the enterprises through diversified channels, and selectively organize and analyze information related to the company based on their professional knowledge, sensitivity to the industry, and experience in the industry. Then they publish research and analysis reports publicly. Thus, they effectively alleviate the problem of information asymmetry caused by the agency problem and protect the interests of investors (especially small- and medium-sized investors) to a certain extent (Fang Junxiong, 2007; Jensen & Meckling, 1976; Pan Yue, Dai Yiyi, & Lin Chaoqun, 2011). At present, domestic and foreign scholars mainly hold two views on the influence mechanism of analyst attention and tracking on earnings management of enterprises, that is, the supervision and pressure effect of analyst attention on earnings management (Wang Shuangjin & Chang Juan, 2020).

Analyst attention has a supervisory effect on the earnings management behavior of the enterprise. The supervisory role of securities analysts in a mature capital market has been widely recognized due to their professionalism, ability to collect information and data, keen insight into the industry, and long-term work experience in following and tracking listed companies (Kryazeva, 2007; Yu Zhongbo, Ye Qiongyan & Tian Gaoliang, 2011; Zhao Yujie, 2013). Gilson, Healy, Noe, and Palepu (2001) believed that analysts could directly or indirectly restrain the improper behavior of enterprise managers, improve the information transparency, and effectively alleviate the information asymmetry problem. Chen, Harford, and Lin (2015) found that when the number of analyst tracking decreased due to the merger of securities firms, earnings management activities of enterprises would increase, which proved that analysts have the role of external supervision. When examining the influence of analyst attention on earnings management, the supervisory effect of analysts is mainly reflected in the accrual earnings management of enterprises. Scholars from home and abroad (Keating, 2000; Tong Dalong & Chen Jiyun 2005) have noticed that managers from listed enterprises utilize the flexible selection of accounting principles, changes in accounting methods, and subjectivity of accounting estimates to implement the manipulation of accrued profits, such as changing the recognition period of income or expense and changing the method of depreciation. Yu (2008) concluded that after solving the endogenous problems between analyst attention and earnings management, the fewer analysts there are, the more accrual earnings management managers would carry out, which fully demonstrates that analysts in the American capital market have a deterrent effect on corporate managers. Li Chuntao, Song Min and Zhang Xuan (2014) pointed out that analysts could effectively restrain the earnings management behavior of leaders in well-known enterprises and reduce the manipulation of accrual earnings management by tracking Chinese listed enterprises. Irani and Oesch (2016) also reached the same conclusion.

As for the influence of analyst attention to accrual earnings management, there are not exactly the same conclusions in previous studies. For example, He Xuefeng, Zhang Long and Wang You (2017) proved that accrual earnings management behavior would increase in the case of increasing analyst attention. Zhao Zaifang (2020) proved an inverted U-shaped relationship between analyst attention and accrual earnings management.

2.2 Research on analyst attention and real earnings management

Domestic and foreign scholars believe that analyst attention has a pressure effect on the earnings management behavior of enterprises. Wiersema and Zhang (2011) and Hazarika, Karpoff, and Nahata (2012) mentioned in their studies that as agents, enterprise managers need to assume certain responsibilities for the earnings level of the enterprise. Managers face pressure to cut pay or be fired if the company's reported earnings fall short of analysts' forecasts. In order to alleviate such pressure and maintain a reputation, managers tend to pay more attention to the market situation and take into account analysts' earnings forecasts to maximize their own interests rather than the interests of shareholders (Graham, Harvey, & Rajgopal, 2005). Li Chuntao et al. (2014) show that if managers fail to achieve analysts' expected profits, stock prices may fall. In order to avoid drastic fluctuations in stock prices, managers will choose to adjust the profits of enterprises according to the earnings level predicted by analysts as the target. Li Chuntao et al. (2014) stated that if managers fail to meet analysts' expected profits, stock prices may fall. In order to avoid drastic fluctuations in the stock market, managers will choose to adjust the profits of enterprises according to the earnings level predicted by analysts as the target. Levitt (1998) mentioned that it is difficult for professional managers to achieve the expected profit of analysts through the improvement of management level, so they have to work hard on earnings management. Therefore, managers' behavior of earnings management is affected by analysts' forecast reports to a certain extent. The pressure effect of analysts is mainly reflected in its promoting effect on real activity earnings management. Graham et al. (2005) adopted the form of questionnaire survey and found that in order to achieve the performance level predicted by analysts, financial managers would also dress up profits through changes in actual business activities. Li Chuntao et al. (2016) believe that managers will carry out more real earnings management activities with the increasing analyst attention in the case of poor business performance and accrual earnings management failing to achieve the purpose of earning under external supervision. Irani and Oesch (2016) show that although analyst attention can reduce accrual earnings management activities, it can promote real earnings management activities. He an Tian (2013) believe that due to the attention of analysts and the pressure to achieve the expected earnings level, managers will strengthen the application of real earnings management while reducing accrual earnings management. Therefore, it leads managers to change from accrual earnings management to real earnings management, and real earnings management is destructive to enterprises. Cohen, Dey, and Lys (2008) pointed out that Sarbanes-Oxley Act strengthened the external supervision of the American capital market, and corporate managers more often chose real earnings management, which is a more covert means, to replace accrual earnings management. Danmeng Li, Jianfang Ye, and Minhui Ye (2015) said that analysts will publish the information of listed companies. If the earnings management behavior of managers is discovered by investors in the capital market, it will cause volatility in the stock price. Therefore, as analysts pay more attention to enterprises, managers tend to choose more covert earnings management means, namely real earnings management. Ye Chengang and Liu Meng (2018) reached a similar conclusion. They believe that the number of analysts is negatively correlated with the accrual earnings management, but positively correlated with the real earnings management.

There are different conclusions about the relationship between analyst attention and real earnings management in the previous research literature. He Xuefeng et al. (2017) show that the real earnings management behavior will decrease in the case of increasing analyst attention. According to the research of Rujun Xu (2019), analysts are concerned about the supervisory effect on accrual and real earnings management. Wang Shuangjin and Chang Juan (2020) believe that analysts' attention to accrual earnings management and real earnings management has a negative effect, and the negative effect on real earnings management is stronger. Zhao Zaifang (2020) proved a positive U-shaped relationship between analyst attention and real earnings management.

To sum up, although predecessors have done a lot of studies on earnings management, there is still no unified conclusion about the influence of analyst attention on accrual earnings management and real earnings management. Is the analyst's attention a restraining or promoting effect on earnings management and is there a substitution or complementary effect between accrual earnings management and real earnings management? What is the influence mechanism of the analyst's attention on the two types of earnings management? This paper tries to solve the above problems.

3 RESEARCH HYPOTHESIS

Securities analysts play an important role in external supervision as well as an information intermediary between enterprises and investors in the capital market (Li Xiaoling & Liu Zhongyan, 2014; Jensen & Meckling, 1976). Analysts analyze, track, and forecast the financial information and stock prices of listed companies by virtue of their own professional qualities, diversified information channels and sources, and strong ability of information collation and analysis. In this way, the information asymmetry between enterprises and external investors can be reduced, and the information related to the intrinsic value of stocks can be provided to investors in the capital market to help investors effectively invest. There are two ways for managers to carry out earnings management: one is accrual earnings management, which adjusts the ending profit mainly through flexible choice of accounting principles, change of balance sheet estimates and accounting methods, correct accounting errors, and other channels. This way only changes the accrued profit of the enterprise, but did not change its cash flow. The second is real earnings management, which manages earnings by changing the strategy of operating activities, so that the business activities of the enterprise deviate from the normal trajectory, which not only changes the cash flow of the enterprise, but also damages the intrinsic value of the enterprise, and has a bad impact on the future development of the enterprise (Wang Liangcheng, 2014). Compared with real earnings management, accrual earnings management is easier to be exposed by external supervision mechanism. Many scholars have found that the attention and tracking of analysts can detect managers' fraudulent behaviors and can also make managers significantly reduce accrual earnings management behaviors, which proves the supervisory effect of analysts on enterprise managers (Knyazeva, 2007; Yu, 2008). Based on this analysis, this paper proposes H1:

H1: The more analysts pay attention to the enterprise, the less accrual earnings management of the enterprise.

In addition to the supervision effect, analysts also have a pressure effect on enterprise managers (Levitt, 1998). Analysts can significantly reduce the accrual earnings management behavior of enterprise managers, so managers need to seek other ways to relieve the pressure brought by the market value of the company, personal reputation, and performance betting. Under the attention and supervision of analysts, there are only two ways for managers to do next, one is to improve earnings quality by improving internal governance and strengthening internal control, or to seek another way of earnings management that is not so easy to be discovered by analysts. Cohen et al. (2008) pointed out that with the in-depth implementation of Sarbanes-Oxley Act, the external regulatory mode in the United States tended to be solidified, and the real earnings management behavior of enterprise managers increased significantly. Chi, Lisic, and Pevzner (2011) found that when external auditors are more professional and rigorous in the audit process, managers prefer real earnings management. Li Zengfu, Dong Zhiqiang and Lian Yujun (2011) also pointed out that real earnings management was more favored by the management because of its concealment.

Based on the above analysis, this paper proposes H2.

H2: The more analysts pay attention to the enterprise, the more real earnings management of the enterprise.

4 RESEARCH DESIGN

4.1 *Sample selection and data sources*

We select Chinese A-share listed companies from 2010 to 2019 as research samples. The data of listed companies are processed as follows: (1) exclude ST or *ST enterprises; (2) the listed companies in the financial industry from the 2012 version of the CSRC (Securities Supervision Commission) industry classification are excluded, because the financial industry has its special nature; (3) excluding the newly listed, delisted, or suspended listed enterprises in that year; (4) eliminate observation values with missing data. In this paper, 14,654 valid samples were obtained. In addition, we winsorized all continuous variables on the 1% and 99% quantiles to offset the effect of extreme values. All the data were obtained from CSMAR database. Stata 16.0 software is used for empirical analysis.

4.2 *Variable definition and measurement*

4.2.1 *Dependent variable*
(1) Accrual earnings management (ABS_DA$_{i,t}$)

There are many models for measuring accrual earnings management. Relevant literature shows that the modified Jones model has the best effect on measuring accrual earnings management (Wang Liangcheng, 2014; Wang Longmei et al., 2021; Wang Shuangjin & Chang Juan, 2020). In this paper, the modified Jones model is selected to calculate accrual earnings management. First, OLS regression was conducted for data from different industries and years according to Equation (1). Second, the coefficients α_1, α_2, and α_3 obtained from Equation (1) are substituted into Equation (2), respectively, to obtain the non-manipulable accrual profit NDA$_{i,t}$. Finally, NDA$_{i,t}$ is substituted into Equation (3) to obtain manipulable accrual profit DA$_{i,t}$.

$$\frac{TA_{i,t}}{A_{i,t-1}} = \alpha_1 \times \frac{1}{A_{i,t-1}} + \alpha_2 \times \frac{\Delta REV_{i,t}}{A_{i,t-1}} + \alpha_3$$
$$\times \frac{PPE_{i,t}}{A_{i,t-1}} + \varepsilon_{i,t} \quad (1)$$

$$NDA_{i,t} = \alpha_1 \times \frac{1}{A_{i,t-1}} + \alpha_2 \times \frac{\Delta REV_{i,t} - \Delta REC_{i,t}}{A_{i,t-1}}$$
$$+ \alpha_3 \times \frac{PPE_{i,t}}{A_{i,t-1}} \quad (2)$$

$$DA_{i,t} = \frac{TA_{i,t}}{A_{i,t}} - NDA_{i,t} \quad (3)$$

wherein TA$_{i,t}$ is the total accrued profit after the net profit of the enterprise minus the net cash flow generated by operating activities; NDA$_{i,t}$ is the non-manipulable accrual profit; DA$_{i,t}$ is the manipulable accrued profit, namely, accrual earnings management, equal to total accrued profit minus non-manipulable accrued profit. This paper focuses on the quantity of earnings management rather than the direction of earnings management (upward or downward earnings management). Therefore, the absolute value of manipulable accruals is taken to measure the accrual earnings management, which is represented by the symbol ABS_DA$_{i,t}$. The higher the absolute value, the more accrual earnings management is performed.

(2) Real earnings management (ABS_REM$_{i,t}$)

This paper adopts the research method of Roychowdhury (2006) to measure real earnings management. Enterprise managers may carry out real earnings management in one or more ways. When managers increase profits through production control, sales control and expense control at the same time, abnormal production cost will increase, but abnormal operating activity cash flow and abnormal discretionary expense R_disexp$_{i,t}$ will decrease. Therefore, these three indicators cannot be directly added up as the total real earnings management level. By referring to previous literature (e.g., Cohen et al., 2008; Zang, 2012), we combined the three indicators into a total indicator to measure the total real earnings management level, namely Equation (7). The formula is as follows:

$$\frac{PROD_{i,t}}{A_{i,t-1}} = \beta_1 \times \frac{1}{A_{i,t-1}} + \beta_2 \times \frac{REV_{i,t}}{A_{i,t-1}} + \beta_3$$
$$\times \frac{\Delta REV_{i,t}}{A_{i,t-1}} + \beta_4 \times \frac{\Delta REV_{i,t-1}}{A_{i,t-1}} + \varepsilon_{i,t} \quad (4)$$

where PROD$_{i,t}$ is the production cost and $\varepsilon_{i,t}$ is the abnormal production cost, namely R_PROXY$_{i,t}$.

$$\frac{CFO_{i,t}}{A_{i,t-1}} = \beta_1 \times \frac{1}{A_{i,t-1}} + \beta_2 \times \frac{REV_{i,t}}{A_{i,t-1}} + \beta_3$$
$$\times \frac{\Delta REV_{i,t}}{A_{i,t-1}} + \varepsilon_{i,t} \quad (5)$$

where CFO$_{i,t}$ is the net cash flow of operating activities and $\varepsilon_{i,t}$ is the cash flow of abnormal operating activities, namely R_CFO$_{i,t}$.

$$\frac{DISEXP_{i,t}}{A_{i,t-1}} = \beta_1 \times \frac{1}{A_{i,t-1}} + \beta_2 \times \frac{REV_{i,t-1}}{A_{i,t-1}} + \varepsilon_{i,t} \quad (6)$$

where DISEXP$_{i,t}$ is the discretionary cost and $\varepsilon_{i,t}$ is the abnormal discretionary cost, namely R_DISEXP$_{i,t}$.

$$REM_{i,t} = R\_PROXY_{i,t} - R\_CFO_{i,t} - R\_DISEXP_{i,t} \qquad (7)$$

REM$_{i,t}$ is for real earnings management. This paper only studies the scale of earnings management. Therefore, the absolute value of REM$_{i,t}$ (namely ABS_REM$_{i,t}$) is taken to measure the real earnings management. The greater the absolute value, the more real earnings management is carried out.

4.2.2 *Independent variables*

The independent variable is analyst attention. Analyst attention is measured by the number of analyst teams that have followed or analyzed public companies in a given year. In line with Li et al. (2016), analyst attention is measured by the logarithm of the number of analysts plus one.

4.2.3 *Control variable*

Based on the research literature of previous scholars (for example, Li Chuntao et al., 2016; Su Chunjiang, 2013), this paper controls the following seven variables that affect earnings management results. They are asset–liability rate, growth rate, big four accounting firms, nature of property rights, shareholding rate of non-controlling shareholders, shareholding rate of senior management, and independent director. In addition, this article sets industry and year as dummy variables. Table 1 shows the variable definition.

4.3 *The empirical model*

This paper builds a multiple linear regression model to test the relationship between analyst attention and the two types of earnings management, as shown below:

We propose model (1) to verify H1:

$$ABS\_DA_{i,t} = \beta_0 + \beta_1 Analyst_{i,t} + \Sigma \beta_m Control_{i,t} + Ind + Year + \varepsilon_{i,t} \qquad (1)$$

We propose model (2) to verify H2:

$$ABS\_REM_{i,t} = \beta_0 + \beta_1 Analyst_{i,t} + \Sigma \beta_m Control_{i,t} + Ind + Year + \varepsilon_{i,t} \qquad (2)$$

where i and t respectively represent the enterprise and the year. ABS_DA$_{i,t}$ represents accrual earnings management. ABS_REM$_{i,t}$ represents real earnings management. Analyst$_{i,t}$ represents analyst attention. $\sum \beta_m Control_{i,t}$ represents control variables, including asset–liability rate (LEV), growth rate (Growth), big four accounting firms (BIG4), nature of property rights (SOE), shareholding rate of non-controlling shareholders (LMS), shareholding rate of senior management (Insider), independent director (ID). IND stands for controlling industry and Year stands for controlling year.

If β_1 in model (1) is less than 0 and significantly correlated, it indicates that the more analysts there are, the less manipulation of enterprise managers on accrual earnings management, which proves that H1 is valid. If β_1 in model (2) is greater than 0 and significantly correlated, it indicates that the higher analysts' attention is, the more real active earnings management of the enterprise is, which proves that H2 is valid.

Table 1. Variable definition table.

Type	Variable	Symbol	Definition
Dependent variable	Accrual earnings management	ABS_DA$_{i,t}$	The modified Jones model is calculated
	Real earnings management	ABS_REM$_{i,t}$	The model proposed by Roychowdhury (2006) is calculated
Independent variable	Analyst attention	Analyst	The logarithm of the number of analysts plus one
Control variable	Asset–liability rate	LEV	Total liabilities/total assets
	Growth rate	Growth	(Current operating income – previous operating income)/previous operating income
	Big four accounting firms	Big4	Dummy variable, if the listed company is audited by the big four accounting firms, the value of BIG4 is 1; otherwise 0
	Nature of property rights	SOE	Dummy variable, state-owned enterprise is 1; otherwise 0
	Shareholding rate of non-controlling shareholders	LMS	The proportion of the total share capital held by the second to tenth largest shareholders
	Shareholding rate of senior management	Insider	Proportion of the total share capital held by senior management
	Independent director	ID	Dummy variable. If the residential address of the independent director is the same as the registration place of the listed company, the value is 1; otherwise 0
	Industry	Ind	Dummy variable
	Year	Year	Dummy variable

Table 2. Descriptive statistics.

Variable	Number	Average	Median	Standard deviation	Minimum	Maximum
Analyst	14,654	2.04	2.08	0.90	0.69	3.83
$ABS\_DA_{i,t}$	14,654	0.05	0.04	0.06	0.00	0.31
$ABS\_REM_{i,t}$	14,654	0.14	0.10	0.14	0.00	0.71
LEV	14,654	0.44	0.44	0.20	0.06	0.86
Growth	14,654	0.22	0.14	0.42	−0.43	2.71
SOE	14,654	0.39	0.00	0.49	0.00	1.00
LMS	14,654	0.24	0.23	0.13	0.02	0.55
Big4	14,654	0.07	0.00	0.26	0.00	1.00
Insider	14,654	0.06	0.00	0.13	0.00	0.58
ID	14,654	0.47	0.00	0.50	0.00	1.00
Report	14,654	2.51	2.57	1.13	0.69	4.78

Table 3. Correlation analysis.

Variable	Analyst	$ABS\_DA_{i,t}$	$ABS\_REM_{i,t}$	LEV	Growth	SOE	LMS	Big4	Insider	Same City
Analyst	1									
$ABS\_DA_{i,t}$	−0.0214*	1								
$ABS\_REM_{i,t}$	0.1184*	0.2743*	1							
LEV	−0.0149	0.0934*	−0.0196	1						
Growth	0.0770*	0.1782*	0.1878*	0.0485*	1					
SOE	−0.0067	−0.0002	0.0132	0.2215*	−0.0354*	1				
LMS	0.1185*	0.0190	0.0521*	−0.1575*	0.1079*	−0.1748*	1			
Big4	0.1502*	−0.0568*	−0.0126	0.1378*	−0.0331*	0.1047*	0.0233*	1		
Insider	0.0258*	0.0141	0.0269*	−0.2662*	0.0577*	−0.2553*	0.2269*	−0.1115*	1	
SameCity	−0.0178	−0.0021	0.0178	−0.0373*	−0.0069	−0.0421*	−0.0347*	−0.0127	0.0783*	1

Note: ***, ** and * indicate significant correlation at 1%, 5% and 10% levels, respectively.

5 EMPIRICAL ANALYSIS

5.1 Descriptive statistics

Table 2 shows the descriptive statistical results. The average value of accrual earnings management ($ABS\_DA_{i,t}$) is 0.0548 and the average value of real earnings management ($ABS\_REM_{i,t}$) is 0.139, indicating that with the increase of analysts' attention, real earnings management is more favored by managers than accrual earnings management. At the same time, the standard deviation of accrual earnings management ($ABS\_DA_{i,t}$) is less than that of real earnings management ($ABS\_REM_{i,t}$), indicating that the dispersion degree of real earnings management in listed enterprises is larger. The average value, minimum value, and maximum value of analyst attention are 2.035, 0.693, and 3.829, respectively, indicating that the sample enterprises are generally concerned by analysts, but the degree of attention varies greatly among companies.

5.2 Correlation analysis

Generally speaking, the Pearson correlation coefficient between variables does not exceed 0.6, which indicates that there is no multicollinearity problem between variables (Li Yingzhao & Liu Min, 2020). Table 3 shows that the Pearson correlation coefficient between any two variables does not exceed 0.3, which proves that there is no multicollinearity problem in this paper. In addition, the correlation coefficient between analyst attention and accrual earnings management is −0.0214, and the correlation is significantly negative at the level of 10%, indicating that the more analyst attention there is, the lower the level of accrual earnings management is, which preliminarily proves that H1 is true. The correlation coefficient between analyst attention and real earnings management is 0.1184, and there is a significant positive correlation at the level of 10%, indicating that the more analyst attention there is, the more the level of real earnings management is, which also preliminarily proves that H2 is true.

5.3 Regression analysis

Table 4 shows that the correlation coefficient between analyst attention and accrual earnings management in model (1) is −0.002, and the correlation is significantly negative at the level of 1%. It indicates that with the increase of analyst attention, under the effect of analyst supervision, managers will reduce accrual earnings management because accrual earnings management is easy to discover. Hypothesis 1 is

Table 4. Regression results.

Variable	Model 1 ABS_DA$_{i,t}$	Model 2 ABS_REM$_{i,t}$
Attention	−0.002***	0.017***
	(0.001)	(0.001)
LEV	0.019***	−0.041***
	(0.003)	(0.006)
Growth	0.021***	0.058***
	(0.002)	(0.004)
SOE	−0.001	0.009***
	(0.001)	(0.002)
LMS	0.011***	0.021**
	(0.004)	(0.009)
Big4	−0.012***	−0.010**
	(0.002)	(0.004)
Insider	0.011***	−0.002
	(0.004)	(0.010)
SameCity	−0.002*	0.000
	(0.001)	(0.002)
Constant	0.044***	0.103***
	(0.002)	(0.004)
Year	YES	YES
Firm	YES	YES
Observations	14,654	14,654
R-squared	0.081	0.103
Adj R-squared	0.0791	0.1008

Note: ***, **, and * indicate significant correlation at 1%, 5%, and 10% levels, respectively.

confirmed. In model (2), the correlation coefficient between analyst attention and real earnings management is 0.017, which is a significant positive correlation at the 1% level, indicating that the existence of analysts does not eliminate the motivation of corporate managers to carry out earnings management. When the analyst pays more attention to the enterprise, the supervision effect on the managers is stronger and the operating space of accrual earnings management will be significantly reduced. Therefore, enterprise managers will try to find another more covert way to carry out earnings management, that is, real earnings management, in order to achieve the expected goals. Hypothesis 2 is also confirmed. The asset–liability rate is significantly positively correlated with accrual earnings management and negatively correlated with real earnings management, indicating that the higher the debt level, the greater the motivation of managers to carry out earnings management (Li Yingzhao & Liu Min, 2020), which is mainly through accrual earnings management rather than real earnings management. The growth rate is significantly positively correlated with accrual earnings management and real earnings management at the level of 1%, indicating that enterprises in the rising period and growth period are more likely to carry out earnings management (Fan Pu, 2020). There is a significant positive correlation between the property right nature of enterprises and the real earnings management at the level of 1%, indicating that managers of state-owned enterprises may choose a more hidden way to earnings management when faced with the performance assessment of

operation and management (Fan Pu, 2020). There is a significant positive correlation between the shareholding rate of senior management and accrued earnings management, indicating that the larger the proportion of senior management ownership, the larger the scale of accrued profits. Independent directors are significantly negatively correlated with accrual earnings management, indicating that independent directors living in the same place as the company's registered address can reduce the accrual earnings management behavior of managers to a certain extent.

5.4 Robustness test

5.4.1 Change the measurement of analyst attention

This paper tests whether the influence mechanism of analyst attention to accrual earnings management and real earnings management is still valid by replacing the measurement of analyst attention. Analyst attention is replaced by report following to measure the attention degree of an enterprise (Shi Yunke, 2019). Report following is measured by the number of research reports issued by analysts on enterprises within a year. The data processing method is the same as analyst attention. The data comes from CSMAR database. The results of the robustness test in Table 5 show that there is a significant negative correlation between the report following and accrued earnings management at the level of 1%, indicating that as more and more analysts issue research reports on companies, companies will reduce the amount of accrued earnings. In addition, report following and real earnings management are significantly positively correlated at the level of 1%,

Table 5. Change the measurement of analyst attention.

Variable	Model 1 ABS_DA$_{i,t}$	Model 2 ABS_REM$_{i,t}$
Report	−0.001***	0.014***
	(0.000)	(0.001)
LEV	0.019***	−0.041***
	(0.003)	(0.006)
Growth	0.021***	0.057***
	(0.002)	(0.004)
SOE	−0.001	0.009***
	(0.001)	(0.002)
LMS	0.011***	0.020**
	(0.004)	(0.009)
Big4	−0.012***	−0.010**
	(0.002)	(0.004)
Insider	0.011***	−0.002
	(0.004)	(0.010)
SameCity	−0.002*	0.000
	(0.001)	(0.002)
Constant	0.043***	0.103***
	(0.002)	(0.004)
Year	YES	YES
Firm	YES	YES
Observations	14,654	14,654
R-squared	0.081	0.104
Adj R-squared	0.0790	0.1020

indicating that when the number of research report increases, real earnings management increases, which means that managers know that when the accrued earnings management is strictly monitored by the external supervision system, they will increase real earnings management. In summary, the results of the robustness test are consistent with the results of the regression analysis.

5.4.2 *Endogeneic test*

Earnings management and analyst attention may have a mutually causal relationship, because analysts are more willing to pay attention to and track those listed companies with high quality of financial information and low level of earnings management (Healy & Wahlen, 1999). Therefore, there may be an endogeneity problem between analyst attention and earnings management. Referring to previous processing methods (e.g., Wang Longmei et al., 2021; Fan Pu, 2020; Li Yingzhao & Liu Min, 2020), explanatory variable, namely analyst attention, and all control variables are processed with a lag of one period in this paper. The robustness test results in Table 6 show that analyst attention has a significant negative correlation with accrual earnings management at the level of 5%, while analyst attention and real earnings management are significantly positively correlated at the 1% level. In summary, the endogeneity test results are consistent with Hypotheses 1 and 2, indicating that the regression results are robust.

Table 6. Endogeneity test.

Variable	Model 1 $ABS\_DA_{i,t}$	Model 2 $ABS\_REM_{i,t}$
L.Attention	-0.001^{**}	0.014^{***}
	(0.001)	(0.002)
L.LEV	0.007^{**}	-0.059^{***}
	(0.003)	(0.007)
L.Growth	0.010^{***}	0.018^{***}
	(0.002)	(0.003)
L.SOE	-0.001	0.007^{**}
	(0.001)	(0.003)
L.LMS	0.001	0.018^{*}
	(0.004)	(0.011)
L.Big4	-0.010^{***}	-0.009^{*}
	(0.002)	(0.005)
L.Insider	0.013^{***}	-0.007
	(0.004)	(0.012)
L.SameCity	-0.001	0.000
	(0.001)	(0.003)
Constant	0.051^{***}	0.121^{***}
	(0.002)	(0.005)
Year	YES	YES
Firm	YES	YES
Observations	10,971	10,971
R-squared	0.048	0.072
Adj R-squared	0.0458	0.0695

6 CONCLUSIONS

We choose Chinese A-share listed companies from 2010 to 2019 as the research samples. From the perspective of long-term equilibrium relationship, this paper studies the influence mechanism of analyst attention on earnings management. The empirical test shows that accrual earnings management and real earnings management are mutually substituted. The specific conclusions are as follows:

(1) Under the principal–agent relationship, when the maximization of shareholders' equity conflicts with the maximization of their own interests, enterprise managers often manipulate earnings for their own interests. Securities analysts analyze and track listed companies based on professional capabilities, resource channels, and work experience. Under the attention of analysts, managers will reduce the manipulation of accrued profits, because accrual earnings management mainly adjusts the company's net profit through the flexible choice of accounting policies, accounting method changes and accounting error correction. These manipulable methods about accrual earnings management are relatively simple, but they are easy to be seen by analysts.

(2) Although enterprise managers face the risk that accrual earnings management is likely to be discovered by external supervisors, managers did not give up on earnings management, because the motivation of managers for earnings management has not been eliminated. Therefore, in order to maintain their own reputation and stabilize the company's stock price and valuation, managers are forced to find a more hidden earnings management path than accrual earnings management, which may be the choice of real earnings management. In other words, analyst attention has a pressure effect on earnings management. Real earnings management essentially changes the business strategy of an enterprise and manipulate earnings through the construction or planning of real business activities. Its manipulable methods are more flexible and covert, which is not easy to be found by external supervision agencies. Therefore, when analysts pay more attention to enterprises, it is bound to cause managers to increase the real earnings management.

REFERENCES

Chen, T., Harford, J., & Lin, C. (2015). Do analysts matter for governance? Evidence from natural experiments. *Journal of financial Economics*, 115(2), 383–410.

Chi, W., Lisic, L. L., & Pevzner, M. (2011). Is enhanced audit quality associated with greater real earnings management? *Accounting horizons*, 25(2), 315–335.

Cohen, D. A., Dey, A., & Lys, T. Z. (2008). Real and accrual-based earnings management in the pre-and post-Sarbanes-Oxley periods. *The accounting review*, 83(3), 757–787.

Danmeng Li, Jianfang Ye, Minhui Ye (2015). Analysts follow up on the impact of earnings management of listed companies. *Foreign Economics and Management*, 37(01), 11–20.

Fan Pu (2020). Product market power, analyst focus and earnings management. *Master's thesis, China University of Mining and Technology.*

Fang Junxiong (2007). The Transparency of Information Disclosure of Chinese Listed Companies and the Forecast of Securities Analysts. *Financial Research*, (06), 136–148.

Gilson, S. C., Healy, P. M., Noe, C. F., & Palepu, K. G. (2001). Analyst specialization and conglomerate stock breakups. *Journal of Accounting Research*, 39(3), 565–582.

Graham, J. R., Harvey, C. R., & Rajgopal, S. (2005). The economic implications of corporate financial reporting. *Journal of accounting and economics*, 40(1–3), 3–73.

Hazarika, S., Karpoff, J. M., & Nahata, R. (2012). Internal corporate governance, CEO turnover, and earnings management. *Journal of Financial Economics*, 104(1), 44–69.

He Xuefeng, Zhang Longjiao, Wang You (2017). Analyst Follow Up, Corporate Nature, and Earnings Management – Based on Accruals and Real Earnings Management. *Accounting Communications*, (30), 19–23+129.

He, J. J., & Tian, X. (2013). The dark side of analyst coverage: The case of innovation. *Journal of Financial Economics*, 109(3), 856–878.

Healy, P. M., & Wahlen, J. M. (1999). A review of the earnings management literature and its implications for standard setting. *Accounting horizons*, 13(4), 365–383.

Irani, R. M., & Oesch, D. (2016). Analyst coverage and real earnings management: Quasi-experimental evidence. *Journal of Financial and Quantitative Analysis*, 589–627.

Jensen, M. C., & Meckling, W. H. (1976). Theory of the firm: Managerial behavior, agency costs and ownership structure. *Journal of financial economics*, 3(4), 305–360.

Keating, P. (2000). Engagement: Australia Faces the Asia-Pacific. *Sydney: Pan Macmillan.*

Knyazeva, D. (2007). Corporate governance, analyst following, and firm behavior. *Working Paper, SSRN. com.*

Levitt Jr, A. (1998). The numbers game. *The CPA Journal*, 68(12), 14.

Li Chuntao, Song Min, Zhang Xuan (2014). Analyst Tracking and Corporate Earnings Management – Evidence from Listed Companies in China. *Financial Research*, (07), 124–139.

Li Chuntao, Zhao Yi, Xu Xin, Li Qingyuan (2016). Pressing the Gourd: Analyst Tracking and Earnings Management Approach Selection. *Financial Research*, (04), 144–157.

Li Xiaoling, Liu Zhongyan (2014). Analyst Focus, Professional Reputation and Accounting Information Transparency. *Journal of Anhui University*, (38)06, 142–149.

Li Yingzhao, Liu Min (2020). Executive Overconfidence, Analyst Tracking and Earnings Management. *Friends of Accounting*, (08), 26–33.

Li Zengfu, Dong Zhiqiang, Lian Yujun (2011). Accrued Project Earnings Management or Real Activity Earnings Management? – Based on the study of China's 2007 income tax reform. *Managing the World*, (01), 121–134.

Pan Yue, Dai Yiyi, Lin Chaoqun (2011). Information is not transparent, and analysts focus on the risk of a slump in individual stocks. *Journal of Financial Research*, (09), 138–151.

Roychowdhury, S. (2006). Earnings management through real activities manipulation. *Journal of accounting and economics*, 42(3), 335–370.

Rujun Xu (2019). Analyst follow up, external audit quality, and earnings management style: Empirical evidence from the perspective of external governance interaction and micro-earnings. *China Certified Public Accountants*, (01), 50–58.

Shi Yunke (2019). "To curry favor" or "to be courteous". *Master's thesis, Dongbei University of Finance and Economics.*

Su Chunjiang (2013). Property Rights, Securities Analyst Tracking and Earnings Management. *Journal of Finance and Accounting*, (22), 14–16.

TONG, D.L., CHEN, J.Y. (2005). Accounting Change, Earnings Management, and Corporate Finance Characteristics: Empirical Evidence from Chinese Listed Companies. *Journal of Economic Management*, (10), 37–44.

Wang Liangcheng (2014). Accruals and Real Earnings Management: Alternative or Complementary. *Financial Theory and Practice*, 35(02), 66–72.

Wang Longmei, Li Mingmin, Tian Jing (2021). Analyst tracking, earnings management and audit opinion buying. *Friends of Accounting*, (01), 133–140.

Wang Shuangjin, Chang Juan (2020). Environmental uncertainty, analyst tracking and earnings management. *Statistics and Decision Making*, 36(19), 141–145.

Wiersema, M. F., & Zhang, Y. (2011). CEO dismissal: The role of investment analysts. *Strategic Management Journal*, 32(11), 1161–1182.

Ye Chenggang, Liu Meng (2018). Analyst Focus, Property Rights Nature and Earnings Management Path. *Journal of Zhongnan University of Economics and Law*, (03), 33–42+159.

Yu Zhongbo, Ye Qiongyan, Tian Gaoliang (2011). External oversight and earnings management – a review of media attention, institutional investors, and analysts. *Journal of Shanxi University of Finance and Economics*, 33(09), 90–99.

Yu, F. F. (2008). Analyst coverage and earnings management. *Journal of financial economics*, 88(2), 245–271.

Zang, A. Y. (2012). Evidence on the trade-off between real activities manipulation and accrual-based earnings management. *The accounting review*, 87(2), 675–703.

Zhao Yujie (2013). Legal environment, analyst follow up and earnings management. *Journal of Shanxi University of Finance and Economics*, 35(01), 73–83.

Zhao Zaifang (2020). Management risk preference, analyst focus on the impact of earnings management. *Master's thesis, Xi'an University of Science and Technology.*

Economic and Business Management – Huang & Zhang (Eds)
© 2022 Copyright the Author(s), ISBN: 978-1-032-06754-4

Labor market analysis within the Slovak healthcare sector

Marcel Kordoš
Alexander Dubček University in Trenčín, Trenčín, Slovak Republic

ABSTRACT: Slovak healthcare sector is currently struggling with many challenges. There is a constant discussion about the need for systemic changes, which would bring not only an increase in the quality of services provided but also better financial coverage. The goal of the paper is based on the labor force situation analysis within the Slovak healthcare sector to figure out the problematic aspects regarding the Slovak healthcare sector labor market and its further development. The data from OECD and Slovak National Health Information Center are to be used. To improve the situation, it is necessary to support the human capital and to eliminate issues such as planning, security, motivation, and stabilization of human resources—high turnover, overloading of current employees in the security system, where the problem concerns not only nurses and social workers but also doctors.

1 INTRODUCTION AND THEORETICAL BACKGROUND

The paper deals with the problematic aspects regarding the Slovak healthcare sector labor market and its further development. Within the theoretical part, the issues of healthcare system within the Slovak national economy structure and Slovak labor force in healthcare sector are to be illustrated. Based on the data from the Medical Yearbook of Slovak Republic published by National Center for Health Information in 2020 and from the OECD data, the issues such as the number of employees in healthcare; the wages and salaries issue in Slovak healthcare sector as well as the structure of healthcare workers in Slovak Republic by gender, occupation, age structure of doctors and nurses; and at last the analysis of healthcare workers according to education are to be observed.

The internal composition of the national economy is represented by the structure of the national economy, and within its assessment, the views of sectoral and territorial structure are presented. The sectoral structure consists of companies with the same or related focus, while individual sectors can be divided into sub-sectors. Healthcare falls under the fifth sector. This sector of development services is represented by services ensuring the improvement of the quality of life, preservation, and cultivation of human potential (Nemec et al. 2021; Zajac et al. 2004). The healthcare system in Slovakia is managed by health insurance companies, which conclude contracts with healthcare providers and individually negotiate the quality, prices, and volumes. The Office for Healthcare Supervision operates as an independent monitoring body for the healthcare market and the Ministry of Healthcare is the main regulatory authority (Hoerbst et al. 2011; Soltes & Gavurova 2014).

The provision of services is decentralized, performed by both public and private providers. They have signed contracts with health insurance companies to be entitled to reimbursement. General practitioners and outpatient specialists can be independent private or public providers. The ownership and management of most public hospitals is also decentralized at the regional level, although through the central state administration, responsibility for the management of one-third of public hospitals is maintained. Health insurance companies have contracts with hospitals and sometimes even directly with departments that cover different types and volumes of healthcare services. All residents should be enrolled in one of the health insurances companies. The share of the population that is not covered is therefore in practice significantly lower than 5%. More than 80% of healthcare expenditures are financed from public sources. Sources of income are mainly contributions paid by employers and employees and represent about two-thirds of total public expenditure on healthcare. The remaining one-third of the total comes from general tax revenues for the payment of contributions for categories of the population, such as dependent family members, students, and pensioners. The largest cost item in Slovak health care system consists of medicines and medical devices and the preventive care is the smallest (Jantosova 2014; Tupa 2020). Pellegrini et al. (2014) argue that during economic contractions, Medicaid and Medicare's share of overall state healthcare spending increases with meaningful effects on the configuration of state healthcare workforces and subsequently, provision of care for populations at-risk for worsening morbidity and mortality.

34

DOI 10.1201/9781003203704-7

Information and data on healthcare workers are obtained through statistical reports in health care, such as the Annual Report on the Number and Structure of Healthcare Workers and the Annual Report on the Number and Structure of Civil Health Workers. The processing of the collection of these reports is carried out in the National Center for Health Information. Healthcare workers are reported as the registered number of employees as of December 31 of the observed year, as natural persons. This number does not include non-registered workers and non-employed workers employed on the basis of agreements and contracts for work performed outside the employment relationship. The professions of healthcare workers are reported in accordance with §27 of Act no. 578/2004 Coll. on healthcare providers, healthcare workers, professional organizations in health care, and on the amendment of certain laws as amended at the time of the observed period.

2 PROBLEM FORMULATION AND METHODOLOGY

The research task of this paper is focused on the assessment how the healthcare sector staff changes are affecting the labor market stabilization within this sector. The goal of the paper is based on the labor force situation analysis within the Slovak healthcare sector to figure out the problematic aspects regarding the Slovak healthcare sector labor market and its further development. To accomplish this goal, methods such as analysis, comparison, synthesis, and logical deduction are to be used. Subsequently, the analysis will lead to synthesis and prognosis by means of abstraction method eliminating the less important factors to set general statements and opinions. Basic data will be drawn from generally accepted institutions, evaluating the Slovak healthcare sector such as OECD, Slovak Ministry of Health, and Slovak National Health Information Center.

3 FINDINGS

Firstly, the number of healthcare employees according to the OECD (2020) data is to be analyzed. In 2019, the density of doctors in Slovakia was similar to the EU average (3.4 doctors per 1,000 inhabitants compared to 3.6), but the number of nurses was below the EU average. Slovakia is one of the few countries that reported a reduction in the number of nurses between 2000 and 2019. In 2019, there was an evident shortage of healthcare workers and their uneven geographical distribution. The density of doctors per 1,000 inhabitants is very high in Bratislava region (6.51). The density in Košice (3.82) and Žilina (3.59) regions is lower, but higher than the national average of 3.4. In the regions of Trnava (2.63), Trenčín (2.54), Prešov (2.93), Nitra (2.72), and Banská Bystrica (2.95), the density is less than three doctors per 1,000 inhabitants

compared to the national average of 3.4. The capital region has considerably more doctors than the rest of the country. Another problem is that doctors are aging as a workforce, and there are legitimate concerns about having enough new doctors available to replace those who will retire in the upcoming years. More than one-third (36%) of all physicians in 2019 were aged 55 and over, which is approximately 6,700 out of 18,600 physicians.

Next step in terms of our observations is the wages and salaries issue in Slovak healthcare sector. According to the NHIC (2020), physicians' and nurses' incomes have grown faster than in other sectors of the economy since 2011, which has made these professions more attractive to medical students and reduced the migration of health professionals to other countries. The average annual salary of doctors increased by more than 50% between 2011 and 2019—EUR 33 000 in 2019, and the salary of nurses increased by approximately 40%—EUR 14 500 in 2019, slightly above the national average wage in 2019 being EUR 14 000.

Regarding the gender structure of medical staff as of December 31, 2019, 110,778 employees were registered in the healthcare system; 23,913 men and 86,865 women worked for healthcare providers or in other healthcare organizations in Slovak Republic (NHIC 2020). Table 1 provides an overview of the number of employees in the period from 2016 to 2019. The number of healthcare workers in 2019 increased by 1,446 persons compared to 2018, which represents an increase of 1.3%.

Table 1. The number of healthcare workers in the period from 2016 to 2019.

Year	2016	2017	2018	2019
Number of employees	107 896	107 729	109 332	110 778
Increase in the number of natural persons	1 214	−167	1 603	1 446
Increase/decrease in %	1,13%	−0,16%	1,47%	1,31%

Source: Own processing by NHIC, 2020.

According to NHIC (2020) data as of December 31, 2019, nurses accounted for 37.3%, doctors 23.2%, paramedics 6.1%, pharmacists 5.3%, general nurses 4.2%, dentists 3.4%, and medical laboratory technicians 3.4%. There were 19,454 doctors registered in Slovakia, which is more than 356.4 doctors per 100,000 inhabitants of Slovak Republic. The rising trend in the number of doctors in the last decade continued in 2019. Since 2010, 1,344 doctors have been added to Slovak healthcare system, which represents an increase of 7.4%. Compared to 2018, the number of doctors in 2019 increased by 1.4% (by 276 persons). The number of dentists grew at a slower pace. At the end of 2019, there were 2,853 dentists in the register, while year-on-year, compared to 2018, their number increased by 2.7% and compared to 2010 by 7.1%. In the observed year 2019, we record 31,309 nurses, which represents 573.6 nurses per 100,000 inhabitants. The number of nurses had a declining trend in the period 2015–2019. The most intensive growth in the last 10 years has been recorded in the profession of nursing. In 2019, there were 64.6 practical nurses per 100,000 inhabitants. Table 2 shows that compared to 2018, there were 219 practical nurses, which in terms of the rate of increase represented an increase of 6.6%.

Table 2. Development of the number of employees in the period from 2015 to 2019.

Year/ the number	Doctors	Dentists	Nurses	Practical nurses
2015	145	5	−262	239
2016	145	54	279	406
2017	-256	22	-451	272
2018	570	56	329	178
2019	276	74	248	219
In total	1 344	190	−1 436	2 097

Source: Own processing by NHIC, 2020.

In terms of the age structure of doctors, the period from 2016 to 2019 was made up of the largest share of doctors over the age of 60, with 10.9% aged 60–64 and 15.5% aged 65 and over. Table 3 indicates that doctors aged 40–49 were also strongly represented, namely, 22.4%, and 30–39 years represented 21.4%. According to Table 3, nurses were the most numerous in the age groups 40–49 years, namely, 37.5% and 50–59 years - 28.0% (NHIC 2020).

Table 3. Age structure of doctors and nurses in the period from 2015 to 2019.

Age group/ percentage	2018		2019	
	Doctors	Nurses	Doctors	Nurses
20–29	11.5	14.2	11.7	16.2
30–39	21.0	21.2	21.4	22.3
40–49	23.1	15.8	22.4	16.4
50–59	17.7	12.7	18.1	11.5
60–64	12.5	15.7	10.9	12.5
65+	14.2	20.6	15.5	21.2

Source: Own processing by NHIC, 2020.

Finally, when it comes to the analysis of healthcare workers according to education, according to NHIC (2020) data as of October 31, 2019, 4,104 Slovak students and 2,784 foreigners were studying at Slovak medical faculties in the general medicine field of study. There were 703 newly admitted students, which was 110 people less than in 2018. In 2019, a total of 938 physicians graduated from the general medicine specialization, of which 354 were foreigners. In the observed year 2019, 662 students of Slovak citizenship and 283 foreigners studied in the field of dentistry. The number of newly admitted Slovak students was

113, and in comparison, with their number in 2018, it remained constant. One hundred and sixty graduates completed their studies in dentistry, including 118 students of Slovak citizenship and 42 foreigners. A total of 1,315 students of Slovak citizenship and 108 foreigners studied pharmaceutical sciences. Two hundred and ninety-nine students of Slovak citizenship were admitted to study pharmacy, which is 16 more than in 2018. Two hundred and forty-nine graduates of Slovak and 15 other citizenship completed their studies. From the study of non-medical sciences at universities, in 2019, the most popular field of study was nursing, both full-time and part-time. In both degrees of study (bachelor and master), 3,712 Slovak students and 951 foreigners of the nursing specialization were qualified to perform the medical profession. A total of 1,081 students completed the nursing field of study. At the same time, another 177 students were preparing for a higher post-secondary specialization study in 2019 in the field of graduated general nurses, and 104 students completed this study.

Table 4. Slovak healthcare sector professions salaries in 2019.

Occupation	Salary in €	Occupation	Salary in €
Nutrition assistant	633 – 1 291	Childbirth assistant	764 – 1 464
Dental hygienist	789 – 1 536	Orderly	623 – 1 010
Chiropractor	732 – 1 232	Public health officer	737 – 1 340
Head nurse	863 – 1 566	Superior nurse	796 – 2 044
Hygienic	655 – 1 244	Nurse	732 – 1 258
Doctor	1 017 – 3 227	Paramedic	843 – 1 723
Practical nurse	709 – 1 202	Dentist	788 – 2 812

Source: Own processing by Ministry of Health, 2021.

As part of the analysis regarding the employees' evaluation in Slovak healthcare sector, Table 4 shows the minimum and the maximum range of salaries in the most common occupations in healthcare. Among the most earning, there are doctors and head nurses. This is mainly due to the lack of doctors, who often go abroad after university graduation, where there are more modernly equipped hospitals and higher salaries. Occupations where there is no condition of education in healthcare, such as the paramedic is one of the least paid places in healthcare. Wage differences depend on labor supply and demand, the cost of living, and the difficulty of work.

The number of jobs in healthcare facilities was only 16,780 in 2005, then increased to almost 20,000 in 2007. In the following years, the number of jobs fluctuated around 19,600. In 2018, there were 19,644 jobs in healthcare facilities. Figure 1 illustrates that the number of doctors in healthcare facilities is slightly growing, which is due to the decision of senior doctors to stay in healthcare and practice their profession despite the possibility of retirement.

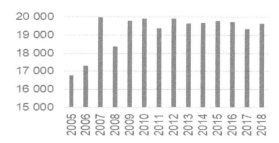

Figure 1. The number of jobs development in medical facilities in Slovak Republic.
Source: Own processing by Ministry of Health, 2021.

4 DISCUSSION

By and large, healthcare is a sector with many highly educated professionals. Many of them get into managerial positions and, in addition to narrowly specialized activities, they also have to perform managerial activities, which they often reach only with their own knowledge, experience, or by completing courses or specialized studies with a focus on management in healthcare. It is not even possible to be surprised by such a situation, as the medical study is really demanding, highly professional, and its study focus is not built on managerial work. In practice, however, these managers lack managerial skills, literally in their very foundations. Therefore, in our opinion, developing certain innovative approaches in management will not be a strength for health managers.

This is not the only reason why the healthcare sector is currently struggling with many problems. There is a constant discussion about the need for systemic changes, which would bring not only an increase in the quality of services provided but also better financial coverage. However, in addition to these macroeconomic reforms, changes are also needed at the micro-level, i.e., at the level of particular health organizations. The management of these facilities should implement many innovative forms of management in their management processes, which would enable the better functioning of individual organizations and ensure their success.

Generally speaking, the main weakness of long-term social and healthcare in Slovak Republic can be described as its insufficient coordination, communication, and cooperation at the level of government regarding the Ministry of Labor and Social Affairs and the Ministry of Health of Slovak Republic. The long-term negative underestimation of the severity of this situation is evident at the system level, in financing as well as in quality assurance. According to Krajnakova and Vojtovic (2020), in the field of human resources and processes, those are mainly:

1. Insufficient support and appreciation of human capital.
2. Problems with planning, securing, motivating, and stabilizing human resources-high turnover, overloading of current employees in the security system, where the problem concerns not only nurses and social workers but also doctors.
3. Insufficient multidisciplinary and interdisciplinary cooperation.
4. Difficult orientation of dependent persons in the health and social system, lack of comprehensive management of aftercare after discharge from hospital, the absence of defined criteria for the results of the quality of healthcare, links to the motivation of providers who are part of the system of its provision, a frequent unethical approach to finding solutions for people who depend on health care, regardless of their condition and needs, and the absence of a holistic approach by various professionals and specialists in the provision of care to people who depend on health care.

To put it in a nutshell, the COVID-19 pandemic reminded us of our strong dependence on healthcare professionals, who are expected to acquire skills and training in infection prevention, quarantine protocols, the use of protective equipment, and clinical and crisis management responsibilities. To meet the needs of healthcare organizations, new digital technologies in healthcare sector must be implemented successfully that improve the quality of care and increase the performance of healthcare systems. This points to a significant skills shortage, which will worsen as a result of demographic aging and the increase in chronic diseases. Bridging this gap is a basic precondition for ensuring a high level of resilience and fairness of national healthcare systems not only in Slovakia but also in other countries of the world.

Our research outcomes correspond with the statements of Tupá (2020b) and Szabo et al. (2020) declaring that medical facilities in Slovak Republic are deeply understaffed. The evolution of the number of nurses employed in the healthcare system by age shows that the situation will continue to deteriorate as a result of their retirement. The inflow of nurses is not sufficient due to the high share of outgoing graduates for work abroad. The situation is exacerbated by the emigration of sisters abroad. The shortage of workers in Slovak healthcare sector has far-reaching consequences, witnessed daily by people seeking help in general and specialist outpatient clinics, hospitals, and other healthcare organizations. In addition, the effects are felt by nurses working for wages below the average gross wage in the national economy, working in 12-hour shifts, half of them being nightshifts, several per month for weekends or holidays and increasing number of patients per nurse on duty, due to which work becomes physically and mentally demanding, leading to stress, work burnout, and others. The numbers of doctors, dentists, or other health professionals are similar. The government is supposed to respond to this unfavorable situation and to ensure a sufficient level of healthcare for all people in Slovakia.

5 CONCLUSIONS

We have arrived at the conclusion that the age structure of doctors and dentists is changing, while the share of doctors in retirement age is growing. In the case of their retirement, the Slovak healthcare system would have big problems. In addition, many students from Slovakia study abroad, and many times remain to work there. On the contrary, foreigners come to us to study, especially from Ukraine, who remain working in Slovak healthcare system. Nurses are also inadequate in the Slovak healthcare system. On the other hand, their level of education is growing. Even in the current situation of the COVID-19 pandemic, it is necessary to invest in the Slovak healthcare system, not only in technical equipment, but especially in staffing. Otherwise, healthcare is in danger of collapsing, and there will be no one to care for the growing aging Slovak population in the future.

Further research will be devoted to exploring the issues such as the healthcare spending on the healthcare workforce composition; the demand on healthcare; a statistical analysis to explain the reasons behind the trends presented on the Slovak healthcare system labor force.

ACKNOWLEDGMENTS

This paper was supported by the Slovak Ministry of Education's grant agency—Slovak Research and Development Agency: "Personnel management processes set-up in hospitals and their impact on the migration of physicians and nurses to work abroad." Project registration number: Reg. no. APVV-19-0579.

REFERENCES

Hoerbst, A., Hackl, W. O., Blomer, R. & Ammenwerth, E. 2011. The status of IT service management in health care – ITIL (R) in selected European countries. *BMC MEDICAL Informatics and Decision Making* 11 Article Number: 76 DOI: 10.1186/1472-6947-11-76

Jantosova, L. 2014. Application of Method Benchmarking in Evaluation Healthcare Facilities in Slovakia. *Aktualne Problemy Podnikovej Sfery 2014*: 153–159.

Krajnakova, E. & Vojtovic, S. 2020. Global Trends in the Labor Market and Balance of Losses and Benefits from Labor Migration. *19th International Scientific Conference Globalization and its Socio-Economic Consequences 2019 – Sustainability in the Global-Knowledge Economy*. Book Series: SHS Web of Conferences Volume: 74, Article Number: 05012. DOI: 10.1051/shsconf/20207405012

National Health Information Center (NHIC). 2019. 2019 Health Yearbook of the Slovak Republic. Bratislava: National Center for Health Information. 227 p. ISBN 978-80-89292-71-4.

Nemec, J., Kubak, M., Donin, G. & Kotherova, Z. 2021. Efficiency of Public Procurement in the Czech and Slovak Health Care Sectors. *Transylvanian Review of Administrative Sciences* 62E: 115–133. DOI: 10.24193/tras.62E.7

OECD/European Observatory on Health Systems and Policies. 2019. Slovakia: Health profile of the country 2019, State of Health in the EU. Brussels: OECD Publishing, Paris/European Observatory on Health Systems and Policies. 24 p. ISBN 9789264999275

Pellegrini LC, Rodriguez-Monguio R, Qian J. 2014. The US healthcare workforce and the labor market effect on healthcare spending and health outcomes *Int J Health Care Finance Econ* 14(2):127–41. DOI: 10.1007/s10754-014-9142-0.

Soltes, V. & Gavurova, B. 2014. Slovak Hospitals' Efficiency – Application of the Data Envelopment Analysis. *Psychology and Psychiatry, Sociology and Healthcare, Education, VOL II*. Book Series: International Multidisciplinary Scientific Conferences on Social Sciences and Arts: 773–784.

Szabo, S., Mihalcova, B., Lukac, J., Gallo, P., Cabinova, V. & Vajdova, I. 2020. Demotivation of Medical Staff in the Selected Health Facility in Slovakia *E & M Ekonomie a Management* 23(2): 83–95. DOI: 10.15240/tul/001/2020-2-006

Slovak Ministry of Health. 2021. Labor Statistics. [on-line] [cit.: 06.12.2021] Retrieved from: https://www.health.gov.sk

Tupa, M. 2020a. Changes in Emmigration of Health Workers in Nuts III. Regions of the Slovak Republic. *RELIK 2020: Reproduction of Human Capital - Mutual Links and Connections*: 579–593.

Tupá, M. 2020b. Personálne zabezpečenie systému zdravotníctva v Slovenskej republike kvalifikovanými sestrami v kontexte pracovnej emigrácie *Zdravotnícke listy* 8(1): 38–46.

Zajac, R., Pazitny, P. & Marcincin, A. 2004. Slovak reform of health care: From fees to systemic changes. *Finance A Uver-Czech Journal of Economics and Finance* 54(9–10): 405–419.

Economic and Business Management – Huang & Zhang (Eds)
© 2022 Copyright the Author(s), ISBN: 978-1-032-06754-4

Real options, firm valuation, and corporate information environment

Yanping Bao
School of Business, Macau University of Science and Technology, Macau, China
Chongqing Finance and Economics College, Chongqing, China

Chan Lyu
School of Business, Macau University of Science and Technology, Macau, China

ABSTRACT: This paper uses the real options model to evaluate the firm value of Chinese A-share listed firms. We find that the value based on the real options model is closed to the intrinsic value of the enterprise, and can explain the variance of stock returns. We further analyze the influence of the corporate information environment on the correlation of real option value, and find that less agency conflict is beneficial to investors' access to relevant information, thereby enhancing the correlation between real-options-based firm value and stock returns. This study has practical significance for understanding the valuation of listed companies and stabilizing the development of capital markets in China.

1 INTRODUCTION

Shanghai and Shenzhen Stock Exchanges were established in 1990. Since then, China's capital market has witnessed 30 years of continuous development and gradual improvement in the institutional system, which has effectively played the role of resource allocation. The stock prices in China's stock market provide information about the listed companies, and the market efficiency has been improving (Carpenter et al., 2020). Investors at all levels pay attention to the intrinsic value of enterprises, which is both an important factor for investors' investment decision-making and a direct indicator affecting the allocation of capital market resources. In the context of the changes in domestic and foreign economic environments and the aggravation of uncertainty, how to evaluate the intrinsic value of enterprises accurately has also attracted the attention of the government regulatory departments.

Firm valuation is a hot research topic for scholars in the field of finance and accounting. In the finance literature, a firm's fundamental value is the present value of the expected future dividend, known as the dividend discount model (Gordon & Shapiro, 1956), which is the benchmark for equity valuation. Meanwhile, in the accounting research literature, the model of valuation takes a slightly different approach. Edwards and Bell (1961) introduced the residual income model for valuation that was developed using accounting numbers and the clean surplus relation assumption (Ohlson, 1995). Burgstahler and Dichev (1997) proposed that the value of a firm depends on the recursion value and the adaptation value. Zhang (2000) developed

the option valuation theoretical model in a more general way and proposed that equity value is convex in both earnings and book value, considering operating efficiency and growth opportunities.

The future investment opportunity can be regarded as a "growth option," which is called a real option because it is based on real assets. The future investment options (either to continue the current operation, change the operating strategy, or even terminate the operation) should theoretically increase the firm value. No matter which decision is taken, managers in the firm are encouraged to achieve the objectives of value-maximization. Real option can also predict the future growth component of firm value (Hiemann, 2020).

The real options theory is an extension of financial options, with the key idea of integrating the option value of future investment decisions into a firm's valuation. The future business strategy may change due to potential investment opportunities. The analytical framework of real options has been applied in explaining the firm valuation based on China's stock market, and the existing literature has discussed in-depth the macro-economic factors, such as growth or abandonment option value Chen et al., 2015; Jin et al., 2010; Xiao et al., 2016; Xinyuan Chen et al., 2013), which may have an impact on real options value. The real option is different from financial option; hence, accurately quantifying the value embedded in the option is difficult. Most of the current literature studies the option value by exploring the convex relation of firm value and net profit. Some studies also try quantifying the option value based on traditional financial option models in valuing particular industries, such as oil, gas, and pharmaceuticals.

DOI 10.1201/9781003203704-8

The information environment of a firm is influenced by the corporate governance, which is regarded as a set of contracts designed to mitigate the agency conflicts between shareholders and managers (Jensen & Meckling, 1976). The agency theory posits firms with less agency conflict generate a better information environment, where more information of the operation and strategies for future development are disclosed to stakeholders. Stakeholders, especially investors, are sensitive to the information related to future development, which may impact their investment decision and the option value. Rao et al. (2018) argued that the efficiency of corporate governance will affect the information environment and that investors pay more attention to the real option value.

In this paper, we first estimate the firm value using a real options model, following the real options model proposed by Hwang and Sohn (2010) who viewed the real option value as an explicit component of abnormal earnings. We then examine whether the firm value can explain the variance of the stock return. We futher examine whether the corporate information environment has an effect in influencing the value relevance of the firm-value based on the real options model.

This paper contributes to the firm valuation literature by providing empirical evidence of applying the option-pricing model in evaluating the firm value based on the Chinese stock market. From the perspective of agency conflict, this paper investigates whether corporate governance affects the value-relevance of real option value. We present evidence that less agency conflict may result in improvement in predicting stock returns.

The remainder of the paper is organized as follows: section 2 develops the research hypothesis; section 3 provides the research design; section 4 describes the data and hypotheses, testing results in this study; and section 5 ends with a conclusion.

2 HYPOTHESIS DEVELOPMENT

2.1 *The value-relevance of real option value*

Evaluating a firm's intrinsic value is essential in investment decision-making in the capital market. Stock is the investors' claim on the future earnings of an entity. The stock prices reflect the investors' expectation of the future dividends and earnings of the firm. Stock returns prediction has long been a hot topic in academic and financial practice. According to Fama and French's (1993) efficiency market hypothesis, in a competitive market with legal laws and transparent information disclosure, all valuable information should be reflected in stock market prices. Moreover, investors will find difficulty in gaining abnormal returns. However, in reality, the capital market is not perfectly competitive, where transaction costs and many market frictions exist. The intrinsic value of an asset may be distorted due to market imperfection. According to the short-term market inefficiency and

long-term market efficiency (Trombley et al., 2003), the market evaluation of a firm may deviate from its intrinsic value in the short term. In addition, the divergence will diminish as more information is disclosed, and the market value will eventually return to its intrinsic value (Frankel & Lee, 1998; Lee et al., 1999).

Investors may earn abnormal returns due to the mispricing mechanism. Specifically, when a firm's value is under-estimated, the value-to-price (V/P) ratio is high, rational investors may buy in the firm's stock at a relatively lower price, and gain positive returns when the price converges to its intrinsic value. By contrast, when the value-to-price (V/P) ratio is lower, the market price of the stock is probably over-estimated, rational investors would sell the stocks to avoid loss when the price is moving downward to its intrinsic value.

Theoretically, a real option is investors' option on the future operation, which generates future operating value. We propose that if the firm value including the real option value reflects the intrinsic value, then the firm value should explain the stock returns. Accordingly, the discussion leads to the first hypothesis of this study:

H1: The value-to-price ratio based on the real options model is positive related to the stock returns.

2.2 *The impact of corporate information environment on the value-relevance*

In order to examine whether corporate governance impacts the value-relevance, this paper takes the information environment into account. The agency theory posits firms with less agency conflict generate a better information environment, where more information of the operation and strategies for future development are disclosed to stakeholders. Stakeholders, especially investors, are sensitive to the information related to future development, which may impact their investment decision and the option value. Rao et al. (2018) argued that the efficiency of corporate governance will affect the information environment and that investors pay more attention to the real option value. The positive relationship between Vf/P and stock returns would be more significant in an information environment that has less agency conflicts.

We propose the second hypothesis in this paper:

H2: The value-relevance of firm value based on real options model is more pronounced for firms with less agency conflicts.

3 RESEARCH DESIGN

3.1 *Firm valuation with real options model*

In estimating the firm value incorporating the real option value, we follow the real options model proposed by Hwang and Sohn (2010) who viewed the real option value as an explicit component of abnormal earnings. The firm valuation $Vf = BV + Vo$, where Vf stands for the firm vale, BV is the book value, and

Vo is the real option value. Vo is estimated by the Black-Scholes Model (Black & Scholes, 1973), and the model in this study is as stated in the following formula (1):

$$Vf = BV_t + Vo_t = BV_t + cE_t * N(d_1)$$
$$- \frac{BV_t}{e^{Rf*T}} * N(d_2) \qquad (1)$$

where cE_t in the Black-Scholes Model representing the current stock price; we use the underlying asset firm value estimated by residual income model as a proxy. $N(d)$ is a normal distribution function, and d_1, d_2 is calculated as follows:

$$d_1 = \frac{\ln\left(\frac{cE_t}{BV_t}\right) + (Rf_t + \sigma^2/2)T}{\sigma\sqrt{T}} \qquad (2)$$

$$d_2 = d_1 - \sigma\sqrt{T} \qquad (3)$$

Rf is the risk-free interest rate, T is the time to maturity (assuming $T = 5$ years), and σ represents the standard deviation of $(cE_t - cE_{t-1})/cE_{t-1}$ for the past 5 years.

3.2 The relationship between firm value and stock returns

We estimate the firm value of listed firms in China's A-share stock market based on the real options value, create a value-to-price ratio Vf/ and examine whether the valuation can explain the variation in stock returns, controlling for other firm risk variables.

$$Return = \alpha_0 + \alpha_1 * \frac{Vf}{P} + \alpha_2 * \frac{BV}{P}$$
$$+ \alpha_k \sum Control_i + \varepsilon \qquad (4)$$

The controlling variables in the regression model include the beta of the individual stock, the size of the firm, profitability (*ROA*), financial leverage (*LEV*), and investment opportunity (*Growth*).

3.3 The effects of corporate information environment

This paper tries to examine whether corporate governance impacts the value-relevance because investors care about the information environment. Following Ang et al. (2000), we use the asset utilization ratio (asset utilization ratio = annual sales/total asset) as the proxy for the agency cost. The asset utilization ratio measures how efficiently and effectively the firm's management deploys its assets. The higher the asset utilization ratio, the more efficient operation is and the less the agency cost (between the management and the shareholders) is.

$$Return = \gamma_0 + \gamma_1 * \frac{Vf}{P} + \gamma_2 * \frac{BV}{P} + \gamma_3 Agency$$
$$+ \gamma_4 * \frac{Vf}{P} * Agency + \gamma_i \sum Control_i + \varepsilon \qquad (5)$$

4 DATA, RESULT AND DISCUSSION

4.1 Descriptive statistics

The financial information for sample firms and market return data are extracted from the China Stock Market Accounting Research database. Consistent with prior studies, we remove the sample firms in the financial industry and firms with missing values. Following Trombley et al. (2003), we further remove sample firms with negative net assets and negative book value to control the outlier effect. We also remove observations with a continuous annual observation of less than five years as we need to calculate the standard deviation of the capitalized firm value (cE), following Hwang and Sohn (2010). The final sample consists of 1,816 listed firms, and 16,802 firm-year observations from 2001 to 2017.

Table 1. Descriptive statistics of variables.

Variables	min	mean	median	max	Std Dev
Vf	0.25	8.37	5.85	431.1	10.1
BV	0.01	4.28	3.75	76.4	2.91
Vf/P	0.1	0.71	0.56	2.76	0.51
BV/P	0.001	0.41	0.36	7.03	0.29
Return	−0.84	0.19	−0.04	11.01	0.78
Beta	0.47	1.12	1.22	3.34	0.25
Size	17.8	22.1	21.93	28.51	1.34
ROA	−0.06	0.07	0.06	0.68	0.59
Lev	0.01	0.48	0.49	0.99	0.19
Growth	−0.97	9.43	0.13	134.6	104.9

The sample contains 1,816 firms with 16,802 firm-year observations from 2001 to 2017.

Table 1 reports the descriptive statistics of the variables. During the sample period, the variables present a right-skewed distribution because the mean values are larger than the median values for all variables. Specifically, the mean of firm value per share is 8.37 estimated by the real options model. The mean of firm value per share is marginally larger than the mean of book value per share (4.28). Meanwhile, the mean values of the value-to-price ratio (Vf/P) is 0.71, indicating the firm undervaluation of the estimated firm value relative to the market price. On average, the book value to price ratio (BV/P) is 0.41, lower than that of Vf/P. Other variables such as stock return, Beta, Size, ROA, Lev and Growth have a similar statistics documented in other studies.

4.2 Hypotheses testing of H1

Table 2 reports the main regression result of the relationship between firm value and stock returns.

We include the BV/P in the regression model because the book value provides the current operating information, which may be reflected in the stock returns, and differs with Vf that is estimated based on future earnings. Trombley et al. (2003) found that when both BV/P and Vf/P are included in the regression model, only the coefficient of BV/P remains significant, whereas the coefficient of V/P losses the significance. The regression results in this study are similar to that of Hwang and Sohn's (2010).

Table 2. Regression results.

Dependent variable: Stock Returns			
(1)	(2)	(3)	(4)
Intercept	$-0.17***$	$-0.19***$	$-0.21***$	2.99***
	(-18.62)	(-20.56)	(-22.5)	(28.8)
Vf/P	0.47***		0.28***	0.25***
	(44.97)		(17.82)	(13.76)
BV/P		0.68***	0.43***	0.67***
		(34.05)	(15.92)	(22.27)
Beta				$-0.33***$
				(-14.13)
Size				$-0.14***$
				(-28.29)
ROA				1.40***
				(12.9)
Lev				0.41***
				(12.48)
Growth				-0.000
				(-0.48)
Adj.R^2	0.098	0.103	0.111	0.157

The sample contains 1,816 firms with 16,802 firm-year observations from 2001 to 2017. The numbers in the parentheses are the t-values. ***, **, and * indicate statistical significance at the 0.01, 0.05 and 0.10 levels, respectively.

We first regress stock returns on value-to-price ratio, and find a siginificant positive relation between firm value and stock return, which supports the first hypothesis in our study. The coefficient of Vf/P in model (1) in Table 2 is 0.47, the coefficient of BV/P in model (1) is 0.68, and both are sigificant at 0.01 level. When the two variables are inclued I model (2), the siginificant positive coefficients remain in the result, indicating that the firm value incorporated real option can explain the variance of stock return, even if book value is controlled.

In model (4), we control for the other possible risk variables. The positive regression coefficients of the main variables (Vf/P and BV/P) are consistent with the existing studies. The results indicate that after controlling for the other risk variables in the models, the value-to-price ratio still plays an important role in explaining the stock returns, and they are not a proxy for the other missing risk variables. Moreover, except for Growth, most of the risk factors are significant in the expected direction.

4.3 Hypotheses testing of H2

In this part, we try to examine whether corporate governance impact the value-relevance because investors care about the information environment. We propose that, as the principal-agent conflict of a firm alleviates, the information environment is conducive to investors'

decision-making, which helps the investors exercise the option value related to the investing firm.

Accordingly, we predict that the coefficient of the interaction Vf/P*Agency is positive. Specifically, in a firm with less agency conflict, the asset utilization ratio is higher; moreover, investors can benefit from the information environment and earn abnormal stock returns. In other words, the positive relation between Vf/P and stock return will be enhanced in firms with a higher asset utilization ratio.

Table 3. Impact of the agency cost on the value-relevance.

Intercept	Vf/P	BV/P	Agency	Vf/P*Agency
2.97***	0.25***	0.69***	$-0.05***$	0.11***
(28.56)	(13.24)	(22.79)	(-2.98)	(5.42)
Beta	Size	ROA	Lev	Growth
$-0.33***$	$-0.14***$	1.38***	0.41***	-0.000
(-14.22)	(-27.99)	(12.56)	(12.17)	(-0.63)

Adj.R^2 0.159
F value $= 384.34$

The independent variable is stock returns. The variable Agency represents the agency cost in a firm. We use the asset utilization ratio (computed as annual sales divided by total assets) as the proxy. The numbers in the parentheses are the t-values. ***, **, and * indicate statistical significance at the 0.01, 0.05 and 0.10 levels, respectively.

Table 3 summarizes the results of the regression model of examining whether the corporate information environment matters. The variable Agency represents the agency cost in a firm, and the asset utilization ratio is used as the proxy. The coefficient of interest is the interaction Vf/P*Agency. As expected, it is positive and significant at the 0.01 level. The enhanced value-relevance based on real options provide empirical evidence for Hypotheses 2 stated in the study. The results show that the alleviated principal-agent conflict may result in an improved information environment, helping investors in investment decision-making. In the environment with less agency conflicts, investors are able to get more information about the firm's operation, and the real options embedded in the firm's future opportunities.

5 CONCLUSION

The firm valuation has been attracting attention from the academic and capital market participants. In recent decades, scholars have attempted to improve the valuation model by examining the dynamic process of investment decisions from the perspective of the real option of future operation. Quantifying the real options accurately is difficult as the real options differ from financial options. Most previous studies have examined the real option value through the convex function of firm value and net profits. This study follows

Hwang and Sohn's (2010) real options model to evaluate the value of China's A-share listed firms from 2001 to 2017. The regression results indicate that the firm value incorporating real option value can explain the variance of the stock return, and the results remain after controlling for other risk factors. In the further analysis section, we also provide evidence that for firms with less agency cost, the information environment can help investors obtain useful information for future investment decision-making and exercising option value. This study provides evidence of the real option value-relevance in China's stock market, which can help investors understand the intrinsic firm valuation from the perspective of real options.

REFERENCES

Ang, J. S., Cole, R., & Lin, J. W. (2000). Agency costs and ownership structure. *The Journal of Finance*, 1(1), 81–106. https://doi.org/10.1111/0022-1082.00201

Black, F., & Scholes, M. (1973). The pricing of options and corporate liabilities. *Journal of Political Economy*, 81(3), 637–657. https://doi.org/10.1086/260062

Burgstahler D. C and Dichev, I. D. 1997. Earnings, adaptation and equity value. *The Accounting Review*, 72(2), 187–215.

Carpenter, J. N., Lu, F., Whitelaw, R. F., Chen, H., Drechsler, I., Goetzmann, W., & Hasbrouck, J. (2020). The real value of China's stock market R. *Journal of Financial Economics*, xxxx, 1–18. https://doi.org/10.1016/j.jfineco.2020.08.012

Chen, C. Y., Chen, P. F., and Jin, Q. 2015. Economic freedom, investment flexibility, and equity value: A cross-country study. *Accounting Review*, 90(5), 1839–1870. doi:10.2308/accr-51034.

Dichev, D. C. B. D. (1997). Earnings, adaptation and equity value. *The Accounting Review*, 72(2), 187–215. https://doi.org/10.1371/journal.pone.0070508

Edwards, E., and P. Bell. 1961. The theory of and measurement of business income. *University of California Press*.

Fama, F., and French, R. 1993. Common risk factors in the returns on stocks and bonds. *Journal of Financial Economics*, 33, 3–56. doi:.10.1016/0304-405X(93)90023-5.

Frankel, R., and Lee, C. M. C. 1998. Accounting valuation, market expectation, and cross-sectional stock returns. *Journal of Accounting and Economics*, 25(3), 283–319. doi:10.1016/S01654101(98)00026-3.

Gordon, M. J., & Shapiro, E. (1956). Capital Equipment Analysis: The Required Rate of Profit. *Management Science*, 3(1), 102–110. https://doi.org/10.1287/mnsc.3.1.102

Hiemann, M. (2020). Earnings and firm value in the presence of real options. *Accounting Review*, 95(6), 263–289. https://doi.org/10.2308/TAR-2017-0019

Hwang, L. S., & Sohn, B. C. (2010). Return predictability and shareholders' real options. *Review of Accounting Studies*, 15(2), 367–402. https://doi.org/10.1007/s11142-010-9119-2

Jensen, Michael C., and William H. Meckling, 1976, Theory of the firm: Managerial behavior, agency costs and capital structure, *Journal of Financial Economics* 3, 305–360.

Lee, C. M. C., Myers, J., & Swaminathan, B. (1999). What Is the Intrinsic Value of the Dow? *The Journal of Finance*, 54(5), 1693–741. https://doi.org/10.1111/0022-1082.00164

Ohlson, J. A. (1995). Earnings, Book Values, and Dividends in Equity Valuation. *Contemporary Accounting Research*, 11(2), 661–687. https://doi.org/10.1111/j.1911-3846.1995.tb00461.x

Qinglu Jin, Shuang Xue, C. G. (2010). Does Market Liberalization Influence Companies? Growth and Liquidation Values? *China Economic Quarterly*, 9(4), 1485–1504. https://doi.org/10.13821/j.cnki.ceq.2010.04.014

Rao, P., Yue, H., & Zhou, X. (2018). Return predictability and the real option value of segments. *In Review of Accounting Studies* (Vol. 23, Issue 1). https://doi.org/10.1007/s11142-017-9421-3

Trombley, A. A. L. H. M. A. (2003). Residual Income Based Valuation Predicts Future Stock Returns: Evidence on Mispricing VS. Risk Explanations. *The Accounting Review*, 78(2), 377–396. https://doi.org/10.2308/accr.2003.78.2.37

Tusheng Xiao, Qinglu Jin, X. C. (2016). Industry Competition and Cost Stickiness: Empirical Tests Based on Real Option Theory. *Journal of Management Sciences in China*, 19(3), 48–63.

Xinyuan Chen, Qinglu Jin, Tusheng Xiao, G. Z. (2013). Industry Competition, Managerial Investment, and Equity Value of Growth/Put Options. *China Economic Quarterly*, 13(1), 305–332. https://doi.org/10.13821/j.cnki.ceq.2014.01.013

Zhang, G. (2000). Accounting Information, Capital Investment Decisions, and Equity Valuation: Theory and Empirical Implications. *Journal of Accounting Research*, 38(2), 271. https://doi.org/10.2307/2672934

Economic and Business Management – Huang & Zhang (Eds)
© 2022 Copyright the Author(s), ISBN: 978-1-032-06754-4

An empirical analysis of the E-commerce impact on social consumption

Guanghai Tang & Hui Zeng
School of Management, Yangtze Normal University, Chongqing, China

ABSTRACT: E-commerce releases the potential of social consumption and promotes the development of social consumption retail. This paper constructs a panel model for empirical research based on the relationship between E-commerce sales, express business income, mobile phone penetration rate, and social consumption retail sales of 31 provinces, municipalities, and autonomous regions in China from 2013 to 2019. The test results show that E-commerce, express business income, science and technology investment, and education investment have a significant impact on social consumption retail sales, and there are certain regional differences. The impact indicators of the eastern region are greater than that of the central and western regions. Especially, the education investment has a negative impact in the western region, but it has a positive impact in the eastern and central regions. Thus, in order to further release the potential of social consumption, we need to strengthen the development of E-commerce, including increasing the construction of mobile E-commerce infrastructure, express service facilities and capacity, and strengthening the investment in education and science and technology in the related fields of E-commerce in the central and western regions.

1 INTRODUCTION

In 2019, the total sales of social consumption retail in 31 provinces, municipalities, and autonomous regions in China, except Hong Kong, Macao, and Taiwan, reached 41.16 trillion yuan. Consumption, investment, and export are the "troika" for modern economic growth. China's economy has entered a new era. How to stimulate domestic demand, promote consumption, and achieve steady economic growth is a hot issue in academic circles. Guan Weihua et al. studied the level of regional social consumption [1]; Zhao Ping and Zhang Bin et al. analyzed the financial policy of social consumption [2], money supply [3], and other important factors; and Hu Daoyin et al. studied the countermeasures to promote regional social consumption [4]. The growth of social consumption or the promotion of social consumption level plays an important role in the economic growth of our country, so we should strengthen or perfect the fiscal and financial policies of consumption.

With the spread of internet technology, the development of online retail has gradually affected the regional consumption pattern [5]. Liu Hu et al. pointed out that the internet is the new driving force of consumption upgrading [6]. While the internet is convenient for online shopping, it also promotes the upgrading of life and security consumption to entertainment consumption and learning consumption [7]. In 2019, the E-commerce sales in China were 16.93 trillion yuan, accounting for 41.13% of the total sales of social consumption retail. E-commerce sales have become one of the main channels of social consumption retail, and

its impact on the total retail sales of social consumption is becoming greater and greater [8]. The rapid growth of mobile E-commerce plays an increasingly important role in activating the traditional consumer retail market. In 2019, the daily online retail sales of Double Eleven exceeded 400 billion yuan, of which 95% of the orders came from mobile terminals. Li Yuhai et al. [9] pointed out that the rise of mobile E-commerce is not an accidental phenomenon. Compared with traditional E-commerce, mobile internet has the characteristics of mobility, immediacy, novelty, randomness, and convenience. When designing and implementing policies to promote social consumption, E-commerce is also innovating the traditional retail model, improving the structure and model of the retail market, and exerting a great influence on the traditional retailers, the market, and consumers [10]. It can be seen that the influence of E-commerce on social consumption has a strong theoretical and practical basis. Regional governments pay more and more attention to E-commerce, online retail, digital consumption, and other new retail modes and channels of social consumption.

In order to reveal the relationship between E-commerce and social consumption retail, a panel data model is established based on the relevant data of 31 provinces, municipalities, and autonomous regions, except Hong Kong, Macao, and Taiwan. This paper makes a comparative analysis of the impact of E-commerce on social consumption retail in eastern, central, and western regions in China, so as to put forward corresponding countermeasures for the development of regional E-commerce, and provide a reference for China's regional E-commerce and digital retail.

44

DOI 10.1201/9781003203704-9

2 MODEL CONSTRUCTION AND DATA DESCRIPTION

2.1 Panel data model

Panel data refers to the repeated observed data of individuals at different time points on the cross section, which is the mixed data of time series and cross section. Using panel data to build a model can increase the observed value to increase the sampling accuracy of the estimator, and at the same time, more dynamic information can be obtained [11].

The general expression of the panel data model is as follows:

$$y_{it} = \alpha_i + \beta_n X_{it} + \varepsilon_{it}, \tag{1}$$

where y_{it} is the regression variable (scalar), α_i is the random variable, X_{it} is the column vector of k*i order regression variables, β is the column vector of k*i order regression coefficients, and ε_{it} is the error term.

2.2 Model construction

In order to investigate the impact of E-commerce on China's social consumption retail, this paper constructs the following model:

$$Cons_{jit} = \beta_0 + \beta_1 X_{it} + \beta_n M_{it} + \mu_i + \varepsilon_{it} \tag{2}$$

Among them, Cons (Consumption) is the explained variable, which represents the total sales of social consumption retail, and j represents the statistical regions of social consumption retail sales, including the whole country, east, middle, and west of China. I represents the province, T represents the time, individual effect and random effect. X is the core explanatory variable of this paper, which is used to reflect the development of E-commerce, and M is the controlled variable.

In addition to Electronic commerce sales (Ecs), the development of E-commerce can also be expressed by Exp (Express Revenue) and the number of online shopping users [8,12]. Among them, E-commerce sales and express revenue indicators have statistical data from 2013 to 2019, while the number of online shopping users lacks direct statistical data, which is generally expressed by internet penetration rate [13]. Since 2013, online shopping users have gradually reflected in the growth of mobile terminals. Therefore, the number of online shopping users can be expressed by the number of mobile users, so Mob is used to measure the number of online shopping users.

The controlled variables mainly include regional economic environment, education investment, science and technology investment, and employment expectation [8].

The regional economic environment is generally expressed in terms of per capita GDP. Preliminary studies have shown that the regional economic environment, especially the local economic environment, has a significant impact on residents' consumption and social consumption [8]. Some studies also take residents' income as the premise of social consumption and retail. Relevant studies also show that the regional per capita income and per capita GDP present synergy. Here, per capita GDP is selected to represent the regional economic environment.

Education input (Edu) is an important factor in social and economic development [14]. Especially in the development of E-commerce and digital commerce, the education investment in internet technology, E-commerce, big data, and other fields directly affects the promotion and application of E-commerce and other digital consumption fields. The per capita investment in education is used to measure the investment in education.

Science and technology input (Sci) is an important foundation for social innovation. Science and technology input can improve the mode, mechanism, and tools of social consumption retail, such as takeaway, crowdfunding, sharing economy and social marketing, and also innovate social consumption products, such as smart phones, e-books, and mobile games [15]. We use the local per capita science and technology expenditure index to measure the investment in science and technology.

Employment expectations are a measure index of people's future income expectations. Confidence in future income will affect the increase of current social consumption proportion, otherwise it will decrease. Scholars often use the urban unemployment rate (UnEmp) to reflect the employment expectation index [16].

The above variables were brought into the model (1). In order to eliminate the heterosexuality, all variables were logarithmically processed to construct the panel model (3).

$$\begin{aligned}
LnCONS = {}& \beta_0 + \beta_1 LnEC_{it} + \beta_1 LnExp_{it} \\
& + \beta_1 LnMob_{it} + \beta_1 LnGDP_{it} \\
& + \beta_1 LnEdu_{it} + \beta_1 LnSci_{it} \\
& + \beta_1 LnUnemp_{it} + \mu_i + \varepsilon_{it}
\end{aligned} \tag{3}$$

2.3 Data description

This paper selects the panel data of 31 provinces, municipalities, and autonomous regions in China, except Hong Kong, Macao, and Taiwan, from 2013 to 2019. All data is obtained from China Statistical Yearbook (2014–2020) and China Economic Network. The relevant data is taken and the influence of price factors is eliminated taking 2013 as the base period. In order to analyze the internal relationship between the data, the descriptive statistical analysis results of each index data are shown in Table 1.

In Table 1, there are big regional differences in E-commerce, express business income, education investment, and scientific and technological investment. The variance of the two indicators, per capita E-commerce sales and per capita express business income, is more than 1.00, and the variance of the two indicators, per

Table 1. Descriptive statistical analysis of data.

	Mean	Std. Dev.	Maximum	Minimum	Probability
LnCons	9.930004	0.460655	11.155300	8.913000	0.069697
LnEcs	8.444457	1.053980	11.588700	5.407200	0.000218
LnExp	4.843835	1.157223	8.577000	2.759600	0.000001
LnMob	4.596886	0.213631	5.244000	4.128300	0.000248
LnGDP	10.868220	0.411474	12.008900	10.047200	0.002452
LnEdu	8.247628	0.957895	11.645900	7.247300	0.000000
LnSci	6.547295	0.996150	9.246600	4.205000	0.109840
LnUnEmp	1.139081	0.226030	1.504100	0.182300	0.000000

capita education expenditure and per capita science and technology expenditure is greater than 0.95. It can be seen that, in addition to the overall impact analysis of E-commerce on social consumption in China, it is necessary to further compare and analyze the effects of regional E-commerce on social consumption from the perspective of eastern, central, and western regions in China.

3 MODEL INSPECTION

3.1 *Impact of E-commerce on social consumption*

The model (3) is first tested by F-statistics to make the choice from the mixed regression effect model and fixed effect model. Then Hausman test is used to make the choice from the random effect model and the fixed effect model. After the test, the model (3) is suitable for the fixed effect model. The inspection results are shown in Table 2.

In Table 2, model ① directly tests the impact of per capita E-commerce sales on per capita total sales of social consumption retail; the model ② is used to test the impact of the three core indicators of E-commerce on the per capita total sales of social consumption retail; the model ③ is the influence of E-commerce on the total retail sales of per capita social consumption by considering the control variables. The R2 of the three models is greater than 0.85, the F value passed the significant level at least 5%, and the fitting degree of each model is very good.

From model ①, the impact of per capita E-commerce sales on the per capita total sales of social consumption retail is significant at the level of 1%, and the coefficient reaches 0.256118, which means that the per capita total sales of social consumption retail will rise by 2.56118% for every 10% increase in per capita E-commerce sales.

In the model ②, the three core indicators of E-commerce have a significant impact on the per capita total sales of social consumption retail, and the coefficients are positive. So the development of internet information technology, the strengthening of E-commerce technology innovation and diffusion, the construction of E-commerce logistics and other infrastructure, the promotion of E-commerce model innovation, and the application of online retail have a good

Table 2. Test results of the impact of E-commerce on social consumption.

Explanatory variable	LnCons		
	Model ①	Model ②	Model ③
C	7.767226***	6.680199***	−1.160215**
	(34.98319)	(7.707687)	(−1.225333)
LnEcs	0.256118***	0.065296**	0.031529*
	(9.756371)	(1.434782)	(0.968484)
LnExp		0.189199**	0.211559**
		(3.801028)	(0.388937)
LnMob		0.387647*	−0.094778*
		(2.621319)	(−0.69146)
LnGDP			0.822412***
			(4.324861)
LnEdu			−0.009366*
			(−0.949932)
LnSci			0.417541***
			(5.260503)
LnUnEmp			−0.026009
			(−0.414372)
R-squared	0.864396	0.908402	0.963448
F	2.039228***	2.184564***	1.723828***
Hausman	0	0	0
Model	FE	FE	FE

Note: '*', '**', '***', respectively, represent the significant level of 10%, 5%, and 1%, and the T-statistic is represented in parentheses, and Fe and RE, respectively, represent fixed effect model and random effect model.

impact and effect on promoting the growth of social consumption retail.

In the model ③, the controlled variables of per capita GDP, per capita education investment, and per capita science and technology investment have significant impact on the total sales of social consumption retail, but the impact of urban unemployment rate is not significant. Among them, per capita GDP and per capita investment in science and technology have a positive impact on the total sales of social consumption retail. However, the per capita education investment has a negative impact. It can be seen that education investment crowded out social consumption, while the new consumption potential brought by education investment is not obvious during 2013–2019.

It can be seen that, as the research results and expectations of Liu Hu [7] and Zhang Hong [12] et al.

indicate, E-commerce has a promoting effect on social consumption. In order to further analyze the impact of various variables and control variables of e-commerce on social consumption, it is necessary to do a comparative study on the eastern, central, and western parts of China.

3.2 Regional difference

In order to further analyze the driving effect of E-commerce on social consumption in China, it is necessary to carry out a comparative study on the eastern, central, and western parts of China. The results are shown in Table 3.

Table 3. Comparative test results of eastern, central, and western regions.

Explanatory variable	Eastern	Central	Western
C	0.561671**	−1.588154**	−1.348381**
	(0.26485)	(−0.681372)	(−1.077029)
LnEcs	0.033066**	0.0308146**	0.021948**
	(0.054589)	(0.545815)	(0.969916)
LnExp	0.373656***	0.347791***	0.023273**
	(2.689205)	(1.280236)	(0.518924)
LnMob	0.377646*	−0.007974*	−0.159233*
	(1.234268)	(−1.566573)	(−0.863644)
LnGDP	0.624605***	0.980898***	0.858883***
	(3.386662)	(4.154334)	(5.633996)
LnEdu	0.060541*	0.055399**	−0.023377***
	(0.330036)	(0.292476)	(−1.717138)
LnSci	0.366158**	0.188884***	0.431093***
	(2.046454)	(1.136691)	(4.389497)
LnUnEmp	−0.102066	0.145712	−0.050533
	(−0.943494)	(0.948383)	(−0.588951)
R-squared	0.966238	0.925724	0.959552
F	1.423688***	2.562779***	1.227848***
Hausman	0	0	0
Model	FE	FE	FE

Note: '*', '*', '*', '*', respectively, represent the significant level of 10%, 5%, and 1%, and the T-statistic is represented in parentheses, and Fe and RE, respectively, represent fixed effect model and random effect model.

The results show that the impact of E-commerce indicators on the total sales of social consumption retail is obviously high in the eastern and low in the western regions.

The impact coefficients of LnEcs on LnCons in the eastern, central, and western regions are 0.033066, 0.0308146 and, 0.021948, respectively. For every 10% increase in E-commerce sales (Ecs) in the eastern region, its impact on social consumption is 0.1% higher than that in the western region; the impact of express income in the eastern and central regions is more obvious than that in the western regions. The impact of express income (Exp) in the eastern region is 10% higher than that in the western region, which is about 16 times; the impact of internet technology and equipment, such as mobile phone on social consumption, is also strengthening. The investment in internet

equipment in the eastern part has a positive impact, while it has a negative effect of crowding out social consumption in the central and western regions.

Compared with the control variables, GDP and other economic environment variables have a significant impact on social consumption; Education investment (Edu) has a positive effect in the eastern and central regions, but it has a negative effect in the western region, which may be related to the brain drain in the western region; Science and technology investment (Sci) has a positive impact on social consumption, and the western is higher than the eastern and central regions, which may be related to the weak foundation of science and technology innovation investment in the western region and the transition of social consumption from survival consumption to development consumption [8].

4 CONCLUSION AND SUGGESTION

Based on the panel data of 31 provinces, municipalities, and autonomous regions, except Hong Kong, Macao, and Taiwan, from 2013 to 2019, this paper finds that the development of E-commerce has a significant impact on the promotion of social consumption in China, and it is higher in the East than in the West; local economic development, education investment, science and technology investment, and other controlled variables have significant effects on promoting social consumption. Based on the relevant test results, the suggestions are as follows:

(1) All localities should strengthen E-commerce development plan, introduce E-commerce incentive policies, vigorously develop E-commerce, and promote social consumption progress to fuel local economic growth. In particular, the western region should develop E-commerce based on local characteristic industries to form E-commerce clusters, learn from the experience of the eastern and central regions, use E-commerce to upgrade the social consumption structure, and promote the economic development.

(2) The development of E-commerce needs to strengthen the construction of logistics infrastructure and express delivery service system. Especially the western express delivery capacity and system is still not perfect, the cost of express service is higher than the middle and east of China, which affects the promotion effect of regional E-commerce on social consumption.

(3) We should further develop internet technology, popularize and upgrade mobile internet devices, innovate E-commerce mode, and promote E-commerce. In particular, the social consumption potential brought by the growth of mobile devices in western region has not been fully released.

(4) Strengthening investment in education, especially popularizing E-commerce sales and consumption skills of rural residents, has a strong driving role in

promoting social consumption. In particular, we should strengthen the investment in E-commerce education and training in the central and western regions to promote the rapid development of regional E-commerce.

ACKNOWLEDGMENT

This work was supported by the research foundation project of Yangtze Normal University (Grants no. 010730095).

REFERENCES

[1] Guan Weihua, Zhou Jing, Lu Yuqi. (2012). Study on the regional pattern change of social consumption levels in China since the reform and opening up [J]. *Geographical Research*, 31 (02), 234–244.

[2] Zhao Ping. (2002). Our positive fiscal policy: effects on pushing consumption demand [J]. *Economic Theory and Business Management*, 11, 18–23.

[3] Zhang Bin, Yin Zhu. (2017). Empirical analysis on the dynamic effect of money supply on social consumption[J]. *Statistics & Decision*, 23, 153–156.

[4] Hu Daoyin, Shen Wen. (2015). Research on consumption promotion strategies of Hubei Province based on retail data of social consumer goods [J]. *Hubei Social Sciences*, 12, 55–60.

[5] Yang Shoude, Zhao Dehai. (2017). Analysis on Influence of Online Retail Development on Regional Consumption Pattern in China [J]. *Journal of Social Sciences*, 10, 61–72.

[6] Liu Hu, Zhang Jiaping. (2016). Driving effects of internet on household consumption [J]. *Journal of Beijing University of Posts and Telecommunications (Social Sciences Edition)*, 18 (03), 14–21.

[7] Liu Hu, Zhang Jiaping. (2016). Is the Internet a new engine for expanding household consumption? Empirical analysis from urban panel data[J]. *Consumption Economy*, 32(02), 17–22.

[8] Liu Hu, Zhang Jiaping. (2016). The influence of Internet on the consumption structure of rural residents and regional differences [J]. *Science of finance and economics*, 04, 80–88.

[9] Li Yuhai, Wang Yinxia. (2015). Analysis of information consumption demand in mobile Internet era [J]. *Library Theory and Practice*, 4, 43–46.

[10] Wang Yu, Li Wei, Zhang Weijin (2019). Research on the Influence Mechanism of Online Retail on Traditional Retailer Innovation [J]. *Management Review*, 31(05):139–146.

[11] Arellano M. (2003). Panel Data Econometrics[M]. *Oxford University Press*, 80–86.

[12] Zhang Hong, Liu Xiuzheng. (2017). The impact of E-commerce on rural economy – based on multiple regression model and cluster analysis [J]. *Jiangsu Agricultural Sciences*, 45 (17), 305–309.

[13] Li Liwei, Li Dandan. (2015) Determinant of mobile Internet Diffusion: empirical research based on country-level cross-sectional data [J]. *Journal of Technology Economics*, 34 (06), 37–42.

[14] Hao Qian. (2021). Analysis of coordination degree between higher education and regional economy [J]. *Statistics & Decision*, 37 (09), 68–70.

[15] Liu Yixuan, He Jianfeng (2020). The impact of science and technology input on industrial structure upgrading: An empirical study based on China's provincial panel data from 2005 to 2016 [J]. *Science and Technology Management Research*, 40 (04), 173–178.

[16] Zhang Huachu. (2015). The impact of unemployment risk on floating population consumption[J]. *Economic Review*, 2, 68–76.

Economic and Business Management – Huang & Zhang (Eds)
© 2022 Copyright the Author(s), ISBN: 978-1-032-06754-4

Study on the trade effects of China's outward foreign direct investment—data from the countries along the Belt and Road

Kai Sun* & Xiaoming Zhang

School of International Economics and Trade, Shandong University of Finance and Economics, Jinan,Shandong, P.R. China

ABSTRACT: To examine the effects of Outward Foreign Direct Investment (OFDI), this paper based on the actual national conditions and relevant endowments of the countries along the Belt and Road (B&R) used an extended gravity model and a systematic GMM to regress the trade effects of OFDI of different investment types. The results showed that China's direct investment in countries along B&R has produced a relatively obvious trade creation effect overall. The market size, population, and natural resources of these countries positively correlate with the trade creation effect, but the correlation of technology level and trade creation effect is weak. The regression of different types of investment reveals that market-seeking and efficiency-seeking OFDI have the largest trade creation effect, followed by resource-seeking OFDI, but technology-seeking OFDI does not have a significant trade creation effect.

Keywords: OFDI; Trade Effect; Investment Motive; Data of Countries along B&R

1 INTRODUCTION

Since the Belt and Road Initiative was proposed, China's investment and trade with these countries has been growing, and bilateral economic cooperation has stepped to a new height. According to the 2019 China Foreign Direct Investment Statistics Bulletin, from 2013 to 2019, China's cumulative direct investment in these countries was US$117.31 billion, and more than 10,000 overseas enterprises were established. In addition, China's total trade in goods with 138 countries along B&R reached US$1.90 trillion, accounting for 41.5% of the total. Thus, the Belt and Road initiative can not only promote China's investment in the countries along the route but also further promote the freedom and facilitation of trade.

Based on literature reviews, there are three main academic views on the trade effect of OFDI: OFDI trade substitution effect (Goh et al., 2012; Helpman et al., 2004; Mundell, 1957), OFDI trade creation effect (Chédor et al., 2002; Kojima & Ozawa, 1984), and the uncertainty of the OFDI impact on trade (Nyen Wong & Khoon Goh, 2013).

There is little literature to analyze the transmission mechanism and internal logic behind the trade effect of OFDI for the actual national conditions and endowments of the countries along B&R. This paper analyzes the mechanism and made a hypothesis on the possibility of OFDI trade effects, explored the overall trade effects of China's direct investment in countries along B&R, and further investigated the trade effects of different investment motives from the perspective of investment motives.

2 THEORETICAL FRAMEWORK AND ASSUMPTIONS

When enterprises make OFDI, they will consider the internal and external environment. Different types of investment will have different effects on imports and exports, which in turn will have different trade effects. The paper draws upon the eclectic theory of international production (Dunning, 1977) and classifies OFDI into three types, consisting of efficiency-seeking, market-seeking, technology-seeking, and resource-seeking, according to different investment motives to analyze the trade effects of OFDI under various investment motives.

2.1 *China's efficiency-seeking investment and trade effects on countries along B&R*

The main investment motive of efficiency-seeking OFDI is to improve enterprise productivity and obtain economies of scope or scale. Because of some factors of production such as labor and land, which are restricted in movement, enterprises transfer their production, lines to the host country to obtain cheap and abundant factors of production. Part of the goods produced by the enterprise will be sold locally to meet the

---

*Corresponding Author

DOI 10.1201/9781003203704-10

previous need of the host country to import this part of products from the home country, which is equivalent to reducing the exports of the home country and generating an export substitution effect. In addition, if the home country shifts its industry to the host country with lower factor costs, the supply of the home country will be reduced and the domestic demand for the product will be met by imports, thus creating an import creation effect for the home country. Based on the analysis above, this paper proposes the following hypothesis:

Hypothesis 1: China's efficiency-seeking investment in countries along B&R generates an export substitution effect, import creation effect, and overall trade creation effect.

2.2 China's market-seeking investment and trade effects on countries along B&R

The main motive of market-seeking investment is to acquire overseas markets or to avoid trade barriers. In recent years, with the continuous upgrading of many industries in China, several industries with competitive advantages in the international market have been spawned, such as large-scale infrastructure, communication construction, high-speed rail, etc., which promotes the export of related electro-mechanical equipment, spare parts, and intermediate goods, generating an export creation effect. On the other hand, these countries, continuously absorbing and imitating technologies, will also produce similar products for re-sale back to China, generating an import creation effect. Based on the above analysis, this paper proposes the following hypothesis:

Hypothesis 2: China's market-seeking investment in countries along B&R generates export-creating effects, import-creating effects, and overall trade-creating effects.

2.3 China's resource-seeking investment and trade effects on countries along B&R

The main investment motive of resource-seeking OFDI is to obtain resources and secure domestic resource supply. For example, in the mining industry, when enterprises make direct investment in the host country, due to the lack of technical capacity in the host country, they will export the corresponding machinery and equipment to the host country, thus expanding the exports of the home country and generating the export creation effect. After acquiring mineral and oil resources, enterprises directly export these resources to the country, thus creating an import creation effect. Furthermore, reprocessing the acquired resources in the host country or applying the extracted resources to reinvest in the related industries in the host country will reduce part of the imports, generating the import substitution effect. Based on the above analysis, this paper proposes the following hypothesis:

Hypothesis 3: China's resource-seeking investment in countries along B&R generates export-creating

effects, import-creating effects, and overall trade-creating effects.

2.4 China's technology-seeking investment and trade effects on countries along B&R

The main investment motive of technology-seeking direct investment is to acquire advanced high technology and related management experience in the host country, most of which are developed countries. After OFDI in the host country, enterprises will, on the one hand, directly import technologically advanced equipment from the host country, creating an import creation effect. On the other hand, after acquiring the relevant technology and management experience, enterprises will break the previously existing technical barriers and upgrade or modify the technology of their products, which will improve the competitiveness of domestic products, indirectly expanding their exports and generating the export creation effect. Based on the above analysis, this paper proposes the following hypothesis:

Hypothesis 4: China's technology-seeking investment in countries along B&R generates export-creating effects, import-creating effects, and overall trade-creating effects.

3 STUDY DESIGN

3.1 Sample selection and data sources

Sixty countries along B&R are selected as the research objects and used in this paper, spanning the period of 2013–2018, as shown in Table 1. And the data are mainly derived from China Statistics Yearbook, China's Foreign Direct Investment Bulletin, World

Table 1. The 60 countries selected for B&R.

Region	Country
East Asia	Mongolia
Southeast Asia	Indonesia, Cambodia, Myanmar, Thailand, Laos, Singapore, Malaysia, Vietnam, Philippines, Brunei
Central Asia	Tajikistan, Kazakhstan, Kyrgyzstan, Uzbekistan, Turkmenistan
South Asia	India, Pakistan, Bangladesh, Pakistan, Sri Lanka, Afghanistan
Western Asia	Oman, UAE, Turkey, Bahrain, Yemen, Kuwait, Syria, Lebanon, Iraq, Qatar, Jordan, Oman, UAE, Turkey, Iran, Saudi Arabia, Israel, Palestine
Commonwealth of Independent States	Russia, Belarus, Georgia, Armenia, Ukraine, Azerbaijan.
Central and Eastern Europe	Czech Republic, Slovakia, Romania, Hungary, Bulgaria, Lithuania, Poland, Latvia, Slovenia, Croatia, Albania, Estonia, Serbia, Macedonia, Bosnia and Herzegovina

Bank, CEPII Database, and World Management Indicator database.

3.2 Model design

Based on the traditional trade gravity model, an extended trade gravity model is constructed to analyze the trade effects of OFDI from China to B&R countries. In order to eliminate the effect of inflation, OFDI data and trade data are deflated in the base period and the unit is unified to US\$ million.

$$LnTT_{ijt} / LnIM_{ijt} / LnEX_{ijt} = \alpha_0 + \alpha_1 LnOFDI_{ijt}$$
$$+ \alpha_2 LnGDP_{jt} + \alpha_3 LnPOP_{jt} + \alpha_4 LnENR_{jt}$$
$$+ \alpha_5 LnRD_{jt} + \alpha_6 LnDIS_{ij} + \alpha_7 BRER_{ijt}$$
$$+ \alpha_8 LnIns_{jt} + \nu t + \mu_{jt} \qquad (1)$$

Where i represents China, j represents the host country, and t represents the year. IM EX and TT represent China's import, export, and export and import (IMP&EXP) to the countries along B&R respectively. Furthermore, OFDI represents the stock of China's direct investment, GDP represents the market size, POP represents the labor force, and ENR represents the natural resources of the host country. RD represents the technology level of the host country. DIS represents the distance between the two countries. BRER represents the exchange rate between the two countries. INS represents the institutional environment of the host country. ν represents the time effect. μ represents the random disturbance term.

3.3 Estimation method

Due to the possible interaction between investment and trade, if the current investment data and trade data are selected, the model may be endogenous, and the regression results of the model may be biased. The Hausman test and the heteroskedasticity robust DWH test are used to verify whether there are endogenous explanatory variables in the model. Both tests significantly rejected the original hypothesis, indicating that the model has endogeneity problems and instrumental variables must be introduced. Further, the White heteroskedasticity test and Wooldridge autocorrelation test were performed on the model, and the results showed that the model has heteroskedasticity as well as autocorrelation.

Considering the advantage of generalized moment estimation (GMM) which allows heteroskedasticity and serial correlation of random error terms, the systematic GMM method among GMM methods is chosen for estimation in this paper. The systematic GMM is chosen because a) years selected in the model are 2013–2018, which are short panel data; and b) the distance variables in the model are time-invariant.

In this paper, the lagged one-period stock of OFDI and the lagged two-period stock of OFDI are selected as the instrumental variables of OFDI stock. To start with, the lagged one-period and lagged two-period

stocks do not affect the current period's imports and exports. Furthermore, the lagged one-period and lagged two-period stocks of OFDI are highly correlated with the current period's stocks of OFDI. The first-stage regression is conducted, and the result shows that the F-statistic is 1586.86 (p = 0.0000), which is significantly greater than 10, indicating that the instrumental variables have good explanatory power for the endogenous variables. In addition, an over-identification test of the instrumental variables shows a P-value of 0.2756, representing the acceptance of the original hypothesis, indicating that the instrumental variables are exogenous and uncorrelated with the disturbance term.

4 ANALYSIS AND TESTING OF EMPIRICAL RESULTS

4.1 Full sample regression

The results of the panel data regression based on the systematic GMM regression method for the 60 countries in the sample are shown in Table 2.

Table 2. Full-sample regression results.

Variables	LnIM	LnEX	LnTT
LnOFDI	0.334***	0.377***	0.332***
	(0.0786)	(0.0661)	(0.0623)
LnGDP	0.4500***	0.314***	0.384***
	(0.0734)	(0.0621)	(0.0585)
LnPOP	0.050	0.374***	0.234***
	(0.0815)	(0.0689)	(0.0645)
LnENR	0.156***	0.174***	0.167***
	(0.0571)	(0.0480)	(0.0258)
LnRD	−0.0161	0.006	−0.0456
	(0.0499)	(0.0420)	(0.0395)
LnINS	1.864***	1.562***	1.598**
	(0.4068)	(0.3421)	(0.0322)
LnBRER	0.009	−0.037	−0.0422
	(0.0439)	(0.0370)	(0.0370)
LnDIS	−0.899***	−0.316*	−0.715***
	(0.2551)	(0.2145)	(0.2018)
R-squared	0.5610	0.6299	0.6134

Note: ***, **, * represent significant at the 1%, 5%, and 10% levels respectively, and standard errors are in parentheses.

Table 2 shows that the coefficients of OFDI are significant at the 1% level in all regression models. For every 1% increase in China's direct investment in the countries along B&R, the import trade with the countries along B&R increases by 0.334%, the export trade by 0.377%, and the import and export (IMP&EXP) trade by 0.332%. This indicates that China's direct investment in countries along B&R has a relatively obvious trade creation effect overall and the export creation effect is slightly larger than the import creation effect.

In terms of other explanatory variables, the host country's market size has a significant positive effect on trade in all three regression models. On the one hand, the huge market size of the host country will attract our investment and other related equipment exports, and on the other hand, the products produced will be sold back to the country, which will have a boosting effect on both imports and exports. The population coefficient is significant at the 1% level in both the export and IMP&EXP models, but not in the import model. The coefficients of natural resources are also positive at the 1% level in all regression models, with coefficients of 0.156, 0.174, and 0.167 respectively. The coefficients of natural resources are smaller than the coefficients of market size and labor force, indicating that the scale of resource-seeking investment is smaller than that of market-seeking investment and efficiency-seeking investment, probably because the market size and labor force are more representatives of China's investment preference in the countries along B&R at this stage. The coefficient of technology level is small and insignificant in all three models because the scale of China's technology-seeking direct investment in the countries along B&R is still relatively small at this stage.

In terms of control variables, the coefficients of the institutional environment of the host country are significantly positive, indicating that a favorable institutional environment has a significant contribution to the trade effect generated by OFDI in China. The positive coefficients in the import model indicate that RMB appreciation has an import-creating effect on the countries along B&R, while the negative coefficients in the export model indicate that RMB appreciation has a suppressive effect on exports. The distance coefficient is larger and significantly negative in each model, indicating that the farther the distance, the smaller the trade effect of China's direct investment in the countries along B&R.

4.2 Sub-sample regression

According to the regional distribution in Table 1, the sample countries selected are shown in Table 3, considering the ranking of countries in terms of the size of investment and trade volume over the years and the market size, labor force, natural resources, and technology level of each country. Table 4 reports

Table 3. Sub-sample countries.

Investment Type	Country
Market-seeking and efficiency-seeking OFDI	Singapore, Myanmar, Thailand, Laos, Malaysia, Indonesia, Philippines, Cambodia, Vietnam, India, Bangladesh, Pakistan
Resource-seeking OFDI	Mongolia, Kuwait, Qatar, Saudi Arabia, UAE, Iran, Turkey, Russia, Kazakhstan, Turkmenistan, Uzbekistan
Technology-seeking OFDI	Singapore, Israel, Poland, Romania, Czech Republic, Hungary, Slovenia

the results of the sub-sample regressions based on different investment motives.

There are both market-seeking and efficiency-seeking types of investment by Southeast Asia and some South Asian countries in China. Therefore, it is difficult to separate the countries in the sample based on a single investment motive. Considering that the main influencing variables of market-seeking and efficiency-seeking are GDP and population, this paper introduces the product of GDP and population as a new explanatory variable in the empirical regression of market-seeking and efficiency-seeking type.

The results of the market-seeking & efficiency-seeking regressions are shown in (a) of Table 4. The coefficients of OFDI in each regression model are significant at the 1% level. The regression results show that for every 1% increase in China's direct investment in market-seeking & efficiency-seeking countries along B&R, it will increase import trade with the countries along B&R by 0.683%, export trade by 0.339%, and IMP&EXP trade by 0.405%. China's

Table 4a. Market-seeking and efficiency-seeking regression results.

Variables	LnIM	LnEX	LnTT
LnOFDI	0.683***	0.339**	0.405***
	(0.1191)	(0.1400)	(0.1007)
Ln(GDP*POP)	0.492***	0.419***	0.441***
	(0.0762)	(0.0892)	(0.0644)
LnENR	0.202***	−0.155**	0.126
	(0.0621)	(0.0726)	(0.234)
LnRD	0.158***	0.294	0.272***
	(0.0233)	(0.2733)	(0.0295)
LnINS	1.370	2.521**	2.187***
	(0.9702)	(1.1354)	(0.8192)
LnBRER	0.174***	−0.194***	−0.183***
	(0.0622)	(−0.0728)	(0.0525)
LnDIS	−9.403**	−13.002***	−11.719***
	(4.1578)	(4.8661)	(3.5110)
R-squared	0.7891	0.7221	0.7642

Table 4b. Resource-seeking regression results.

Variables	LnIM	LnEX	LnTT
LnOFDI	0.407***	0.313***	0.344**
	(0.0263)	(0.0346)	(0.0314)
LnGDP	0.389***	0.361***	0.374***
	(0.0725)	(0.0935)	(0.0924)
LnPOP	0.164	0.221*	0.249*
	(0.182)	(0.1242)	(0.1383)
LnENR	0.286***	0.235***	0.254***
	(0.0365)	(0.0429)	(0.0726)
LnRD	0.037	−0.125*	−0.063
	(0.4652)	(0.0694)	(0.3647)
LnINS	1.125***	1.168***	1.135**
	(0.3521)	(0.0694)	(0.0674)
LnBRER	0.025**	−0.055	−0.0412
	(0.0114)	(0.0524)	(0.0653)
LnDIS	−1.589***	−1.241***	−1.015*
	(0.2651)	(0.3218)	(0.2454)
R-squared	0.6642	0.6658	0.6737

Table 4c. Technology-seeking regression results.

Variables	LnIM	LnEX	LnTT
LnOFDI	0.022	−0.050**	−0.030
	(0.3497)	(0.0243)	(0.0242)
LnGDP	0.673***	0.759***	0.805***
	(0.2446)	(0.1706)	(0.1691)
LnPOP	−0.141	0.598***	0.371**
	(0.3005)	(0.2096)	(0.2077)
LnENR	0.061	−0.038	−0.008
	(0.1545)	(0.1077)	(0.1068)
LnRD	0.509	0.971	0.804
	(0.4745)	(0.9642)	(0.8654)
LnINS	0.271	1.405***	1.032**
	(0.7347)	(0.5125)	(0.5079)
LnBRER	0.209***	0.137***	0.172***
	(0.3713)	(0.0269)	(0.0257)
LnDIS	−3.428***	−2.153***	−2.678***
	(0.8734)	(0.6093)	−0.6038
R-squared	0.8805	0.8882	0.8889

Note: ***, **, * represent significant at the 1%, 5%, and 10% levels respectively, and standard errors are in parentheses.

investment in market-seeking & efficiency-seeking countries along B&R has a significant export-creating and import-creating effect, which contradicts Hypothesis 1 but is consistent with Hypothesis 2. The reason for the violation of Hypothesis 1 may be that the sample of market-seeking countries and efficiency-seeking countries along B&R overlap, i.e., a country has both motives for investment. First, efficiency-seeking investment replaces the portion of exports to the host country by transferring the domestic production line for production and sales in the host country. Second, market-seeking OFDI establishes a production base in the host country and at the same time expands part of its exports to the product in question. The reason for the larger import coefficient may be the following: The host country of market-seeking investment, after gradually mastering the production technology exported by China, starts to produce similar products back to China. Additionally, the efficiency-seeking investment builds production plants in the host country, and China also imports products to the host country to meet domestic needs, so the two import creation effects are superimposed, thus the import coefficient is larger. In addition, the coefficients of the interaction term between market size and population are significant and significantly larger than the coefficients in the full sample regression, indicating that the larger the interaction term is, the more significant the trade creation effect is for direct investment.

The results of the resource-seeking regressions are shown in (b) of Table 4, which shows that there is a significant positive relationship between OFDI and trade. For every 1% increase in Chinese direct investment in resource-seeking countries along B&R, the import, export, and IMP&EXP of the countries along B&R increase by 0.407%, 0.313%, and 0.344% respectively. China's OFDI along B&R has a significant trade creation effect, which is consistent with Hypothesis 3.

The results of the technology-seeking regression are shown in (c) of Table 4. The coefficients are 0.022, −0.05, and −0.03 respectively, and only import trade passes the significance test. China's investment in technology-seeking countries along B&R has an import creation effect and an export substitution effect, which partially contradicts Hypothesis 4. The possible reasons for this are the following: 1) the small scale of China's efficiency-seeking investment at this stage, and 2) the time lag of technology absorption after China imports advanced technology equipment from the host countries, which cannot improve the competitiveness of domestic products in a short period, and thus the trade effect generated by direct investment is not significant.

4.3 Robustness tests

To confirm the robustness of the model, the regression method of the empirical model is changed from GMM to conventional panel data regression, and the explanatory variables are changed to OFDI current stocks. The regression results shown in Table 5 indicate that the signs and the coefficients of the variables are consistent with those of the full-sample regression, suggesting that the empirical model of this paper is robust and feasible.

Table 5. Robustness regression results.

Variables	LnIM	LnEX	LnTT
LnOFDI	0.109**	0.169***	0.148***
	(0.0654)	(0.0248)	(0.0305)
LnGDP	0.204***	0.126***	0.183***
	(0.0459)	(0.0370)	(0.0417)
LnPOP	0.243**	0.569***	0.431***
	(0.1268)	(0.0976)	(0.0898)
LnENR	0.116**	0.102***	0.104***
	(0.0671)	(0.0302)	(0.0237)
LnRD	−0.051	0.023	−0.040
	(0.0479)	(0.0384)	(0.0378)
LnINS	2.072***	1.609***	1.857***
	(0.5809)	(0.4557)	(−0.4344)
LnBRER	0.044	−0.053	0.063
	(0.0715)	(0.0550)	(0.0504)
LnDIS	−1.034**	−0.481**	−0.871***
	(0.4628)	(0.3552)	(0.3241)
R-squared	0.5263	0.5312	0.5958

Note: ***, **, * represent significant at the 1%, 5%, and 10% levels, respectively, and coefficients in parentheses are standard errors.

5 CONCLUSION AND INSIGHTS

China's direct investment in countries along B&R has produced a relatively obvious trade creation effect on imports, exports, and IMP&EXP. The larger the market size, the larger the population, and the richer the natural resources of the countries along B&R, the more obvious the trade creation effect of OFDI is, while the

53

level of technology is not obvious to the trade creation effect of direct investment. The institutional environment has a facilitating effect on the trade creation effect of direct investment, the influence of exchange rate is not significant, and the geographical distance has a suppressing effect, which means that China's OFDI may prefer countries with a better institutional environment and closer geographical distance.

The trade creation effects generated by different investment types are differentiated. Market-seeking and efficiency-seeking OFDI generate the most obvious trade creation effect, followed by resource-seeking OFDI. The trade creation effect of technology-seeking OFDI is not obvious, probably because of the small scale of efficiency-seeking investment in China at this stage, and the time lag of technology absorption after importing advanced technology equipment from the host country, which cannot improve the competitiveness of domestic products in a short period. This paper will try to solve the following problems in the follow-up study. First, in terms of sample selection, the samples selected only include the countries joined in the early stage of B&R. Second, the overall discussion on the trade effect of OFDI only stays at the macro-level and does not go further to the micro-level.

REFERENCES

Chédor, S., Mucchielli, J. & Soubaya, I. (2002), "Intra-firm trade and foreign direct investment: an empirical analysis of French firms", *Multinational firms and impacts on employment, trade and technology*, 84–100.

Goh, S. K., Wong, K. N. & Tham, S. Y. (2012), "Does Outward FDI Matter in International Trade? Evidence from Malaysia".

Helpman, E., Melitz, M. J. & Yeaple, S. R. (2004), "Export Versus FDI with Heterogeneous Firms", *The American economic review*, Vol. 94 No. 1, pp. 300–316.

Kojima, K. & Ozawa, T. (1984), "Micro- and macroeconomic models of direct foreign investment: Toward a synthesis", *Hitotsubashi journal of economics*, Vol. 25 No. 1, pp. 1–20.

Mundell, R. A. (1957), "International trade and factor mobility", *the American economic review*, No. 3, pp. 321–335.

Nyen Wong, K. & Khoon Goh, S. (2013), "Outward FDI, merchandise and services trade: evidence from Singapore", *Journal of business economics and management*, Vol. 14 No. 2, pp. 276–291.

Economic and Business Management – Huang & Zhang (Eds)
© 2022 Copyright the Author(s), ISBN: 978-1-032-06754-4

The comparative studies of Great Divergence from 1850 to 1914

Yifei Liu
University of Edinburgh, UK

ABSTRACT: Great Divergence is a significant change in economic history. From the 19th century onwards, the old wealthy civilisation such as Qing China fell behind. And the Western world gradually becomes the world economic centre. This paper will explain the reasons for Great Divergence through comparative studies. The paper will compare countries' real GDP per capita in the sample to show that nations embracing new technology will have a higher GDP per capita. Second, the paper will demonstrate that countries with a higher educational attainment rate usually have higher real GDP per capita. Finally, this paper shows that different population growth rate also contributes to the differences in economic growth. The Cobb–Douglas function is used to explain the impact of various factors on the economy. The research result is also in line with Kenneth Pomenranz's idea.

1 INTRODUCTION

The purpose of this paper is to explore why the level of real GDP per capita in countries within the sample is very different from 1850 to 1914. All countries in the sample are cherry-picked and have their implication. The nations selected for comparison are China, United States, United Kingdom, Germany, and Japan. China represents a nation that refuses to embrace the outcomes generated from the Industrial Revolution. The United Kingdom is the nation that started the Industrial Revolution but did not participate as much as Germany and the United States in the Second Industrial Revolution. Japan will be compared with China since Japan had quite similar conditions with China before the Meiji Restoration. Nevertheless, up to 1914, Japan became an industrial country with relatively high real GDP per capita and a coloniser, while China ended up as a semi-colonial and semi-feudal nation with a low GDP per capita. Similarly, Hong Kong and Taiwan will also be brought into comparison with China since their economic condition changed dramatically after the coloniser annexed them.

2 LITERATURE REVIEW

Great Divergence is a significant change in economic history. From the 19th century onwards, the old wealthy civilisation such as Qing China and Tokugawa Japan fell behind. And Western countries such as the United Kingdom and the United States occupied the dominance of the world. And industrial revolution was the beginning of the turning point. Currently, economic historians have proposed several reasons for Great Divergence. Kenneth Pomeranz believed that colonisation and industrialisation were

the main reasons for the Great Divergence. Colonisation brought a plenty of resources to Europe, which was necessary for the Industrial Revolution [1]. Gregory Clark has shared a similar view. He pointed out that the railway and steamboat generated from the Industrial Revolution sped up the transportation of goods and the dissemination of information, resulting in Great Divergence [2]. Justin yifu Lin argued that China had experienced enormous population growth before the 14th century, which brought high economic growth in China. However, population growth slowed down in China from the 18th century onwards, which decreased its productivity. In comparison, Europe was undergoing high population growth in the 18th century and technological breakthroughs that achieved sustained economic growth [3]. Furthermore, Geoffrey Jones argues that education also played a role in Great Divergence because the rise in education level cultivated much-skilled labour, contributing to high economic growth [4].

3 METHODOLOGY

This paper uses quantitative methods to address the question of why did Great Divergence happen? In order to explore the reason for the Great Divergence, the economic data of the countries in the sample will be combined with historical events that occurred during the same period for analysis. This paper will use the real GDP per capita as a measure of economic development. And the data is from the Maddison database, which provides information on comparative economic growth and income level from 1800 to 2020. The line chart of real GDP per capita data will compare different nations' financial conditions in different years. Special attention will be paid to the changes

DOI 10.1201/9781003203704-11

in economic growth between different countries to demonstrate how technology changes the national economic strength. In addition, a linear regression line will be made between education data and real GDP per capita, which comes from Barro-Lee Educational Attainment, to see the interaction between them. Finally, this paper will explore the correlation coefficient between population and real GDP per capita to find their relationship. However, secondary literature will be missed using the quantitative method since the results from the linear regression line will produce outcomes. And the missing secondary literature will be the biggest limitation for using this approach for this paper. The Cobb–Douglas function will be used to show that technology, education, and population are the factors accounting for Great Divergence in economic history. $Y = K^\alpha [E * N]^{1-\alpha}$ and $dY/Y = dK/K = n + g$ [5] (Y represents aggregate income, production, or GDP, N represents the population, E refers to the technology, K refers to the capital, n is the growth rate of population, and g is the growth rate of technology). The basic idea is that the technological growth rate (E & g) including education level measured by average years of total schooling and population growth rate (N, n) account for the difference in real GDP per capita among sampling countries. The paper will compare countries' real GDP per capita in the sample to test the assumption that nations embracing new technology will typically have a higher GDP per capita. Second, the paper will demonstrate that countries with a higher educational attainment rate usually have higher real GDP per capita. This paper will use average years of total schooling to indicate education level since it can represent the whole population. Finally, this paper will show that the population growth rate also contributes to the high real GDP per capita and how the population growth rate interacts with technology levels.

4 INDUSTRIAL REVOLUTION

4.1 Technology – industrial revolution in west

Technological breakthroughs will constantly improve the economy's development in both the short term and the long term. As the Cobb–Douglas function is shown above, an increase in E or g will also increase Y. Also, as modernisation theory suggests, a nation will develop rapidly as it adopts advanced technologies. During the Great Divergence, the West embraced technological advancements in fields including railways, steamship, metallurgy, and agriculture to a greater extent than the East. Within sectors of agriculture, commerce, and energy, technology contributed to greater industrialisation and economic complexity [6]. A nation that joins the Industrial Revolution and utilises the Industrial Revolution's outcomes should be a nation with high real GDP per capita. As we saw in Figure 1, the United Kingdom had the highest real GDP per capita before 1880. The United Kingdom was where the Industrial Revolution started, and as Figure 1 suggests,

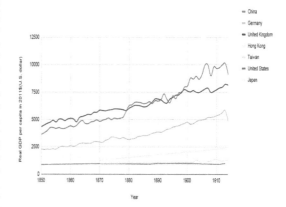

Figure 1. GDP per capita (1850–1914).

Table 1.

Name of the country	Real GDP per capita growth rate from 1850 to 1880 measured in 2011 US dollar	Real GDP per capita growth rate from 1880 to 1914 measured in 2011 US dollar
United Kingdom	0.384349%	0.355845%
United States	0.394552%	0.536232%

the United Kingdom was one of the wealthiest nations from 1850 to 1914.

However, the United Kingdom was gradually exceeded by the United States from 1880 onwards. This is mainly because the United States was the leading country driving the Second Industrial Revolution. The United Kingdom did not innovate as much as the United States did in the Second Industrial Revolution. Similarly, we can also see from Table 1 that before 1880, the economic growth rates of the United Kingdom and Germany were almost the same. Nevertheless, after 1880 (when the Second Industrial Revolution began), the economic growth rate of Germany (another leading country in the Second Industrial Revolution) was much faster than the economic growth rate of the United Kingdom.

4.2 Technology – the fall of China

China was seen as a prosperous nation in the world before the 19th century. As Jack A. Goldstone mentioned, China reached its "efflorescence", which refers to the period of significant expansion in economy and population during the High Qing period (1680–1780) and had an economy and living standard comparable to the United Kingdom [7]. However, as Figure 1 illustrates, from 1850 to 1914, China's real GDP per capita only consisted of a fifth of the real GDP per capita in the United Kingdom. The main reason behind this is the failure of China to join the Industrial Revolution.

From 1757 onwards, China adopted its isolationism policy which cut itself off from other countries. The core concept of isolationism is to refuse new technology. David Landes pointed out that the East had spectacular innovations and inventions before, but innovations seemed to stop, and the East started to sustain what they already had [8]. Hong Kong is a fair comparison with China since Hong Kong was gradually ceded to the United Kingdom from 1841 onwards. The main component of Hong Kong was ceded to the United Kingdom in the Treaty of Peking in 1860. As Hong Kong became part of the British empire, Hong Kong passively accepted some Industrial Revolution outcomes and achieved a higher economic growth rate than China. As Figure 1 suggests, the real GDP per capita of Hong Kong was higher than its motherland China from 1860 to 1914. So, technology indeed explains the divergence between the nations which joined the Industrial Revolution and the countries which did not.

5 EDUCATION

5.1 Education theory

In addition to technology, education also explains the difference in real GDP per capita within the sample. According to the research conducted by Professor Fabrizio Carmignani, an one per cent increase in education expenditure of GDP increases GDP growth by 0.9 percentage points [9]. Education will enable people to master science and technology better and improve work efficiency. Education next has discovered that each additional year of average schooling in a country increased the average 40-year growth rate in GDP by about 0.37 percentage points [10]. Education level represented by average years of schooling can be seen as part of E in the Cobb–Douglas function $Y = K^{\alpha}[E * N]^{1-\alpha}$ or part of K, seen as human capital. Education is also included in g (technology) in the function $dY/Y = dK/K = n + g$, which describes the GDP change in the long run. As we saw in Figure 2, it is easy to realise that nations with higher average years of schooling have higher real GDP per capita.

When we compare Figures 1 and 2, we realise that the rank of GDP per capita and average years of total schooling are roughly the same. The United States, Germany, and the United Kingdom had the highest average years of total schooling in the sample and were also the nations with the highest real GDP per capita. Moreover, China, which had the lowest years of schooling, also had the lowest real GDP per capita. Justin yifu Lin has argued that the Chinese imperial examination system, which only tests the ability to write literature, destroys Chinese education since it prevents Chinese students from learning science courses such as mathematics. In comparison, science was taught in most European nations at that time, and education in the West encourages innovation, which cultivates many talents and skilled labour [11].

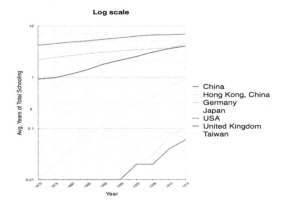

Figure 2. Average years of total schooling (1870–1915).

5.2 Comparative studies between China and Japan in education

Before 1870, Japan held a similar political structure and isolationism policy to China. Also, Japan did not fully join the Industrial Revolution. As Figure 1 suggests, Japan's real GDP per capita was low and had nearly 0 growth rate before 1870. Nevertheless, things changed quickly after the 1870s, which was the time the Meiji Restoration began. One of the core aims of the Meiji Restoration was educational reform. The educational system "gakuse" was implemented in 1872, which requires all children over the age of six, no matter which gender, to complete primary school [12]. Meanwhile, the Meiji government hired teachers from Western nations to teach the science disciplines in Japan. Japan also sent many students to the United States, Germany, and the United Kingdom to learn the new knowledge generated from the Industrial Revolution. We can find the corresponding evidence from Figure 2, which shows that Japan's average years of total schooling rose quickly from the 1870s. Moreover, we can also see the real GDP per capita growth rate in Japan accelerate from the 1870s onwards in Figure 1. Besides, Japan defeated China in the Sino-Japanese war in 1894 and annexed Taiwan as a colony. Since Japan brought its education system to Taiwan, we also see in Figures 1 and 2 that from 1900 onwards, the average total years of schooling in Taiwan rose higher than mainland China, and so does the real GDP per capita.

5.3 Linear regression for education

To further demonstrate the argument that education will influence real GDP per capita, Figures 3–8 show the linear relationship between education and real GDP per capita. Those figures show a clear positive relationship between education and real GDP per capita. Almost every nation has a strong coefficient correlation rate (R^2 is between 0.9 and 1) between education and real GDP per capita, except for China due to only a small change in average total schooling from 1870 to

Figure 3. The relationship between educational attainment rate and real GDP per capita in China from 1870–1910.

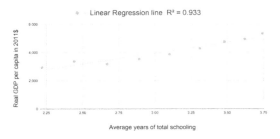

Figure 4. The relationship between educational attainment rate and real GDP per capita in Germany from 1870 to 1910.

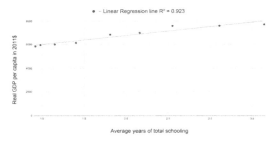

Figure 5. The relationship between educational attainment rate and real GDP per capita in United Kingdom from 1870 to 1910.

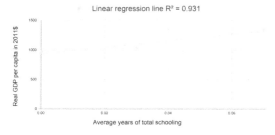

Figure 6. The relationship between educational attainment rate and real GDP per capita in Taiwan from 1870 to 1910.

1914. And there is also a relatively strong positive relationship between education and average years of total schooling in China since the correlation coefficient is still 0.531.

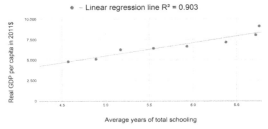

Figure 7. The relationship between educational attainment rate and real GDP per capita in United States from 1870 to 1910.

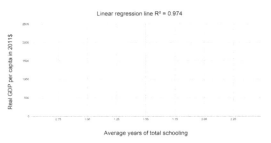

Figure 8. The relationship between educational attainment rate and real GDP per capita in Japan from 1870 to 1910.

6 POPULATION GROWTH

Furthermore, population growth will also account for the difference in real GDP per capita. The population is represented by N in the function $Y = K^{\alpha} [E * N]^{1-\alpha}$ and n in the function $dY = dK = n + g$. China has experienced stuck in population growth from 19th century onwards. On the contrary, after the new world was discovered, America provided abundant primary resources, which led to a high population growth rate in Europe [13].

As we see from Table 2, the countries with a higher population growth rate (the United States, Germany, and the United Kingdom) had a higher real GDP per capita. And China, with the lowest population growth rate, also had the lowest real GDP per capita. The relationship between population growth and real GDP per capita can also be found in Figures 9, 10, 11, and 12, which show the strong linear relationship between population level and real GDP per capita with correlation coefficients between 0.9 and 1. Population growth alone will drive economic growth to a certain extent. More importantly, population growth should also be accompanied by an increase in technological and educational levels. Since productivity increases with technological and educational levels, the marginal product of labour will increase. Thus, the faster growth of the population will contribute to real GDP per capita by increasing returns to scale. Therefore, nations that had higher real GDP per capita from 1850 to 1914 not only had a higher population growth rate but also had advanced technology and a higher educational attainment rate.

Table 2.

Name of the country	Population growth rate from 1850 to 1914	Real GDP per capita at 1914 measured in 2011 US dollar	Real GDP per capita growth rate from 1850 to 1914 measured in 2011 US dollar
China	0.0727%	985	0.12%
Japan	0.642061%	2358	0.637375%
United States	3.219889%	9096	1.054405%
United Kingdom	0.876962%	8131	0.6941%
Germany	0.95863%	4876	1.142355%

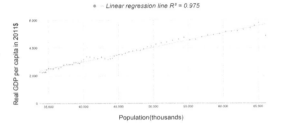

Figure 9. The relationship between population and real GDP per capita in Germany from 1850 to 1914.

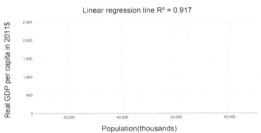

Figure 12. The relationship between population and GDP per capita in Japan from 1850 to 1914.

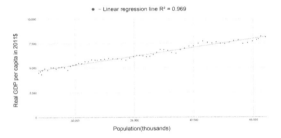

Figure 10. The relationship between population and real GDP per capita in United Kingdom from 1850 to 1914.

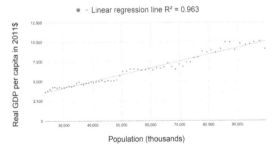

Figure 11. The relationship between population and GDP per capita in United States from 1850 to 1914.

7 CONCLUSION

From the earlier discussion, we see that the Great Divergence that appeared in economic history originated from the Industrial Revolution. Simultaneously, sustained population growth and increased education level also explain the Great Divergence to a certain extent. And this finding is in line with previous research conducted by Kenneth Pomeranz. However, most of the prior research is qualitatively based, which is different from the approach used in this paper. This paper failed to find the correlation among three factors and did not demonstrate how those three factors interact. So, further research should be focused on the correlation and causation among technological levels, education levels, and population growth. In addition, more nations such as Russia and Turkey should be brought into the sample since they are also representative countries in Great Divergence. Furthermore, other possible factors for Great Divergence, such as geographic factors and property rights, should be analysed to find their causation.

REFERENCES

[1] Kenneth Pomeranz, *The Great Divergence: China, Europe, and the Making of the Modern World Economy*, Princeton University Press (2000)

[2] Gregory Clark; Feenstra, Robert C. (2003), "Technology in the Great Divergence", in Bordo, Michael (ed.), *Globalisation in Historical Perspective*, University of Chicago Press, 277

[3] Justin Yifu Lin (1995), "The Needham Puzzle: Why the Industrial Revolution Did Not Originate in China", *Economic Development and Cultural Change*, **43** (2): 269–292

[4] Geoffrey Jones, "Business History, the Great Divergence and the Great Convergence." working paper 18-004, 2017

[5] Nills Gottfries, Macroeconomics (Basingstoke: Palgrave Macmillan 2013), 151

[6] Korotayev, Andrey; etal "Phases of global demographic transition correlate with phases of the Great Divergence and Great Convergence". *Technological Forecasting and Social Change*. **95**: 163–169

[7] Jack A. Goldstone, 'Efflorescences and Economic Growth in World History: Rethinking the "Rise of the West" and the Industrial Revolution,' *Journal of World History* 13, no. 2 (2002) page 323–379

[8] David Landes, "Why Europe and the West? Why Not China?", *Journal of Economic Perspectives*, **20** no. 2 (2006): 3–22

[9] Fabrizio Carmignani, "Does government spending on education promote education growth?" accessed August 3rd 2018 https://theconversation.com/does-government-spending-on-education-promote-economic-growth-60229

[10] Google, "Education and economic growth", accessed August 3rd 202, https://www.educationnext.org/education-and-economic-growth/

[11] Justin Yifu Lin, "Demystifying the Chinese Economy", *Cambridge University Press* (2006), Preface xiv

[12] He xiaofei, Education reform in Meiji Restoration period of Japan, *Journal of humanity first normal college* 7 (2007), 1

[13] Kenneth Pomeranz, "The Great Divergence: China, Europe and the Making of the Modern World Economy." *Princeton University Press 2009*

Economic and Business Management – Huang & Zhang (Eds)
© 2022 Copyright the Author(s), ISBN: 978-1-032-06754-4

The analysis of inter-industry VaR on China stock markets—based on the GARCH-EVT-copula model

Feifan Jiang & Yucan Liu

School of Economics and Management, Nanjing University of Science and Technology, Nanjing, China

ABSTRACT: The GARCH-EVT-copula model can fit the finance asset time series better, which has the peak and thick tail of the series, and can accurately describe the complex correlation among the time series of financial assets. This paper, we choose the daily closing price of Wind's first-level industry index from January 1, 2010 to May 31, 2021, and calculate the daily return rate of the industrial index. We calculate the value at risk (VaR) of the industry index by the GARCH-EVT-copula model, and the predicted VaR effect is evaluated by the Kupiec-Test. This paper compares the accuracy of VAR calculated by the GARCH-EVT-copula model and empirical return data, and also compares the performance of the GARCH-EVT-copula model under different distributions.

1 INTRODUCTION

1.1 *Background*

Risk measurement of the stock market has always been a focus of academic research. Nowadays, financial innovation and derivative instruments are increasingly diversified, which brings more complicated uncertainty factors. There is a complex correlation in different industries and different markets. Volatility of one industry may make a deep impact on other industries. There are many studies about the risk measurement, risk management, risk diversification and so on. The evidence has shown that the distribution of the time series for finance assets has the characteristics of sharp peak and thick tail. Extreme value theory focuses on the tail of the series and does not need to fit the whole distribution of the series. Therefore, extreme value theory is widely used in the analysis of the return time series. The GPD model is the most commonly used model in extreme value theory, and the GPD model requires that the series' distribution is independent, identical and without autocorrelation. According to Adesi et al. (2002), they obtained the residuals by regressing on return series, then normalized the residuals, the residuals were divided by the estimated daily volatility, $z_t = \varepsilon_t / \sigma_t$, and the series, z_t, met the requirements of the GPD model. Chan and Gray (2006) found that the series, z_t, could be obtained from the residual of the GARCH model, so they built the GARCH-EVT model to fit the return series of financial assets.

1.2 *Literature review*

Our goal is to analyze the joint VaR of any two wind one-level industries, we need to describe the correlation between two industries, and we chose the copula function. The copula function is a precise tool to analyze the correlation between two financial assets' return series. Xiao Y (2020) studied the risk spillovers of the Chinese stock market to major East Asian stock markets during turbulent and calm periods, and employed the Markov regime-switching model, the extreme value theory (EVT) and the vine copula function to model their multivariate dependence structures and compute the CoVaR in direct and indirect ways. Ali Chebbi and Amel Hedhli (2020) employed GARCH-EVT-copula to model the dependence between the marginal distributions of returns and forecast the VaR. Haiying, Ying, Yiou and Xunhong W (2021) proposed a new approach to the study of financial contagion and contagion channels in the forex market by using a dynamic mixture copula-extreme value theory (DMC-EVT) model. Zhu Mengnan and Duan Hongjun (2019) used it to measure the risk of foreign exchange market with consideration of two risk factors, interest rate and exchange rate.

GARCH-EVT-copula model takes advantages in predicting the return of financial assets and measuring the risk. It focuses on the upper and lower ends of the series and reduces the error on assumption of the series distribution. And, copula function is used to measure the correlation between the series. It can describe the linear and nonlinear correlation between series more accurately. Therefore, we use GARCH-EVT-copula model to measure VaR among 9 Wind one-level industries. First, in the sample, we use GARCH-EVT to fit the return series, then use the copula function to describe the correlation between any two industries, and last, we predict and calculate the VaR out-of-sample. The results show that the VaR calculated by the GARCH-EVT-copula model is more accurate than that obtained by empirical data.

This paper is arranged as follows: section one is the instruction, which introduces the background, the goals, and the literature reviews, Section two is the

DOI 10.1201/9781003203704-12

61

Table 1. The descriptive statistical analysis.

	mean	Standard deviation	Skewness	Kurtosis	JB statistic	P value
r1	−0.0003	0.0165	−0.7069	8.5451	3779.58	0.001
r2	0.0002	0.0183	−0.8401	7.9520	3156.13	0.001
r3	0.0002	0.0175	−0.8902	9.1742	4765.52	0.001
r4	0.0002	0.0171	−0.8839	8.6804	4084.77	0.001
r5	0.0006	0.0164	−0.6825	7.3998	2449.27	0.001
r6	0.0005	0.0175	−0.6168	7.3977	2407.75	0.001
r8	0.0004	0.0212	−0.6488	6.4419	1561.65	0.001
r9	−0.0001	0.0202	−0.2896	7.1116	1989.90	0.001
r11	0.0001	0.0186	−0.5766	7.1378	2129.59	0.001

research design. Section three is empirical part, including the descriptive statistics, relevant tests, obtaining the new interest series, calculating VaR of inter-industry, and testing and evaluating the results. Section four is the conclusion.

2 RESEARCH DESIGN

The GPD model requires that the series does not have autocorrelation and is independently and identically distributed. According to the research of Adisi et al. (2002), we use the GARCH model to fit the original return series in the sample, and then calculate the new interest series Z_t by the residuals.

Extreme value theory pays close attention to the extreme cases that have a small probability of occurrence but will make a great loss once they occur, and modeling is only carried out for the tail of the series. The GPD model is the most widely used model in extreme value theory, which was firstly proposed by Pickands. We use theGPD model to fit the series Zt.

In order to describe the correlation structure between industries, we use the copula function. Sklar (1959) proposed the famous Sklar theorem: assuming that F is a joint distribution function, and its edge distribution functions are respectively: $F1(.)...,Fn(.)$, then, there must be a $CopulaC$, that makes $F1 (x1, x2,... xn)=C(F1(x1), F2(x2),... , Fn(xn))$, to the whole $X1, X2... , xn$. There are several kinds of copula function, we use Gaussian and t copula.

After we get the parameters of the GARCH-EVT-copula model in the sample, then we predict the joint VaR between industries in the sample. Value at risk is the maximum possible loss of financial assets over a given period and a given certain level of confidence. The expression is: $prob(\Delta P > VaR) = 1 - c$. ΔP is the loss of financial assets in a certain time interval, and VaR is the maximum loss at the confidence level c. Kupiec-failure frequency test method is often used to check the accuracy of the estimated VaR.

3 EMPIRICAL ANALYSIS

3.1 *Data samples and analysis*

We selected the daily closing prices of Wind's first-level industry indexes from January 1, 2010 to May 31, 2021, including energy index, materials index, industrial index, optional consumption index, daily consumption index, medical consumption index, information technology index, telecommunications service index, and real estate index, and calculate the daily logarithmic return rate, ri, and $i = 1, 2, 3, 4, 5, 6, 8, 9, 11$, correspond to the last digit or two digits of the 9 industry index codes respectively. The samples were divided into in-sample and out-of-sample. In the sample: from January 1, 2010 to December 31, 2017, 1,942 close price data; out of sample: from January 1, 2018 to May 31, 2021, 827 close price data. We use them to train the model and predict VaR, test the model performance respectively.

We make the descriptive statistical analysis and JB normality test for the return series. Results are shown in Table 1, rejecting the JB test, which means the series has an obvious feature of sharp peak and thick tail.

Table 2 shows the results of some tests. The ADF test, autocorrelation test and ARCH effect test were carried out. The results show that, at the confidence level of 99%, the null hypothesis is rejected, indicating that the series has stable auto-correlation and has the ARCH effect.

3.2 *In-sample regression*

The above analysis shows that the original return series don't meet the assumptions of the GPD model. According to the ACF and PACF diagrams of the series, we find that the lag order of the residual term is big, so we use the GARCH(1,1) model to obtain the residual. The coefficients of variance equation of the GARCH model are shown in Table 2. According to the estimated results of the GARCH(1,1) model, except that the probability of the volatility of energy index return rate r1 being affected by its own volatility is 71.61%, the probability of other index return rate volatility being affected by its own volatility is more than 90%, indicating that the volatility of return rate has an obvious aggregation phenomenon, and a large part of the current period's return rate fluctuations will continue in the next period.

Then we standardize the residual term: $Z_t = \varepsilon_t/\sigma_t$, and the new interest series Z_i, $i= 1,2,3,4,5,6,8,9,11$ is obtained. Through the Ljung-Boxq test and BDS test, the new interest series Zi doesn't have autocorrelation

Table 2. ADF test, LBQ test and ARCH effect test.

	ADF test		LBQ test		ARCH effect test	
	ADF	P value	LBQ	P value	ARCH	P value
r1	−50.3186	0.001	59.5185	0.000	192.0800	0.000
r2	−47.9918	0.001	61.2641	0.000	336.3263	0.000
r3	−47.7757	0.001	63.8938	0.000	327.0040	0.000
r4	−48.4157	0.001	64.8432	0.000	308.9407	0.000
r5	−49.0046	0.001	58.2229	0.000	245.3728	0.000
r6	−48.1841	0.001	72.7513	0.000	320.9333	0.000
r8	−47.9055	0.001	53.2059	0.000	296.0287	0.000
r9	−50.0827	0.001	41.6181	0.003	246.9585	0.000
r11	−50.3908	0.001	39.8281	0.005	131.9308	0.000

Table 3. GARCH (1,1) model coefficients.

		ω	β	α
r1	Coefficient	2.6931E-05***	0.7161***	0.1941***
	P value	0.0000	0.0000	0.0000
r2	Coefficient	3.1214E-06***	0.9377***	0.0530***
	P value	0.0008	0.0000	0.0000
r3	Coefficient	1.8136E-06***	0.9478***	0.0454***
	P value	0.0048	0.0000	0.0000
r4	Coefficient	1.5860E-06***	0.9396***	0.0547***
	P value	0.0062	0.0000	0.0000
r5	Coefficient	2.7233E-06***	0.9205***	0.0681***
	P value	0.0020	0.0000	0.0000
r6	Coefficient	1.5221E-06**	0.9406***	0.0539***
	P value	0.0033	0.0000	0.0000
r8	Coefficient	3.0781E-06***	0.9461***	0.0454***
	P value	0.0004	0.0000	0.0000
r9	Coefficient	6.5214E-06***	0.9177***	0.0646***
	P value	0.0000	0.0000	0.0000
r11	Coefficient	2.0753E-06**	0.9383***	0.0572***
	P value	0.0199	0.000	0.0000

***present reject the null hypothesis in 99% confidence level, ** present reject the null hypothesis in 95% confidence level.

Table 4. LBQ test of the series Z_i.

	LBQ-statistic	P value
Z1	20.6949	0.4153
Z2	14.7698	0.7894
Z3	14.9453	0.7795
Z4	11.7312	0.9250
Z5	9.4437	0.9772
Z6	14.8961	0.7823
Z8	9.0327	0.9825
Z9	15.2842	0.7599
Z11	9.2530	0.9798

and is independently and identically distributed. The results are shown in Tables 3 and 4.

We use the GPD model to fit the upper and lower tails, and use a 10% over-threshold ratio (N_μ/N) to estimate the parameters. ξ^L and ξ^U represent the lower tail and upper tail shape parameters, respectively. β^L and β^U represent lower tail and upper tail size parameters, respectively. The middle part of the Z_t is fitted by normal distribution as usual, and mu and sigma represent the mean and standard deviation of the normal distribution parameters, respectively. The results are shown in Table 5.

Figure 1 shows the fitting CDF distribution curve and empirical CDF distribution curve of energy index as examples. The dotted line is the empirical CDF distribution curve, and the solid line is the fitting CDF distribution curve. It is obvious that the GPD model has a better performance on fitting the tail.

Next, we use the Gaussian-copula function and t-copula function to describe the correlation between any two industrial index interest series, respectively. According to the results, the correlation coefficient

Table 5. BDS test of the series.

Dimension		2	3	4	5	6
BDS-statistic	Z1	0.0045	0.0068	0.0071	0.0047	0.0028
	Z2	0.0016	0.0015	0.0037	0.0046	0.0052
	Z3	0.0019	0.0016	−0.0017	−0.0010	−0.0016
	Z4	−0.0001	−0.003	−0.0001	−0.0003	−0.0001
	Z5	0.0022	0.0060	0.0111	0.0111	0.0117
	Z6	0.0054	0.0085	0.0095	0.0096	0.0098
	Z8	−0.0002	−0.0004	−0.0001	−0.0002	−0.0003
	Z9	0.0010	0.0019	0.0030	0.0044	0.0041
	Z11	0.0087	0.0146	0.0143	0.0096	0.0066
P value	Z1	0.1280	0.1434	0.2051	0.4233	0.6148
	Z2	0.5912	0.7372	0.4979	0.4173	0.3407
	Z3	0.4311	0.6710	0.7139	0.8414	0.7236
	Z4	0.9413	0.9211	0.9055	0.8922	0.8803
	Z5	0.4747	0.2114	0.0527	0.0630	0.0429
	Z6	0.0411	0.0423	0.0592	0.0668	0.0513
	Z8	0.9742	0.9654	0.9585	0.9527	0.9475
	Z9	0.7064	0.6423	0.5376	0.3897	0.4040
	Z11	0.0427	0.0534	0.0634	0.0454	0.1550

Table 6. Extreme value distribution parameter estimation results.

	Lower Tail Parameters		Normal Distribution Parameters		Upper Tail Parameters	
	ξ^L	β^L	mu	sigma	ξ^U	β^U
Z1	0.0982	0.7038	0.0049	1.0019	−0.0590	0.6475
Z2	−0.0731	0.7717	−0.0078	0.9902	−0.0556	0.4151
Z3	−0.0274	0.8099	0.0031	0.9993	0.0548	0.3404
Z4	−0.0322	0.7909	0.0034	1.0037	−0.0558	0.4023
Z5	0.0218	0.6528	0.0152	0.9992	−0.2108	0.5294
Z6	−0.0407	0.7387	0.0035	0.9980	−0.1665	0.5622
Z8	−0.0256	0.7194	0.0080	0.9999	−0.1380	0.4141
Z9	−0.1491	0.7905	0.0079	1.0008	0.0567	0.6259
Z11	0.0152	0.7280	−0.0009	1.0007	−0.0804	0.5876

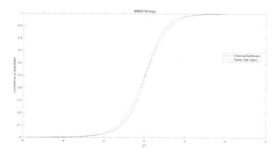

Figure 1. The empirical CDF curve and the fitting CDF curve of energy index and daily consumption index.

3.3 Predicting the VaR out-of-sample

And now, we can use the GARCH-EVT-copula model, which has been trained in the sample, to estimate the VaR of the sample.

The copula function describes the correlation, and Monte Carlo simulation predicts the return series of the portfolio. Nine industry indexes can produce 36 portfolios. Table 6 shows that under the t-distribution, the GARCH-EVT-copula model fits better and the estimated VaR is more accurate. In order to prove the GARCH-EVT-copula model performs better, we use empirical data to calculate VaR and make a comparison. The result is placed in Table 2 too. The advantage of the GARCH-EVT-copula model is proved. The average proportion of the VaR for the Kupiec test obtained from empirical data is 60.38%. The GARCH-EVT-copula model has a better performance, and the results further verify that the model under t distribution performs better than under the normal distribution (Table 7).

between any two first-level industries is above 0.53, and the largest is 0.8009, which is between the material index and the industrial index, which indicates that there is a high correlation between various industries.

Table 7. Kupiec test result.

Distribution	Confidence Level	GARCH-EVT-copula model		Empirical Data	
		VaR mean	The Proportion of the VaR passed the test	VaR mean	The Proportion of the VaR passed the test
normal	99%	−0.0353	66.76%	−0.0390	54.10%
	95%	−0.0211	66.67%	−0.0303	52.11%
t	99%	−0.0335	75.00%	−0.0366	69.08%
	95%	−0.0204	69.44%	−0.0284	66.24%

4 CONCLUSION

Through the GARCH-EVT-copula model, we analyze the joint VaR of nine Wind first-level industry indexes. The results show that the GARCH-EVT-copula model performs better on fitting the return series, and at the same time, the model under t distribution has a slightly better effect than that under normal distribution. The prediction accuracy of the two kinds of distribution in 36 portfolio series, composed by nine industries, is about 70%. Compared with empirical data, the VaR obtained by the GARCH-EVT-copula model is more accurate. Of course, the GARCH-EVT-copula model in this paper still can be improved in some respects. In terms of fitting the series, it can be more accurate to improve the calculation accuracy of VAR.

According to the conclusions, we give some suggestions for risk supervision. First, we should focus on extreme risks, with a minimum probability of occurrence; once they happen, the losses will be huge. Second, we should take into consideration the correlation between upstream and downstream industries. Last, we should pay attention to the impact on related industries when we carry out regulation in one industry.

REFERENCES

G B Adesi, Kostas G & Les Vosper. 2002. Backtesting derivative portfolios with filtered historieal simulation (FHS). *European financial management*, 8: 31–58.

Ali Chebbi & Amel Hedhli. 2020. Revisiting the accuracy of standard VaR methods for risk assessment: Using the Copula–EVT multidimensional approach for stock markets in the MENA region(J). *The Quarterly Review of Economics and Finance*, 10:1–16.

Chan K F & Gray P. 2006. Using extreme value theory to measure value-at-risk for daily electricity spot prices(J). *International Journal of Forecasting*, 2: 283–300.

Haiying W, Ying Y, Yiou Li & Xunhong W. 2021. Financial contagion and contagion channels in the forex market: A new approach via the dynamic mixture copula-extreme value theory(J). *Economic Modelling*, 94:401–414.

Xiao Y. 2020. The risk spillovers from the Chinese stock market to major East Asian stock markets: A MSGARCH-EVT-copula approach. *International Review of Economics & Finance*, 65: 173–186.

Zhu M N & Duan H J. 2019. Risk Measurement of China's Foreign Exchange Reserve Market – Based on Copula-EVT-GARCH Model Integrated Analysis of Interest Rate and Exchange Rate Risk (in Chinese) (J). *Journal of Xiamen University*, 3:56–67.

Economic and Business Management – Huang & Zhang (Eds)
© 2022 Copyright the Author(s), ISBN: 978-1-032-06754-4

The effect of managerial ownership on corporate value

Yanlin Zhang & Yucan Liu
Nanjing University of Science and Technology, Nanjing, China

ABSTRACT: Corporate governance mechanisms, such as equity incentives, have led many managers to own shares in publicly traded companies. Based on the data of A-share listed companies from 2008 to 2019, we find that there is a negative relationship between managerial ownership ratio and Tobin's Q, an indicator of corporate value. Such a relationship is more obvious in listed companies with poor liquidity and small size.

1 INTRODUCTION

For many listed enterprises in China, the management of the enterprise is often the founder of the enterprise, and the major shareholders of such companies are also the management, so the management of the company owns many shares. With the improvement of corporate governance in China, equity incentives, such as employee stock ownership plans, also make the management hold more shares. Therefore, it is necessary to study the influence of managerial ownership ratio on corporate value and discuss the role of managerial ownership in corporate governance.

2 LITERATURE REVIEW

At present, scholars' conclusions on the impact of managerial ownership on enterprise value are inconsistent.

Some scholars believe that managerial ownership will not significantly affect corporate value. Wang and Chen (2014) selected the GEM data from 2009 to 2012 and used principal component analysis to measure the enterprise value, and found that the managerial ownership ratio had no significant influence on the enterprise value.

However, some scholars believe that corporate value is positively correlated with managerial ownership. Darlene Dacia Septiana and Ernie Riswandari (2020) found that there was a positive correlation between the company value and the proportion of managerial ownership.

There are also scholars who believe that managerial ownership has a negative impact on corporate value. Fabisik Kornelia et al. (2021) used a variety of methods to make a regression and found that the higher the proportion of management shares in the American market, the lower the value of the company, as represented by Tobin's Q.

Some scholars believe that different managerial ownership ranges have different influences on companies. Morck et al. (1988) believed that the cut-off point for the impact of management shareholding on enterprise value is 5% and 25%. Xu Lin, Zhu Chunxi and Dong Yongqi (2018) found that managerial ownership has a positive impact on corporate value as a whole. Moreover, managerial ownership has the characteristics of intervals, and different intervals have different influences: When the managerial ownership ratio ranges from 0 to 13.4%, from 31.3% to 58.7% and exceeds 79.5%, the managerial ownership ratio has a positive impact on the company value; when the managerial ownership ratio ranges from 13.4% to 31.3% and from 58.7% to 79.5%, the managerial ownership ratio has a negative impact. In state-owned enterprises, the incentive effect of managerial ownership is stronger. Yi Chuilin (2009) selected the data of listed companies in the Shanghai and Shenzhen stock markets in 2008 and found that there was a cubic curve relationship between managerial ownership ratio and company value. When the managerial ownership ratio is below 23.84% and above 60.55%, the increase of managerial ownership will increase the value of the company. While the increase of managerial ownership will decrease the value of the company when the managerial ownership is between 23.84% and 60.55%. Syed Moudud Ul Huq, Tanmay Biswas, and Shukla Proshad Dola (2020) selected data from Bangladesh and found that there is a U-shaped relationship between managerial ownership ratio and corporate value. Low managerial ownership ratio has a positive effect on corporate value, while higher managerial ownership damages corporate value. Tan Qingmei, Liu Yaguang, and Ma Mingze (2013) selected the data from 2002 to 2010 and found that product competition would affect the relationship between Tobin's Q and managerial ownership. Managerial ownership showed an inverted U-shaped relationship with Tobin's Q, and the turning point was about 6.7%. When the shareholding ratio is low, there is convergence effect of interests, which increases the enterprise value. When the growth reaches a certain level, the management defense dominates, and higher managerial ownership will destroy the enterprise value.

DOI 10.1201/9781003203704-13

The influence of managerial ownership on enterprise value may be related to financing constraints and technological innovation. Ji Weili and Fan Weichao (2021) found that there is an inverted U-shaped relationship between management shareholding ratio and enterprise innovation investment. For state-owned enterprises, management equity incentive can significantly affect innovation, while high shareholding ratio will destroy innovation. Therefore, management shareholding ratio should be kept within an appropriate range. Fan Haifeng and Zhou Xiaochun (2020) selected samples from 2012 to 2015 and found that there was a U-shaped relationship between managerial ownership and financing constraints, and an inverted U-shaped relationship between managerial ownership and R&D investment and innovation efficiency. Chen Xiding, Dai Xiaozhen, and Zhang Fangfang (2018) found that the management shareholding ratio would improve the technological innovation efficiency of listed companies, and such a positive influence was more obvious in enterprises with low agency cost.

3 DATA PREPARATION

Relevant data of listed companies in China from 2008 to 2019 were selected as samples, and companies in the financial industry and public facility management industry were excluded. Except for Sigma, which is from Wind database, all the other data are from CSMAR database.

With reference to Fabisik Kornelia et al. (2021), different variables were set as shown in the Table 1 below.

Tobin's Q is used as the proxy variable of enterprise value, because compared with accounting indicators such as return on equity, Tobin's Q is more able to reflect market expectations and enterprise prospects. So Tobin's Q is more forward-looking and more able to represent the market value of enterprises.

As can be seen from Table 2, during the 12 years from 2008 to 2019, the number of listed companies in China keeps increasing, and the management shareholding ratio presents an overall growth trend. This is because many newly listed companies implement equity incentives, and the management shareholding ratio is high, which raises the average shareholding ratio. With the gradual maturity of China's stock market, the stock liquidity is increasing, and the average age of companies is increasing. In contrast, Tobin's Q, an indicator of corporate value, shows no obvious trend.

4 EMPIRICAL PROCESS

4.1 *Relationship between Tobin's Q and management shareholding ratio*

According to Fabisik Kornelia et al. (2021), in the lifecycle theory, firms with high liquidity tend to be successful firms, which means they tend to have a high Tobin's Q. In the Chinese stock market, successful firms also tend to have big size. Decreases in ownership are also related to liquidity, so firms with a high Tobin's Q tend to have low managerial ownership. Our prediction is that:

H1: There is a negative relationship between managerial ownership and Tobin's Q.

H2: The negative relationship between managerial ownership and Tobin's Q is more obvious in large firms with high liquidity.

In order to study the relationship between Tobin's Q and management shareholding ratio, we refer to the practice of Fabisik Kornelia et al. (2021) and set up the regression model (Table 3).

In addition to the regression of the total sample of all companies, subsamples with management shareholding are selected for regression in this section. As can be seen from the total sample regression results, the proportion of management shareholding significantly negatively affects Tobin's Q, which means that in general, the higher the proportion of management shareholding, the lower the company value. The result is in line with the prediction of Fabisik Kornelia et al. (2021). When the square term of managerial ownership is added, the coefficient of ownership is still significantly negative and becomes larger and more significant, while the coefficient of the square term is significantly positive. At this point, the turning point is 37.93%. In the total sample, there are a total of 3,961 companies with the managerial ownership ratio exceeding 37.93%. It accounts for 14.44% of the total sample, which means that most companies' management shareholding ratio has a negative relationship with the company value, while a few companies have a positive relationship. After segmenting the management shareholding ratio, the regression coefficient of 0% to 5% shareholding ratio is significantly positive, the regression coefficient of 5% to 25% shareholding ratio is significantly negative, and the regression coefficient of more than 25% shareholding ratio is positive and significant at the significance level of 10%. This indicates that among different management shareholding ratios, the influence of management shareholding ratio on Tobin's Q varies in different directions.

After the sample without managerial ownership is deleted, the coefficient of ownership in the first column is more significant, and the negative relationship between ownership ratio and Tobin's Q is more obvious in panel B. In the second column, the coefficient of ownership is −1.13 and the coefficient of square term is 1.30. At this point, the turning point is 43.46%. There are 3,076 companies exceeding the turning point, accounting for 19.07% of the subsample.

This regression result supports the entrenchment effect: with the increase of the shareholding ratio of senior executives, senior executives' control over the enterprise is continuously enhanced, and external restraint on them is weakened. As a result, senior executives further pursue personal interests and increase agency costs. Therefore, the higher the management shareholding ratio, the lower the enterprise value.

Table 1. Variable definition table.

Variable	Description
Ownership	Management shareholding ratio of listed companies.
Ownership 0% to 5%	=5% if ownership$\geq$5%,
	=0 if ownership$\leq$5%.
Ownership 5% to 25%	=20% if ownership$\geq$25%,
	=ownership-5% if 5%$\leq$ownership$\leq$25%,
	=0 if ownership<5%.
Ownership over 25%	=ownership-25%if ownership$\geq$25%
	=0 if ownership$\leq$25%.
Ownership wedge	Ownership wedge$_t$ = ownership$_t$-ownership$_{2008}$.
LN(S)	The logarithm of operating revenue.
K/S	The ratio of fixed assets to sales revenue.
I/K	The ratio of capital expenditure to fixed assets.
SIGMA	The standard deviation of residual of CAPM model.
Amihud	Amihud represents illiquidity.
Tobin's Q	The ratio of market value of A and B shares to total assets.

Table 2. Descriptive statistics.

year	n	Tobin's Q		Managerial ownership		Amihud	
		mean	median	mean	median	mean	median
2008	1398	1.53	1.22	0.03	0.00004	0.31	0.19
2009	1458	2.83	2.02	0.04	0.00003	0.10	0.04
2010	1599	2.64	2.03	0.06	0.00003	0.04	0.04
2011	1944	1.94	1.44	0.10	0.00008	0.08	0.06
2012	2189	1.80	1.37	0.13	0.00021	0.12	0.09
2013	2301	2.14	1.53	0.12	0.00036	0.07	0.06
2014	2287	2.40	1.79	0.12	0.00070	0.05	0.04
2015	2366	3.49	2.45	0.12	0.00264	0.10	0.03
2016	2608	2.76	2.04	0.12	0.00517	0.04	0.02
2017	2882	2.13	1.67	0.14	0.00909	0.18	0.02
2018	3379	1.65	1.33	0.15	0.01718	0.08	0.05
2019	3378	1.95	1.49	0.14	0.01619	0.05	0.04

4.2 Influence of liquidity, size and management shareholding ratio on Tobin's Q

According to liquidity theory, larger and more mature companies with less information asymmetry are more liquid, investors are more interested in such companies, and the Tobin's Q is higher. Therefore, we further classify the company's liquidity and size. The top 25% of the company's size from large to small is defined as large company, the bottom 25% as small company. The top 25% of the company's illiquidity is defined as high liquid company, and the bottom 25% as low liquid company. The dummy variables are set respectively. In order to explore the influence of liquidity, size, and managerial ownership on Tobin's Q of the company, regression is conducted with the interaction item of the variable ownership of management.

The results of panel A in Table 4 show that the coefficient of management shareholding ratio is still significant after considering enterprise size and liquidity. The coefficient of dummy variable of small size is significantly negative, indicating that small size

enterprises tend to have lower Tobin's Q. In column (4) regression, the coefficient of large size dummy variable is significantly positive, while in column (3) regression, although the coefficient of large-scale dummy variable is not significant, it is also positive, which indicates that large-scale enterprises tend to have higher Tobin's Q value and higher enterprise value. In column (1) and (3), the coefficient of dummy variable with high liquidity is significantly positive, indicating that enterprises with higher liquidity have higher Tobin's Q value. In column (2) and (4), the coefficient of dummy variable with low liquidity is significantly negative, indicating that enterprises with poor liquidity have lower Tobin's Q value.

In panel B, column (2) shows that the interaction term doesn't influence the significance of managerial ownership and high liquidity dummy variable. The interaction term is significantly positive, indicating that high liquidity can alleviate the negative impact of management shareholding ratio on Tobin's Q to a certain extent. In column (3), both the dummy variable

Table 3.   Regression results of Tobin's Q and management shareholding.

Panel A: All firms

Ownership	−0.32**	−1.10***	
	(−2.43)	(−2.67)	
Ownership^2		1.45**	
		(2.01)	
Ownership 0% to 5%			7.95***
			(4.00)
Ownership 5% to 25%			−3.31***
			(−5.09)
Ownership over 25%			0.60*
			(1.78)
LN(S)	−12.22***	−12.19***	−12.24***
	(−51.47)	(−51.25)	(−51.42)
(LN(S))^2	0.26***	0.26***	0.26***
	(48.18)	(47.95)	(48.12)
K/S	−0.54***	−0.54***	−0.54***
	(−17.90)	(−17.93)	(−17.77)
(K/S)^2	0.002***	0.002***	0.002***
	(13.56)	(13.58)	(13.44)
I/K	0.0001	0.0001	0.0001
	(0.85)	(0.85)	(0.85)
SIGMA	0.01***	0.01***	0.01***
	(8.20)	(8.21)	(8.18)
Observations	27424	27424	27424
R-squared	0.20	0.20	0.20
Year FE	Yes	Yes	Yes
Industry FE	Yes	Yes	Yes

Panel B: Firms that have managerial ownership

Ownership	−0.40**	−1.13***	
	(−2.73)	(−2.49)	
Ownership^2		1.30*	
		(1.70)	
Ownership 0% to 5%			8.43***
			(3.87)
Ownership 5% to 25%			−3.23***
			(−4.82)
Ownership over 25%			0.41
			(1.16)
LN(S)	−14.35***	−14.32***	−14.38***
	(−43.11)	(−42.95)	(−43.09)
(LN(S))^2	0.31***	0.31***	0.31***
	(40.92)	(40.73)	(40.90)
K/S	−0.99***	−1.00***	−0.98***
	(−15.13)	(−15.18)	(−14.86)
(K/S)^2	0.05***	0.05***	0.05***
	(7.89)	(7.92)	(7.74)
I/K	−0.0006	−0.0006	−0.0005
	(−0.30)	(−0.30)	(−0.28)
SIGMA	0.01***	0.01***	0.01***
	(6.47)	(6.49)	(6.44)
Observations	20773	20773	20773
R-squared	0.18	0.18	0.18
Year FE	Yes	Yes	Yes
Industry FE	Yes	Yes	Yes

***,**and* indicate statistical significance of the coefficient at the 1%, 5% and 10% levels, respectively.

with low liquidity and the management shareholding ratio are significantly negative. The interaction term coefficient is significantly negative, indicating that the negative influence of management shareholding ratio on Tobin's Q is mainly explained by the interaction term. Low liquidity often makes it difficult for the management to sell their own stocks for cash, thus owning a higher proportion of shares. At the same

Table 4. The effect of managerial ownership, size and liquidity on Tobin's Q.

Panel A

	(1)	(2)	(3)	(4)
Ownership	−0.27*	−0.28*	−0.31**	−0.29**
	(−1.84)	(−1.87)	(−2.13)	(−2.01)
Small size	−0.27***	−0.21**		
	(−3.19)	(−2.43)		
Big size			0.13	0.21**
			(1.34)	(2.18)
High liquidity	0.55***		0.54***	
	(7.25)		(7.05)	
Low liquidity		−0.57***		−0.59***
		(−7.64)		(−7.93)
LN(S)	−14.63***	−14.97***	−14.10***	−14.51***
	(−40.10)	(−41.16)	(−41.87)	(−42.92)
$(LN(S))^2$	0.32***	0.32***	0.30***	0.31***
	(38.25)	(39.53)	(38.96)	(40.14)
K/S	−1.06***	−1.05***	−1.04***	−1.05***
	(−15.88)	(−15.74)	(−15.54)	(−15.67)
$(K/S)^2$	0.05***	0.05***	0.05***	0.05***
	(8.31)	(8.19)	(8.20)	(8.20)
I/K	−0.0007	−0.0008	−0.0007	−0.0009
	(−0.36)	(−0.41)	(−0.36)	(−0.44)
SIGMA	0.01***	0.01***	0.01***	0.01***
	(6.62)	(6.60)	(6.51)	(6.53)
Observations	20773	20773	20773	20773
R-squared	0.18	0.18	0.18	0.18
Year FE	Yes	Yes	Yes	Yes
Industry FE	Yes	Yes	Yes	Yes

Panel B   The effect of liquidity on Tobin's Q

	(1)	(2)	(3)	(4)
Ownership	−0.32**	−0.69***	−0.31**	0.24
	(−2.19)	(−4.48)	(−2.12)	(1.39)
High liquidity	0.56***	0.25***		
	(7.37)	(2.86)		
Low liquidity			−0.59***	−0.28***
			(−8.02)	(−2.97)
High liquidity*Ownership		2.88***		
		(7.36)		
Low liquidity*Ownership				−1.61***
				(−5.64)
LN(S)	−14.16**	−14.42***	−14.62***	−14.68***
	(−42.47)	(−43.06)	(−43.77)	(−43.96)
$(LN(S))^2$	0.31***	0.31***	0.32***	0.32***
	(39.95)	(40.57)	(41.51)	(41.73)
K/S	−1.02***	−1.01***	−1.02***	−1.01***
	(−15.57)	(−15.43)	(−15.55)	(−15.39)
$(K/S)^2$	0.05***	0.05***	0.05***	0.05***
	(8.12)	(8.01)	(8.05)	(7.96)
I/K	−0.0006	−0.0007	−0.0007	−0.0007
	(−0.32)	(−0.35)	(−0.38)	(−0.36)
SIGMA	0.01***	0.01***	0.01***	0.01***
	(6.50)	(6.49)	(6.51)	(6.47)
Observations	20773	20773	20773	20773
R-squared	0.18	0.18	0.18	0.18
Year FE	Yes	Yes	Yes	Yes
Industry FE	Yes	Yes	Yes	Yes

(Continued)

Table 4. The effect of managerial ownership, size and liquidity on Tobin's Q.

Panel C   The effect of size on Tobin's Q

	(1)	(2)	(3)	(4)
Ownership	−0.38***	−0.52***	−0.34**	0.55***
	(−2.59)	(−3.45)	(−2.35)	(3.04)
Big size	0.24**	0.11		
	(2.51)	(1.06)		
Small size			−0.29***	0.26**
			(−3.44)	(2.43)
Big size*Ownership		1.83***		
		(3.66)		
Small size*Ownership				−2.40***
				(8.32)
LN(S)	−14.22***	−14.33***	−14.86***	−14.79***
	(−42.25)	(−42.42)	(−40.82)	(−40.69)
$(LN(S))^2$	0.31***	0.31***	0.32***	0.32***
	(39.53)	(39.71)	(39.26)	(39.23)
K/S	−1.03***	−1.02***	−1.03***	−1.01***
	(−15.33)	(−15.17)	(−15.49)	(−15.16)
$(K/S)^2$	0.05***	0.05***	0.05***	0.05***
	(8.06)	(7.98)	(8.10)	(7.93)
I/K	−0.0007	−0.0007	−0.0007	−0.0006
	(−0.37)	(−0.35)	(−0.34)	(−0.29)
SIGMA	0.01***	0.01***	0.01***	0.01***
	(6.50)	(6.46)	(6.61)	(6.74)
Observations	20773	20773	20773	20773
R-squared	0.18	0.18	0.18	0.18
Year FE	Yes	Yes	Yes	Yes
Industry FE	Yes	Yes	Yes	Yes

time, low liquidity stocks also often have poor corporate performance and are less attractive to investors. Therefore, the negative correlation between Tobin's Q and management shareholding ratio is more obvious in companies with low liquidity.

In the regression results of panel C, column (1) shows that large companies tend to have higher Tobin's Q. In column (2), the interaction coefficient between dummy variables of large-scale companies and the proportion of managerial ownership is significantly positive, which indicates that when the size of companies with managerial ownership is large, the negative effect of managerial ownership on enterprise value will be suppressed to some extent. The results in columns (3) and (4) show that small companies tend to have lower Tobin's Q value, and in small companies, the negative effect of management shareholding ratio on corporate value will be enhanced.

The reason is that when stock liquidity is poor, the reduction of management holdings is likely to bring huge stock price fluctuations, and it is difficult for management to reduce holdings. Therefore, companies with poor stock liquidity tend to have higher managerial ownership, and managerial ownership has a more significant negative effect on Tobin's Q.

5   CONCLUSIONS

In general, there is a negative relationship between managerial shareholding ratio and Tobin's Q, that is, the higher the managerial shareholding ratio is, the lower the company value will be. When Tobin's Q takes total assets as the denominator, there is a quadratic positive relationship between managerial shareholding ratio and Tobin's Q, and some companies are on the right side of the U-shaped curve. The negative effect of managerial ownership on Tobin's Q is more obvious in small firms with low liquidity. The characteristics of high liquidity and large scale can offset this kind of negative effect.

REFERENCES

Chen Xiding, Dai Xiaozhen, & Zhang Fangfang. (2018). A study of the influence of managerial ownership on firm's innovation efficiency. *Science Research Management*, 39(05), 11–18.

Fabisik Kornelia, Fahlenbrach Rüdiger, Stulz René M. & Taillard Jérôme P. (2021). Why are firms with more managerial ownership worth less?. *Journal of Financial Economics* (3), doi:10.1016/J.JFINECO.2021.02.008.

Fan Haifeng, & Zhou Xiaochun. (2020). A research on the effect mechanism of managerial ownership on innovation performance—The mediating role based on financial constraints. *Science Research Management*, 41(03), 52–60.

Ji Weili, & Fan Weichao. (2021). Is a higher management shareholding ratio conducive to innovation? - Research based on different ownership and industry background. *Friends of accouting*, 4(14), 46–53.

Morck, R., Shleifer, A., & Vishny, R. W. (1988). Management ownership and market valuation: An empirical analysis. *Journal of financial economics* 20, 293–315.

Moudud-Ul-Huq, S., Biswas, T., & Dola, S. P. (2020). Effect of managerial ownership on bank value: insights of an emerging economy. *Asian Journal of Accounting Research*, ahead-of-print(ahead-of-print).

Septiana, D. D., & Riswandari, E. (2020). The role of investment opportunities, managerial ownership, capital structure on corporate value. *EAJ (Economics and Accounting Journal)*, 3(2), 138–145.

Tan Qingmei, Liu Yaguang, & Ma Mingze. (2013). Managerial ownership, product market competition and firm value: evidence from panel data of Chinese listed firms. *Journal of Tianjin University (social science)*, 15(02), 97–103.

Wang Xiaowei, & Chen Fengbo. (2014). Ownership structure and enterprises' value of growth enterprise market listed companies. *Journal of Management Science*, 27(06), 40–52.

Xu Lin, Zhu Chunxi, & Dong Yongqi. (2018). Study on the relationship between the characteristics of management shareholding range and the value of listed companies. *Wuhan Finance Monthly*, 4(08), 43–48.

Yi Chuilin. (2009). An empirical analysis on managerial ownership and corporate value – Based on data set of listed companies from Shanghai and Shenzhen stock exchange. *Industrial Economics Research*, 4(06), 60–64.

Economic and Business Management – Huang & Zhang (Eds)
© 2022 Copyright the Author(s), ISBN: 978-1-032-06754-4

The analysis of the impact of Shenzhen-Hong Kong stock connect on the stock market co-movement between the mainland and Hong Kong—based on the GARCH-copula model

Xunjun Zhang & Yucan Liu
School of Economics and Management, Nanjing University of Science and Technology, Nanjing, China

ABSTRACT: The introduction of Shenzhen-Hong Kong Stock Connect has further expanded the opening of the mainland's capital market and strengthened the cross-straits stock market co-movement effect. In this paper, Shanghai Stock Index, Shenzhen component Index and Hang Seng Index are selected, and December 5, 2016 is taken as the time cut-off point to select the daily return before and after the launch of Shenzhen-Hong Kong Stock Connect. The GARCH-Copula model is used to analyze the co-movement effect between mainland and Hong Kong stock markets. It is found that after the introduction of Shenzhen-Hong Kong Stock Connect, the co-movement between the two stock markets has been strengthened, and the co-movement between the Shanghai stock market and the Hong Kong stock market is stronger than that between the Shenzhen stock market and the Hong Kong stock market.

1 INTRODUCTION

After the reform and opening up, China's economy has developed rapidly and the capital market has been continuously opened to the outside world.

In particular, the introduction of Shenzhen-Hong Kong Stock Connect has expanded the openness of China's inland market and promoted the interconnection between China's mainland and Hong Kong stock markets. It not only has a profound impact on the promotion of economic exchanges between the mainland and Hong Kong, but also consolidates Hong Kong's position as an international financial center, and enhances the economic and non-economic cooperation between the mainland and Hong Kong. Understanding the impact of Shenzhen-Hong Kong Stock Connect on the stock market interaction between the mainland and Hong Kong will help investors to further understand the interaction between stock prices of the two places and optimize their investment portfolio. It also helps the government departments to formulate policies more in line with the rules of market operation and promote the stable economic development of the two inland ports.

Research on co-movement originated from abroad. Eun and Shims (1989) studied many developed stock markets, such as in the USA and Japan, by using cointegration analysis and the Granger causality test, and found that information transmission between stock markets of different countries was very rapid, and it could be completed within one or two days. Gebka and Serwa (2007) analyzed the stock volatility in emerging economies such as Central and Eastern Europe,

Southeast Asia, and Latin America, and found that the impact of the stock market in the same economic region was greater than that of the international stock market. Sharma and Bodla (2011) used variance decomposition and Granger causality test to analyze the interaction effect among the stock markets of India, Pakistan and Sri Lanka, and believed that there were multiple interaction effects among South Asian countries, especially Among India, Pakistan and Sri Lanka. Shahzad et al. (2016) conducted the ARDL bound test, DLOS valuation, vector error test and Granger causality test on indexes such as Dow Jones 600, and analyzed the co-movement effect between stock markets in South Asia and developed countries, through the study, they found that the stock markets in South Asia are closely linked with each other. Zhang (2017) built a micro model of retail investors' decision-making behavior and found that there is a linkage relationship between Shanghai and Shenzhen stock markets in both the long and short term; the returns of the two stock markets are not independent of each other, but have a very important influence on each other. Hou and Lu (2019) analyzed the correlation between Shanghai and Shenzhen stock markets by establishing the Copula-GARCH model, and found that the returns of Shanghai and Shenzhen stock markets had a strong correlation, and that the description of problems was more accurate than the binary normal Copula model and the t-Copula model. Li (2021) established the VEC model to analyze the characteristics of the cointegration between the mainland stock market and the Hong Kong stock market before and after the introduction of Shanghai-Hong Kong Stock

DOI 10.1201/9781003203704-14

Connect and Shenzhen-Hong Kong Stock Connect, it was found that there was a long-term co-integration relationship between the mainland stock market and the Hong Kong stock market before and after the epidemic.

The research of domestic and foreign scholars all show that the development of stock markets in different parts of the world is influenced by the stock markets in other regions, and at the same time, it also has an important influence on other stock markets. Stock markets in different parts of the world influence each other and develop together, which is of great significance to the research on the correlation between stock markets.

This paper combines theoretical and empirical methods, and analyzes the interlinkage between the mainland and Hong Kong stock markets by establishing the GARCH-Copula model, and makes a quantitative study on the basis of previous qualitative analysis.

This paper consists of four chapters. The first chapter introduces the research background, research significance, research methods and the main content of the paper. The second chapter makes a theoretical analysis of the causes of the interlinkage between the mainland and Hong Kong stock markets. In chapter three, the GARCH-Copula model is established to study the impact of Shenzhen-Hong Kong Stock Connect on the stock market co-movement between Mainland and Hong Kong. The fourth chapter draws conclusions and provides reasonable suggestions.

2 EMPIRICAL ANALYSIS

2.1 *Theoretical basis*

Scholars have different opinions on the causes of co-movement. The main one is the efficient market hypothesis proposed by the famous US scholars Eugene Malkiel and Fama (1970). That is, on the premise that if the market is rational enough, the market price can fully and quickly reflect all the relevant information contained in the market. According to the theory, the completeness of capital market information and the behavior of investors in the market are the important basis for judging whether a security market is efficient or not. With the development of economy and the introduction of a series of interconnection policies, the transparency of information is constantly improved, the investors of the two places have a deeper understanding of the information of the two places' stock markets, and the co-movement of the two places' stock markets is constantly strengthened.

Second is the rapid development of economic integration. Economies around the world are increasingly interconnected, and the economies of all regions have become an indispensable part of global economic development. According to the theory of comparative advantage, free trade between different regions is conducive to improving the welfare of citizens in different regions. Economic globalization makes capital factors in different regions flow across borders on a global scale. Under the background of economic globalization, the two regions with an open economy are closely connected to each other. In recent years, the implementation of various trade and financial measures in the two inland ports has made the relationship between them deeper.

Based on the theoretical analysis of the co-movement between mainland and Hong Kong stock markets before and after the introduction of Shenzhen-Hong Kong Stock Connect, the following assumptions are put forward:

Hypothesis 1: The co-movement between the mainland and Hong Kong stock markets is weakened after the launch of Shenzhen-Hong Kong Stock Connect.

Hypothesis 2: The co-movement between the mainland and Hong Kong stock markets has not changed after the launch of Shenzhen-Hong Kong Stock Connect.

Hypothesis 3: The co-movement between the mainland and Hong Kong stock markets has been enhanced after the launch of Shenzhen-Hong Kong Stock Connect.

2.2 *Data*

This paper takes the introduction date of Shenzhen-Hong Kong Stock Connect as the node, December 5, 2016, and divides the time period into: from January 4, 2013 to December 5, 2016, and from December 6, 2016 to June 30, 2021, six subsequences: SHI1, SHI2, SZI1, SZI2, HSI1, and HSI2; and if there are days when the mainland and Hong Kong stock markets don't open at the same time, we will take them out. There were 6009 groups of observations obtained.

Before and after the introduction of Shenzhen-Hong Kong Stock Connect, the return series of Shanghai Stock Index, Shenzhen component Index and Hang Seng Index show the obvious characteristics of sharp peak and thick tail, and all of them do not obey the normal distribution. Therefore, it can be seen that the normal distribution cannot well describe the distribution characteristics of the return series of the three stock markets in each stage. And through the ADF test, it can be seen that at the confidence level of 1%, the rate sequences are all stable.

2.3 *Marginal distribution model*

The distribution of rate series shows the characteristics of bias, fluctuation cluster, peak and thick tail, etc. The GARCH model can make a good description of the volatility of financial time series. In addition, there is an autocorrelation between the return rate in each stage, and the time series selected by the sample have all passed the ARCH effect test. Therefore, this paper intends to use the GARCH model to fit the edge distribution of the stock index in each stage.

In this paper, the Copula-GARCH (1,1) model is selected to study the relationship between Shanghai Securities Composite Index, Compositional Index of

Table 1. ARCH test.

	H	stat	P value
SHI1	1	43.4826	0.000
SHI2	1	7.0007	0.001
SZI1	1	42.2382	0.000
SZI2	1	6.2837	0.001
HSI1	1	23.3824	0.000
HSI2	1	41.3223	0.000

Table 2. GARCH (1,1) model coefficients.

		ω	β	α
SHI1	Coefficient	1.6110E-06*	0.9269***	0.0644***
	t-Statistic	1.6805	134.45	8.8753
SHI2	Coefficient	1.9943E-06**	0.8747***	0.1195***
	t-Statistic	2.3236	98.787	13.5091
SZI1	Coefficient	2.2832E-06*	0.9287***	0.0652***
	t-Statistic	1.5801	110.00	7.3665
SZI2	Coefficient	6.2773E-06***	0.8710***	0.1017***
	t-Statistic	6.3969	55.2704	7.9895
HSI1	Coefficient	6.8863E-06***	0.8666***	0.0748***
	t-Statistic	6.6491	33.6903	4.3425
HSI2	Coefficient	1.8805E-06*	0.9354***	0.0503***
	t-Statistic	1.8932	103.346	5.7464

***present reject the null hypothesis in 99% confidence level,
** present reject the null hypothesis in 95% confidence level.
* present reject the null hypothesis in 90% confidence level.

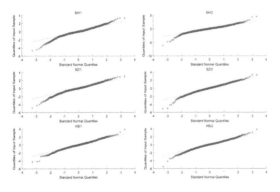

Figure 1. The Q-Q diagram of GARCH (1,1) model.

Shenzhen Stock Market and Hang Seng Index before and after the introduction of Shenzhen-Hong Kong Stock Connect. Table 2 shows the parameter estimation results of the GARCH (1,1) model. It can be seen from the Q-Q figure in Figure 1 that the GARCH (1,1) model adopted in this paper has a good fitting effect.

As the results in Table 3 show, the processed residual sequences all meet the conditions of independent distribution, so the new residual sequence is normalized to make it satisfy the conditions of independent distribution on (0,1). The new data obtained meet the conditions of Copula model.

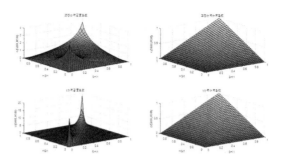

Figure 2. Density function and distribution function.

Table 3. The result of the Q test.

	Residual		Residual square	
	stat	H	stat	H
SHI1	22.62	0	26.11	0
SHI2	14.16	0	13.79	0
SZI1	24.28	0	22.17	0
SZI2	14.96	0	18.66	0
HSI1	12.55	0	21.85	0
HSI2	18.22	0	12.20	0

Table 4. Euclidean distance comparison between the Copula model and t-Copula model.

	SHI-HSI		SZI-HSI	
Copula model	before	after	before	after
Copula model	1.23	0.69	1.52	1.15
t-Copula model	1.29	0.76	1.58	1.24

Figure 2 shows the density function diagram and distribution function diagram. This paper only takes the Shanghai stock market and Hong Kong stock market in the first stage as an example to draw the diagram. The square Euclidean distance can be used to evaluate the fitting effect of the model. The smaller the distance is, the better the fitting effect is. As shown by the result in Table 4, in either case, the Euclidean distance of the bivariate normal Copula is smaller, indicating that the bivariate normal Copula is fitting the case better. Meanwhile, as can be seen from Figure 2, the density function graph of the binary normal Copula has a thicker tail, which can better describe the tail correlation between variables. At the same time, Kendall rank correlation coefficient and linear correlation coefficient are the same no matter which model is adopted. Clearly, after the introduction of Shenzhen-Hong Kong Connect the co-movement between the mainland and Hong Kong stock market really has been enhanced. At the same time, through the comparison the co-movement between Shanghai stock market and Hong Kong stock market, Shenzhen stock market and Hong

Kong stock market, we can find that the co-movement between the Shanghai stock market and the Hong Kong stock market is better. This indicates that the mainland stock market has the ability to predict the Hong Kong stock market to a certain extent, and this predictive ability has been enhanced after the introduction of Shenzhen-Hong Kong Stock Connect. Meanwhile, the Shanghai stock market has a stronger predictive ability for the Hong Kong stock market, which may be due to the effect of the Shanghai-Hong Kong Stock Connect before the Shenzhen-Hong Kong Stock Connect.

3 CONCLUSIONS

3.1 *Conclusions*

This paper analyzes the co-movement between the mainland and Hong Kong stock markets before and after the introduction of Shenzhen-Hong Kong Stock Connect, and draws the following conclusions.

In this paper, the GARCH(1,1) model was established to fit the marginal distribution of return rate, and the bivariate normal Copula and t-copula were used to fit the correlation, respectively. And we find the normal Copula has a better fitting effect through the Euclidean distance. At the same time, through the comparison of the co-movement between the mainland and Hong Kong stock markets before and after the introduction of Shenzhen-Hong Kong Stock Connect, it can be found that the co-movement between the mainland and Hong Kong stock markets has indeed been enhanced by the introduction of Shenzhen-Hong Kong Stock Connect, and the co-movement between the Shanghai stock market and Hong Kong stock market is stronger. This may be due to the fact that the introduction of Shanghai-Hong Kong Stock Connect has a strong promoting effect on the co-movement of the Shanghai stock market and the Hong Kong stock Market. Shenzhen-Hong Kong Stock Connect is similar to Shanghai-Hong Kong Stock Connect, so investors' reaction to Shenzhen-Hong Kong Stock Connect is not as strong as to Shanghai-Hong Kong Stock Connect.

3.2 *Advices*

For investors, due to the differences between the mainland and Hong Kong, investment philosophy differ, therefore, when faced with a new investment market and investment mechanism, investors must first to learn both trading systems, and grasp both connectivity mechanisms of investment opportunity, seize the investment opportunities, and build high-quality portfolios, so as to achieve maximum profit.

For policy makers, the implementation of Shenzhen-Hong Kong Stock Connect strengthens the correlation between the mainland and Hong Kong. When formulating and issuing policies, relevant national departments should fully consider the possible co-movement of the policies, not only the impact of the policies on the stock market in mainland China, but also the possible impact on the capital market in Hong Kong, and the timing of the policy release should be carefully considered, too. After the implementation of the policy, the co-movement between the mainland and Hong Kong stock markets will not magnify the impact and bring negative effects to the two places, and it is also necessary to prevent the co-movement between the mainland and Hong Kong from neutralizing the impact of the policy and making the policy fail to achieve the expected effect after the implementation. Therefore, before formulating relevant policies, policy makers should have a good understanding of the joint movement of the mainland and Hong Kong stock markets in advance, and do research to ensure the effective implementation of the policies.

REFERENCES

Bartosz Gebka & Dobromil Serwa. 2007. Intra and interregional spillovers between emerging capital markets around the World(J). *Research in International Business and Finance* 21(2): 203–221.

Burton, G. Malkiel & Eugene F. Fama. 1970. Efficient Capital Markets: A Review of Theory and Empirical Work. *Journal of Finance* 25(2): 383–417.

Cheol S Eun & Sangdal Shim. 1989. International transmission of stock market movements(J). *The Journal of Financial and Quantitative Analysis* 24(2): 241–256.

Gagan Deep Sharma & B.S. Bodla. 2011. Inter-linkages among stock markets of South Asia(J). *Asia-Pacific Journal of Business Administration* 3(2): 132–148.

Meng Zhang. 2017. Research on the linkage effect of Shanghai and Shenzhen stock markets – microcosmic basis and empirical test(J). *Technical economics and Management research* (3): 3–7. (in Chinese)

Syed Jawad Hussain Shahzad & Memoona Kanwal & Tanveer Ahmed & Mobeen Ur Rehman. 2016. Relationship between development, European and South Asian stock markets: a multivariate analysis(J). *South Asian Journal of Global Business* 5(3): 385–402.

Xing Li. 2021. Analysis on the joint activity of A shares and H shares under the background of Shanghai-Shenzhen-Hong Kong Stock Connect(J) *Technology and Economic Guide* 29(04): 211–212. (in Chinese).

Yezi Hou & Junxiang Lu. 2019. Correlation analysis of Shanghai and Shenzhen stock markets based on Copula-GARCH Model(J). *Journal of Xi 'an University of Technology* 39(1): 7–11. (in Chinese)

Economic and Business Management – Huang & Zhang (Eds)
© 2022 Copyright the Author(s), ISBN: 978-1-032-06754-4

The impact of logistics performance on China's cross-border e-commerce trade

Hehua Li & Yuqing Xia

School of Economics and Management, Shanghai Polytechnic University, Shanghai, China

ABSTRACT: Cross-border e-commerce (CBEC), a new engine of foreign trade under the epidemic, is highly dependent on international logistics. Although recent studies deal with the impact of logistics on international trade, this impact on electronic commerce is still an open research question. Moreover, these studies usually do not consider the influence of all components of the logistics on trade. This paper, therefore, aims at identifying the role of logistics performance in cross-border e-commerce imports and exports between China and Central and Eastern European Countries (CEE) in the Belt and Road Initiative. Using an extended gravity model, we examine whether the indicators of the World Bank Logistics Performance Index (LPI), adopted as a proxy of logistics efficiency, are an important determinant of bilateral e-commerce trade facilitation. The results lead to the conclusion that the logistics performance has statistically significant and positive correlation with cross-border e-commerce, especially on exports. Specifically, great importance was placed more on the customs, followed by shipment, infrastructure, and services. Factors like tracing and timeliness have the least importance.

1 INTRODUCTION

The spread of the epidemic continues to promote the transformation of online consumption habits, the digitalization of the Internet has accelerated, and the penetration rate of e-commerce has further increased. In recent years, cross-border e-commerce has become an increasingly important pillar of China's foreign trade (Lai Youwei 2014). According to customs statistics, imports and exports of China's cross-border e-commerce totaled 1.69 trillion yuan in 2020, up 31.1 percent year-on-year. E-commerce exports were 1.12 trillion yuan, up 40.1 percent on a yearly basis while imports stood at 570 billion yuan, up 16.5 percent. From the perspective of cross-border e-commerce destination countries, in addition to developed countries such as the European Union, the United States, and Japan, under the promotion of the Belt and Road Initiative, emerging markets such as Central and Eastern European countries, Southeast Asia, and Africa have risen rapidly, with huge trade potential (Zhang Yabin 2016). However, the logistics infrastructure of these countries and regions is generally insufficient or has been built for a long time, and needs to be rebuilt or updated. So how much influence does logistics performance have on China's cross-border e-commerce import and export trade? Which aspects of logistics are more relevant to e-commerce foreign trade? These issues are of great significance to the development of China's e-commerce foreign trade.

Based on these problems, this article intends to use the extended trade gravity model to find out the main factors affecting CBEC, and explore whether or how the logistics performance affects China's cross-border e-commerce import and export trade specifically.

To this end, the rest of this paper will proceed as follows: section two discusses the previous reviews; section three is about empirical analysis; while section four draws conclusions and makes some suggestions.

2 LITERATURE REVIEW

2.1 *The factors affecting cross-border e-commerce*

In response to the above-mentioned problems, many scholars have conducted related investigations and discussions. Tinbergen (1962) proposed that the decisive factors affecting bilateral trade flow are the economic volume of bilateral countries and the trade distance between the two countries. Besides that, there are other important factors such as national population, national logistics level, geographic factors (whether it is coastal or not), political factors (join the Economic Cooperation Organization or to sign a free trade agreement), cultural factors (language), and so on (Kuang Zengjie 2019). Thinking of CBEC, a new way of international trade, some scholars add new factors like the level of national e-commerce development, network coverage, and payment, etc. Wang Junjuan (2021) found that national informatization level (measured by the proportion of Internet users) has a great impact on cross-border e-commerce. Luo Na (2018) believed that Networked Readiness Index reflects the level of national e-commerce development. Ai Weina (2016) thought that cross-border payment is a bottleneck in developing CBEC.

DOI 10.1201/9781003203704-15

According to the research of the above scholars, it can be found that the economic sizes, distance between two countries, and population are generally considered to be important factors of CBEC. Others like language and national logistics haven't been universal truths yet. However, studies specifically investigating the relation between logistics and e-commerce, commonly acknowledged as critical, seem to be lacking and many contributions are descriptive (Maria Giuffrida et al. 2017). Therefore, more experiments are needed to prove whether or how national logistics affects cross-border e-commerce.

2.2 *Logistics performance index (LPI)*

Hollweg (2009) concluded that there is a significant positive correlation between international trade and logistics performance. To measure the level of logistics development in a country, the international logistics performance index (LPI) is usually used. International logistics performance is an important indicator reflecting the level of logistics development and trade facilitation of a country (Wang Dongfang, 2018), from six aspects (customs, shipment, infrastructure, services, tracing and timeliness). There are also scholars using Principal Component Analysis to independently construct a trade facilitation index system (Kong Qingfeng 2015). Empirical models that study the correlation between international trade and national logistics levels usually include an enhanced gravity model of trade and Global Trade Analysis Project (GTAP). For example, Zhao Yanan (2020) uses an extended trade gravity model to empirically explain the influencing factors of CBEC volume scale between "Belt and Road" countries and China.

Based on previous studies, this article intends to use logistics performance index from 2010 to 2018, published by the World Bank as an important indicator to measure logistics performance. We will describe and analyze the logistics performance index of China and the Central and Eastern European Countries, and explore the current status and problems of logistics performance in these countries; then, logistics performance indicators are added to the extended trade gravity model to explore whether the logistics performance affects China's cross-border e-commerce import and export trade.

3 EMPIRICAL ANALYSIS

3.1 *Overview of logistics performance in China and 17 CEE countries*

From 2010 to 2018, the LPI of CEE countries is low, only slightly higher than the global average, but overall it is rising. China's LPI is generally higher than the global average, and the ranking continues to rise, and the logistics level gap between China and the top ten developed countries has been narrowing. In 2018, China's LPI score was 3.61, ranking 26th in the world (Figure 1).

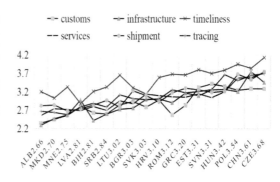

Figure 1. Comparison of logistics performance among China and 17CEE countries (2018).

Taking the latest data (2018) as an example, the countries on the horizontal axis are ranked from low to high in terms of comprehensive logistics performance, and China ranks between Poland and the Czech Republic. From the perspective of sub-indices, the timeliness scored the highest in each country, and performed best in the six sub-indexes of logistics performance; followed by tracing and shipment. Therefore, the 17 CCE countries should pay more attention to the two aspects of customs and infrastructure to promote their logistics performance.

3.2 *Constructing a gravity model of trade*

The trade gravity model was first introduced into the field of international trade by Tinbergen (1963), and many scholars have conducted in-depth research on the model and extended it on the basis of the original one. Based on literature review, this paper selects six main factors affecting international trade: the economic sizes, distance between two countries, logistics performance, population, e-commerce development and policy. The regression equation is constructed below:

$$lnEXP_i(INP_i) = \beta_0 + \beta_1 lnGDP_i + \beta_2 lnDIS_i \\ + \beta_3 lnPOP_i + \beta_4 lnLPI_i + \beta_5 lnNRI_i \\ + \beta_6 PLY_i + \varepsilon_i$$

In the formula, $\beta_1 - \beta_6$ represent coefficients, while β_0 is a constant term, and ε_i is the error term. The data sources and explanation of other variables in the equation are shown in Table 1.

In this study, we use ordinary least squares (OLS) with panel data in spss to examine the weight of six main factors affecting China's cross-border e-commerce. First, select the basic two variables (economic size and the distance between the two countries) in the regression model, and then gradually introduce more variables to it. The results are in Table 2 (exports) and Table 3 (imports) for easy comparison.

In order to further study the impact of different aspects of LPI on China's cross-border e-commerce export trade, this article introduces six sub-indexes of LPI into the regression model: efficiency of customs clearance process (CEI); quality of trade and

Table 1. Explanation of variable indicators.

Index	Variable	Description	Data source
Import	INP	e-commerce import	iResearch
Export	EXP	e-commerce export	iResearch
Product	GDP	gross Domestic Product	World Bank
Distance	DIS	between Beijing and the capital	CEPII
Population	POP	domestic population	World Bank
Logistics	LPI	logistics performance index	World Bank
E-commerce	NRI	Network Readiness Index	Technology Report
Policy	PLY	Free Trade Partner China	FTA Network

Table 2. Regression results of e-commerce exports.

Model	1	2	3	4	5
Independent variable					
lnGDP	0.967***	0.825***	0.584***	0.559***	0.529***
	[14.223]	[9.768]	[6.666]	[7.582]	[7.166]
INDIS	-5.198***	-4.513***	-2.981**	-3.101**	-2.941**
	[-3.192]	[-2.835]	[-2.096]	[-2.593]	[-2.499]
INPOP		0.259***	0.177**	0.349***	0.315***
		[2.665]	[2.044]	[4.454]	[3.991]
INLPI			4.268***	1.914**	1.690**
			[5.115]	[2.367]	[2.107]
INNRI				4.106***	3.726***
				[5.850]	[5.209]
PLY					0.335*
					[1.983]
_cons	41.549***	33.602**	20.248	15.712	15.897
	[2.765]	[2.270]	[1.535]	[1.414]	[1.457]
N	85	85	85	85	85
adj. R-sq	0.797	0.811	0.856	0.898	0.902
r^2	0.801	0.817	0.862	0.904	0.909
F	165.417	120.852	125.334	148.749	129.212

***, **, *represent P<0.01, P<0.05, P<0.1.

transport-related infrastructure (TII); frequency with which shipments reach consignee within scheduled or expected time (TDI); competence and quality of logistics services (LQI); ease of arranging competitively priced shipments (IFI); and ability to track and trace consignments (TSI). The results are shown in Table 4.

3.3 Results

It can be seen from the Table 2 that with the gradual addition of independent variables, the R-squared values are higher. LPI ranks third among all influencing factors, and its elasticity coefficient to export trade is 1.69, indicating that if the logistics performance of 17 CEE countries increases by 1%, China's cross-border e-commerce export will grow 1.69 %. In addition, these factors have passed the 10% significance test.

From the results in Table 4, it can be seen that, the influence of each sub-indicator on China's e-commerce export is positive and they are then ranked by their weight:

customs > shipment > infrastructure > services > tracing > timeliness.

In Table 3, when other factors remain unchanged, LPI ranks fourth among all influencing factors, and its elasticity coefficient to import trade is 0.411, indicating that by improving logistics performance of CEE countries by 1%, China's e-commerce import trade will increase by 0.411 %.

By comprehensive analysis and comparison, it can be found that the logistics performance of CEE countries have statistically significant and positive correlation with China's cross-border e-commerce, especially on exports.

Four sub-indexes of LPI (customs, shipment, tracing, and timeliness) pass the significance level of 5% and the coefficients of each sub-indicator are between 0.5 and 1.6, larger than the those of economy, population, and policy factors (smaller than national e-commerce development level and geographic location). It shows that the prosperity of cross-border e-commerce exports is inseparable from the improvement of the logistics performance of trading countries, and the improvement of each sub-indicator will further reduce costs. Each improvement will bring about a significant increase in China's cross-border e-commerce export trade.

Table 3. Regression results of e-commerce imports.

Model	1	2	3	4	5
Independent variable					
lnGDP	0.949***	0.701***	0.506***	0.483***	0.372**
	[8.592]	[5.148]	[3.209]	[3.167]	[2.588]
INDIS	−9.723***	−8.529***	−7.286***	−7.395***	−6.787***
	[−3.675]	[−3.320]	[−2.845]	[−2.987]	[−2.967]
INPOP		0.451***	0.384**	0.541***	0.411***
		[2.877]	[2.471]	[3.335]	[2.680]
INLPI			3.463**	1.324	0.472
			[2.305]	[0.791]	[0.303]
INNRI				3.733**	2.291
				[2.568]	[1.648]
PLY					1.273***
					[3.873]
_cons	79.142***	65.297***	54.460**	50.336**	51.039**
	[3.242]	[2.734]	[2.293]	[2.187]	[2.406]
N	85	85	85	85	85
adj. R-sq	0.641	0.67	0.687	0.707	0.751
r^2	0.649	0.682	0.702	0.725	0.769
F	75.94	57.879	47.05	41.593	43.305

***, **, *represent P<0.01, P<0.05, P<0.1.

Table 4. Weights to the six components of the LPI.

Model	1	2	3	4	5	6
Independent variable						
lnGDP	0.532***	0.539***	0.585***	0.570***	0.548***	0.551***
	[7.437]	[7.564]	[8.413]	[8.129]	[7.706]	[7.809]
INDIS	−2.902**	−3.098***	−2.886**	−3.181***	−2.451*	−2.937**
	[−2.492]	[−2.673]	[−2.251]	[−2.695]	[−1.962]	[−2.492]
INPOP	0.368***	0.324***	0.355***	0.343***	0.344***	0.347***
	[4.921]	[4.212]	[4.574]	[4.415]	[4.508]	[4.564]
INNRI	3.466***	3.429***	4.351***	3.954***	3.909***	4.104***
	[4.678]	[4.493]	[6.610]	[5.575]	[5.695]	[6.237]
PLY	0.264	0.282	0.378**	0.301*	0.306*	0.27
	[1.524]	[1.638]	[2.206]	[1.687]	[1.778]	[1.529]
INCEI	1.658**					
	[2.435]					
INTII		1.489**				
		[2.299]				
INTDI			0.566			
			[1.006]			
INLQI				1.268		
				[1.538]		
INIFI					1.517**	
					[2.021]	
INTSI						1.264**
						[2.077]
_cons	15.26	17.807	14.196	17.171	10.745	15.006
	[1.409]	[1.653]	[1.179]	[1.559]	[0.927]	[1.365]
N	85	85	85	85	85	85
adj. R-sq	0.903	0.903	0.897	0.899	0.901	0.901
r^2	0.91	0.91	0.905	0.906	0.908	0.908
F	131.778	130.674	123.301	125.636	43.305	

***, **, *represent P<0.01, P<0.05, P<0.1.

4 CONCLUSIONS

4.1 Conclusions

The results lead to the conclusion that the logistics performance of CEE countries has positive correlation with China's cross-border e-commerce both on exports and imports. Specifically, it has a much greater impact on exports than on that on imports. The top three most influential factors on cross-border e-commerce exports are the e-commerce development, population, and logistics performance, which is completely different from imports (distance between two countries, e-commerce development and policy are the top three factors, while logistics performance ranks fourth).

Logistics performance can be divided into six specific area: customs, shipment, infrastructure, services, tracing, and timeliness. According to the results, customs is the most influential factor. Shipment ranks second, while infrastructure is the third. Others like services, tracing, and timeliness have the least importance.

4.2 Suggestions

Since the launch of the "17+1 Cooperation," China and CEE countries have cooperated in various fields such as railways, highways, bridges, ports, aviation and so on. The completion of the Hungary-Serbia Railway, China-Europe Express Line, Serbia E763 Expressway, Montenegro North-South Expressway, and other projects are bound to enhance the local foundation construction, improving the level of logistics development and strengthening the commercial ties between China and European countries. To create an intercontinental logistics chain connecting Europe and Asia, it is necessary to promote the construction of optical cables, submarine cables, cloud computing, big data centers and other infrastructures, construct "logistics information ports," and establish logistics big data calculation and analysis centers to provide services for various logistics applications.

Besides that, focus should be on reducing documents, optimizing processes, improving timeliness, and reducing costs to accelerate the efficiency of customs clearance processes and to enhance the level of trade facilitation with Central and Eastern Europe. First, take the cross-border e-commerce customs clearance as the entry point, with the help of big data, thoroughly break down the information barriers among customs clearance, inspection, taxation, foreign exchange, business, goods, and financing, and establish a full data chain cross-border comprehensive security system for border e-commerce. The second is to effectively establish a cooperation platform between the Chinese customs and the customs of Central and Eastern European countries, improve and unify the regulatory rules and standards, clarify legal responsibilities, and simplify the customs clearance process.

4.3 Study limitations and opportunities for future work

The number of samples is relatively small because of limited time and effort. More factors such as language and geographical environment could be considered in the impact of cross-border e-commerce in the future.

ACKNOWLEDGMENT

Joint Higher Education Project in Central and Eastern European Countries, China Education Association for International Exchange, No. 201910.

REFERENCES

Hollweg C, Wong MH. 2009. Measuring Regulatory Restrictions in Logistics Services[R]. *ERIA Discussion Paper Series*.

Kong Qingfeng & Dong Hongwei. 2015. Research on the Measurement of the Level of Trade Facilitation and the Trade Potential of "One Belt One Road" Countries [J]. *International Trade Issues*, {4}(12): 158–168.

Kuang Zengjie & Gao Jun. 2019. Research on the Trade Potential between China and Central and Eastern European Countries under the "One Belt and One Road" Initiative [J]. *Statistics and Decision*, 35(13): 122–124.

Lai Youwei & Wang Kaiqian. 2014. Development patterns, obstacles and next steps of China's cross-border e-commerce [J]. *Reform*, {4}(05): 68–74.

Luo Na & Luo Lejuan. 2018. An Empirical Study on the Impact of One Belt One Road -based Cross-border E-commerce on China's Import and Export Trade [J]. *Business Economics Research*, {4}(20): 132–134.

Maria Giuffrida et al. 2017. Cross-border B2C e-commerce to Greater China and the role of logistics: a literature review[J]. *International Journal of Physical Distribution & Logistics Management*, 47(9): 772–795.

Tinbergen, J. 1962. An analysis of world trade flows[J]. *Shaping the World Economy*, 5(1):27–30.

Wang Dongfang & Dong Qianli & Yu Lixin. 2018. Logistics performance of countries and regions along the "Belt and Road" and China's foreign trade potential [J]. *China Circulation Economy*, 32(02): 17–27.

Wang Junjuan. 2021. The trade facilitation effect of my country's cross-border e-commerce development – Based on the empirical analysis of countries along the "Belt and Road" [J]. *Business Economics Research*, (02): 70–73.

Weina Ai & Jianzheng Yang & Lin Wang. 2016. Revelation of cross-border logistics performance for the manufacturing industry development[J]. *Int. J. of Mobile Communications*, 14(6): 593–609.

Yanan Zhao. 2020. Influencing Factors of Cross-Border E-Commerce Trade between China and "Belt and Road" Coastal and Inland Countries[J]. *Journal of Coastal Research*, 103(sp1): 70–73.

Zhang Yabin & Liu Jun & Li Chenglin. 2016. Silk Road economic belt of trade facilitation measures and trade potential in China [J]. *Finance & Economics*, {4} (05): 112–122.

Economic and Business Management – Huang & Zhang (Eds)
© 2022 Copyright the Author(s), ISBN: 978-1-032-06754-4

Research on the optimization path of catastrophe insurance business development from the perspective of the Guangdong-Hong Kong-Macao Greater Bay Area linkage

Xue Dang
South China Business College, Guangdong University of Foreign Studies, Guangzhou, China

ABSTRACT: Catastrophe insurance reflects its necessity in the disaster environment and economic construction needs. Guangdong, Hong Kong, and Macao, as an integrated mechanism of economic linkage in the Bay Area of China, must start from a unified and centralized perspective in response to catastrophe risks and build an integrated catastrophe commercial insurance system. In this paper, the authors have discussed regarding the optimization of the current development path of commercial catastrophe insurance, and jointly building a catastrophe mechanism with "system freedom and diversified insurance types" in the form of linkages between banks and insurance companies to ensure that the catastrophe insurance commercial systems form pilot areas with demonstration effects.

1 INTRODUCTION

Catastrophe insurance has a wide range of components and subjects, which directly leads to the development and formation of the commercialization model of catastrophe insurance. It needs to be based on the macro- and micro-perspectives. The simultaneous intervention of the government and the market has been the inevitable direction in the continuous evolution of catastrophe insurance. In this dynamic evolution process, due to factors such as insensitivity of information and narrow access to common knowledge among individuals, cognitive biases are likely to occur under risk perception differences. Therefore, in the commercialization of catastrophe insurance, the vacuum zone for consumers should also be restricted and regulated to achieve the dynamic game balance of catastrophe insurance commercialization.

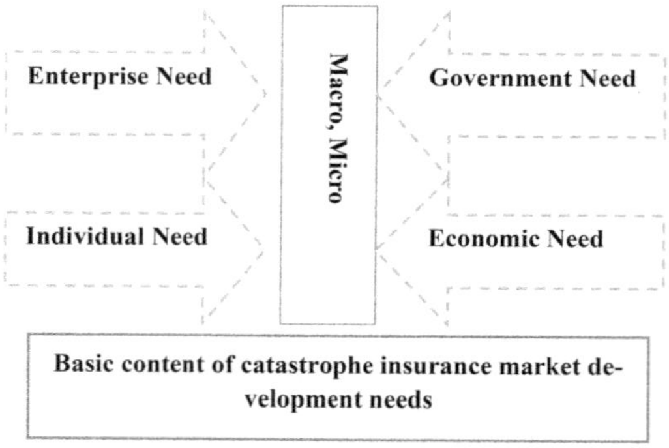

Figure 1. Basic content of catastrophe insurance needs.

2 COMPARISON OF RESEARCH AND DEVELOPMENT STATUS AT HOME AND ABROAD

The connotation and extension of catastrophe insurance demand are quite different from traditional insurance. The realization of catastrophe insurance driven by the concept of "risk insurable" is not just a matter of paper. At this stage, many countries are using the government, insurance companies, banks, and other departments to build an integrated catastrophe insurance system. However, in terms of the coverage and protection capabilities, it is slightly inadequate in our country. Zhang Yunxia (2020) proposed the application of earthquake-based commercial insurance in future national governance based on topography of the western region, but the system has not yet been developed. Song Qingqing (2020) assesses precise catastrophes from the perspective of huge low-quality disasters in rural Gansu Province. The current academic research on catastrophe insurance focus on the value evaluation and application evaluation, and it has not yet been formally implemented. As shown in Figure 1, how the catastrophe insurance market builds a system that balances its market demand, government demand, and enterprise demand, and implants it into our country's economic system, is also an academic focus issue [1].

82

DOI 10.1201/9781003203704-16

3 DEVELOPMENT STATUS OF CATASTROPHE INSURANCE IN THE GREATER BAY AREA

3.1 *The catastrophe insurance mechanism is launched due to frequent disasters*

The economic linkage of Guangdong, Hong Kong, and Macao drives the economic development of the region in a coordinated manner. Similar geographic and meteorological environments in the Guangdong-Hong Kong-Macao Greater Bay Area (hereinafter referred to as GBA) have led to very similar types of regional catastrophes. The GBA sit on the Pearl River system, and the climate type is subtropical monsoon climate. The winter is warm and there is little rain, and the summer is vulnerable to natural disasters such as typhoons, cold waves, heavy rainfall, and floods. In order to reduce the economic damage coefficient of the disasters under the catastrophic environment, and to jointly promote the economic axis effect in GBA, the Guangdong Provincial Water Resources Department issued a cooperative project "Flood risk and catastrophe insurance in GBA" in June 2019, which attempts to use the joint intervention of insurance companies, banks, and the government to control the risks caused by floods. On January 16, 2020, the Shenzhen Banking and Insurance Regulatory Bureau held the 19th Guangdong-Hong Kong-Macao-Shenzhen Joint Conference on Insurance Regulatory Supervision. The meeting focused on the "GBA Planning Outline" and proposed policies for the implementation of catastrophe insurance and bonds in GBA, and combined the meteorological situation, topography, and landforms of Guangdong, Hong Kong, and Macao in this policy as well as economic characteristics, correlation analysis of the overall planning direction of catastrophe insurance or financial product projects. Guangdong Province issued the "Catastrophe Insurance Pilot Work Plan" in 2015, and proposed basic policies for catastrophe insurance claims in prefecture-level cities, pointing out the prefecture-level city can obtain a catastrophe claim amount of 10 million yuan, and the catastrophe insurance claim amount of a low-level city exceeds 30 million yuan, and the prefecture-level city shall bear it.

Disasters have distinct regional characteristics in GBA. The overall construction of catastrophe insurance mechanism is still in the preliminary stage and targeted in catastrophe insurance supply. When invested in collective enterprises or in cities, the insurance coverage group has a larger margin [2].

3.2 *Promotion of commercial catastrophe insurance products in a pilot form*

The launch of commercial catastrophe insurance products in GBA at this stage will be carried out on a small scale in the form of pilot projects. The catastrophe insurance compensation was the fastest case for the first domestic catastrophe compensation. In July 2016, Zhanjiang, Shaoguan, Meizhou and Shanwei, Guangdong Province, Maoming, Shantou, and Heyuan have successively signed catastrophe insurance policies, triggering 12 catastrophe claims in the same year. Guangzhou launched a pilot project for catastrophe insurance in 2019, uniting PICC P&C, Pacific Insurance, and Ping An Insurance as a co-insurance. The catastrophe index is selected with the typhoon and heavy rainfall as the disaster factors, and the premium is divided by 1:1 according to the districts and cities, and the compensation amount is directly paid to the government. In 2020, continuous heavy rain in Guangzhou triggered the index threshold to obtain the highest insurance claim amount so far in the catastrophe insurance. On May 21, 2020, the catastrophe insurance co-insurance delivered 13.34 million Yuan to the Guangzhou Monetary Authority. In 2019, Macao launched catastrophe property insurance products for small and medium-sized enterprises to compensate for their losses. Hong Kong plans to jointly issue catastrophe securities with mainland security companies in 2021.

The commercial catastrophe insurance claims work is carried out later than the government catastrophe claims work. The compensation objects of commercial catastrophe insurance claims are still mainly enterprises or cities, and there is a gap in insurance coverage [3].

Looking at the basic overview development of catastrophe insurance in GBA, we can understand that the overall time for the implementation of various catastrophe insurance policies or products is lacking. The catastrophe insurance plan began in 2016, and some policies officially landed in 2019. In the short term, there are many aspects in the construction of a catastrophe insurance system which deserve optimization.

4 ANALYSIS ON THE DEVELOPMENT OF CATASTROPHE INSURANCE BUSINESS IN THE GREATER BAY AREA

The development cycle of catastrophe insurance business in GBA is relatively short, and the system has not yet been fully implemented. Based on the long-term development perspective of catastrophe insurance, the three regions will cover individuals in the process of commercialization. The above-mentioned problems in the establishment of a catastrophe insurance system must be resolved in order to deepen the institutionalization of problems, the restricted supply in the development, and the lack of legal protection systems and regulations for catastrophe insurance.

4.1 *Individual coverage under catastrophe insurance*

The ultimate influence of catastrophes in GBA is not directly manifested in collectives or enterprises. It can have an impact on the actual lives of everyone in the three regions. In the actual implementation of insurance, individuals have completely ignored the impact. The comprehensive perception of risks, combined with the gaps of individual consumers and the theoretical conflicts, the actual coverage of catastrophe insurance still has the following contradictions in the context of frequent natural disaster. Under the influence of short-sighted behaviors, people are interested in catastrophe insurance or related financial products. For rational people, the occurrence of events in the short term will cause individuals to worry about risks and excessive emotions. The factors that guide individuals to pay attention to catastrophes are not reasonable, but once the disaster is over, short-sighted behavior is difficult to have an impact, and catastrophe insurance has become a waste product in consumer judgment. This behavior mode is affected by the level of individual risk perception. Consumers' own risk perception level is relatively low. The control of catastrophe risk rests on the frequency of catastrophes, personal preferences, economic strength, and other factors. Individuals find it difficult to make rational decisions of the actual losses, which leads to great obstacles for the commercialization of catastrophe insurance [4].

4.2 *Constrained supply of catastrophe insurance in the Greater Bay Area markets*

It is necessary to fully examine the constraints of catastrophe insurance on the market supply in GBA. The overall supply of catastrophe insurance to the market is also subject to strong restraint effects. The restraints are embodied in technical, financial, and contractual conditions.

4.2.1 *Technical constraints*
The biggest technical problem is that the impact of catastrophes on individuals or enterprises is not relevant and does not comply with the law of large numbers. The loss and direct impact on property are difficult to correlate with effective correlation factors. For insurance companies, floods, typhoons, landslides, and other disaster losses caused by heavy rainfall in GBA over the years are difficult to accurately characterize and count. In the process of constructing actuarial models, the fluctuation of frequency data and the estimation of loss data will directly cause the evaluation results to be inaccurate. For insurance companies, the difficulty of calculating the pricing data conditions of the actuarial model, as well as technical construction and operational problems such as the evaluation of the possible future mega-disasters, are all problems faced by catastrophe insurance when it is fully put into the market and landed [5].

Therefore, in the process of commercialization of catastrophe insurance in GBA, it can only cover small areas in a small-scale pilot form, and it is impossible to find an effective way to achieve full coverage of catastrophe insurance in the three regions.

4.2.2 *Financial constraints*
Financial constraints mean that the final disaster claim amount and expenses of catastrophe insurance cannot be borne by any insurance company in GBA at this

stage. In the market supply, the absolute indicators required are the amount of natural disaster losses and net assets of insurance companies, combined with the basic situation of the current development of catastrophe insurance in the three regions. Take the PICC Property and Casualty Company, Ping An Insurance Company, and Pacific Insurance Company as examples, the net assets of the three companies in the joint guarantee body were 55.88 billion Yuan in 2010. In 2010, the natural disaster loss in Guangdong Province was as high as 17.82 billion Yuan, which directly shows that the current insurance companies themselves are severely restricted in their economic power to pay for catastrophe insurance. The rigid financial constraints are also an obstacle to the effective implementation and promotion of catastrophe insurance.

4.2.3 *Contract constraints*
The catastrophe itself has short-term effects. The so-called short-term effect means that the catastrophe can only show a certain demand effect in a short time, and under the changes of the meteorological environment, the catastrophe insurance premium itself shows certain volatility. However, at the current stage, there is no obvious and effective difference between the catastrophe insurance contract signing method and the traditional property insurance contract signing method. The conflict between catastrophe instability and current contract stability has caused that catastrophe insurance affects the stability of insurance companies, which affects the stability of funds [6].

4.3 *Legal protection system for catastrophe insurance*

The catastrophe system actually traces its source, which includes the State Council, the earthquake relief department, the flood control and drought relief headquarters, the disaster reduction committee, and all administrative organizations under the prefecture-level cities. The system also includes social organizations. For all public property and private economy, the system needs to ensure the integrity of public property and private property during disasters from the perspective of macro-prevention and control. Thus, catastrophe relief and command in GBA also include three links: pre-prevention and control, operation during the event, and relief after the event. Among the current three links, catastrophe relief operations already include all departments and levels as for social and economic operations. However, the follow-up of relevant laws has been slow to effectively advance. The construction of the catastrophe insurance legal system is the guarantee for the commercialization of catastrophe insurance. However, its legal structure still has deficiencies in the following aspects:

4.3.1 *Lack of legislation causes failure of commercial market control*
The catastrophe insurance system itself has strong external feature, that is, the behavior of the insurance

The development of catastrophe insurance commercialization

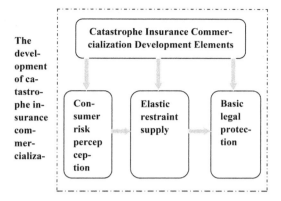

Figure 2. Defects in the commercialization of catastrophe insurance in the Greater Bay Area.

subject will directly affect other insurance subjects or individuals, eventually leading to the failure of the insurance market, which will result in the delay of catastrophe insurance into small groups. The lack of the GBA in the catastrophe-related legal system is also a key reason for the difficulty of commercialization. Looking at the improvement of the foreign catastrophe insurance system, the follow-up of relevant legal systems has effectively guaranteed the value of catastrophe insurance, such as the "Natural Disaster Insurance Compensation System" passed by the French Congress and the "Flood Insurance Reform Act" passed by the US Congress.

4.3.2 Low level of legislation related to catastrophe insurance

Let us analyze the content of legislation related to catastrophe insurance in GBA. At present, regional government regulations such as notifications, project participation, and decisions exist for regional catastrophe insurance issues. The legislative content itself is not constructive in the promotion of catastrophe insurance. According to opinions, most of the legislative content is of poor operability, and the initiative of the legal level exhibits strong bottom level, randomness, and insecure nature. As shown in Figure 2, it is difficult to improve the public's risk perception and promote the commercialization of catastrophe insurance.

5 ANALYSIS ON THE OPTIMIZATION PATH OF CATASTROPHE INSURANCE IN THE GREATER BAY AREA

In the commercialization of catastrophe insurance in GBA, the participants are individuals, governments, and enterprises. At present, the development of catastrophe insurance is still in its infancy, there are deficiencies in the construction of catastrophe insurance at all levels, and that makes overall reconstruction and planning more difficult. Thus, it is necessary to use existing resources and models to advance layer by layer, coordinate the commercial development in the right direction, and use existing system's advantages and expand the commercialization. At the same time, only under the unified cooperation of individuals, enterprises, and the government can the overall catastrophe insurance in GBA play a linkage promotion effect. Based on the above two elements, the following suggestions are made:

5.1 The construction of a long-term catastrophe insurance system with linkage effects

The construction of a long-term catastrophe insurance system in GBA needs to consider the needs of the current catastrophe insurance system from the macro-level, as well as the economic linkage effect of the regions to create a long-term catastrophe linkage with characteristics of its insurance system. The first is the design of the long-term catastrophe insurance system. Currently, the three regions mostly focus on short-term insurance policy decisions. The government's catastrophe insurance and the period for small and medium-sized enterprises are relatively short within 2 years. The stress response of the disaster market has directly stimulated the increase in the number of catastrophe insurances in the regions.

Secondly, we should consider the above-mentioned constraints on the supply of catastrophe insurance in GBA. Technical constraints in the construction of long-term systems need to get rid of the traditional property insurance actuarial pricing model, and insurance companies need to associate short-term insurance policy decisions with long-term insurance activities, which is, short-term insurance needs to adopt a 1-year system, and long-term insurance needs to stimulate continuous insurance purchase behaviors of policyholders. The following methods can be used: 1) In the actuarial pricing model, premium discount activities can be introduced. For example, under the conditions of enterprise or individual docking, if an individual or enterprise wants to renew the catastrophe insurance for the next year, they can enjoy the premium in the catastrophe insurance pricing for the next year with discount from 1% to 5%. Attention should be paid that the latest meteorological disasters, geological disasters, and various disasters will be used to calculate the premium pricing for the next year, which can effectively shorten the actuarial period to ensure the stability of reserve. 2) The government launches tax incentives under catastrophe mode or products, such as individuals, can introduce catastrophes under deferred tax. This policy ensures that individuals can use year-on-year tax incentives to purchase related catastrophe insurance products in the process.

A natural downward trend is shown in Figure 3. Only by continuing the short-term insurance policy can we build a long-term insurance policy.

Finally, integrate the economic development characteristics of GBA into long-term catastrophe insurance products with regional characteristics. The economic development of these regions is synergistic, and long-term catastrophe insurance should be integrated.

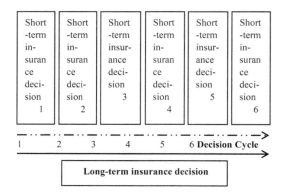

Figure 3. The establishment of a long-term insurance mechanism for catastrophe insurance.

Regional economic characteristics can be set in the long-term public catastrophe insurance claims or funds of the three regions. For example, the high-tech industries can activate the public catastrophe insurance fund or claim settlement mechanism after a catastrophe to take advantage of the economic linkage characteristics of the three regions.

5.2 *The construction of a catastrophe insurance system under government-led model*

Based on the analysis above at this stage, the government of the GBA is indeed guiding the commercial development of catastrophe insurance in the region, but there are still many shortcomings in its top-level design work. It needs to be revised from the following levels to ensure that the public will not have cognitive or behavioral deviations on catastrophe insurance:

In the current GBA, disaster subsidy shows a certain crowding-out effect on catastrophe insurance. The so-called crowding-out effect is that the disaster protection system itself excludes the intervention of catastrophe insurance, but in the actual catastrophe insurance process, disaster subsidies and catastrophe insurance are not mutually squeezed out. From the perspective of the financial constraints, the current economic strength of catastrophe insurance companies in our country is far from being able to bear the economic losses caused by catastrophes in local areas. The catastrophe insurance business system under the government-led model is actually a top-down commercial development path design. As the top-level design, the government needs to lead and correct the development of the catastrophe insurance market. Therefore, the only way to fully utilize the mobility of government disaster subsidies is to allow catastrophe insurance to fill in the unreached part of disaster subsidies under the current system and model in the form of missing and filling vacancies.

The functional complementarity of disaster subsidies and catastrophe insurance can effectively fill the blanks and vacancies. For example, the government's disaster subsidies to the people will not evaluate the loss of individuals or enterprises in the disaster, but will be more fair and just. The method of granting uniform subsidies in the form of subsidies directly caused some people with severe economic losses after the disaster occurred. They can only rely on government subsidies during periods of excessive disasters. It is difficult to mitigate the losses caused by disasters in a true sense or extent. Under this circumstance or premise, catastrophe insurance companies can effectively intervene in the form of commercialization, evaluate disaster economic losses, provide secondary claims, and cover gaps in the current disaster relief system.

5.3 *The establishment of a joint mechanism for insurance companies*

In the current administrative and economic environments of GBA, the government must use government means to promote its development. In the process of commercialization of catastrophe insurance, the government's industry policy support for catastrophe insurance can be driven by insurance company cash subsidies and tax incentives. From the perspective of the existing system in the GBA, the government can join more insurance companies to participate in catastrophe insurance work. At this stage, only three insurance companies are involved in catastrophe claims. The number of companies and total assets cannot really play an effective role. However, expand the number of insurance companies to participate in the catastrophe insurance project and bring more established insurance companies into the catastrophe insurance project. So that the large number of co-insurance bodies can downgrade the insurance company's own catastrophe claims risk.

6 CONCLUSION

In summary, the overall problems faced by the Guangdong-Hong Kong-Macao Greater Bay Area in the development of catastrophe insurance commercialization at this stage are mostly macro-organizational and macro-oriented issues. The commercialization cycle of catastrophe insurance is relatively short, leading to important corrections of detailed issues. It is far lower than the design and planning of framework issues. It can also be seen that the overall practical experience of catastrophe insurance in China's insurance market is far from forming a guiding theory and experience. Catastrophe insurance plays a major role in China's social system. Development is still in the stage of crossing the river by feeling for the stones. As an important mainstay in driving China's economic development, Guangdong, Hong Kong, and Macao Greater Bay Area also need to try their best to actively explore and make achievements in the field of catastrophe insurance, and seek a variety of catastrophe insurance commercialization. They also need to seek ways to truly encourage the awareness of catastrophe insurance to be deeply rooted in the hearts of the people, and to set a good example.

ACKNOWLEDGMENT

A special acknowledgment should be shown to the support by the "Research on the Influencing Factors and Optimization Countermeasures of Catastrophe Insurance Purchase Behavior from the Perspective of Guangdong-Hong Kong-Macao Greater Bay Area Interaction" of Guangdong Province Ordinary University Characteristic Innovation Project in 2020 (2020WTSCX149).

REFERENCES

[1] Chen, W. 2019. Catastrophe insurance guarantees the housing safety of people in deeply impoverished areas – Taking the residential earthquake catastrophe insurance for urban and rural residents in Sichuan Province as an example, *Shanghai Insurance*, vol. 07, pp. 42–43.

[2] Guo, J.L. & Zhu, J.J. 2020. The important role of commercial insurance in the major epidemic prevention and control system[J]. *China Insurance*, (02): 8–12.

[3] Song, Q.Q. 2020. Analysis on the necessity of agricultural catastrophe insurance development in Gansu Province under targeted poverty alleviation, *Journal of Lanzhou Institute of Technology*, vol. 27, pp. 99–104.

[4] Zhang, Y.X. 2020. The role and value of commercial insurance in national governance from the perspective of earthquake insurance, *China Insurance*, vol. 05, pp. 28–31.

[5] Zheng, X.L. 2019. Research on Public Catastrophe Insurance-Based on the perspective of Hainan people's livelihood security and Ningbo's public catastrophe insurance experience, *National Circulation Economy*, vol. 22, pp. 152–154.

[6] Zhou, X.Y. & Wang, H.Y. 2019. Typhoon Catastrophe Insurance Premium Pricing Research-Taking Shanghai as an Example, *2019 China Insurance and Risk Management International Annual Conference*. pp. 1011–1018.

Economic and Business Management – Huang & Zhang (Eds)
© 2022 Copyright the Author(s), ISBN: 978-1-032-06754-4

Financing difficulties and solutions in the development of rural tourism

Xiaoling Hu
A College of Management, Wuhan Technology and Business University, Wuhan, China

ABSTRACT: With the increase in the development of rural tourism, it is very important to scientifically identify and solve the financing problems faced in the development of rural tourism. This thesis analyzes the current equity structure, leasing, financing, and land transfer issues in the development of rural tourism, and puts forward rural financing countermeasures.

1 INTRODUCTION

The development of rural tourism promotes agricultural production and farmers' income, which is closely related to the rural revitalization strategy. The No. 1 document of the Party Central Committee stated that the country's resources and funds are gradually tilted toward the countryside, and it is necessary to vigorously support the development of the countryside. Rural tourism is a new sector of tourism, and rural tourism has a vernacular nature. The development of farmhouses, ecological farms, modern agricultural technology demonstration parks, large farms, ancient villages, and folk cultural villages in the countryside all require financing environment and financing strategies. At present, the state has issued policies to support rural tourism, which is in full swing. Rural tourism has also improved the living environment and the relationship between people and land in the countryside. However, in the process of its development, rural tourism requires a lot of financing for different projects, which are currently facing financing difficulties. Therefore, it is particularly important to study the financing of rural tourism.

2 THE DILEMMA OF RURAL TOURISM FINANCING

2.1 *The issue of shareholding structure*

2.1.1 *Underdeveloped joint-stock cooperative system*

The laws and regulations of rural tourism joint-stock cooperative enterprises are not clear. For example, the "General Principles of the Civil Law" and the "Regulations on Rural Enterprises" do not stipulate the legal status of rural joint-stock cooperative enterprises. Some local laws and regulations stipulate that rural joint-stock cooperative enterprises can obtain legal person status, but the enforcement power is insufficient and the relevant content in those legal documents is not clear. Moreover, the country's operating principles for rural tourism joint-stock cooperative enterprises are not uniform. The actual operation process of rural joint-stock cooperative enterprises is unscientific and inaccurate. For example, the content of the legislative documents such as the principle of property rights, the principle of public accumulation and the principle of distribution of rural tourism joint-stock cooperative enterprises lack consistency, and it leads to difficulties for the person in charge of the enterprise to grasp the connotation of the joint-stock cooperative system. In addition, the rights and obligations of the shareholders of rural tourism enterprises are not clear. At present, neither national nor local legislative document outlines the rights and obligations of stakeholders, and the two documents have not clearly shown any distinction. Some chapters of the document mention the shareholders' right to distribute profits, but they are far from adequate.

Besides, there is a contradiction between the shareholding system and the cooperative system of the rural tourism enterprises. The shareholding system is a form of a capital union based on large-scale social production, reflecting the trend of capital accumulation. The joint-stock cooperative system of rural tourism enterprises requires mutual assistance and cooperation among the relevant stakeholders, and all members to work together and manage democratically. For example, the distribution of dividends according to shares and capital distribution in rural tourism enterprises is a departure from the cooperative system.

2.1.2 *The property right system needs to be improved*

First, the subject of the property rights of rural land is not clear. The rural land law "Constitution," "Land Management Law," and the "Rural Land Contract Law" have defined land ownership in villages, mainly including collective economic organizations, village and peasant collectives, villager groups, and rural and

88

DOI 10.1201/9781003203704-17

peasant collective economic organizations. The main body of collective land management is the village committee and the village and township farmers' collective economic organization, which is both the administrative body and the right body, and the villagers' autonomous organization is the same. Unclear rural land responsibilities have led to low rural collective responsibility awareness. Small-scale decentralized management in rural areas results in high land development costs and low land utilization efficiency, making it difficult to form large-scale industrialized operations. The reason for the scattered management of rural land is that the property rights of land use are not clear and the property rights of rural land have not been modernized. The industry and scale of rural tourism and the intensiveness of land are in contradiction with the land system. The diversification of the subject of land ownership causes the land rights to belong to different subjects, leading to the defects of the rights of each subject. In fact, the control of rural collective land in the countryside belongs to the government, and farmers cannot be in a dominant position in terms of the rural tourism development.

Second, the boundaries of the right to use rural land need to be clear. Because of the unclear property rights of rural land, farmers tend to avoid government approval when using land, and privately expand the scale of land to develop tourism projects. Rural tourism operators lease the rural collective economy, or contract, or cooperate with villagers to obtain land. In the process of land development, it may happen that without the approval procedure for land transfer, the land use may be changed privately, and hotels and restaurants may be built. There is even a misrepresentation of business content, with the help of rural tourism construction to engage in real estate development. Villagers and village committees may also rent, sell, and transfer collective land ownership without authorization. These phenomena have restricted the development of rural tourism.

Third, the incompleteness of the rural land property rights system has resulted in unfair income distribution and unclear responsibilities for violations of the law. If rural tourism is managed well and benefits are abundant, farmers, farmersbution of tourism revenue; if there are financing problems in rural tourism development, the government will be held accountable for illegal land use. When sharing the risk of rural tourism land property rights, the problem of evasive responsibility arises from multi-stakeholders. Therefore, rural tourism land rights need to be resolved gradually.

2.1.3 *Incomplete property rights*

The use and management of rural land is under the jurisdiction of local governments and agricultural departments. The rural tourism land has not formed a joint force to strictly supervise it. It is difficult for the central government to evaluate local agricultural land and cultivated land through performance evaluation and conduct index evaluation. The central government hopes to realize the rational distribution of land resources and form some comprehensive economic, social and ecological benefits of rural land. In order to increase local fiscal revenues, local governments sometimes use public power to compete with farmers collectively for land, use leases instead of requisitions, repossess the land, enter into transactions with real estate developers, and start tourism and commercial development after transferring the land to obtain benefits. The national law does not clearly define the expropriation of rural collective land and rural tourism land, causing the local governments to abuse the expropriation power. Because of the lack of a legal system, the government and developers may use space in the rural tourism land market. To standardize the allocation of rural land resources and protect rural tourism land, it is necessary to improve the laws and regulations on tourism land.

2.2 *Lease issues*

2.2.1 *The problem of ideas*

The separation of ownership and use rights of rural collective land has prompted the rural tourism land to be circulated before it can be used. However, China restricts the use of collective land and adopts farmland protection. Rural tourism land needs to be approved by the government, and the development of rural tourism projects often requires government recruitment tender. Therefore, to ensure the demand for rural tourism land and to carry out large-scale operations, a perfect rural land transfer market is needed. However, when the local governments expropriate collective land in rural areas, they give farmers a small amount of compensation; while developing the tourism sector by means of projects, they transfer the land to developers at a high price. The huge "scissors" benefit the local governments and tourism developers from this behavior which destroys the rural tourism land market. Rural tourism development needs to pass through the formal circulation market and the invisible market, such as the unreasonable land acquisition compensation system, which makes farmers circumvent the law, circumvent the legal channels of local governments and directly engage in land transactions with developers. Due to the weak legal awareness of farmers, signing land transfer contracts with developers is in a passive situation. Villagers want to take the initiative in land transfer and protect their legal rights and interests but in fact, because they illegally transfer land and sign false contracts with developers, the losses outweigh the gains, and the farmers lose their land without gaining any benefits.

Due to the conservative ideas of the villagers, the collective interest orientation of farmers, and the government's compulsory participation, most land transfers are spontaneous or administrative actions, and they are not used to promote rural tourism development and economic prosperity through collective land transfers. Villagers are at a disadvantage in the land transfer, and the value of rural land tourism development cannot be realized.

2.2.2 Decentralized funds

Capitalization brings about the lack of decision-making power and control power of villagers. Rural tourism organizations dominated by the labor union of laborers and the capital union of laborers dominate capital, but not capital dominates labor. Rural laborers exercise democratic management decision-making power, distribute according to the contribution of enterprise laborers (shareholders), and receive only limited interest. In rural tourism joint-stock cooperative enterprises, the opposition between capital and labor should be actively sublated, and collective ownership can be effectively realized. There are very few classic enterprises in the rural areas of China as joint-stock cooperative enterprises. In particular, rural tourism in ethnic minority areas has insufficient democratic decision-making and fund allocation. The proportion of labor unions in the rural tourism industry is small, and most of the funds given rely on project financing granted by the government and foreign companies. Rural tourism labor union is sometimes a labor–employment relationship. This has led to the weakening of the control and decision-making power of rural tourism villagers' joint-stock cooperative enterprises.

The management cost of rural tourism enterprises reduces the performance of the shareholding cooperative system. The reduction of transaction costs is the driving force for scattered operators to join the rural tourism joint-stock cooperative enterprise. In practice, the establishment of a rural tourism enterprise will bring a lot of management costs, which will also offset foreign transaction costs, and reduce transaction costs so that the income of the villagers is lower than the income recorded before joining the enterprise, which also reduces the enthusiasm of farmers. Rural tourism shares cooperation made into a beautiful "ideal"

2.2.3 Factors of production are not concentrated

It is difficult for rural land elements to form a scale because of their scattered elements. "Nongjiale is actually an extension of the traditional family sideline business model." The management system with farmers as the basic production unit restricts the large-scale operation of rural tourism. Specifically, it is difficult to plan land, have a large-scale and attractive ecological agricultural landscape, build tourism public infrastructure service facilities, and fully share the existing facilities. In the face of scattered production factors, the shareholding cooperative system gives full play to its advantages: In the rural tourism shareholding cooperative system, farmers use capital, technology, land, labor and other production factors as equity to invest in enterprises, absorbing investment from foreign companies, and rural tourism companies gather various production factors and integrated production and operation management to obtain economic benefits.

Rural tourism financing can realize investment in rural tourism projects, get rid of the situation of only "service" projects, and broaden product sales channels. At the same time, it can improve the hardware quality of the service, provide a good "living" environment for tourists, and increase their satisfaction. The concentration of technology can improve the marketization level of rural tourism, improve operating efficiency, promote product innovation, and improve services. To realize the unified planning of rural tourism, a large-scale ecological agricultural landscape can be formed through the agglomeration of rural land, which provides conditions for the large-scale operation of collective land.

2.3 Financial issues

Rural tourism operators are not satisfied with rural tourism financing. For example, the amount of small loans is low, and large amounts of financing require mortgages, and many rural tourism financing difficulties. For example, the farming industry of rural tourism has a long production cycle, and the introduction of new varieties or the use of new technologies by producers requires a long time to experiment. Nowadays, the financial institutions in towns and villages have a short period of financing, and some financing periods are half a year or a year. There is a phenomenon that short-term loans are used for long-term investment projects. At the same time, the country's financial institutions have low interest rates on loans, which creates an alternative mode of rural tourism financing other than borrowing from relatives and friends. Due to information asymmetry, national financial institutions did not investigate the household income, behavior patterns, and integrity status of lenders. Due to the possibility of moral hazard in the financing process, loan policies in rural tourism enterprises are strict, the process of getting a loan is complicated, and multiple materials need to be provided, which takes a long time. This causes villagers to disagree with the country's financial institution loans.

Farmers lack loan collateral, yet its ownership is required as a guarantee. In order to avoid risks, national financial institutions need to provide an equivalent collateral to secure the loans. However, the economic conditions of the villagers are not enough, and it is difficult to guarantee the mortgage. Moreover, the villagers' land and houses belong to collective property rights and cannot be bought or sold. The National Commercial Bank does not accept the "two-rights mortgage financing" model. If the villagers default, the mortgage problem is not easily solved. Due to the lack of products of financial institutions, the products of the villagers' loans are insufficient, and they cannot satisfy the villagers' loans. Financial institutions have insufficient product R&D and no innovation. For example, the rural credit cooperatives and the Postal Savings Bank serve local farmers, and getting loans is simple. However, the loan amount is low, and the unsecured loan amount is controlled at about 20,000 yuan, and the maximum is not higher than 50,000 yuan. In fact, the development of rural tourism in rural villages requires a high amount of rural tourism loans and a large amount of financing. At present, the national financial institutions provide few products to villagers, and the loan business cannot match the actual needs of rural tourism development, so financial institutions need to improve their products.

2.4 Circulation area

First, the touristic circulation of rural land has aggravated rural social conflicts. At present, there are four aspects: the unfair distribution of economic overflow caused by the circulation of rural land tourism, the village committee, township government or tourism developer collecting the value-added income caused by the circulation of land, and the villager group being in a passive position. Villagers have no legal awareness of land property rights, and legal contracts are not signed between the subjects of land transfer, which is conducive to disputes over interests and property rights. In addition, the problem of staying behind in rural areas has emerged. Furthermore, after the land is transferred, the surplus rural labor force leaves the countryside, and there are only the elderly and children in the rural areas.

Second, the natural and cultural landscape of the countryside has been devastated. Rural tourism forms the attraction of rural customs through the combination of agricultural production landscape and rural characteristics of humanities and natural resources. However, some rural tourism projects only attach importance to commercial functions and neglect the creation of good rural landscapes and customs. The individual landscapes are destroyed hence the incapability of attracting city tourists to visit and enjoy the tourism area for a long time.

Third, the transfer of the rural tourism financing land may undermine the sustainable development of the rural areas. At present, most rural tourism does not consider the local landscape, comprehensive value and carrying capacity of the land, and even overuse and development of land, development of real estate, and malicious competition in scenic spots. Due to the blind pursuit of high-end star hotels, the area of the cultivated land has been continuously reduced, which is not conducive to the sustainable development of rural tourism.

3 CONCLUSIONS

3.1 Formulating laws and regulations for rural joint-stock cooperative enterprises

The state formulates special laws for rural tourism joint-stock cooperative enterprises but, to make such laws work efficiently the following suggestions are worth considering. The state should clearly stipulate the legal status of rural joint-stock cooperative enterprises and their establishment, modification, termination, liquidation, etc. through laws; at the same time, it is necessary to stipulate the organization and articles of association of rural tourism enterprises, and the relationship between members and enterprises; it is crucially important to regulate the shares and circulation, finance and distribution. These laws make rural tourism joint-stock cooperative enterprises become entities that develop the market economy, independently operate and manage, and are open to cooperation.

3.2 Headings changing the leasing model in rural tourism financing

First, clarify the property rights of rural tourism land. China's social system determines that land ownership cannot be fully granted to farmers. In view of the national conditions, China has begun to implement the "three-rights separation" of rural contracted land. According to the policy of "implementation of collective ownership, stabilization of rural households' contracting rights, and deregulation of land management rights," the country has been transferring land management rights in an orderly manner. The land management right of the contracted land shall be operational in accordance with the law to enable the rational development and utilization of rural tourism land. Second, the local government performs its own functions to solve the problem of unclear ownership of the villagers' land property rights, improve rural land property rights, and implement rural household registration planning. The local government shall use the provisions of the Agricultural Land Compensation Law to compensate farmers based on the land acquired for rural tourism development. If property rights disputes occur between the farmers and rural collectives, the local government should assume its responsibilities in verifying and confirming the ownership of the property rights; if the government mediation is invalid, the villagers can use their legal rights to confirm the disputed land property rights.

3.3 Listing and numbering changing the financial support for rural tourism

First, the amount of funds required for rural tourism projects is large at present, and financing urgently needs to be strengthened to encourage and support the supply of financing in multiple ways to achieve diversification of financing channels. Second, an improvement of the rural credit guarantee system is essential. That is, gradually improve the rural credit loan system to effectively reduce the financing difficulties of the rural tourism development projects. Third, explore the application of emerging technologies in rural project financing. With the rapid development of big data, internet +, tourism +, etc., new technology and the old ones are applied, and traditional problems are gradually solved. For example, with the help of blockchain, enter the rural credit system, fully standardize the storage of personal information, and authorize departmental information to be updated in the public chain for related institutions to gradually improve the rural credit system.

3.4 Equations changing the land transfer strategy of rural tourism financing

The improvement of the land circulation system can focus on the following aspects: First, the circulation process of rural land tourism should be changed. At present, in the development of rural tourism land, the relevant management departments ought to actively communicate, clarify the planning approval management procedures, and improve the development procedures of rural tourism land. The local government has stepped up supervision over the circulation, planning, development, utilization and operation of rural tourism land, and the next task is to put an end to illegal activities such as random replacement and expansion of land use area. Second, the legal system for regulating the circulation of rural land needs to be put in place. It is imperative for the local government to regulate the legality, integrity and equality of rural land transfer from the legal standpoint. Effective measures to safeguard the legitimate rights and interests of all parties involved in transactions should be used, and the rights and interests of the farmers need to be protected. Third, the process of rural land transfer has to be standardized. When introducing rural agricultural production entities, the qualifications of agricultural companies should be thoroughly examined and approved, and private capital access need to be strictly enforced; secondly, the transfer price of the land management rights to protect the rights and interests of farmers and agricultural enterprises should be regulated; finally, the government should strengthen tracking and order the rural tourism companies to correct behavior if violations are found, immediately restore the original appearance of the land after use, and the enterprise should be ordered to compensate the farmers if the land is no longer suitable for farming. Fourth, the distribution of rural land tourism circulation income should be improved and the interests of farmers ought to be safeguarded. The government should establish land appraisal agencies and regulatory agencies to protect the legitimate interests of the farmers.

ACKNOWLEDGMENT

This work was financially supported by Wuhan Technology and Business University project the "List of high-quality off-campus practice bases of 2019 – Xiamen Yuanchang Kempinski Hotel" (PZ201909), one of the onthe-field work results. This work was financially supported by Hubei Provincial Department of Education project "Hundred Schools and 100 Counties-Action Plan for Universities to Serve Rural Rejuvenation Science and Technology Support – Research on Cultural Tourism Brand Building and Promotion of Yandi Shennong's Hometown Scenic Spot Based on Rural Revitalization (BXLBX0984)" one of the onthe-field work results.

REFERENCES

Arie Reichel, Oded Lowengart, Ady Milman. Rural tourism in Israel: service quality and orientation. [J]. *Tourism Management*, 2000, 21(5): 451–459.

Aliza Fleischer, Anat Tchetchik. Does rural tourism benefit from agriculture? [J]. *Tourism Management*, 2005, 26(4): 493–501.

Daniele Vieira do Nascimento. Exploring climate finance for tourism adaptation development: an overview[J]. *Worldwide Hospitality and Tourism Themes*. 2016, Vol. 8 (No. 5): 593–605.

Daniel Badulescu, Adriana Giurgiu, Nicolae Istudor, Alina Badulescu. Rural tourism development and financing in Romania: A supply-side analysis[J]. *Agricultural Economics*. 2015, 61(2): 72–80.

Kesar Vinay, Soodan Vishal. A Study on Role of Sustainable Rural Tourism in Economic Development of Local Communities: A Case of Jammu Region[J]. *Asian Journal of Research in Social Sciences and Humanities*. 2017, Vol. 7(No.4): 170–176.

Prof. Parag A. Gadve. A study on Need of Financial Support to Rural Tourism Intermediaries in India[J]. *Imperial Journal of Interdisciplinary Research*. 2017, Vol. 3 (No. 9): 1115–1117.

Economic and Business Management – Huang & Zhang (Eds)
© 2022 Copyright the Author(s), ISBN: 978-1-032-06754-4

Analyst coverage, corporate governance, and firms' innovation output: Evidence from China

Yang Yang
International Business School, Beijing Foreign Studies University, Beijing, P.R. China

ABSTRACT: This paper studies the effect of analyst coverage on firms' innovation output in China. Using data of listed firms from 2003 to 2017, this study finds evidence that analyst coverage is positively related to firms' innovation output. To establish causality, the paper uses both an instrumental approach and a difference-in-differences approach. The identification methodologies suggest a positive effect of analyst coverage on firms' innovation output. On the basis of the features of corporate governance in China, the paper attributes this positive result to the governance role of analyst coverage and identifies three channels through which it boosts corporate innovation. When firms lack managerial ownership, stock incentive schemes, and independent directors, the positive effect of analyst coverage on firms' innovation output is more pronounced. The evidence is consistent with the hypotheses that analyst coverage reduces the agency cost and increases firms' long-term performance measured by innovation output. This study provides a novel perspective to study the effect of analyst coverage on firms' innovation.

Keywords: Analyst coverage, corporate governance, innovation

1 INTRODUCTION

Innovation is an important engine of economic growth (Solow 1957) and is the key to firms' long-term profitability (Arrow 1962; Schumpeter 1942). Financial economists research multiple factors which influence firms' investment decisions on innovation activities (Holmstrom 1989). In recent years financial intermediaries' role on firms' innovation has attracted scholars' attention. He and Tian (2013) revealed the effect of analyst coverage on firms' innovation. Aghion et al. (2013) and Brav et al. (2017) studied the impacts of institutional investors and hedge funds on corporate innovation. Analyst coverage has multiple theoretical mechanisms affecting corporate innovation.

Existing literature identifies two effects of analyst coverage on corporate innovation. The information effect (Guo et al. 2019) means that analyst coverage mitigates information asymmetry between firm managers and financial investors. By conducting due diligence and publishing reports, analysts help to avoid the undervaluation of firms' innovation investment, reducing the risk of hostile takeovers and encouraging managers to undertake corporate innovation activities. Analyst coverage also has a pressure effect on corporate innovation. To satisfy the earnings forecasts made by financial analysts, managers tend to focus on routine tasks that generate cash flow in the short term instead of investing in innovation projects (He & Tian 2013).

In this paper, I contribute to the understanding of the effect of analyst coverage on firms' innovation by introducing the corporate governance effect of analyst coverage based on the evidence from China. As external governors, financial analysts mitigate listed firms' agency cost (Chen et al. 2015) and firms with lower agency cost have higher level of innovation output (Francis & Smith 1995). To further identify the channels through which analyst coverage serves as a governance mechanism and generates a positive effect on corporate innovation, I analyze the features of corporate governance in China, which are different from those in America and other developed economies in various aspects (Jiang & Kim 2015). This paper focuses on three corporate governance mechanisms: managerial ownership, stock incentive schemes, and independent directors. Because the financial market in China began to develop later than its counterpart in developed economies, internal corporate governance mechanisms that resolve the agency problem are relatively scarce. Therefore, analyst coverage in China substitutes for internal governance mechanisms to resolve the agency problem and to increase firms' innovation output. Additionally, other external corporate governance mechanisms including legal environment, institutional investors, and the market for corporate control in China are weaker compared with those in developed countries, which allows analyst coverage to generate a comprehensively positive effect on corporate innovation in China, and thus makes China a typical setting to study the governance effect of analyst coverage on corporate innovation.

The baseline result shows that analyst coverage (measured by the number of research reports published

DOI 10.1201/9781003203704-18

by analysts on a firm) is positively correlated with the firm's patent output number, but analyst coverage is likely to be endogenous. There might be omitted variables that correlate both with analyst coverage and with innovation output (i.e., resignation of star managers excelling in handling technical and managerial issues, which reduces a firm's analyst coverage and the firm's innovation output simultaneously). In addition, reverse causality might also bias the result (i.e., firms with higher innovation productivity attract more analyst coverage). To establish causality, I use two identification methods.

My first identification method is to construct an instrumental variable, expected coverage, based on the sizes of brokerage houses, and to use two-stage least squares (2SLS) regressions. The method is introduced by Yu (2008). Since the size of a brokerage house is mainly determined by its profitability and the brokerage size affects the brokerage house's analyst coverage business, expected coverage is exogenous to firms' innovation activities and is qualified for being an instrumental variable. The result of 2SLS regressions establishes the positive effect of analyst coverage on firms' innovation output and reveals the direction of the bias if endogeneity remains uncontrolled.

My second identification strategy is to use a merger event of two brokerage houses as a quasi-natural experiment (Hong & Kacperczyk 2010). The brokerage merger is a strategic decision based on industrial competition. A series of adjustments for staff in the newly established brokerage house directly affect firms' analyst coverage but are exogenous to firms' innovation productivity. The result of the difference-in-differences (DID) method shows that the brokerage merger causes a decrease in analyst coverage of the firms tracked by the two merged brokerage houses and that the exogenous decrease in analyst coverage results in a relative reduction in innovation output for the treatment group (i.e., firms whose analyst coverage is negatively affected by the brokerage merger) compared with that for the control group (i.e., firms whose analyst coverage is not affected by the brokerage merger). The result of DID analysis supports the positive effect of analyst coverage on firms' innovation output.

After establishing causality, I conduct several robustness checks including altering the regression model, the main explanatory variable, lag period, and the dependent variable. The results of robustness checks are consistent with that of the baseline regression.

In the final part of this paper, I examine the underlying corporate governance channels through which analyst coverage increases firms' innovation output. First of all, I study the managerial ownership. I find that the positive effect of analyst coverage on firms' innovation output is larger for the firms with lower level of managerial ownership compared with those with higher level of managerial ownership. The existence of manger-owners helps resolve the agency conflict by aligning the interest of mangers and shareholders (Han et al. 2006). Analyst coverage substitutes

for managerial ownership. By reporting on firms' productivity and making disclosure to investors, analysts can serve as an external governance mechanism. By influencing investors' decisions, analysts directly exert pressure on shareholders. Shareholders set performance requirements for managers. Shareholders and managers act collectively to enhance firms' value measured by innovation output. In this way analyst coverage aligns the interest of managers and shareholders, reduces the agency cost, and boosts firms' innovation output. Next, I find that analyst coverage's positive impact on corporate innovation is larger for the firms without option incentive schemes compared with those with option incentive schemes. Tian and Meng (2018) find that option incentive schemes encourage managers to undertake risk in the short run and to pursue long-term return of innovation. Analyst coverage substitutes for option incentive schemes. By reporting on firms' innovation productivity, analyst coverage helps to avoid the undervaluation of R&D investment, encouraging managers to undertake short-term risk of innovation activities. If R&D investment is successful in the long run, analyst coverage influences investors to invest heavily in firms with high innovation productivity, rewarding both managers and shareholders. Finally, I study the ratio of the number of independent directors to the number of total directors in firms' boards and find that analyst coverage generates a larger positive impact on firms' innovation output for firms with a lower ratio of independent directors compared with those with a higher ratio of independent directors. Independent directors monitor firms' operation on behalf of shareholders and prevent managers from making decisions that erode firms' value (Li & Xu 2014). Analyst coverage substitutes for the supervisory role of independent directors. Analysts are independent from managers and responsible to investors. By conducting due diligence and publishing research reports, analysts monitor managers on behalf of investors, encouraging managers to maximize firms' value measured by innovation output.

The rest of the paper is organized as follows. Section 2 presents a literature review and develops theoretical hypotheses. Section 3 presents variable measurement and sample selection. Section 4 discusses the results of baseline regression, causality identification, and robustness checks. Section 5 discusses the corporate governance channels through which analyst coverage affects corporate innovation. Section 6 includes the discussion and conclusion.

2 LITERATURE REVIEW AND HYPOTHESIS DEVELOPMENT

2.1 *Literature review*

This paper contributes to the academic field of finance and innovation. The literature in this field can be categorized into three parts from micro to macro perspectives. First of all, the literature of micro-perspective combining firm-level characteristics with corporate innovation includes the effects of venture capital (Kortum & Lerner 2000), option incentive schemes (Chang et al. 2015), analyst coverage (He & Tian 2013), and overvaluation of shares (Dong et al. 2017) on firms' innovation. Next, from the meso-perspective, product market competition (Aghion et al. 2005), the cycle of venture capital (Nanda & Rhodes-Kropf 2013), regulations of the banking industry (Benfratello et al. 2008), and corporate taxation (Atanassov & Liu 2016) have impacts on firms' investment in innovation activities. Finally, from the macro-perspective, demographic features (Derrien et al. 2018) and laws and regulations (Moser 2005) can affect firms' innovation productivity. This paper is closely related to two papers by He and Tian (2013) and Guo et al. (2018). He and Tian's (2013) study shows that analyst coverage in America reduces firms' innovation output by imposing the pressure of earnings forecasts on corporate managers. Guo et al.'s (2018) work further identifies the information and pressure effects on firms' internal and external innovation strategies. I contribute to this literature by studying the governance effect of analyst coverage on firms' innovation output measured by the number of patents and by identifying the specific channels through which analyst coverage generates the governance effect on firms' innovation in China.

This paper also adds to the literature that studies the governance role of financial analysts. Many scholars have discovered that financial analysts help reduce information asymmetry, generate accurate earnings forecasts, and serve as external monitors for corporate managers (Brennan & Subrahmanyam 1995; Hong et al. 2000; Yu 2008). Through the mechanisms above, financial analysts influence firms' investing and financing decisions as well as the price and liquidity of shares (Bradley et al. 2003; Irvine 2003; Chang et al. 2006; Derrien & Kecskes 2013; Kelly & Ljungqvist 2011). Chen et al.'s (2015) study shows that analysts have a positive monitoring effect on listed firms. With more analysts covering the firms, firm shareholders attach greater importance to internal cash flow and CEOs receive less excessive compensations and undertake fewer value-destroying M&A deals. The study of Gentry and Shen (2013) has the same conclusion as that of Chen et al. (2015). Derrien and Kecskes' (2013) study finds that analyst coverage helps curb the capital cost and increases M&A investment. This paper contributes to this strand of literature by studying the corporate governance effect of analysts on firms' innovation.

This study also contributes to the literature focusing on the effect of corporate internal governance on firms' innovation. Ownership structure and boards of directors are the two most important internal governance mechanisms affecting corporate innovation. First of all, the existing literature proves that ownership concentration has a positive impact on corporate innovation because large shareholders attach great important to listed firms' market value and

they have strong motivation to invest in innovation projects which generate high expected return (Baysinger et al. 1991; Belloc 2012; Lee 2005). In addition, large shareholders' attitudes towards innovation differ according to their identities. Institutional investors encourage managers to invest in long-term innovation projects because they gain economy of scale from investing a large amount of capital (Black 1992) and they particularly evaluate the return of long-term projects rather than fluctuations of asset price in the short run (Black 1992; Kochhar & David 1996). Non-financial entities encourage investment in innovation activities due to reciprocal trade relationships and synergy effects between investors and invested companies (Jaffe 1986). Foreign investors provide cutting-edge technology and encourage innovation activities because when MNEs invest in companies in host countries, they need to cultivate technological edges of invested firms over other domestic competitors (Chang 1995). Manager-owners help resolve the agency conflict between shareholder and managers and maximize shareholder profit by undertaking R&D activities (Hill & Snell 1988; Latham & Braun 2009). Next, boards of directors are important organizations for firm's internal governance (Fama & Jensen 1983) and they influence corporate innovation. Independent directors reduce the agency cost by monitoring managers (Peng 2007) and maximize shareholder profit by adding innovation activities. They also help firms attract external investment and raise the speed of knowledge absorption (Fried et al. 1998) to increase firms' value measured by innovation output (Kosnik 1990). This study finds evidence that analyst coverage substitutes for internal governance mechanisms and generates a positive effect on firms' innovation output.

2.2 Hypothesis development

This study proposes that analyst coverage can increase firms' innovation output by reducing the agency cost. The study of Jensen and Meckling (1976) shows that when the agency cost incurred by the separation of ownership from managerial authority is higher, managers hold a higher proportion of firms' shares to monitor business activities more effectively. Francis and Smith's (1995) study uses firms' innovation activities as the setting to study the agency cost, because compared with routine business activities firms' innovation activities have higher agency cost due to their higher complexity. Francis and Smith's study shows that the firms with higher percentage of managerial ownership have more innovation output because the managers holding higher percentage of firms' shares are motivated to a greater extant to monitor innovation activities and this mechanism reduces the agency cost of innovation activities. Therefore, if analyst coverage serves as an external governance mechanism that resolves the agency conflict, it may have a similar effect on corporate innovation as managerial ownership does. Jensen and Meckling (1976) maintain that analysts can mitigate the agency cost through external monitoring because financial analysts with professional knowledge and skills are qualified to serve as external monitors. Chen et al. (2015) find that financial analysts monitor listed firms through direct and indirect channels. By tracking firms' financial reports regularly and raising questions to the managers in earnings announcement conferences, analysts can play a direct role in detecting frauds in listed firms (Dyck et al. 2010). Analysts also serve as an indirect monitoring role by publishing research reports and by being interviewed by media (Miller 2006), transmitting the information of public firms to investors and helping identify misbehaviors of managers. Chen et al. (2015) find that analyst coverage's monitoring mechanism reduces CEOs' excessive compensations, value-destroying activities as well as earnings management. Analyst coverage also makes shareholders attach greater importance to internal cash flow. Based on the theoretical analysis above, I propose that by serving as an external governance mechanism, analyst coverage reduces the agency cost and enables listed firms to generate more innovation output. In addition, the comprehensive effect of analyst coverage on firms' innovation output in China may be positive. Wang et al.'s (2021) study shows that investors in China respond positively to the research reports published by financial analysts. This means that through affecting the decisions of investors, analyst coverage in China plays a supervisory role effectively in monitoring firms' behaviors. Also because of relatively scarce internal and external corporate governance mechanisms in China (Jiang & Kim 2015), analyst coverage may serve as a prominent external governance mechanism positively affecting corporate innovation output. Taken together, I make the baseline hypothesis.

H1: By serving as an external governance mechanism, analyst coverage reduces the agency cost and increases firms' innovation output in China.

This study should also examine the specific channels through which analyst coverage exerts the governance effect on firms' innovation output in China. The first channel is substituting for managerial ownership and aligning the interest between managers and shareholders. Based on the existing literature, managerial ownership has two potential effects on firms' value. On the one hand, managerial ownership has an effect of interest alignment and resolves the agency conflict between managers and shareholders (Jensen & Meckling 1976). On the other hand, manager-owners may have entrenchment behaviors and increase the agency cost (Fama & Jensen 1983; Morck et al. 1988). The literature based on the evidence in China suggests that when the percentage of managerial ownership is between 8% and 25%, the entrenchment effect is more prominent, otherwise the effect of alignment of interest is more pronounced (Han et al. 2006). Kim and Jiang's (2015) study shows that managerial ownership is scarce in Chinese listed firms, with only 3% on

average. The descriptive statistics table of this paper also shows that the mean of managerial ownership in Chinese listed firms is approximately 7%, which means the effect of alignment of interest overwhelms the entrenchment effect. In addition, listed firms in China have high degree of ownership concentration (Jiang & Kim 2015). The largest shareholder within a firm can enhance monitoring managers and get rid of the entrenchment effect of managerial ownership (Demsetz 1986) with his or her stronger voting power (Shleifer & Vishny 1986). Therefore, managerial ownership in China is an effective but scarce corporate governance mechanism which resolves the agency conflict Analyst coverage may make up for managerial ownership and align the interest between managers and shareholders. Through publishing research reports on firms and influencing investors' decisions, analysts impose pressure directly on shareholders Shareholders set performance requirements for managers. Therefore, under analyst coverage managers and shareholders take uniform actions including innovation activities to maximize firms' value Taken together, I have the second hypothesis.

H2: Analyst coverage aligns the interest of managers and shareholders as managerial ownership does, and it has a larger positive effect on the innovation output of firms with less percentage of managerial ownership.

The next channel through which analyst coverage has a governance effect on firms' innovation output is making up for option incentive schemes in listed firms and encouraging managers to undertake risk in the short run and to pursue long-term return. Based on the existing literature, option incentive has a positive effect on firms' long-term performance measured by innovation output through three mechanisms (Tian & Meng 2018). First of all, option incentive schemes protect managers from the loss incurred by the fall of share price and bring managers considerable gain if share price rises due to successful innovation activities. Next, option incentive schemes usually have long term of validity and thus can motivate managers and technical staff to devote themselves in long-term R&D activities (Lv et al. 2011). Finally, by relating managers' return to fluctuations in share price, option incentive schemes encourage managers to undertake risk (Armstrong & Vashishtha 2012) and thus have a positive effect on innovation (Holmstrom 1989). Greater fluctuations in share price mean higher value of stock options. Undertaking risk in share price is beneficial to increasing managers' wealth. However, according to the study of Jiang and Kim (2015), although option incentive schemes are becoming more effective in motivating managers to pursue long-term value for firms after the split-share structure reform in 2005, they only take up a small part of total compensation packages for listed firms' managers in China. Analyst coverage may substitute for option incentive schemes and incentivize managers to undertake innovation activities by encouraging managers to undertake short-term risk and pursue long-term innovation return. By publishing research reports on listed firms' innovation productivity, financial analysts help avoid undervaluation of firms' innovation investment in the short run. When innovation activities are successful in the future, financial market gives high valuation for firms' shares under analyst coverage and managers are rewarded for high performance. Thus, I have the third hypothesis.

H3: Analyst coverage encourages managers to undertake short-term risk and to pursue innovation return in the long run as option incentive schemes do, and it has a larger positive effect on innovation output of the firms without option inventive schemes.

The final channel through which financial analysts serve as a governance mechanism and increase corporate innovation output is substituting for independent directors' supervisory role. Prior literature proves that independent directors are an internal corporate governance mechanism that identifies managers with poor performance (Weisbach 1988) and motivates managers to improve performance (Stiglitz & Weiss 1983) and that enhances firms' value (Jenwittayaroje & Jiraporn 2019). Through the mechanisms above, independent directors resolve the agency conflict including the erosion of firms' value (Holmstrom 1979; Holmstrom & Milgrom 1991). Balsmeier et al.'s (2017) study shows that through getting rid of managers' misbehaviors, independent directors generate a positive impact on firms' innovation output. In China, Li and Xu (2014) prove that independent directors can reduce the agency cost of listed firms by using strategic control measures to monitor managers and to mitigate the risk of executive successions. In addition, according to the regulation of China Securities Regulatory Commission (CSRC), independent directors are not allowed to hold more than 1% of firms' total shares or to become the top ten largest shareholders of firms. The regulation ensures that independent directors serve as an effective monitoring mechanism to moderate the agency cost of listed firms. However, Jiang and Kim's (2015) study shows that many listed firms know the supervisory role of independent directors and maintain only the minimum number of independent directors to meet the requirement of CSRC. Therefore, external analysts may make up for independent directors that are effective but restrained by listed firms. Financial analysts are independent from listed firms' managers and only responsible to investors, so they are able to monitor firms' managers as effectively as independent directors do by detecting managerial misbehaviors and reporting on managers' performance. Consequently, managers avoid behaviors that harm firms' value and take actions including innovation activities to improve firms' performance and to maximize investors' profit. Taken together, I have the fourth hypothesis.

H4: Analysts monitor managers as independent directors do, and analyst coverage has a larger positive impact on the innovation output of the firms with less percentage of independent directors in boards.

3 VARIABLE MEASUREMENT AND SAMPLE SELECTION

3.1 *Variable measurement*

3.1.1 *Dependent variables*

For the innovation output, I use more observable patent output number to measure firms' successful innovation activities. To effectively calculate the number of patents of listed firms, I count in firm's patents that are officially granted by China National Intellectual Property Administration (CNIPA). Using the number of patents to measure firms' innovation output is a standardized method in the literature focusing on corporate innovation (Aghion et al. 2005; Nanda & Rhodes-Kropf 2013). In addition, according to the patent law in China, patents are categorized into invention patents and utility model patents. Compared with utility model patents, invention patents have longer period of protection due to their higher level of creativity and complexity. I refer to the studies of Jiang et al. (2020), using invention patents that are officially granted by CNIPA as a rigorous measure of firms' innovation output. Because of the right skewness of the patent number, I use the natural logarithm of the number of invention patents as the main measure of innovation output in my analysis. To avoid losing firm-year observations with zero patents, I plus one to the actual number of patents when calculating the natural logarithm. Additionally, it costs firms a period of time to develop invention patents, so I choose the lag period of two years for the innovation output. Taken together, I use $LnInvention_{i,t+2}$ to measure the innovation output of the firm i in the $t + 2^{th}$ year. In robustness checks, I also use the natural logarithm of one plus the number of utility model patents, $LnUtility_{i,t+2}$, and the natural logarithm of one plus the sum of two types of patents, $LnUI_{i,t+2}$, as dependent variables. I also change the lag period to one year for the innovation output, using $LnInvention_{i,t+1}$ as the dependent variable.

3.1.2 *Explanatory variables*

As for the main explanatory variable, analyst coverage, I use the number of research reports on firms published by financial analysts in a period of time. This measure is highly related to that in the study of He and Tian (2013), in which analyst coverage is measured by the number of financial analysts track-ing the firms in a period of time. The number of re-search reports on firms can directly reflect the atten-tion they receive in the financial market. I use the natural logarithm of one plus the number of re-search reports, $LnReport_{i,t}$, to measure analyst coverage due to right skewness of the number of research reports. To avoid losing observations with zero report numbers, I plus one to the actual number of reports in the calculation. In robustness checks, I return to the method in He and Tian's (2013) study and use the natural logarithm of one plus the number of analysts tracking the firm, $LnAnalyst_{i,t}$, as the explanatory variable.

Table 1. Variable measurement.

Variable	Measurement
$LnInvention_{i,t+2}$	The natural logarithm of one plus the number of invention patents that are officially granted by CNIPA to the firm i in the tth year.
$LnUtility_{i,t+2}$	The natural logarithm of one plus the number of utility model patents that are officially granted by CNIPA to the firm i in the tth year.
$LnUI_{i,t+2}$	The natural logarithm of one plus the number of utility model patents and invention patents that are officially granted by CNIPA to the firm i in the tth year.
$LnReport_{i,t}$	The natural logarithm of one plus the number of research reports published by analysts on the firm i in the tth year.
$LnAnalyst_{i,t}$	The natural logarithm of one plus the number of analysts tracking the firm i in the tth year.
$ExpCoverage_{i,t}$	The expected coverage on the firm i in the tth year speculated on the basis of the sizes of brokerage houses.
$DID_{i,t}$	The dummy variable that is 1 if the firm i is in the treatment group and the tth year is after the merger.
$ManaOwn_{i,t}$	The percentage of the firm i's shares held by managers in the tth year.
$Option_{i,t}$	The dummy variable that is 1 if the firm i has enforced option incentive schemes in the tth year.
$IndDir_{i,t}$	The ratio of the number of independent directors to the number of total directors of the firm i's board in the tth year.
$ROA_{i,t}$	The ratio of net profit to the total asset value of the firm i in the tth year.
$LnAge_{i,t}$	The natural logarithm of one plus the number of years the firm i has been listed for in the tth year.
$Size_{i,t}$	The natural logarithm of the total asset value adjusted by the consumer price index (CPI).
$Leverage_{i,t}$	The ratio of the total liability value to the total asset value of the firm i in the tth year.
$TobinQ_{i,t}$	The Tobin's Q value of the firm i in the tth year.
$Fixed_{i,t}$	The ratio of the net value of fixed assets to the total asset value of the firm i in the tth year.

3.1.3 Instrumental variable, difference-in-differences effect and channel variables

To establish causality, I construct an instrumental variable, $ExpCoverage_{i,t}$, based on the sizes of brokerage houses, and a DID effect, $DID_{i,t}$, based on the exogenous shock. The methods to construct the instrumental variable and the DID effect will be elaborated in the fourth section.

To test the channels through which analyst coverage serves as a governance mechanism and increases innovation output, I identify three channel variables. The first one is managerial ownership, $ManaOwn_{i,t}$, measured by the ratio of the number of shares held by managers to the number of total shares of the firm i in the tth year. The next one is the option incentive scheme, $Option_{i,t}$, measured by a dummy variable that is 1 if the firm i has enforced an option incentive scheme in the tth year and is 0 if the firm i doesn't have any option incentive scheme in the tth year. The final one is the ratio of independent directors, $IndDir_{i,t}$, measured by the ratio of the number of independent directors to the number of total directors in the board of the firm i in the tth year.

3.1.4 Control variables

In this study, there are a vector of firm-level characteristics that have an impact on firms' innovation productivity. The firm-level characteristics include listed firms' size measured by the natural logarithm of the total asset value adjusted by the consumer price index (CPI), return on assets (ROA) measured by the ratio of net profit to the total asset value, leverage ratio measured by the ratio of the total liability value to the total asset value, fixed asset ratio measured by the ratio of the net value of fixed assets to the total asset value, Tobin's Q value and the corporate age measured by one plus the natural logarithm of the number of years the firm has been listed for. Table 1 contains the measurement of the variables used in this paper.

3.2 Sample selection and descriptive statistics

The data in this study are sourced from China Stock Market Accounting Research (CSMAR) database. The period of the sample is from 2003 to 2017. The consumer price index (CPI) used to adjust total asset value is sourced from National Bureau of Statistics of China. Because the business model of listed firms in the financial sector basically do not rely on innovation output, I delete the listed firms in the financial sector from the sample. Sector classification standards are made by China Securities Regulatory Commission (CSRC) and the data of sectors are sourced from RESSET database. In addition, I delete the firm-year observations in which leverage ratio is larger than 1 and the firm-year observations in which the listed firms are specially treated. To avoid the impact of extreme values, I winsorize all continuous variables at the 1st and 99th percentile. Table 2 contains descriptive statistics.

4 BASELINE RESULT, CAUSALITY IDENTIFICATION, AND ROBUSTNESS CHECKS

4.1 Baseline result

To examine the effect of analyst coverage on firms' innovation output, I construct the fixed-effect model

Table 2. Descriptive statistics.

	(1)	(2)	(3)	(4)	(5)
Variable	Number of observations	Mean	Standard deviation	Minimum	Maximum
$LnInvention_{i,t+2}$	12,520	1.340	1.316	0	5.088
$LnUtility_{i,t+2}$	12,520	2.200	1.570	0	6.023
$LnUI_{i,t+2}$	12,520	2.606	1.489	0	6.373
$LnReport_{i,t}$	12,520	2.371	1.079	0.693	4.718
$LnAnalyst_{i,t}$	12,316	1.990	0.862	0.693	3.784
$ExpCoverage_{i,t}$	12,520	12.43	17.48	0	109.8
$DID_{i,t}$	12,520	0.042	0.202	0	1
$ManaOwn_{i,t}$	12,001	0.0699	0.140	0	0.587
$Option_{i,t}$	12,520	0.133	0.339	0	1
$IndDir_{i,t}$	12,520	0.373	0.0674	0	0.571
$ROA_{i,t}$	12,520	0.0500	0.0487	−0.265	0.198
$LnAge_{i,t}$	12,520	1.776	0.901	0	3.258
$Size_{i,t}$	12,520	21.95	1.295	19.30	26.67
$Leverage_{i,t}$	12,520	0.423	0.204	0.0521	0.936
$TobinQ_{i,t}$	12,520	1.983	1.209	0.894	8.251
$Fixed_{i,t}$	12,520	0.239	0.160	0.00188	0.736
Number of Company	2433	2433	2433	2433	2433

based on the panel data. The firm fixed effect and the year fixed effect are simultaneously controlled for. Robust standard errors are clustered by firm. The coefficient of $LnReport_{i,t}$ represents the effect of analyst coverage on firms' innovation output and is the focus of this study.

Table 3 presents the result of the baseline regression. Column (1) is the result of the regression without controlling for firm-level characteristics. Column (2) presents the result with the full set of control variables. Both regressions control for the firm and year fixed effects. Standard errors are clustered by firm. As is shown in the two columns of Table 3, the coefficients of $LnReport_{i,t}$ are positive and have significant levels at 1% and 5%. Therefore, analyst coverage has a significantly positive relationship with firms' innovation output in China.

4.2 Causality identification

The baseline result may be biased due to endogeneity issues. There might be omitted variables that influence both firms' analyst coverage and their innovation output. To establish causality, I use two identification strategies: an instrumental variable (IV) and a difference-in-differences (DID) approach.

4.2.1 Instrumental variable

The qualified instrumental variable in this study should have an impact on analyst coverage but is not correlated with firms' innovation output. Therefore, according to the study of Yu (2008), I speculate firms' expected analyst coverage on the basis of the sizes of brokerage houses and define it as $ExpCoverage_{i,t}$. Yu

Table 3. Baseline result.

	(1)	(2)
Dependent Variable	$LnInvention_{t+2}$	$LnInvention_{t+2}$
LnReport	0.059***	0.035**
	(0.014)	(0.014)
ROA		0.532*
		(0.279)
Leverage		−0.056
		(0.129)
TobinQ		0.019
		(0.013)
Size		0.163***
		(0.040)
LnAge		0.091**
		(0.037)
Fixed		0.414***
		(0.137)
Constant	0.185	−3.467***
	(0.256)	(0.898)
Firm fixed effect	Yes	Yes
Year fixed effect	Yes	Yes
Observations	12,520	12,520
R^2	0.361	0.365
Number of Company	2433	2433

Robust standard errors clustered by firm are displayed in parentheses. ***, **, and * indicate significance at the 1%, 5%, and 10% level, respectively.

(2008) maintains that the sizes of brokerage houses in each year is determined by their profitability and performance which are exogenous to firms' innovation productivity and output. In this study, I use the

Table 4. IV 2SLS.

	(1)	(2)	(3)
	First-stage	Second-stage	OLS
Dependent Variable	$LnReport_t$	$LnInvention_{t+2}$	$LnInvention_{t+2}$
ExpCoverage	0.013*** (0.001)		
LnReport		0.199*	0.035**
		(0.107)	(0.016)
Controls	Yes	Yes	Yes
Firm fixed effect	Yes	Yes	Yes
Year fixed effect	Yes	Yes	Yes
Observations	10,181	10,181	10,181
F-statistic	247.030		
Kleibergen-Paap rk LM statistic	199.151		
Cragg-Donald Wald F-statistic	223.910		
Kleibergen-Paap Wald rk F-statistic	247.035		
R^2		0.378	0.389
Number of Company	2001	2001	2001

Robust standard errors clustered by firm are displayed in parentheses. ***, **, and * indicate significance at the 1%, 5%, and 10% level, respectively.

total number of research reports each brokerage house publishes in each year to gauge their sizes.

$$ExpCoverage_{i,t,j} = \left(\frac{Brokersize_{t,j}}{Brokersize_{0,j}} \right) * Report_{i,0,j} \quad (1)$$

$$ExpCoverage_{i,t} = \sum_{j=1}^{n} ExpCoverage_{i,t,j} \quad (2)$$

The calculation method of the instrumental variable is shown in the equations (1) and (2). $Brokersize_{t,j}$ and $Brokersize_{0,j}$ are the numbers of total research reports published by the brokerage house j in the tth year and in the base year. I use the midterm in the sample, year 2010, as the base year. $Report_{i,0,j}$ is the number of research reports on the firm i published by the brokerage house j in the base year. $ExpCoverage_{i,t,j}$ is the expected number of research reports on the firm i published by the brokerage house j in the tth year speculated on the basis of the brokerage house j's relative size in the tth year. The relative size is the ratio of the brokerage house j's size in the tth year to that in the base year. The instrumental variable $ExpCoverage_{i,t}$ is the total expected number of research reports published on the firm i by all brokerage houses in the tth year. Under the calculation method, the relative size of all brokerage houses in the base year is 1, which makes firms' expected coverage equal to actual coverage. Therefore, referring to the studies of Yu (2008) and He and Tian (2013), I exclude the firm-year observations in the year 2010 when conducting 2SLS regressions. I regress $ExpCoverage_{i,t}$ on the main explanatory variable $LnReport_{i,t}$ which may be endogenous and conduct the second-stage regression on the dependent variable $LnInvention_{i,t+2}$.

The column (1) in Table 4 presents the first-stage regression result. The control variable set and

fixed effects are the same with those in the baseline regression. Standard errors are clustered by firm. The coefficient of $ExpCoverage_{i,t}$ is positive and has a significant level at 1%. In addition, I test for under-identification and the weak instrument. The value of Kleibergen-Paap rk LM statistic is 199.151. Thus, the instrumental variable $ExpCoverage_{i,t}$ is highly correlated with $LnReport_{i,t}$. The model in this study uses one instrumental variable to examine one possibly exogenous variable. Based on the rule of thumb I find that the value of F-statistic is 247.030, much larger than 10, so I reject the null hypothesis that the instrumental variable is weak. Additionally, I check the values of the Cragg-Donald Wald F statistic and the Kleibergen-Paap Wald rk F statistic and examine them according to the Stock-Yogo critical value for weak instrument tests. The values of two statistics above are 223910 and 247035 respectively, much larger than the Stock-Yogo critical value of 16.38. Therefore, the null hypothesis that the weak instrument exists is rejected. Taken together, $ExpCoverage_{i,t}$ is an effective instrumental variable.

The column (2) in Table 4 reports the result of the second-stage regression. The main explanatory variable is the fitted value of $LnReport_{i,t}$ generated in the first-stage regression. Consistent with the baseline result, the coefficient of the fitted value of $LnReport_{i,t}$ in the second-stage regression is positive and has a significant level at 10%. The result confirms that analyst coverage has a positive and statistically significant causal effect on firms' innovation output in China.

To gauge the direction of the bias incurred by endogeneity issues, I conduct an OLS regression with the same sample in 2SLS regressions and compare the results. As is shown in the column (3), the coefficient of $LnReport_{i,t}$ (0.035) in the OLS regression is smaller than that (0.199) in the second-stage regression, so the actual effect of analyst coverage on firms' innovation output is underestimated due to endogeneity issues. Some omitted factors may negatively affect firms' analyst coverage and innovation output simultaneously. The resignation of star managers with high performance is an instance among them. Star managers who excel in handling technical and managerial issues attract more attention from financial analysts and increase firms' innovation output. When star managers resign from firms, firms' analyst coverage and innovation output decrease. Therefore, when I rule out the correlation between analyst coverage and the error term in the baseline model, the actual effect of analyst coverage on firms' innovation output is larger.

4.2.2 Difference-in-differences

Next, I use a difference-in-differences (DID) approach based on an exogenous shock, the merger between two brokerage houses in China. The merger directly affects analyst coverage on firms but is exogenous to firms' innovation productivity and output. Kelly and Ljungqvist (2012) maintain that when two brokerage houses merge, analysts reporting on the same firms become redundant, so the newly established brokerage house lays off some analysts whose report targets overlap with those of others. This results in a decrease in analyst coverage of firms which are tracked by two merged brokerage houses. Kelly and Ljungqvist (2012) rigorously verify that the merger events among brokerage houses are not correlated with characteristics of firms being tracked. Additionally, Hong and Kacperczyk's (2010) study shows that newly merged brokerage houses lay off analysts due to corporate culture shocks and organizational adjustments, which are not correlated with characteristics of firms being tracked. In this study, I use the merger between SNENYIN & WANGUO Securities limited corporation and HONGYUAN Securities limited corporation in the year 2015 to build up the DID effect. The merger deal is negotiated because of business strategies of two companies rather than the features of firms they track, so the merger directly affects firms' analyst coverage but is exogenous to firms' innovation productivity and output.

The DID effect is constructed as follows. This study focuses on the innovation output of firms in treatment and control groups three years before the merger and three years after the merger. According to the CSMAR database, the new brokerage house SHENWAN HONGYUAN Securities limited corporation published research reports in early 2015. To more accurately gauge the effect of the brokerage merger on firms' innovation output, I treat year 2015 as the year after the merger. Therefore, year 2015 to 2017 is the period after the merger and year 2012 to 2014 is the period before the merger. The method of constructing treatment and control groups resembles that by Guo et al. (2019). Guo et al. (2019) maintain that brokerage mergers result in a decrease in analyst coverage due to the overlap of analysts' targets, so the firms in the treatment group should be reported by original brokerage houses before the merger and be reported continuously

Table 5. Difference-in-difference estimation.

	(1)	(2)
Dependent variable	LnReport$_{t+1}$	LnInvention$_{t+2}$
DID effect	−0.256***	−0.230**
	(0.058)	(0.094)
Controls	Yes	Yes
Firm fixed effect	Yes	Yes
Year fixed effect	Yes	Yes
Observations	8294	9860
R^2	0.109	0.411
Number of Company	2135	2377

Robust standard errors clustered by firm are displayed in parentheses. ***, **, and * indicate significance at the 1%, 5%, and 10% level, respectively.

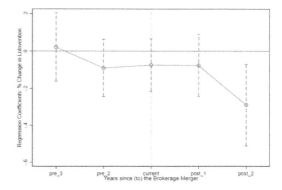

Figure 1. The dynamic effect of brokerage merger on corporate innovation output.

by the new brokerage house after the merger. However, according the study of Hong and Kacperczyk (2010), analyst coverage can also be negatively affected by other factors in the brokerage mergers including corporate culture clashes and organizational adjustments. The new brokerage firm may cease reporting on listed firms the original brokerage firms track. Therefore, to more accurately measure the effect of the brokerage merger on analyst coverage and firms' innovation output, I count the firms in the treatment group if they are reported by both brokerage firms in the three-year period before the merger. Other listed firms outside of the treatment group are counted in the control group.

Then I examine the effect of the brokerage merger on analyst coverage and firms' innovation output. Table 5 shows that the merger event has a significantly negative impact on firms' analyst coverage and innovation output. The result supports the positive causal relationship between analyst coverage and firms' innovation output.

Finally, to check how the brokerage merger affects corporate innovation before and after 2015, I use an event study to test for the parallel trend assumption. Referring to the study of Wang (2013), I chose 2014 as the base year and drop the observations in 2014 to avoid collinearity. The result is shown in the Figure 1. The horizontal axis measures the number of years since the merger event took place. The plots connected by the solid line indicate changes in $LnInvention_{i,t}$ compared to the period before the brokerage merger. The event study controls for firm and year fixed effects. The dotted lines indicate the 95% confidence intervals where standard errors are clustered at the firm level. As is shown in the Figure 1, the brokerage merger event generates a significantly negative effect on corporate innovation output two years after 2015. The lag period is consistent with that in the baseline regression. In the years when the brokerage merger has not generated its effect on corporate innovation, the treatment and control groups are comparable. Taken together, the parallel trend assumption holds.

4.3 Robustness checks

In this part I conduct a series of robustness checks for the baseline result. First of all, I conduct a Poisson regression using the number of invention patents. The column (1) of Table 6 shows the result of the Poisson regression. The IRR of $LnReport_{i,t}$ is significantly positive. There is a difference in the numbers of firm-year observations between the Poisson regression and the OLS regression. This is because in non-linear fixed-effects models, conditional estimators exclude observations with which the outcome does not vary. Next, I use the natural logarithm of the number of financial analysts tracking the listed firm i in the tth year, $LnAnalyst_{i,t}$ to measure firms' analyst coverage. To avoid losing observations with zero analysts, I add one to the actual number of analysts tracking the firm when calculating the natural logarithm. As is shown in the column (2) of Table 6, the coefficient of $LnAnalyst_{i,t}$ is significantly positive. Then I alter the lag period of the dependent variable. The column (3) presents the result of lagging invention patent output for one year. The coefficient of $LnReport_{i,t}$ is still significantly positive. Finally, this study also uses different types of patents to measure firms' innovation output. As is stated before, patents in China are categorized into invention patents and utility model patents. Invention patents are more complex and creative than utility model patents. The column (4) shows the result of the regression on the natural logarithm of one plus the number of utility model patents of the firm i in the $t + 2^{th}$ year and the column (5) shows the result of the regression on the natural logarithm of one plus the sum of invention patents and utility model patents of the firm i in the $t + 2^{th}$ year. The coefficients of $LnReport^{i,t}$ in the two models are significantly positive.

5   GOVERNANCE CHANNELS OF ANALYST COVERAGE

After proving that analyst coverage has a positive impact on firms' innovation output in China, I further explore the specific channels through which analyst coverage serves as a governance mechanism and increases firms' innovation output in this section.

5.1 Managerial ownership

As I stated in hypothesis 2, analyst coverage may make up for managerial ownership by generating an interest-alignment effect and positively affect innovation. Analyst coverage imposes pressure on shareholders by influencing investors' decisions and shareholders make requirements for managers to improve firms' performance. Under the coverage of analysts, managers and shareholders take uniform actions including innovation activities to maximize firms' performance and value.

To examine hypothesis 2, I construct the interaction term of analyst coverage and managerial ownership, $LnReport_{i,t}*ManaOwn_{i,t}$, to see the difference in the effect of analyst coverage on innovation output of firms with different levels of managerial ownership. The firm and the year fixed effects are simultaneously controlled for. Robust standard errors are clustered by firm. The coefficient of the interaction term is the focus.

Table 6.   Robustness checks.

	(1)	(2)	(3)	(4)	(5)
Dependent variable	Invention$_{t+2}$	LnInvention$_{t+2}$	LnInvention$_{t+1}$	LnUtility$_{t+2}$	LnUI$_{t+2}$
LnReport	1.015***		0.043***	0.060***	0.057***
	(0.006)		(0.013)	(0.014)	(0.014)
LnAnalyst		0.046***			
		(0.018)			
Controls	Yes	Yes	Yes	Yes	Yes
Firm fixed effect	Yes	Yes	Yes	Yes	Yes
Year fixed effect	Yes	Yes	Yes	Yes	Yes
Observations	11,503	12,316	14,140	12,520	12,520
R^2		0.368	0.357	0.280	0.220
Number of Company	1827	2418	2622	2433	2433

Robust standard errors clustered by firm are displayed in parentheses. ***, **, and * indicate significance at the 1%, 5%, and 10% level, respectively.

Table 7. Governance channels of analyst coverage.

	(1)	(2)	(3)
Dependent variable	LnInvention$_{t+2}$	LnInvention$_{t+2}$	LnInvention$_{t+2}$
Channels	Managerial Ownership	Option Incentive	Independent Directors
LnReport	0.044***	0.049***	0.196***
	(0.016)	(0.015)	(0.057)
ManaOwn	0.376		
	(0.269)		
LnReport*ManaOwn	−0.174*		
	(0.091)		
Option		0.151	
		(0.096)	
LnReport*Option		−0.076**	
		(0.037)	
IndDir			1.143***
			(0.380)
LnReport*IndDir			−0.428***
			(0.147)
Controls	Yes	Yes	Yes
Firm fixed effect	Yes	Yes	Yes
Year fixed effect	Yes	Yes	Yes
Observations	12,001	12,520	12,520
R^2	0.365	0.366	0.366
Number of Company	2416	2433	2433

Robust standard errors clustered by firm are displayed in parentheses. ***, **, and * indicate significance at the 1%, 5%, and 10% level, respectively.

The column (1) of Table 7 shows that the coefficient of $LnReport_{i,t}*ManaOwn_{i,t}$ is significantly negative. It means that analyst coverage has a larger positive effect on the innovation output of the firms with lower level of managerial ownership. The result is consistent with hypothesis 2.

5.2 Incentive option schemes

In hypothesis 3, by mitigating the risk of innovation activities in the short term and increasing managers' innovation return in the long run, analyst coverage may substitute for option incentive schemes to encourage managers to undertake innovation activities. Research reports published by analysts help to avoid the under-valuation of firms' innovation investment. When successful innovation output is reported by analysts, firms' shares are highly valued and managers are rewarded for high performance.

To examine hypothesis 3, I construct the interaction term of analyst coverage and option incentive, $LnReport_{i,t}*Option_{i,t}$, to see the difference in the effect of analyst coverage on innovation output of firms with or without option incentive schemes. The firm and the year fixed effects are simultaneously controlled for. Robust standard errors are clustered by firm. The coefficient of the interaction term is the focus.

The column (2) of Table 7 shows that the coefficient of $LnReport_{i,t}*Option_{i,t}$ is significantly negative. It means that analyst coverage generates a larger positive effect on the innovation output of the firms without option incentive schemes. The result is consistent with hypothesis 3.

5.3 Independent directors

As is mentioned in hypothesis 4, financial analysts may substitute for independent directors' supervisory role to monitor managers on behalf of investors and positively affect innovation. Because of analysts' independence, they can supervise managers as effectively as independent directors do by publishing research reports and conducting due diligence. Thus, managers avoid behaviors that erode the firm's value and take actions including technical innovation to maximize investors' profit and to improve the firm's performance.

To examine hypothesis 4, I construct the interaction term of analyst coverage and the ratio of the number of independent directors to the number of total directors on the firm's board, $LnReport_{i,t}*IndDir_{i,t}$, to see the difference in the effect of analyst coverage on innovation output of firms with different ratios of independent directors. The firm and the year fixed effects are simultaneously controlled for. Robust standard errors are clustered by firm. The coefficient of the interaction term is the focus.

The column (3) of Table 7 shows that the coefficient of $LnReport_{i,t}*IndDir_{i,t}$ is significantly negative. It means that analyst coverage has a larger positive effect on the innovation output of the firms with lower ratio of independent directors. The result is consistent with hypothesis 4.

6 CONCLUSION AND DISCUSSION

In this paper, I study the effect of analyst coverage on firms' innovation output measured by the number of invention patents in China. I find that the listed firms covered in more research reports published by financial analysts generate more invention patents. Next, I use an instrumental variable and a difference-in-differences method to establish causality. Then a series of robustness checks are conducted. Finally, I examine three corporate governance channels through which analyst coverage resolves the agency conflict and increases innovation output. The evidence is consistent with the governance hypothesis of analyst coverage in China. My study provides a new corporate governance perspective to study the effect of analyst coverage on firms' innovation.

There are two fields that are worth being studied in the future. First of all, although this study finds that in China, the comprehensive effect of analyst coverage on firms' innovation output is positive and there are corporate governance channels through which analyst coverage generates the positive effect, analyst coverage might have other mechanisms which generate negative impacts on firms' innovation output. The pressure effect of analyst coverage on innovation output examined by He and Tian (2013) in the American setting might exist in China. Next, this study examines the positive effect of analyst coverage on firms' innovation on the basis of corporate level data. It is also important for policy makers to know whether the whole financial and capital market system generates a positive effect on the innovation output of all walks of life.

Finally, the practical implications of this study are as follows. Individual and institutional investors in China can invest in the firms that are intensively covered, because these firms benefit from the governance effect of analyst coverage and will have better long-term performance measured by innovation output. The government should attach importance to the governance role played by financial analysts and encourage the robust development of brokerage houses.

REFERENCES

Aghion, P., Bloom, N., Blundell, R., Griffith, R., Howitt, P., 2005. Competition and innovation: an inverted-U relationship. *Quarterly Journal of Economics* 120(2), 701–728.

Aghion, P., Reenen, J., Zingales, L., 2013. Innovation and institutional ownership. *American Economic Review* 103(1), 277–304.

Armstrong, C., Vashishtha, R. 2012. Executive Stock Options, Differential Risk-taking Incentives, and Firm Value. *Journal of Financial Economics* 104(1), 70–88.

Arrow, K., 1962. Economic welfare and the allocation of resources for invention. In: Nelson, R.R. (Ed.), *The Rate and Direction of Inventive Activity: Economic and Social Factors*. Princeton University Press, Princeton, pp. 609–626.

Atanassov, J., Liu, X., 2016. Corporate income taxes, pledgeable income and innovation. Working paper, University of Nebraska.

Balsmeier, B., Buchwald, A., Stiebale, J., 2014. Outside directors on the board and innovative firm performance. *Research Policy* 43(10), 1800–1815.

Baysinger, B., Kosnik, R., Turk, T., 1991. Effects of board and ownership structure on corporate R&D strategy. *Academy of Management Journal* 34(1), 205–214.

Belloc, F., 2012. Corporate governance and innovation: a survey. *Journal of Economic Surveys* 26(5), 835–864.

Benfratello, L., Schiantarelli, F., Sembenelli, A., 2008. Banks and innovation: Microeconometric evidence on Italian firms. *Journal of Financial Economics* 90(2): 197–217.

Black, B., 1992. Agents watching agents: the promise of institutional investor voice. *UCLA Law Review* 39, 811–893.

Bradley, D., Jordan, B., Ritter, J., 2003. The quiet period goes out with a bang. *The Journal of Finance* 58(1), 1–36.

Brav, A., Jiang, W., Ma, S., Tian, X., 2018. How does hedge fund activism reshape corporate innovation? *Journal of Financial Economics* 130(2), 237–264.

Brennan, M., Tamarowski, C., 2000. Investor relations, liquidity, and stock prices. *Journal of Applied Corporate Finance* 12 (4), 26–37.

Chang, S., 1995. International expansion strategy of Japanese firms: capability building through sequential entry. *Academy of Management Journal* 38(2), 383–407.

Chang, X., Dasgupta, S., Hilary, G., 2006. Analyst coverage and financing decisions. *The Journal of Finance* 61(6), 3009–3048.

Chang, X., Fu, K., Low, A., Zhang, W., 2015. Non-executive employee stock options and corporate innovation. *Journal of Financial Economics* 115(1), 168–188.

Chen, T., Harford, J., Lin, C., 2015. Do analysts matter for governance? Evidence from natural experiments. *Journal of Financial Economics* 115(2), 383–410.

Demsetz, H., 1986. Corporate control, insider trading, and rates of return. *American Economic Review* 76(2), 313–316.

Derrien, F., Kecskes, A., 2013. The real effects of financial shocks: evidence from exogenous changes in analyst coverage. *The Journal of Finance* 68(4), 1407–1440.

Derrien, F., Kecskes, A., Nguyen, P., 2018. Labor force demographics and corporate innovation. Working paper.

Dong, M., Hirshleifer, D., Teoh. S., 2017. Stock market overvaluation, moonshots, and corporate innovation. Working paper, University of California, Irvine.

Dyck, A., Morse, A., Zingales, L., 2010. Who blows the whistle on corporate fraud? *The Journal of Finance* 65(6), 2213–2253.

Fama, E., Jensen, M., 1983. Separation of ownership and control. *Journal of Law and Economics*, 26(2), 301–325.

Francis, J., Smith A., 1995. Agency costs and innovation some empirical evidence. *Journal of Accounting and Economics* 19(2–3), 383–409.

Fried, V., Bruton, G., Hisrich, R., 1998. Strategy and the board of directors in venture capital-backed firms. *Journal of Business Venturing* 13(6), 493–503.

Gentry, R., Shen, W., 2013. The impacts of performance relative to analyst forecasts and analyst coverage on firm R&D intensity. *Strategic Management Journal* 34(1), 121–130.

Guo, B., Pérez-Castrillo, D., Toldrà-Simats, A., 2019. Firms' innovation strategy under the shadow of analyst coverage. *Journal of Financial Economics* 131(2), 456–483.

Han L., Li K., Song L., 2003. Managerial ownership and firm value: Empirical evidence based on the convergence of interest effects and the entrenchment effects. *Nankai Business Review* 9(4), 35–41.

He, J., Tian, X., 2013. The dark side of analyst coverage: The case of innovation. *Journal of Financial Economics* 109(3), 856–878.

Hill, C., Snell, S., 1988. External control, corporate strategy, and firm performance. *Strategic Management Journal* 9(6), 577–590.

Holmstrom, B., 1979. Moral hazard and observability. *The Bell Journal of Economics* 10(1), 74–91.

Holmstrom, B., 1989. Agency costs and innovation. *Journal of Economic Behavior and Organization* 12(3), 305–327.

Holmstrom, B., Milgrom, P., 1991. Multitask principal agent analyses: Incentive contracts, asset ownership, and job design. *Journal of Law, Economics, and Organization* 7(Sp), 24–52.

Hong, H., Kacperczyk, M., 2010. Competition and bias. *Quarterly Journal of Economics* 125(4), 1683–1725.

Hong, H., Lim, T., Stein, J., 2000. Bad news travels slowly: size, analyst coverage, and the profitability of momentum strategies. *The Journal of Finance* 55(1), 265–295.

Irvine, P., 2003. Incremental impact of analyst initiation of coverage. *Journal of Corporate Finance* 9(4), 431–451.

Jaffe, A., 1986. Technological opportunity and spillovers of R&D: evidence from firm's patents, profits and market value. *American Economic Review* 76(5), 984–1001.

Jensen, M., Meckling, W., 1976. Theory of the firm: managerial behavior, agency costs, and ownership structure. *Journal of Financial Economics* 3(4), 305–360.

Jenwittayaroje, N., Jiraporn, P., 2019. Do Independent Directors Improve Firm Value? Evidence from the Great Recession. *International Review of Finance* 19(1), 207–222.

Jiang, F., Kim, K., 2015. Corporate governance in China: A modern perspective. *Journal of corporate finance* 32, 190–216.

Jiang, J., Jiang, X., Yi, Z., 2020. Efficiency of Corporate Innovation: The Impact of Controlling Shareholders' Stock Pledge. *Journal of Financial Research* 2, 128–146.

Kelly, B., Ljungqvist, A., 2012. Testing asymmetric-information asset pricing models. *The Review of Financial Studies* 25(5), 1366–1413.

Kochhar, R., David, P., 1996. Institutional investors and firm innovation: a test of competing hypotheses. *Strategic Management Journal* 17(1), 73–84.

Kortum, S., Lerner, J., 2000. Assessing the contribution of venture capital to innovation. *The RAND Journal of Economics* 31(4), 674–692.

Kosnik, R., 1990. Effects of board demography and directors' incentives on corporate greenmail decisions. *Academy of Management Journal* 33(1), 129–150.

Latham, S., Braun, M., 2009. Managerial risk, innovation, and organizational decline. *Journal of Management* 35(2), 258–281.

Lee, P., 2005. A comparison of ownership structures and innovations of US and Japanese firms. *Managerial and Decision Economics* 26(1), 39–50.

Li, W., Xu, J., 2014. Board's Independence, CEO Succession and the Scope of Strategic Change: An Empirical Research on the Effectiveness of Independent Directors. *Nankai Business Review* 17(1), 4–13.

Lv, C., Zheng, H., Yan, M., Xu, J., 2009. The design for listed companies' system of stimulation by stock option and purchase: Is it an incentive or welfare? *Management World* 9, 133–147.

Miller, G., 2006. The press as a watchdog for accounting fraud. *Journal of Accounting Research* 44(5), 1001–1033.

Morck, R., Shleifer, A., Vishny R., 1988. Management Ownership and Market Valuation: An Empirical Analysis. *Journal of Financial Economics* 20 (1–2), 293–315.

Moser, P., 2005. How do patent laws influence innovation? Evidence from nineteenth-century world's fairs. *American Economic Review* 95(4), 1214–1236.

Nanda, R., Rhodes-Kropf, M., 2013. Investment cycles and startup innovation. *Journal of Financial Economics* 110(2), 403–418.

Peng, M., 2004. Outside directors and firm performance during institutional transitions. *Strategic Management Journal* 25(5), 453–471.

Schumpeter, J., 1942. *Capitalism, Socialism, and Democracy*. Harper and Brothers, New York.

Shleifer, A., Vishny, R., 1986. Large shareholders and corporate control. *Journal of Political Economy* 94(3), 461–488.

Solow, R., 1957. Technological change and the aggregate production function. *Review of Economics and Statistics* 39(3), 312–320.

Stiglitz, J., Weiss, A., 1983. Incentive effects of termination: Applications to the credit and labor markets. *American Economic Review* 73(5), 912–927.

Tian X., Meng Q., 2018. Do stock incentive schemes spur corporate innovation? *Nankai Business Review* 21(3), 176–190.

Wang Y., Wang J., Zhao Y., 2021. Stock recommendations and recommendations change of analysts and market response in China. *Management Review* 33(2), 3–14.

Wang, J., 2013. The Economic Impact of Special Economic Zones: Evidence from Chinese Municipalities. *Journal of Development Economics* 101, 133–147.

Weisbach, M., 1988. Outside directors and CEO turnover. *Journal of Financial Economics* 20, 431–460.

Yu, F., 2008. Analyst coverage and earnings management. *Journal of Financial Economics* 88(2), 245–271.

Economic and Business Management – Huang & Zhang (Eds)
© 2022 Copyright the Author(s), ISBN: 978-1-032-06754-4

The impact of green finance on the value of Chinese photovolatic enterprises in the context of COVID-19—based on the research of listed photovoltaic enterprises

Feifan Wang*

Business Department, Nanjing University, Jiangsu, China

ABSTRACT: Under the double whammy of the COVID-19 epidemic and the new photovoltaic policy, Chinese photovoltaic enterprises are facing a sharp drop in profits and even loss, directly reflected in the volatility of stock prices. In this context, this paper selects 50 Chinese photovoltaic enterprises listed on A-shares as samples and uses stock prices and derivative data to explore the impact of green financial policies on the value of Chinese photovoltaic enterprises under the background of the epidemic. The results show that the value of Chinese listed photovolatic enterprises with green financial support is more stable during the epidemic period. Under the background of the epidemic, green finance has a positive impact on the value of Chinese photovoltaic enterprises. Finally, some suggestions are put forward according to the results.

1 INTRODUCTION

At present, China's photovoltaic industry is in a period of rapid growth, and photovoltaic enterprises with core technologies spring up like mushrooms. The photovolatic industry is leading China's new energy industry to the forefront of the world, but the sudden COVID-19 has made most enterprises face a sharp decline in profits or even loss. At the peak of epidemic, the efficiency of enterprises returning to work was not high, which had a strong negative impact on new energy industry. Due to the need of epidemic prevention and control and the increase of the health security of necessary inputs, enterprises' production costs have risen sharply. Furthermore, photovoltaic enterprises also face challenges like a power imbalance between supply and demand and the New Deal of subsidies.

Green finance refers to economic activities aimed at supporting environmental improvement, tackling with climate change and efficient use of resources. Among the several forms of green financial policies to support the new energy industry, green credit and bonds are widely used. After the Overall Plan for Ecological Civilization System Reform issued by the CPC Central Committee and The State Council in 2015 clearly proposed the construction of green financial system, green financial policies have been in the process of steady progress. Its capital aggregation effect, investment orientation and scientific and technological innovation effect have a large supporting role for the new energy industry (Wang Zhiguo 2019). Therefore, as a major branch of the new energy

industry, photovolatic industry can benefit from this policy.

From the perspective of research objects, most of the previous studies focused on the relationship between the epidemic and the new energy industry as a whole, or the relationship between green finance and the new energy industry, while few papers focused on the relationship between green finance and photovolatic enterprises in the context of the epidemic. As an early developing part of China's new energy industry, photovoltaic enterprises have a relatively mature and independent market system compared with other new energy enterprises. This paper conducts a separate study on them, to a certain extent, to fill in the blank of previous studies. In addition, in terms of research methods, the number of listed photovoltaic enterprises in the past is small, which leads to the lack of sufficient data in the horizontal and vertical direction. The samples of 50 photovolatic enterprises selected in this paper have complete data in the past two years and have strong research value, which provide a new entry point for subsequent research.

This paper empirically analyzes the effect of green financial policies on the sustainable development of enterprises, combined with the epidemic factor. On the one hand, it tries to quantify the impact of the epidemic on photovoltaic enterprises; on the other hand, it tries to make the research more practical and reference value. The content of this paper is in line with the theme of green development. To some extent, it can bring some consideration to the government, enterprises and investors. The government can further plan and implement green finance policies based on the research conclusions of this paper; Enterprises can

---

*Corresponding Author

106

DOI 10.1201/9781003203704-19

understand the supporting role of policies and actively make sustainable development programs; Investors can use this article to understand the market trend and make good investment strategies.

2 LITERATURE REVIEW

2.1 *Foreign literature*

In terms of the policies of green finance supporting photovoltaic and other new energy enterprises, Alagappan et al. (2011) believe that the development of new energy industry cannot be separated from the support of industrial policies. Borenstein (2012) and Jenner et al. (2013) questioned the effect of industrial policy. Hscher et al. (2014) believed that providing subsidies to upstream industries of new energy industry is better than providing subsidies to downstream industries, which can reduce costs and improve their competitiveness. As for the investment and financing of financial institutions in the new energy industry, Ali (1981), through the study of the oil crisis, proposed that the development of the new energy industry should be mainly through the investment and financing support channels such as the World Bank and funds. By collating the data of photovoltaic industry, Derrick (1998) found that the development of new energy industry was slow due to the lack of correct financing mechanism. Jeucken (2010) believed that all countries should meet the requirements of sustainable economic and environmental development through the green financial means of financial institutions. Scholtens (2006) believed that it was the social responsibility of financial institutions to support the development of green finance and promote economic development and environmental protection through the innovation of green financial instruments. Szabo and Waldau (2008) believed that the financing burden of enterprises could be reduced through market competition.

2.2 *Domestic literature*

In terms of policy support, Yuan Zhao et al. (2005) classified new energy industrial policies and put forward policy support suggestions. Songwan Liu (2009) believed that the government should use financial funds to support the development of new energy industry. Xiaoqiong Gao (2010) believed that the development of China's new energy industry is still in its early stage, and it needs policy support to help solve the financing problem and promote the combination of new energy industry and finance. Xianxiang Lu et al. (2012) believed that the government should create a mechanism combining encouragement and restriction for the policy support of the new energy industry. Yahong Zhou et al. (2015) believed that the development of new energy industry could be promoted through government tax policies and subsidies. In terms of investment and financing of financial institutions, Junwen Fu et al. (2007) pointed out that financial

institutions should actively expand energy financial products and improve the financial service system. Liuqin Chen (2011) believed that commercial banks should establish policy-based financial organizations to help the development of new energy industry and create a good investment and financing atmosphere. Anbao Tang et al. (2016) found that China's financial institutions do not have enough financing for the new energy industry, and the financing gap needs to be filled. Zhenzhi Zhao et al. (2020) believed that green finance can provide financing channels according to the characteristics of new energy industry and solve the problem of capital chain turnover of enterprises.

3 DATA ANALYSIS AND MODEL CONSTRUCTION

3.1 *Sample selection*

By July 6, 2020, China has a total of 147 listed photovoltaic enterprises, the overall market value has reached 1,213 billion yuan, among which a total of 63 enterprises listed in Shanghai and Shenzhen stock exchange, accounting for less than half. This paper takes 50 sample enterprises, all of which were listed before December 31, 2018. Firstly, the information disclosure degree of listed enterprises is higher and easier to collect than that of unlisted enterprises. Second, because of the emerging industry of photovoltaic listed enterprises, the government, the market and investors pay much attention to their data quality, which is more complete and real, more reference value than the unlisted enterprises; Third, the long-term existence of the enterprise in terms of enterprise value is more representative. In this paper, Stata and Eviews are mainly used for data processing and chart making. The data are all from Polaris Solar Photovoltaic network, Great Tide Information network and RESSET database.

Considering the representativeness, authenticity and availability of data, this paper mainly uses stock price data to calculate and obtain stock price index and logarithmic return form of stock price index for further research. The full sample data summarizes the market value of photovoltaic enterprises before and after the epidemic; The group sample data are mainly used to analyze whether the photovoltaic enterprises with and without green financial support have different performance in value under the background of the epidemic.

3.2 *Variable*

The meanings of variables in this paper are shown in Table 1, where T represents the period from the prevention and control of COVID-19 to the full resumption of work in low-risk areas, i.e., January 20, 2020 to February 20, 2020. In the group sample, the support group (gf10, GF10) is composed of 10 A-share listed photovoltaic enterprises supported by green financial

Table 1. Variable meaning.

Variable	Variable meaning
gf50	A full sample index of corporate share prices
gf10	Support group sample company stock price index
gf40	Blank group sample company stock price index
GF50	A full sample corporate stock price index logarithmic return
GF10	Support group sample company stock price index logarithmic return
GF40	Blank group sample company stock price index logarithmic return
CN19	Epidemic factor

Table 2. Basic statistics of logarithmic return sequence for full sample and group sample.

Variable	S.D.	Average	Skewness	Kurtosis
GF50	0.020	0.001	−0.671	5.906
GF10	0.022	0.001	−0.716	5.751
GF40	0.021	0.001	−0.440	5.275

Table 3. ADF test results of full samples, support group and blank group.

Variable	ADF	10%level	Result
GF50	−18.60323	−2.570999	Yes
GF10	−18.21188		Yes
GF40	−19.28288		Yes

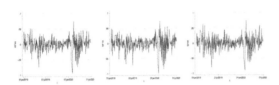

Figure 1. Return on stock price index for full sample and group sample firms.

policies, and the remaining enterprises constitute the blank group (gf40, GF40).

3.3 Equations

In order to explore the overall impact of the epidemic on listed photovoltaic enterprises and the different impacts on the support group and the blank group, this paper mainly constructs the GARCH (1,1) model, which takes the full sample stock return rate and the group sample stock logarithmic return rate as the explained variable and the epidemic factor as the explanatory variable:

$$GF_t = \alpha_0 + \alpha_1 \cdot CN19 + u_t, u_t \in N(0, \sigma_t^2)$$
$$\sigma_t^2 = \beta_0 + \beta_1 \cdot u_{t-1}^2 + \beta_2 \sigma_{t-1}^2 \quad (1)$$

Formula (1) is applicable to both the full sample and the group sample. GF can be substituted by GF50, GF10 and GF40 to represent the logarithmic return rate of the stock price index of the full sample, the support group and the blank group respectively. CN19 represents the epidemic factor, which is a dummy variable; T represents a trading day, and its domain is 361 trading days from January 1, 2019 to June 30, 2020.

4 EMPIRICAL ANALYSIS

4.1 Descriptive statistical analysis

Figure 1 shows that the return rate of the sample companies' stock price index has the volatility aggregation, which is the strongest on the first trading day after the Spring Festival in 2020, that is to say, the sample photovoltaic enterprise value changes greatly on February 3, 2020. In theory, the COVID-19 pandemic has led to a downturn in market sentiment, which is closely related to price-earnings ratios, leading to a sharp decline in stock prices (Gaofeng Gu 2020).

The statistical description results of the full sample and group sample show that the sequences of GF50, GF10 and GF40 samples have a spike (Kurtosis>3) and a right Skewness<0 distribution. Combined with the Jarque-Bera test, the sequences of the three groups do not follow the normal distribution. In addition, the mean value of GF10 is lower than that of GF40, indicating that the fluctuation range of the support group is smaller and the performance is more stable than that of the blank group. Since the profitability and sustainable development ability of the enterprises supported by green financial policies are prominent, the support group is more likely to get the attention of the government and investors, and attaches more importance to the steady improvement of enterprise value, and thus has a more stable performance in the value fluctuation.

4.2 Stationarity test and autocorrelation

Unit root test is performed on the full sample, support group and blank group respectively, and the test results are summarized as shown in Table 3. The test values of GF50, GF10 and GF40 are −18.6, −18.21 and −19.28, respectively, all less than the critical value at the significance level of 1%, 5% and 10%, negating the null hypothesis of unit root test, that is, there is no unit root in the three groups, indicating that GF50, GF10 and GF40 are stable time series.

4.3 Sequence correlation and ARCH testing

In this paper, the residual square autocorrelation results are used as the test sequence for the existence of conditional heteroscedasticity, namely ARCH effect. Table 4 is the partial results of the test for full sample.

In Table 4, the p-value of the full sample sequence is less than 0.05 from the 5th order.

Table 4. The squared autocorrelation of residual in the full sample sequence.

Lags	AC	PAC	Q-Stat	Prob
1	0.099	0.099	3.596	0.058
2	0.087	0.078	6.363	0.042
3	0.047	0.032	7.186	0.066
4	0.013	−0.001	7.250	0.123
5	0.176	0.171	18.638	0.002
6	0.018	−0.016	18.751	0.005
7	0.182	0.162	30.946	0.000
8	0.092	0.053	34.105	0.000
9	0.021	−0.013	34.265	0.000
10	0.187	0.152	47.357	0.000

Table 5. Regression results of GARCH model with full sample with epidemic factor added.

Variable	Coefficient	Std. Error	z-Statistic	Prob.
CN19	−0.015087	0.003623	−4.163830	0.0000
Variance Equation				
C	0.000009	0.000005	1.687464	0.0915
RESID(−1)^2	0.106544	0.027048	3.939065	0.0001
GARCH(−1)	0.874610	0.031381	27.870940	0.0000

The P-value of the support group and the blank group is less than 0.05 from the 1st and 10th order, respectively. The test values significantly indicate the existence of autocorrelation, ARCH effect exists in both the full sample and the group sample sequence, which meets the requirements of fitting GARCH model.

4.4 *GARCH model estimation with dummy variables*

Because the ARCH effect exists in the sample sequence, GARCH model can be used for effective regression. In this paper, the full sample regression is first used to analyze the overall impact of the epidemic on photovoltaic enterprises, and then the group sample regression is used to compare and analyze the impact of green finance on the value of photovoltaic enterprises under the background of the epidemic.

Table 5 shows the regression results of the full samples. In the table, the coefficient of the epidemic factor of the dummy variable is -0.015 and p value is 0.000, indicating that the coefficient of CN19 is significantly negative. In the regression model (1) is not significant, which has been eliminated here; The residual terms and GARCH terms in the table are significant, indicating that the regression results of GARCH (1,1) model are good. The ARCH effect of the full sample sequence has been eliminated after regression.

The regression results of group sample show that the coefficients of the support group (GF10) and the blank group (GF40) are −0.011 and −0.014, respectively, indicating that the samples of the support group are relatively less affected by the epidemic. In terms of P value, at 5% significance level, the blank group

is more significant, indicating that the blank group is more sensitive to epidemic factors. The ARCH effect test of the support group and the blank group can pass the test with the P value of 0.2219 and 0.5517. There is no ARCH effect in the support group and the blank group. When other conditions are equal, the support group is less affected by the epidemic than the blank group, which theoretically indicates that the value of photovoltaic enterprises supported by green financial policies is more stable during the epidemic period, and the green financial policies makes the enterprises have more survival strength in the face of black swan events. In the long term, green financial policies enable enterprises to have the ability of sustainable development (Lin Zou et al. 2019).

In conclusion, the height of the epidemic on China pv enterprises has significant negative effects, but the opportunities and challenges coexist, effective prevention measures and relative support policy making enterprises in the outbreak time presents the good development trend. The photovoltaic enterprises that had the support of the green financial development perform more steadier, which have the better ability of sustainable development.

5 CONCLUSIONS AND SUGGESTIONS

In this paper, GARCH model regression results are used to conclude that green finance is a completely favorable policy for photovoltaic enterprises. In the face of the epidemic, enterprises with policy support have a more stable performance in value. Part of the reason is that the enterprises supported by green finance have strong management capabilities, emergency management plans and funds, and they can also reasonably allocate production resources and realize effective capital turnover during the epidemic. The other reason is the capital gathering, investment orientation and scientific and technological innovation effect brought by green financial support, which enable these enterprises to have sufficient cash flow in the epidemic and thus maintain steady operation (Wang Zhiguo 2019).

Regardless of the impact of COVID-19, green finance is a rare opportunity for photovoltaic enterprises. However, the surprise of COVID-19 will make the government, enterprises and investors understand the important help of green finance policies for enterprises to fight risks, operate steadily and develop sustainably. In the post-epidemic era, this paper gives some suggestions on how the government should implement green financial policies, how the photovoltaic enterprises should seize the favorable policies, and how investors should distinguish the advantages and disadvantages of enterprises.

First, the government needs to strengthen the supervision of green credit and green bonds. It can cooperate with major financial institutions to create a unified information disclosure portal or add relevant columns to the existing portal for enterprises to learn about it. At the same time, a special group of green finance can be

Table 6. Comparison of GARCH model regression results of group sample after adding epidemic factors.

Variable	Coefficient	Std. Error	z-Statistic	Prob.
CN19	−0.011594	0.004592	−2.524946	0.011600
		GF10 Variance Equation		
C	0.000012	0.000006	1.939971	0.052400
RESID(−1)^2	0.114920	0.029805	3.855757	0.000100
GARCH(−1)	0.860343	0.030775	27.955560	0.000000

Variable	Coefficient	Std. Error	z-Statistic	Prob.
CN19	−0.014268	0.003563	−4.004169	0.000100
		GF40 Variance Equation		
C	0.000010	0.000006	1.589356	0.112000
RESID(−1)^2	0.092350	0.026647	3.465654	0.000500
GARCH(−1)	0.889402	0.032838	27.084830	0.000000

established to understand the financing needs of target enterprises and summarize experience and lessons.

Second, enterprises should take the initiative to understand the policy orientation, obtain financing information, actively fulfill social responsibilities, and further expand the reputation of enterprises to develop high-quality demanders.

Third, investors can understand the ESG rating data of photovoltaic enterprises through relevant databases. Different rating agencies have different rating methods, and investors can make comparative analysis. Under the guidance of policies, domestic enterprises begin to pay attention to the undertaking of corporate social responsibility. Some photovoltaic enterprises have shown outstanding performance in poverty alleviation projects, and investors can also focus on their ability to fulfill social responsibility and sustainable development.

Considering that this paper mainly focuses on the relationship between the epidemic factor, green finance and the value of photovoltaic enterprises, the subsequent research can start from the theory of stock price formation, and further analyze the mechanism of green finance's influence on the value change of photovoltaic enterprises in China under the background of the epidemic. At the same time, more factors affecting stock return could be included to explore the impact of green finance on the value changes of photovoltaic enterprises in different sizes, reputations and regions under the background of the epidemic.

REFERENCES

L. Alagappan and R. Orans and C.K. Woo. What drives renewable energy development? [J]. *Energy Policy*, 2011, 39(9): 5099–5104.

Anbao Tang, Fengyun Li, Financing constraints, government subsidies and investment efficiency of new energy enterprises: Based on heterogeneous bilateral stochastic frontier model [J]. *Industrial technical economy*, 2016, 35(08):145–153.

Bert Scholtens. Finance as a Driver of Corporate Social Responsibility[J]. *Journal of Business Ethics*, 2006, 68(1): 19–33.

Derrick. Financing mechanisms for renewable energy[J]. *Renewable Energy*, 1998, 15(1).

Gaofeng Gu. Outbreak of stock investment strategy under discussion [EB/OL]. (2020–03) [in the 2020–08]. https://mf.ecust.edu.cn/news/detail/cat/10/nav/xmxw/code/mfin.news.kx/id/2-4271338.

Jeucken Marcel. Sustainable Finance and Banking: The Financial Sector and the Future of the Planet[M]. *Taylor and Francis*: 2010-09-23.

Junwen Fu, Yongzhi Fan, Strategic thinking on building financial support system of energy industry [J]. *Soft Science*, 2007, pp. 92–101.

Liaqat Ali. Financing New and Renewable Sources of Energy [J]. *Economic and Political Weekly*, Vol. 16(20), 1981: 913–921

Liuqing Chen, Research on the development trend of new energy industry at home and abroad [J]. *Environmental Economy*, 2011, pp. 36–42.

X X Lu, Y Wang. On the fiscal and tax policy support system for developing low-carbon economy in foreign countries [J]. *Economic and Management Review*, 2012(2):13–21.

Severin Borenstein and Meghan R. Busse and Ryan Kellogg. Career Concerns, Inaction and Market Inefficiency: Evidence From Utility Regulation[J]. *The Journal of Industrial Economics*, 2012, 60(2): 220–248.

Steffen Jenner and Felix Groba and Joe Indvik. Assessing the strength and effectiveness of renewable electricity feed-in tariffs in European Union countries[J]. *Energy Policy*, 2013, 52: 385–401.

Yuan Zhao, Lisha Hao, World new energy policy framework and formation mechanism. *Resources Science*, 2005, (05):62–69.

Zhenzhi Zhao, Zhang Lu, Current situation and improvement suggestions of green financing of new energy enterprises [J]. *Modern commerce & trade industry*, 2020, 41(25):1–2.

Zhiguo Wang. Research on green finance supporting new energy industry development [D]. *Tianjin University of Finance and Economics*, 2019.

Y H Zhou, et al. "Government support and new industrial development: A case study of new energy." *Economic Research journal* 50.06(2015):147–161. doi: CNKI: SUN: JJYJ.0.2015-06-012.

L Zou, Li Y and Ren Y, et al. The impact of green finance policy on sustainable development of enterprises: a case study of Jiangsu province [J]. *Finance and Economics*, 2019, pp. 103–106.

Economic and Business Management – Huang & Zhang (Eds)
© 2022 Copyright the Author(s), ISBN: 978-1-032-06754-4

Study on the relationship between capacity regulation, internal control and economic benefits in China's iron and steel industry

Yu Chen
Nantong Institute of Technology Business School, Nantong, China

Xueyi Zhu
College of Economic Management, China University of Mining and Technology, Xuzhou, China

ABSTRACT: In recent years, the iron and steel industry has achieved satisfactory results in de-capacity. How this effect affects the economic benefits of listed companies in iron and steel industry is the goal of this paper. This paper collects the data of de-capacity index in iron and steel industry from 2013 to 2018, collecting the data of internal control and improving quality and efficiency of 32 listed companies in iron and steel industry from 2014 to 2018, and using regression analysis method to determine the impact of de-capacity and internal control on the economic benefits of listed companies in iron and steel industry. Empirical research shows that the 5-year task of de-capacity in the iron and steel industry has been completed in 3 years, which has promoted the ratio of return on common stockholder's equity of the iron and steel industry's superior companies to rise continuously; the bigger the internal control index of the listed companies in the iron and steel industry, the better the economic benefits of the company; under the background of de-capacity, the listed companies in the iron and steel industry have increased the sales revenue of products and accelerated the process of capital turnover and improving profitability will promote the economic efficiency of the company. The listed companies in the iron and steel industry should be guided by the world steel market demand, based on the high-quality transformation and development, enhance the scientific and technological attractiveness and innovation of iron and steel products, and lead the continuous, healthy, and high-quality development of the iron and steel industry.

Keywords: de-productivity; internal control; economic benefits; iron and steel listed companies.

1 RAISING QUESTIONS

The steel output produced by China's steel industry exceeds the effective market demand, which is known as "steel overcapacity." For more than 20 years, the Chinese government has made four efforts to adjust the steel overcapacity: (1) Adjustment of steel capacity in 1999: in August 1999, the State Economic and Trade Commission issued the Catalogue for The Prevention of Redundant Construction in Industrial and Commercial Investment (the first batch), which restricted redundant investment in 17 industries such as steel and coal, but the problem of redundant construction in steel and other industries was not completely under control. According to the data released by China's National Bureau of Statistics, steel production is mainly reflected by pig iron, crude steel, and steel output. In 1998, China's steel output was 341.60 million tons, and in 2002 it rose to 545.73 million tons, with an average annual increase of 12.4%. (2) Steel capacity adjustment in 2003: in 2003, the State Council of China successively issued proposals on restraining blind investment in iron, steel, cement, electrolytic aluminum and other industries, and called

for speeding up the restructuring of industries with overcapacity. The policy has played a role in regulating the balance of supply and demand in the steel market for several years. However, affected by the US financial crisis in 2008, the policy of "expanding domestic demand" implemented by the Chinese government accelerated again, this has further expanded the production capacity of steel, cement and other industries. In 2008, China's steel output reached 1.5859 billion tons, with an average annual increase of 16.6% based on that of 1998. (3) Steel capacity adjustment in 2009: on September 26, 2009, the State Council of China forwarded the Notice of Several Opinions on Curbing Overcapacity and Redundant Construction in Some Industries and Guiding the Healthy Development of Industries to further restrict the blind expansion of industries with overcapacity such as iron, steel and cement. The implementation of this policy has produced obvious effects. Although China's steel output reached 2.52992 billion tons by the end of December 2015, compared with the steel production base in 1998, the annual average increase rate is 12.5%, which is 4.1 percentage points lower than the previous stage 16.6% (1998–2008). (4) Steel capacity adjustment in

DOI 10.1201/9781003203704-20

2016: by the end of 2015, the Chinese government had measured specific data on steel overcapacity (Review and Trend Analysis Report of Iron and Steel Industry in 2018, no date). On February 1, 2016, the State Council issued document No. [2016]6 "Opinions on Eliminating Surplus Capacity in the Iron and Steel Industry and Achieving Development Without Distress," which states that "From 2016 onwards, the crude steel capacity shall be reduced by 100 million-150 million tons in five years." The macro-control target has been well implemented with the efforts of governments at all levels: During 2016–2018, the steel industry reduced its crude steel capacity by 65 million tons, 50 million tons (Fan, no date), and 30 million tons respectively (Iron and Steel Industry Will Continuously Consolidate Iron and Steel Production Achievements in 2019, no date). The country is expected to reach the goal of reducing 150 million tons of steel capacity by 2018, which is ahead of the schedule time 2020. From 2019 to 2020, China's iron and steel industry has reached a balance of supply and demand.

Looking back at the actual situation of the Chinese government's regulation of steel capacity, we cannot help but ask three questions: (1) Does the Chinese government's regulation of steel capacity undermine the function of the market in regulating steel capacity? No, it is the Chinese government's macro-regulation of steel production capacity which fits the changes of market supply and demand that makes up for the market regulation failure and makes the steel industry develop normally and healthily. Therefore, it is the "two hands" of the market and the government that are adjusting the changes of steel production capacity. (2) The market and the government have forced the steel industry to adjust its steel production capacity, and whether the steel enterprises have strengthened their internal management and control to absorb the adverse effects of external pressure or no? (3) The market and the government forced the iron and steel industry to adjust its iron and steel production capacity. Has the economic benefits of iron and steel enterprises been affected? In order to summarize the effective experience, reveal the deep-level problems and seek for a new way for the transformation and development of iron and steel enterprises, this paper collects the data of regulating the capacity of iron and steel industry in China from 2013 to 2020 and the actual data of strengthening internal control and improving quality and efficiency from 2014 to 2020.

2 RESEARCH STATUS OF ADJUSTING PRODUCTION CAPACITY AND STRENGTHENING INTERNAL CONTROL IN CHINA'S IRON AND STEEL INDUSTRY

2.1 Research status of regulating production capacity in China's iron and steel industry

On CNKI, we searched the contents of relevant periodicals with "De-productive Capacity" and "Iron and Steel Industry" as "title." The research results are as follows: Jia Shuaishuai et al. study the trend and de-productive effect of China's iron and steel prices under the background of de-capacity (Jia & Sun, 2017). It is concluded that the macro-control of iron and steel capacity in the iron and steel industry has achieved phased effects: The prices of relevant products have stabilized and rebounded, and the capacity utilization rate has improved. Deng Zhongqi et al. estimated the degree of overcapacity in China's steel industry and studied the effectiveness of the capacity reduction policy (Deng, Liu, & Pang, 2018). It is considered that the capacity utilization rate in most provinces and cities in China showed an upward trend first and then a downward trend from 2001 to 2016. China's capacity removal policy is effective in the short term, but the long-term effect is not obvious. Liu Xianwei et al. have studied the relationship between the efficiency of iron and steel industry and the development of high quality (Liu & Liu, 2019). It is considered that the efficiency of the iron and steel industry has achieved obvious results, and the overall benefit of the industry has increased steadily. However, the tasks of transformation and upgrading of the iron and steel industry and the development of high quality are still arduous. Lu Kefan has studied the capacity reduction measures of the steel industry in the United States (Lu, 2017). The enlightenment is that the steel industry must have the thinking and self-confidence of the international development strategy to meet the challenges of the domestic and foreign market environment. We should give full pay to the decisive role of the market and strengthen the main responsibility of the enterprise. We should coordinate, supervise, and guide the iron and steel industry to reduce production capacity; we should pay attention to overseas markets and promote international production capacity cooperation.

2.2 Research status of strengthening internal control in China's iron and steel industry

The research on internal control in China's iron and steel industry focuses on its relationship with economic benefits. Zhao Xiaoxi studied the structural adjustment and de-capacity of the iron and steel industry and believes that strengthening internal control can improve the internal management level and corporate governance structure and better form state-owned capital, an effective regulatory mechanism for production (Zhao, 2019). Wang Rui believes that iron and steel enterprises strengthen internal control, promote internal resource optimization, ensure and improve product quality, reduce production cost, accelerate capital flow, and increase enterprise profits (Wang, 2018). Hong Yuying believes that the de-productivity should first start from enterprise production and operation-procurement business (Hong, 2019). Reasonable and effective control of enterprise procurement business can ensure product quality, appropriately reduce enterprise procurement costs, and reduce procurement business risks, so as to increase enterprise operating profits and enhance enterprise value.

The above studies have gathered the focus of capacity adjustment of the steel industry: environmental background of capacity adjustment, capacity surplus test, the effect of capacity adjustment, price trend in capacity adjustment, international experience of capacity adjustment, etc. At the same time, steel enterprises under external pressure study the relationships between strengthening internal control and improving economic efficiency. These studies have a good guiding effect on the transformation and development of Chinese steel enterprises. However, it is necessary to further study the relationships between regulating iron and steel production capacity and strengthening internal control, and the joint effect of regulating capacity and strengthening internal control on the economic benefit of iron and enterprises.

The report of the 19th National Congress of the Communist Party of China proposed for the first time the construction of a modern economic system. Through the transformation of development mode, optimization of economic structure, and transformation of growth momentum, China can achieve the high-quality economic development from the high-speed economic growth. The marginal contribution of the article is to propose that listed companies in the steel industry should base on high-quality transformation and development, enhance the innovation of steel products, establish a performance-centric internal control evaluation system, and promote the continuous, healthy, and high-quality development of the steel industry.

3 RESEARCH DESIGN

3.1 Research mechanism analysis and research frame design

The relationship between capacity adjustment, internal control and economic benefits of China's iron and steel industry is highlighted in two aspects: one is that the Chinese government regulates the capacity, which forces the iron and steel enterprises to strengthen internal control. From the macro-control level, the government has solved the problem of balance between supply and demand of iron and steel production capacity, which brings the following benefits: eliminating backward production capacity, such as banning inferior steel, rapidly occupying the market with high-quality production capacity, and improving the supply environment; at the same time, the balance of supply and demand of iron and steel production is realized, and the price of iron and steel returns to the rational level, which provides an orderly and equal competitive environment for iron and steel enterprises. Second, from the level of iron and steel enterprises, enterprises reduce the output of iron and steel, focus on improving the quality of products, to provide better products for the market; at the same time, the internal departments of the enterprise reduce the level of material consumption, back-calculate the product cost as the control standard, control the product cost to the minimum limit, so as to reduce the output without reducing the sales income, reduce the output without reducing the profit level, so as not only to reduce the economic benefits but also improve the operating efficiency from the whole management mechanism inside the enterprise. Therefore, see Figure 1 for the mechanism and research framework of adjusting production capacity, strengthening internal control and economic benefits.

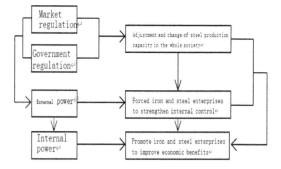

Figure 1. Mechanism relationship and research framework of regulating production capacity, strengthening internal control and economic benefits in iron and steel industry.

3.2 Setting and evaluation of adjustable production capacity index in China's iron and steel industry

3.2.1 Setting indicators from the perspective of market regulation

From the point of view of market regulation of iron and steel capacity, market demand for iron and steel capacity is the basis of iron and steel production. The market includes domestic market and foreign market; product production includes product output growth and product inventory. Therefore, the following three indicators should be designed:

First, the growth rate of steel production. It refers to the ratio of the increase in steel output of the current year over the previous year to the steel output of the previous year. According to the data released by China's National Bureau of Statistics, steel output is reflected by the total of pig iron, crude steel, and steel products.

The second is the growth rate of steel inventory. It refers to the ratio of the amount increased by the inventory balance of iron and steel products in the current year over the previous year to the inventory balance of iron and steel products in the previous year. In order to reflect the inventory of all iron and steel products, the State Bureau of Statistics of China regularly publishes the inventory cost data of "finished products" of ferrous metal smelting and rolling processing enterprises (reflected in 100 million yuan). Ferrous metal smelting and rolling processing enterprises are an industry under the category of manufacturing industry. In fact, they are iron and steel production enterprises.

Third, the growth rate of net export of steel. The products exported by China's iron and steel industry mainly fall into three categories: pig iron and mirror iron, billet and rough forgings, and steel. Steel products imported by China are mainly steel. Exports minus imports equal net exports. In order to correspond to the export product index, the author selects "net export growth rate of steel" as an important index for the iron and steel industry to adjust production capacity. The net export volume of steel refers to the net amount of steel export quantity minus steel import quantity. The growth rate of net export of steel refers to the ratio of the increase in net export of steel in the current year over the previous year to the net export of steel in the previous year.

3.2.2 Setting indicators from the angle of government regulation

From the point of view of government regulation and control of iron and steel production capacity, the government will issue steel production capacity regulation documents and take measures, which will inevitably change the whole society's iron and steel production capacity. Therefore, the following indicators are set as a sign of whether the government's regulation of iron and steel production capacity is effective (followed by the indicator sequence number in 3.2.1).

Fourth, steel capacity regulation. Before 2016, i.e., 2014–2015 selected in the paper, China's iron and steel overcapacity was with a value of 1; from 2016 onwards, in the year when the government's capacity reduction task is completed, the index is taken as 0. On the contrary, if it is taken as 1, the value from 2016 to 2020 will be 0. The adjusted capacity index data of China's iron and steel industry from 2013 to 2020 collected and sorted according to the above indicators are shown in Table 1.

It can be seen from Table 1 that under the regulation of market and government, the annual average increase rate of China's steel output in 2013–2020 is only 3.32%, which is 2.32% lower than the annual average increase rate of China's GDP in the same period. The annual average inventory of finished products of iron and steel enterprises is decreasing by 1.85%, which indicates that the inventory is decreasing continuously; net steel exports are declining, with an average annual decline of 5.1%. Therefore, except that the net steel export volume of China's steel industry is affected by the "trade war" of the western countries, other adjustment and control indicators of the steel industry are in good trend, and the government has achieved the expected target.

3.3 Setting and evaluation of intensified internal control index for listed companies in China's iron and steel industry

In order to evaluate the internal control level of the enterprise, in 2011, the first professional organization with internal control and risk management as its main business direction, Debo Enterprise Risk Management Technology Co., Ltd. was established in Shenzhen. The company has established a DIB database. The database reflects the internal control and risk management of Chinese listed companies on the basis of foreign Audit Analytics Database. Among them, the "internal control database" is created by the independent research of DIBO Big Data Research Center. From the perspective of internal control of five elements (internal environment, risk assessment, control activities, information and communication, internal supervision), it designs and constructs nine sub-databases such as internal control evaluation information database and internal control index database. It objectively reflects the internal control level of listed companies in China, and is the first and most professional authoritative internal control information database in China. It has been recognized by high-end professionals in the field of internal control research in China, and has been widely used (Chi, 2011). The author refers to the "internal control index" of 32 listed companies in the iron and steel industry from 2014 to 2020 in the DIB database, divides the internal control index of each listed company by 100, and obtains a new internal control index less than 1, so as to match with the following model data. From 2014 to 2020, the average value of internal control index of listed companies in China's iron and steel industry (divided by 100) is shown in Table 2.

It can be seen from the data in Table 2 that the internal control index of the iron and steel industry is U-shaped from 2014 to 2020, and the overall effectiveness is continuously increasing, with an annual increase of 1.39%.

3.4 Model settings

3.4.1 Setting of the explained variable

The economic benefits of listed companies in China's iron and steel industry can be reflected by setting a "return on net assets" index. Because the shareholder of a listed company is the owner of the company, the net income obtained by the company every year (period) belongs to the owner through the indicator of "net assets" (also known as "owner's equity"), and the "return on net assets" reflects the goal that the shareholder of the company pursues "maximization of owner's equity." This indicator is reflected by ROE.

3.4.2 Interpreting variable settings

The first is the production index of iron and steel capacity, which refers to the output of iron and steel produced by iron and steel enterprises and their growth, and is reflected by the "growth rate of iron and steel output" (GrSteel); the second is that the government regulates the steel capacity index, which is reflected by the "steel capacity regulation and control degree" (RegSteel); the third is the internal control index, which is reflected by the internal control index (IntContr).

3.4.3 Adjust variable settings

Regulatory variables are variables that regulate the relationship between a dependent variable and an independent variable. The steel industry regulates capacity

Table 1. 2013–2020 adjusted capacity indicators of China's iron and steel industry.

				Market regulation				
Year	Total steel production (10,000 tons)	Steel production growth rate (%)	Finished product inventory of iron and steel enterprises (Billion Yuan)	Steel inventory growth rate (%)	Net export steel (10,000 tons)	Net export growth rate of steel (%)	Government regulation Steel capacity regulation
	1	2=this year 1/last year 1	3	4=this year 3/ last year 3	5	6=this year 5/last year 5	7
2013	260664.31		2782.87		4825		
2014	266118.53	2.09%	2835.13	1.88%	7935	64.46%	1
2015	252992.21	−4.93%	2429.09	−14.32%	9962	25.55%	1
2016	255801.72	1.11%	2461.06	1.32%	9531	−4.33%	0
2017	263078.07	2.84%	2508.76	1.94%	6211	−34.83%	0
2018	284178.80	8.02%	2298.00	−8.40%	5616	−9.58%	0
2019	300848.21	5.87%	2276.96	−0.92%	5199	−7.43%	0
2020	327718.30	8.93%	2305.90	1.27%	3344	−35.68%	0
Annual increase	3.32%	–	−1.85%	–	−5.10%	–	–

Data source: Annual China Statistical Yearbook; Inventory data of "ferrous metal smelting and calendering industrial enterprises" and "finished products" determined by iron and steel enterprises in China Statistical Yearbook.

Table 2. 2014–2020 average internal control index of listed companies in China's iron & steel industry.

Year	2014	2015	2016	2017	2018	2019	2020	Annual increase rate (%)
Internal control index (Reduced 100 times)	0.6462	0.601	0.5323	0.5834	0.5818	0.5367	0.7022	1.39%

Data source: Dibo database (http://www.dibdata.cn).

in addition to controlling the source of steel production (reflected by "Steel output growth rate"), domestic steel market effective need (reflected by "steel production capacity control degree"), but also to observe the inventory of steel products, because the supply exceeds the demand, the products that cannot be sold out will be left in the warehouse and increase the inventory, using InvSteel as the adjusting variable can reflect its special relationship with the economic benefits of iron and steel enterprises; at the same time, the change of production capacity in steel industry is also affected by the international environment. The relationship between net steel export and the economic benefits of steel enterprises is investigated by using "net steel export growth rate" (ExpSteel) as the adjustment variable.

3.4.4 Setting of control variables
The economic benefits of listed companies in China's iron and steel industry are not only influenced by externally regulated production capacity but also influenced by internal control factors (Wang, 2018). The control indicators include: (1) total asset growth rate (GroAsset), which is a symbol of the expansion of production scale. (2) The growth rate of operating income (GroReven) is the premise and foundation for the survival and development of enterprises. (3) Total Asset Turnover (AssetTur) is a measure of a company's

capital operating capacity (performance). (4) Net operating cash flow per share (CashFlow) is an indicator of a company's cash flow level (performance). (5) Sales Cost Rate (ReveCost), which is the proportion of operating costs in operating revenue, reflects the consumption of product costs incurred by the enterprise in creating operating revenue. The less the cost consumption in the enterprise's product revenue, the better the economic benefit of the enterprise.

3.4.5 Model construction
Based on the above analysis, the following two models are set up for regulating the production capacity and strengthening the relationship between internal control and economic benefits in China's iron and steel industry:

(1) Explain the variable model, see model 1:
$$ROE = \alpha 0 + \alpha 1 GroSteel + \alpha 2 RegSteel + \alpha 3 IntContr + \alpha 4 GroAsset + \alpha 5 GroReven + \alpha 6 AssetTur + \alpha 7 CashFlow + \alpha 8 RevCost$$
(Model 1)

(2) Adjust the variable model, see model 2:
$$ROE = \beta 0 + \beta 1 InvSteel + \beta 2 ExpSteel + \beta 3 IntContr + \beta 4 GroAsset + \beta 5 GroReven + \beta 6 AssetTur + \beta 7 CashFlow + \beta 8 RevCost$$
(Model 2)

Table 3. Model variable definition table.

	Variable name	Symbol	Variable definition
Explained variable	Return on net assets	ROE	Current net profit ÷ [(owner's equity at the beginning of the year + owner's equity at the end of the year) ÷ 2]
	Growth rate of steel production	Greyscale	The growth rate of steel production in Table 1 is allocated to each listed company by year
Explain variable	Regulation degree of steel production capacity	System	In Table 1, the regulation degree of steel production capacity is allocated to each listed company by year
	Internal control index	IntContr	"Internal control index" of each company in DIB database ÷ 100
Moderator variable	Inventory growth rate of iron and steel products	InvSteel.	The inventory growth rate of iron and steel products in Table 1 is allocated to each listed company by year
	Growth rate of net export of steel	Exposure	In Table 1, the growth rate of steel net export is allocated to each listed company by year
	Growth rate of total assets	Greyscale	Total assets at the end of the period ÷ total assets at the beginning of the period – 100%
	Growth rate of operating revenue	GroReven	Current operating income ÷ previous operating income – 100%
Control variable	Total asset turnover (Times)	AssetTur	Current operating income ÷ total assets at the end of the period
	Net operating cash flow per share	CashFlow	Net cash flow from current operating activities ÷ total equity at the end of the period
	Cost of sales ratio	RevCost	Current operating cost ÷ current operating income
Dummy variable	Year	Year	Seven annual dummy variables are set according to the sample from 2014 to 2020 They are respectively allocated to 32 listed companies in the iron and steel industry

3.4.6 *Model variable definition*

The definitions of variables determined from model 2 of model 1 above are shown in Table 3.

4 MODEL APPLICATION

4.1 *Sample selection and data sources*

The explaining variables and adjustment data related to steel capacity in Table 3 are sourced from Table 1, and the internal control index is sourced from the DIB database; the explained and controlled variables are taken from the 2014 to 2020-year balance sheet, profit statement and cash flow statement of 32 listed companies in the iron and steel industry (excluding "St Fushun" company) from the website of "zhongcai.com" from 2014 to 2020.

4.2 *Descriptive statistics*

Descriptive statistics are carried out according to the constructed model, model 2 and the collected sample data. The results are shown in Table 4.

From the descriptive statistics in Table 4, the average net asset profit rate of 32 listed companies in the steel industry in 2014–2020 is 0.0704; the average growth rate of steel output is 0.0337; the average degree of regulation of iron and steel capacity is 0.1507; the average internal control index is 0.6126; the average growth rate of steel product inventory is −0.0250; the average net export growth rate of steel is 0.0015; the average growth rate of total assets is 0.1178; the average

growth rate of operating income is 0.2179; the average turnover rate of total assets is 0.9457; the average net operating cash flow per share is 0.8947; the average cost of sales rate is 0.8900. All variable values are in the normal range.

4.3 *Regression analysis*

See Table 5 for regression results of models 1 and 2 of factors affecting economic benefits of 32 listed companies in China's iron and steel industry from 2014 to 2020.

Table 5. Regression analysis of influencing factors Model 1 and Model 2 of economic benefits of Chinese iron and steel listed companies from 2014 to 2020.

It can be seen from the regression results in Table 5 that the significance coefficients of all independent variables of models 1 and 2 to the explained variable "return on net assets" are less than 0.1 except the growth rate of operating income is greater than 0.1 (0.737 and 0.583, respectively), that is, seven of the eight independent variables of model 1 or model 2 in Table 5 pass the significance test. The specific analysis based on the regression results of model 1 is as follows:

(1) The analysis of the adjustment index of steel production capacity: The growth rate of steel output is significantly positively correlated with the net asset return rate of listed companies in the steel industry at the level of 5%, that is, the listed companies in the steel industry effectively control the steel output so that it meets the demand of the steel market. The stronger the demand, the more the output increases, and the better

Table 4. Descriptive statistics of sample variables.

	N	Minimum value	Maximum	Average	Standard deviation
Return on net assets	219	−0.9688	1.4669	0.0704	0.2245
Growth rate of steel production	219	−0.0493	0.0893	0.0337	0.0441
Steel capacity adjustment	219	0.0000	1.0000	0.1507	0.3586
Internal control index	219	0.0000	0.9816	0.6126	0.1924
Inventory growth rate of iron and steel products	219	−0.1432	0.0194	−0.0250	0.0596
Growth rate of net export of steel	219	−0.3568	0.6446	0.0015	0.3291
Growth rate of total assets	219	−0.6855	9.6652	0.1178	0.6924
Growth rate of operating revenue	219	−0.9743	27.5218	0.2179	1.8902
Total asset turnover	219	0.1167	2.4643	0.9457	0.4126
Net operating cash flow per share	219	−1.7764	5.7810	0.8947	0.8877
Cost of sales ratio	219	0.6713	1.3959	0.8900	0.0821
Valid n (listwise)	219				

Table 5. Regression analysis of influencing factors Model 1 and Model 2 of economic benefits of Chinese iron and steel listed companies from 2014 to 2020.

Variable	Explained variable: Return on net assets	
	Explaining Variable Model 1	Moderator Variable Model 2
Constant	1.002***	0.977***
	(6.920)	(7.105)
Growth rate of steel production	0.607**	
	(2.267)	
Steel capacity regulation	−0.051*	
	(−1.655)	
Growth rate of steel products inventory		0.330*
		(1.801)
Growth rate of net steel exports		−0.124***
		(−3.654)
Internal Control Index	−0.254***	−0.235***
	(−4.427)	(−4.179)
Total Assets Growth Rate	−0.030*	−0.026*
	(−1.892)	(−1.668)
Growth rate of operating income	−0.002	−0.003
	(−0.337)	(−0.550)
Total Asset Turnover	0.155***	0.151***
	(5.460)	(5.485)
EPCF	0.059***	0.061***
	(4.577)	(4.843)
Ratio of Sales to Cost	−1.106***	−1.066***
	(−7.668)	(−7.714)
N	218	218
R2	0.532	0.553
Adj R2	0.514	0.536
F Value	29.810***	32.448***

Note: The value in brackets is T coefficient; ***, **, * represent significance levels of 1, 5, and 10%, respectively.

the economic benefits of the enterprise. The regulation degree of iron and steel production capacity is significantly negatively correlated with the return on net assets of listed companies in the iron and steel industry at the level of 10%, that is, the greater the regulation degree of the government on the iron and

steel production capacity, the more the restriction on the production of the iron and steel products of the listed companies, the worse the economic benefits of the enterprises.

It should be noted that the adjustment variables "steel product inventory growth rate" and "steel net export growth rate" are significantly related to the economic benefits of listed companies in the steel industry, and the correlation coefficients are 1.801 and −3.654, respectively, but the correlation degree is lower than the correlation coefficient 2.367 of the steel output growth rate and the correlation coefficient −1.655 of the steel output capacity control degree. This indicates that the explanatory variables "steel output growth rate" and "steel production capacity control degree" play a main role in the economic benefits of listed companies in the steel industry, and the adjustable variables "steel product inventory growth rate" and "steel net export growth rate" play a supplementary role in the economic benefits of listed companies in the steel industry.

(2) The internal control index was negatively correlated with ROA at 1% level. This indicates that under the background of external compression of steel production capacity, if the internal control of listed companies in the steel industry is more rigid, the internal economic vitality will be smaller, and the economic benefits of enterprises will be worse.

(3) The turnover rate of total assets and the net cash flow per share were significantly positively correlated with the rate of return on net assets at the level of 1%. This shows that in the background of government and market regulation of steel production capacity, enterprises can bring positive benefits by accelerating capital turnover and increasing net cash flow per share.

(4) The growth rate of total assets, cost of sales, and return on net assets are significantly negatively correlated. This shows that in the context of the government and the market regulating steel production capacity, the expansion of asset scale and lax cost control will reduce the economic benefits of enterprises. Regression analysis also shows that the growth rate of operating income is negatively correlated with

117

the return on net assets, but it is not significant. This shows that the excess capacity of iron and steel and the increase of sales of iron and steel products will reduce the market price and affect the economic benefits of enterprises.

5 ROBUSTNESS TEST

In order to test the reliability of the research conclusion of the model and avoid the occurrence of endogenous variables, the robustness of the model should be carried out. The most commonly used test method of robustness in economic management is "variable substitution method." The thesis chooses "return on asset return rate" to replace the explained variable "net asset return rate" in models 1 and 2, and explaining variables, adjustment variables, and control variables remain unchanged. The results obtained through regression analysis are shown in Table 6.

It can be seen from the robustness test in Table 6 that "return on total assets" is used to replace "return on net assets" for regression analysis. After the test of model 1, the nature of positive and negative correlation of variables (number of indicators) has not changed; six passed the significance of independent variables among eight, only the "total asset growth rate" significance coefficient 0.919, greater than 0.1, did not pass the significance test, which may be the reason that both the control variable and the explained variable have the "total asset" indicator. The regression results of model 1 are robust and reliable. From the robustness results of model 2, the properties of positive correlation and negative correlation are only "total." The positive and negative directions of other variables do not change; the significance of the eight independent variables passed five (the original model 2 passed seven), and the total asset growth rate and the steel product inventory growth rate did not pass the significance test, which may be caused by the co-linearity of "total asset" and "inventory commodity" in the control variables and the explained variable "total asset." But in general, the regression results of model 2 are robust and reliable.

6 INTERMEDIATE VARIABLE TEST

Both models 1 and 2 are set with "internal control index" explanatory variables. Whether this indicator is a "intermediary variable" needs to be tested: if the "internal control index" is used as the dependent variable, and the steel output growth rate, steel capacity control degree, steel product inventory growth rate, and steel net export growth rate are used as the independent variables, the "internal control index" is used as the intermediary variable. See Table 7 for inspection results.

From the results of regression analysis in Table 7, it can be seen that the "regulation degree of steel production capacity" and "growth rate of steel net export"

Table 6. Robustness test results of Models 1 & 2 of Chinese listed iron & steel companies from 2014 to 2020.

Variable	Explained variable: Return on net assets	
	Test the results of model 1	Test the results of model 2
Constant	0.385***	0.393***
	(10.922)	(11.492)
Growth rate of steel production	0.176**	
	(2.702)	
Steel capacity regulation	−0.013*	
	(−1.714)	
Growth rate of steel products inventory		0.016
		(0.348)
Growth rate of net steel exports		−0.029***
		(−3.404)
Internal Control Index	−0.025***	−0.023*
	(−1.816)	(−1.634)
Total Assets Growth Rate	−0.0004	0.0001
	(−0.102)	(0.021)
Growth rate of operating income	−0.001	−0.001
	(−1.010)	(−1.053)
Total Asset Turnover	0.058***	0.058***
	(8.351)	(8.499)
EPCF	0.006***	0.006***
	(1.980)	(2.087)
Ratio of Sales to Cost	−0.426***	−0.433***
	(−12.136)	(−12.607)
N	218	218
R2	0.659	0.661
Adj R2	0.646	0.648
F Value	50.813***	51.095***

Note: The value in brackets is T coefficient; ***, **, * represent significance levels of 1, 5, and 10%, respectively.

are significantly correlated with the internal control index at the levels of 5% and 10%, respectively, indicating that the Chinese government's regulation of the domestic steel market and the changes in the international environment of steel products have a significant effect on the strengthening of internal control measures of iron and steel enterprises. The growth rate of iron and steel output is positively correlated with the internal control index of listed companies in the iron and steel industry, but it is not significant. The growth rate of iron and steel product inventory is negatively correlated with the internal control index of listed companies in the iron and steel industry, but it is not significant. The two significantly correlated T coefficients totaled 4.295 (2.353 + 1.942) is much greater than the total T coefficient of two insignificant correlations −0.319 (0.043-0.361), that is, the significant correlation accounts for the main body, so the "internal control index" is an intermediary variable, that is, the government and the market regulate the iron and steel production capacity, promote the iron and steel enterprises to strengthen internal management, and then promote the improvement of enterprise economic benefits.

Table 7. Results of intermediary variable test of Models 1 and 2 of Chinese steel listed companies from 2014 to 2020.

Variable	Explained variable: Return on net assets	
	Test the results of model 1	Test the results of model 2
Constant	0.599*** (33.936)	0.610*** (43.401)
Growth rate of steel production	0.012 (0.042)	
Steel capacity regulation	−0.086* (2.353)	
Growth rate of steel products inventory		−0.800 (−0.361)
Growth rate of net steel exports		0.078* (1.942)

7 RESEARCH CONCLUSIONS AND ENLIGHTENMENT

7.1 Study conclusion

(1) From 2013 to 2020, China's iron and steel industry achieved good results in adjusting production capacity: from 2013 to 2015, the growth rate of China's total iron and steel output continued to decline; from 2016 to 2020, the 5-year task of reducing iron and steel production capacity determined by the Chinese government was completed in only 3 years, the supply and demand relationship in the iron and steel market rebounded steadily, and the growth rate of iron and steel products inventory of iron and steel enterprises continued to decline. However, the deficiency is that the growth rate of net steel export also shows a downward trend affected by the international "trade war" (Hong, 2019).

(2) From 2014 to 2020, China's iron and steel industry regulated production capacity to promote the listed steel companies to strengthen internal management, and improved the level of internal control by stimulating internal vitality to absorb the external adverse effects. From 2014 to 2020, the internal control index of listed companies in China's iron and steel industry rose continuously in, with an average annual increase of 1.39%, which laid a foundation for the high-quality transformation and development of the iron and steel industry and the further improvement of economic benefits.

(3) From 2014 to 2020, the listed companies in China's iron and steel industry will not seriously affect the economic benefits due to the government's regulation of excess capacity. On the contrary, the government's "retreat for progress" policy provides good conditions for enterprises to transform the economic benefit mechanism (Chi, 2011). The outstanding performances are as follows: the total asset turnover of listed companies in the iron and steel industry is accelerating, the net operating cash flow per share is increasing, and the sales cost rate is declining. These achievements have brought "positive energy" to the improvement of economic benefits of listed companies in China's iron and steel industry (Zhu, 2017): the average net asset profit margin of 32 listed companies has increased from - 1.25% in 2014 to 9.31% in 2020.

7.2 Study enlightenment

Under the pressure of the Chinese government and the market to regulate the iron and steel production capacity, there are three main strategies for Chinese iron and steel enterprises: one is to deal with the dialectical relationship between the "retreat and advance" of the iron and steel production capacity: remove the backward production capacity such as inferior steel and reduce the excess capacity and high energy consumption capacity of oversupply (Zhu & Zhu, 2019). This is the performance of "retreat," but it improves the supply quality of steel products and promotes the internal transformation of iron and steel enterprises. It is cost-effective for iron and steel enterprises to exchange temporary "pain" for long-term "effect" (Zhu & Zhu, 2021). Second, we should dissolve the unfavorable factors into favorable factors (Ren, 2017). In the face of all kinds of adverse effects caused by the external regulation of production capacity, the key point of the iron and steel enterprises is to establish and implement the internal control system, which is the fundamental plan of the long-term development of the company (Gao & Zhu, 2021). Third, we should grasp the relation between supply and demand of steel product market: when the external market, including the international market, exceeds demand, the focus of our work is not only to reduce steel production capacity, but also to improve the quality of supplied products; when the supply of steel products is less than the demand, it is not only necessary to increase the supply at any time but also to highlight the scientific and technological attraction and innovation of steel products, so that the steel industry can develop continuously, healthily, and with high quality (Lv & Zhu, 2020).

ACKNOWLEDGMENT

Fund Project: Jiangsu Province "13th Five-Year Plan" Key Construction Discipline Project (SJY 201609); Jiangsu province university of humanities social science off-campus research base-Tonghu industry coordinated development research base project (project number: SJSZ 201716); The Fourth Economic Census of Nantong Bureau of Statistics (JP2006).

REFERENCES

Chi, G. (2011) 'Function Positioning and System Construction of Internal Control Index of Chinese Listed Companies', *Management World*, (6), pp. 172–173.

Deng, Z., Liu, M. and Pang, R. (2018) 'Study on Estimating Overcapacity of China's Iron and Steel Industry and Effectiveness of Capacity Removal Policy', *Journal of China University of Geosciences (Social Science Edition)*, 18(6), pp. 131–142.

Fan, R. (2018) Target Determination of Steel and Coal Capacity in 2018. Available at: http://www.80sd.org/caijing/2018/03/05/26564.html (Accessed: 5 March 2018).

Gao, Y. and Zhu, X. (2021) 'Study on the Relationship between Production Capacity and Economic Benefit in the Steel Industry', *Price Theory and Practice*, (2), pp. 64–67.

Hong, Y. (2019) Research on Internal Control of Purchasing Business of Y Steel Company.

Iron and Steel Industry Will Continuously Consolidate Iron and Steel Production Achievements in 2019 (2019) Ministry of Industry and Information Technology. Available at: http://www.360kuai.com/pc/9eb3522f8cd7cd99b? cota=4&sign=360_57c3bbd1&refer_scene=so_1. (Accessed: 9 January 2019).

Jia, S. and Sun, H. (2017) 'Research on the Trend of China's Iron and Steel Price under the Background of Production Capacity', *Price Theory and Practice*, (9), pp. 64–67.

Liu, X. and Liu, L. (2019) 'Research on Production Efficiency and High Quality Development of Iron and Steel Industry', *Economic Review*, (2), pp. 41–48.

Lu, K. (2017) 'Measures to Remove Capacity of American Iron and Steel Industry and Enlightenment', *Macroeconomic Studies*, (10), pp. 108–112.

Lv, Y. and Zhu, X. (2020) 'A Study on the Relationship between Production Capacity, Risk Avoidance and Stock Value - A Case Study of Steel Listed Companies', *Wuhan Finance Monthly*, (12), pp. 57–63.

Ren, J. (2017) 'The Impact of China's Iron, Steel and Coal Production on Employment: An Empirical Analysis Based on Input-Output Table', *Macroeconomic Studies*, (10), pp. 83–91.

Review and Trend Analysis Report of Iron and Steel Industry in 2018 (2019) Docin. Available at: https://www.docin.com/p-2230103233.html (Accessed: 15 July 2019).

Wang, R. (2018) 'Discussion on the Construction of Internal Control in Iron and Steel', *Metallurgical Financial Accounting*, (11).

Zhao, X. (2019) 'Deepening the Reform of the Management System of State-owned Enterprises and Releasing the Innovation Vitality', *Volkswagen Investment Guide*, (11).

Zhu, L. (2017) Study on Supporting Theory and Operational Efficiency of Capitalization of Coal Resources. B*eijing: China Economic Publishing House*.

Zhu, L. and Zhu, X. (2019) 'Energy policy, market environment and the economic benefits of enterprises: evidence from China's petrochemical enterprises', *Natural Hazards*, 95(12), pp. 113–127.

Zhu, L. and Zhu, X. (2021) 'Pry Effect of Coal Industry Capacity Removal and Asset Structure Adjustment on Coal Economy', *Resources Science*, 43(2), pp. 316–327.

Economic and Business Management – Huang & Zhang (Eds)
© 2022 Copyright the Author(s), ISBN: 978-1-032-06754-4

Political economic capacity traps on the development of Indonesia's international hub ports

Zamroni Salim*
Research Center for Economic, National Research and Innovation Agency (BRIN), Indonesia
(ORCID: 0000-0002-8028-0860)

ABSTRACT: Investment in seaport development is crucial to support economic growth, especially in the countries experiencing under-investment infrastructure problems. Political economic traps exist in Indonesia to develop its international hub ports (IHPs). Solid and continuous political will and business–government collaboration to develop integrated IHPs are still in question under the traps of imbalance cargoes, inadequate infrastructure facilities, and lack of proper industrial zones. The country also faces a development dilemma as a seaport is a sensitive national security and sovereignty issue and causes the pressures for the national government to reluctantly deliver the projects to private sectors even though the country has been under-investment in the maritime sector.

Keywords: International Hub Port; Political Economic Capacity Traps; Indonesia; Development Dilemma

1 INTRODUCTION

Competitiveness of seaports initially stems from economies of scale based on primary production factors (capital, land, labor) to economies of scale based on advanced production (service) factors [1]. Improvement in the quality of port infrastructure and its supporting industries would bring the most significant benefits to the economy and provide crucial nodes for global production networks, trade [2], [1] the creation of added value and employment in related sectors [3]. Investment in the transportation sector is significant to support growth, especially in countries experiencing infrastructure problems [4].

Seaport development is crucial for Indonesia as the largest archipelago country in the world. The president of the Republic of Indonesia, Mr. Joko Widodo, has promoted seaports to foreign direct investment (FDI) since his first lead in 2014 under the Global Maritime Fulcrum (GMF) policy. Under the second phase of his administration (2019–2024), Mr. Joko Widodo has taken earnest invitations to foreign investors followed by adequate regulations.

This paper examines the political economic capacity traps on the development of Indonesia's international hub ports (IHPs). The paper discusses the planning and running of projects, including the problems and dilemmas that may exist. From the political economic capacity traps, two strategic IHP development projects in Indonesia are analyzed, i.e., Kuala Tanjung and Bitung IHPs.

2 POLITICAL ECONOMIC CAPACITY TRAPS

Indonesia, as a lower middle-income country (lower-middle income with a gross national income (GNI) per capita of $3,870 as of July 1, 2021, compared to the previous status as upper-middle-income with a GNI per capita of $4,050 last year [5]), needs to pay attention to the middle-income trap primarily related to infrastructure development. Infrastructure is critical to get out of the middle-income trap [6]. The quality and level of cooperation between the government and the private sector determine the innovation capabilities, the increasing domestic production, and the country's ability to avoid the income trap [7]. Once the country is trapped, it is not easy to upgrade its level to the upper-middle-income class [4].

The country needs to enable efficient and dynamic targeted policy interventions to increase regional competitiveness and avoid the trap [4]. In addition, the country also needs longer solid political will and business–government collaboration [8]. Indonesia has lost more than 1% of additional gross domestic product (GDP) growth due to under-investment in infrastructure, and problems with transportation are among the worst obstacles [9].

Political economic capacity traps are related to design policy with medium and long-term seaport development time preferences. The capacity trap in this study is adapted from the capacity traps of security by Takeuchi, Murotani, and Tsunekawa [10]; in this study, the capacity trap is directed to the capacity of a country in designing integrated seaports development. The political economic capacity trap problem involves

---

*Corresponding Author

DOI 10.1201/9781003203704-21

a vicious circle between the lack of capacity to establish continued seaport development and the difficulty in establishing sustainable economic growth.

2.1 Political trap: continuing political supports

Seaport development is ideally supported by continuous political legitimacy. Under the GMF, the seaport development program only lasted in the first period of Joko Widodo's administration (in 2014–2019), then disappeared in his second presidency (2019–2024). The GMF was only a political clause that echoed at the beginning of the government and not supported by a strong brand strategy; it was not an R&D-based policy concept [11]. The GMF was a popular maritime policy without a clear strategy and was not properly delivered by the relevant ministries and government agencies. Joko Widodo's high-cost maritime industry policy is still in the planning stage and unclear enough to be implemented [12].

The GMF is to improve the country's inter-island connectivity, which aligns with China's 21st Belt Road Initiative (BRI) to have global maritime connectivity [13]. The absence of sustainable political support means that the change of government has not been accompanied by the continuation of the previous development program. Efforts to develop the maritime sector began with the MP3EI Program in 2011. The project started running, but when the previous administration ended, the MP3EI stopped suddenly and was replaced politically by the GMF in 2014.

The political capacity traps of seaport development are associated with the legitimate policy for marine infrastructure development. It is only based on lucratively political slogans [14], the absence of sustainable political support, and not based on R&D and mature national policies.

2.2 Economic traps: partial IHP development

IHP development must be an integrated development in the maritime industry that connects various supporting seaports (peripheries) and various industrial centers in the surrounding areas. The underlying concept of this development is a supply- and-demand-based business. The surrounding areas in the region must also grow and develop together to keep the supply and demand and the balance cargoes (unloading and loading activities) of the IHP.

Development of IHP needs comprehensive business calculation and R&D-based policy concepts. It also needs attention to the demand and supply of potential products and services across borders, supporting industrial zones in the vicinity regions and seaport interchange connections with international shipping lines.

To improve its inter-islands and global connectivity, Indonesia needs to develop IHP and transshipment ports to attract cargo volumes. Integration of IHP, its spokes, other supporting hinterland facilities, and manufacturing in the regions can support domestic and international trade [15], [16]. The efficiency and effectiveness of seaports depend on how these seaports are connected to global value chains in the global transshipment network and with hinterland transportation [15].

The operation of an IHP in a particular area has a positive economic impact on regional development. Even though the results of seaport development do not always provide equal positive economic impacts for each area/region or country, it depends on many determinants such as complexity in seaport reforms, coordination between local and regional, institutional coordination [17]. Other determinants of regional economic growth must also be considered, such as human capital and investment in R&D that support the implementation of new technological advancements to increase the effectiveness, efficiency, and general competitiveness of IHP operations [18].

The IHP is not a partial development from the surrounding regions; the manufacturing industry should grow around the hub ports. If the supply–demand business in transshipment principle is achieved (with the balance cargoes), the IHP has succeeded in adapting its functions as the agent of change in the country's economy.

The economic capacity trap often comes with partial seaport development. The government often sees seaport infrastructure as just physical construction and pays less attention to the carrying capacity of the supporting industrial zones in the hinterlands [19].

3 KUALA TANJUNG AND BITUNG IHP PROJECTS

Indonesia is on the way to build IHPs to complement the existing international ports (Belawan, Tanjung Priuk, Tanjung Perak and Makassar) due to their limited capacities. So, the government is trying to develop new IHPs, namely Kuala Tanjung, Bitung and Sorong (Papua). In this study, Kuala Tanjung and Bitung which are two of the three new IHPs developed under the National Strategic Project (Decree of the Indonesian Minister of Transportation Number KP 432, 2017) are analyzed.

3.1 Kuala Tanjung IHP

The Kuala Tanjung IHP is being built since 2015 as an ambitious maritime project of President Joko Widodo to develop Indonesia as a GMF. Kuala Tanjung IHP multipurpose terminal has a container capacity of 600,000 TEUs (twenty-foot equivalent units), and the liquid and dry bulk capacity reached 3.4 million tons and 1.5 million tons, respectively [20]. The Kuala Tanjung IHP has not significantly accompanied the special economic zone (SEZ) Sei Mangkei as an integrated IHP development [21].

The government has assigned a state-owned enterprise, Pelindo, and Indonesia Asahan Aluminium to start the projects to improve maritime connectivity, logistics centers, industrial and regional development.

Pelindo I has invited investors to join the operation, where the business scheme offered is the sale of management rights (right to operate) to potential investors with a period of 15–20 years. So far, prospective investors entering Kuala Tanjung are from the Netherlands (Port of Rotterdam Authority) and China (Zhejiang Provincial Seaport Investment & Operation Group Co. Ltd) [23].

3.2 Bitung IHP

Bitung IHP was also part of the GMF project. Pelindo IV controls Bitung IHP and several ports in Eastern Indonesia. Bitung SEZ is designed as an industrial, export, and logistic development zone by utilizing Bitung IHP as the entrance and exit point for domestic and cross-border trade.

Bitung IHP has not played a significant role in the Asia-Pacific region yet [24]. The existence of international shipping companies can be used as an indicator of the success of the port development. For example, Maersk Line – Sea Transportation Company – Cargo which serves the Bitung route and connects it with other countries (exports–imports) started in 2014, but then in 2016, Maersk Line has started to reduce its operations [25], [26] and finally, the company stopped its operations in Bitung in 2017. This withdrawal shows that Bitung has not been an ideal IHP yet. The existing international shipping lines, both to Indonesia via Surabaya and Jakarta and Australia via the Maluku Sea and the Sulawesi Sea, have not seen Bitung Port as a destination/transit point for international shipping. Bitung Port is just a docking yard for national/inter-island shipping lines, especially from Maluku and South and Southeast Sulawesi.

The political trap comes up with the facts that maritime development projects are no longer a national strategic project, in Indonesia's corridors as a GMF [14] and inefficient sea highway programs (by subsidies) [27]. The economic trap occurs as their respective SEZs have not yet run as proper supporting industries [21]. There are not enough supporting industries in the vicinity areas in Sumatera Island, except for some CPO processing industries. So does the Bitung SEZ [24]. The IHP can operate well if it is supported by industrial zones to meet the supply and demand of cargo (balanced cargoes) services for international shipping lines.

Figures 1 (Kuala Tanjung IHP) and 2 (Bitung IHP), taken on August 16, 2021, show the flows of no significant international shipping lines during the pandemic to and from the hub ports. For comparison, see other shipping lines that involve other routes in the Ports of Singapore and Malaysia across the Malacca Strait. The pictures explain that there has been no international shipping line that serves except for regular national ships that stop by. It means that supply and demand between loading and unloading port services and users of international shipping services do not occur at these ports yet.

From the analysis of the two IHPs, we can wrap up that IHP development in Indonesia is inseparable from

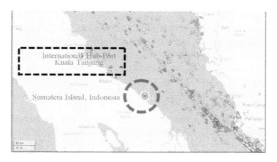

Figure 1. Shipping line across Kuala Tanjung international hub port. Source: [22].

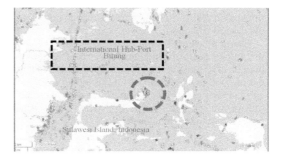

Figure 2. Shipping line across Bitung international hub port. Source: [22].

the development of hinterland and inter-island connectivity. They need support from industrial development in the surrounding areas. Moreover, IHP connectivity with international shipping lines is purely a business activity based on supply and demand, not a political slogan without a strong and continuous political will.

4 PROBLEMS AND IHP DEVELOPMENT DILEMMA

Privatization is a way to reduce the macroeconomic problems of crowding out; relying solely on state enterprises could cause private (foreign) investors' reluctance to enter into integrated seaport development. The methods to finance the seaport development projects from the MP3EI to GMF were available in the markets, but the most preferred one by the Government of Indonesia was the framework for public–private partnerships (PPPs) [28].

However, the PPP has not created a substantial infrastructure output and services yet, and the progress remains slow with less ability to attract investment because of the challenges in their implementation and coordination [9] and the limited capacity of domestic banks [16]. It is necessary to assess the PPP scheme and review the share of ownership and responsibility among the stakeholders. Planning and building an IHP need to pay attention to the demand and supply of products, traffic of international shipping lines, national and international fleet readiness, industrial support zones, and logistics activities in remote areas [29]. Overall, regulations and institutions are the most binding constraint to economic growth due to the lack of strategic alignment, weak supervision, overlapping institutional responsibilities with corruption, and bureaucratic inefficiency [30], [31].

There are some dilemmas in building seaports in Indonesia. On the one hand, Indonesia requires large investment funds; on the other hand, the seaport is a sensitive national security and sovereignty issue. As such, the cooperation of the GMF and BRI has been highlighted as economic cooperation in maritime development and trade and about naval power presence and international influence of China in the international arena [32], [33]. The same perspective has been the case for Indonesia.

The government's reluctance to open wider FDI in the seaport sector in Indonesia can be seen from the high level of government ownership, the limited number of foreign ownership of no more than 49% [34], and the view that privatization causes the government to lose control of the sea transportation sector which poses a risk to national sovereignty.

5 CONCLUSIONS

Political economic traps exist in Indonesia when the country has been developing its national strategic projects of Kuala Tanjung and Bitung IHPs. A political capacity trap occurs because maritime development projects are no longer a national strategic project under GMF policy, inefficient sea highway programs, and other infrastructure policies. There has been no solid and continuous political will and business–government collaboration to develop integrated IHP. The economic trap can be identified by the absence of international shipping lines anchored at the two IHPs. With the under-investment status, the ambitious IHP projects face the economic capacity traps of imbalance cargoes, the existing SEZ not functioning properly, regional insufficient infrastructure facilities, and lack of industrial areas in supporting hinterlands. The country also faces a seaport development dilemma, as foreign investment in seaports is a sensitive national security and sovereignty issue. This dilemma pressures the national government to be reluctant to open the projects properly to private sectors even though the country has been under-invested in the IHP development. Indonesian government should make long-term sustainable maritime development policies that can ensure that the change of presidency does not mean the termination of maritime development policies. The policy must emerge as laws or higher regulations that guarantee its sustainability. While considering national security, the PPP scheme should be reviewed and the share of private sector ownership should be increased to make maritime infrastructure development more attractive to investors.

REFERENCES

[1] J. Monios and G. Wilmsmeier, "Between path dependency and contingency: New challenges for the geography of port system evolution," *J. Transp. Geogr.*, vol. 51, pp. 247–251, 2016.

[2] Z. H. Munim and H.-J. Schramm, "The impacts of port infrastructure and logistics performance on economic growth: the mediating role of seaborne trade.," *J. Shipp. Trade*, vol. 3, no. 1, 2018.

[3] M. H. Yudhistira and Y. Sofifiyandi, "Seaport Status, Access, and Regional Development in Indonesia," *Work. Pap. Econ. Bus.*, vol. V, no. 1, 2016.

[4] European Commission, "Falling into the Middle-Income Trap: A Study on the Risks for EU Regions to be Caught in a Middle-Income Trap. *Final Report*, Contract No. 2018CE16BAT055," 2020.

[5] Bloomberg, "Indonesia Loses Upper-Middle Income Status Amid Pandemic," *Bloomberg*, Aug. 07, 2021.

[6] S. Setiawan, "Middle Income Trap and Infrastructure issues In Indonesia: A Strategic Perspective," Int. J. *Econ. Financ. Issues*, vol. 7, no. 4, pp. 42–48, 2017.

[7] E. Kang, Nahee & Paus, "The Political Economy of the Middle Income Trap: The Challenges of Advancing Innovation Capabilities in Latin America, Asia and Beyond," J. *Dev. Stud.*, 2019.

[8] R. Doner and B. Schneider, "The Middle-Income Trap More Politics than Economics," *World Polit.*, vol. 1, no. 37, 2016.

[9] World Bank, "Indonesia: Avoiding The Trap." Development Policy Review 2014, *World Bank*, Jakarta, 2014, [Online]. Available: https://www.worldbank.org/content/dam/Worldbank/document/EAP/Indonesia/Indonesia-development-policy-review-2014-english.pdf.

[10] S. Takeuchi, R. Murotani, and K. Tsunekawa, "Capacity Traps and Legitimacy Traps: Development Assistance and State Building in Fragile Situations," in Catalyzing Development: A New Vision for Aid, & J. W. Kharas H., Makino K., Ed. *Brookings Institution Press*, 2011, pp. 127–154.

[11] E. Laksmana, "Indonesia as 'Global Maritime Fulcrum': A Post-Mortem Analysis Asia Maritime Transparency Initiative." CSIS, 2019, [Online]. Available: https://amti.csis. org/Indonesia-As-Global-Maritime-Fulcrum-a-Post-Mortem-Analysis/.

[12] L. Suryadinata, "The Growing 'Strategic Partnership' Between Indonesia and China Faces Difficult Challenges," 2017.

[13] A. Lalisang and D. S. C. Candra, "Indonesia's Global Maritime Fulcrum & China's Belt Road Initiative A match made at sea?," *Friedrich-Ebert-Stiftung (FES)*, 2020.

[14] A. N. P. Pikoli, "Critical Analysis of Indonesia's Global Maritime Fulcrum under Joko Widodo: Problems and Challenges," *Publik (Jurnal Ilmu Adm.*), vol. 10, no. 1, 2021.

[15] O. Merk, "The Competitiveness of Global Port-Cities: Synthesis Report," 2013. doi: https://dx.doi.org/10.1787/5k40hdhp6t8s-en.

[16] C. Duffield, S. Wahyuni, D. Parikesit, K. Hui, and S. Wilson, "Potential Infrastructure Enhancements for Ports and Cities: Conclusions, Future Research and Policy Concepts," in Infrastructure Investment in Indonesia: A Focus on Ports, 1st ed., S. (Ed.. Duffield, C (Ed.). Hui, K (Ed.). Wilson, Ed. Open Book Publishers, 2019, pp. 327–341.

[17] M. Brooks, "A new direction or stay the course? Canada's port-specific challenges resulting from the

port reform program of the 1990s," *Res. Transp. Bus. Manag.*, vol. 22, pp. 161–170, 2017.

[18] G. Mudronja, A. Jugović, and D. Škalamera-Alilović, "Seaports and Economic Growth: Panel Data Analysis of EU Port Regions," *J. Mar. Sci. Eng.*, vol. 8, no. 12, p. 1017, 2020.

[19] T. Herdian, "Pembangunan Tujuh Pelabuhan Indonesia sebagai Hub Internasional," *Supply Chain Indonesia*, 2019.

[20] Bisnis, "Pemerintah Tetapkan 7 Pelabuhan Hub, Ini Respons Asosiasi Logistik Indonesia," *Jakarta*, Feb. 17, 2019.

[21] A. A. Baeha, "Optimalisasi Kelembagaan KEK dalam Pengelolaan KEK Sei Mangkei Berdasarkan Peraturan Pemerintah Nomor 29/2012 tentang KEK Sei Mangkei," *Theses, Universitas Sumatera Utara*, 2018.

[22] Marinetraffic.com, "Marine Traffic," *Data accessed 2021-08-16*, 2021. marinetraffic.com (accessed Aug. 16, 2021).

[23] Maritime Coordinating Minister of Indonesia, "Kemenko Marves Kawal Realisasi Investasi di Pelabuhan dan Kawasan Industri Kuala Tanjung," *Maritime Coordinating Minister of Indonesia*, 2020. https://maritim.go.id/kemenko-marves-kawal-realisasi-investasi-pelabuhan-kawasan-industri/ (accessed Aug. 01, 2021).

[24] KSP, "KSP Temukan Permasalahan di KEK Bitung.," 2020. https://ksp.go.id/ksp-temukan-permasalahan-di-kek-bitung.html.

[25] S. Hidayat et al., "ASEAN - China Connectivity Development," *Jakarta*, 2016.

[26] Supply Chain Indonesia, "Pengapalan Langsung: 2017, Pelindo IV Siap Luncurkan Tiga Direct Call," Dec. 02, 2016. https://supplychainindonesia.com/pengapalan-langsung-2017-pelindo-iv-siap-luncurkan-tiga-direct-call/.

[27] Bisnis.com, "Dinilai Tidak Efisien, DPR Belum Setuju Kelanjutan Program Tol Laut," Jun. 19, 2019.

[28] J. Kaur, "Evaluating Port Reform in Indonesia: A case study of the Ports of Tanjung Priok and Tanjung Emas," *Murdoch University*, 2018.

[29] H. Nur, T. Achmadi, and K. Mercy, "Analysis of Seven International Indonesian Hub Ports Policy Development Impact on Shipping and Port Sector," in Analysis of Seven International Indonesian Hub Ports Policy Development Impact on Shipping and Port Sector, 2020, p. 557.

[30] Z. Salim, "Indonesia's Ways to Sustainable Economic Growth and Development," in *Handbook of Emerging Economies*, I. R. L. (Edt), Ed. Routledge, 2014.

[31] M. Hidayat, A. N. Saputro, and B. F. Maula, "Indonesia Growth Diagnostics: Strategic Priority to Boost Economic Growth," 2018.

[32] M. Duchâtel and A. S. Duplaix, "Blue China: Navigating the Maritime Silk Road to Europe." *European Council on Foreign Relation*, 2018.

[33] G. Nabbs-Keller, "The contending domestic and international imperatives of Indonesia's China challenge," *Aust. J. Def. Strateg. Stud.*, vol. 2, no. 2, pp. 189–214, 2020.

[34] Z. Salim, N. Pranata, and A. Tobing, "Maritime Logistics In ASEAN: An Investment Guidebook," *Jakarta*, 2017. [Online]. Available: http://www.habibiecenter.or.id/img/publication/f1bf617f99aab572b9518f2bf7fb8e39.pdf.

Economic and Business Management – Huang & Zhang (Eds)
© 2022 Copyright the Author(s), ISBN: 978-1-032-06754-4

Hospitality and tourism under COVID-19: A bibliometric analysis

Shan (Anna) Wang & Jose Weng Chou Wong*

Faculty of Hospitality and Tourism Management, Macau University of Science and Technology, Taipa, China

ABSTRACT: The purpose of this paper is to explore the knowledge infrastructure of tourism research under COVID-19 based on a bibliometric analysis. Two hundred and seventy articles published in hospitality and tourism journals are applied to examine tourism research distribution in the era of COVID-19 by using the software HistCite. The findings of bibliometric analysis involve authors, journals, institutions, countries, and trending development in this field. The results revealed eight research themes: (1) marketing promotion under crisis, (2) human rights, (3) hospitality workforce, (4) travel and lifestyle change, (5) e-tourism, (6) sustainability, (7) travel risk and perception, and (8) tourism education. The identification of COVID-19 research draws attention on research gaps and future opportunities.

1 BACKGROUND

Tourism is one of the most fundamental sections for the economic growth of the regions (Ivanov & Webster, 2007). Since the first reported case of COVID-19 in 2019, the tourism industry has been changed globally from both micro- and macro-perspectives in a few months (Xu et al., 2020). Tourists feel insecure to travel during COVID-19 (Neuburger & Egger, 2020). For example, Shamshiripour, Rahimi, Shabanpour, and Mohammadian (2020) reported that people's travel habits have changed as COVID-19 experienced several stages.

In the beginning, researchers focused on the effects of COVID-19 on the hospitality and tourism fields (De Vos, 2020). At present, researchers have extended their studies from different perspectives, such as tourist attitude (Bae & Chang, 2020), hospitality employees (Lai & Wong, 2020), city crisis management (Stephens et al., 2020). Because the research related to COVID-19 has a growth trend, there is a need for researchers to understand core knowledge which will help them to have an overview in this field.

To achieve the objective of this study, a bibliometric analysis by HistCite will be introduced in the next section "Methodology," to find highly cited articles in this field after classifying articles published in hospitality and tourism field from Web of Science. Next, in the "Results" section, the researcher's institutions, journals, and countries distribution will be presented in the table format to identify the overall situation of COVID-19 tourism research. Third, citation analysis and research themes will be discussed. Finally, this paper will present the conclusion and implications.

---
*Corresponding Author

2 METHODOLOGY

The bibliometric analysis is to systematically classify articles within journals, themes, publication years, authors, institutions, and explore research performance (Okumus, Koseoglu, & Ma, 2018). Generally, the bibliometric analysis consists of three steps: data selection, citation analysis, and content analysis. This methodology section will introduce the first step. All articles are selected from Web of Science database, imported to HistCite, and citation content is analyzed. Researchers firstly input keywords "COVID-19" in the Web of Science and categorize them into hospitality, leisure, and tourism fields. Other forms of articles, such as conference proceedings and books, are not included in this study. Bibliometric analysis in this review includes the most cited 30 articles to explore its research trending. All citation analyses based on articles are updated before April 11, 2021. For the second (citation analysis) and third steps (content analysis), the Result section will present them.

3 RESULT

This section firstly presents the descriptive analysis, including trending articles, top 10 institutions involved in COVID-19 tourism research, followed by SSCI (Social Science Citation Index) journals. In addition, it includes citation analysis of trending articles. By content analysis, researcher quantified the research presence and summarized the research themes. We identified 270 tourism articles relevant to COVID-19 in total. Thus, statistics, ranking, and tables are outlined in the following paragraphs.

3.1 Top 10 trending articles

Table 1 provides the most cited 10 articles with local citation score (LCS), global citation score (GCS), local citation reference (LCR), and citation reference (CR). The articles were sorted by local citation scores (LCS) because this allows researchers to locate literature quickly in a field and find out what is the most relevant article in the latest literature and research direction. This trending article lists by LCS identify both where the topic of this study came from and where it is going to, thus, demonstrating a significant influence on COVID-19 research.

Table 1. Top 10 trending articles.

No.	Title	LCS	GCS	LCR	CR
1	Pandemics, tourism and global change: a rapid assessment of COVID-19	63	292	0	118
2	Pandemics, transformations and tourism: be careful what you wish for	26	79	1	133
3	Effects of COVID-19 on hotel marketing and management: a perspective article	25	43	1	57
4	Hospitality, tourism, human rights and the impact of COVID-19	18	37	0	32
5	COVID-19's impact on the hospitality workforce—new crisis or amplification of the norm?	12	22	1	95
6	Reset redux: possible evolutionary pathways towards the transformation of tourism in a COVID-19 world	11	40	1	21
7	COVID-19: potential effects on Chinese citizens' lifestyle and travel	11	45	0	71
8	COVID-19: from temporary de-globalization to a re-discovery of tourism?	9	32	0	28
9	From high-touch to high-tech: COVID-19 drives robotics adoption	9	35	0	57
10	Lessons from COVID-19 can prepare global tourism for the economic transformation needed to combat climate change	8	33	1	39

3.2 Descriptive analysis of COVID-19 research

To include more specific analysis of COVID-19 research in tourism field, this study firstly identified section of "where" and "who." In other words, it is significant to know where the COVID-19 research came from and who studied them. Table 2 shows the top 10 institutions where COVID-19 research with records (Recs), total local citation score (TLCS), and total global citation score (TGCS) were published. Hong

Table 2. Top 10 institutions.

No.	Institution	Recs	TLCS	TGCS
1	Hong Kong Polytech Univ	12	7	89
2	Univ Cent Florida	10	0	19
3	Kyung Hee Univ	9	3	22
4	Univ Johannesburg	9	41	111
5	Univ Greenwich	8	5	16
6	Univ Surrey	8	89	400
7	Griffith Univ	7	0	9
8	Sejong Univ	7	1	4
9	Sun Yat Sen Univ	6	0	39
10	Univ Queensland	6	12	34

Table 3. Top 10 countries.

No.	Country	Recs	TLCS	TGCS
1	USA	74	31	204
2	Peoples Republic of China	49	54	245
3	UK	48	142	621
4	Australia	37	61	288
5	South Korea	25	9	70
6	Canada	19	103	499
7	Spain	18	7	74
8	New Zealand	17	110	440
9	Italy	13	12	86
10	South Africa	10	41	128

Kong Polytech University has the most studies (12), followed by University Central Florida (10) and Kyung Hee University (9).

Table 3 summarizes geographical locations of COVID-19 research. USA (74) is the most frequent research destination, followed by China (49) and UK (48), showing that the results are consistent with previous research that USA and China are the top two areas focusing in COVID-19.

Table 4 shows all SSCI journals with COVID-19 topic. Among these, the most published journals are International Journal of Hospitality Management (62), followed by Current Issues in Tourism (45) and Tourism Geographies (30).

3.3 Citation analysis

Aiming to figure out the research stream, this study uses HistCite™to conduct the core structure and analyze content from interrelated articles. HistCite shows 30 articles and the links between them which are most cited, indicating their importance in COVID-19 research. The number of articles which have the most LCS is shown in Table 1. For example, the article with highest citations is "Pandemics, tourism and global change: a rapid assessment of COVID-19," published by Gössling, Scott, and Hall (2020). This article has 63 LCS, 292 GCS, and 118 CR. Therefore, this paper can be considered as the most important and central article in COVID-19 field.

Table 4. SSCI Journals with COVID-19 topics.

No.	Journal	Recs	TLCS	TGCS
1	International Journal of Hospitality Management	62	0	145
2	Current Issues in Tourism	45	7	132
3	Tourism Geographies	30	103	507
4	International Journal of Contemporary Hospitality Management	24	76	145
5	Journal of Sustainable Tourism	17	63	312
6	Tourism Economics	12	0	23
7	Leisure Sciences	8	0	12
8	Sport in Society	6	1	10
9	Tourism Review	6	11	45
10	Journal of Hospitality and Tourism Management	5	4	13
11	Tourism Management Perspectives	5	0	27
12	Annals of Tourism Research	4	0	51
13	European Sport Management Quarterly	4	0	2
14	Journal of Destination Marketing & Management	4	0	7
15	Journal of Hospitality & Tourism Research	4	0	2
16	Tourism Management	4	0	37
17	Information Technology & Tourism	3	7	30
18	International Journal of Sport and Exercise Psychology	3	0	18
19	International Journal of Tourism Research	3	1	14
20	Journal of Travel Research	3	0	7
21	Leisure Studies	3	0	1
22	Journal of Sport and Health Science	2	0	21
23	Journal of Travel & Tourism Marketing	2	0	0
24	Psychology of Sport and Exercise	2	0	6
25	Communication & Sport	1	0	0
26	International Review for The Sociology of Sport	1	0	7
27	Journal of Hospitality Marketing & Management	1	0	0
28	Journal of The Philosophy of Sport	1	0	0
29	Journal of Vacation Marketing	1	0	0
30	Scandinavian Journal of Hospitality and Tourism	1	0	0
31	Sport Education and Society	1	0	7
32	Sport Psychologist	1	0	0
33	Tourist Studies	1	0	0

According to the topics and contents of these most cited 30 articles, they can be classified as two research hotspots. Hotspot A (articles cited from No. 1 in Table 1) discussed the strategic development of tourism issues and risk perception under COVID-19. These authors argue that tourism under COVID-19 has been transformed, thus tourists' risk perception improves to a greater level. Most articles under this hotspot are conceptual articles. Hotspot B (articles cited from No. 2 in Table 1) discussed tourism sustainability under COVID-19. Also, most articles under this category are conceptual articles.

Although research hotspots are found by the HistCite network, there is a need to identify more specific themes, so that scholars can understand the core knowledge and direction for future research.

3.4 Research themes

The results of hotspot help us to identify eight research themes: (1) marketing promotion under crisis, (2) human rights, (3) hospitality workforce, (4) travel and lifestyle change, (5) e-tourism, (6) sustainability, (7) travel risk and perception, and (8) tourism education. Marketing management articles discussed hotels and tourism marketing management practices under COVID-19. For example, Jiang and Wen (2020) discussed artificial intelligence, hygiene, cleanness, and health care are main practices during COVID-19. Human rights include articles of the right to participate in activities during COVID-19. For example, Baum and Hai (2020) revealed that the rights to participate in hospitality and tourism have been challenged, especially in parts of Asia, Europe, and North America. Hospitality workforce includes employees' intention and attitude toward working in the sensitive environment. Travel and lifestyle change refer to tourists' intention to go to travel and their change in travel habits. E-tourism refers to articles of online tourism with high-tech skills which can avoid people's contact. Articles of sustainability include climate change, environmental sustainability under COVID-19, and tourism recovery after COVID-19. Travel risk and perception include people's psychological activities, and these articles mostly apply quantitative analysis to study their perception to travel. Tourism education includes the change in education formats during COVID-19 as most education institutions changed their courses with online classes.

4 DISCUSSION AND CONCLUSION

COVID-19 has brought huge impact in hospitality and tourism field, and an increasing number of COVID-19 research in hospitality and tourism field has been transformed. At the beginning of COVID-19, researchers pay attention on tourism issues of COVID-19 and its difference than past crisis. With the development of COVID-19, more research focuses on tourists' risk perception and workers' perception to hospitality and tourism field. Then, more researchers pay attention on pandemic and epidemic, discussing tourism recovery strategies.

The results demonstrate the potential of bibliometric analysis on tourism literature and provide insights of COVID-19 research structure. Eight research themes are identified: (1) marketing promotion under crisis, (2) human rights, (3) hospitality workforce, (4) travel and lifestyle change, (5) e-tourism, (6) sustainability, (7) travel risk and perception, and (8) tourism education. These research themes provide a broader perspective and are likely to increase in future research. Also, the results identified the major scholar communities and helped the readers to understand social structure of COVID-19 research. Third, the results help researchers to know research frontier by authors and trending articles, which are likely to be the focus of future research. Fourth, there are many conceptual articles with geography, climate, and resilience. These studies more likely focus on the period before COVID-19 epidemic, thus signifying the great opportunity that connects these fields with post-COVID-19 era.

The findings have implications for COVID-19 research as well as the study of knowledge development in this field. In tourism, bibliometric analysis by HistCite provides comprehensive view of the research structure and insights of authors, communities, and trending works. Second, the trends and insights provide opportunities for future research, which suggests future research could follow theoretical way to analyze post-COVID-19 issues and sustainable recovery strategies.

Despite these contributions, this study also has its limitations. First, the use of software "HistCite" may have limitations. A single database of WoS may not be comprehensive. In the future study, researchers can consider other software with several databases. Second, the results may have limitations. The results of this study are from HistCite and researchers' analysis. For future research, expert group or other software (e.g., VOSviewer) can be applied to robust the results. Third, this study included published articles until April 2021. In the future study, it is necessary to repeat bibliometric analysis after COVID-19 has completely gone.

ACKNOWLEDGMENT

The research is supported by Higher Education Fund of the Macao S.A.R. Government (TET-MUST-2020-03).

REFERENCES

Bae, S. Y., & Chang, P.-J. (2020). The effect of coronavirus disease-19 (COVID-19) risk perception on behavioural intention towards 'untact'tourism in South Korea during the first wave of the pandemic (March 2020). *Current Issues in Tourism*, 1–19.

Baum, T., & Hai, N. T. T. (2020). Hospitality, tourism, human rights and the impact of COVID-19. *International Journal of Contemporary Hospitality Management*.

De Vos, J. (2020). The effect of COVID-19 and subsequent social distancing on travel behavior. *Transportation Research Interdisciplinary Perspectives, 5*, 100121.

Gössling, S., Scott, D., & Hall, C. M. (2020). Pandemics, tourism and global change: a rapid assessment of COVID-19. *Journal of Sustainable Tourism, 29*(1), 1–20.

Ivanov, S., & Webster, C. (2007). Measuring the impact of tourism on economic growth. *Tourism Economics, 13*(3), 379–388.

Jiang, Y., & Wen, J. (2020). Effects of COVID-19 on hotel marketing and management: a perspective article. *International Journal of Contemporary Hospitality Management*.

Lai, I. K. W., & Wong, J. W. C. (2020). Comparing crisis management practices in the hotel industry between initial and pandemic stages of COVID-19. *International Journal of Contemporary Hospitality Management*.

Neuburger, L., & Egger, R. (2020). Travel risk perception and travel behaviour during the COVID-19 pandemic 2020: a case study of the DACH region. *Current Issues in Tourism*, 1–14.

Okumus, B., Koseoglu, M. A., & Ma, F. (2018). Food and gastronomy research in tourism and hospitality: A bibliometric analysis. *International Journal of Hospitality Management, 73*, 64–74.

Shamshiripour, A., Rahimi, E., Shabanpour, R., & Mohammadian, A. K. (2020). How is COVID-19 reshaping activity-travel behavior? Evidence from a comprehensive survey in Chicago. *Transportation Research Interdisciplinary Perspectives, 7*, 100216.

Song, H., & Witt, S. F. (2006). Forecasting international tourist flows to Macau. *Tourism Management, 27*(2), 214–224.

Song, H., Wong, K. K., & Chon, K. K. (2003). Modelling and forecasting the demand for Hong Kong tourism. *International Journal of Hospitality Management, 22*(4), 435–451.

Stephens, E. H., Dearani, J. A., Guleserian, K. J., Overman, D. M., Tweddell, J. S., Backer, C. L., … Bacha, E. (2020). COVID-19: crisis management in congenital heart surgery. *World Journal for Pediatric and Congenital Heart Surgery, 11*(4), 395–400.

Xu, B., Gutierrez, B., Mekaru, S., Sewalk, K., Goodwin, L., Loskill, A., …Cobo, M. M. (2020). Epidemiological data from the COVID-19 outbreak, real-time case information. *Scientific data, 7*(1), 1–6.

Economic and Business Management – Huang & Zhang (Eds)
© 2022 Copyright the Author(s), ISBN: 978-1-032-06754-4

The effect of video attributes on memorable short video experience and intention to visit: The case of tiktok

Xiaopeng (Bella) Bai & Fang Hong*
Faculty of Hospitality and Tourism Management, Macau University of Science and Technology Taipa, Macau, China

ABSTRACT: In the era of experience economy, memorable experiences have received substantial attention in the last decade. As one of the most influential determinants attracting tourists in the destination, the studies of tourists' experience are increasing significantly. However, the studies of online experience are still underexplored, especially incorporating the emerging phenomena of short video. Hence, this study attempts to examine the short video attributes that influence memorable short video experience. This study proposed a conceptional model based on the existing literature, and the survey will be performed on potential tourists who have watched short video of popular city, Chongqing. PLS-SEM will be utilized to testify the proposed hypotheses. Given that there are few studies related to memorable experience on short video, this study will expand the understandings of theory and provide practical guidelines to destination managers.

1 INTRODUCTION

With the development and maturity of the tourism market, the competition among destinations has become more and more fierce, especially among the homogenized products (Hudson & Ritchie, 2009). As Pine and Gilmore (1998) mentioned, "experiences" become the fourth economic offering in addition to commodities, goods, and services. Destinations are therefore paying more attention to distinguish themselves by providing pleasant and memorable experiences, and to build their own unique competitiveness (Deutsch & Pierce, 2014; Kim, 2018).

With the advancement of information technology, potential tourists can gain experience by exploring the destinations through internet, and the presence of information is not limited with texts and pictures. For example, the high-speed WiFi makes potential tourists to acquire intuitionistic destination information via short videos on smartphone, which are thereby affecting their travel decisions (Dwityas & Briandana, 2017). At the same time, the rich information on internet has also brought tourism destinations big challenges. The insipid video styles and unstructured designs are now difficult to attract the attention of potential tourists (Pan, 2011). Therefore, it is important to provide the memorable short video experience to attract potential tourists.

However, the current research on memorable tourism experiences (MTEs) mainly focus on the actual experience stage of during and after the travel. The studies on pre-travel stage, especially on the online

experience of short videos, are still unclear (Kim, Ritchie & McCormick, 2012; Wong, Lai & Tao, 2019). Moreover, previous studies have indicated that the visual, musical, and cultural attributes of short video stimulate the senses and memory of potential tourists and have the direct impact on their behavioral intentions (Kim, 2014; Rajaguru, 2014). Therefore, the purpose of this research is to examine the effect of above attributes on potential tourists' memorable short videos experience and its consequences of intention to visit.

The contributions of this study are threefold. First, this study examines the factors of short video attributes that are extracted from existing literature. Second, this study contributes to the theory of memorable tourism experiences by enriching its content with online experience. Third, the results of this study provide implications for video producers and DMO managers that creating memorable short videos should be in three aspects: visual, music and culture. To increase the destination competitiveness, they should come up with strategies to gain view flows and attract potential tourists.

2 THEORETICAL BACKGROUND AND HYPOTHESIS DEVELOPMENT

2.1 The construct of short video attributes

2.1.1 Visual effect
When the potential tourists watch the destination short video, the visual factors can effectively convey the destination image, which has an important impact on

---

*Corresponding Author

the potential tourists' experience perception (Montgomery, 2010). For example, in one destination, the presented magnificent landscape, local architecture, and interesting activities will all provide potential tourists with a distinctive visual enjoyment, making them have a memorable video experience or subsequent behavioral intention for the destination (Wan et al., 2020). Therefore, it is important for tourism market to make effective use of visual effects and fully present destination experience (Stepchenkova & Zhan, 2013).

Based on the existing literature, we argued that memorable short video should take visual effect into account. In addition, the attractiveness of visual effect can also be improved through the color and clarity, which are conducive to enhance potential tourists' memorable experience and visit intention (Fei, Jiang & Mao, 2017).

2.1.2 *Music effect*

Music is an auditory image composed of sound structure. It is an artistic form that expresses people's thoughts, feelings, social reality, and it is also one of the most instantly touching art forms (Deutsch & Pierce, 2014).

Music is considered as probably the most stimulating component of a video and can be a key "catalyst" (Hecker & Marketing, 1984). Music in short video has ability to create potential tourists a memorable experience atmosphere and evoke wonderful feelings or pleasures (Oh, Ahn & Baek, 2015). Moreover, Su (2011) further indicated that local music can be used to attract tourists to the place of origin if it is successfully raised to the level of imagery (Hudson et al., 2015).

Based on the existing literature, this study argued that destination marketers can harness the power of music effects to create memorable short videos with distinctive music (Ting et al., 2020).

2.1.3 *Cultural effect*

Culture includes various special activities, interests, and attractions in tourist destinations. It is an important aspect of tourists' experience and provides a driving force for travel decision (Ramkissoon & Uysal, 2011). Cultural experience meets the motivation of tourists to seek valuable and authentic experiences. Therefore, it is necessary to constitute a memorable cultural experience for tourists (Kim, 2014). For destination video marketers, it is significant to demonstrate local cultural atmosphere by creating a memorable viewing experience (Smith, 2015).

At the same time, in view of the short-term characteristics of short videos, it is particularly important to use clear style positioning and cultural display to leave viewing memories for potential visitors (Edney, Dimmock & Boyd, 2021). Based on the current literature, this study suggests that the cultural content of short videos should be embedded in the local lifestyle, unique history, and other colorful cultural factors.

Unique cultural characteristics will help to create the memorable short video experience (Chen & Rahman, 2018).

2.2 *Memorable short video experience*

Pine and Gilmore (1998) put forward the concept of experience economy, which indicated that the world economy has shifted from being based on products and services to being based on experience. Therefore, many service organizations are emphasizing on providing pleasant experiences to their customers (Kim, 2018). Hence, the concept of experience economy becomes more meaningful for destination positioning and marketing (Tan 2016).

Especially with the development of modern communication and social media, the use of vivid short videos on recording and sharing travel experiences has gradually become sought after (Wong, Lai & Tao, 2020) Potential tourists can also preview the destination's memorable scenery, food, activities, culture, and other content through online short videos (Shani et al., 2010). Meanwhile, the video experience shows a variety of sensory experiences (Rajaguru, 2014), and they contribute to creating various memories for potential tourists. Above all, unique destination style positioning and multi-sensory atmosphere rendering help potential tourists produce a memorable experience (Ernawadi & Putra, 2020). When the video is memorable enough, it will inspire tourists' intention to make an actual visit to the destination (Kim, 2018).

2.3 *The construct of intention to visit*

Chen, Shang, and Li (2014) addressed that visiting intention is the result of a psychological process, which contains the dual components of psychology and behavior. Also, Jang et al. (2009) further suggest that intention to visit is an important outcome variable as it has a great correlation with actual travel behavior. Destinations that are negatively perceived may be eliminated from the tourist decision-making process, while destinations that are positively perceived are more likely to be selected (Molinillo et al., 2018). As Rajaguru (2014) argued, intention to visit emphasizes that a tourist's commitments, which is an important predictor that will lead to actual travel behavior in the future.

2.4 *Hypotheses development*

Some existing literature support the relationship between video attributes and memorable short video experiences. For instance, Fei's (2017) research indicated that well-produced videos represent the diversity of sensory experiences, produce excellent visual effects, and attract potential tourists. At the same time, it uses the performance in the prediction of visual memory close to the human level to inspire the potential tourists to have a memorable short video experience (Loureiro, Stylos & Bellou, 2021). This is consistent with the research proposed by Pera and

Viglia (2016) to explore the relationship between video narrative and experience.

According to the discussion above, the following hypotheses are proposed:

H1. Visual effect positively influences potential tourists' memorable short video experience.
H2. Music effect positively influences potential tourists' memorable short video experience.
H3. Cultural effect positively influences potential tourists' memorable short video experience.

The current theoretical content also supports the relationship between memorable short video experience and intention to visit. For instance, Kim (2018) argues that memorable travel experiences are the most influential key to behavioral intentions. At the same time, the research of Rajaguru (2014) also addresses that potential tourists' perception of tourism videos is directly related to their intention to visit. Therefore, following hypothesis is proposed:

H4. Potential tourists' memorable short video experience positively influences intention to visit.

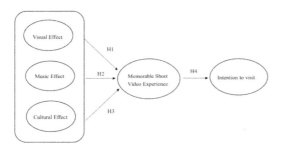

Figure 1. A proposed hypothetical model.

3 METHOD

In this study, the research site will be set to be an internet celebrity city—Chongqing in China. The three different themes of short videos with over 100 million views in "tiktok" will be selected in this study; the three research themes include "Hongyadong", "Chongqing Food" and "Liziba Light Rail Station", which are popular tourism sites in Chongqing.

As "tiktok" users are almost active online users, this study will select online audience among Chinese tiktok users. The professional survey website "Sojump.com" will be used and the questionnaire will be distributed through online links and QR code to the tiktok users who watched those three videos. The screening questions will be set to "Have you watched the short 'tiktok' destination video" and "Have you watched the video of the above themes in Chongqing" to filter valid respondents.

After collecting the questionnaire, PLS-SEM will be used to perform validity and reliability analysis and testify the proposed hypotheses.

4 DISCUSSION AND CONCLUSION

This paper will extend the theoretical concept of memorable tourism experience from the perspective of online short video. Taking the example of destination short travel videos in Chongqing, the proposed relationship among three attributes of destination short video, memorable short video experiences and intention to real visit will be examined. While most MTEs studies focus on tourists experience during and post-stages, few studies examined the effect of travel short video on pre-stage memorable tourism experience. Therefore, it is necessary to explore whether watching online travel video experience in pre-travel stage has impact on actual visit. A broader understanding of MTEs may help scholars discover new research fields and help practitioners gain more competitive advantages from the perspective of online marketing. Meanwhile, this study will identify the sub-dimensions of three primary effects of destination short video (visual, musical and cultural) and rebuild the measurement items for each factor. The proposed model of memorable short video experience will enrich MTEs theory for future research.

In addition, this study may offer guidelines for practitioners. For example, for video makers, attractive short videos can be produced from visual, musical and cultural perspective, creating a memorable experience for potential tourists and attracting viewing flow; for DMO managers, the results of the study may also give them guidelines of how to better promote their destination market under fierce competition.

ACKNOWLEDGMENT

The research is supported by Higher Education Fund of the Macao S.A.R. Government (TET-MUST-2020-03).

REFERENCES

Chen, H., & Rahman, I. (2018). Cultural tourism: An analysis of engagement, cultural contact, memorable tourism experience and destination loyalty. *Tourism Management Perspectives*, 26, 153–163.

Chen, Y. C., Shang, R. A., & Li, M. J. (2014). The effects of perceived relevance of travel blogs' content on the behavioral intention to visit a tourist destination. *Computers in Human Behavior*, 30, 787–799.

Deutsch, D., & Pierce, J. R. (2014). The climate of auditory imagery and music. In *Auditory imagery* (pp. 249–272). Psychology Press.

Dwityas, N. A., & Briandana, R. (2017). Social media in travel decision making process. *International Journal of Humanities and Social Science*, 7(7), 291–292.

Edney, J., Dimmock, K., & Boyd, W. E. (2021). Understanding Diver Behavior on Underwater Cultural Heritage: Enriching the Observation Record Using Video Methods. *Sustainability*, 13(10), 5601.

Ernawadi, Y., & Putra, H. T. (2020). Antecedents and consequences of memorable tourism experience. *Dinasti*

International Journal of Management Science, 1(5), 676–684.

Fei, M., Jiang, W., & Mao, W. (2017). Memorable and rich video summarization. *Journal of Visual Communication and Image Representation*, 42, 207–217.

Hecker, S. (1984). Music for advertising effect. *Psychology & Marketing*, 1(3–4), 3–8.

Hudson, S., & Ritchie, J. B. (2009). Branding a memorable destination experience. The case of 'Brand Canada'. *International Journal of Tourism Research*, 11(2), 217–228.

Jang, S., Bai, B., Hu, C., & Wu, C. M. E. (2009). Affect, travel motivation, and travel intention: A senior market. *Journal of Hospitality & Tourism Research*, 33(1), 51–73.

Kim, J. H. (2018). The impact of memorable tourism experiences on loyalty behaviors: The mediating effects of destination image and satisfaction. *Journal of Travel Research*, 57(7), 856–870.

Kim, J. H., Ritchie, J. B., & McCormick, B. (2012). Development of a scale to measure memorable tourism experiences. *Journal of Travel research*, 51(1), 12–25.

Kim, J.-H. (2014). The antecedents of memorable tourism experiences: The development of a scale to measure the destination attributes associated with memorable experiences. *Tourism Management*, 44, 34–45.

Loureiro, S. M. C., Stylos, N., & Bellou, V. (2021). Destination atmospheric cues as key influencers of tourists' word-of-mouth communication: Tourist visitation at two Mediterranean capital cities. *Tourism Recreation Research*, 46(1), 85–108.

Molinillo, S., Liébana-Cabanillas, F., Anaya-Sánchez, R., & Buhalis, D. (2018). DMO online platforms: Image and intention to visit. *Tourism management*, 65, 116–130.

Montgomery, R. L. (2010). Terms of Response: Language and the Audience in *Seventeenth-and Eighteenth-Century Theory*. Pennsylvania: Pennsylvania State Press.

Oh, S., Ahn, J., & Baek, H. (2015). The effects of social media on music-induced tourism: A case of Korean pop music and inbound tourism to Korea. *Asia pacific journal of information systems*, 25(1), 119–141.

Pan, S. (2011). The role of TV commercial visuals in forming memorable and impressive destination images. *Journal of Travel Research*, 50(2), 171–185.

Pera, R., & Viglia, G. (2016). Exploring how video digital storytelling builds relationship experiences. *Psychology & Marketing*, 33(12), 1142–1150.

Pine, B. J., and J. H. Gilmore. 1998. "Welcome to the Experience Economy." *Harvard Business Review* 76 (4): 97–105.

Rajaguru, R. (2014). Motion picture-induced visual, vocal and celebrity effects on tourism motivation: Stimulus organism response model. *Asia Pacific Journal of Tourism Research*, 19(4), 375–388.

Ramkissoon, H., & Uysal, M. S. (2011). The effects of perceived authenticity, information search behaviour, motivation and destination imagery on cultural behavioural intentions of tourists. *Current Issues in Tourism*, 14(6), 537–562.

Rasoolimanesh, S. M., Seyfi, S., Hall, C. M., & Hatamifar, P. (2021). Understanding memorable tourism experiences and behavioural intentions of heritage tourists. *Journal of Destination Marketing & Management*, 21, 100621.

Shani, A., Chen, P. J., Wang, Y., & Hua, N. (2010). Testing the impact of a promotional video on destination image change: Application of China as a tourism destination. *International Journal of Tourism Research*, 12(2), 116–133.

Smith, S. (2015). A sense of place: Place, culture and tourism. *Tourism Recreation Research*, 40(2), 220–233.

Stepchenkova, S., & Zhan, F. (2013). Visual destination images of Peru: Comparative content analysis of DMO and user-generated photography. *Tourism management*, 36, 590–601.

Su, X. (2011). Commodification and the selling of ethnic music to tourists. *Geoforum*, 42(4), 496–505.

Ting, W. A. N. G., Tao, X. U. E., Fang, W. A. N. G., & WU, B. H. (2020). The International Effect of Destination Involvement Based on Empathy from Anti-epidemic Music Video on Behavioral Intention. *Journal of Southwest University*, 42(9), 26–39.

Wan, C. B., Chow, K. K., de Bont, C. J., & Hekkert, P. (2020). Finding synergy between oral and visual narratives on memorable and meaningful tourism experiences. *Information Technology & Tourism*, 22(1), 107–130.

Wong, J. W. C., Lai, I. K. W., & Tao, Z. (2019). Memorable ethnic minority tourism experiences in China: a case study of Guangxi Zhuang Zu. *Journal of Tourism and Cultural Change*, 17(4), 508–525.

Wong, J. W. C., Lai, I. K. W., & Tao, Z. (2020). *Sharing memorable tourism experiences on mobile social media and how it influences further travel decisions. Current Issues in Tourism*, 23(14), 1773–1787.

An economic theoretical analysis of collusive behavior: Based on the international iron ore industry as an example

Yixuan Zhang
Durham University Business School, Durham University, Durham, UK

ABSTRACT: This paper will take the international iron ore industry as an example to focus on the collusion between oligopolists. At present, the global iron ore market is an oligopoly market, with a few companies controlling iron ore production volume and market transaction prices. This paper mainly analyzes the game process and results of oligopolists in the international iron ore industry, and explains the causes of collusion and its impact on the economy and society. The research shows that the oligarchic collusion in the international iron ore market has largely promoted the formation of invisible cartels, strengthened industry barriers, and caused economic welfare losses, price discrimination and other adverse effects. As the world's largest importer of iron ore, China is currently suffering from serious difficulties. Therefore, this paper also puts forward some feasible suggestions to improve the existing situation and break the collusion.

Keywords: Collusive Behavior; Game Theory; Nash Equilibrium; International Iron Ore Industry

1 INTRODUCTION

Collusion is generally regarded as a kind of consensus reached by competing companies through some means, which may be the output produced or the price charged (Levenstein & Suslow, 2006). As an important market behavior, collusion is often studied in an oligopoly market. Oligopoly consists of a small number of sellers and has a high degree of inter-company dependence (Mankiw, 2015). In order to pursue economic interests, enterprises may form cartels, which take joint actions through collusion. This paper will take the international iron ore industry as an example to study its possible collusion in the seaborne trade market. Through exploring the game process between the giants of the enterprise, this paper will mainly analyze the possible causes of collusion and its influence on economic welfare.

2 CASE ANALYSIS

In the international iron ore market, Brazil's Vale, Australia's Rio Tinto, BHP, and FMG are the four major iron ore exporters, accounting for nearly 70% of the world's total iron ore seaborne trade exports (Yang & He, 2016). According to the comparison of the export volume of major global iron ore companies, the iron ore exports of the four major iron ore producers in 2019 totaled 1.05 billion tons, accounting for 66% of the total global iron ore export volume (Worldsteel, 2019). With the improvement of enterprise production

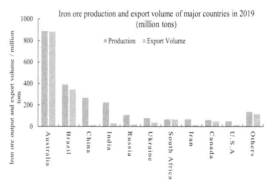

Figure 1. Iron ore production and export volume of major countries in 2019 (Worldsteel, 2019).

capacity in recent years, it is expected to exceed 70% or even achieve a higher proportion. In addition, data from the World Steel Association (Figure 1) shows that global iron ore production is mainly concentrated in Australia (891 million tons), Brazil (395 million tons), China (266 million tons), etc. Among them, Australia and Brazil are the countries with the most iron ore exports, and their combined exports account for about 77% of global exports. But in China, India, Russia, and other producers, their iron ore production mainly meets the domestic steel production demand.

Therefore, these four major producers dominate the supply of global iron ore seaborne trade market, forming an oligopoly situation in which a few enterprises monopolize most of the market. In the long term, the trading price and production volume of the iron ore seaborne market will be controlled by the four giants. In this situation, there is a great temptation for the four oligopolists to collude in order to avoid price competition. They are likely to collude to obtain monopoly prices and pursue the maximization of the mutual interests of enterprises. In the following part, this paper will assume iron ore oligopolist A and oligopolist B to analyze the possible game process between the enterprises.

3 GAME THEORY AND NASH EQUILIBRIUM

Nash equilibrium explores the case of non-collusion, in which a company judges the decision that is best for itself by assuming other competitors' possible actions (Sloman, Hinde & Garratt, 2013). In the process of the game between enterprises, the optimal strategic combination (Nash equilibrium) will be formed eventually, and neither party will change the strategy alone (Nezarat & Dastghaibifard, 2015). Actually, in oligopoly markets, companies often face two options: collusion and non-collusion (Sloman, Hinde & Garratt, 2013). However, there are conflicts between cooperation and self-interest among oligopoly companies, which usually face the prisoner's dilemma. Therefore, this paper simulates the game process of iron ore seaborne trade market. Assuming iron ore oligopolists A and B, the following economic analysis is conducted:

Under this assumption, if the firms A and B choose high yield (50 tons of iron ore) at the same time, each one will earn $1,700. When the firm A/B chooses to produce 50 tons of iron ore, and the other firm B/A chooses to produce 40 tons of iron ore profit of choosing high yield is $2200, while the choice of low yield earns $1600. If both firms A and B choose a low-yield 40 tons, they will gain $2,000 each.

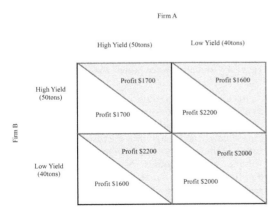

Figure 2. Game model of firms A and B.

Under the situation of non-collusion, from the perspective of firm A, when B makes a choice to produce 50 tons, A chooses to produce 50 tons with a profit of $1,700 and 40 tons with a profit of $1600, so A will choose high yield (50 tons). If B chooses low yield, the comparison shows that A also chooses high yield in order to gain more profits. Similarly, no matter firm A keeps high or low yield, the best choice for B is also high yield. Therefore, in the course of the game between the two sides, the final Nash equilibrium of the prisoner's dilemma is that both A and B choose high yield (50 tons of iron ore), with a profit of $1,700 each. However, in this case of non-collusion, oligopoly companies A and B achieve suboptimal results. In fact, if enterprises A and B collude and choose low production at the same time, they will achieve a win-win situation (each one's profit = 2000).

Combined with the actual situation of oligopoly in iron ore seaborne market, the four giants occupy most of the market share and have full motive to collude. Companies can raise the market prices by controlling the supply of iron ore in the seaborne market. In this situation, four iron ore giants united to form a cartel, producing and pricing like monopolists, and finally obtaining monopoly profits. For other production enterprises with less output, their production decisions cannot affect market prices, and only as the receiver of the price. However, the collusion between the oligopolists is likely to be unstable. Facing the temptation of self-interest, companies may act unilaterally to obtain higher profits (Feuerstein, 2005). As a result, the iron ore oligopolists may collude to form monopoly price while also being driven by self-interest, privately increasing production in an attempt to capture a larger share of the market.

4 REASONS FOR COLLUSIVE BEHAVIOR

First of all, through collusion, oligopolists can achieve monopoly production and monopoly price, so as to ensure the maximization of common interests in the market (Mankiw, 2015). According to the analysis of the game model, the oligopolists in the iron ore seaborne market have strong motivation to collude in order to maximize profits. Since the iron ore oligopolists occupy the absolute advantage in the supply of seaborne market, they can be regarded as an actual monopolist when colluding. For the four oligopolists, the main purpose that they may collude into a cartel is to obtain the maximum monopoly benefit. As shown in Figure 3, it can be seen that the demand curve of iron ore slopes to the lower right after forming a cartel. Therefore, the marginal revenue (MR) faced by enterprises is less than the price of iron ore (P). They will choose the output (Q) when the marginal revenue equals the marginal cost (MR=MC), and determine the price according to the intersection of the output and the demand curve (Sloman, Hinde & Garratt, 2013). According to the results in Figure 3, the monopoly price of iron ore cartel will be higher than marginal cost and marginal revenue. At this time, oligopolists collude and form a cartel to ultimately mutually maximize profits.

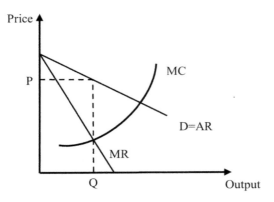

Figure 3. Production and price selection of collusion (cartel).

Secondly, the small number of oligopolies and high industrial concentration are conducive to promoting collusive stability (Levenstein & Suslow, 2006). At present, there are only a few oligopolists in the seaborne iron ore market, but they have the majority of the market share, which provides favorable conditions for the formation of stable collusion to avoid price wars between each other. In addition, the higher the homogeneity of the product, the more likely it is to achieve a uniform price target (Sloman, Hinde & Garratt, 2013). Iron ore production has the characteristics of homogeneity, which promotes the establishment of output or price agreement, colluding to form a cartel. Moreover, collusion is more likely to be formed when market entry barriers are high and there is less threat from new entrants (Sloman, Hinde & Garratt, 2013). The iron ore industry has high barriers to entry due to the geographical characteristics of the distribution of iron ore resources. Iron ore oligopolies have obvious cost and resource advantages, which are easy to produce collusion and monopolize the seaborne trade of iron ore. Furthermore, international iron ore export mainly adopts the way of annual agreement pricing (Yang & He, 2016). It provides an opportunity for oligopoly companies to collude with each other in terms of pricing and output, form a cartel alliance, and maintain a higher monopoly price than the non-collusion. Therefore, based on the above analysis, it can be seen that in the iron ore seaborne market, there is a strong motive for the oligopolies to collude, as well as the possibility of maintaining the long-term stability of colluding. Iron ore oligopolists form cartel through collusion, which is conducive for the firms in achieving their purpose of obtaining the high profits of monopoly.

5 ECONOMIC IMPACT OF COLLUSIVE BEHAVIOR

When oligopolists collude to form a cartel, the economic impact is mainly reflected in the reduction of efficiency (Beyer, Kottmann & Blackenburg, 2018). In other words, it will inevitably result in the loss of welfare. In this situation, the colluding oligopolies will determine the output and price like the monopolist. Thus, the effect on economic welfare is similar to that of monopoly (Beyer, Kottmann & Blackenburg, 2018).

This paper uses a simple hypothesis model (marginal cost remains constant) to compare and analyze the impact of iron ore oligopolies on welfare under the condition of collusion and non-collusion. Although the oligopolists have self-interest and try to increase the supply, they will not expand their output to a state of perfect competition (Mankiw, 2015). If the output is increased too much, the price of iron ore will fall and the total profit will decrease. Therefore, even if there is no collusion, the final Nash equilibrium formed by iron ore firms through the game is higher than the price level of perfect competition but lower than the monopoly price.

According to Figure 4, it is assumed that the price is P^o when the oligopolies do not collude. At this point, the consumer surplus is the area of the triangle P^oAD. When oligopolistic enterprises collude, it will realize monopoly and set a monopoly price P^m, in which the consumer surplus will be the area of P^mAB. Compared with non-collusion, consumer surplus reduced the area of the trapezoidal $P^o P^m$BD. However, monopoly leads to higher prices, the profit of the producers (monopoly profit) is the rectangular $P^o P^m$BC. Therefore, compared with the case of non-collusion, cartel collusion leads to a further increase in welfare loss, that is, the area of triangle BCD.

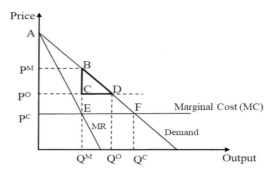

Figure 4. Welfare loss (collusion versus non-collusion).

Based on the analysis of the seaborne iron ore trade market, its consumers are iron ore importing countries. As the world's largest steel producer, China relies heavily on foreign iron ore resources. Currently, China is the country with the largest iron ore import volume, which accounts for a large proportion and highly depends on the seaborne trade market (Yang & He, 2016). Since 2017, China's iron ore imports have maintained a high level of around 1.10 billion tons (Figure 5), constantly driving up the demand for iron ore seaborne and iron ore prices.

As a result, the potential for an invisible cartel in iron ore exports leaves China at a persistent disadvantage in price game and affects overall economic interests

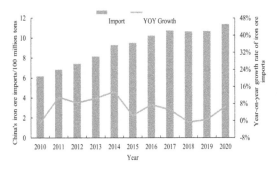

Figure 5. China's iron ore imports from 2010 to 2020. (National Bureau of Statistics, 2020).

(Yang & He, 2016). Additionally, collusive behavior of oligopolists will further enhance industry barriers and restrict consumers' choice of products.

6 CONCLUSION AND RECOMMENDATION

This research focuses on the current situation of the iron ore seaborne trade, analyzes the economic principle of collusion, and further explores its economic impact. Through simulating the game process, it has demonstrated the yield and profit that the oligopolists can achieve under non-collusion and collusion, as well as the conflicts that exist in obtaining private profits and collusion. Moreover, combined with the diagram analysis, this paper also explains the motivation of oligopolistic collusion and the main economic impact. Compared with non-collusion, collusive behavior will cause more welfare loss. Although no clear agreement has been found to prove that the iron ore oligopoly companies formed a cartel organization, this paper still researches on the possibility of hidden cartel. In fact, four iron ore giants have strong market share and favorable conditions for collusion and stability. Therefore, they have a great temptation to collude, form a cartel, seek the interests of monopolists, and maximize the common interests. In future research, this issue is worth further analysis and exploration.

Meanwhile, due to the potential influence of oligarchic collusion, China, as the largest demand country for iron ore, has been constantly frustrated in the price game. Consequently, this paper puts forward corresponding feasibility suggestions for reference. Firstly, it is necessary to establish a relatively open and transparent iron ore pricing mechanism and use index pricing methods such as iron ore futures price index to make the price more effectively reflect the actual situation of the market. In addition, the relevant international laws and regulations should be improved to reduce the opportunity of iron ore oligopoly price discrimination and protect the interests of all parties in the market. Finally, China should enhance the competitiveness of enterprises, accelerate industrial transformation and upgrading, improve the utilization efficiency of resources, and reduce excessive dependence on iron ore resources. By improving the supply capacity of the domestic iron ore market, China can more effectively break the monopoly of the international oligopoly market and enhance its voice in the international iron ore market, thus lowering the price of iron ore market.

REFERENCES

Beyer, C., Kottmann, E., & Blackenburg, K.V. (2018). The Welfare Implications of the European Trucks Cartel. *MAGKS Papers on Economics*, (18), pp.1–12.

Feuerstein, S. (2005). Collusion in Industrial Economics—A Survey. *Journal of Industry, Competition and Trade*, (5), pp.163–198.

Levenstein, M.C., & Suslow, V.Y. (2006). What Determines Cartel Success? *Journal of Economic Literature*, 44(1), pp.43–95.

Mankiw, N.G. (2015) *Principles of Economics.* 7th edn. Cengage Learning.

National Bureau of Statistics. 2020. Available at: http://www.stats.gov.cn/ (Accessed 4th September 2021).

Nezarat, A., & Dastghaibifard, G. (2015). Efficient Nash Equilibrium Resource Allocation Based on Game Theory Mechanism in Cloud Computing by Using Auction. *PLoSONE*, 10(10): e0138424.

Sloman, J., Hinde, K., & Garratt, D. (2013). *Economics for Business.* 6th edn. Pearson Education Limited.

Worldsteel (2019). "Steel Statistical Yearbook 2019". Available at: www.worldsteel.org (Accessed 3rd September 2021).

Yang, L. M., & He, Z. J. (2016). Game and Strategy of China in the World's Negotiation of Iron Ore Price. *2016 International Conference on Industrial Informatics-Computing Technology, Intelligent Technology, Industrial Information Integration (ICIICII)*, pp.360–363.

Economic and Business Management – Huang & Zhang (Eds)
© 2022 Copyright the Author(s), ISBN: 978-1-032-06754-4

Research on the construction of brand stories of a regional brand of agricultural products under the background of the internet

Chunmei Chen, Sifan Pei, Xinyu Jiang* & Wenlong Lu
School of Business and Tourism, Sichuan Agricultural University, Chengdu, China

ABSTRACT: Brand story is an important way to shape and spread the regional brand of agricultural products. This article takes 28 brand stories of fruit regional brands of top 100 regional public brands of agricultural products in China as the research object and uses Nvivo12plus software to analyze the text characteristics from brand stories' four elements which include messages, conflicts, events, and characters about the brand stories. It finally summarizes the building law of brand stories, provides a reference for the construction of brand stories of regional brand of agricultural products, and promotes the communication of regional brand of agricultural products effectively.

1 INTRODUCTION

With the rapid development of internet, consumers' receiving of information is highly saturated, and traditional advertising methods are difficult to stimulate the audience's interest. However, Wang Tao et al (2011) pointed out that the legend, twists and turns, conflict, drama, dissemination and inheritance of the story make it the most effective and lasting tool to seize the hearts of the people [1].

How to build a good brand story? It should not only contain a message but also consider sending this message to the plot stored in the receiver's memory. Fog et al (2005) said that the plot with conflicting points can be more attractive to consumers, and the occurrence of the plot requires the actions of characters [2]. The four elements of the story are message, plot, conflict, and character. Tungate (2008) said that the message is the core message that the brand delivers to consumers reflecting the narrator's views and opinions [3] Vincent (2002) said that the plot includes the beginning, middle, and end of the story, which is linked by different events [4] Martin (1990) pointed out that the conflict is the driving force of a good story [5]. Fog et al (2005) believed that the character is a promoter or main interpreter of the story [2].

For regional brand of agricultural products, most of them have regional characteristics and historical background. Brand stories include regional stories, product stories, brand stories, and so on. So, what are the characteristics of the four elements of brand stories of regional brand of agricultural products? What is the construction pattern of the brand story?

Based on the above research motives, this article collects 28 brand stories of fruit regional brands on the

internet and uses Nvivo12plus software to analyze the text characteristics from brand stories' four elements which include messages, events, conflicts, and characters about brand stories. It summarizes the building law of brand stories, provides a reference for the construction of regional brand of agricultural products.

2 RESEARCH DESIGN

2.1 Source of research date

This paper takes brand stories of regional brand of agricultural products as the research object. First, we found the list of top 100 regional public brands of agricultural products in China. Second, we chose 28 brand stories of fruit regional brands. Finally, 28 brand stories of fruit regional brands are retrieved and collected from relevant websites by using selected regional brand of agricultural products and brand stories as keywords.

2.2 Research methods and tools

This research mainly uses qualitative research methods, selects 28 brand stories texts of fruit regional brands as the research data source. Pan Baocheng & Song zhanmei (2021) used Nvivo12plus software to encode the collected story texts, determine nodes, select key nodes, analyze, and summarize them [6]. Nvivo12plus software is very common in qualitative research, which can process text, audio, video, pictures, web pages, or social media. The information points related to the research topic are encoded and summarized. According to Jiang xin (2017) NVivo software can enhance the rigor, reliability, and interest of qualitative research [7].

*Corresponding Author

138

DOI 10.1201/9781003203704-25

2.3 Data analysis process

There are two main coding methods commonly used in Nvivo12plus software. Sun Lixin and Song Yuxin (2020) said that the first way is from coarse to fine, which forms a research framework according to the research theme and codes the theme to form several sub-nodes [8]. Xieyu and Chen faxiang (2020) said that the second way is to start from the details, which determines nodes according to text contents and then integrates them to form related categories [9]. This study adopts the first encoding method, and the specific analysis process is as follows: (1) We organize the collected 28 agricultural product regional brand stories and import them into NVivo12plus software. (2) We establish four nodes of messages, conflicts, events, and characters according to the elements of brand stories. (3) We read the texts of brand stories word by word to clarify the contents covered by the four elements in brand stories. (4) We read contents of the four elements carefully and extract some subject words as a sub-node. (5) We read contents of each sub-node carefully and extract topic words as the secondary sub-node until the contents of each node are completely independent. (6) Finally, the construction pattern of regional brand stories of agricultural products is summarized by comparing the numbers of event types at different stages of brand stories.

3 ANALYSIS OF RESEARCH RESULTS

3.1 Analysis of word frequency characteristics of brand story texts

Xie yu and Chen faxiang (2020) said that word frequency is the number of words appearing in story texts. Its level will reflect the importance of specific words in brand stories [9]. Wu junqi and Wang wei (2021) said that counting the frequency of occurrence of words can reflect the most concerned indicators in the story [10]. The word cloud is a very intuitive presentation of the word frequency of a specific word, and the size of words represents the word frequency of the word. Figure 1 shows the word cloud of brand stories, in which 30 words with the highest frequency of occurrence are selected.

After classifying high-frequency words, it can be found that brand, development, industry, China, and agricultural products are high-frequency keywords, which shows the important position of the development of agricultural products industry. Moreover, production, technology, planting, bases, varieties, fruit farmers, enterprises, sales, markets, countries, and standardization drive the development of regional brand of agricultural products in brand stories.

3.2 Element analysis of regional brand story of agricultural products

In this study, four nodes are formed by Nvivo12plus qualitative text encoding, and the number of texts and reference point values are shown in Table 1.

Table 1. Number of texts and references of nodes.

Name of Nodes	Number of texts	References
Message	28	112
Conflict	26	76
Character	28	193
Event	28	284

3.2.1 Message

The encoding of the message is shown in Table 2. There are 4 first-level sub-nodes of characteristics, inheritance, innovation, and honor; 12 second-level sub-nodes; and 112 references. Among them, the references of characteristics are the most, including three secondary nodes of excellent varieties (EV), rich nutrition (RN), and green health (GH); by transmitting the characteristics of branded agricultural products in the region and distinguishing them from other brands, a unique image is created. Inheritance includes two secondary nodes of planting inheritance (PI) and cultural inheritance (CI), conveying the long history of the regional brand and catering to the psychological demands of consumers. Innovation includes variety cultivation innovation (VCI), planting technology innovation (PTI), quality and safety system innovation (QSSI), and business strategy innovation (BSI). This means that innovation is an important support for the development of regional brand of agricultural products and a driving source for continuous development and growth. Honor includes titles, geographical indication products (GIP), and awards, which means that regional brand of agricultural products have high recognition.

The values in parentheses: the number of texts before the comma is the number of texts of the brand story of the content of the node, and the reference point after the comma is the number of occurrences of related content under the node. The following table is the same.

Figure 1. Brand stories word cloud.

Table 2. Number of nodes, texts, and references contained in the message node.

Name of Node	First-level sub-nodes	Second-level sub-nodes	Number of texts and references
Message (28,112)	Characteristics (26,45)	EV	(26,28)
		RN	(11,11)
		GH	(6,6)
	Inheritance (13,17)	PI	(10,10)
		CI	(7,7)
	Innovation (20,23)	VCI	(4,4)
		PTI	(10,10)
		QSSI	(2,2)
		BSI	(7,7)
	Honor (15,27)	Titles	(10,15)
		GIP	(5,6)
		Awards	(6,6)

3.2.2 Conflict

In the tree node conflict, no obvious conflicts were found, but they contained turning points. The encoding of the conflict is shown in Table 3. There are 3 primary sub-nodes for government intervention, technical support, and policy change; 7 secondary sub-nodes; and 76 references. Among them, the references of government intervention are the most, including two secondary nodes of supporting policies (SP) and measures. Through government intervention, the scale of planting can be expanded and the development of regional brands of agricultural products can be promoted. Technical support includes two secondary nodes of production technology (PT) and cultivation technology (CT). The introduction of new technologies is conducive to providing consumers with better quality agricultural products. Strategy change includes three secondary nodes of production strategy change (PSC), e-commerce platform sales (EPS), and publicity and marketing (PAM). Through strategy change, it is helpful to improve the visibility of regional brands of agricultural products and promote

Table 3. Number of nodes, texts, and references contained in the conflict node.

Name of Node	First-level sub-nodes	Second-level sub-nodes	Number of texts and references
Conflict (26,76)	Government intervention (21,34)	SP	(5,5)
		Measures	(19,29)
	Technical support (12,16)	PT	(9,9)
		CT	(6,7)
	Strategy change (18,26)	PSC	(5,7)
		EPS	(7,8)
		PAM	(10,11)

the development of regional brands of agricultural products.

3.2.3 Character

The encoding of the character is shown in Table 4. Huang Xiangfang (2021) said that there are 5 first-level sub-nodes of company organizations, fruit farmers, governments, other social public organizations, and consumers; 15 second-level sub-nodes; and 188 references [11]. Company organizations include three secondary nodes of cooperative unified management (CUM), enterprise market development (EMD), and farm participation (FP). Through the joint efforts of the company organization, the development of the brand is promoted. Fruit farmers include five secondary nodes of creating companies (CC), actively planting (AP), learning technology (LT), selling products (SEP), and benefiting products (BP). Fruit farmers actively learn technology and participate in the standardized production of agricultural products, which ensures the stable supply of agricultural products quality and is conducive to the sustainable development of regional brands of agricultural products. The references of government are the most, including supportive policies (SP), service measures (SM), and preferential measures (PM). Government is the promoter and guide of regional brand construction of agricultural products. Governments promote the development of regional brands of agricultural products by creating a good development environment. Other public organizations include Technical guidance for scientific research institutions (TGFSRI) and business organizations promote sales (BOPS). Consumers include celebrity advocacy (CD) and loyal customers (LC). The narration of celebrities in the story can make the

Table 4. Number of nodes, texts, and references contained in the character node.

Name of Node	First-level sub-nodes	Second-level sub-nodes	Number of texts and references
Character (28,193)	Company organizations (20,35)	CUM	(8,9)
		EMD	(15,20)
		FP	(6,6)
	Fruit farmers (21,43)	CC	(3,4)
		AP	(4,4)
		LT	(13,14)
		SEP	(4,6)
		BP	(15,15)
	Government (23,65)	SP	(5,5)
		SM	(23,54)
		PM	(6,6)
	Other social public organizations (18,26)	TGFSRI	(12,14)
		BOPS	(12,12)
	Consumers (14,19)	CD	(10,12)
		LC	(7,7)

story humane. The description of ordinary consumers is less.

3.2.4 Event

The encoding of the event is shown in Table 5. There are 4 first-level sub-nodes, 11 second-level sub-nodes, and 284 references. Regional-related events include two secondary nodes of the natural environment (NE) and historical heritage (HH). Through the transmission of the special environment and historical heritage of the region, the uniqueness of agricultural products is highlighted. Product-related events include three secondary nodes of product naming (PN), product efficacy (PE), and product technology innovation (PTI). They can transmit the excellent quality of agricultural products. The references of brand-related events are the most, including brand origin (BO), brand development (BD), brand promotion (BP), and brand honor (BH), which means that the brand concept and value. Human-related events include internal staff (IS) and consumers. The events of internal staff can show the core concept of the brand and corporate culture. Bruce (2001) said that consumers' events can cause consumers' resonance [12].

Table 5. Number of nodes, texts, and references contained in the event node.

Name of Node	First-level sub-nodes	Second-level sub-nodes	Number of texts and references
Event (28,284)	Regional-related events (25,43)	NE HH	(23,29) (13,14)
	Product-related events (27,56)	PN PE PTI	(4,5) (22,30) (16,21)
	Brand-related events (28,140)	BO BD BP BH	(13,15) (23,66) (20,34) (16,25)
	Human-related events (20,45)	IS Consumers	(15,31) (10,14)

3.3 The construction pattern of brand stories of regional brand of agricultural products

The development of regional brands of agricultural products is divided into three stages: the early stage, the middle stage, and the late stage. By coding stories, this study summarizes what stories are told at different stages.

From the data in Table 6, the story types of agricultural regional brands at different stages can be concluded as shown in Figure 2. In the early stage, they mainly talk about natural environment, historical heritage, product naming, product efficacy, and brand

Table 6. The number of nodes, texts, and references in event nodes at different stages.

Event types	Early brand	Mid-term brand	Late brand
NE	(23, 28)	(1, 1)	(0, 0)
HH	(13, 14)	(0, 0)	(0, 0)
PN	(4, 5)	(0, 0)	(0, 0)
PE	(17, 22)	(3, 3)	(4, 4)
PTI	(0, 0)	(14, 16)	(5, 5)
BO	(13, 15)	(0, 0)	(0, 0)
BD	(4, 4)	(15, 25)	(20, 37)
BP	(0, 0)	(8, 10)	(18, 24)
BH	(0, 0)	(5, 6)	(15, 19)
IS	(4, 4)	(5, 8)	(11, 19)
Consumers	(2, 2)	(2, 2)	(8, 10)

origin. In the middle stage, they mainly talk about product technology innovation, brand development, and brand promotion. In the late stage, they mainly talk about brand development, brand promotion, brand honor, internal staff, and consumers.

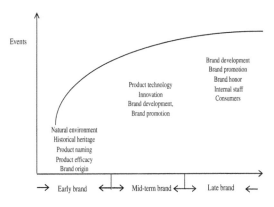

Figure 2. Event types of agricultural regional brands at different stages.

4 DISCUSSIONS AND PROSPECTS

4.1 Discussions and prospects

This study provides a specific value reference for the construction of regional brand stories of agricultural products from messages, conflicts, events, and characters. In terms of messages, four aspects including characteristics, inheritance, innovation, and honor can be considered, especially characteristics and innovation. The characteristics reflect the uniqueness of the agricultural products and establish a unique brand image in the minds of consumers. The innovations convey the spirit and concept of the brand, and encourage consumers to love the brand and then recognize the brand. In terms of conflicts, there are three aspects which are the driving forces to promote the development of regional brands of agricultural products: government intervention, technical support, and policy change. Among them, government intervention is the most referenced aspect. In terms of characters, including company organizations, fruit farmers, governments, industry associations, other social public organizations, and consumers, governments and fruit growers are the most referenced and industry associations and consumers are less referenced. But the stories of consumers are more likely to cause consumption resonance with the audience. This is a problem that needs attention in the process of building a brand story. In terms of events, there are regional-related events, product-related events, brand-related events, and human-related events. And there are fewer human-related events, which may change with the development of regional brands of agricultural products. At different stages of the development of regional brand of agricultural products, the distribution of events is different, and the continuity in time is not strong, and the narrative structure of the story is linear.

4.2 *Research limitations and prospects*

This research combines the results and software from a previous research for analysis. However, the research sample is fruit, and there are some doubts about whether other types of agricultural products have universal significance. Through research, it is found that most consumers in the story are celebrities, and there are few ordinary consumers. The emotionality of the story needs to be strengthened. Future research can be done from the perspective of brand story types and brand story functions to obtain more in-depth research conclusions.

ACKNOWLEDGMENTS

This is a scientific research project of Sichuan Provincial Education Department: Research on Influencing Factors, Mechanism and Construction Countermeasures of Regional Brand Equity of Sichuan Agricultural Products (18SB0520). This project is funded by Research Center for Sichuan Liquor Industry Development of Sichuan University of Science & Engineering (CJY21-03).

REFERENCES

[1] Wang Tao, Zhou Ling, Peng Chuanxin, et al (2011). Storytelling Brand: Brand Narrative Theory of Constructing and Disseminating Stories -A Case Study of Daphne Brand. *Journal of Management World*, (03),112–123.

[2] Fog K, Budtz C, Yakaboylu B. (2005). Storytelling: Branding in Practice. *Berlin: Springer*.

[3] Tungate M. (2008). Fashion brands: branding style from Armani to Zara. *Kogan Page*.

[4] Vincent L. (2002). Legendary Brands: Unleashing the Power of Storytelling to Create a Winning Market Strategy. *Chicago:Dearborn*.

[5] Martin, W. (1990). Recent theories of narrative. *Beijing: Peking University Press*.

[6] Pan baocheng, Song zhanmei. (2021) Policy Analysis and Reflection on Promoting the Development of Care Services for Infants under 3 Years Old in China—Based on the NVivo Analysis of the Policy Text of 28 Provincial Implementation Opinions. *Journal of Shaanxi Xueqian Normal University*, 37(07):8–17.

[7] Jiang Xin. (2017). Research on the Opening and Sharing Policies ofScientific Data of Foreign Funding Agencies—A Policy Text Analysis Based on NVivo 12. *Journal of Modern Information*, 40(08):144–155.

[8] Sun Lixin,Song Yuxin. (2020). Research Progress and Future Prospects of Learning Society in China£Content Analysis Based on NVivo. *Modern Distance Education*, (06):3–8.

[9] Xie yu, Chen faxiang. (2020). The Policy Analysis of College Mental Health Education in China Based on the Tool of NVivo. *Heilongjiang Researches on Higher Education*, 38(07):145–149.

[10] Wu Junqi, Wang Wei. (2021). A Comparative Analysis of Professional Development Standards for Primary and Secondary School Teachers. *Modern Education Management*, (05),77–85.

[11] Huang Xiangfang. (2021). Research on the Cooperative Construction Mode and Mechanism of Multi Subject Agricultural Products Regional Brand in Xiangxi Prefecture. *Modern Agriculture Research*, 27(01):12–14.

[12] Bruce D. (2001). Storytelling wins hearts: Ten tips for creating captivating brand stories. *Marketing Magazine*, 106(9): 26.

Economic and Business Management – Huang & Zhang (Eds)
© 2022 Copyright the Author(s), ISBN: 978-1-032-06754-4

Research on the influence of leverage ratio on the credit risk of commercial banks based on entropy weight method

Yuhong Tao
Sumitomo Mitsui Banking Corporation (China), Shanghai, China

ABSTRACT: Entropy method refers to a method that is capable of effectively constructing comprehensive evaluation indexes. In accordance with this method, the evaluation of abstract transactions can be carried out in an objective and systematical way with the integration of the principle of information entropy and relevant indexes. The calculation of relevant indicators through entropy weight method excels in the measurement of credit risk. On the basis of theories of leverage ratio regulation and credit risk management of commercial banks, this thesis focuses on the empirical analysis on the relevant data of 21 listed commercial banks in China from 2014 to 2019 after the exclusion of the impact imposed by the epidemic. Survey has been carried out on the relationship between leverage ratio and bank credit risk and the influence of leverage ratio on China's commercial bank credit risk management from both micro- and macroperspectives. In accordance with the conclusion drawn in this thesis, suggestions were put forward for the supervision policies of commercial banks, which means to provide practical references for the credit risk management of commercial banks and better formulation of relevant supervision policies.

1 INTRODUCTION

China has long witnessed the banking industry taking a crucial role in the reform of the financial industry. However, in comparison with other international commercial banks holding the same asset scale, the proportion of the off-balance sheet business of the banking industry at home remains relatively low, while the loan business still plays a role as the major source of asset and profit.

From a comprehensive view, the banking industry at home has embarked on the concept of total risk management. However, different from the banking industry of other mature and developed countries, one of the most challenging risks that the commercial banking industry confronting at home is still credit risk, in particular the risk related to credit. Such phenomenon is in line with the reality in China, where the commercial banks continue to give priority to credit business and see a relatively single type of business. The financial crisis that took place in the year 2008 has brought to the table the disadvantages of the application of single capital adequacy ratio index by domestic commercial banks for the capital regulation, which provided a cradle of the *2010 Version of the Basel III*. It was the first time to add the leverage ratio index into the regulatory index, which means greater importance has been attached to the index of leverage from the government regulators in China. Commercial banks are in essence institutions responsible for

risk management. Among all the difficulties faced by China's commercial banks, one prominent challenge is that the management competence of their own credit risks is bound to be highly relevant to the operating conditions and the stability of the entire national financial system.

2 LITERATURE REVIEW

Ma Bin and Fan Rui (2019) took advantage of the dynamic panel model GMM estimation method to realize the test on the data of 16 listed banks in China from 2007 to 2016. In such case, the non-performing loan ratio was picked up as the measurement standard of credit risk of commercial banks. In accordance with the results, the credit risk continued to crop up, during which process the leverage ratio regulation played an effective role in dealing with the crisis confronted by relevant commercial banks. In accordance with Blum (2007), the improvement of the supervision of leverage ratio is conducive to leveling up the competence of banks to improve their net asset value, better facilitating banks to report their risks in real time, thus to guide the banks to deal with their off-balance sheet risks. Lu Lu and Yang Wenhua (2020) pointed out that based on the research carried out, the introduction of leverage ratio regulation is prone to increase the risk preference of some banks from a broad perspective

DOI 10.1201/9781003203704-26

143

and realize the mitigation of systemic risk in the long run.

Robert (2013) also pointed out that the regulation of leverage ratio has demonstrated a good effect for the government to further regulate the behaviors of commercial banks and decrease the risks that commercial banks are getting trapped by. In accordance with Mirza and Strobel (2013), the leverage ratio regulation plays a crucial role in controlling and managing the systemic risk of commercial banks. In addition, Liu Ping and Liang Yu (2011) once carried out the research on macro subjects, when it was found that there remains a long-term and stable correlation between the non-performing loan ratio (of state-owned commercial banks and joint-stock commercial banks) and a variety of indicators, including gross domestic product (GDP), the consumer price index (CPI), the growth of money supply (M2), loan interest rate, financial institutions in all kinds of loan growth, the growth rate of total retail sales of social consumer goods, the import and export growth, the total fixed asset investment growth, and other macroeconomic indicators.

These days have witnessed few discussions and talks in terms of the influence of leverage ratio on the credit risk of China's commercial banks. In addition, when conducting the analysis of credit risk, most of the researchers prefer to focus on a single index, such as non-performing loan ratio or provision coverage to measure. However, the overall credit risk of commercial banks has been overlooked, which has not been well understood and identified. In the empirical analysis, some researchers chose to classify the data of commercial banks in accordance with the division of state-owned commercial banks and joint-stock commercial banks. However, the results tell that no obvious difference can be found when it comes to the influence of leverage ratio on these two types of commercial banks.

3 DATA AND MODELS

3.1 Selection of data and indicators

Against the backdrop of the outbreak of COVID-19 in the year of 2020, significant transformation and changes took place on the credit data of commercial banks with the adjustments of relevant policies launched by the Central Bank. In order to mitigate the influence of data during the epidemic on this study, 21 listed commercial banks from 2014 to 2019 were selected as sample data for the analysis ②. All the selected bank data samples include on one hand state-owned commercial banks, and on the other hand joint-stock commercial banks as well as city commercial banks, which have accounted for the vast majority of China's commercial banks in terms of accumulated assets and operating performance. In comparison with other smaller banks, the selected banks enjoy superior and much stabler competence of credit risk management, which is regarded as the symbol of the overall competence of the banking industry in China.

Table 1. Range of data selection.

Types of banks	Name of banks
Large scaled state-owned commercial banks	Industrial and Commercial Bank, Agricultural Bank, Construction Bank, Bank of China, Bank of Communications
Joint-stock commercial bank	China Merchants Bank, Shanghai Pudong Development Bank, China Citic Bank, China Everbright Bank, Huaxia Bank, Minsheng Bank, China Guangfa Bank, Industrial Bank, Ping A Bank, Zheshang Bank, Bohai Bank
City Commercial Bank	Bank of Jiangsu, Bank of Ningbo, Bank of Shanghai, Bank of Beijing, Bank of Nanjing

In accordance with the basic theory of information in physics, the smaller the information entropy of an index is, the more information it is expected to offer, and it is expected that the greater the weight it takes in the comprehensive evaluation. The entropy method is capable of calculating the weight of each index among the comprehensive index, which has been frequently applied as the foundation for the realization of the comprehensive evaluation of multiple indexes. Five metrics that are most commonly used for loan credit risk evaluation, namely, reserve ratio, provision coverage, non-performing loan ratio, the single biggest customer loan proportion, as well as the 10 largest customer loan proportion ① are selected and applied to calculate the specific weights of indicators through the entropy method, which refers to the overall level of credit risk management of commercial bank, thus to measure the credit risk of each commercial bank in a comprehensive and effective way.

3.2 Processing of indicators in line with entropy method

3.2.1 Forward (standardized) treatment of indictors

Considering that differences take place among these indicators in the dimensional terms, it is required to standardize them, thus to eliminate the influence between dimensions. The credit risk indicators of commercial banks can be classified and processed respectively. In this thesis, the loan provision ratio and provision coverage ratio were set as positive indicators, while the non-performing loan ratio, the loan ratio of single largest customer, and the loan ratio of the largest 10 customers were set as negative indicators. The treatment methods are as follows:

$$\tilde{x}_{ij} = \frac{x_{ij} - \min(x_{ij})}{\max(x_{ij}) - \min(x_{ij})} \tag{1}$$

$$\tilde{x}_{ij} = \frac{\max(x_{ij}) - x_{ij}}{\max(x_{ij}) - \min(x_{ij})} \qquad (2)$$

In the formula, x_{ij} refers to the actual value of the indicator; Min (x_{ij}) refers to the minimum of all data for this metric; Max (x_{ij}) refers to the maximum value of all data for this metric.

3.2.2 Entropy value and weight of indicators

$$E_J = -k \sum_{i=1}^{m} p_{ij} \ln p_{ij} \qquad (3)$$

In the formula,
where $k = 1/\ln m$;
E_j refers to the entropy value of index;
M refers to the total number of data;
P_{ij} refers to the weight of the treated index that is calculated in Formula (3–4).

$$p_{ij} = x_{ij} / \sum_{i=1}^{m} x_{ij} \qquad (4)$$

$$W_j = (1 - E_j) / \sum_{j=1}^{5} (1 - E_j) \qquad (5)$$

In the formula, Wj refers to the due weight of indicators.

Table 2. Weight assigned to each indicator.

Indicator	Weight
Loan provision ratio	0.1827
Provision coverage	0.5706
Non-performing loan ratio	0.0897
Single largest customer loan ratio	0.1094
Ten customers with the largest scale loan ratio	0.0476

Data source: Calculation in accordance with the formula given above

From where it is safe to draw the conclusion that, in accordance with the above process and calculation, the comprehensive measurement index of commercial bank credit risk can be obtained.

3.3 Establishment of multiple linear regression model

3.3.1 Construction of the basic model

The sample data of the 21 banks picked up, on the one hand, cover the cross-sectional data, on the other hand, contain the time series, which manages to form the balanced panel data. Hence, panel data model was applied by this empirical analysis to realize the implementation of empirical research on the relationship between leverage ratio and credit risk. The basic model is static panel data model, which can be expressed as:

$$Y_{it} = \alpha_i + \beta X_{it} + u_{it} \qquad (6)$$

In the formula, $I = 1, 2, 3...N$; $T = 1, 2, 3...T$. N refers to the number of sectional data, T refers to the number of time series, X refers to the explanatory variable, β refers to the regression coefficient, Y refers to the explained variable, α refers to i different individuals with i different intercept terms, and U refers to the random disturbance terms. In addition, in accordance with the research and analysis of relevant literature, GDP was taken as a control variable for considering that there is a strong correlation between GDP and the non-performing loan ratio of banks. M2 refers to the total supply of money and social funds, which is believed to show a great influence on the credit scale of commercial banks. The two indicators mentioned above were picked up as macroeconomic variables and were carefully added into the model. In addition, as many studies have proved a strong and close correlation between capital adequacy ratio and credit risk of commercial banks, index of capital adequacy ratio is also included in the control variable for regression.

Table 3. Definitions of variables in the model.

Types	Sign	Index	Definition
Explained variable	F	Credit risk index	Credit risk composite index calculated by entropy method
Explanatory variables	LEV	Leverage ratio	Tier 1 Capital – Tier 1 Capital deduction/Adjusted balance of off-balance sheet assets *100%
Control variables	CAR	Capital adequacy ratio	Capital/risk - weighted assets
	lnM2	Growth rate of broad money quantity	Year-on-year growth rate of money supply
	LnGDP	Economic growth rate	Year-on-year GDP growth rate

Table 4. Descriptive statistical results of variables.

| | Minimum | Maximum | Mean value | Standard deviation | The median | Kurtosis | | Kurtosis | |
						Statistic	Standard error	Statistic	Standard error
Comprehensive index of credit risk	2.02	5.48	3.14	0.82	2.82	0.94	0.22	−0.14	0.43
Leverage ratio	3.53	8.31	5.91	1.02	5.62	0.06	0.22	−0.47	0.43
Capital adequacy ratio	10.50	17.52	12.92	1.54	12.27	0.69	0.22	−0.07	0.43
The GDP growth rate	6.10	7.30	6.73	0.36	6.76	0.23	0.22	−0.36	0.43
M2 growth rate	8.17	13.34	10.25	1.82	11.01	0.46	0.22	−1.14	0.43

Data source: Calculation in accordance with SPSS 23

3.3.2 *Descriptive statistical results of variables*

As can be seen from the table, the credit risk composite index calculated by the entropy weight method sees fluctuations within the range from 5.48% to 2.02%. In accordance with the weighted calculation, the index demonstrated a relatively stable situation with small standard deviation. The volatility of leverage ratio was relatively high, which could be strongly associated with the fact that commercial banks mean to control the size of their own capital, thus to meet the minimum standard after the launch out of new leverage ratio regulation measures in China. Meanwhile, what is worth mentioning is that the capital adequacy ratio presents a large fluctuation, with a range of 7.02%. The median is biased to the minimum value, and the skewness also stands at a state of negative bias.

3.3.3 *Test of stationarity, collinearity, heteroscedasticity, and autocorrelation of sample data*

In accordance with the Fisher-PP test of the model, no unit root process for all variables can be found, and the data were stable. For collinearity, the test of variance inflation factors is applied in this study. VIF values of variables are all less than 5, which means no serious multicollinearity problem can be found in sample data. Heteroscedasticity can be found in the cross-section data of the sample data. GLS is a unique method of OLS under linear conditions, which makes it possible to correct heteroscedasticity and sequence dependence of random terms in linear models. Hence, this thesis adopted cross-section weights method for GLS, in which case the challenge of heteroscedasticity in the subsequent application of individual fixed effect model can be well resolved. Given the panel applied in this study is short, together with the small time span, it means less information can be obtained that is contained in each individual. In accordance with it, it is impossible to discuss if there is any autocorrelation within the disturbance terms. Hence, it is generally assumed that the disturbance term is subject to independent homodistribution.

3.3.4 *The selection of the model*

In accordance with the likelihood test and Wald test, the two sorts of tests tend to adopt the fixed effect model, while in comparison, the Hausman test is more inclined to apply the random utility model. Given the divergences and differences that emerge among different test results generated by different models, the two models are expected to be applied for regression in the follow-up, and comparison will be made to show the similarities and differences of the output results of the two models.

The empirical model of this thesis is:

$$F_{it} = \alpha_i + \beta_1 LEV_{it} + \beta_2 CAR_{it} + \beta_3 GDP_{it} + \beta_4 M2_{it} + u_{it}$$

Table 5. Model test results.

	Likelihood test	Hausman test	Wald test
Test statistics	Cross-section F(20,80)=14.243 Prob=0.0000	Cross-section random=0.0000 Prob=1.0000	F(1,121)-statistic=13.3552 Prob=0.0004

Data source: Calculation in accordance with Eviews 10

3.3.5 Regression results of the model

(1) Random effects model

Table 6. Estimation results of random effect model.

F	Coefficient	t	P
C	5.35111	3.3059	0.0012
LEV	−0.3658	−3.5007	0.0007
CAR	0.1411	2.2433	0.0267
lnGDP	−0.1802	−1.1309	0.2603
lnM2	−0.0637	−2.5994	0.0105

Data source: Calculation in accordance with Eviews 10

(2) Fixed effects model

Table 7. Estimation results of fixed effect model.

F	Coefficient	t	P
C	6.8523	6.7534	0.0000
LEV	−0.2743	−5.2793	0.0000
CAR	0.0103	0.2935	0.7697
lnGDP	−0.2421	−2.8561	0.0052
lnM2	−0.0574	−6.1191	0.0000

Data source: Calculation in accordance with Eviews 10

In terms of the comparison of the two models, the fitting degree of the fixed effect model is superior to that of the random effect model, among which the adjusted R2 of the fixed effect model reached 0.858 and the DW value reached 1.374, which proved that the fixed effect model enjoys better properties compared with the random utility model. In terms of the regression results of the two models, the leverage ratio of the two models has a significant negative impact on the credit risk of commercial banks at the significance level of 1%. The increase of leverage ratio will inevitably contribute to the rise of the credit risk level of commercial banks and the rise of the difficulty of management. This can be largely attributed to the simple reason that as the commercial banks attach much more importance to the leverage ratio of themselves in the capital and the ratio of net worth, at the same time, cast no eye to their credit business risk, the provision will be largely reduced. In addition, the ignorance on the quality of its net assets is also expected to make their loans endure excessive concentration on a few large customers, thus to lead to the significant increase of bad loans. All the factors will inevitably directly contribute to the increase in credit risk.

4 CONCLUSIONS

This thesis mainly focuses on the balanced panel data of commercial banks from 2014 to 2019 before the outbreak of COVID-19 and after the revision of the leverage ratio management measures, thus carrying out the research on the relationship between leverage ratio and the credit risk level of banks.

From the overall perspective of commercial banks, the leverage ratio shows a negative impact on the credit risk index of commercial banks in accordance with the calculation by entropy method. As the improvement of the regulatory level of the leverage ratio is expected to give a cut on the operating performance of commercial banks, the latter would make arduous efforts to level up the risks confronted once the requirements of the regulatory level of leverage ratio can be met. Among all the commercial banks selected to study in this thesis, a large amount of them witness the significant rise of concentration degree with the increase of leverage ratio. In addition, most of the commercial banks selected see their provision coverage fall or remain stable, which also means that from a general view, the banks' provisions have decreased in China. In such a case, it is safe to draw the conclusion that the leverage ratio regulation has imposed a negative impact on credit risk management in the country.

In terms of the relationship between macroeconomic environment and credit risk level, the M2 growth rate in China shares a positive correlation with the credit risk level of commercial banks, which means that the credit measurement of commercial banks is typically pro-cyclical. When the inflation rate remains low, the enterprise will find their benefits increase, which will lead to much more optimistic borrower's solvency. In such a case, the non-performing loan ratio decreased, together with the reduction of non-performing loans, thus to increase the rate of provision for coverage and provision for loan, and commercial banks can lend loan to more enterprises, contributing to the decrease of two concentration index and the reduction of the credit risk level of the commercial bank.

In accordance with the above conclusions, the following two suggestions are put forward.

(1) A more reasonable regulatory system should be established for the management of the leverage ratio of commercial banks. To achieve the realization of preventing the increase of credit risks of commercial banks, the market calls for a more flexible and comprehensive regulatory system, thus to provide restrictions for banks and refrain them from taking on high risks and excessive expansion, as well as prevent the emergence of regulatory arbitrage contributed by the decline of profits due to excessive supervision. The implementation effect of leverage ratio regulatory tools should be attached significant importance and be properly evaluated, and the effectiveness, practicability, and applicability of policy application should also be given priority. The innovation of regulatory early-warning mechanisms should be further enhanced. If it is necessary, the classification of commercial banks should be done in a more detailed way before the implementation of supervision which is highly relevant to the actual situation.

(2) It is of paramount importance to take into consideration the impact of macroeconomic policies on commercial banks. Great efforts will be made to strengthen the mechanism of information exchange and policy coordination between regulators and banks and level up the guidance of macroeconomic policies, thus to maximize the effectiveness of policies. The research and analysis of macroeconomic policies and macroeconomic situation should be further developed, thus providing macroeconomic guidance for the credit policies of commercial banks.

① The index calculation method is in accordance with the *Measures for Information Disclosure of Commercial Banks*.

② Data sources are from annual reports of commercial banks.

REFERENCES

Bluhm M, Faia E, Krahnen J P. Monetary Policy Implementation in an Interbank Network: The Effects on Systemic risk[R]. *SAFE Working Paper Series* 46, 2014.

Blum, J. M.. Why Basel II May Need a Leverage Ratio Restriction[J]. *Journal of Banking & Finance*, 2008(32): 1599–1707.

Dong Jingwen. Research on the Effectiveness of New Leverage Ratio Regulation on Credit Constraints of Listed Commercial Banks [J]. *Southern Finance*, 2014(09): 24–27+7.

Li Cheng. *Journal of Shanghai Lixin University of Accounting and Finance*, 2019(03): 64–77.

Li Hongmei, Li Jian. Analysis of the Impact of Macroeconomic Factors on the Credit Risk of Commercial Banks [J]. *Economist*, 2010(03): 202–204.

Liu Ping, LIANG Yu. Analysis of the Impact of Macroeconomic Factors on Credit Risk of Commercial Banks [J]. *Regional Financial Research*, 2011(02): 45–50.

Lu LU, Yang Wenhua. Can Leverage Ratio Regulation Effectively Reduce Systemic Risk in the Banking System? – Simulation Analysis in Line with Endogenous Network Model [J]. *Finance and Economics Research*, 2020, 46(02): 52–66.

Ma Bin, FAN Rui. The Influence of Leverage Ratio Regulation on Credit Risk of Listed Commercial Banks in China: System GMM Estimation in Accordance with Dynamic Panel Model [J]. *Economic Problems*, 2019(01): 41–47.

Mirza A, Strobel F. Leverage Requirements and Systemic Risk[R]. *Working Paper*, 2013.

Robert, J. A Leverage Ratio Rule for Capital Adequacy[J]. *Journal. of Banking and Finance*, 2013(3): 973–976.

Song K. Macroprudential Policy, Leverage Ratio and Bank Risk Taking [C]. *International Monetary Research Institute, Renmin University of China*, 2019: 1891–1910.

Wu X D. Credit Risk Management of Commercial Banks under the Condition of "Deleveraging" [J]. *Modern State-owned Enterprises Research*, 2018(02): 202.

Xia Min, Wang Rui. *Journal of Hebei University of Economics and Business (Comprehensive Edition)*, 2019, 19(03): 56–63.

Zheng Zhen. Regulation of Leverage Ratio of Commercial Banks: Policy Logic, Basic Status Quo and Optimization Strategy [J]. *Financial Economics*, 2019(18): 114–115.

Economic and Business Management – Huang & Zhang (Eds)
© 2022 Copyright the Author(s), ISBN: 978-1-032-06754-4

Research on two-stage price volatility of Beijing carbon market

Junyun Cai
School of Economics and Management, Nanjing University of Science and Technology, Nanjing, China

ABSTRACT: This paper takes the formal establishment of the national carbon market at the end of 2017 as the demarcation point, uses MATLAB tools to conduct an empirical study on the volatility of the two-stage carbon price daily return sequence of the Beijing carbon market, and establishes the two-stage fitting through model identification and ranking. The model and Monte Carlo simulation were performed to compare the two-stage volatility. It was found that the second stage, which was more impacted by extreme events, had higher volatility. The paper also emphasizes the importance of risk prevention and control mechanisms in order to have a beneficial impact on the mature operation of the national carbon market.

1 INTRODUCTION

With the rapid development of the carbon market in recent years and the formal establishment and operation of our country's national carbon market, the research on the fluctuation characteristics of the carbon market's yield will help us deeply understand the development and implementation of the carbon market in order to rationalize the predictions of future development trend.

From the pilot market to the national carbon market, as the first batch of construction, the Beijing carbon market has always reached 100% compliance rate and transactions are relatively active, and its prices are representative. This paper will conduct an empirical study on the price volatility of the Beijing carbon market from the two stages before and after the establishment of the national carbon market, analyze and compare its development and changes, in order to have a beneficial impact on the mature operation of the national carbon market.

2 LITERATURE REVIEW

2.1 *Research based on GARCH model*

Benz and Trueck (2006) found through empirical analysis that in the EU carbon emissions trading system, the carbon spot price series showed an obvious "spike and thick tail" phenomenon. Oberndorfer (2008) established a GARCH model to examine the relationship between the fluctuation of EUA yield and the stock price of the power industry. Chen and Wang (2010), Chevallier (2011), and Wu et al. (2016) used the EGARCH model to measure EUA volatility. Zhang and Wei (2011) conducted an empirical analysis on the operating characteristics of the EU ETS carbon futures

market by introducing research methods such as the GED-GARCH model.

2.2 *Research based on the combination of multiple models*

Benz and Stefan (2009) constructed the AR-GARCH model and the Markov mechanism conversion model. Wu et al. (2011) constructed the T-GARCH model and the nonlinear Markov mechanism conversion model in the linear measurement model. Daskalakis et al. (2009) used an empirical study on the pricing model of cost-of-carrying futures. Liu and Guo (2011) used SV-N, SV-T, SV-MN, and leverage-SV models to simulate the volatility of EUA carbon prices. Gao and Guo (2012) used wavelet analysis and VAR model to study the EU ETS market operation mechanism, the law of price fluctuations, and market efficiency. The studies of these scholars all show that the leverage effect of the carbon trading market is obvious.

3 DATA AND SOURCES

3.1 *Choice of carbon price data*

This paper uses the establishment of a national carbon market at the end of 2017 as the demarcation point, and conducts a two-stage research and analysis on the price volatility of the Beijing carbon market. The period from November 2013 to December 2017 is selected as the first stage, and that from January 2018 to June 2020 is selected as the second stage. The daily carbon price data comes from the China Carbon Emissions Trading Network. The carbon price range in the first stage is mainly 30–60 yuan and that in the second stage is mainly 50–90 yuan which fluctuates more. Among them, in April 2020, due to the impact

DOI 10.1201/9781003203704-27

149

of COVID-19 on the global economy, the carbon price once fell below 20 yuan which was far from the main range price. The calculation results in this paper are realized by MATLAB.

3.2 Descriptive statistics

In order to better analyze the volatility of the return rate series, this paper uses descriptive statistical indicators to analyze the basic characteristics of the two-stage carbon price daily return volatility. The descriptive statistics of the daily return rate of the two-stage carbon price are shown in Table 1.

Table 1. Descriptive statistics of the daily rate of return of the two-stage carbon price.

Stage	Value	Mean	Maximum	Minimum
1	1199	0.00004	0.4645	−0.4848
2	598	0.00091	1.5388	−1.5388

Stage	S.D.	Skewness	Kurtosis	JB test
1	0.0537	−0.7233	19.8003	ans = 1
2	0.1073	−0.1907	142.9272	ans = 1

It can be seen from Table 1 that the average daily rate of return of carbon prices in the two stages of the Beijing carbon market is close to 0 and both are greater than 0, indicating that the carbon prices in the two stages are both rising, and the average value of the second stage is significantly greater than that of the first stage. In terms of standard deviation, the larger value in the second stage indicates greater volatility. From the perspective of skewness, the skewness of the daily rate of return of the carbon price in the two stages is less than 0, showing a clear left-biasing trend, indicating that the rate of return is often lower than the average. From the perspective of kurtosis, both of them are obviously greater than 3, and the kurtosis of the second stage is much higher than the first stage, indicating that the second stage carbon price return is more concentrated. On the whole, the two-stage carbon price return has the characteristic of peak and thick tail, and the JB test value of the two-stage data is 1, indicating that the two-stage carbon price return rejects the assumption of normal distribution.

4 EMPIRICAL STUDY

4.1 Test of stationarity of daily return series

Compared with the observation method test which can only roughly judge stationarity, the unit root test is more accurate and reliable because of the statistical test using statistics. The initial unit root test is generally completed by the DF test, and later higher order time series have higher requirements for testing as the research continues to deepen. Therefore, the ADF test extended by Dickey and Fuller on the basis of the DF test is widely used. The "adftest" function judges

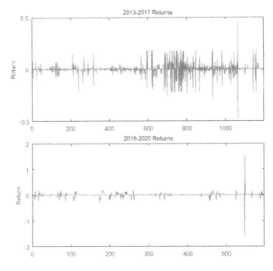

Figure 1. Two-stage carbon price daily yield trend.

whether the data is stable. The output results of the "adftest" function of the two-stage data are all 1, which indicates that the two-stage carbon price daily rate of return series are all stationary series. The volatility trend of the two-stage carbon price daily yield series is shown in Figure 1.

4.2 Model identification and ordering

From the above analysis, we can know that the two-stage carbon price daily rate of return series are stable. In the following, we use the "autocorr" and "parcorr" functions to test the autocorrelation and partial autocorrelation of the two-stage data to determine the form and order of time series model.

After model calculation, the autocorrelation lag order of the first-stage carbon price daily rate of return sequence is 2nd order, and the partial autocorrelation lag order is 3rd. The ARMA (2,3) model is established according to the final prediction error (FPE) value of 0.002557 and the mean square error (MSE) value of 0.002536. The same as above, the second-stage has an autocorrelation lag of order 1, and a partial autocorrelation lag of order 2. The ARMA (1,2) model is established according to the FPE value of 0.01039 and the MSE value of 0.01028.

4.3 Model diagnostic test

According to the ARMA (2,3) model and the ARMA (1,2) model established in the first stage and the second stage, respectively, the white noise test of its residual sequence is carried out. If the residual sequence is not a white noise sequence, it means that there is some valuable information in it, and the model needs further improvement. Thus we first use the "resid" function to generate residual series for the two models, and then use the "lbqtest" function to test the autocorrelation of the residual series, and the "archtest" function to test the ARCH effect of the residual series. Then we judge whether there is valuable information waiting to be discovered in the residual sequence of the two-stage carbon price daily return rate.

The output results of the autocorrelation LBQ test and the ARCH effect test of the residual sequence of the ARMA (2,3) model in the first stage are both 1, indicating that the residual sequence has autocorrelation and the ARCH effect, and the model needs to be improved accordingly. The second stage is the same. In addition, the ARCH effect tests of 10, 15, and 20 lag orders were performed on the corresponding model residual sequences of the two stages respectively, and the output results were all 1, indicating that the two-stage carbon price daily rate of return sequence has a high-order ARCH effect, that is, the GARCH effect. Therefore, we consider establishing the GARCH model further.

4.4 GARCH modeling

The GARCH model is derived from the extension of the constraints of the ARCH model. For the two-stage carbon price daily return rate series, GARCH (1,1), GARCH (1,2), and GARCH (2,1) models are established respectively.

In the output results of the first stage, the GARCH (1,2) model shows that the estimation is unstable, so the "lratiotest" function is used to compare the GARCH (1,1) model and the GARCH (2,1) model, and the results of output show that the GARCH (2,1) model has a higher degree of fitting. Therefore, the GARCH (2,1) model is selected for the first stage of the carbon price daily return sequence. The model fitting results are shown in Table 2. The same as above, the ARCH (1) model is selected for the second-stage carbon price daily rate of return sequence, and the model fitting results are shown in Table 3.

Table 2. The first stage GARCH (2,1) model fitting parameters.

	Value	Standard error	T-statistic
Constant	0.00002	0.000001	13.6344
GARCH (1)	0.0715812	0.0189135	3.78467
GARCH (2)	0.847366	0.0182265	46.4909
ARCH (1)	0.0810523	0.00269718	30.0508

Table 3. The second stage ARCH (1) model fitting parameters.

	Value	Standard error	T-statistic
Constant	0.00708485	0.000271594	26.0861
ARCH (1)	0.162845	0.0521816	3.12073

From Table 2, the first stage GARCH (2,1) model fits the sum of the GARCH term coefficients to 0.9189472, indicating that the current variance shock still has a great impact on the next period, and more than 90% of the shocks still exist in the next period. The sum of the coefficients of the GARCH term and the ARCH term is 0.9999995, which is less than 1 and satisfies the parameter constraints and is very close to 1. It is difficult to eliminate the internal situation, and shocks play an important role in all future predictions.

From Table 3, the fitting effect of the ARCH (1) model in the second stage is not very good. It may be due to the extreme impact caused by COVID-19 in April 2020, which produced extreme values and lowered the fitting effect.

4.5 Monte Carlo simulation

We use the "simulate" function to perform Monte Carlo simulations on the two-stage daily carbon price return series and explore and compare the fluctuations of the respective models of the two-stage carbon price daily return series. The number of Monte Carlo simulation paths are all 500, and the simulation results are shown in Figure 2.

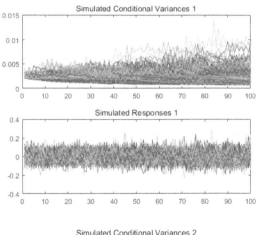

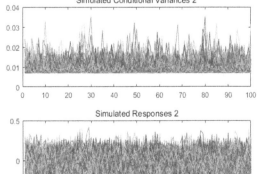

Figure 2. Two-stage Monte Carlo simulation results.

According to the results of the two-stage Monte Carlo simulation, the fluctuation range of the daily carbon price return sequence in the second stage is significantly greater than that in the first stage. Price volatility has also increased, and carbon market risk prevention and control mechanisms are particularly important.

5 CONCLUSIONS

The research on the volatility characteristics of the carbon market yield will help us deeply understand the development and implementation of the carbon market, so as to make reasonable predictions about the future development trend. In addition, volatility represents the uncertainty and irregularity of ups and downs, which can reflect market risk to a certain extent. Researching the characteristics of volatility that change over time is a prerequisite for further research on the risk value of the entire market. This paper took the formal establishment of the national carbon market at the end of 2017 as the demarcation point, conducted an empirical study on the volatility of the two-stage carbon price daily return sequence of the Beijing carbon market, established a two-stage fitting model through model identification and order determination, and conducted a Monte Carlo simulation to compare the fluctuations in the two stages. By combining data descriptive statistics and model empirical analysis, results have been obtained.

First, the performance characteristics of the daily rate of return of carbon prices in the two stages of the Beijing carbon market are different. The price range of the first stage is significantly smaller than that of the second stage, indicating that carbon trading is more active after the national carbon market is officially established, and the price range will rise accordingly. The kurtosis of the second stage is much higher than that of the first stage, indicating that the carbon price of second stage is more concentrated, and includes extreme values more obviously.

Second, the two-stage carbon price daily rate of return sequence of the Beijing carbon market both showed obvious peak and thick-tail fluctuations, and the first stage had significant volatility persistence characteristics. What is more, external shocks from the previous period will aggravate the volatility of the current daily yield, and the duration of the volatility is generally longer which is not conducive to the stability of carbon prices.

Third, the design of mechanisms for preventing extreme risks in the carbon market is particularly important. An analysis of the volatility of the two-stage daily carbon price return sequence of the Beijing carbon market shows that the second stage, which is more affected by extreme events, has greater volatility, which indicates that the impact of extreme events will significantly increase carbon market risks and is not conducive to national carbon. The development and smooth operation of the market and the optimal design of risk prevention and control mechanisms play an important role in enhancing market confidence and giving full play to the effects of the carbon market.

REFERENCES

Benz, E. & Stefan, T. 2009. Modeling the price dynamics of CO2 emission allowances. *Energy Economics*, 31(1): 4–15.

Benz, E. & Trueck, S. 2006. CO2 emission allowances trading in Europe – Specifying a new class of assets. *Investment Management & Financial Innovations*, 4(3): 30-40.

Chen, X.H. & Wang, Z.Y. 2010. An empirical study on the price mechanism of European carbon emissions trading. *Science & Technology Progress and Policy*, 27(19): 142–147.

Chevallier, J. 2011. Detecting instability in the volatility of carbon prices. *Energy Economics*, 33(1): 99–110.

Daskalakis, G., et al. 2009. Modeling CO2 emission allowance prices and derivatives: Evidence from the European trading scheme. *Journal of Banking & Finance*, 33(7): 1230–1241.

Gao, Y. & Guo, K. 2012. Global carbon trading market structure and its price characteristics: Taking the European climate trading system as an example. *Studies of International Finance*, 12: 82–88.

Liu, W.Q. & Guo, Z.H. 2011. EU ETS carbon emission futures market risk measurement: An empirical analysis based on SV model. *System Engineering*, 10: 14–23.

Oberndorfer, U. 2008. EU Emission Allowances and the Stock Market: Evidence from the Electricity Industry. *Zew Discussion Papers*, 68(4): 1116–1126.

Wu, H.Y., et al. 2011. Research on the dynamic effects of the international carbon market: based on the ECX CER market. *Journal of Shanxi University of Finance and Economics*, 9: 18–24.

Wu, Z.X., et al. 2016. Research on EU ETS price volatility and risk based on different distribution EGARCH models. *Mathematics in Practice and Theory*, 24: 10–16.

Zhang, Y.J. & Wei, Y.M. 2011. Mean reversion of international carbon futures price: An empirical analysis based on EU ETS. *Systems Engineering-Theory & Practice*, 31(2): 214–220.

Economic and Business Management – Huang & Zhang (Eds)
© 2022 Copyright the Author(s), ISBN: 978-1-032-06754-4

Differential game research on fresh food supply chain based on fresh-keeping efforts

Lihong Deng & Chaoyan Peng
School of Economics and Management, Harbin Engineering University, Harbin, China

ABSTRACT: As a necessity of people's lives, fresh food occupies an important position in people's lives. However, fresh food is not easy to preserve. The natural attributes of corrosion are obvious, the supply chain node enterprises lack the awareness of preservation, and the cost of preservation and transportation is high. Fresh foods are prone to deterioration and loss from the supplier to the consumption stage, reducing the quality of fresh foods. Low-quality fresh food cannot meet the needs of fresh consumers. In response to this situation, this article studies a supply chain composed of retailer and supplier. The supplier is responsible for the supply and preservation of fresh food, and the retailer is responsible for sales. Aiming at the characteristics of the decrease in freshness over time, this paper designs a market demand function that is inversely proportional to the price of fresh food and directly proportional to the freshness, and constructs a supply chain structure that takes into account the freshness of supplier. This paper establishes a differential game model, and finally compares the equilibrium solutions under the two modes of centralized decision-making and decentralized decision-making. By comparing the two models, the freshness of freshness suppliers, the freshness of fresh food, the selling price, and the difference in supply chain profits. This study has the following conclusions: compared with the decision-making model, the supplier under the centralized decision-making model has greater freshness preservation, higher freshness, and greater supply chain profits. Finally, the conclusions of the model are verified by sensitivity analysis.

Keywords: Fresh food supply chain; Differential game; Fresh-keeping effort

1 INTRODUCTION

With the development of the economy, the consumption level of residents has also increased rapidly. Residents' demand for fresh food increases. Because of this, the government has also increased its attention on fresh products, and the academic community has also increased research on fresh products following the policy. However, the storage and transportation of fresh food requires special preservation measures, and the current preservation methods in China are not perfect; the fresh food is prone to deterioration and serious losses in the process of circulation from the supplier to the consumer. Therefore, driven by the goal of maximizing the overall profit of the supply chain, saving resources, and effectively meeting consumer needs, improving fresh-keeping technology and controlling losses have become indispensable parts of the fresh-food supply chain [1-4]. At present, the fresh supply chain scholars mainly focus on the coordination of the fresh supply chain, the preservation of fresh products, pricing, and ordering. In the literature on pricing issues, there is more and more research on dynamic pricing strategies and joint pricing decisions for fresh agricultural products. Herbon et al. [5] determined

the dynamic price and the best replenishment plan by studying the dynamic pricing of perishables. Ghoreishi et al. [6] considered the inflation and customer return, and studied the optimal pricing and replenishment strategies. In terms of dynamic pricing, Wang et al. [1] designed a dynamic pricing strategy. None of the above-mentioned documents considered the impact of preservation efforts when studying pricing issues.

There are also individual studies that analyze the impact of efforts on supply chain revenue. Wang [7] analyzed the impact of these two factors on freshness from the perspective of suppliers' fresh-keeping efforts and transportation time, and constructed a centralized decision-making model and a decentralized decision-making model. It also analyzes and compares the prices of fresh products, the efforts of suppliers to keep produce fresh, and the profits of the supply chain [8], based on the theory of consumer utility, and on this basis, considering price integration and logistics cooperation. The impact of product freshness and product price on consumer purchase intention was analyzed, a pricing coordination model was established, and a revenue sharing contract and linearity were established. The compensation contract model was coordinated, and the optimal solution of the

DOI 10.1201/9781003203704-28

153

two coordination strategies was obtained. Wang et al. [9] considered the "double loss" in quantity and quality of fresh agricultural products in the transportation and circulation to be an optimized three-level cold chain inventory model in which freshness affects demand. Yan et al. [10] analyzed the attributes of fresh agricultural products, and then comprehensively considered the impact of fair behavior and the attributes of fresh agricultural products on the fresh supply chain. Cao et al. [11] established a decentralized model and a centralized decision-making model, and then analyzed the profits of the two models. The study found that the centralized decision-making model has relatively less free-riding behavior, which is more conducive to increasing supply chain profits.

To sum up, the existing literature is rich in the research direction and content of the fresh food supply chain, but mainly analyzes the income, pricing, and coordination strategies of each member of the supply chain, such as wholesale prices and retail prices. However, the existing literature lacks consideration of the dynamic game process, that is, the game in continuous time and the research process of constantly changing freshness. In the fresh food supply chain coordination, the coordination contract plays an important role. Product freshness is an important factor affecting market demand. Existing research lacks consideration of consumer psychology, and most of them only consider the impact of product prices on market demand. This article comprehensively considers factors such as inter-enterprise game behavior and product freshness, and establishes two game models of suppliers and retailers for comparative analysis. On this basis, this article can improve the way retailers and suppliers manage the fresh food supply chain.

2 MODEL CONSTRUCTION AND ASSUMPTIONS

This article establishes a fresh food supply chain consisting of supplier S and retailer R. In this article, it is assumed that the freshness of fresh products will decrease as time increases. Freshness and the selling price of fresh food retailers affect the demand for food. In the supply chain of this article, fresh food retailers are connected to the consumer market, and based on the forecast market's demand for fresh food, they then order a corresponding amount of fresh food from the supplier, and the fresh food supplier is responsible for the fresh food delivery. At the same time, due to the characteristics of fresh foods, i.e., that they are prone to spoilage and rot, and the quality is greatly affected by the environment, suppliers adopt certain preservation methods to delay fresh foods from becoming stale and ensure the quality of fresh foods. The cost of preservation efforts made is borne by the supplier alone. In the fresh food supply chain, the supplier's profit is represented by $\pi_G(t)$, the retailer's profit is represented by $\pi_L(t)$. The total profit of the supply chain is represented by $\pi_a(t)$. The decentralized decision-making model is denoted by the superscript d, and the centralized decision-making model is denoted by c.

2.1 Basic assumptions

Hypothesis 1: Referring to the Albert [12] market demand function model, the sales price of fresh food and the freshness of fresh food affect market demand. According to this, the following function is used to express the market demand of fresh food:

$$D(t) = a - bp(t) + k\theta(t) \qquad (1)$$

Among them, a is the market size of fresh food, b and k respectively represent the elasticity coefficient of market demand to price and freshness, then $a > 0$, $b > 0, k > 0, a - bc_0 > 0$.

Hypothesis 2: Learning from the research of Ouardighi [13], we assume that the freshness of fresh food is a state variable $\theta(t)$, the following state equation represents its change process:

$$\dot{\theta}(t) = e(t) - \delta\theta(t) \qquad (2)$$

Among them, $\theta(t)$ is the freshness value of fresh food at time t, the initial freshness of fresh food is $\theta(0) = \theta_o$, $e(t)$ represents the freshness preservation effort of the supplier at time t; δ is the rate of decrease in freshness over time, including the negative effects caused by various factors such as insufficient technical level and incomplete equipment.

Hypothesis 3: Drawing on the assumption of the relationship between results and input in the literature [14], the relationship between preservation cost and preservation effort is expressed as:

$$c(e) = ue^2(t)/2 \qquad (3)$$

The cost of preservation efforts is represented by $c_{(e)}$, and the cost coefficient of preservation efforts is represented by u.

Hypothesis 4: We assume that the unit cost of fresh produce is fixed and does not change to C_0 with the freshness. The retailer obtains the wholesale price g(t) from the supplier, and the retailer sells it to the consumer at the retail price p(t), and does not include cost of sales.

2.2 Model establishment

2.2.1 Centralized decision-making

From the overall perspective of the supply chain, maximizing the profit of the supply chain is the goal of the centralized decision-making model. Its instantaneous profit expression is:

$$\pi(t) = [P(t) - C_0] D(t) - ue^2(t)/2 \qquad (4)$$

Under the centralized decision model, in order to maximize the overall profit of the supply chain, it is necessary to find the best supplier's fresh-keeping effort and the most favorable selling price $p(t)$ in a continuous period of time $t \in [0, +\infty)$. The objective function is:

$$\max \int_0^{+\infty} \pi(t)e^{-\rho t}dt \qquad (5)$$

s.t $\dot{\theta}(t) = e(t) - \delta\theta(t)$

Among them, ρ represents the discount rate, which is greater than 0. Next, we find the price $P(t)$, when the objective function value is maximized. The value of freshness preservation effort is $e(t)$. The corresponding present value Hamilton function is:

$$(A = [p(t) - C_0][a - bP(t) + k\theta(t)] - ue^2(t)/$$
$$2 + \lambda_1(t)[e(t) - \delta\theta(t)] \qquad (6)$$

The shadow price of the state variable $\theta(t)$ is $\lambda_1(t)$. The function of common state equation and the first-order conditional equation that maximize the present value of the Hamiltonian are:

$$\partial A/\partial p = a - 2bp(t) + k\theta(t) + bC_0 = 0 \qquad (7)$$
$$\partial A/\partial e = \lambda_1(t) - ue(t) = 0 \qquad (8)$$
$$\lambda_1(t) = (\rho + \delta)\lambda_1(t) - kp(t) + kC_0 \qquad (9)$$

The pricing strategy of the fresh food supply chain under the centralized decision-making model can be obtained from equation (7), namely:

$$P(g) = (a + k\theta(t) + bC_0)/2b \qquad (10)$$

It can be obtained from the pricing formula (10) that the market price of fresh products will increase with the increase in freshness, namely: $\partial p/\partial\theta > 0$ Next, we further study the law of changes in preservation efforts, find the derivative of the time t for the first-order conditional formula (8), and then substitute it into formula (9). After calculation, we can get:

$$\dot{e}(t) = (\rho + \delta)e(t) - k[a + k\theta(t) - bc_0]/2bu \qquad (11)$$

From formula (11) $\partial\dot{e}/\partial\theta < 0$, it can be seen that the changes in preservation efforts is negatively correlated with the change of freshness, so when the freshness reaches the optimal level, the preservation effort will remain stable, and the corresponding preservation effort will no longer change, that is, $\theta(t) = \theta^*, \partial e/\partial\theta = 0$. Next, we construct a fresh food supply chain control system and calculate its equilibrium solution. At the same time, through equations (2) and (11), the dynamic control system of the management level of the fresh food supply chain can be obtained, namely:

$$\begin{cases} \dot{\theta}(t) = e(t) - \delta\theta(t) \\ \dot{e}(t) = (\rho + \delta)e(t) - \frac{k[a+k\theta(t)-bc_0]}{2bu} \end{cases} \qquad (12)$$

Through the above formula, the following equilibrium solutions can be obtained:

$$e^c = \frac{\delta k(a - bc_0)}{2bu\delta(\rho + \delta) - k^2}, \theta^c = \frac{k(a - bc_0)}{2bu\delta(\rho + \delta) - k^2},$$

Where $2bu\delta(\rho + \delta) - k^2$ is greater than 0 ;

$$P^c = \frac{u\delta(\rho + \delta)(a + bc_0) - C_0k^2}{2bu\delta(\rho + \delta) - k^2}$$

$$D^C = \frac{bu\delta(\rho + \delta)(a - bc_0)}{2bu\delta(\rho + \delta) - k^2}$$

$$\pi_a^c = \frac{u\delta^2(a - bC_0)^2[2bu(p + \delta)^2 - k^2]}{2[2bu\delta(\rho + \delta) - k^2]^2}$$

2.2.2 Decentralized decision

In the case of decentralized decision-making, this article assumes that the leader of the fresh food supply chain is the supplier. The order of the game between fresh food retailers and suppliers is: the first step is for the supplier to determine the wholesale price of fresh food and the degree of fresh-keeping effort; the second step is for the retailer to determine the market price after the supplier's decision. We use inverse induction to solve the model solution, and let $\pi_G(t)$ denote the instantaneous profit of the fresh food supplier under the differential game model, and $\pi_L(t)$ respectively denote the instantaneous profit function of the fresh food retailer. According to the above assumptions, we can get:

$$\pi_G(t) = [g_{(t)} - c_0][a - bp(t) + k\theta(t)]$$
$$- ue^2(t)/2 \qquad (13)$$
$$\pi_L(t) = [P(t) - g_{(t)}][a - bp(t) + k\theta(t)] \qquad (14)$$

Suppliers dominate the fresh produce supply chain and are the first to predict the market price of fresh produce. Therefore, we must first find the market price of the product. Take the partial derivative of equation (14) and set its value to 0 , it can be solved:

$$p(\theta, g) = [a + k\theta(t) + bg(t)]/2b \qquad (15)$$

From equation (15), we get, $\partial p/\partial\theta > 0, \partial p/\partial g > 0$, the above two ine- qualities indicate the market price of fresh food is positively correlated with freshness and wholesale prices. Next, we list the objective function of fresh food supplier. Fresh food suppliers seek to the best wholesale price and preservation within a continuous time $t \geq 0$, so as to maxistion the discount value of their profits. Therefore, tuting equation (15) into equation (13) and ing equation (1), the function can be obtained as lows: $\max \int_0^{+\infty} \pi_G(t)e^{-\rho t}dt$ $\theta(t) = e(t) - \delta\theta(t)$ qualities indicate the market price of fresh food is positively correlated with freshness and wholesale prices. Next, we list the objective function of the fresh food supplier. Fresh food suppliers seek to find the best wholesale price and preservation effort within a continuous time $t \geq 0$, so as to maximize the discount value of their profits. Therefore, substituting equation (15) into equation (13) and combining equation (1), the function can be obtained as follows: can Due to space limitations, we only give the equilibrium solution in this case. Its calculation process is like centralized mode. The solutions are as follows:

$$max \int_0^{+\infty} \pi_G(t)e^{-\rho t}dt$$
$$\dot{\theta}(t) = e(t) - \partial\theta(t) \tag{16}$$

Due to space limitations, we only give the equilibrium solution in this case. Its calculation process is like centralized mode. The solutions are as follows:

$$g^d = \frac{2\delta u(a + bc_0) - c_0 k^2}{4b\delta u(\rho + \delta) - k^2}$$

$$p^d = \frac{u\delta(\rho + \delta)(3a + bc_0) - k^2 c_0}{4b\delta u(\rho + \delta) - k^2}$$

$$D^d = \frac{bu\delta(\rho + \delta)(a - bc_0)}{4b\delta u(\rho + \delta) - k^2}$$

$$\pi_G^d = \frac{u\delta^2 (a - bc_0)^2 \left[4bu(\rho + \delta)^2 - k^2\right]}{2\left[4b\delta u(\rho + \delta) - k^2\right]^2}$$

$$\pi_L^d = \frac{bu^2\delta^2(\rho + \delta)^2 (a - bc_0)^2}{\left[4b\delta u(\rho + \delta) - k^2\right]^2}$$

3 RESULT ANALYSIS

Comparing the equilibrium solutions under centralized and decentralized decision-making, the following proposition can be obtained.

Proposition 1: The freshness supplier's optimal preservation effort under the decentralized decision-making model is lower than the optimal preservation effort under the centralized decision-making model, namely $e^c > e^d$.
Prove: make $B = e^c - e^d$.

$$B = \frac{bu\delta^2 k(\rho + \delta)(a - bc_0)}{\left[2bu\delta(\rho + \delta) - k^2\right]\left[4b\delta u(\rho + \delta) - k^2\right]}$$

because $2bu\delta(\rho + \delta) - k^2 > 0$, $4b\delta u(\rho + \delta) - k^2 > 0$, $a - bc_0 > 0$, so B > 0, so $e^c > e^d$.

Proposition 2: Compared with the decentralized decision-making model, the centralized decisionmaking model improves the optimal product freshness, which is : $\theta^c > \theta^d$.
Prove: We bring the values of θ^c and θ^d into θ^c/θ^d,

$$\frac{\theta^c}{\theta^d} = \frac{4b\delta u(\rho + \delta) - k^2}{2b\delta u(\rho + \delta) - k^2} > 1$$

so $\theta^c > \theta^d$, The proposition is proved.

Proposition 3: The optimal total profit of fresh food channels is satisfied, $\pi_a^c > \pi_a^d$.
Prove : let $C = \pi_a^c - \pi_a^d$,

$$C = \frac{bu^2\delta^2 (a - bc_0)^2 (\rho + \delta)\left\{bu\delta(\rho + \delta)\left[2bu\delta(\rho + \delta)^2 + k^2(2\rho - \delta)\right] - \rho k^4\right\}}{\left[2bu\delta(\rho + \delta) - k^2\right]^2 \left[4b\delta u(\rho + \delta) - k^2\right]^2}$$

because $bu\delta(\rho + \delta)^2 > bu\delta^2(\rho + \delta)$, $2bu\delta(\rho + \delta) - k^2 > 0, 2bu\delta(\rho + \delta)^2 + k^2(2\rho - \delta) > 2\rho k^2$, then there is $bu\delta\rho + \delta)\left[2bu\delta(\rho + \delta)^2 + k^2(2\rho - \delta)\right] > \rho k^4$, then $C > 0$. The proposition is proved.

From the above analysis, it can be seen that the total profit of the fresh food channel and the preservation of freshness under decentralized decision-making has not yet reached best state. To promote further cooperation between the fresh food supply chain members, the centralized control model tends to develop.

4 SENSITIVITY ANALYSIS

In order to verify the above assumptions, the model parameters are assigned and sensitivity analysis is carried out. This article sets a=100, b=10, $C_0 = 5$, p=0.3, $\delta = 0.2$, k=1, $u = 1$. The cost coefficient of u

as a supplier's preservation technology is an important parameter of this article, because it affects the freshness of the product and the price of the product by influencing the supplier's freshness investment level. Therefore, we use $u = 1$ as the basis and change its value to study the influence of u value on the equilibrium solution.

Table 1 shows the influence of value on the equilibrium solution. It can be found that under the decentralized mode and the centralized mode, with the increase of u, the freshness of the suppliers, the product freshness, commodity prices, and the overall profit level of the supply chain show a downward trend. The increase in the cost coefficient of preservation efforts represents an increase in the cost of each unit of the supplier's preservation efforts. Therefore, the supplier will reduce the investment in preservation efforts, and the freshness of the product will decrease accordingly. It can be derived from the price expression that the price of a product is directly proportional to the freshness, and the price also increases as the freshness increases. The market demand of the product is directly proportional to the freshness of the product and inversely proportional to the selling price. The decrease in demand caused by the decline in freshness is greater than the increase in demand caused by the decline in prices, so the demand for goods decreases. As market demand decreases and prices drop, the total profit of the supply chain also decreases.

Table 1. The effect of preservation effort cost coefficient u on equilibrium solution

u	e^c/e^d	θ^c/θ^d	p^c/p^d	π_a^c/π_a^d
0.8	16.7/4.6	83.3/22.7	11.7/10.5	333.3/90.9
0.9	12.5/3.9	62.5/19.2	10.6/10.2	246.1/83.2
1	10/3.3	50/16.7	10/10	200/77.8
1.1	8.3/2.9	41.7/14.7	9.6/9.9	171.9/73.8
1.2	7.1/2.6	35.7/13.2	9.3/9.7	153.1/70.6

5 CONCLUSIONS

This paper comprehensively considers the supplier's freshness effort, product freshness, and game behavior among participants in the fresh food supply chain, formulates a differential game model that takes into account the freshness effort, compares the equilibrium solution under the centralized and decentralized modes, and adopts data analysis to verify the model. The research of this paper draws the conclusion: compared with the decentralized decision-making model, the supplier of the centralized decision-making model has higher investment in preservation efforts, higher product freshness, and greater total profit in the fresh food supply chain. Therefore, the following points are made. Recommendation: under the decentralized model, enterprises in all links cannot guarantee the freshness of fresh food under the premise of maximizing their own interests. The increase in the freshness of fresh food plays an important role in increasing the overall income of the supply chain. The article recommends that members of the supply chain strengthen cooperation and reduce gaming. Strengthening cooperation between enterprises can not only increase the profit of the supply chain, but also increase the freshness of fresh food, satisfies consumers' requirements for fresh food quality, and meets their own goal of pursuing profits. This article does not consider the situation of incomplete information, it is a game based on the assumption of complete information. We can continue to learn in future research.

REFERENCES

[1] Wang D P, Chen L, Li F. Supply chain coordination of agricultural product under random yield[J]. *Control and Decision*, 2012, 27(6): 881–885.

[2] Wang X, Li D. A dynamic product quality evaluation based pricing model for perishable food supply chains[J]. *Omega*, 2012, 40(6): 906–917.

[3] Song H, Gao X. Green supply chain game model and analysis under revenue-sharing contract[J]. *Journal of Cleaner Production*, 2017, 170: 183–192.

[4] Soto-Silva W E, Nadal-Roig E, González-Araya M C, et al. Operational research models applied to the fresh fruit supply chain[J]. *European Journal of Operational Research*, 2016, 251(2): 345–355.

[5] Herbon A, Khmelnitsky E. Optimal dynamic pricing and ordering of a perishable product under additive effects of price and time on demand[J]. *European Journal of Operational Research*, 2017, 260(2): 546–556.

[6] Ghoreishi M, Mirzazadeh A, Weber G W. Optimal pricing and ordering policy for non-instantaneous deteriorating items under inflation and customer returns[J]. *Optimization*, 2014, 63(12): 1785–1804.

[7] Wang Daoping, Zhu Mengying, Wang Ting ting. Research on the Cost Sharing Contract of Ecological Supply Chain Fresh-keeping Efforts[J]. *Industrial Engineering and Management*, 2020, v.25; No.141(02): 40–47.

[8] Chen Yiming, Zhang Qiongsi, Fan Chen, et al. Fresh food supply chain coordination strategy research under the background of channel integration [J]. *Economic Mathematics*, 2020, 037(001): 43–47.

[9] Wang Shuyun, Fan Xiaoqing, Ma Xueli, et al. Three-level cold chain inventory optimization model considering commodity freshness and quantitative loss[J]. *Journal of System Management*, 2020, v.29(02): 212–219.

[10] Yan B, Wu J, Jin Z, et al. Decision-making of fresh agricultural product supply chain considering the manufacturer's fairness concerns[J]. *4OR*, 2020, 18.

[11] Cao Yu, Wu Kan, Xiong Shouyao. A Study on Fresh-keeping Efforts and Order Pricing in the Fresh Food Supply Chain[J]. *Operations Research and Management*, 2019, 028(010): 100–109.

[12] Albert Y Ha, Tong S, Zhang H. Sharing demand information in competing supply chains with production diseconomies[J]. *Mathematics of Operations Research*, 2011, 57(3): 566–581.

[13] F E Ouardighi. Supply quality management with optimal wholesale price and revenue sharing contracts: A two-stage game approach[J]. *International Journal of Production Economics*, 2014, 156(oct.): 260–268.

[14] Sun Yuling, Hong Meina, Shi Kunran. Fresh agricultural product supply chain revenue sharing contract considering fairness concerns[J]. *Operations Research and Management*, 2015, 24(6): 103–111.

Economic and Business Management – Huang & Zhang (Eds)
© 2022 Copyright the Author(s), ISBN: 978-1-032-06754-4

Research on the effect of RCEP on China's manufacturing trade—based on the dynamic recursive GTAP model

Nina Zhu
School of Economics and Management, Beijing University of Technology, Beijing, China

Lixing Lv*, Siyi Huang & Kunyao Gong
Beijing-Dublin International College, Beijing University of Technology, Beijing, China

ABSTRACT: RCEP as a mega-FTA plays an important role in the world trade, especially for China. In this paper, China's manufacturing trade networks from 2022 to 2057 are established using expanded GTAP model (Tenth Version) with dynamic recursion method. The paper also constructs two new models which are baseline model and tariff shocked model. By using these two models, it draws out dynamic trends of RCEP countries' manufacturing trade volume, complementarity, export advantages, and additionally estimates net trade effects that are brought out by the force of RECP. The results show the following: First, the total volume of manufacturing trade within RCEP region will expand from 1.77 trillion US dollars in 2022 to 3.54 trillion US dollars in 2040. For China, tariff reduction will boost the volume of China's high-quality manufacturing exports. Second, the trade complementarity between China and some Association of Southeast Asian Nations (ASEAN) countries will decline in short term and go up in medium and long run. Last, trade complementarity between China and Japan/South Korea will continue to increase.

1 INTRODUCTION

On November 15, 2020, China with Japan, South Korea, New Zealand, Australia, and 10 ASEAN countries formally signed the agreement of Regional Comprehensive Economic Partnership (RCEP). Since these 15 countries cover almost 30% of the world's population, GDP and trade flow, RCEP has been the largest FTA in the world. Therefore, research on the net trade effect of RCEP is of much significance.

This article expands GTAP model with dynamic recursion method, specifically it first builds up a baseline model to simulate macroeconomic changes under RCEP condition then establishes a tariff shock model to calculate effectiveness of RCEP tariff reduction. Based on these analyses, it predicts the dynamic trend of RCEP trade volume, trade complementarity, and export advantages of the manufacturing industry for the next 36 years and estimates the net effects of RCEP. The marginal contributions of this article are mainly four points: first, it calibrates consecutive timestamps of GTAP baseline model with dynamic recursive. This method can promise to get real effect with the shock of policy under consistent macroeconomic conditions changing. Second, it does not aggregate production departments and regions in order to get detailed information under the modeling process. Third, this article uses real tariff reduction data of RCEP to conduct

shock analysis. Finally, this article plugs extended modeling results into UN Comtrade Database and forks the entire database into baseline and tariff shock scenarios for the next 36 years.

2 LITERATURE REVIEW

Due to lack of data on tariff concession and the ambiguity of policy implementations, early researches on RCEP topic usually focus on qualitative analysis. Athukorala (2016) found that RCEP could help East Asian countries become more integrated by increasing intra-regional trade. He also argued that the reduction of tariff had potential force to improve manufacturing competitiveness in this region through vertically specialized production. In recent 10 years, many scholars had started to make comparisons with different economic effects of RCEP and some other Free Trade Agreements (FTAs), like Asia-Pacific. Wilson (2015) stated that 'the role of ASEAN,' 'US-China geopolitical rivalries' and 'defensive concerns' were the three main factors, and these things determined how the governments who are in the overlapping areas made their own decisions. Hamanaka (2014) emphasized that opposing RCEP's economic framework with Trans-Pacific Partnership (TPP) was incorrect, as the essential parts of both agreements were dual control over 'membership' and 'agenda.'

Since RCEP was signed last year, some scholars have begun to make quantitative analysis of RCEP

---
*Corresponding Author

158

DOI 10.1201/9781003203704-29

effects on this regional economy by using Computable General Equilibrium model. Li, Wang, and Whalley (2016) used CGE model to compare effects of RCEP, CJK FTA, China-TPP, China-US FTA, and China-India FTA. They concluded that among all these mega deals, RCEP and China-TPP agreements would yield the highest benefits for China's welfare and trade. By adopting the GTAP model, Li and Moon (2018) found that RCEP would improve trade volume for both China and South Korea to around 8 billion dollars and 2.5% and their national income would also increase 1.5% and 0.6% respectively. A study by Rahman and Ara (2015) showed us the signing of TPP, TTIP, and RCEP would seriously harm the current interests of South Asian countries outside these FTA regions. Mahadevan and Nugroho (2019) examined whether the benefits brought out by signing of RCEP agreement can offset the detrimental effects of Sino-US trade war by using dynamic GTAP model.

3 MODELING AND DATA

3.1 *Model design*

This article uses GTAP model as its benchmark. The GTAP model is constructed based on general equilibrium theory. This model starts with simulating the changes in international and domestic prices caused by the exogenous policy changes. Price changing will bring out further changes in other variables such as consumption, production, investment, savings, and the use of producing factors. GTAP model can finally capture the impact of above changes over entire economic system.

First, this article separates 15 member countries and aggregates other countries as the rest of the world, then retains 65 production departments. Most of the existing studies have constructed highly aggregated GTAP models, the previous method just analyzes the trends of variables. The advantage of this paper is that it is able to keep the details of the GTAP models, and the output data of models will not be distorted due to excessive aggregation. Second, it calibrates the baseline GTAP model with dynamic recursion. For a single timestamp, this paper improves the method of Walmsley, Dimaranan, and McDougall (2006), using macroeconomic variables of GDP, GDI, population, skilled labor, and unskilled labor to update the original GTAP model. At the same time, the tariff will be updated through the built-in module of GTAP model. In order to comply with the principle that shocking of tariff concession should be carried out under consistent macroeconomic conditions, this article uses recursive method to extend single calibration to the time series. However, most of the existing studies only update the baseline once, which can only ensure the first tariff shock complies with the above-mentioned principles. Third, this article establishes tariff shock GTAP model. This process uses RCEP tariff concession of HS commodities (6-digit data) to shock GTAP baseline model

with corresponding years to ensure the model's authenticity and accuracy. Finally, this article plugs forecast trade changing data into UN Comtrade Database. Most of current researches on GTAP model just satisfied with the data of direct output, and the database generated in this paper can be used for the other bilateral trade research.

Basically GTAP model is a very comprehensive system consisting of many nonlinear equations and is based on the price change rate, which describes the supply, demand, exchange, and distribution processes in this economic system. The shocking process of this paper first deals with tariff reduction problem and then finds a new equilibrium point which is equivalent to changing initial solution of some equations, and finally obtains variation on the other variables. Specifically, the W.B. Gragg method with 16-32-48 steps of automatic precision is used to solve the model in this article. The main reason to use multi-step solution is to avoid linearization errors, which can improve accuracy of our solutions At the end, all GTAP models included in this paper have achieved more than nine points in overall variables accuracy and overall data accuracy measured by modified Chernoff statistic.

3.2 *Modeling*

3.2.1 *Baseline model*

This article assumes that countries will complete approval of RCEP agreement in 2022, which means macroeconomic changes from 2014 to 2022 will be used to shock the benchmark GTAP model. Then the tariff adjustment module will be used to adjust the tariff changes from 2014 to 2021. After constructing the first timestamp of the baseline GTAP model in 2022, this article will build up timestamp from 2023 to 2057 on the GTAP baseline model. This process can be expressed as Equation (1). It can be noted that the tariff adjustment module was only used in the construction of the 2022 baseline GTAP model because the article assumes that no more new RTA agreements from 2022 to 2057.

$$F_B\left(X_{t,B}, Y_{t,B}{}^*\right) = F_B\left(X_{t-1,B} * x_{t-1,B}, Y_{t-1,B}\right) \quad (1)$$

F_B represents the nonlinear equation system of the baseline GTAP model, $X_{t,B}$ and $Y_{t,B}$ represent the exogenous variables and the endogenous variable vector in the baseline model equation system at time t, represents the vector in equilibrium, and x is the shock variable vector.

3.2.2 *Tariff shocked model*

Then this article explores the continuous impact of RCEP throughout the shock baseline model with real tariff changes to different corresponding years. This process can be described by Equation (2).

$$F_S\left(TMS_{t,S}(i,r,s), X_{t,S}^C, Y_{t,S}^*\right)$$
$$= F_S\left(TMS_{t,B}(i,r,s)\right.$$
$$\left. * \left(tms_{t,S}(i,r,s)+1\right), X_{t,B}^C, Y_{t,B}\right) \quad (2)$$

$TMS_{t,S}(i,r,s)$ is the change in tariff on imports of i sector from r region into s region level variable vector in the tariff shocked GTAP model at moment of $t \cdot X_{t,S}^C$ is the other endogenous variable in the equation system except the tariff rate, and tms is the tariff shock vector.

3.2.3 UN Comtrade database extension

Last step is plugging forecast data of changes into UN Comtrade database. Output data are equivalent to forking the entire database into baseline and RCEP tariff shock scenarios and continued for 36 years.

$$X_{t,B}(j,r,s) = X_{t-1,B}(j,r,s) * (q \times s_{t,B}(j,r,s) + 1) \quad (3)$$

$$X_{t,s}(j,r,s) = X_{t,B}(j,r,s) * (q \times s_{t,S}(j,r,s) + 1) \quad (4)$$

X is the export value, and qxs is the percentage change in the export value predicted by GTAP.

3.3 Data description and indicators

3.3.1 Data description

Data used in this article come from the tenth edition of GTAP database, EconMap database, RCEP tariff agreement documents, and UN Comtrade Database, from which GTAP SAM data, EconMap macroeconomic level variable forecast sequence (2010-2057), RCEP tax reduction rules, and HS (2002) bilateral trade data are selected.

3.3.2 Selection of indicators

As shown in Equation (5), Equation (6), and Equation (7), this article uses trade complementarity index to measure consistency between main export product of China's manufacturing industry and main import product of RCEP partner countries. TCI index is based on Revealed Comparative Advantage Index and proposed by Finger and Kreinin (1979), which measures degree of two countries or regions' import and export.

$$TCI(j,r,s) = RCA_x(r,j) \times RCA_m(s,j) \quad (5)$$

$$RCA_x(r,j) = \frac{\sum_s X(j,r,s)}{\sum_{s,j} X(j,r,s)} \Bigg/ \frac{\sum_{r,s} X(j,r,s)}{\sum_{j,r,s} X(j,r,s)} \quad (6)$$

$$RCA_m(s,j) = \frac{\sum_r X(j,r,s)}{\sum_{r,j} X(j,r,s)} \Bigg/ \frac{\sum_{r,s} X(j,r,s)}{\sum j,r,s} X(j,r,s) \quad (7)$$

TCI (j,r,s) is the trade complementation index between r area and s area on commodity j, and $RCAx(r,j)$ is the export comparative advantage of commodity j in r area and $RCAm(s,j)$ is the import comparative advantage of commodity j in s area.

This article also uses Equation (8) to measure the net trade effect of trade complementarity brought out by RCEP.

$$TCI_{t,N}(j,r,s) = \frac{TCI_{t,s}(j,r,s) - TCI_{t,B}(j,r,s)}{TCI_{t,B}(j,r,s)} \quad (8)$$

$TCI_{t,N}(j,r,s)$ is the net effect of trade complementarity brought by the RCEP of the r area and the s area on the commodity j.

4 MANUFACTURING TRADE FORECASTING

4.1 Manufacturing trade

4.1.1 Trade volume

The volume of manufacturing trade between China and other 14 countries will increase year by year. ASEAN and South Korea will be the top two trading partners of China from 2022 to 2057. Bilateral trade volume between Japan-China and Australia-China will be relatively small, and their growth rates will be relatively slow. New Zealand does not show evident growth with China during the time sequence. The results are shown in Figure 1. It can be seen that China is going to continue to keep close trade ties with ASEAN in the future. This confirms the testification that eastern countries are moving to the upper level of global industrial chains. Traditional markets are still in Europe and America; in the next 30 years, the largest demanding market is likely to locate in China-ASEAN region. This will help to re-build the global industrial chain and supply chain system.

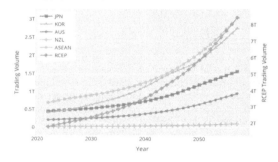

Figure 1. Manufacturing trade volume sequence between China and RCEP members.

4.1.2 Trade complementarity

According to Figure 2, manufacturing trade complementarity of New Zealand-China will constantly increase, but of the other countries will decrease and finally drop to below 1.0 in 2055. RCEP agreement will help New Zealand integrate into regional manufacturing cooperation well because of the excellent division of labor and better exertion of its advantages in high-end technology fields. On the one

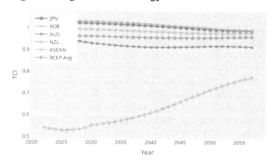

Figure 2. Manufacturing trade complementarity sequence between China and RCEP members.

hand, China will possess more competitive industries, which makes its trade complementarity with many other countries gradually decline. On the other hand, Figure 2 also indicates that RCEP will possibly bring negative effects of product homogeneity. This will lead to a negative consequence that under the condition of low market share of high-tech products, China's market share of low-end products may be seized by ASEAN.

4.2 Mechanical applications, electrical equipment, and automobile trade

This paper chooses 3 years 2022, 2040, and 2057 as short-term, medium-term, and long-term. Based on simulation results, China's export advantage will mainly concentrate on mechanical and electrical processed products. Only to Laos, Myanmar, and Vietnam will China have comparative advantages in automobile manufacturing. In the short-medium term, China's high-ranking export products to other RCEP countries will be telephone sets (HS 8517), electronic integrated circuits (HS 8542), and other labor-intensive products. In the long term, insulated wire, cable, and other electric conductors (HS 8544) will increase to the top fifth. There is no sign indicating that RCEP will promote Chinese electrical and mechanical industrial chains. More details can be seen in Table 1.

China, Japan, and South Korea will strengthen their relationship on the electrical and mechanical industry chain. Japan lies in the upstream position, South Korea lies in the middle-stream, and China lies in downstream. China's comparative export advantages to Japan will focus on transmission apparatus for radio-broadcasting or television (HS 8525) and automatic data processing machines and units thereof (HS 8471) in 2022. China's advantages to Korea will concentrate on telephone sets (HS 8517) and electronic integrated circuits (HS 8542). Japan's most significant export advantage will be motor cars (HS 8703). Its semiconductor devices (HS 8541) always have a high export volume. South Korea's electronic integrated circuits (HS 8542) export advantage will be more competitive. The details can be seen in Tables 1 and 2.

4.2.1 Export advantage

It can be concluded that, for the electrical and mechanical manufacturing chain, Japan will provide materials of diodes and semiconductors for integrated circuits; South Korea will process these raw materials into electrical integrated circuits, and China will assemble the intermediate products into final goods. Additionally, rank data of 3 years present that RCEP will not change the industrial positions of China, Korea, and Japan.

GTAP simulation result shows ASEAN countries will still be the processor of low-end products and the

Table 1. Forecast of China's advantages of export commodities

			AUS	BRN	IDN	JPN	KHM	KOR	LAO	MMR	MYS	NZL	PHL	SGP	THA	VNM
2022	Rank 1	Commodity (HS)	8471	8471	8525	8525	8517	8517	8517	8481	8542	8471	8542	8542	8525	8517
		Export Volume (B)	8.196	.024	2.810	19.639	.130	8.439	.105	.256	7.062	1.070	.904	4.869	4.699	8.747
	Rank 2	Commodity (HS)	8525	8525	8471	8471	8447	8542	8704	8711	8471	8525	8473	8471	8471	8525
		Export Volume (B)	5.197	.017	2.223	19.090	.095	8.379	.044	.143	2.099	.583	.493	2.823	3.885	2.824
	Rank 3	Commodity (HS)	8517	8517	8517	8541	8452	8471	8544	8716	8473	8517	8471	8525	8473	8542
		Export Volume (B)	2.272	.011	1.644	7.002	.074	7.206	.036	.116	1.777	.280	.352	2.664	1.910	1.605
	Rank 4	Commodity (HS)	8544	8415	8529	8517	8537	8544	8521	8704	8525	8516	8517	8473	8517	8471
		Export Volume (B)	1.119	.011	.967	6.213	.063	3.915	.032	.097	1.424	.137	.341	2.601	1.665	1.483
	Rank 5	Commodity (HS)	8516	8426	8474	8544	8544	8541	8714	8701	8529	8467	8544	8517	8542	8473
		Export Volume (B)	.855	.005	.583	4.407	.055	3.163	.025	.073	1.112	.114	.333	1.125	1.455	1.184
2040	Rank 1	Commodity (HS)	8471	8471	8525	8525	8447	8517	8517	8481	8542	8471	8542	8542	8525	8517
		Export Volume (B)	24.312	.062	7.343	40.119	.479	32.822	.293	.419	17.365	2.677	1.803	7.274	12.215	15.114
	Rank 2	Commodity (HS)	8525	8525	8471	8471	8517	8542	8704	8716	8471	8525	8473	8471	8471	8525
		Export Volume (B)	15.415	.044	5.809	38.997	.471	32.590	.166	.344	5.160	1.458	1.188	4.217	10.099	4.880
	Rank 3	Commodity (HS)	8517	8517	8517	8708	8452	8471	8521	8704	8473	8517	8544	8473	8708	8542
		Export Volume (B)	6.738	.029	4.296	15.229	.375	28.029	.088	.287	4.459	.701	.957	4.176	5.202	2.773
	Rank 4	Commodity (HS)	8544	8415	8529	8541	8537	8544	8705	8711	8525	8516	8471	8525	8473	8471
		Export Volume (B)	4.058	.022	2.527	14.303	.364	18.613	.085	.246	3.502	.517	.702	3.980	4.693	2.562
	Rank 5	Commodity (HS)	8708	8426	8502	8517	8714	8541	8714	8701	8708	8544	8517	8517	8517	8473
		Export Volume (B)	3.490	.010	1.663	12.692	.351	12.300	.084	.215	2.806	.342	.679	1.680	4.327	2.455
2057	Rank 1	Commodity (HS)	8471	8471	8525	8525	8517	8517	8517	8716	8542	8471	8542	8542	8525	8517
		Export Volume (B)	51.065	.142	15.192	61.459	.572	58.713	.406	1.669	28.091	5.014	1.528	9.543	15.611	17.287
	Rank 2	Commodity (HS)	8525	8525	8402	8471	8537	8542	8704	8704	8471	8525	8544	8471	8471	8525
		Export Volume (B)	32.378	.101	12.052	59.740	.464	58.297	.261	1.395	8.348	2.731	1.311	5.533	12.907	5.582
	Rank 3	Commodity (HS)	8517	8517	8471	8708	8447	8471	8544	8701	8708	8517	8704	8525	8708	8504
		Export Volume (B)	14.153	.067	12.020	31.625	.365	50.138	.153	1.043	6.867	1.313	.993	5.221	11.612	3.386
	Rank 4	Commodity (HS)	8544	8415	8404	8541	8544	8544	8705	8711	8525	8516	8504	8473	8544	8542
		Export Volume (B)	10.237	.033	9.356	21.911	.362	33.403	.134	.673	5.665	1.289	.897	3.549	7.013	3.172
	Rank 5	Commodity (HS)	8516	8528	8517	8517	8502	8541	8521	8481	8504	8544	8473	8536	8501	8471
		Export Volume (B)	7.827	.015	8.888	19.443	.316	22.003	.122	.607	4.622	.854	.786	2.735	6.513	2.930

Table 2. Forecast of export advantages of RCEP countries

			AUS	BRN	**CHN**	IDN	JPN	KHM	KOR	LAO	MMR	MYS	NZL	PHL	SGP	THA
2022	Rank 1	Commodity (HS)	8703	8548	**8517**	8703	8703	8529	8542	8529	8525	8542	8504	8542	8542	8471
		Export Volume (B)	.268	.065	**74.936**	1.544	24.608	.576	80.522	.251	.017	51.673	.046	15.171	26.422	11.059
	Rank 2	Commodity (HS)	8708	8708	**8542**	8532	8542	8544	8517	8544	8431	8541	8418	8471	8471	8542
		Export Volume (B)	.247	.012	**73.059**	1.345	17.807	.505	14.599	.023	.008	7.715	.040	5.091	4.137	9.974
	Rank 3	Commodity (HS)	8431	8414	**8471**	8471	8708	8501	8708	8714	8518	8471	8544	8473	8523	8704
		Export Volume (B)	.235	.012	**71.566**	1.144	17.311	.267	5.805	.013	.006	6.059	.037	4.248	3.116	5.748
	Rank 4	Commodity (HS)	8407	8431	**8525**	8708	8708	8518	8534	8504	8426	8517	8428	8541	8541	8473
		Export Volume (B)	.180	.009	**53.605**	1.029	6.575	.080	5.035	.005	.005	3.132	.034	2.733	2.466	4.838
	Rank 5	Commodity (HS)	8704	8703	**8473**	8544	8479	8454	8703	8541	8536	8473	8415	8517	8517	8703
		Export Volume (B)	.137	.009	**33.335**	.958	4.877	.061	5.031	.004	.005	2.818	.029	1.279	.962	4.457
2040	Rank 1	Commodity (HS)	8703	8548	**8471**	8703	8703	8712	8542	8529	8525	8542	8418	8542	8542	8704
		Export Volume (B)	.458	.013	**157.933**	2.977	26.634	4.486	205.825	1.243	.008	44.698	.040	15.132	.871	13.693
	Rank 2	Commodity (HS)	8708	8414	**8517**	8708	8708	8544	8517	8714	8431	8541	8708	8471	8471	8703
		Export Volume (B)	.439	.004	**147.841**	1.977	18.888	.314	37.135	.657	.050	6.894	.040	4.967	.135	10.622
	Rank 3	Commodity (HS)	8431	8431	**8542**	8419	8542	8714	8703	8544	8426	8471	8428	8473	8523	8708
		Export Volume (B)	.258	.003	**141.226**	.980	15.336	.179	13.010	.089	.005	5.776	.037	3.958	.095	9.080
	Rank 4	Commodity (HS)	8704	8430	**8525**	8409	8479	8501	8534	8504	8518	8473	8415	8541	8541	8471
		Export Volume (B)	.236	.003	**116.884**	.836	6.780	.151	12.717	.020	.003	4.259	.036	2.735	.077	9.013
	Rank 5	Commodity (HS)	8407	8708	**8473**	8714	8456	8408	8541	8541	8443	8517	8419	8708	8704	8542
		Export Volume (B)	.233	.002	**61.741**	.687	5.883	.069	12.206	.014	.003	3.109	.025	1.279	.034	8.289
2057	Rank 1	Commodity (HS)	8708	8548	**8471**	8703	8542	8712	8542	8529	8431	8542	8708	8542	8542	8704
		Export Volume (B)	.616	.000	**226.798**	3.382	18.002	18.002	346.485	.791	.000	35.535	.481	20.463	.420	29.190
	Rank 2	Commodity (HS)	8703	8414	**8525**	8708	8703	8408	8517	8714	8426	8541	8418	8471	8471	8703
		Export Volume (B)	.581	.000	**173.083**	2.477	41.596	1.447	63.327	.250	.000	6.928	.400	5.599	.068	23.704
	Rank 3	Commodity (HS)	8431	8430	**8517**	8409	8708	8714	8703	8544	8525	8471	8415	8541	8541	8708
		Export Volume (B)	.439	.000	**167.139**	1.102	30.696	.821	43.644	.061	.000	6.713	.381	3.993	.037	21.888
	Rank 4	Commodity (HS)	8704	8431	**8542**	8704	8541	8711	8708	8504	8708	8473	8428	8473	8523	8471
		Export Volume (B)	.316	.000	**149.313**	.480	27.846	.123	31.586	.014	.000	5.613	.356	3.032	.033	11.528
	Rank 5	Commodity (HS)	8471	8412	**8544**	8419	8479	8715	8525	8541	8430	8517	8716	8708	8704	8542
		Export Volume (B)	.261	.000	**90.108**	.475	26.365	.050	24.634	.006	.000	4.522	.247	2.858	.027	11.010

supplier of raw natural materials. The reason is that the tariff concessions of the vast majority of products have relatively the same period, same direction, and the same degree in most RCEP countries. Especially the long tax exemption span will leave sufficient adjustment time for each industry to rebalance the supply and demand market. The competition and the complimentary pattern will also not change much in the RCEP region in the future.

4.2.2 Trade complementarity

According to Table 3, for mechanical applications (HS 84), only Japan, South Korea, the Philippines, and Thailand will maintain good trade complementarity with China. Among these countries, Japan will have the strongest complementarity. The net effect of RCEP tariff exemption will make the complementarities of China-Japan and China-South Korea fall, with adverse effects reaching -6% and -15%, respectively, in 2057. However, the net effect will be positive on the trade complementarity of China-Philippines and China-Thailand.

According to Table 4, for electrical equipment (HS 85), Japan, South Korea, Malaysia, Philippines, and Vietnam will maintain good trade complementarity with China. In the shocked scenario, the complementarity of China-South Korea and China-Philippines will increase in the medium and long term. The net effect of RCEP will negatively impact the trade complementarity of China-Japan and China-Vietnam in the whole time series.

According to Table 5, for automobiles (HS 87), Japan, Cambodia, and Thailand will have stable trade complementarity with China in the future. The trade complementarity between China and Cambodia will be extremely low in 2022, only accounting for 0.2, but it will rise to 4.271 in 2040 and finally to 6.45 in 2057, showing an incredible increasing rate. The tariff reduction brought by RCEP will positively affect the trade complementarity of China-Japan in the short and medium-term but will drop it in the long term.

Overall, the complementarity rates of HS 84, HS 85, HS 87 between China and Korea and Japan at

Table 3. Forecast of commodity HS 84 trade complementarity between RCEP countries and China

	2022			2040			2057		
	Baseline	Net effect (%)	Shocked	Baseline	Net effect (%)	Shocked	Baseline	Net effect (%)	Shocked
AUS	.067	5.786	.070	.065	10.409	.072	.062	11.450	.069
BRN	.066	−9.240	.060	.031	−8.508	.028	.000	−6.031	.000
IDN	.366	1.623	.372	.259	8.605	.281	.091	25.061	.114
JPN	1.185	.191	1.188	2.053	−.312	2.046	5.280	−5.606	4.984
KHM	.118	−8.462	.108	.050	−8.669	.046	.417	−15.085	.354
KOR	.638	−.819	.633	1.105	−10.261	.991	2.312	−14.969	1.966
LAO	.008	13.196	.009	.015	23.089	.019	.006	34.062	.008
MMR	.008	−11.905	.007	.012	−29.260	.008	.000	16.902	.000
MYS	.567	−1.077	.561	.614	.871	.619	.806	3.062	.831
NZL	.112	3.073	.116	.128	−8.271	.118	.706	−9.079	.642
PHL	1.422	8.631	1.544	1.723	6.465	1.834	1.940	3.139	2.001
SGP	.181	4.620	.190	.003	5.027	.003	.001	2.450	.001
THA	1.437	5.417	1.515	1.450	2.808	1.491	1.730	1.323	1.753
VNM	.462	−9.373	.418	.522	−9.913	.470	.735	−10.276	.659

162

Table 4. Forecast of commodity HS 85 trade complementarity between RCEP countries and China

	2022			2040			2057		
	Baseline	Net effect (%)	Shocked	Baseline	Net effect (%)	Shocked	Baseline	Net effect (%)	Shocked
AUS	.018	7.568	.020	.014	8.659	.015	.016	−2.441	.016
BRN	.058	13.158	.066	.019	7.966	.020	.000	−.946	.000
IDN	.350	7.252	.375	.152	15.750	.176	.014	18.331	.017
JPN	.919	−1.663	.904	1.197	−1.926	1.174	3.236	−15.690	2.728
KHM	1.669	−3.330	1.613	.244	−4.808	.232	.004	−8.030	.004
KOR	1.968	−3.682	1.896	3.833	2.185	3.916	4.347	−10.641	3.884
LAO	.219	27.999	.280	.671	40.560	.943	.254	41.242	.359
MMR	.009	.264	.009	.009	−17.467	.008	.000	27.219	.000
MYS	1.965	6.753	2.098	1.845	6.182	1.959	1.523	−3.926	1.464
NZL	.042	4.365	.044	.034	−8.507	.031	.227	−20.712	.180
PHL	2.545	4.758	2.666	3.688	2.196	3.769	4.877	−8.361	4.469
SGP	.532	6.733	.568	.009	4.665	.010	.004	−4.028	.004
THA	.941	8.692	1.023	.859	7.558	.924	.916	−4.013	.879
VNM	1.824	−.307	1.818	2.782	−1.203	2.748	3.247	−10.972	2.890

baseline will increase from short term to long term. The net effects brought by RCEP can only slightly reduce China's dependence on above two countries. China will confront the challenge of the technological monopoly from developed countries for a long time. Tariff concession cannot bring down the technical barriers; on the contrary, it will further fix the original division of labor and cooperation that has already been established in East Asia. For China, the best way to break down the technical barriers always originates from its own technological innovation.

Table 5. Forecast of commodity HS 87 trade complementarity between RCEP countries and China

	2022			2040			2057		
	Baseline	Net effect (%)	Shocked	Baseline	Net effect (%)	Shocked	Baseline	Net effect (%)	Shocked
AUS	.076	2.798	.078	.066	15.892	.077	.045	11.002	.050
BRN	.074	−1.319	.073	.010	7.716	.011	.000	2.762	.000
IDN	.598	−2.279	.584	.471	14.214	.537	.264	21.466	.321
JPN	3.021	2.178	3.087	2.700	3.051	2.783	2.301	−5.763	2.168
KHM	.246	−5.544	.232	3.535	20.805	4.271	6.199	4.042	6.450
KOR	.726	−2.571	.708	.779	−11.225	.692	1.324	−18.424	1.080
LAO	.049	11.120	.055	.527	76.942	.933	.108	79.916	.194
MMR	.002	−10.627	.002	.003	−1.065	.003	.000	33.697	.000
MYS	.217	−8.921	.197	.228	18.351	.270	.218	19.193	.260
NZL	.037	−.421	.037	.049	−3.229	.047	.260	−9.778	.234
PHL	.281	−14.720	.240	.409	1.328	.414	.718	−.013	.718
SGP	.015	−3.107	.015	.001	16.368	.001	.001	10.006	.001
THA	2.498	−7.404	2.313	2.834	6.334	3.014	3.828	2.410	3.920
VNM	.266	−22.123	.207	.151	−12.093	.133	.178	−12.652	.156

5 CONCLUSIONS AND SUGGESTION

5.1 Conclusion

Based on the above analysis, total manufacturing trade volume within RCEP region will expand. The trade value will increase from less than 2 trillion dollars in 2022 to 3.6 trillion dollars in 2040, and finally to 8 trillion dollars in 2056. As far as the tariff reduction degree is concerned, it will continuously increase from 2022 to 2057, the multilateral trade relationship between China and other RCEP members will become closer. China's comparative industrial advantages in fundamental manufacturing will further increase its trade surplus. China's trade complementarity with other members will decline.

For the electrical, mechanical, and automobile manufacturing industries, China will present weak complementarity with most of the ASEAN countries but strong complementarity with Japan and Korea in both baseline model and tariff shocked model. The net trade effect of RCEP will make trade complementarities between China-Japan and China-Korea slightly reduce.

The simulation results indicate that China's comparative industries will still focus on low-tech, labor-intensive products in the medium and long term. The top five export products will not change in the future. This will hinder the upgrade of China's position in the global industrial chain.

5.2 Suggestion

The level of economic development among RCEP member countries is different. The competition and complementarity in major manufacturing industries also coexist in the RCEP region. Based on the above analysis, China should make use of successful experience in the construction of China-ASEAN FTA to promote industrial cooperation with other countries. For instance, boosting the export of Chinese manufactured goods into ASEAN market and the imports of ASEAN's raw materials into China is a practical strategy to achieve a win-win situation. Additionally, emerging comparative advantage of ASEAN countries in resource-intensive and labor-intensive industries can push China to eliminate backward industry and upgrade its industrial structure effectively.

Furthermore, China should concentrate on solving the problem of less competencies in high technology industries. This paper has shown that China's advantages of core products of HS 84, HS 85, and HS 87 are weaker than Japan and Korea. The key point to improve competencies is to encourage and promote technological innovation. The Chinese government should promulgate related laws to strengthen the protection on the intellectual property rights. It is also recommended to actively absorb qualified foreign investment into high value-added products and encourage communication and cooperation between China's high-tech companies with Japan and Korea. In these ways, China will update its industrial structure at a larger pace and up forward its position in the global industrial chain.

ACKNOWLEDGMENTS

This work was sponsored by *Xing Huo Fund* for undergraduate students in Beijing University of Technology (Grant no. XH-2021-37-01).

REFERENCES

Athukorala, P.-c. (2016). Global production sharing and Asian trade patterns: Implications for the Regional Comprehensive Economic Partnership (RCEP). *Global Economic Cooperation*, 241–253.

Finger, J. M. & M. E. Kreinin (1979). A measure of export similarity and its possible uses. *The Economic Journal 89(356)*, 905–912.

Hamanaka, S. (2014). Tpp versus rcep: Control of membership and agenda setting. *Journal of East Asian Economic Integration 18(2)*, 163–186.

Li, C., J. Wang, & J. Whalley (2016). Impact of mega trade deals on China: A computational general equilibrium analysis. *Economic Modelling 57*, 13–25.

Li, Q. & H. C. Moon (2018). The trade and income effects of rcep: implications for china and Korea. *Journal of Korea Trade*.

Mahadevan, R. & A. Nugroho (2019). Can the regional comprehensive economic partnership minimise the harm from the united states - china trade war? *The World Economy 42(11)*, 3148–3167.

Rahman, M. M. & L. A. Ara (2015). Tpp, ttip and rcep: implications for South Asian economies. *South Asia Economic Journal 16(1)*, 27–45.

Walmsley, T. L., B. V. Dimaranan, & R. A. McDougall (2006). A baseline scenario for the dynamic gtap model. *Dynamic modeling and applications for global economic analysis*, 136.

Wilson, J. D. (2015). Mega-regional trade deals in the asia-pacific: choosing between the tpp and rcep? *Journal of Contemporary Asia 45(2)*, 345–353.

Economic and Business Management – Huang & Zhang (Eds)
© 2022 Copyright the Author(s), ISBN: 978-1-032-06754-4

Cost leadership strategy, diagnostic control style and firm performance

Weixiang Sun & Cheng Li
Macao University of Science and Technology, Macao, China

ABSTRACT: Whether an enterprise can formulate a suitable strategy is an important prerequisite for the continuous improvement of firm performance. We adopt primary data using 427 questionnaires for the survey and use SPSS software to study the relationship between cost leadership strategy, diagnostic control style and firm performance. The research results show that cost leadership strategy can effectively improve firm performance. Moreover, the diagnostic control style plays a positive intermediary effect between the cost leadership strategy and firm performance, which means that the cost leadership strategy can exert a positive impact on firm performance through the diagnostic control style. Our study reveals the influence mechanism of cost leadership strategy and diagnostic control style on firm performance, thus providing a path to effectively improve firm performance. At the same time, it also enriches the literature on enterprise strategy, management control style and firm performance.

Keywords: cost leadership strategy, diagnostic control style, firm performance, influence mechanism.

1 INTRODUCTION

Enterprises need to clarify which Enterprise strategy is suitable for them? The successful formulation and implementation of Enterprise strategy has a positive impact on firm performance, which has been widely recognized by scholars at home and abroad and the industry (Allen et al. 2006; Hill 1988; Rubach & McGee 2004; Sands 2006). Enterprise strategy is often divided into two types: cost leadership strategy and differentiation strategy. According to JE Leo (1982) and Porter (2011), enterprises that adopt differentiation strategy are different from those that adopt cost leadership strategy. An enterprise with a differentiation strategy can produce unique products, so it can demand high prices from customers. Enterprises that adopt a cost leadership strategy tend to produce standardized products and gain market share and make profits by setting product prices lower than those of competitors. Besanko et al. (1996) believed that enterprises adopting differentiation strategy set product prices higher than competitors, while enterprises adopting cost leadership strategy did the opposite. At present, there are abundant literature and theoretical basis on the research of differentiation strategy on firm performance. Research on cost leadership strategy is relatively scarce. This study focuses on the impact of cost leadership strategy on firm performance.

When reading related literature, I found an interesting question. In the field of management accounting, some scholars have recognized the need to use the style of management control as a research variable to expand the relationship between Enterprise strategy and firm performance (Simons 1987, 1990). The literature on management control style mainly focuses on the relationship between its internal elements (Bedford 2015), such as the relationship between diagnostic control style and interactive control style, and the relationship between diagnostic control style and boundary control. Our study does not relate the internal elements of management control style. Instead, the diagnostic control style in the management control style is regarded as a formal feedback system for monitoring firm performance and correcting deviations from pre-set goals (D&Amp & Acierno 2016; Simons 2008; Widener 2007). Our research has enriched the literature in this area from the original scholars focusing on the correlation of internal elements of the management control style to the discussion of the economic consequences of the management control style.

On the basis of previous research, this study explores the factors affecting firm performance. We investigate the impact of cost leadership strategy and diagnostic control style on firm performance, and the internal relationship between the three. Specifically, this study seeks to answer two questions. The first is whether the cost leadership strategy adopted by enterprises can directly affect the performance of enterprises, whether there is an indirect impact. The second, if there is indirect influence, can diagnostic control style play a mediating role in the impact path of cost leadership strategy on firm performance?

This paper consists of five parts. The first part is the introduction. The second part is the research hypothesis. The third part is questionnaire design and data collection. The fourth part is the empirical results. The last part is the research conclusion.

DOI 10.1201/9781003203704-30

2 THEORETICAL ANALYSIS AND RESEARCH HYPOTHESIS

The proper application of cost leadership strategy can bring substantial profits to enterprises (Rubach & McGee 2004). From the perspective of general strategy theory, enterprises with cost leadership strategy tend to focus on mass production of standardized products, which are not innovative and do not require much innovation (Porter 1985b). Enterprises with cost leadership strategy improve their performance through advantages in unit profit rate and market share. From the aspect of unit profit rate, enterprises improve the profit rate of each unit product by adopting lower production cost, such as reducing design cost, using the cheapest labor force and reducing raw material procurement cost. Rugman and Hodgetts (1995) research shows that the cost control of enterprises with cost leadership strategy mainly focuses on sales expenses, administrative expenses, and expenditures for providing production services and R&D services. Wheelen and Hunger (2002) believed that enterprises with cost leadership strategy should reduce costs in product design and production. Eraslan (2008) believes that enterprises with cost leadership strategy can always maintain competitive advantages in the capital market because these enterprises sell goods and provide services at the lowest price, use the lowest cost raw materials and the cheapest labor force, and reduce transportation costs to the lowest level. From the aspect of market share, Enterprises can obtain price competitive advantage by cost advantage and sell products to customers at a low price in the market to improve the market share of their products. Enterprises can obtain price competitive advantage by virtue of cost advantage. Then, they sell the goods to customers at low prices in the market to increase the market share of the business. Johnson et al. (2008) showed that when an enterprise wants to gain competitive advantages through cost leadership strategy, and its cost benefits come from economies of scale. Especially in the context of frequent market price fluctuations, enterprises applying cost leadership strategy have strong competitive advantages (Johnson et al. 2008; Thompson & Strictland 1996). Therefore, combining these two aspects, we believe that cost leadership strategy can effectively improve firm performance. Therefore, hypothesis H1 is proposed:

H1: Cost leadership strategy is positively correlated with firm performance.

The diagnostic or interactive application of enterprise strategy to management control style can improve firm performance (Abernethy & Brownell 1999; Henri 2006; Simons 1995, 2008). If enterprises with cost leadership strategy choose an interactive control style, they may not be able to maintain unit profit margins and market share advantages in order to obtain better firm performance. Enterprises adopting interactive control style need frequent communication or meetings between management and subordinates, which may lead to the decline of production efficiency for enterprises that obtain market share by producing standardized products at low prices (Porter 1998). The diagnostic control style is an attractive system for organizations that have a daily production order. Enterprises with cost leadership strategies tend to do repetitive tasks and produce standardized products (Miller 1988). Therefore, enterprises with cost leadership strategy should choose diagnostic control style in order to achieve the pre-established performance goals. What they need is a formal control system that has the property of adjusting policies through feedback on results. The diagnostic control method has exactly this attribute. The feedback mechanism of diagnostic control style is to find out the differences by observing the completion of the task and comparing the previously set goals after the task is completed, so as to understand the deficiencies of the enterprise, make adjustments in which areas, and reformulate policies to ensure more successful actions in the future (Mundy 2010). The diagnostic control style is suitable for enterprises that adopt cost leadership strategies. It helps employees tune out distractions and focus on work. The quality of products can be guaranteed, and the production activities of enterprises can be carried out smoothly. Therefore, we believe that cost leadership strategy promotes diagnostic control style. Therefore, hypothesis H2 is proposed:

H2: Cost leadership strategy is positively correlated with diagnostic control style.

Organizations that choose diagnostic control have clear enterprise goals and transparent and open work processes. Their employees have reached a consensus on the desired goals and work together to achieve them (Adler & Chen 2011; Widener 2007). How does diagnostic control style improve firm performance? Unproductive discussions arising from diagnostic mechanisms may occur when managers' preferences are unstable or enterprise objectives are unclear (Chapman 1997). Diagnostic control styles often find deficiencies by comparing desired goals to actual results. Enterprises with diagnostic control style attract the attention of management through feedback, and then adjust policies to improve firm performance. Therefore, we believe that diagnostic control style can promote firm performance. Therefore, hypothesis H3 is proposed:

H3: Diagnostic control style is positively correlated with firm performance.

3 QUESTIONNAIRE DESIGN AND DATA COLLECTION

We collected data on cost leadership strategy, diagnostic control style and firm performance by sending questionnaires to the management of Chinese manufacturing enterprises. The SPSS statistical software was used for data processing (Hayes 2018). The specific situation of questionnaire design and data collection is as follows:

3.1 Questionnaire design

The variables in this study were cost leadership strategy, diagnostic management control style, and firm performance. According to the questionnaire developed by Henri (2006), a total of 7 questions are set for firm performance. The measurement items of firm performance are divided into financial and non-financial levels. Financial indicators include return on investment, market share, overall profitability and sales growth rate. Non-financial indicators include new product introduction to market, employee turnover and customer retention. There are 5 measurement items for diagnostic control style, as shown in Table 1. The measurement items of cost leadership strategy are 4 questions, including product and service cost, low selling expenses, low price and control cost. In order to reduce the possibility of common method deviations, this study uses a seven-point scale of Likert scale to measure the degree of the variable (Podsakoff et al. 2003). Respondents only need to choose a score for each question that best suits the situation of their enterprise. The score ranges from 1 to 7 to indicate the degree from minimum to maximum.

Table 1. Measurement items of diagnostic control style.

NO.	Measurement item
1	Senior management uses administrative controls to track progress and monitor results
2	Senior managers will formulate plans through management control to ensure that the operational direction is consistent with the strategic plan.
3	Senior managers will evaluate performance through management control
4	Senior managers will find major deviations and implement corresponding measures through management control
5	Senior managers will use management control to match performance measurement with enterprise strategy

3.2 Data collection

A total of 427 valid questionnaires were collected in this study, as shown in Table 2. There are 140 grassroots managers, accounting for 33%. There are 120 middle managers, accounting for 28%. There are 96 department heads, accounting for 23%. There are 53

senior managers, accounting for 12%. There are 18 chief executives, accounting for 4%. Data sources are mainly from grassroots and middle managers and department heads. Since most of the information and data about firm performance are controlled by these managers, this study takes these groups as the survey objects. The results are reliable.

4 EMPIRICAL RESULTS

4.1 Factor analysis

Prior to factor analysis, KMO and Bartlett sphericity tests are required to determine whether the data are suitable for factor analysis.

As can be seen from Table 3, the P value of Bartlett's sphericity test is less than 0.05, indicating a significant relationship between variables. KMO value is 0.918, greater than 0.7, indicating that this study can be performed factor analysis.

Table 3. KMO and Bartlett tests.

KMO Measure of Sampling Adequacy		0.918
Bartlett Test of Sphericity	Chi square	5665.836
	df	231
	Sig.	0.00

Table 4 shows that the cumulative variance contribution rate is 66.195%, which is greater than the standard line of 40%, indicating that these three factors can represent three different variables and explain their respective degrees of variation.

As can be seen from the rotated factor matrix table in Table 1 in the appendix, the factor coefficients of the measurement items are all greater than 0.5, indicating that the measurement items can effectively measure the corresponding variables. The measurement items used in this study to measure cost leadership strategy, diagnostic control style and firm performance can effectively measure their respective variables, and there is no need to delete items.

4.2 Reliability analysis

It can be seen from Table 5 that the Cronbach Alpha coefficient of the cost leadership strategy is 0.712, which is greater than the 0.7 standard line, and reaches

Table 2. Distribution of survey objects.

Type	Number	Proportion	Type	Number	Proportion
Grassroots managers	140	33%	State-owned enterprise	43	48%
Middle managers	120	28%	Private enterprise	41	45%
Department heads	96	23%	Foreign Enterprise	6	7%
Senior managers	53	12%			
CEO	18	4%			
Total	427	100%	Total	90	100%

Table 4. Explanation table of total variance.

| Factor | Initial eigenvalue | | | After rotation | | |
	Total	Variance %	Cumulative contribution rate	Total	Variance %	Cumulative contribution rate
1	12.177	57.626	57.626	12.677	54.941	54.941
2	1.826	8.299	65.925	1.326	6.028	60.969
3	1.416	6.438	72.363	1.150	5.226	66.195

the reliability standard, indicating that the cost leadership strategy's measurement items are consistent among themselves. In addition, the Cronbach Alpha coefficients of the diagnostic control method and firm performance are 0.946 and 0.930, respectively, which reaches a relatively high level of reliability, indicating that there is consistency between the diagnostic control method and the measurement items of firm performance.

Table 5. Summary table of reliability analysis coefficients.

Variable	Number	Cronbach Alpha coefficient
Cost leadership strategy	4	0.712
Diagnostic control style	5	0.946
Firm performance	7	0.930

4.3 Descriptive statistics

Table 6 shows the basic information of the three variables. In terms of standard deviation and variance, the variation degree of the three variables is relatively small. The average values of cost leadership strategy, diagnostic control style and firm performance are 4.9759, 5.4736 and 5.4513 respectively, all greater than 3.5, indicating that in the effective samples of the survey, more enterprises prefer to adopt cost leadership strategy and diagnostic control style, and their performance is higher than the average level.

4.4 Correlation analysis

It can be seen from Table 7 that the correlation coefficients are all less than 0.7, indicating that there is no multicollinearity problem among variables. The correlation coefficient between cost leadership strategy

and diagnostic control style is 0.315, and the P value is less than 0.01, indicating that there is a significant positive relationship between cost leadership strategy and diagnostic control style. The correlation coefficient between cost leadership strategy and firm performance is 0.171, and the P value is greater than 0.01, indicating that there is a significant positive relationship between cost leadership strategy and firm performance. The correlation coefficient of diagnostic control style to firm performance is 0.462, p value is less than 0.01, indicating that the correlation between diagnostic control style and firm performance is very significant.

Table 7. Correlation coefficient table.

Variable	Cost leadership strategy	Diagnostic control style	Firm performance
Cost leadership strategy	1	0.315** (0.00)	0.171** (0.001)
Diagnostic control style	0.315** (0.00)	1	0.462** (0.00)
Firm performance	0.171** (0.001)	0.462** (0.00)	1

Note: ***, ** and * indicate that the regression coefficients are significant at the level of 1%, 5% and 10% respectively.

4.5 Regression results

4.5.1 Test of goodness for fit

We used the PROCESS (Version 3) program developed by Hayes (2018) in SPSS statistical software to study the degree of fitting of the overall model. The square of multiple correlation coefficient is represented by R squared, and the value range is 0 to 1. The larger the value is, the better the fitting degree of the overall model is. It can be seen from Table 8 that R squared is 0.2205, indicating that the overall model fits well.

Table 6. Descriptive statistics.

Variable	Num	min	max	average	Standard Deviation	Variance
Cost leadership strategy	405	1.25	7	4.9759	1.07653	1.159
Diagnostic control style	405	1.60	7	5.4736	1.05672	1.117
Firm performance	403	2.00	7	5.4513	1.08312	1.173

Table 8. Summary of multiple correlation coefficients of the overall model.

R	R^2
0.4696	0.2205

Table 11. Regression results of diagnostic control style and firm performance.

Variable	coeff	se	t	p	LLCI	ULCI
Constant	2.5776	0.2834	9.0945	0.0000	2.0204	3.1348
Diagnostic	0.3896	0.0579	6.7254	0.0000	0.2757	0.5034

4.5.2 *Hypothesis test results*

It can be seen from Table 9 that the correlation coefficient is 0.172 and the P value is less than 0.05, rejecting the original hypothesis H0 and proving that there is a significant positive correlation between cost leadership strategy and firm performance, which means that cost leadership strategy can effectively improve firm performance. Hypothesis 1 is valid. This is consistent with the conclusions of Porter (1985) and Li, C. & Li, J. (2008).

Table 9. Regression results of cost leadership strategy and firm performance.

Variable	coeff	se	t	p
Constant	4.596	0.252	18.237	0.0000
Cost leadership strategy	0.172	0.050	3.472	0.001

As can be seen from Table 10, p value is less than 0.01. The correlation coefficient is 0.3075. In addition, LLCI=3.4705 and ULCI=4.4036 are both greater than 0, and the confidence interval at 99% confidence level does not contain 0, indicating that null hypothesis H0 can be rejected at 99% confidence level. Hypothesis H2 is proved to be valid, indicating a significant positive correlation between cost leadership strategy and diagnostic control style.

Table 10. Regression results of cost leadership strategy and diagnostic control style.

Variable	coeff	se	t	p	LLCI	ULCI
Constant	3.9370	0.2373	16.5899	0.0000	3.4705	4.4036
Cost leadership strategy	0.3075	0.0467	6.5849	0.0000	0.2157	0.3993

As can be seen from Table 11, p value is less than 0.01. The correlation coefficient was 0.3896. In addition, LLCI=0.2757 and ULCI=0.5034 are both greater than 0, and the confidence interval at 99% confidence level does not contain 0, indicating that null hypothesis H0 can be rejected at 99% confidence level. Hypothesis H6 is established, indicating that diagnostic control style can effectively improve firm performance

To sum up, the empirical results show that cost leadership strategy can effectively improve firm performance. Meanwhile, cost leadership strategy can exert a positive impact on firm performance through diagnostic control style. Diagnostic control style plays a good mediating role between the cost leadership strategy and firm performance.

Table 12. Regression results of the indirect impact of cost leadership strategy and firm performance.

Variable	Effect	BootSE	BootLLCI	BootULCI
Cost-Diagnostic-Performance	0.1191	0.0280	0.0697	0.1795

Next, we further verify the influence path and extent of the diagnostic control style (Diagnostic) on the relationship between cost leadership strategy (Cost) and firm performance (Performance). It can be seen from Table 12 that the confidence interval is [0.0697,0.1795], and its confidence interval does not contain 0, indicating that the diagnostic control style has an intermediary effect.

5 CONCLUSIONS

The hypotheses proposed in this study about the correlation between cost leadership strategy, diagnostic control style and firm performance have been verified. The conclusion of this study is that cost leadership strategy can effectively improve firm performance, at the same time, cost leadership strategy can play a positive impact on firm performance through diagnostic control style. Diagnostic control style plays a positive mediating role between cost leadership strategy and firm performance. Porter (1985), Li, C. & Li, J. (2008) proposed that cost leadership strategy can improve firm performance, which has been proved in this study. Cost leadership strategy can directly play a positive impact on improving firm performance, which indicates that cost leadership strategy can obtain market share by selling goods at low prices and achieve small profits and high turnover. Cost leadership strategies can also have a positive impact on firm performance through a diagnostic control style (Bedford 2015). The diagnostic control style helps managers quickly discover their shortcomings, improves the efficiency of the enterprise in solving problems, and promotes the improvement of firm performance. Enterprises with cost leadership strategies need to adopt more formal control systems to eliminate interference when producing standardized products, so as to improve firm performance to a greater extent (Melek & Semih 2016). In the future, on the basis of this study, variables of environmental uncertainty can be introduced to enrich the relevant literature on enterprise strategy and performance from a dynamic perspective.

ACKNOWLEDGMENTS

The authors thank the anonymous reviewers for their useful comments on the earlier version of this article.

CONFLICTS OF INTEREST

The authors declare no conflict of interest.

REFERENCES

Adler, P. S., & Chen, C. X. (2011). Combining creativity and control: understanding individual motivation in large-scale collaborative creativity. *Accounting Organizations & Society*, 36(2), 63–85.

Allen, D. G. & Shore, L. M. & Griffith, R. W. (2003). The role of perceived organizational support and supportive human resource practices in the turnover process, *Journal of Management*, 29(1), 99–118.

Bedford, & David, S. (2015). Management control systems across different modes of innovation: implications for firm performance. *Management Accounting Research*, 28, 12–30.

Besanko D, Kanatas G. (1996). The regulation of bank capital: Do capital standards promote bank safety? [J]. *Journal of financial intermediation*, 5(2): 160–183.

Caroline, Bingxin, Li, Julie, Juan, & Li. (2008). Achieving superior financial performance in China: differentiation, cost leadership, or both? *Journal of International Marketing*, 16(3), 1–22

Chapman, C. S. (1997). Reflections on a contingent view of accounting. *Accounting, organizations and society*, 22(2), 189–205.

D&Amp, L., & Acierno. (2016). "Levers of Control: How Managers Use Innovative Control Systems to Drive Strategic Renewal" by Robert Simons.

Eraslan, İ. H. (2008). The effects of competitive strategies on firm performance: A study in Turkish textile and apparel industry considering the mediating role of value chain activities (Unpublished doctoral dissertation). *Boğaziçi University Social Sciences Institute*, İstanbul.

Hayes, A. F. (2018). *PROCESS macro for SPSS and SAS*. The PROCESS macro for SPSS and SAS. Introduction to mediation, moderation, and conditional PROCESS analysis, second edition: A regression-based approach.

Henri, J. F. (2006). Management control systems and strategy: a resource-based perspective. *Accounting Organizations & Society*, 31(6), 529–558.

Hill, C. W. L. (1988). Differentiation versus low cost or differentiation and low cost: Contingency framework, *Academy of Management Review*, 13(3), 401–412.

Johnson, G. & Scholes, K. & Whittington, R. & Fréry. F. (2008) Strategique, 8e edition, *Paris: Pearson Education*.

Leo, J. E. (1982). Competitive strategy: techniques for analysing industries and competitors porter, Michael e. free press (Macmillan), New York, 396 pages, $17.95. *Industrial Marketing Management*, 11(4), 318–319.

Margaret, A., Abernethy, and, Peter, & Brownell. (1999). The role of budgets in organizations facing strategic change: an exploratory study. *Accounting Organizations & Society*, 24(3), 189–204.

Melek, Eker & Semih, Eker. (2016). The Effects of Interactions between Management Control Systems and Strategy on Firm Performance: An Empirical Study. *Business and Economics Research Journal*, 7(4), 123–141

Miller, D. (1988). Relating Porter's business strategies to environment and structure: Analysis and performance implications. *Academy of management Journal*, 31(2), 280-308. Mundy, J. (2010). Creating dynamic tensions through a balanced use of management control systems. *Accounting Organizations & Society*, 35(5), 499–523.

Podsakoff, P. M., Mackenzie, S. B., Lee, J. Y., & Podsakoff, N. P. (2003). Common method biases in behavioral research: a critical review of the literature and recommended remedies. *J Appl Psychol*, 88(5), 879–903.

Porter, M. E. (1985). Competitive advantage: Creating and sustaining superior performance. *New York: The Free Press*.

Porter, M. E. (1998). Clusters and the new economics of competition (Vol. 76, No. 6, pp. 77–90). *Boston: Harvard Business Review*.

Porter, M. E. (2011). Competitive Advantage. *Peking University Press*.

Rubach, M. J & McGee, J. E. (2004). Responding to increased environmental hostility: A study of the competitive behavior or small retailers, *Journal of Applied Business ResearchS*, 13(1): pp. 83–94.

Rugman, A. M., Hodgetts, R. M., Management, M., & McGrawHill. (1995). *International Business: A Strategic Management Approach*.

Sands, J. (2006). Strategic Priorities, Management Control Systems and Managerial Performance: An Empirical study (Unpublished PhD thesis), *Griffith University: Australia*.

Simon, R. (1995). Levers of Control: How Managers Use Innovative Control Systems to Drive Strategic Renewal. *Harvard Business School Press*.

Simons, R. (1987). The role of management control systems and business strategy: an empirical analysis. *Accounting Organizations & Society*, 12(4), 357–374.

Simons, R. (1990). The role of management control systems in creating competitive advantage: new perspectives. *Accounting, Organizations and Society*, 15(1), 127–143.

Simons, Robert, & L. (2008). Control in an age of empowerment. *Harvard Business School Press Books*.

Thompson, A. A., & Strickland, A. J. (1996). Strategic management: Concepts and cases. (9th ed.). *USA: Irwin McGraw-Hill*.

Wheelen, T., & Hunger, J. D. (2002). Strategic Management and Business Policy Prentice Hall.

Widener, S. K. (2007). An empirical analysis of the levers of control framework. *Accounting Organizations & Society*, 32(7–8), 757–788.

APPENDIX

Table 1.   The rotated factor matrix table.

	Factor			
	1	2	3	4
return on investment	.872	.146	.095	.054
sales growth rate	.863	.185	.118	.033
overall profitability	.860	.147	.108	.003
market share,	.859	.161	.059	.034
customer retention	.807	00.219	.116	.040
new product introduction to market	.803	00.139	00.198	.013
employee turnover	.644	.075	.138	.147
Senior managers will formulate plans through management control to ensure that the operational direction is consistent with the strategic plan.	.207	.840	00.280	.079
Senior managers will evaluate performance through management control	.247	.832	.285	.098
Senior management uses administrative controls to track progress and monitor results	.191	.832	.241	.086
Senior managers will use management control to match performance measurement with enterprise strategy	.216	.822	.343	.101
Senior managers will find major deviations and implement corresponding measures through management control	.270	.783	.323	.135
low price	.069	.026	-0.012	.819
Low selling expenses	.173	-.076	.045	.775
control cost	-0.044	.362	.276	.631
product and service cost	-0.022	.341	.171	.594

Extraction method: principal component analysis.
Rotation method: Kaiser normalized maximum variance method.
A. Rotation converges after 5 iterations.

Economic and Business Management – Huang & Zhang (Eds)
© 2022 Copyright the Author(s), ISBN: 978-1-032-06754-4

Digital transformation of agricultural enterprises during COVID-19: The design of a recommendation technology

Lewei Hu*

School of Business, Institute of Intelligent Decision-making, Jianghan University, Wuhan, China

ABSTRACT: China is a large agricultural country. The agricultural industry occupies a large proportion in the state economy, and the development of electronic commerce of agricultural products enterprises is particularly important. At present, agricultural enterprises are in the critical period of digital transformation. The purpose of this study is to analyze and design the recommended technology in the context of agricultural e-commerce platforms, which not only improve the profits of agricultural enterprises, but also provide support for enterprises to further integrate into e-commerce platforms.

Keywords: agricultural firms, digital transformation, recommendation technology, COVID-19

1 INTRODUCTION

In recent years, with the popularization and application of the Internet and computers, we have ushered in the era of big data, and e-commerce has gradually integrated into the lives of ordinary people. According to the latest data from the China Internet Network Information Center (CNNIC) in 2021, China has 989 million Internet users, with an Internet penetration rate of 70.4 percent. Among them are 309 million rural Internet users, with a penetration rate of 55.9 percent. China is a large agricultural country with a mostly rural population. With excellent natural conditions and the support of national policies, e-commerce of agricultural products has developed more rapidly, bringing hope to farmers with agricultural products as their main income and speeding up the pace of rural economic development. At present, various e-commerce platforms of various sizes recommend and display the products they sell to users through various technologies. However, these e-commerce platforms (e.g., The products recommended by Taobao or JD.com) are usually based on large and comprehensive categories of products, so it is impossible to grasp the detailed attributes of the products for recommendation. However, agricultural products pay special attention to the details of the products, and consumers attach great importance to the details of the origin, nutritional value, transgenic and other aspects of the agricultural products when choosing and buying. At the same time, product recommendation needs to be associated with user behaviors. Users leave abundant behavior data (such as browsing, liking, forwarding, commenting, purchasing, etc.) when they choose and purchase agricultural products on the e-commerce platforms. However, the current mainstream recommendation technologies mainly focus on the relevance of browsing and purchasing behaviors of users, while ignoring the relevance of other user behaviors and products, resulting in inaccuracy of product recommendation. Therefore, in the face with the abundant agricultural products, consumers are often unable to find suitable agricultural products through e-commerce platforms. Just like shopping guides in offline physical stores, intelligent recommendation imperceptibly provides consumers with purchase suggestions and product recommendations. The agricultural products industry has undergone great change and information is everywhere Under the support of the government's strong preferential policies, how to develop agricultural economy and how to improve the profits of agricultural products enterprises are very important. Therefore, based on the characteristics of agricultural products e-commerce intelligent recommendation technology analysis has a very important practical significance.

2 DEVELOPMENT STATUS OF AGRICULTURAL PRODUCTS ENTERPRISES

According to Alibaba's agricultural products e-commerce report, the turnover of agricultural products reached 200 billion yuan in 2019. As of April 25, 2020, more than 250,000 tons of unsalable agricultural products had been removed on Taobao and Tmall during the epidemic. Meanwhile, live broadcast of agricultural products has played a role, with sales of live broadcast agricultural products increasing 1.4

---

*Corresponding Author

times year-on-year in the first quarter of 2020 [1]. At present, the recommendation modules of agricultural products of e-commerce are attached to comprehensive e-commerce platforms, and there are few studies on the recommendation algorithms of independent e-commerce platforms of agricultural products. Therefore, it is difficult for agricultural products producers and marketing enterprises to sell products more effectively.

3 RESEARCH STATUS OF RECOMMENDATION SYSTEM TECHNOLOGY

In China, the recommendation algorithm is most widely used in entertainment and sales. Software such as Tik Tok, Kuaishou, Taobao and Alibaba all use recommendation theory to enable users to get information they are interested in [2]. With its intelligent recommendation system, Tik Tok has become the first-class volume platform in China. Many anchors and bloggers shoot small videos to catch people's attention and gain traffic and fans' popularity. The most important algorithms used by most e-commerce platforms are recommendation technologies based on association rules and recommendation algorithms based on collaborative filtering.

4 PRINCIPLE OF AGRICULTURAL PRODUCT RECOMMENDATION TECHNOLOGY BASED ON COLLABORATIVE FILTERING ALGORITHM

This paper is based on the content and the collaborative filtering recommendation algorithm, combining analysis of agricultural enterprises of recommendation technology. The biggest advantage of a content-based recommendation algorithm is that it is simple in principle and does not need to consider the relationship between target users and other users [3]. It only needs to conduct interest modeling according to the historical behavior data of users, and the recommendation effect is also good. Recommendations can be improved by adding an item attribute dimension. Different from content-based recommendation algorithms, collaborative filtering algorithms can share the experience of others and tap the potential interests of users, making recommendations more efficient. These two traditional algorithms simply recommend items to target users based on users' evaluation of items and users' neighbors, which ignores users' preference for details of item attributes.

4.1 Agricultural product recommendation technology in e-commerce platform

4.1.1 Diversity of consumer behavior

With the rise of Internet big data, e-commerce platforms can support users' various behaviors, such as searching, browsing, collecting, purchasing, sharing, evaluation, etc. Increasingly diversified behaviors make recommendation algorithms more accurate and efficient.

Agricultural products are different from other items. In order to obtain users' preference for agricultural products, explicit collection is not allowed. Excessive collection of user information will make users feel that their privacy security cannot be guaranteed and give rise to resistance, and they may make malicious comments instead. Therefore, it is necessary to analyze users' preference for agricultural products through implicit feedback information of user behavior.

The historical behavior data introduced in this paper can be divided into five specific historical behaviors: browsing, collecting, purchasing, purchasing and evaluating. The more behaviors users have for an item, the more interested users are in the item. Threshold values are designed in algorithm analysis to determine whether users like the item or not.

4.1.2 Characteristics of agricultural products

When consumers choose agricultural product, they can notice the attribute characteristic of the agricultural product especially [4]. The production date and shelf life of agricultural products are related to the health of users, so the characteristics of agricultural products are an important basis for the recommendation system of agricultural products for users. Every article has its own characteristics, such as clothing, whose attributes can be divided into brand, material, style, technology, applicable group, etc. These attributes represent the keywords that consumers prefer to the attributes of goods, and the collection of extracted attribute keywords becomes the label of target consumers.

4.1.3 Compound similarity calculation

In this paper, content-based recommendation algorithm and collaborative filtering algorithm are combined [5]. The similarity calculation of the recommendation algorithm is divided into two parts: one is to calculate the similarity between items based on the user's historical behavior data; the other is to calculate the similarity between items based on the attribute characteristics of the agricultural product itself; finally, the similarity matrix is taken as the mean of the sum of the two, which makes the algorithm more complicated.

4.1.4 Similarity calculation between agricultural products

1. Calculation of item similarity based on consumer behavior data

   The collected historical behavior data of users for agricultural products are expressed by a scoring matrix. Specific behaviors include browsing, collecting, adding to shopping cart, purchasing, and evaluating. When a user has a certain behavior with an item, it means that the user has a rating of +1 for this item.

Table 1. Consumer behavior data.

Behavior	Eggplant	Cabbage	Apple	Chicken
user1	browse collect		browse collect	
user2	browse collect adding to shopping cart buy		browse collect adding to shopping cart	browse collect adding to shopping cart buy
user3	browse			

Convert it into a user item scoring table, as shown in the following table:

Table 2. User-agricultural product scoring matrix.

rating	eggplant	cabbage	apple	chicken
user1	2	0	2	0
user2	4	0	3	4
user3	1	0	0	0

According to the scores in the table, set a score greater than or equal to 2 as like, which can be transformed into a user item preference matrix, as follows:

Table 3. User-agricultural product preference matrix.

preferences	eggplant	cabbage	apple	chicken
user1	like		like	
user2	like		like	like
user3				

According to the cosine similarity formula between items, the similarity matrix of agricultural products is obtained, as shown in the table below

Table 4. Similarity matrix one of agricultural products.

similarity_1	eggplant	cabbage	apple	chicken
eggplant	1	0	1	0.5
cabbage	0	1	0	0
apple	1	0	1	0.5
chicken	0.5	0	0. 5	1

2. Content-based agricultural products similarity calculation

The agricultural product attribute matrix is constructed as follows in table 5.

The calculation of similarity between users or items is the basis for generating recommendation results. The cosine similarity calculation method requires the value of a single value. There are two data types of agricultural product attributes: continuous and discrete. Continuous data should be discretized and split, and the discrete data can be directly converted into matrix elements. The value of the element is 1 or 0, indicating whether it has the corresponding attribute.

Table 6. Similarity matrix two of agricultural products.

similarity_2	eggplant	cabbage	apple	chicken
eggplant	1	0.6	0.2	0.4
cabbage	0.6	1	0.4	0.2
apple	0.2	0.4	1	0.2
chicken	0.4	0.2	0.2	1

3. Calculate the comprehensive similarity between items

Add the matrices in Tables 4 and 6 to obtain the average value to obtain the final similarity matrix.

Table 7. Final similarity matrix of agricultural products.

SIM	eggplant	cabbage	apple	chicken
eggplant	1	0.3	0.6	0.45
cabbage	0.3	1	0.2	0.1
apple	0.6	0.2	1	0.35
chicken	0.45	0.1	0.35	1

Finally, recommend one or more items with the highest similarity with the items loved by the user to the target user.

5 APPLICATION PROCESS OF AGRICULTURAL PRODUCT RECOMMENDATION TECHNOLOGY

The process of agricultural product recommendation model based on user behavior and item attributes is shown in the Figure 1:

Table 5. Agricultural product attribute matrix.

	type	place	Year of production	Shelf life	Genetically modified
eggplant	vegetable	southwest	2021	3 days	no
cabbage	vegetable	east	2021	2 days	yes
apple	fruit	central south	2021	7days	yes
chicken	poultry	northwest	2021	3months	no

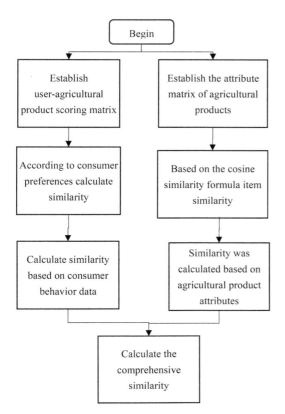

Figure 1. Flow chart of agricultural product recommendation model.

As shown in the figure above, the agricultural product recommendation model process based on collaborative filtering is proposed in this paper. The similarity calculation of this recommendation technology integrates user behavior and agricultural product attributes. Firstly, the user-agricultural product scoring matrix is constructed according to the historical behavior data of users; the similarity of agricultural products is calculated based on the user preference; and the similarity of agricultural products itself is calculated according to the commodity attribute matrix.

The two similarity degrees are integrated into the final similarity, and the recommendation result is finally generated.

6 CONCLUSIONS

COVID-19 has caused serious damage to China's agricultural products enterprises, and agriculture is the foundation of national stability. Based on this, this study analyzes a recommendation technology based on agricultural products, which aims to help China's agricultural enterprises make more effective digital transformation.

ACKNOWLEDGEMENTS

This research has been supported by grants from the Institute of Wuhan Studies fund under Grant IWHS20202057 and the High-level talent fund of Jianghan University under Grant 1001/08580001 and the National Social Science Foundation of China 72171102

REFERENCES

[1] Wu, C.H., S.C. Kao, and J.S. Lin, Determinants of bidding behaviours on live broadcast auction platforms: Goal desire perspective. *International Journal of Consumer Studies*, 2021. 45(5) p. 1079–1102.
[2] Chen, Y., Research on personalized recommendation algorithm based on user preference in mobile e-commerce. *Information Systems and E-Business Management*, 2020. 18(4) p. 837–850.
[3] Wang, G., et al., A content-based weighted granularity sequence recommendation algorithm. *Computer Engineering and Science*, 2018. 40(3) p. 564–570.
[4] Chen, Y.H., et al., How do product recommendations affect impulse buying? An empirical study on WeChat social commerce. *Information & Management*, 2019. 56(2) p. 236–248.
[5] Singh, N., N. Sinha, and F.J. Liebana-Cabanillas, Determining factors in the adoption and recommendation of mobile wallet services in India: Analysis of the effect of innovativeness, stress to use and social influence. *International Journal of Information Management*, 2020. 50 p. 191–205.

Economic and Business Management – Huang & Zhang (Eds)
© 2022 Copyright the Author(s), ISBN: 978-1-032-06754-4

An empirical study of skewness on stock returns forecast

Cancan Yang & Yucan Liu
Nanjing University of Science and Technology, Nanjing, Jiangsu, China

ABSTRACT: The traditional CAPM model assumes that the returns on the securities market strictly follow a normal distribution, and the actual securities returns tend to exhibit asymmetric characteristics, so higher-moment risk factor should also be included in the pricing model. This article aims to investigate the role of stock skewness in predicting excess returns. It selects monthly data of A-shares in the Shanghai and Shenzhen stock markets from January 2005 to December 2019, and uses Fama and MacBeth regression to analyze the constructed prediction model. The research results show that there is a significant negative correlation between the monthly skewness of stocks and expected excess returns. Investors' preference for positively skewed stocks makes them have a lower risk premium. This negative correlation is still robust after introducing control variables and testing the sub-samples.

Keywords: Asset pricing; Stock skewness; Excess returns

1 INTRODUCTION

Profitability, liquidity and risk are the three most important characteristics of financial instruments, among which the relationship between risk and return is undoubtedly one of the core issues in financial research. The traditional CAPM model test effect of real earnings is more and more ragged, because only when the probability distribution of return on assets is normal, can asset risk be completely identified by return variance or standard deviation. However, in fact, the distribution of the return often does not meet the normal hypothesis.

Kraus and Litzenberger (1976) first added the system skewness factor into the CAPM model, believing that investors prefer positive skewness, and developed the third-moment CAPM model. Siddique and Harvey (1999) assumed that returns follow the non-central t-distribution under the maximum likelihood framework, and found a significant negative correlation between conditional skewness and returns through studies on daily, weekly and monthly returns. In real life, a large number of investors hold incompletely diversified portfolios, so many scholars have also studied the pricing problem of idiosyncratic skewness. Boyer et al. (2010) estimate expected idiosyncratic skewness through the cross-sectional model and found the negative correlation between expected idiosyncratic skewness and expected return rate in the American market, and showed that expected idiosyncratic skewness helps to explain the "idiosyncratic volatility puzzle" discovered by Ang et al. (2006). Zheng et al. (2013) studied the relationship between stock expected idiosyncratic skewness and expected return

rate in China's A stock market, and found that there is a significant negative correlation between them. Yao et al. (2019) thought this phenomenon reflected the strong gambling atmosphere of the Chinese stock market, and believe that it is caused by the irrationality of individual investors and the restriction of market arbitrage.

As for total skewness, its proxy variable can be the realized skewness constructed based on historical data. Amaya et al. (2011) found that the realized skewness constructed by the high-frequency returns of individual stocks and the stock returns of the next week have a significant negative correlation on the cross-section. The proxy variable can also be risk neutral skewness. Conrad et al. (2013) extracted the expected skewness risk from the option price of individual stocks and founf that it has a significantly negative correlation with the future return rate of stocks.

Why is positive skewness always associated with lower expected returns? Harvey and Siddique (2000) believe that limited liability and agency issues will lead to asymmetric returns and make investment managers prefer stocks with high skewness. The empirical results of Jondeau et al. (2019) show that the average monthly skewness of companies can well predict future market returns, and believe that this negative correlation is related to tail risk, crash risk and investors' gambling psychology, which is also consistent with Kumar's (2009) view that individual investors prefer lottery stocks.

China's stock market is not only an emerging market, but also vulnerable to risks from various aspects due to the limitation of arbitrage space and the strong gambling atmosphere. Understanding the relationship

176

DOI 10.1201/9781003203704-32

between stock returns skewness and expected returns can help us to better grasp the influencing factors of stock expected returns. However, there are few studies on whether skewness of China's stock market has a predictive ability beyond the CAPM model and Fama-French's three-factor model for future returns, which is also the research direction of this paper.

The remainder of the paper proceeds as follows. Section 2 is the research scheme design; orrelated variables and correlated model are constructed in this part. Section 3 is empirical analysis, which mainly presents results of model regression and the robustness test. Section 4 is the conclusion.

2 RESEARCH SCHEME DESIGN

2.1 Variable construction

In this paper, monthly excess returns of the4 CAPM model and Fama-French's three-factor model are taken as explained variables. The rolling regression method is adopted to calculate the coefficient of individual stocks, and the time window is from t-36 to t-1. The original return is a logarithmic return. Then the coefficients are substituted into the following formula to obtain the monthly excess return rate:

$$R_{1(i,t)} = r_{(i,t)} - r_{f(t)} - \beta_{m(i,t)} R_{m(t)} \tag{1}$$

$$R_{2(i,t)} = r_{(i,t)} - r_{f(t)} - \left[\beta_{MKT(i,t)} MKT_t + \beta_{SMB(i,t)} SMB_t + \beta_{HML(i,t)} HML_t \right] \tag{2}$$

where $r_{(i,t)}$ is the monthly return of the stock i in month t, $r_{f(t)}$ is the risk-free rate of return in month t, and MKT_t SMB_t HML_t are the average market return factor, market value factor and book-to-market ratio factor of A-shares in the t month, respectively.

This paper studies the prediction effect of total skewness and constructs the monthly skewness of stocks using the high-order moment method of samples. For stock i, the monthly skew at period t is as follows:

$$skew = \frac{\frac{1}{n}\sum_{i=1}^{n}(x_i - \bar{x})^3}{\left[\frac{1}{n}\sum_{i=1}^{n}(x_i - \bar{x})^2\right]^{3/2}} \tag{3}$$

where n is the number of samples, and is the mean of daily return rate

As for control variables, this paper takes the natural logarithm of the market value, $Size_{i,t}$=ln $MV_{i,t}$, to measure the market value of the company, and the MV is in CNY. $BM_{i,t}$ is used to represent the book-to-market ratio of stock i at the end of month t, equal to shareholders' equity divided by the company's market value. $Turn_{i,t}$ are used to represent the monthly turnover rate of tradable shares, which is the sum of the daily turnover rate of tradable shares.

2.2 Model construction and research methods

Regress all the stocks in China's A-share market according to the following model:

$$R_{1(i,t+1)} = \beta_0 + \beta_1 Skew_{i,t} + \gamma\, Control_{i,t} + \varepsilon_{i,t} \tag{4}$$

$$R_{2(i,t+1)} = \gamma_0 + \gamma_1 Skew_{i,t} + \gamma\, Control_{i,t} + \varepsilon_{i,t} \tag{5}$$

where $R_{1(i,t+1)}$ and $R_{2(i,t+1)}$, respectively represent the excess return of stock i based on the CAPM model and Fama-French's three-factor model in month $t+1$. $Skew_{i,t}$ and $Control_{i,t}$ represent the monthly skewness and control variables of stock i in month t.

Considering that the number of stocks in the A stock market is not the same every month, the general panel analysis will lead to inaccurate results. Therefore, this paper adopts the Fama and MacBeth regression. The FM regression method is as follows:

$$\begin{cases} \bar{b} = \frac{1}{T}\sum_t \hat{b}_t \\ Var\,(b) = \sum_t \frac{1}{T-1}(\hat{b}_t - \bar{b})^2 \\ t_b = \frac{\bar{b}}{\sqrt{Var(b)/T}} \end{cases} \tag{6}$$

where $\hat{b}$ represents the coefficient estimated in cross-sectional regression, and T represents the number of samples used in cross-sectional regression. If $\bar{b}$ is positive and t_b is statistically significant, it indicates that there is a positive correlation between the explanatory variable and explained variable.

2.3 Selection of sample data

The data for this article are from Resset. This paper selects all A-share stocks in Shanghai and Shenzhen stock markets as the research object. Since the reform of non-tradable shares in China's stock market officially began in 2005, the benchmark sample period selected is from January 2005 to December 2019, with a total of 180 monthly data over 15 years. After calculating the coefficients of 36 months rolling regression, the sample period of excess monthly returns finally used is from January 2008 to December 2019, with 144 monthly data.

3 EMPIRICAL ANALYSIS

3.1 Data description

Skewness is a high-order description of return rate. In this paper, monthly skewness is calculated based on the daily return rate of stocks of more than 3000 companies from December 2007 to November 2019. Table 1 shows the descriptive statistics of these company's monthly characteristic variables.

As can be seen from the table, R_1 skewness is 1.474, R_2 skewness is 1.353, and the mean value of the unprocessed original monthly return skewness is −0.01, indicating that the actual monthly stock returns

Table 1. Descriptive statistics of data.

Variable	Mean	Std	Min	Max	Skew	Kurt
R_1	0.456	10.90	−161.4	252.7	1.474	11.10
R_2	−0.142	10.79	−86.83	179.5	1.353	9.334
skew	−0.010	0.735	−3.870	4.281	0.048	1.028
Size	22.36	1.075	18.13	28.36	0.787	1.877
BM	0.391	0.267	0.0001	12.50	2.593	53.29
Turn	41.78	41.20	0.0003	717.1	2.624	11.89

R_1 and R_2 are given as percentages.

in China's A stock market are generally left skewed. However, the excess return after CAPM model and Fama-French's three-factor model is skewed to the right. For the selected control variables, combining skewness and kurtosis, it can be seen that the market value basically obeys the normal distribution, the book-to-market ratio and the turnover rate present obvious "peak fat tail" distribution.

3.2 Fama and MacBeth regression

In this section, 144 months of data from January 2008 to December 2019 are used. The excess return after 36 months of rolling according to CAPM model and three-factor model is taken as the explained variable, monthly skewness is taken as the explanatory variable, and $Size_{i,t}$, $BM_{i,t}$ and $Turn_{i,t}$ are introduced as control variables. In Fama and MacBeth regression, first of all, according to the regression model (4,5), the cross-sectional regression of all individual stocks at each monthly time point is conducted. Due to space limitation, specific monthly regression results are not shown here. Complete regression results can be requested from the author. In order to obtain a more accurate overall judgment, we used Fama and MacBeth regression method in formula (6) to calculate $\bar{b}$ and t_b of each variable. The Fama and MacBeth regression results are shown in Table 2.

Table 2. Cross-sectional regression results of expected excess returns of stocks.

	CAPM excess returns		Three-factor excess return	
Skew	−0.49***	−0.31***	−0.35***	−0.25***
	(−3.56)	(−2.82)	(−3.19)	(−2.63)
Size		−0.67***		−0.31***
		(−4.46)		(−3.78)
BM		0.27		1.21***
		(0.48)		(3.25)
Turn		−0.022***		−0.026***
		(−8.15)		(−9.45)
R²	0.55	5.69	0.35	2.77

t_b statistics are in parentheses. R^2 is the average value of adjusted R^2 of the monthly regression model. ***,** and * respectively indicate that the coefficients are significant at the significance level of 1%,5% and 10%.

As can be seen from Table 2, the mean value of the regression coefficient is significantly negative at the 1% significance level even if the control variables are added, indicating that at the level of individual stocks, skewness does have a predictive effect on earnings, and the higher the skewness, the lower the expected return. The mean values of adjusted R^2 of the multivariate prediction model based on the CAPM model and three-factor model reached 5.69% and 2.77% respectively, indicating that the model can significantly improve the actual excess returns.

For the control variable, the mean of $Size_{i,t}$ and $Turn_{i,t}$ coefficient are both negative under the excess returns based on the two models, and the mean value of $BM_{i,t}$ coefficient is positive, which is in line with the expectation, indicating that small size, high book-to-market ratio and low turnover rate usually mean higher expected excess returns.

3.3 Robust test

3.3.1 Classification by market

For the two markets of Shanghai Stock Exchange and Shenzhen Stock Exchange, there are certain differences in the bidding system, the relationship between skewness and excess returns may also be different. The regression results by market classification are shown in Table 3.

Table 3. Regression results of stock expected excess returns classified by market.

	Shanghai _R_1	Shenzhen _R_1	Shanghai _R_2	Shenzhen _R_2
Skew	−0.44***	−0.53***	-0.31***	−0.40***
	(−10.93)	(−13.31)	(−6.91)	(−9.17)
Size	-0.61***	−0.73***	−0.32***	−0.32***
	(−24.07)	(−22.74)	(−11.72)	(−9.42)
BM	0.28***	-0.03	1.20***	0.09
	(2.62)	(-0.26)	(10.10)	(0.66)
Turn	−0.01***	−0.01***	−0.02***	−0.02***
	(−15.00)	(−13.95)	(−23.54)	(−28.71)
R²	0.70	0.60	0.80	0.85

For the explanation of the table, see Table 2.

As can be seen from Table 3, the regression coefficient of skewness under the two models has statistical significance at 1% level in both Shanghai stock Market and Shenzhen Stock market. This indicates that the negative correlation between skewness and expected returns is very robust. In addition, it can also be seen that skewness has a greater impact on expected excess returns in the Shenzhen market, and the t value of the variable regression coefficient is also larger. The coefficient of $BM_{i,t}$ has a statistical significance of 1% in Shanghai stock market, but it is not significant in Shenzhen stock market, indicating that the "book-to-market ratio" may not be valid in Shenzhen stock market.

3.3.2 *Classification by time*

The stock market crash around the end of 2015 is, in a sense, a concentrated release of the long-term contradiction in the A-share market. Since 2016, regulatory authorities have begun to carry out more comprehensive governance of the stock market. Therefore, this paper takes the beginning of 2016 as the basis for division. The samples are divided into the period I from January 2008 to December 2015 and the period II from January 2016 to December 2019.

As can be seen from Table 4, the negative correlation between skewness and expected excess returns is also quite robust in the sub-samples divided by time. The regression coefficient of skewness and the t value are larger in period I, indicating that the negative correlation between skewness and expected returns is more obvious in period before 2016.

Table 4. Regression results of stock expected excess returns classified by time.

	period I $\_R_1$	period II $\_R_1$	period I $\_R_2$	period II $\_R_2$
Skew	−0.66***	−0.39***	−0.46***	−0.27***
	(−14.47)	(−11.42)	(−9.89)	(−6.71)
Size	−0.72***	−0.12***	−0.35***	−0.15***
	(−26.00)	(−4.11)	(−12.37)	(−4.52)
BM	0.11	0.51***	1.24***	0.09
	(0.92)	(5.09)	(9.87)	(0.73)
Turn	−0.009***	−0.019***	−0.022***	−0.021***
	(−13.29)	(−23.62)	(−29.30)	(−22.45)
R^2	0.68	0.70	0.93	0.69

For the explanation of the table, see Table 2.

4 CONCLUSIONS

The purpose of this paper is to study the predictive ability of stock skewness to excess returns and test whether investors prefer positively skewed stocks. The sample selects stock data of China's A-share market from January 2005 to December 2019. The excess return after 36 months of rolling according to CAPM model and Fama-French's three-factor model is the explained variable, the monthly skewness of individual stocks is the explanatory variable, and the market value, book-to-market ratio and turnover rate are introduced as control variables. The multivariate linear prediction model is established, and Fama and Mac-Beth regression method is used for empirical analysis of the model.

Previous studies generally proved that skewness is negatively correlated with expected original returns. The contribution of this article is to clearly prove that there is a significant negative correlation between stock return skewness and expected excess return in China's A-share market whether it is the excess return based on the CAPM model or the Fama-French three-factor model. This forecasting ability is still significant after controlling other predictors of China's stock market. The robustness tests of subsamples classified by market and time are also passed. In the Shenzhen market and in the period I from 2008 to 2016, skewness has a greater impact on expected excess returns, and the regression coefficient is also more significant.

Based on the empirical results, we want to give investors a sincere suggestion. If you want to win excess returns, don't blindly pursue the stocks with positive skewness in previous period. Many investors prefer these stocks, so they are overvalued and tend to have a lower risk premium in the future. In short, in the investment market, following the public is not a good choice.

REFERENCES

Amaya, D., Christoffersen, P., Jacobs, K. & Vasquez, A. 2011. Do Realized Skewness and Kurtosis Predict the Cross-Section of Equity Returns? *CREATES Research Papers* 118(1):135–167.

Ang, A., Hodrick, R. J., Xing, Y. & Zhang, X. 2006. The Cross-Section of Volatility and Expected Returns. *The Journal of Finance* 61(1):259–299.

Boyer, B., Mitton, T. &Vorkink K. 2010. Expected Idiosyncratic Skewness. *Review of Financial Studies* 23(1): 169–202.

Conrad, J., Dittmar, R. F. & Ghysels, E. 2013. Ex Ante Skewness and Expected Stock Returns. *The Journal of Finance* 68(1):85–124.

Harvey, C.R & Siddique, A. 2000. Conditional Skewness in Asset Pricing Tests. *The Journal of Finance* 55(3):1263–1295.

Jondeau, E., Zhang, Q. & Zhu, X. 2019. Average skewness matters. *Journal of Financial Economics* 134(1): 29–47.

Kraus, A. & Litzenberger, R.H. 1976. Skewness Preference and the Valuation of Risk Assets. *The Journal of Finance* 31(4):1085–1100.

Kumar, A. 2009. Who Gambles in the Stock Market? *The Journal of Finance* 64(4): 1889–1933.

Siddique, A.R & Harvey, C.R. 1999. Autoregressive Conditional Skewness. *Social Science Electronic Publishing* 34(4):465–487.

Yao, S., Wang, C., Cui, X. & Fang, Z. 2019. Idiosyncratic Skewness, Gambling Preference, and Cross-section of Stock Returns: Evidence from China. *Pacific-Basin Finance Journal* 53: 464–483.

Zheng, Z. L. & Wang, L. 2013. Is Idiosyncratic Skewness Priced? *Journal of management science* 16(05): 1–12.

Economic and Business Management – Huang & Zhang (Eds)
© 2022 Copyright the Author(s), ISBN: 978-1-032-06754-4

Moderating role of marketization process in the analyst tracking and corporate social responsibility

Zhuo Zhang & Jing Song
School of Business, Macau University of Science and Technology, Taipa, China

Yu Song
School of Business, Xi'an Polytechnic University, Xi'an, China

ABSTRACT: Over the past few years, corporate social responsibility has been one of the hot topics in the field of accounting or finance. According to the analyzed data of publicly traded companies from 2010 to 2019, we established a multiple linear model to empirically test the impact of analyst tracking on fulfillment of corporate social responsibility. And also, we discuss the moderating effect of marketization process on the relationship between analyst tracking and corporate social responsibility. The research indicates that both analyst tracking and marketization process can enhance enterprises' fulfillment to social responsibility, and at the same time, marketization process, as a moderating effect, can effectively strengthen the relationship between two factors. The research enriches the impact factors of corporate social responsibility and forces business to fulfill more corporate social responsibility.

1 INTRODUCTION

China's economy has grown rapidly since the reform. Enterprises always search for profit maximization as the primary goal of development under the tide of rapid economic development However, companies often ignore the social and environmental problems caused by development [1], such as market disorder, information distortion, energy exhaustion and water pollution. Business, especially publicly traded companies, have to think about how to solve these problems while the public gradually concerned about such problems That is, effective solutions to these problems are fulfillment of corporate social responsibility [2]. According to the requirements of the CSR, the public business has to disclose the performance of corporate social responsibility in the note disclosure of the Financial Statement if any. Statistics of responsibility rating in 2020 indicate that corporate social responsibility report disclosure shows a rapid growth trend. The number of companies disclosed in 2010 compared to 2019 doubled. Social responsibility has become a very important part of enterprise management [3] Based on this trend, many scholars gradually focus on how to fulfill corporate social responsibility when enterprises expand [4]. From the current research, there are two kinds of driving factors: internal factors and external factors. The internal factors focus on the research of company's financial characteristics and corporate governance characteristics influence over CSR On the

other hand, the external factors discuss about the institutional environment and the government policy of the capital market influence over CSR [5].

To address this problem, our study intends to explore how analyst tracking frequency affects corporate social responsibility (CSR) of the enterprise. On the other hand, we also examine another external governance factor, how marketization process may influence the relationship between analyst tracking and CSR.

The logical connection between analyst tracking, market process, and CSR can provide a new idea for undertaking CSR. It is easier for regulatory authorities to influence corporate social responsibility information disclosure behavior by formulating relevant institutional norms, so as to ensure the simultaneous implementation of economic benefits and corporate responsibility.

2 LITERATURE REVIEW AND HYPOTHESES

2.1 *Analyst tracking and corporate social responsibility*

As we know, there are agency problems and information asymmetry between business management and information users in the capital market based on the agency theory and signal transmission theory. Another group, analysts, serves as an intermediary to help information users to make decisions of investment by providing an effective analysis report. Analysts analyze business financial statements and related business information to produce a reference report for users. As an information intermediary, analysts can use their professional skills to collect and analyze the financial reports and prospectus publicly released by enterprises, dig for some hidden information, track enterprises, and disclose some business problems for using in decision-making. Studies have shown that analysts deliver incremental information to the capital markets, with higher information credibility and more readability, thus enhancing market information transparency [6]. In addition, analysts play another important role in the capital market, one of the external supervisors. Analysts track the target enterprises, and they have some responsibilities to expose a lot of problems during their analysis. As the frequency of analyst tracking increases, management can feel the pressure of external supervision, which forces enterprise management to assume corporate social responsibility, and take the initiative to disclose social responsibility information to the public. Studies show that the level of corporate environmental responsibility information disclosure and the level of environmental responsibility information disclosure quality will be significantly improved [7]. Therefore, analyst tracking, as an external governance mechanism, is mainly through the effective acquisition, analysis, and interpretation of information, to affect the corporate social responsibility of efforts.

Based on the theory of "complete information hypothesis" an analyst, one of the market participants, must have complete recognition of knowledge given the economic environment. Analysts need to look at the details of all companies, including fulfillment of CSR. Analysts can influence CSR by tracking all relevant information about the company The more frequently analysts track, the better the business fulfill the CSR [8].

Analyst tracking affects CSR in two main ways: one is information access. Corporate financial information and non-financial information will be reviewed frequently when analysts are interested in a business. More and more comprehensive and detailed information of fulfillment of business CSR is concerned with the increase in the number of analyst tracking The company has to worry about the potential negative impact of the analyst's disclosure on the company Another one is professional interpretation. There are problems such as corporate social responsibility information, which is difficult to be quantified Lack of unified standardization and poor comparability can increase the difficulty to understand corporate social responsibility for information users [9]. Analysts have strong professional analytical skills. They are more professional, independent, and objective in interpretation of business information than auditing or other governance departments. The key reason is that they have no interest correlation with the company. With the increase in the number of tracking people, analysts can transmit much more information to information users, and then facilitate them to understand any more of business CSR Conversely, the company will actively fulfill its responsibilities to grab shareholders' hearts.

The more frequent the analysts track, the stronger the business management fulfill the CSR. So, the first hypothesis is proposed:

H1: Analyst tracking has a positive impact on corporate social responsibility.

2.2 Marketization process and corporate social responsibility

An enterprise's cognition level and performance of social responsibility will be greatly affected by the marketization process in the region where the enterprise is located. Marketization process is the external market environment faced by enterprises, and the influence path of corporate social responsibility is generally in four dimensions: 1. Regional education level. The higher the level of education, the more advanced the idea of social responsibility of the public recognition [10]; 2. intensity of government intervention. The less government intervention in the region, the freer are the capital markets. In the free market, enterprises are faced with more competition from similar enterprises. In order to seek more support and recognition from external investors and customers, enterprises may actively undertake corporate social responsibility and improve their corporate social responsibility [11,12]; 3. regional legal system level. Areas with a relatively sound legal system will restrict corporate behavior from the institutional aspect, and enterprises will realize the undertaking and disclosure of social responsibility within the scope permitted by law to promote the implementation of social responsibility [13,14]; 4. public awareness. The higher the degree of marketization, the more social responsibility awareness of the public, to assume the role of "supervisor," promote enterprises to fulfill, and disclose more social responsibility. So the second hypothesis is proposed:

H2. Regional marketization process has a positive impact on corporate social responsibility.

2.3 The moderating effect of marketization process on the relationship between analyst tracking and corporate social responsibility

A large number of literature has shown that the marketization process will have a certain impact on the third-party supervision agencies outside the enterprise and the own behavior within the enterprise [15]. The higher the marketization degree, the better the market environment, the more complete the relevant legal system, the higher the information transparency, which is conducive to the analysts' more convenient access to the relevant information of the enterprise. The management gradually finds that whether the information in the market is positive (or negative) will have a positive (or negative) impact on the stock price, corporate reputation, and product competitiveness of the enterprise. Fulfilling corporate social responsibility and actively disclosing social responsibility information may become the choice for target enterprises to convey positive image to the market. With the continuous improvement of marketization, analysts will continue to strengthen the tracking of corporate social responsibility, and enterprises are more likely to consciously or forced to fulfill their social responsibility. So the third hypothesis is proposed:

H3. The increasing marketization process has a positive impact on the relationship between analyst tracking and corporate social responsibility.

3 MODELING AND VARIABLE DEFINITION

We constructed three models: Model (1), Model (2), and Model (3) based on our three hypotheses:

$$CSR = \beta_0 + \beta_1 Follow + \beta_2 Size + \beta_3 Roa +$$
$$\beta_4 Leverage + \beta_5 Age + \beta_6 GrowthRate$$
$$+ \beta_7 LHRate + \Sigma Year + \Sigma Industry + \varepsilon_1 \ (1)$$

$$CSR = \beta_0 + \beta_1 Index + \beta_2 Size + \beta_3 Roa$$
$$+ \beta_4 Leverage + \beta_5 Age + \beta_6 GrowthRate$$
$$+ \beta_7 LHRate + \Sigma Year + \Sigma Insustry + \varepsilon_1 \ (2)$$

$$CSR = \beta_0 + \beta_1 Follow + \beta_2 Index + \beta_3 Follow^*Index$$
$$+ \beta_4 Size + \beta_5 Roa + \beta_6 Leverage$$
$$+ \beta_7 Age + \beta_8 GrowthRate + \beta_9 LHRate$$
$$+ \Sigma Year + \Sigma Industry + \varepsilon_1 \qquad (3)$$

The i,t in the model represents the enterprise and the year, respectively; the CSR stands for corporate social responsibility; Follow on behalf of the analyst tracking, Index represents the process of marketization, Follow*Index represents the interaction terms for analyst tracking and the marketization process. Other variables represent the company size (Size), return on assets (Roa), asset-to-liability ratio (Leverage), time of listing (Age), total assets turnover (Growth Rate), largest shareholder shareholding (LH Rate), industry (Industry), year (Year). Table 1 shows the detailed variable definitions.

4 DATA AND DATA ANALYSIS

This paper adopts A-share listed companies in Shanghai and Shenzhen stock markets from 2010 to 2019 as the research samples, with data from Hexun database, GTD database, and Fan Gang's Report on Market Indexes by Provinces in China.

4.1 Descriptive statistics

Table 2 reports the descriptive statistics. The mean value of CSR is 27.36, indicating that our corporate

social responsibility index is low while enterprises are not strong enough to fulfill their social responsibilities. Meanwhile, the minimum value of -18.45 and the maximum value of 88 show the degree of social responsibility performance between different enterprises. Analyst tracking with an average of 1.538 shows that the number of analyst tracking companies is small. Also, the minimum value of 0 and the maximum value of 4.331 show that there are still large differences in the intensity of being tracked between enterprises. The average value of the marketization process is 7.015, the minimum value is -1.142, and the maximum value is 10.92. It means that there are large differences in the marketization process between regions, which will lead to unbalanced development among regions. The average value of return on assets (ROA) is 0.0334, indicating that the profitability of the sample enterprises is low. The average value of leverage is 0.482, and the standard deviation is 0.264, indicating that the overall financial risk of sample enterprises is relatively high, and the gap between samples is quite obvious. Analysis of other control variables is also available.

Table 1. Variable definition.

Variables	Name	Variable	Definition
Dependent Variable	Corporate Social Responsibility	CSR	CSR rating (HeXun Database)
Independent Variable	Analyst tracking	Follow	Log (The numbers of analysts tracking the same public company +1)
Moderator	Marketization process	Index	Report on Market Index by Province in China (Gang Fan, 2018)
	Business Size	Size	Ln(Total Assets)
	Return on Assets	ROA	Net Income/ Total Assets
Control Variables	Asset– Liability Ratio	Leverage	Total Liabilities/ Total Assets
	Time to market	Age	Number of years on the market
	Asset Turnover	Asset growth rate	Sale Revenue/ Total asset turnover days
	Shareholding ratio of the largest shareholder	Largest Holder Rate	Number of shares held by the largest shareholder of the company/ Total shares
	Industry	Indcd	Dummy variable
	Year	Year	Dummy variable

182

4.2 Analysis of correlation

Pearson correlation matrix report indicates the correlation coefficients of all variables below 0.3. The data follow a normal distribution. And there is no serious multicollinearity problem.

4.3 Regression analysis

Table 3 shows the results of regression by running the data of 8520 samples.

In the regression analysis in Table 4, Model 1, the regression coefficient between analyst tracking and CSR is 2.126 and passed the significance test, indicating a significant positive correlation with CSR, where the more the number of analyst tracking, the more social responsibility companies take on, consistent with Hypothesis 1.

In the regression analysis of Table 4, Model 2, the regression coefficient between index and corporate social responsibility is 5.761, and the significance test shows that the marketization process and corporate social responsibility are significantly positively related, that is, the higher the degree of marketization process of the enterprise location, the more the social responsibility of the enterprise will assume, consistent with Hypothesis 2.

In the regression analysis of Table 4, Model 3, the correlation coefficient of the interaction term Follow*Index of the marketization process is 0.324, and the significance test positively regulates the relationship between analyst tracking and corporate social responsibility. The marketization process will create a good corporate location environment, prompting analysts to increase tracking to improve corporate social responsibility, which is consistent with Hypothesis 3.

The empirical study indicates that there is a positive correlation between analyst tracking and corporate social responsibility, the marketization process has a positive correlation for corporate social responsibility, and the marketization process has a positively moderate relationship between analyst tracking and corporate social responsibility.

5 ROBUSTNESS TEST

We replaced Roe with Roa, and the independent director ratio IIN replaced the largest shareholder

Table 2. Descriptive statistics report

Variables	Number	Mean	Median	Std.	Min	Max
CSR	8,520	27.36	23.070	18.59	−18.45	88
Follow	8,520	1.538	1.609	1.185	0	4.331
Index	8,520	7.015	6.980	2.003	−1.420	10.92
Size	8,520	22.57	22.410	1.485	16.52	28.64
Roa	8,520	0.0334	0.028	0.104	−3.501	3.876
Leverage	8,520	0.482	0.487	0.264	0.00836	11.99
Age	8,520	13.38	14.000	6.231	0	29
Growth Rate	8,520	0.636	0.514	0.551	0.00057	10.59
LH Rate	8,520	35.85	34.020	15.47	0.290	89.09

Table 3. Regression report.

Variables	CSR		
	Model 1	Model 2	Model 3
Follow	2.126*** (9.70)		−0.114 (−0.16)
Index		5.761*** (3.69)	2.141** (1.98)
Follow * Index			0.324*** (3.30)
Roa	16.78*** (10.67)	55.56*** (17.61)	16.65*** (10.59)
LH Rate	0.0722*** (2.98)	0.0532** (2.23)	0.0724*** (2.99)
Age	−1.576*** (−18.16)	−1.532 (−0.98)	−1.496*** (−16.11)
Leverage	−5.063*** (−6.29)	−15.06*** (−10.33)	−4.969*** (−6.17)
size	3.949*** (11.27)	6.057*** (16.99)	3.954*** (11.29)
Growth Rate	1.306** (2.28)	3.281*** (4.63)	1.200** (2.28)
constants	−46.92*** (−6.44)	−80.46658*** (−7.56)	−63.24653*** (−5.90)
Numbers	8520	8520	8520
R2	0.3418	0.3224	0.3448
Adj R2	0.3356	0.3161	0.3385
Year Fixed	YES	YES	YES
Industry Fixed	YES	YES	YES

*** 1% level of significance.
** 5% level of significance.
* 10% level of significance.

Table 4. Robustness test

	CSR		
Variables	Model 1	Model 2	Model 3
Follow	3.087*** (14.57)		0.478 (0.66)
Index		2.843** (2.54)	2.392** (2.16)
Follow*Index			0.379*** (3.77)
Roe	−0.0259* (−0.36)	−0.0577* (−0.79)	−0.0239* (−0.33)
IIN	4.258** (1.21)	3.425** (0.96)	4.280** (1.21)
Age	0.0991*** (2.92)	0.117*** (3.41)	0.0893*** (2.63)
Leverage	1.165* (1.69)	0.968 (1.38)	1.161* (1.68)
Size	−1.789*** (−11.73)	−1.894*** (−12.26)	−1.766*** (−11.59)
Growth Rate	1.089*** (2.89)	1.239*** (3.24)	1.155*** (3.06)
constants	62.50*** (17.16)	50.29*** (5.69)	44.72*** (5.12)
Numbers	8520	8520	8520
R2	0.2947	0.2076	0.3011
Adj R2	0.2880	0.2000	0.2944
Year Fixed	YES	YES	YES
Firm Fixed	YES	YES	YES

shareholding ratio LH rate in order to further test the robustness of the previous regression. The empirical results are shown in Table 4. The result is consistent with that of the previous regression In conclusion, H1, H2 and H3 can be verified while replacing some different variables. The robustness test improves the reliability of our results.

6 CONCLUSIONS

Attracting analysts to track and promote the marketization process in the location of enterprises is an important path to improve corporate social responsibility, but also an external governance force to promote the benign development of enterprises and enhance market competitiveness. The main findings are given in the following paragraphs.

Firstly, as an important information intermediary in the capital market, analysts promote the information transmission between investors and enterprises and play an important role in promoting the development of enterprises. Analysts have a certain restraint and supervision effect on management. The results show that analyst tracking significantly improves corporate social responsibility, even after controlling for possible endogenous problems between the two.

Secondly, the marketization process is conducive to the fulfillment of corporate social responsibility. When the legal environment is better, the external pressure is smoothly transmitted, and the government's supervision is in place, the company's commitment and performance of social responsibility will be improved.

Thirdly, the marketization process, as an external factor, will further promote analysts to track the impact on CSR performance through the pressure of institutional environment.

Both external supervision (analyst tracking) and strengthening of external governance (marketization process) are conducive to the fulfillment of corporate social responsibility.

The limitation of our study is mainly reflected in the shortage of samples. In particular, the disclosure of corporate CSR in the past 2 years (2020 and 2021) was not included in our study.

REFERENCES

[1] Stuebs, M., & Sun, L. (2015). Corporate governance and social responsibility. *International Journal of Law and Management*, 57(1), 38–52.

[2] Montiel, I. (2008). Corporate Social Responsibility and Corporate Sustainability: Separate Pasts, *Common Futures Organization & Environment* 21(3), 245–269.

[3] L. J. Ma, Z. H. Yi, & C. Zhang. (2019). Is the cheap talk still justified? Analyst Report Text [J]. *Management World* 35 (07): 182–200.

[4] C. Cai, K. F. Zheng, Y. Chen, & P. Wang (2019). Study on the Impact of Government Environmental Audit on Corporate Environmental Responsibility Information Disclosure–Based on empirical evidence of "Three Rivers and Three Lakes" Environmental Audit [J]. *Audit research* (06): 3–12.

[5] Williams, Daniel W. (2000). The effects of corporate governance on firm credit ratings[J]. *Journal of Accounting and Economics* 42(1).

[6] Sun, J., & Liu, G. (2016). Does analyst coverage constrain real earnings management? *The Quarterly Review of Economics and Finance*, 59, 131–140.

[7] Y. Y. Liu, & Y. Tian. (2019). Financial statements misstatement, risk and voluntary disclosure of–based on Corporate Social Responsibility Report [J]. *Accounting Research* (04): 26–35.

[8] Sun, J., & Liu, G. (2016). Does analyst coverage constrain real earnings management? *The Quarterly Review of Economics and Finance*, 59, 131–140.

[9] L. J. Xia, & Y. Q. Fang. (2005). Government control, governance environment, and corporate value–from

empirical evidence from the Chinese securities market [J]. *Economic Research*, (05): 40–51.

[10] Natale, S. M., & Doran, C. (2012). Marketization of education: An ethical dilemma. *Journal of Business Ethics*, 105(2), 187–196.

[11] Zhao, Wang, & Deng. (2019). Interest Rate Marketization, Financing Constraints and R&D Investments: Evidence from China. *Sustainability (Basel, Switzerland)*, 11(8), 23–11.

[12] Yuan, B., Li, C., & Xiong, X. (2021). Innovation and environmental total factor productivity in China: the moderating roles of economic policy uncertainty and marketization process. *Environmental Science and Pollution Research International*, 28(8), 9558–9581.

[13] Dobers, P. (2009). Corporate social responsibility: management and methods. *Corporate Social Responsibility and Environmental Management*, 8(4), 185–191.

[14] Rigoberto Parada Daza, J. (2009). A valuation model for corporate social responsibility. *Social Responsibility Journal*, 5(3), 284–299.

[15] Shi, G., Sun, J., Zhang, L., & Jin, Y. (2017). Corporate social responsibility and geographic dispersion. *Journal of Accounting and Public Policy*, 36(6), 417–428.

Economic and Business Management – Huang & Zhang (Eds)
© 2022 Copyright the Author(s), ISBN: 978-1-032-06754-4

Research on the co-agglomeration and spatial similarity of producer services and manufacturing industries in Jiangxi

Shenglan Huang
Jiangxi Normal University, China

ABSTRACT: Based on the enterprise data of the second national economic census of China in 2008, this paper analyzes the spatial synergy between the five producer services and three manufacturing industries in Jiangxi Province by using the methods of nuclear density and geographic detector from the perspective of spatial similarity. Based on the county scale, this paper discusses the co-agglomeration of producer services and manufacturing industries in Jiangxi Province from the industry level. There is a certain spatial similarity between the spatial layout of producer services and manufacturing industries in Jiangxi Province from the perspective of spatial layout of industrial agglomeration centers. The region with the highest spatial similarity between producer services and manufacturing industries is concentrated in Nanchang, and the spatial similarity between producer services and manufacturing industries in Jingdezhen, Xinyu, Shangrao, Jiujiang, Yingtan, Yichun, Ji 'an, Ganzhou, Pingxiang and Fuzhou is low. On the whole, Jiangxi's transportation, warehousing and postal industries are highly similar to manufacturing industries, and the financial industries are similar to capital-intensive and labor-intensive manufacturing industries. The layout of information transmission, computer service and software industries and leasing and business services has high spatial similarity with the layout of capital and technology-intensive manufacturing industries. Differences in government planning and the flexibility of enterprise layout are important factors which affect the spatial similarity between producer services and manufacturing industries.

1 INTRODUCTION

In recent years, geographical agglomeration of manufacturing industries has become increasingly prominent. Driven by the construction of industrial parks, economic circles and economic belts, the manufacturing industries in various regions of China develop rapidly. Nevertheless, Jiangxi's manufacturing industries still have the problem of insufficient driving force. During the 13th Five-Year Plan period in Jiangxi, while emphasizing that the manufacturing industries should take the road of industrial agglomeration and cluster development and build advanced manufacturing base in the central China, it was also emphasized that the development level of services should be improved, productive services and manufacturing industries should be integrated, and the productive services should be promoted to specialization and high-end value chain extension. Recently, the People's Government of Jiangxi Province issued the Jiangxi Province's 14th Five-Year Plan for high-quality manufacturing industries development, which further clarified the main objectives of high-quality manufacturing industries development in Jiangxi Province during the 14th Five-Year Plan period, so as to achieve new upgrading of industrial structure, build advanced manufacturing clusters and upgrade the modernization level of industrial chain and supply chain. In view

of this, based on the perspective of regional industrial co-agglomeration of producer services and manufacturing industries, this paper reexamines the regional spatial problems of co-agglomeration of producer services and manufacturing industries in Jiangxi, and explores the influence degree of co-agglomeration of producer services and manufacturing industries, with a view to providing favorable policy suggestions for the development of producer services and manufacturing industries in Jiangxi.

2 LITERATURE REVIEW

The research on the relationship between producer services and manufacturing industries is a hot spot in academic circles. In China, the list of representative literature of coagglomeration of producer services and manufacturing industries is as follows: Chen (2018) found that the geographical agglomeration degree of manufacturing industries and producer services in three northeastern provinces was increasing. Gao et al. (2018) analyzed the spatial pattern evolution and its driving mechanism by using the data of prefecture-level cities in the Yangtze River Economic Belt and pointed out that the spatial trend of high in the northeast, uplift in the middle and low in the southwest and collaborative development showed

186

DOI 10.1201/9781003203704-34

a continuous spatial agglomeration trend. Zhao et al. (2018) took Beijing-Tianjin-Hebei urban agglomeration as the research object and made a quantitative analysis on the industrial connection and spatial interaction between producer services and manufacturing industries, and found that the relationship between supply and demand was the basic motivation for their spatial agglomeration, and externalities such as knowledge spillovers and labor pool sharing were also the reasons for their spatial agglomeration. An et al. (2017) conducted a dynamic study on the spatial relationship between producer services and manufacturing industries from 2003 to 2014 based on 113 cities in coastal areas, and showed that the spatial difference between producer services and manufacturing industries had a significant expansion trend, and the spatial relationship between subsectors of producer services and manufacturing industries could be divided into four types: completely identical, completely opposite, identical in the north–south direction and opposite in the east–west direction. Zhang et al. (2017) analyzed the spatial correlation and spillover effects of collaborative agglomeration between manufacturing industries and producer services and found that the spatial correlation degree of coagglomeration between manufacturing industries and producer services was not high, and coagglomeration had spatial spillover effect and spatial feedback mechanism, and knowledge spillover, technological innovation and hierarchical division of labor had a positive impact on the synergy between manufacturing industries and producer services. Sun et al. (2021) applied the grey GM (1,N) model and showed that industrial innovation capability and environmental regulation had significantly promoted the synergy between producer services and manufacturing industries, while transaction costs and tax competition had inhibitory effect on the synergy between them. Zhong et al. (2021) used enterprise micro big data from the perspective of spatial similarity and found that the layout of manufacturing industries and productive service in Guangzhou was similar in space, and industrial development history, service function characteristics of industries and layout flexibility of private enterprises were important factors that affected the spatial similarity between producer services and manufacturing industries.

The research on the relationship between producer services and manufacturing industries in China mainly reflected the degree of co-agglomeration between industries based on employment data, but it was less used to analyze the co-agglomeration relationship between producer services and manufacturing industries by micro-data of enterprises. This paper draws a lesson from the research ideas of Zhong et al. (2021) and takes Jiangxi's producer services and manufacturing industries as the research object. Based on the national economic census database in 2008, this paper uses Python to obtain the latitude and longitude information of Baidu Map corresponding to the geographical location of producer services and manufacturing enterprises in Jiangxi Province, and which is transformed into longitude and latitude information of WGS1984 coordinate system. Then we can get the geographical position information of 18,156 enterprises in 5 producer services and 3 manufacturing industries in Jiangxi Province in 2008. By using nuclear density and geographic detector analysis methods, this paper discusses the spatial co-agglomeration relationship between manufacturing and producer services in Jiangxi Province, and further explains the reasons for the differences in the degree of co-agglomeration between producer services and manufacturing industries in Jiangxi Province.

3 DATA AND RESEARCH METHODS

3.1 *Data*

In this paper, Jiangxi Province is taken as the research area, and the spatial data of producer services and manufacturing enterprises at the county level are used for analysis. There are 100 county-level areas in the database of Jiangxi Economic Census in 2008. In the aspect of industry selection, referring to Xie (2003) classification method of industrial industries according to factor intensity, 30 manufacturing industries were divided into labor-, capital-, capital and technology-intensive industries, and other industries. In this paper, labor-intensive manufacturing, capital-intensive manufacturing, and capital and technology-intensive manufacturing are selected as the research objects of manufacturing industries, and three major manufacturing industries are sorted out according to the four-digit codes of national economy industries in the database. Among them, labor-intensive manufacturing industries include agricultural and sideline foodstuffs processing industry; food manufacturing industry; beverage manufacturing industry; tobacco products industry; textile industry; textile and garment, shoes, and hats manufacturing industry; leather, fur, feather (down), and its products industry; wood processing and wood, bamboo, rattan, brown, and grass products industry; and furniture manufacturing industry. Capital-intensive manufacturing industries include paper and paper products, printing and recording media reproduction, cultural and educational sporting goods, chemical raw materials and chemical products, rubber products, plastic products, nonmetallic mineral products, ferrous metal smelting and rolling processing, nonferrous metal smelting and rolling processing, and metal products. Capital and technology-intensive manufacturing industries include petroleum processing, coking and nuclear fuel processing industries; pharmaceutical manufacturing; chemical fiber manufacturing industry; general equipment manufacturing industry; special equipment manufacturing industry; transportation equipment manufacturing industry; electrical and equipment manufacturing industry; manufacturing of communication equipment, computers, and other electronic equipment; instrument and culture; office machinery manufacturing industry. The five productive services include transportation, warehousing and postal services; information transmission, computer services and software industry; finance; leasing and business services; and scientific research and technical services.

In this paper, the geographic location information of 18,156 enterprises in the above 8 industries are sorted, and the geographic coordinates of each enterprise are searched through Baidu Map API and converted into spatial point data files.

3.2 Research methods

3.2.1 Nuclear density analysis method
Kernel density estimation is a nonparametric estimation method for estimating probability density function, which can be used to estimate unknown density function and calculate the density of spatial elements in surrounding areas. There is a positive correlation between the value of kernel density and the degree of spatial element agglomeration, that is, the higher the value of kernel density, the higher the degree of spatial element agglomeration. According to Wang (2019), the specific formula is as follows:

$$f(x,y) = \frac{1}{nh^2} \sum_{i=1}^{n} K\left(\frac{x - x_i}{h}\right) \tag{1}$$

In the formula, $f(x,y)$ is the kernel density value of spatial position (x,y), n is the number of research objects, $k(.)$ is a kernel density function, and h is the bandwidth and a smoothing parameter.

3.2.2 Geographic detector analysis method
Wang et al. (2017) pointed out that geographic detector was a statistical method to detect spatial heterogeneity and explain the driving factors behind it. This method can detect not only numerical data but also qualitative data. The application of geographic detector is based on the assumption that the influence of independent variables on dependent variables is due to the similarity of spatial distribution between independent variables and dependent variables. The factor detection method in geographic detector can detect the influence of factor X on Y in spatial differentiation. In this paper, referring to Zhong et al. (2021), we quantitatively analyzed the association degree between producer services and manufacturing industries by using geographic detectors, and explored the influence degree of five producer services on the spatial differentiation of three manufacturing industries, and measured it with q value. The specific formula is as follows:

$$q_{X,Y} = 1 - \frac{\sum\limits_{i=1}^{n} N_{X,i}\sigma^2_{Y_{X,i}}}{N\sigma^2_Y} \tag{2}$$

In this formula, $q_{X,Y}$ stands for x's interpretation of y, x stands for a productive service industry, y stands for a manufacturing industry, n stands for the number of samples in the whole region, $N_{X,i}$ stands for the number of samples in a certain sub-region i, n stands for the total number of sub-regions, stands for the discrete variance of manufacturing enterprises in the whole region, and stands for the discrete variance of manufacturing enterprises in sub-region i. The larger the value of q, the greater the influence of a producer service X on the spatial differentiation of Y distribution in a manufacturing industry, and the greater the influence of producer service X on the spatial agglomeration of manufacturing Y.

4 SIMILARITY ANALYSIS

According to the number of county-level regional enterprises in Jiangxi Province, the spatial distribution pattern of five major productive services and three major manufacturing enterprises in Jiangxi in 2008 was visually analyzed using kernel density analysis tool of ArcGIS10.2 software, which reflected the characteristics of industrial spatial distribution, as shown in Figure 1. It can be seen from Figure 1 that the producer services and manufacturing enterprises in Jiangxi Province are mainly concentrated in Nanchang, and Nanchang has become the central city of major industrial clusters. It can be seen that Nanchang, as the provincial capital, has played a leading role in the development of producer services and manufacturing industries. However, the agglomeration development of producer services and manufacturing industries in Nanchang does not radiate well to the surrounding cities. The layout of producer services and manufacturing enterprises in neighboring cities of Nanchang, such as Jiujiang, Yichun, Yingtan, Shangrao, and Fuzhou, is relatively scattered, and the characteristics of industrial agglomeration are not obvious.

According to the agglomeration of producer service enterprises, the enterprise layout of transportation, warehousing and postal services has obvious agglomeration phenomenon in 11 cities of Jiangxi Province, among which Nanchang, Yichun, and Jiujiang are the three major agglomeration areas of transportation, warehousing and postal services in Jiangxi Province. The agglomeration of financial industry can be divided into three echelons. The first echelon is Nanchang. Shangrao and Jiujiang are the second echelon, and Yichun and Ganzhou are the third echelon. The agglomeration of enterprises in science and technology industries is still centered on Nanchang, and the other 10 cities also show an agglomeration trend, but the agglomeration degree of enterprise layout is not high. The layout of enterprises in information transmission, computer service and software industries is mainly concentrated in Nanchang, while Ganzhou and Jingdezhen show a certain gathering trend. The other cities have no obvious agglomeration characteristics. Besides Nanchang as the core area of agglomeration,

Ganzhou also presents a certain agglomeration phenomenon, but its performance is not obvious, and the enterprise layout of other cities is more dispersed.

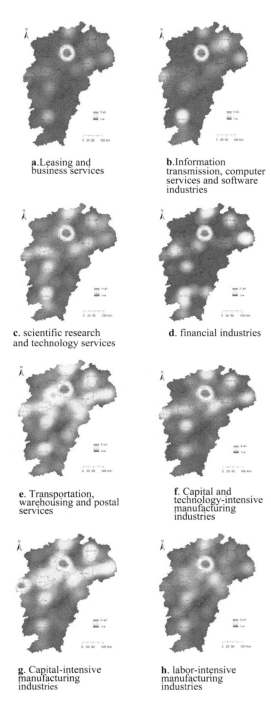

a. Leasing and business services
b. Information transmission, computer services and software industries
c. scientific research and technology services
d. financial industries
e. Transportation, warehousing and postal services
f. Capital and technology-intensive manufacturing industries
g. Capital-intensive manufacturing industries
h. labor-intensive manufacturing industries

Figure 1. Nuclear density distribution of five major producer services and three major manufacturing enterprises in Jiangxi Province in 2008.

From the perspective of the agglomeration of manufacturing enterprises, labor-intensive manufacturing enterprises have a very obvious agglomeration phenomenon in Nanchang, while they also show a certain agglomeration phenomenon in Fuzhou, Ji'an, Ganzhou, and Jiujiang, but the degree of agglomeration is not high; capital-intensive manufacturing industries are the industries with the highest concentration of enterprises in manufacturing industries, with Nanchang and Pingxiang as the main concentration core areas. Jingdezhen, Shangrao, Xinyu, and Fuzhou have a certain degree of agglomeration, while Jiujiang, Ji'an, Yichun, and Ganzhou enterprises have certain agglomeration characteristics, but the degree of agglomeration is relatively low. Technology-intensive manufacturing enterprises have formed a concentrated core area in Nanchang, while Jiujiang, Jingdezhen, Shangrao, Pingxiang, Fuzhou, Xinyu, Ji'an, and Ganzhou have a certain degree of agglomeration in some urban areas, but the degree of agglomeration is not high.

From the similarity of the overall distribution of producer services and manufacturing enterprises, there is a certain similarity in the spatial distribution of the location of producer services and manufacturing clusters. Among them, transportation, warehousing and postal services and capital-intensive manufacturing enterprises have obvious agglomeration characteristics and high degree of agglomeration. In addition, through visual comparison, it is not difficult to find that there is a high similarity between transportation, warehousing and postal industry and manufacturing industries; the layout of financial industries is similar to capital-intensive manufacturing industries and labor-intensive manufacturing industries; and the layout of information transmission and computer services and software industries is similar to capital and technology-intensive manufacturing industries.

5 COMPARISION OF THE INFLUENCE DEGREE OF CO-AGGLOMERATION

The results of kernel density analysis show that there is a certain spatial similarity between producer services and manufacturing industries in Jiangxi, especially between leasing and business services and capital and technology-intensive manufacturing industries. This paper assumes that the layout of manufacturing enterprises will be affected by the layout of producer service enterprises. At the county level, the influence of various industries of producer services on the spatial layout of the three major manufacturing industries is measured by using geographic detectors. The q value of the detection result of the geographic detector is shown in Table 1.

From Table 1, it can be seen that at the significance level of 99%, the five major producer services in Jiangxi Province have a significant impact on the layout of manufacturing industry. Among producer

Table 1. The results of geographic detectors for producer services and manufacturing industries in Jiangxi Province.

Industries	Transportation, warehousing and postal services	Financial industries	Scientific research and technology Service	Information transmission, computer services and software industries	Leasing and business services
Labor-intensive manufacturing industries	0.3832***	0.2045***	0.3807***	0.3948***	0.3952***
Capital-intensive manufacturing industries	0.4323***	0.3132***	0.4295***	0.4405***	0.4417***
Capital and technology-intensive manufacturing industries	0.4879***	0.3223***	0.5038***	0.5134***	0.5153***

Note: ******* indicate significant correlation when the confidence level is 99%, 95%, and 90%, respectively.

services, leasing and business services have the highest q value, which indicates that leasing and business services have the greatest influence on manufacturing layout and their spatial similarity is the largest. Information transmission, computer services and software industries have the second influence on manufacturing layout, followed by transportation, warehousing and postal services and scientific research and technical services. The financial industries have the smallest q value, the financial industries have the smallest influence on manufacturing layout, and the spatial similarity between financial industries and manufacturing industries is the lowest.

Producer services can not only provide services for the manufacturing industries, but also show a certain degree of followship in spatial layout. From the analysis of spatial distribution similarity between producer services and manufacturing industries in Jiangxi, it can be seen that there is a certain degree of spatial similarity between producer services and manufacturing industries in Jiangxi. Leasing and business services show strong spatial followship with manufacturing spatial layout, while financial industries have weak spatial followship with manufacturing spatial layout. The reason is that leasing and business services are the result of deepening social division of labor. Leasing and business services mainly provide services for production and business activities, and leasing and business services can reduce transaction costs and improve productivity by improving the degree of specialization. The more the economy develops, the finer the social division of labor, and the greater the demand for leasing and business services. In the process of developing manufacturing industries in Jiangxi, the government attached great importance to the development of leasing and business services,

and provided many policy supports for their development. In addition, in order to reduce transaction costs and provide better services for production and business activities, enterprises are usually close to the production enterprises when they choose a site. So it shows that leasing and business services have strong spatial followship with manufacturing spatial layout. However, financial industries have a higher entry threshold, and financial industries are less flexible in layout. It shows that the spatial similarity between financial industries and manufacturing industries is low. As emerging service industries, information transmission, computer service and software industries, as well as scientific research and technology services, are playing an increasingly important role in the development of Jiangxi manufacturing industries and have gradually penetrated into the development of Jiangxi manufacturing industries, showing certain followship and similarity in spatial layout. Transportation, warehousing and postal services are traditional service industries, and they have played an important role in the development of Jiangxi's manufacturing industries. Under the action of government planning and the flexibility of enterprise layout, they have a high degree of agglomeration and have a high spatial similarity and followship with the manufacturing layout.

6 CONCLUSIONS

There is a strong correlation between producer services and manufacturing industries, which is reflected not only in the production function of products but also in the spatial layout. Based on the data of enterprises at county level, this paper discusses the spatial relationship between producer services and manufacturing industries in Jiangxi by industry, and it combines the nuclear density and geographic detector analysis methods. This paper analyzes agglomeration and spatial similarity of Jiangxi producer services and manufacturing industries. It provides a new idea for studying the spatial synergy agglomeration of Jiangxi producer services and manufacturing industries.

Through the research, it is found that Jiangxi's producer services and manufacturing industries are mainly concentrated in Nanchang, while the concentration in other cities of Jiangxi is relatively low. Among producer services, transportation, warehousing and postal services have a relatively high degree of agglomeration, while among manufacturing industries, capital-intensive manufacturing industries have a relatively high degree of agglomeration. According to the similarity of spatial layout, there is a high similarity between transportation, warehousing and postal industries and manufacturing industries. The layout of financial industries is similar to capital-intensive manufacturing and labor-intensive manufacturing. There is a high similarity between the layout of information transmission, computer services and software industries and the layout of capital technology intensive manufacturing. According to the influence degree of the spatial distribution of Jiangxi's producer services and manufacturing industries, Jiangxi's producer services show a spatial followship with manufacturing industries, among which leasing and business services have strong followship with manufacturing industries, while the financial industries have relatively weak followship with manufacturing industries.

Although the existing research methods have not verified the existence of spatial followship between producer services and manufacturing industries, there are certain spatial similarities between producer services and manufacturing industries in Jiangxi Province in terms of spatial layout, and the difference in spatial similarity is related not only to the nature of industries, but also to government planning and the flexible layout of enterprises, and it shows that Jiangxi producer services have a followship with the manufacturing industries to a certain extent.

ACKNOWLEDGMENTS

This project was funded by the Social Science Planning Project of Jiangxi Province "Research on the Regional Spatial Reconstruction of Co-agglomeration of Producer Services and Manufacturing Industries" [No.17YJ32].

REFERENCES

An, S.W. & Chang, R.X. 2017. Dynamics of spatial relation between producer services and manufacturing in coastal area of China. *China Soft Science* (11): 101–110.

Chen, Y. 2018. Spatiotemporal evolution of manufacturing and producer services co-agglomeration empirical study based on the data of the prefecture level city of three provinces in northeast China. *Regional Economic Review* (03): 33–41.

Gao, S.H., Liu C.J. & Chen G.L. 2018. Study on collaborative agglomeration of producer services and manufacturing industries an empirical analysis on the Yangtze River economic belt. *Journal of Technical Economics & Management* (04): 122–128.

Sun, Z., Yang, S. & Liu J.Y. 2021. Calculation of the degree of synergy and integration between producer service industry and manufacturing industry and its determinants. *China Soft Science* (07): 31–39.

Wang, F.H. 2019. *Quantitative methods applications in GIS*. Beijing: The Commercial Press.

Wang, J.F. & Xu, C.D. 2017. Geodetector: Principle and prospective. *Acta Geographica Sinica* 72(1): 116–134.

Xie, J.G. 2003. Foreign direct investment and China's export competitiveness *World Economy Studies* (07): 34–39.

Zhang, H., Han, A.H. & Yang, Q.L. 2017. Spatial effect analysis of synergetic agglomeration of manufacturing and producer services in China. *The Journal of Quantitative & Technical Economics* 34(02): 3–20.

Zhao, J.H., Feng, J. & Zhang, J.F. 2018. Quantitative analysis of co-agglomeration of producer service sectors and manufacturing industry in Beijing metropolitan area. *Urban Development Studies* 25(04): 62–68.

Zhong Y, Zhao B.L. & Li H. 2021. Co-agglomeration and spatial similarity: based on the analysis of manufacturing and producer services in Guangzhou, China. *Scientia Geographica Sinica* 41(3): 437–445.

Economic and Business Management – Huang & Zhang (Eds)
© 2022 Copyright the Author(s), ISBN: 978-1-032-06754-4

Financial flexibility, R&D investment and corporate value: Evidence from new energy companies in China

Junyi Li, Yumeng Fan, Han Jin & Chang Deng
Yunnan University, Kunming, China

ABSTRACT: This paper takes new energy companies listed in China from 2013 to 2019 as samples to study the correlation between financial flexibility, R&D investment and corporate value, as well as the mediating effect of R&D investment on the relationship between financial flexibility and corporate value. The results show that the financial flexibility of new energy companies is positively correlated with corporate value, and R&D investment plays a mediating role in this relationship. This paper reveals that managers need to pay attention to the management of financial flexibility when making their business strategy, and take advantage of financial flexibility to support the development of innovation activities, to achieve sustainable and steady development of companies and the financial goal of maximizing corporate value.

Keywords: Financial flexibility; R&D investment; corporate value; mediating effect

1 INTRODUCTION

The 19th CPC National Congress proposed to promote the revolution of energy production and consumption, and build a clean, low-carbon, safe and efficient energy system. This provides the development direction for the domestic energy industry, and brings a new starting point for the development of new energy.

New energy is one of the emerging industries of strategic importance in China. The state has clearly proposed to develop new energy and related industries during the 14th Five-Year Plan period. Promoting the development of new energy industry is not only the need of national strategy but also the inevitable requirement of global energy revolution. New energy is a technology-intensive industry. Companies need to strengthen their competitiveness and sustainable development ability and promote added value through active innovation activities. However, in view of the high risk of R&D, when companies face the situation of insufficient internal financing and high external financing cost, they are prone to give up the investment. Further, empirical evidence shows that the management of financial flexibility can improve companies' competence of risk resistance and bring about the improvement of corporate value.

China's new energy industry is currently in the stage of rapid development. Effective management of corporate financial resources and innovation activities is beneficial to the sustainable development of companies and the realization of the financial goal of maximizing corporate value. By studying new energy companies listed in China, this paper hopes to explore the correlation between financial flexibility, R&D investment and corporate value; act as a reference for financial management and business strategy decision-making of new energy companies; and ultimately contribute to the sustainable development of China's new energy industry and the realization of the financial goal of maximizing corporate value.

The innovation of this paper lies in focusing the study on the relationship between financial flexibility, R&D investment and corporate value on China's new energy industry, which makes the study of this paper more targeted. Moreover, an internal mechanism of financial flexibility affecting corporate value is studied, which enriches the research results in related fields.

2 LITERATURE REVIEW

Financial flexibility which is regarded as an emergency after-action behavior of companies was proposed by Heath (1978) in his study. It enables companies to overcome situations where current cash inflows are insufficient to cover future cash outflows without having a significant impact on current and future earnings and stock price. On the one hand, financial flexibility can help companies reduce risk and avoid getting into trouble when adverse shocks occur; on the other hand, companies can use financial resources in a timely manner when investment opportunities arise (Gamba &

192

DOI 10.1201/9781003203704-35

Triantis 2008). Theoretically, financially flexible companies show sufficient cash reserves and lower financial leverage on their reports, which makes their financial policies flexible (Marchica 2010). Simultaneously, companies can reserve the financing capacity to cope with the uncertainty of the business environment by using their residual borrowing power and idle funds (Zeng et al. 2011). Given that financial flexibility enables companies to resist risks and in a timely manner use financial resources to invest, financial flexibility can bring value growth to listed companies (Gamba & Triantis 2008). The study takes China's biomedical industry, Hengrui Medicine, China's listed companies on GEM and listed companies in China's A stock market as research objects, and verify this point of view through empirical analysis (Chen 2020; Song 2021; Yao 2020; Yu 2020).

R&D plays an important role in the sustainable development of companies and the formation of their core competitiveness. Moreover, most research results show that the improvement of corporate investment in R&D contributes to the increase of corporate value (Olibe 2010; Xu 2010). However, the high investment, high risk and high secrecy of innovation activities often make companies reduce the support for R&D when the owned capital is insufficient (Song 2021). This will not only affect the future business growth from the perspective of enterprise competitiveness, but also reduce investors' confidence in the company's development, thus affecting the realization of the financial goal of corporate value maximization. Financial flexibility can enable companies to use cash reserves or lowcost loans to fund innovation projects when there is a funding gap, which is conducive to the smooth development of innovation activities (Zhang & Zhang 2007). Further, the existence of financial flexibility increases the probability of managers passing high-risk projects (Steensma & Corley 2001).

On the whole, there are many studies on the relationship among financial flexibility, R&D investment and corporate value in the existing literature. Moreover, most literatures demonstrate the promoting effect of financial flexibility and R&D investment on corporate value theoretically. However, in the case that most of the literature has reached similar conclusions, some studies have found inconsistent results from different perspectives and on different research objects. Richardson's (2006) study shows that high cash reserves damage corporate value. The study of Chen et al. (2016) reveals that R&D investment has no significant impact on corporate value. Meanwhile, there is little literature on the relationship between financial flexibility, R&D investment and corporate value of new energy companies in China, as well as the internal mechanism of financial flexibility affecting corporate value of new energy companies. Therefore, this paper hopes to provide empirical reference for theoretical research in related fields and the realization of sustainable innovation-driven development of rapidly developing new energy companies by studying this issue.

3 RESEARCH DESIGN

3.1 Theoretical analysis and hypothesis formulation

The function of financial flexibility is mainly reflected in the resistance to external adverse events and the timely utilization of potential investment opportunities. It can be regarded as an option with both value-preserving and value-adding capabilities, so that companies can release the current reserves of financial flexibility in the future to realize the improvement of corporate value (Sun 2020). Meanwhile, according to the signaling theory proposed by Spence (1973), in the case of information asymmetry, the financial information provided by the company will affect investors' evaluation of the enterprise. The existence of financial flexibility of a company enables the company to have higher cash reserves or lower financial leverage, or both, thus conveying a signal of good financial condition to investors, which can enhance investors' confidence and improve their evaluation of corporate value. Based on the above analysis, this paper proposes the following hypotheses:

H1: For new energy companies in China, financial flexibility is positively correlated with corporate value.

According to the signaling theory, as the information provided by companies, the investment in R&D conveys the signal of the enhancement of innovation ability of companies, the expected improvement of competitiveness and the improvement of revenues to investors. Such information, when taken into account in valuation, tends to increase investors' estimates of corporate value. Based on the value chain theory of Porter (1985), innovation ability of companies has an influence on the value creation of company's various business links. The innovation ability of a company will be reflected in its operating performance and growth ability, and then affect its value. Under the increasingly fierce market competition, R&D plays an increasingly important role in the sustainable development of new energy companies which are in a technology-intensive industry.

H2: R&D investment of new energy companies in China is positively correlated with corporate value.

According to the pecking order theory proposed by Myers and Majluf (1984), and in view of the potential adverse impact of external financing on innovation activities of companies which is of strong confidentiality, companies' ability of internal financing has a great impact on R&D investment. When the company has a high cash reserve, the high liquidity and low cost of corporate funds can support the development of innovation activities. When the company is faced with the insufficiency of owned capital, its remaining borrowing power which derives from low financial leverage, to a certain extent, can improve the credit rating, which is conducive to borrowing for innovation activities at a low cost. Simultaneously, by reducing worries about future financing problems, the flexibility of corporate financial policies can improve the possibility of companies' passing innovation projects. Meanwhile, the cash reserve of companies can significantly reduce the risk assessment of managers for innovation projects (Song 2021).

H3: Financial flexibility of new energy companies in China is positively correlated with R&D investment.

On the basis of the above analysis, this paper deems that financial flexibility will affect the corporate value, as well as R&D investment. Further, in view of the positive impact of R&D investment on corporate value, it is considered that R&D investment plays a mediating role in the mechanism of financial flexibility on corporate value.

H4: R&D investment of new energy companies in China has a mediating effect in the mechanism of financial flexibility on corporate value.

3.2 Measurement of variables

3.2.1 Dependent variable

Based on existing studies, this paper selects Tobin's Q, as proposed by James Tobin (1969) to measure the value of companies. Tobin's Q covers a combination of historical data and investors' future expectations. To some extent, it is objective.

3.2.2 Independent variables

(1) Financial flexibility

Based on the research method of Zeng (2011), this paper uses the sum of cash reserve flexibility and financing flexibility in debt to measure the financial flexibility of the company. Among them, cash reserve flexibility is equal to corporate cash ratio minus the industry average cash ratio; financing flexibility in debt is equal to the greater of zero and the industry average asset-liability ratio minus corporate asset-liability ratio.

(2) R&D investment

Based on the reference of existing studies, this paper adopts the indicator of R&D investment ratio (RDR) which is equal to the amount invested in R&D divided by operating income, to measure the level of corporate R&D investment, which can facilitate horizontal comparison between companies. This indicator is calculated by dividing R&D investment by operating income.

3.2.3 Control variables

To rule out alternative explanations, we referred to previous researches and used a comprehensive set of control variables. They are corporate size (SIZE), rate of revenue growth (RRG), return on equity (ROE), largest shareholder ratio (BIG1), independent director ratio (IDR), this study also includes the year dummies (YEAR) and industry dummies (INDUSTRY).

3.3 Definition of variables

Table 1. Variable description.

	Variables	Measurement
Dependent Variable	TQ	Corporate market value/asset replacement cost

Table 1. Variable description.

Independent variable	FF		The sum of cash reserve flexibility and financing flexibility in debt
	RDR		R&D investment divided by operating income
Control variables	SIZE		The logarithm of total assets
	RRG		(Current period operating income minus previous period operating income) divided by operating income in previous period
	ROE		Net profit scaled by owner's equity
	BIG1		The largest shareholder's squared shareholding ratios
	IDR		The number of independent directors/board of directors
	YEAR		Dummy variable, the control variable of year
	INDUSTRY		Dummy variables, indicating the category of industry which is based on the Guidelines for Industry Classification of Listed Companies (revised in 2012) issued by CSRC

3.4 Model specification

In order to test the four hypotheses proposed in this paper, the following model is used for the regression analysis of samples in subsequent empirical tests.

Model (1) is used to test the influence of financial flexibility on R&D investment:

$$RDR = \alpha + \beta_1 FF_{i,t} + \gamma_1 Control_{i,t} + \varepsilon \qquad (1)$$

Model (2) is used to test the influence of financial flexibility on corporate value:

$$TQ = \alpha + \beta_1 FF_{i,t} + \gamma_1 Control_{i,t} + \varepsilon \qquad (2)$$

Model (3) is used to test the influence of R&D investment on corporate value:

$$TQ = \alpha + \beta_1 RDR_{i,t} + \gamma_1 Control_{i,t} + \varepsilon \qquad (3)$$

Model (4) is used to test the mediating effect of R&D investment on the relationship between financial flexibility and corporate value:

$$TQ = \alpha + \beta_1 FF_{t,t} + \delta_1 RDR_{u,t} + \gamma_1 Control_{t,t} + \varepsilon \quad (4)$$

In the above four models, γ_1 is the row vector, referring to $[\beta_2 + \beta_3 + \beta_4 + \beta_5 + \beta_6]$, $Control_{i,t}$ is the column vector, referring to $[SIZE_{i,t} + RRG_{i,t} + ROE_{i,t} + BIG1_{i,t} + IDR_{i,t}]^T$ and then $\gamma_1 Control_{i,t}$ is $\beta_2 SIZE_{i,t} + \beta_3 RRG_{i,t} + \beta_4 ROE_{i,t}$ $\beta_5 BIG1_{i,t} + \beta_6 IDR_{i,t}$. Among them, i is the company number, t is the year, α is the intercept term, and ε is the residual term of the equation. In addition, year and industry are controlled by setting dummy variables in equations.

4 EMPIRICAL TEST

4.1 Sample selection and descriptive statistics

Table 1 shows the statistical descriptive of the study variables. Samples of this paper are Chinese new energy companies (excluding ST companies and date without relevant variables value) listed on the Shenzhen and Shanghai stock exchanges between 2013 to 2019. And the relevant variables in this paper were shrunken by 1% up and down. Finally 837 valid sample data were collected.

Table 2. Statistical descriptive of the study variables.

Variable	N	Mean	Std. Dev.	Min	Max
TQ	836	1.774	0.830	0.842	5.388
RDR	836	3.550	2.778	0.020	14.530
FF	836	−0.251	0.598	−1.930	3.949
SIZE	836	22.794	1.229	20.287	26.360
RRG	836	0.180	0.377	−0.561	2.253
ROE	836	0.052	0.126	−0.666	0.339
BIG1	836	33.178	13.892	8.720	67.390
IDR	836	0.367	0.046	0.333	0.500

The results show that the mean value of financial flexibility is −0.251. Overall, the financial flexibility of new energy companies is low.

4.2 Relevance analysis

This paper tests the correlation of the variables and makes a preliminary test of the proposed hypothesis.

From the table, it can be found that the Pearson correlation coefficient and Spearman correlation coefficient show a significant positive correlation between R&D investment (RDR) and Tobin Q value (TQ). The Pearson correlation coefficient between financial flexibility (FF) and TQ (0.126) is significant at level 1%, while the Pearson correlation coefficient between FF and RDR (0.082) is significant at level 5% and level 10% of their Spearman correlation coefficient (0.063). These results tentatively verify the four hypotheses proposed in this paper.

4.3 Results and analysis

According to the model established in this paper, the results are shown in Table 4 after regression.

Table 4. Results of regression testing analysis.

Variable	(1)	(2)	(3)	(4)
	RDR	TQ	TQ	TQ
FF	0.828***	0.100**		0.079*
	(4.957)	(2.119)		(1.658)
RDR			0.028**	0.025*
			(1.973)	(1.687)
SIZE	−0.546***	−0.360***	−0.357***	−0.347***
	(−6.172)	(−14.399)	(−13.311)	(−13.082)
RRG	−0.692***	−0.110**	−0.087	−0.092*
	(−3.606)	(−2.094)	(−1.594)	(−1.717)
ROE	0.344	0.702***	0.711***	0.694***
	(0.476)	(3.333)	(3.322)	(3.237)
IDR	1.783	1.521***	1.484***	1.476***
	(0.902)	(2.845)	(2.824)	(2.810)
BIG1	0.012*	0.002	0.001	0.001
	(1.846)	(0.825)	(0.604)	(0.682)
Constant	10.921***	8.811***	8.711***	8.540***
	(6.033)	(16.804)	(15.136)	(15.080)
Industry	Yes	Yes	Yes	Yes
Year	Yes	Yes	Yes	Yes
N	836	836	836	836
R-squared	0.436	0.470	0.472	0.474

Note(s): ***, **, * are respectively Significant at the 0.1, 0.05, 0.01 level.

Column (1) presents the regression result of model (1). It shows that the financial flexibility of new energy listed companies is positively related to R&D investment at 1% significance level with a coefficient value of 0.828. The results indicate that new energy companies with high financial flexibility generally have greater investment in innovation activities. With financial flexibility, while making decisions, companies can give more considerations to their long-term development, rather than worrying too much about its capital chain in a short-term. According to the result, H3 is verified.

Table 3. The correlation matrix for the key variables.

	TQ	RDR	FF	SIZE	RRG	ROE	BIG1	IDR
TQ	1	0.357***	0.054	−0.615***	0.005	0.075**	−0.101***	0.077**
RDR	0.309***	1	0.063*	−0.333***	−0.029	−0.032	−0.171***	0.118***
FF	0.126***	0.082**	1	−0.125***	−0.036	0.028	−0.083**	0.021
SIZE	−0.527***	−0.350***	−0.167***	1	0.076**	0.226***	0.141***	−0.033
RRG	−0.025	−0.080**	−0.001	0.049	1	0.293***	0.041	−0.034
ROE	0.044	−0.021	0.021	0.157***	0.259***	1	0.135***	−0.010
BIG1	−0.078**	−0.099***	−0.067*	0.166***	0.049	0.079**	1	−0.078**
IDR	0.100***	0.121***	0.006	−0.018	−0.057*	0.006	−0.058*	1

Note(s): The lower triangle region presents the Pearson correlation coefficient and the upper triangle region presents the Spearman correlation coefficient.

Column (2) presents the regression result of model (2). It shows that the financial flexibility of new energy listed companies is positively related to corporate value at 5% significance level with a coefficient value of 0.100. The results show that new energy companies with high financial flexibility also perform better in corporate value growth. It can better resist internal and external risks, which is conducive to the sound operation of companies.

Companies with financial flexibility can disclose information that shows a good financial situation and a low level of risk, which sends a positive signal to the market and investors. At the same time, it can enable companies to carry out low cost internal and external financing. To a certain extent, it is conducive for companies to seize investment opportunities in a timely manner and relatively improve the level of income. Based on the result, H1 is verified.

Column (3) presents the regression result of model (3). It shows that the R&D investment of new energy listed companies is positively related to corporate value at 5% significance level with a coefficient value of 0.028.

The results show that the market and investors have timely feedback on the innovation activities of companies, while benefiting from positive R&D investment, the expected level of income of companies has increased to some extent, which in turn is positively reflected in the assessment of the corporate value. According to the result, H2 is verified.

Column (4) is the test result of model (4) for the mediating effect of corporate R&D investment on financial flexibility and corporate value. After adding R&D investment as a mediating variable to the regression model (2), R&D investment is positively correlated with corporate value at the 10% significance level with a regression coefficient value of 0.025, and the financial flexibility is positively correlated with corporate value at the 10% significance level with a regression coefficient of 0.079.

Combining the regression tests of columns (1) and (2), it can be found that the regression coefficient values of the main explanatory variables of each regression equation are significant, thus indicating that R&D investment satisfies the condition proposed by Baron and Kenny (1986) as a mediating variable. The financial flexibility significantly affects corporate value as well as R&D investment. In the co-regression of these three variables, there shows a significant correlation between R&D investment and corporate value. It is confirmed that mediating effect of R&D investment on the relationship between financial flexibility and corporate value exists. Furthermore, the total effect of financial flexibility on corporate value is 0.100, while the direct effect is 0.079 and the mediating effect of R&D investment is $0.828 \times 0.025 = 0.0207$, from which the proportion of the mediating effect of R&D investment to the total effect can be calculated as $0.0207/0.100 = 20.7\%$.

The results show that companies with financial flexibility can help them achieve their financial goals

of value growth by strengthening their investment attitudes in R&D investment and supporting the development of this activity. Thus, H4 is verified.

Overall, financial flexibility has a direct positive impact on the improvement of corporate value while it has an indirect positive impact on corporate value through R&D investment. The improvement of financial flexibility of companies conveys a favorable signal to the market and investors, allows companies to allocate financial resources timely for investment at a lower cost, especially for R&D investment, and makes companies better able to mitigate the impact of risk and reduce the impact on corporate value. And thus it enhances investor's assessment of the value of the company, the level of corporate income and its competitiveness in the market competition.

5 CONCLUSIONS

This paper investigates the correlation between financial flexibility, R&D investment and corporate value, as well as the mediating effect of R&D investment on the tie between financial flexibility and corporate value with a sample of new energy companies listed in China between 2013 and 2019. The main findings are as follows.

(1) Financial flexibility (FF) is positively related to R&D investment for China's new energy companies. FF has a significant regression coefficient of 0.828, which indicates that FF has a major impact on R&D investment. Further, the level of FF influences the attitude toward decision-making of R&D investment. Companies with high FF are better able to withstand financial risks during long-term operations and have lower financing costs. Thus, they can become more positive in making R&D investment decisions.

(2) Financial flexibility (FF) is positively related to corporate value for China's new energy companies. Firms with high FF have good liquidity, which conveys a positive signal to the market, thereby facilitating investment activities. Also, high FF will contribute to the growth of corporate value and help firms withstand and mitigate the impact of sudden crises.

(3) In China's new energy companies, R&D investment works as a mediator among the effects of financial flexibility and corporate value. FF leads to more R&D investment. The continuity of R&D activities has been enhanced and the anti-risk ability has also been ensured. Further, R&D will increase the value-added of business activities, and contribute to the growth of corporate value.

It is important for new energy companies to take advantage of their financial flexibility, so that financial management contributes to the growth of corporate value. This will increase firms' sustainable development ability. Companies should plan their financial flexibility as they create strategies and make business decisions, in addition to allocating resources to marketing, R&D, and operations, while avoiding overinvesting in particular business activities.

It is also important for companies to maintain surplus reserves above the minimum cash holdings and to reduce their financial leverage appropriately over the long term. By actively managing financial flexibility, organizations should look for internal and external investment opportunities, provide more support for R&D in line with their development, and make full use of available financial resources.

In this paper, financial flexibility is measured only from two common perspectives, cash and liabilities. In the future research, flexibility in equity can be introduced in order to comprehensively reflect the financial flexibility of companies. This paper only studies the investment of innovation activities of new energy companies. Researchers can take the output of innovation activities to study the influence of financial flexibility in the process of corporate innovation activities from capital input to outcome output. In addition, agency cost can be considered in future research on the issues related to financial flexibility and corporate value of new energy companies in China.

ACKNOWLEDGMENT

This work was supported by 2021 Yunnan Province Undergraduate Innovation Training Program (202110 673033), and 2021 Undergraduate Innovation Training Program of Yunnan University (S202110673065).

REFERENCES

Aimin Zeng, Yuanlve Fu, Zhihua Wei. Impact of Financial Crisis, Financial Flexibility and Corporate Financing Behaviors: Evidence from Chinese Listed Companies[J]. *Journal of Financial Research*, 2011(10): 155–169.

Anna Song. Financial Flexibility, Technological Innovation and Corporate Value: Based on the Empirical Research of the Biomedical Industry[D]. *Zhejiang University*, 2021.

Baron R M & Kenny D A. The moderator–mediator variable distinction in social psychological research: Conceptual, strategic, and statistical considerations. *Journal of Personality and Social Psychology*,1986, 51(6): 1173–1182.

Ehie I C & Olibe K. The effect of R&D investment on firm value: An examination of US manufacturing and service industries[J]. *International Journal of Production Economics*, 2010, 128(1): 127–135.

Gamba A & Triantis A. The Value of Financial Flexibility[J]. *The Journal of Finance*, 2008, 63(5): 2263–2296.

Haofan Sun. Life Cycle, Financial Flexibility and Firm Value[D]. *Shanghai University of Finance and Economics*, 2020.

Heath L C. Financial reporting and the evaluation of solvency[J]. Accounting Research Monograph, *New York: American Institute of Certified Public Accountants* 1978, 1(3): 1–153.

Jinyong Chen, Menghan Yuan, Xiangxi Tang. Will R&D Input Increase Enterprise Value? - From the Perspective of Innovation Input and Output[J]. *Science and Technology Management Research*,2016, 36(11): 8–14.

Marchica M & Mura R. Financial Flexibility, Investment Ability, and Firm Value: Evidence from Firms with Spare Debt Capacity[J]. *Financial management*, 2010, 39(4): 1339–1365.

Myers S C & Majluf N S. Corporate Financing Decisions When Firms Have Information Investors Do Not Have[J]. *Journal of Financial Economics*,1984, 13(2): 187–221.

Porter ME. Competitive Advantage: Creating and Sustaining Superior Performance[M]. *Simon & Schuster Inc*, 1985.

Qian Chen. Study on the Influence of Hengrui Medicine's Financial Flexibility on Enterprise Value[D]. *Qingdao University of Science & Technology*, 2020.

Qing Yu. Research on the Influence of Financial Flexibility and Technological Innovation on the Value Creation of High-tech Enterprises[D]. *Jilin University*, 2020.

Richardson S. Over-investment of free cash flow[J]. *Review of Accounting Studies*, 2006, 11(2–3): 159–189.

Songye Yao. An Empirical Study of Financial Flexibility, Corporate Governance and Corporate Value: Based on the Nature of Property Rights[D]. *Northeast Forestry University*, 2020.

Spence A M. Job Market Signaling[J]. *Quarterly Journal of Economics*, 1973(3): 355–374.

Steensma H K & Corley K G. Organizational Context as a Moderator of Theories on Firm Boundaries for Technology Sourcing[J]. *Academy of Management Journal*, 2001, 44(2), 271–291.

Tobin J A. General Equilibrium Approach to Monetary Theory. *Journal of Money, Credit and Banking*,1969, 1: 15–29.

Xin Xu, Qingquan Tang. Financial Analysts Following and Corporate R&D Activities: A Study on Chinese Securities Marke[J]. *Journal of Financial Research* 2010(12): 173–189.

Zongyi Zhang, Mei Zhang. Empirical Research on the Relationship between Corporate Governance and R&D Investment in the High-Tech Enterprises, 2007(05): 23–26+116.

Economic and Business Management – Huang & Zhang (Eds)
© 2022 Copyright the Author(s), ISBN: 978-1-032-06754-4

Study on supply chain logistics ecosystem under the background of big data

Xudong He, Yubo Sun & Fengzhao Chen
Xuzhou University of Technology, Jiangsu, China

ABSTRACT: With the rapid development of the Internet and big data technology, many enterprises in the supply chain are more closely related to each other, forming a symbiotic and mutually beneficial supply chain ecosystem based on leading enterprises. It is of great significance to study the supply chain logistics ecosystem for solving the ecological and network development problems of enterprises. This paper takes the supply chain logistics ecosystem as the research object, combines it with the ecosystem theory, evolutionary game, and other research methods, and compares the characteristics and operation mechanism of the natural ecosystem. It makes an in-depth study on the internal composition, operation mode, population relationship, evolution process, and collaborative relationship of the supply chain logistics ecosystem.

1 INTRODUCTION

With the rapid development of the application of big data technology, logistics is experiencing the transformation process from the primary state to the advanced state of service specialization and characteristics. Similar to the biological world, in the long-term development process, logistics gradually forms an ecosystem with its stakeholders and the surrounding environment, which depend on and influence each other, and constantly exchange material, energy, and information. The ecosystem is characterized by openness, diversity, self adaptation, and self-organization evolution. The application of "big data" technology not only provides the possibility of mutual benefit and symbiosis between individuals, populations, and external environment in a logistics ecosystem, but also becomes a new way for logistics enterprises to create value. Therefore, it is a new trend to study supply chain logistics from the perspective of an ecosystem.

2 LITERATURE REVIEW

2.1 *Research status of industrial ecosystem*

In the 1980s, Freeman (1989) [1], Moore (1993) [2], and Erkman (1997) [3] used ecological theory to study the evolution and regulation of industrial economic organization, which provided a new way of thinking and path for the study of industrial organization management. There are two main research directions of industrial ecosystem at home and abroad: one is the research on the evolution mechanism of the industrial ecosystem, including the connotation, characteristics, and structure of industrial ecosystem, focusing on

qualitative research. The other is the research on the development evaluation of the industrial ecosystem, including the health evaluation, collaborative evaluation, and efficiency evaluation of an ecosystem, focusing on quantitative research. The representative figures of foreign scholars mainly include Allen and Sriram (2000) [4], Malerba (2002) [5], Adner (2006) [6], etc.; domestic scholars mainly include Wu Shaobo (2014) [7], Chen Yantai (2015) [8], Li Weiliang [9], Li Qiwei (2016) [10], and Sun Yuan (2017) [11], who have studied the industrial innovation ecosystem from different perspectives.

2.2 *Research status of logistics ecosystem*

The research direction of the logistics industry ecosystem at home and abroad mainly includes the following three aspects.

The research on the co-evolution of logistics ecosystem includes the co-evolution path of the modern logistics industry and advanced manufacturing industry; the symbiotic system model of joint development of manufacturing industry and logistics industry; the research on the collaborative relationship and growth evolution mechanism of logistics service supply chain nodes. The representative scholars are Peng Benhong (2009) [12], Wang Zhenzhen, Chen Gongyu (2009) [13], Ding Chaoxun, Qin Ligong (2011) [14], Yan Fei, Dong Qianli (2012) [15], Xue Xiaofang (2016) [16], etc.

The research on the logistics industry cluster ecosystem includes the development path of the cluster ecosystem; the evolution mode of urban agglomeration logistics ecosystem; the self-organization evolution mechanism of the urban logistics industry cluster ecosystem. Representative scholars include

Wang Xuhui, Zhang Qilin (2013) [17], Zhou Lingyun et al. (2013) [18], and Cao Yujiao et al. (2015) [19].

The research on the regional logistics ecosystem includes the regional logistics co-evolution process and collaborative model research; regional logistics system co-evolution mechanism; regional logistics subject order and behavior model; logistics ecosystem formation mechanism and influencing factors research. Representative scholars include Zhou Lingyun et al. (2013) [20], Zhou Lingyun, Zhou Jun (2014) [21], and Fan, Junjie [22].

2.3 Review of logistics ecosystem research

From the perspective of research: most of the research is mainly from the perspective of regional logistics, logistics industry cluster, manufacturing and logistics industry collaboration, e-commerce ecosystem.

From the perspective of research direction: there are more qualitative researches on the evolution mechanism, characteristics and structure of logistics ecosystem. There is less research on the operation, driving mechanism, and operation status evaluation of logistics ecosystem.

From the level of research: at present, the logistics ecosystem mainly focuses on qualitative research, less quantitative research, less systematic, comprehensive, and in-depth study of the logistics ecosystem, and the existing research practice guidance is limited. The research trends are logistics ecosystem research and e-commerce ecosystem research based on big data technology and internet thinking.

3 SUPPLY CHAIN ECOSYSTEM

3.1 Concept of supply chain logistics ecosystem

The supply chain logistics ecosystem under the background of big data application should be an information exchange platform based on the Internet and big data technology. The interaction within the ecosystem is carried out through the platform, including resource exchange, value distribution, and information transmission. The supply chain logistics ecosystem is composed of logistics demanders (consumers), logistics suppliers (logistics enterprises), logistics policy service providers (governments), logistics information technology service providers (platforms), logistics financial service providers (banks), etc.

A supply chain logistics ecosystem usually has the following characteristics: (1) hierarchy. (2) organic and holistic. (3) dynamic. (4) openness. (5) self-organization.

Under the effect of "big data," logistics ecosystem presents a new development trend. In the era of "big data," information exchange and sharing between logistics enterprises are more convenient and fast. The interaction between the logistics ecosystem and the external environment is becoming more and more frequent under the industrial integration promoted by

"big data," and the value association between industries has a new form of expression. If big data is compared to an industry, the key to making profits in this industry lies in improving the "processing ability" of data. Through the "processing data" added value can be achieved. Therefore, in the context of "big data," data information has become an important emerging factor of production, which will change the management mode of logistics enterprises and innovate the profit mode of logistics enterprises.

3.2 Types and structure of supply chain logistics ecosystem

3.2.1 Population classification of supply chain logistics ecosystem

Based on ecosystem theory and business ecosystem theory, enterprises with different scales but similar functions can be regarded as the same population. Different populations undertake different functions, and their status in the ecosystem is also different. Accordingly the population in the supply chain logistics ecosystem is divided into: (1) Leader population, referring to the core enterprise of the supply chain logistics ecosystem, which is the leader and ruler of the supply chain logistics ecosystem. (2) Core group, referring to the logistics enterprises that provide logistics services and provide the logistics services required by key groups. The timeliness of logistics services determines the speed and quality of logistics activities in the whole supply chain. (3) Key population, referring to the other main bodies connected by the supply chain logistics services, and is the main demand side of logistics services, mainly including suppliers, manufacturers, channel providers and retailers. (4) Supporting population, referring to the supporting service enterprises that are absorbed into the ecosystem to meet the needs of the ecosystem population. (5) Parasitic species, referring to the institutions or enterprises that provide value-added services to both sides of the supply chain.

3.2.2 Structure of supply chain logistics ecosystem

The supply chain logistics ecosystem is mainly dominated by the core enterprises of the supply chain. It is the collaborative and integrated operation among the members of the supply chain around the logistics needs of the core enterprises of the supply chain. It mainly includes the following structures: first, the supply chain logistics ecosystem is dominated by the transportation enterprises, which are the leading groups and mainly provide the trunk transportation and distribution logistics services. The second is the supply chain logistics ecosystem dominated by warehousing enterprises, which undertake the operation and management of the whole system. The third is the supply chain logistics ecosystem dominated by express enterprises, which undertake the operation and management of the whole system. The fourth is the supply chain logistics ecosystem dominated by retail enterprises. Through the combination of third-party logistics, fourth-party logistics, and e-commerce platforms, it constantly provides scientific and intensive supply chain solutions according to the changes of supply and demand. The fifth is the supply chain logistics ecosystem dominated by production enterprises, which forms the ecological model of collaborative development through complementary advantages, resource sharing, and competition and cooperation among various species.

4 STUDY ON RELATIONSHIP BETWEEN SPECIES & POPULATIONS

4.1 *Analysis of cooperation strategies among species*

An ecosystem is an organic whole composed of biological population and environment. The population and environment in the system coordinate with each other, forming the value-added effect of the whole ecosystem, and then form the coordinated development effect of various groups and environment. In the supply chain logistics ecosystem, the core species, key species, and leading species are symbiotic to a certain extent, and the symbiotic intensity is different. Therefore, the study of the relationship between species, first of all, assumes that there is a certain degree of symbiotic relationship between species, and using this premise, it studies the strength of the symbiotic relationship between species; the stronger the symbiotic relationship, the closer the relationship between species. The description of symbiotic relationship strength among species in a supply chain logistics ecosystem can be studied by measuring the logistics-related relationship and non-logistics-related relationship between species.

The cooperation strategy between species is directly proportional to the strength of symbiotic relationship between them, and has a one-to-one matching strategy in theory. According to the symbiotic strength of species, the cooperative relationship between species is divided into highly embedded cooperative relationship, strategic cooperative relationship, cooperative partnership relationship, contractual relationship, and loose cooperative relationship.

For example, a complete set of logistics services includes transportation, warehousing, packaging, loading and unloading, circulation processing, logistics operation management, and logistics information communication. No logistics enterprise can complete the customer's service demands alone. Only by cooperating with other kinds of enterprises and establishing long-term and stable cooperative strategic relationships, can it meet the customer's additional needs in time, and thus enhance customer loyalty.

Therefore, the transportation enterprises should achieve collaborative communication with the storage enterprises to ensure that the volume and arrival time of goods will not bring trouble to the storage enterprises. At the same time, the packaging materials and forms of goods should also meet the requirements of efficiency and safety in the transportation process. The storage enterprises should achieve collaborative communication with the distribution enterprises to ensure that there is enough storage space and timely distribution of goods. The idea of cooperation among different species in other types of logistics population is similar, that is, symbiosis, win-win, and co-evolution.

To form such a collaborative system, the most important thing is information collection, analysis, sharing, and communication. Each species in the logistics ecosystem will integrate and analyze the collected data information, and use the non-relational data analysis technology of "big data" to optimize their business processes, strengthen collaboration, and achieve the goal of overall optimization and win-win.

4.2 *Co-evolution among populations*

Co-evolution shows the interaction between different species. The process of evolution is the process of mutual adaptation between species, and also the result of species coexistence. There is both coordination and competition among populations in the supply chain logistics ecosystem, but there must be coordination among the core population, key population, and leading population. However, whether the coordination is high or low depends on the cost and benefit of coordination.

Assuming that there is a low degree of synergy between two species, A and B, both of them can obtain certain benefits. When there is a high degree of synergy, both parties need to pay a high degree of synergy costs, such as increasing the cost of facility transformation, while obtaining the additional benefits brought by the high degree of synergy. The income matrix [23] is shown in Tables 1 and 2.

Table 1. Income matrix of population A and B.

		B	
		high degree of collaboration	low degree collaboration
A	high degree of collaboration	$A + \beta_A N - C_{AB}$ $B + \beta_B N - C_{BA}$	$A - C_A$ B
	low degree of collaboration	A $B - C_B$	A B

It is assumed that the probability of highly cooperative selection of population A is x, and the probability of low cooperative selection is 1-x. The probability of high coordination for population B is y, and the probability of low degree collaboration is 1-y. The benefits of the highly collaborative strategy selected by population A are as follows:

$$U_{1A} = y(A + \beta_A N - C_{AB}) + (1-y)(A - C_A)$$

The profit of the low degree cooperative strategy selected by population A is:

$$U_{2A} = yA + (1-y)A$$

Therefore, the expected return of a can be obtained:

$$\bar{U}_A = XU_{1A} + (1-X)U_{2A}$$

By copying the dynamic equation:

$$F(A) = \frac{dx}{dt} = x(1-x)[y(\beta_A N - C_{AB} + C_A) - C_A]$$

Similarly, the dynamic equation of population B is:

$$F(B) = \frac{dy}{dt} = y(1-y)[x(\beta_B N - C_{BA} + C_B) - C_B]$$

Let F(A) and F(B) be 0, the result can be obtained:

$$x = 0, x = 1, y* = C_A/(\beta_A N - C_{AB+}C_A)$$
$$y = 0, y = 1, x* = C_B/(\beta_B N - C_{BA} + C_B).$$

Table 2. Symbol meaning.

Symbols	Meaning
A	The profit of population A in low degree cooperation
B	The income of population B in low degree of cooperation
C_{AB}	The extra cost of A and B when they are highly collaborative
C_{BA}	The extra cost of high synergy between B and A
N	When A and B choose to cooperate, the increase in the overall ecosystem benefits
β_A	When A choose to cooperate with B increasing proportion of income
β_B	When B choose to cooperate with A increasing proportion of income
C_A	The potential cost of population A cooperating with others
C_B	The potential cost of population B cooperating with others

Then, the partial derivative of F (A) to x:

$$\frac{\partial \frac{dx}{dt}}{\partial x} = (1 - 2x)[y(\beta_A N - C_{AB} + C_A) - C_A]$$

(1) If $y* = C_A/(\beta_A N - C_{AB+}C_A)$, Then the dynamic equation of population a is equal to 0, and it is stable no matter what value is taken.

(2) when $0 < y* < C_A/(\beta_A N - C_{AB+}C_A)$, if $x = 0$ then

$$\frac{\partial \frac{dx}{dt}}{\partial x} < 0, \text{ if } x = 1 \text{ then } \frac{\partial \frac{dx}{dt}}{\partial x} > 0$$

So $x = 0$ is a stable solution. At this time, population A will not choose the highly cooperative strategy, while population B will have the behavior of "free riding" to obtain additional benefits. At this time, B is the parasitic population of A, and A will not ignore it, so this relationship will soon break up, and eventually both sides choose a low degree of cooperation.

(3) when $C_A/(\beta_A N - C_{AB} + C_A) < y* < 1$, if $x = 0$, then

$$\frac{\partial \frac{dx}{dt}}{\partial x} > 0, \text{ if } x = 1 \text{ then } \frac{\partial \frac{dx}{dt}}{\partial x} < 0$$

So $x = 1$ is a stable solution. At this time, population A will choose the highly cooperative strategy, and the probability that population B will choose the highly cooperative strategy is greater than that. As the energy exchange between the two sides becomes more and more frequent, the interactive relationship becomes more and more closer, and finally develops into a highly collaborative relationship.

Similarly, we can discuss the cooperative strategy selection process of population B. The above analysis shows that there are five equilibrium points in the cooperative model of population A and B: $O(0,0) P(1,1) N(1,0) M(0,1)$ and

$$E\left(\frac{C_B}{\beta_B - C_{BA} + C_B}, \frac{C_A}{\beta_A - C_{AB} + C_A}\right).$$

Expressed as Jacobian matrix:

$$\begin{bmatrix} (1 - 2x)[y(\beta N - & x^n - x) \\ C + C) - C1 & [y(\beta N - C + C) \\ y(1 - y)[x(\beta N - & (1 - 2y)[x(\beta N - \\ C + C) & C + C) - C] \end{bmatrix}$$

When $\beta_A N - C_{AB} > 0$ and $\beta_B N - C_{BA} > 0$. The benefit of high synergy is greater than the cost of low synergy, and the populations in the ecosystem tend to choose the strategy of high synergy

5 CONCLUSIONS

In the process of frequent interaction, the population of supply chain logistics ecosystem gradually evolves to the equilibrium point of low or high collaboration, which is a dynamic process. Because there is always the leading role of the leading population in the ecosystem, the core population and the key population will gradually tend to a high degree of synergy. Aiming at the process that tends to be highly collaborative, this paper discusses the cost and benefit of being highly collaborative.

(1) From the perspective of high synergy cost, when the high synergy cost rises and the high synergy

benefit remains unchanged, the probability of low synergy among populations will increase. In order to promote the high degree of collaboration among the populations within the ecosystem, the cost of a high degree of collaboration should be reduced.

(2) From the perspective of synergy benefits, when the benefits of high synergy increase and the cost of high synergy remains unchanged, the probability of selecting high synergy strategies among populations will increase. In order to promote the high synergy among populations, the leader population should take various measures to increase the high synergy benefits.

(3) From the perspective of synergy benefit, when the net benefit of high synergy is higher than that of low synergy, the probability of selecting high synergy strategy among populations will increase. In order to promote the high synergy among populations, the leader population should take measures to enhance the net income of high synergy.

(4) The co-evolution relationship between populations mainly depends on the cooperative net income. Therefore, the net profit of collaboration among populations in the supply chain ecosystem becomes the driving force of population collaboration, and the evolution process of the supply chain system model also depends on the net profit of collaboration.

Therefore, the leader population in the supply chain logistics ecosystem needs to be clear about the convergence point of the income between the populations when constructing the coordination strategy among the populations, so that the coordination among the populations can be in a relative equilibrium point. For example, in the supply chain ecosystem of express enterprises, the express enterprise population and the e-commerce platform enterprise population are in a high degree of synergy, because the synergy benefits are much higher than the synergy costs. The high degree of collaboration between the manufacturing enterprise population and its upstream suppliers and downstream customers can effectively reduce inventory costs, prevent the bullwhip effect of demand amplification, and reduce the operation costs of the supply chain.

The collaboration among different types of logistics enterprise groups needs to use information data, and take information transmission and information sharing as the main way of collaboration among various groups in the logistics ecosystem. The accurate analysis and prediction ability of "big data" can meet the needs of real-time dynamic monitoring of demand changes of logistics functional enterprises by supporting population; "big data" has the dynamic allocation function of resources, which makes the deployment of functional logistics enterprises by logistics integrators more reasonable, and makes the species cooperation mode in logistics ecosystem more diversified and high-value.

ACKNOWLEDGMENTS

This research was funded by a research granted from Key Projects of Natural Science Research of Jiangsu Higher Education Institutions (18KJA12001) (20KJA120003), and Jiangsu Water Conservancy Science and Technology Project (2019059), whose support are greatly appreciated.

REFERENCES

[1] Freeman J, Hannan M T. Organizational ecology [M]. Boston: *Harvard University Press*, 1989.

[2] Moore J F. Predators and prey: A new ecology of competition [J]. *Harvard Business Review*, 1993, 71(3): 75–86.

[3] Erkman S. Industrial ecology: Anhistorical view [J]. Cleaner Production, 1997, 5(2): 23–25.

[4] Roert H, Allen Ram D, Sriram. The role of standards in innovation [J]. *Technological Forecasting and Social Change*, 2000, 64(2–3):171–181.

[5] Malerba F, Mani S. Sectoral systems of innovation and production in developing countries[M]. *UK: Edward Elgar Publishing Limited*, 2009.

[6] Adner R. Match your innovation strategy to your innovation ecosystem [J]. *Harvard Business Review*, 2006, 84(4):98–107.

[7] Wu Shaobo. Research on knowledge input incentive of collaborative innovation in innovation ecosystem of strategic emerging industries [J]. *Science and technology management*, 2013, 34(9): 71–76

[8] Chen Yantai, et al. Analysis on value creation and acquisition mechanism of industrial innovation ecosystem – cross case analysis based on China's electric vehicles [J]. *Scientific research management*, 2015(1).

[9] Li Weiliang. Construction and Countermeasures of industrial innovation ecosystem based on supply and demand coordination [J]. *East China economic management*, 2016 (11).

[10] Li Qiwei. Connotation, source and formation of knowledge advantage in industrial innovation ecosystem [J]. *Scientific management research*, 2016(05): 53–56.

[11] Sun Yuan. Research on industrial innovation ecosystem from the perspective of symbiosis[J]. *Journal of Henan Normal University (philosophy and social sciences)*, 2017(01): 127–134.

[12] Peng Ben Hong. Research on the co evolution of modern logistics industry and advanced manufacturing industry [J]. *Science and technology and management*, 2009.

[13] Wang Zhenzhen, Chen Gongyu. Research on the CO opetition model of the joint development of manufacturing industry and logistics industry from the perspective of industrial ecosystem [J]. *Economy and management*, 2009(7).

[14] Ding chaoxun, Qin Ligong. Ecological integration path and evolution of logistics industry [J]. *Ecological economy*, 2011(1): 277–281.

[15] Yan Fei, Dong Qianli. Analysis on collaborative relationship and growth evolution mechanism of logistics service supply chain nodes [J]. *Journal of Beijing Jiaotong University (SOCIAL SCIENCE EDITION)*, 2012(4).

[16] Xue Xiaofang. Research on collaborative logistics ecosystem under the background of "big data" [J]. *Logistics engineering and management*, 2015(09): 1–3.

[17] Wang Xuhui, Zhang Qilin. Research on shipping cluster ecosystem: a case study of Dalian shipping service industry [J]. *Research on financial issues*, 2013(10).

[18] Zhou Lingyun, et al. Evolution mechanism and path of regional logistics micro main body aggregation based on ecological perspective [J]. *China's circulation economy*, 2013(9).

[19] Cao Yujiao et al. research on Symbiosis Model of logistics and economic symbiosis system of Urban Agglomeration Based on L-V model [J]. *Economic system reform*, 2015(5).

[20] Zhou Lingyun, Zhou Jing, Gu Weidong. Research on the order and behavior mode of regional logistics subject from the perspective of ecology [J]. *Frontier forum*, 2013(02), 24–28.

[21] Zhou Lingyun, Zhou Jun. evolution mechanism of regional logistics ecosystem based on compound logistic development mechanism [J]. *Ecological economy*, 2014(6): 142–145.

[22] Fan J, Zhou L, Cao Y, et al. Health evaluation of a regional logistics industrial ecosystem in China based on fuzzy matter-element analysis method [J]. *Journal of Intelligent & Fuzzy Systems*, 2016, 31(4): 2195–2202.

[23] Hao Cheng. Research on collaborative evolution of logistics ecosystem of platform e-commerce enterprises [D]. *Jiangxi: Jiangxi University of Finance and economics*, 2019.

Economic and Business Management – Huang & Zhang (Eds)
© 2022 Copyright the Author(s), ISBN: 978-1-032-06754-4

Consumer empowerment, enterprise life cycle, and R&D

Chan Lyu, Zihan Yang & Yang Huang
School of Business, Macau University of Science and Technology, Macau, China

ABSTRACT: This study examines the association between the enterprise life cycle and R&D. This paper finds that the resource base and competitive advantages allow mature firms to invest more in R&D than firms at other stages of the enterprise life cycle. We further examine the role of consumer empowerment in explaining the relation between the enterprise life cycle and R&D. Our results show that consumer empowerment moderates the association between them. These findings are robust when subjected to a series of tests. The significance of this paper has the following aspects First, it helps to provide strategic guidance for enterprise R&D. Second, it helps enterprises fully recognize and effectively use the power of consumers. Third, the research on enterprise R&D from the perspective of enterprise life cycle enriches the relevant theories of the influencing factors of enterprise investment. Fourth, this paper extends the application scope of consumer empowerment and enriches the theory of consumer empowerment to a certain extent.

1 INTRODUCTION

In the past few decades, scholars' interest and debate on the concept of "consumer empowerment" have increased rapidly. The European Commission Institute (Nardo, Loi, Rosati, & Manca, 2011) conducted a questionnaire survey of consumers in 29 European countries (EU 27 plus Iceland and Norway), resulting in a report on consumer empowerment (Special Eurobarometer n.342), ranking consumers in various countries.

The resulting consumer empowerment index is divided into three main areas: (1) consumer skills: consumer basic digital and financial skills and identification (e.g., Simple interest calculation, Do you know the organic vegetable logo); (2) consumer information level: consumer knowledge of their rights (e.g., How long you can have and return a product if you're not satisfied with it, Do you read carefully when signing the contract); (3) consumer's ability to complain (Consumer response to misinformation and fraud, Choose the right solution). The report also illustrates the relationship between the individual characteristics of consumers and their degree of empowerment Having identified education, age, gender and internet use as the most critical social factors for consumer empowerment, the discussion on consumer protection was facilitated.

In enterprises with different life cycles, R&D may be different, and consumer empowerment also has an important impact on enterprise R&D. This paper makes an empirical study on consumer empowerment and re-examines the entry point of considering enterprise R&D from a new perspective, which enriches

the influencing factors of enterprise R&D. It is of guiding significance to urge enterprises to pay more attention to the strength of consumers and to establish a long-term mechanism of communication with consumers.

At present, there are two main viewpoints on the relationship between growth enterprises and mature enterprises and R&D. The first view is that the R&D of mature enterprises is greater than that of the growth period. Jawahar and Mclaughlin (2001) believed that the demand for R&D investment is the strongest in the initial and growing period, but the scale of the enterprise is small, the risk of operation is large, the market share is not high, and the visibility of the enterprise is low. The problem of information asymmetry in mature enterprises will be alleviated, if the external financing conditions are good and the cash flow is abundant, which is the most favorable period for enterprises to carry out innovative activities.

The second view is that the R&D of the growing enterprise is greater than the mature period. Liang Lai Yin and Han Mixiao (2007) made an empirical study on R&D investment in high-tech enterprises in China and the United States from the perspective of enterprise life cycle and found that from the growth period to the mature period, the intensity of R&D investment in enterprises showed a downward trend. This view is more practical in high-tech industries, and there is less consideration of the practical problems faced by enterprises in financing, so the author thinks that the first view is more reliable.

Academic circles have not yet reached an agreement on the concept of consumer empowerment Shankar, Cherrier, and Canniford (2006) believe that consumer

204

DOI 10.1201/9781003203704-37

empowerment is to transfer the power of enterprise production and development agreement from the original operator to the consumer, and consumer empowerment is equivalent to the increase in consumer choice. But this definition is very narrow: First, consumers are not only entitled to choose but they can also influence the whole process of production and marketing through evaluation, complaints and other means. Second, consumer empowerment is not only the increase of its power but also the promotion of power.

2 LITERATURE REVIEW AND HYPOTHESIS DEVELOPMENT

2.1 *Association between the life cycle and R&D*

Enterprises in different life cycles have different R&D. Cumming and Johan (2010) point out that the various decisions of enterprises in the same life cycle have universal laws, while those in different life cycle stages show many differences in capital allocation efficiency, financing constraints, dividend policy, innovation ability, and so on. Enterprise R&D has the characteristics of high initial investment in R&D, high risk in R&D process, and high information asymmetry. In addition, intangible assets cannot obtain mortgage loans in banks, so it is difficult for enterprises to finance R&D investments.

Combined with the actual situation, financing constraints are also the real problems of European enterprises. Bronwyn et al.'s (2016) and Michele et al.'s (2010) analysis of the European enterprises by the Ministry of Macroeconomics and the Ministry of Investment in Berlin, respectively, shows that European enterprises are likely to have problems in obtaining credit and external financing obstacles, and European R&D companies face financing constraints far greater than their American competitors.

When enterprises are in the mature period, their financing pipeline is richer, the ability of continuous supply of funds is stronger, and they have a stronger attraction to high-tech talents. The confidentiality of technical information is more guaranteed. Enterprises have stronger economic strength, stronger ability to bear the uncertainty of R&D investment and stronger ability to resist risks.

This paper proposes hypothesis one:

H1: Compared with the growth period, the mature enterprise R&D investment is more.

2.2 *Enterprise life cycle and R&D: Moderating role of consumer empowerment*

Guo Guoqing (2010) believes that consumer empowerment is a dynamic process of comprehensive improvement of enterprise rights and functions. Consumer empowerment will have an impact on enterprise R&D, but there will be some differences in different life cycles.

When enterprises are in the growth period, its emphasis is on rapid development, consumers control the direction of enterprise development, strategic planning plays a small role. Therefore, the impact of consumer empowerment on enterprises is relatively small compared with maturity. When the enterprise is in the mature period, the development is basically stable, its resources enter the stage of product differentiation and efficiency improvement. As far as the enterprise is concerned, determining the direction of development is conducive to consumers to put forward opinions on specific products and services; from the consumer's point of view, the choice of consumers is limited to a certain range, and it is easier to make suggestions to enterprises. To sum up, hypothesis two is proposed:

H2: Compared with growth period, the positive correlation between consumer empowerment and R&D investment in mature enterprises is higher.

3 RESEARCH DESIGN

3.1 *Measurement of variables*

The main model of this paper uses the ratio of R&D to income to measure the investment of enterprise innovation. This study adopts the method of measuring life cycle proposed by Anthony and Ramesh (1992), combines with the actual situation, removes the index of enterprise age, and changes capital expenditure into investment cash flow. Finally, the comprehensive score of sales income growth rate, dividend payment, investment cash flow, and asset ratio is used to divide the enterprise life cycle. Here, we use the EU's Consumer Empowerment Report scoring to measure consumer empowerment.

3.2 *Empirical model*

In this paper, the model 1 is proposed to test Hypothesis 1. Among them, R&D R represents the ratio of R&D to income, MATURE represents the mature, i says the business, and t indicates the year. Control variables are as follows: DECLINE is the corporate recession, SIZE is the natural logarithm of a company's assets, ROA is the return on assets, LEV is the asset-liability ratio, OCF is the return on operating cash flow, EBIT_R is the profit margin before sales interest and tax; AG GDP is the per capita GG GDP growth rate; LIST for market size.

Based on the model of Chen Shen et al. (2016), the model 2 is proposed to verify Hypothesis 2. Among them CONSUMER represents consumer increase right 2 When $\alpha > 0$ in model 2, the $\alpha_2 + \alpha_3 > \alpha_2$, shows that the positive correlation between consumer empowerment and R&D is higher in mature enterprises.

$$R\&D\_R = \alpha_0 + \alpha_1 MATURE + \alpha_2 DECLINE \\ + \alpha_3 SIZE + \alpha_4 ROA + \alpha_5 LEV$$

$$+ \alpha_6 OCF + \alpha_7 EBIT_R + \alpha_8 AG$$
$$+ \alpha_9 GG + \alpha_{10} LIST$$
$$+ \sum INDUSTRY$$
$$+ \sum YEAR + \varepsilon \qquad (1)$$

$$R\&D\_R = \alpha_0 + \alpha_1 MATURE$$
$$+ \alpha_2 CONSUMER + \alpha_3 MATURE$$
$$* CONSUMER + \alpha_4 DECLINE$$
$$+ \alpha_5 DECLINE * CONSUMER$$
$$+ \alpha_6 SIZE + \alpha_7 ROA + \alpha_8 LEV$$
$$+ \alpha_9 OCF + \alpha_{10} EBIT_R + \alpha_{11} AG$$
$$+ \alpha_{12} GG + \alpha_{13} LIST$$
$$+ \sum INDUSTRY$$
$$+ \sum YEAR + \varepsilon \qquad (2)$$

4 SAMPLE SELECTION AND DESCRIPTIVE STATISTICS

4.1 Sample selection

In this paper, 28 listed companies in Europe from 2000 to 2018 are selected as the initial samples, and Malta is excluded because of the small amount of data. In order to ensure the rationality of the data, this paper selects the initial samples according to the following steps: (1) excluding companies with less than one year's listing time; (2) excluding ST, *ST listed companies with abnormal operating conditions; (3) excluding financial insurance and enterprises that cannot be classified. In order to remove the influence of extreme value, the continuous variable was treated with 1% winsorize, and the final observed value was 20048.

Table 1. Descriptive statistical analysis.

Var	Obs	Min	Max	Mean	SD
R&D_R	20,048	−0.240	9.163	0.105	0.352
R&D_A	18,130	0.000	3.139	0.053	0.086
MATURE	20,048	0.000	1.000	0.526	0.499
LIFE1	24,189	0.000	1.000	0.083	0.276
CONSUMER	20,048	2.402	2.884	2.765	0.274
DECLINE	20,048	0.000	1.000	0.360	0.480

4.2 Descriptive statistics

According to Table 1, the average value of innovation input (R&D_R) of the expanded variables is 0.105 and median is 0.021. Besides, R&D (R&D_R) minimum is -0.240 and the maximum is 9.163, showing a large gap (9.163-(-0.24)=9.403). This indicates that there is a large gap in R&D investment (R&D_R) of listed conventions in European countries.

4.3 Correlation

The Pearson correlation analysis of key variables is given. The coefficient of enterprise innovation input (R&D_R) and mature enterprise (MATURE) is 0.125, which is significantly positive at 1% level. In addition, correlation analysis also determines pollution.

5 MULTIPLE REGRESSION RESULTS

5.1 Regression results

The first column of Table 2 reveals the regression results of enterprise life cycle and innovation input. The adjustment in this study is 56.12, which indicates that the model fitting effect is good. The results show that the correlation coefficient of the mature (MATURE) enterprise is significantly positive at 5% level. This shows that compared with the growth enterprises, the R&D investment of the mature enterprises of 28 listed conventions in Europe is greater.

Table 2. Regression results.

R&D_R	Model 1	Model 2
Cons	−0.018	−0.229***
	(0.023)	(0.047)
MATURE	0.012**	0.010**
	(0.005)	(0.005)
CONSUMER		0.006***
		(0.002)
MATURE*CONSUMER		0.009**
		(0.004)
DECLINE	−0.011***	−0.013**
	(0.005)	(0.006)
DECLINE*CONSUMER		−0.019***
		(0.004)
SIZE	0.006***	0.006***
	(0.000)	(0.001)
ROA	0.004***	0.005***
	(0.001)	(0.000)
LEV	0.001***	0.001***
	(0.000)	(0.000)
OCF	−0.138***	−0.142***
	(0.016)	(0.017)
EBIT_R	−0.502***	−0.501***
	(0.004)	(0.004)
AG	0.026 ***	0.013 **
	(0.005)	(0.006)
GG	0.094	0.128
	(0.083)	(0.083)
LIST	−0.005**	−0.004**
	(0.002)	(0.002)
Industry	control	control
Year	control	control
Obs	20048	20048
F	524.31***	469.86***
Adj − R^2(%)	56.12	56.26

Std. Error in brackets. *** $p < 0.01$. ** $p < 0.05$. *$p < 0.10$.

The second column of Table 2 reveals the relationship between consumer empowerment, business life cycle, and innovative investment. If the enterprise is in a growth period, at the level of 1%, the marginal effect of consumer empowerment on enterprise R&D is CONSUMER. If the enterprise is in maturity, MATURE*CONSUMER coefficient is significantly positive at 5% level. To sum up, Hypothesis 2 is proved.

5.2 Robustness test

This paper replaces the measurement of enterprise life cycle and R&D, and tests the robustness of the conclusion. First of all, the way to measure the life cycle of an enterprise is replaced, and the cash flow method (Dickinson, 2011) is used to distinguish the life cycle of an enterprise. Variable MATURE is replaced by LIFE1 and DECLINE is replaced by LIFE2. And then, the way to measure enterprise R&D is replaced by the ratio of R&D to total assets. Variable R&D_R is replaced by R&D_A. The test results are consistent with the above.

6 CONCLUSIONS

This paper studies the relationship between consumer empowerment, enterprise life cycle, and innovation input through 20048 data samples from 28 EU countries from 2000 to 2018. According to the research hypothesis one, it is determined that compared with the growth period, the enterprise R&D in the mature period is more. According to Hypothesis 2, it is determined that compared with the growth period, the positive correlation between consumer empowerment and R&D in mature enterprises is higher.

This paper summarizes the development ways of enterprise innovation and studies the influencing factors of enterprise R&D, provides the basis for enterprises to make innovative investment decisions, causes enterprises to attach importance to consumers, and promotes the protection of consumer rights and interests.

REFERENCES

Anthony, J., and K. Ramesh. (1992). Association between accounting performance measures and stock prices. *Journal of Accounting and Economics* 15 (2–3): 203–227.

Avi Shankar, Helene Cherrier & Robin Canniford (2006). Consumer empowerment: a Foucauldian interpretation. *European Journal of Marketing*, (9/10):1013–1030.

Bronwyn H. Hall, Pietro Moncada-Paternò-Castello, Sandro Montresor & Antonio Vezzani (2016) Financing constraints, R&D investments and innovative performances: new empirical evidence at the firm level for Europe, *Economics of Innovation and New Technology*, 25:3, 183–196.

Chen Chen, Li Zhe and Wang Lei (2016). Management control, enterprise life cycle and real earnings management. *Management science*, 29 (04): 29–44.

Cumming D, Johan S. (2010). Phasing out an inefficient venture capital tax credit. *Journal of Industry, Competition and Trade*, 10(3–4):227–252.

Guo Guoqing, Li Guangming (2010). The latest development of consumer empowerment theory and its enlightenment. *China's circulation economy*, 24 (08): 58–61.

Jawahar I M, Mclaughlin G L. (2001) Toward a Descriptive Stake Holder Theory: An Organizational Life Cycle Approach. *Academy of Management Review*, 26(3): 397–414.

Liang Laixin, Han Mixiao (2007). A comparative empirical study of R&D investment between China and the United States based on the life cycle of high-tech enterprises. *Science and Technology Management Research*, 2007(08): 109–111. (In Chinese)

Michele Cincera and Julien Ravet, (April 2010). Financing constraints and R&D investments of large corporations in Europe and the USA. Retrieved from http://iri.jrc.es/.

Nardo, Michela and Loi, Massimo and Rosati, Rossana and Manca, Anna Rita. (April 2011). *The Consumer Empowerment Index*. A measure of skills, awareness and engagement of European consumers. Retrieved from https://mpra.ub.uni-muenchen.de/30711/.

Victoria Dickinson (2011) Cash Flow Patterns as a Proxy for Firm Life cycle. *The Accounting Review*, 86(6)1969–1994.

Economic and Business Management – Huang & Zhang (Eds)
© 2022 Copyright the Author(s), ISBN: 978-1-032-06754-4

Survival of self-employment under COVID-19—evidence from Slovakia

Miroslava Knapková
Faculty of Economics, Matej Bel University in Banská Bystrica, Slovakia

ABSTRACT: Self-employment represents an important part of the Slovak economy. It is also one of the areas most affected by COVID-19 pandemic. The aim of the article is to analyze the short-term effects of COVID-19 pandemic on self-employment (represented by tradesmen) in Slovakia. The article focuses on the number of newly established trades, number of terminated trades, including number of bankrupted trades in the period from 2017 to 2021. The article also analyses the total unemployment rate in pre-COVID period (second half of 2019) and in the COVID period (until February 2021). Results indicate a stable unemployment rate until April 2020 (at around 5%). The second quarter of 2020 is not only the beginning of the unemployment rate increase (for more than 1.5 percentual points) but also the period of the changes in establishing and terminating the trades. The lowest number of new tradesmen were established in the second quarter of 2020. However, the rising unemployment was subsequently reflected in the unusual growth in the number of new self-employed, peaking in the fourth quarter of 2020, when the highest number of trades was established (opposite situation than before the pandemic).

1 INTRODUCTION

Self-employment as part of small- and medium-sized enterprises (SME) in Slovakia is considered as part of the entrepreneurship and self-employed person as person, who gain income from business activities (act 461/2003 Coll. On Social insurance). The most common form of self-employment is a trade business. A trade is a systematic activity performed independently by an entrepreneur (trader), in his own name and on his account, conducted for the purpose of earning profits or to achieve a measurable positive social impact. Trader shall be a natural person older than 18 years of age, with the full capacity to act and must possess integrity (act no. 455/1991 Coll. Trade Business Act). This paper examines the short-term effects of COVID-19 pandemic on self-employment (represented by tradesmen) in Slovakia. The paper is divided into four parts: literature review (including literature gap and paper's main research idea), materials and data sources, results, and discussion (focusing on state measures to support self-employment, unemployment rate and the number of new, extinct, and bankrupted tradesmen), and conclusions.

2 LITERATURE REVIEW

There are only few studies focusing on the so-far influence of COVID-19 pandemic on self-employment and its various economic features. Authors Blundell

and Machin (2020) analyzed weekly worked hours and monthly income in April 2019 and April 2020 in the United Kingdom. Authors Beland, Fakorede, and Mikola (2020) analyzed a number of active business owners before and during COVID-19 (May 2019–May 2020) in Canada. The influence of reductions of hours of work and the associated income reductions on the subjective well-being of self-employed in the United Kingdom were analyzed by Yue and Cowling (2021). Besides worked hours, Kalenkoski and Pabilonia (2020) focused also on the changes in unemployment in the USA. Graeber et al. (2021) focused on the gender gap and reduction of income of the self-employed persons in Germany. International Labor Organization and World Bank elaborated a series of analysis of the COVID-19 pandemic on the world of work (including self-employment). They also identified indicators that could be used to assess short-term, mid-term, and long-term effects of the pandemic on the employment and self-employment. Those indicators are loss of working hours, unemployment, underemployment and job losses, registered employment, GDP per person employed, and mortality rate of enterprises (World Bank 2020a, 2020b, 2020c).

Most of the so-far research of COVID-19 influence on self-employment is either theoretical or based on the small research sample questionnaire (mostly focusing on the reduction of working time and consequently reduction of the income). Because of the relatively short period of COVID-19 pandemic, research based on the analysis of empirical statistical data is

208

DOI 10.1201/9781003203704-38

missing. Research of the impact of COVID-19 on self-employment in Slovakia is missing at all. This paper tries to fill the gap in so far the research and to offer development of self-employment under COVID-19 pandemic based on the official secondary data, covering the whole self-employment in Slovakia. Based on the literature review and availability of the official data, the article focuses on the analysis of the unemployment rate (registered unemployment) and mortality of enterprises (particularly tradesmen as the most common part of self-employment). Mortality includes the overall mortality (without considering the reason for the termination of the self-employed person), as well as forced termination because of economic problems (bankruptcy of tradesmen as sole proprietors).

3 MATERIALS AND DATA SOURCES

In this paper, the author analyzes the development of selected indicators related to self-employment in the years 2017–2021. Data of all indicators are processed as quarterly data, starting from the second quarter of 2017 (Q2 2017) (in 2021, the last data are for the first quarter, corresponding to the situation on 31.3.2021). The reason for starting with the second quarter of 2017 is the fact that there was a change in the bankruptcy legislation at the beginning of 2017 which significantly influenced the number and methodology of recording bankruptcies. Time series thus contain data for a total of 16 time periods (quarters). In the case of the registered unemployment rate, the data are monthly, covering the second half of 2019, the whole of 2020, and January and February 2021 (to describe the situation just before the start of the pandemic and during the pandemic; altogether 20 monthly time periods).

Quarterly data on the number of newly established trades, number of extinct trades, and number of bankrupt trades are processed according to Finstat data (www.finstat.sk). Monthly data on the registered unemployment rate are processed based on the official statistics of the Ministry of Labor, Social Affairs and Family of the Slovak Republic (www.upsvr.gov.sk).

4 RESULTS AND DISCUSSION

4.1 *State measures to protect self-employment*

The first official occurrence of COVID-19 disease in Slovakia was in March 2020. On 12th March 2020, the extraordinary situation and consequently emergency situation were declared and the first state measures to protect and to support the private sector were adopted. From 16th March 2020, all retail establishments and all establishments providing services were closed (Regulation of the Public Health Office no. OLP/ 2595/2020). To minimize the negative impact of coronavirus and quarantine measures in the field of law, the National Council adopted an act no. 62/2020

Coll. on certain emergency measures in relation to the spread of the dangerous human disease COVID-19 and the judiciary. These measures include the non-expiry of legal deadlines, the failure to conduct court hearings, as well as the prevention of the exercise of liens and auctions.

Based on the Government regulation no. 131/2020 Coll. on the Maturity of Social Insurance Premiums in the event of an extraordinary situation declared in connection with COVID-19, the self-employed persons have the right to apply for the postponement of payment of obligatory social insurance levies (all monthly payments for March 2020–March 2021 were postponed to June 2021). From 17th June 2020, self-employed persons can claim reimbursement of part of the rent for leased facilities which they cannot effectively use in connection with COVID-19 (up to 50% of the rent; amendment to the Act no. 71/2013 Coll. on the provision of subsidies within the competence of the Ministry of Economy of the Slovak Republic).

Starting from the 6th April 2020, self-employed persons can apply for financial aid within the project "First aid" (www.employment.gov.sk). The "First aid" is a project covered by 85% from the European Union budget (as part of the Human resources operational program) and by 15% from the Slovak state budget. For the financial aid from 330 to 870 euro (the average wage in 2019 in Slovakia was 1,133 euro) can apply: 1. The self-employed person which at the time of the declared emergency situation interrupted the performance or operation of self-employment on the basis of a decision of the Public Health Office of the Slovak Republic or 2. Self-employed person whose sales decreased by at least 20%.

Besides the above-mentioned direct support of self-employment, the Act no. 67/2020 Coll. on Certain Extraordinary Measures in the Financial Area in Relation to the Spread of Dangerous Infectious Human Disease COVID-19 introduced an indirect support of self-employment. The support includes guarantees for loans and the payment of interest on a loan, as part of the financial assistance to support the maintenance of operations in small or medium-sized enterprises.

Thanks to these measures, which were taken immediately after the declaration of the emergency situation, it is still possible to keep the level of self-employed persons at a stable level in Slovakia, what we are pointing out in the next part of the article.

4.2 *Development of unemployment*

According to the guidelines of ILO and World Bank (World Bank 2020a, 2020b, 2020c), we use the unemployment rate rather than the employment rate when analyzing the short-term effects of the COVID-19 pandemic. Before the COVID-19 pandemic, the registered unemployment was relatively stable (varying from 4.92% in November and December 2019 to 5.19% in March 2019), at the level of a natural rate of unemployment. Immediately after the declaration of an emergency situation (second half of March 2020), the unemployment rate started to increase. In April 2020, the unemployment rate increased by almost 1.5 percentual points, and it continued to rise until July 2020 (7.65%). In the period between the 14th June 2020 and 30th September 2020, there was a release period, without any specific restrictions on operations and trades, which was also reflected in a slight decline in the registered unemployment rate (we can observe a one-month delay in the response of the unemployment rate to the changes in the state measures against COVID-19). It means a decrease of the unemployment rate in August, September, and October 2020 (the minimum of 7.35% in October 2020). Consequently, with the new wave of COVID-19 pandemic and new restrictions in the operation of enterprises, the unemployment rate started to rise again, reaching 7.9% in February 2021 (Figure 1).

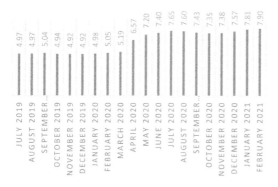

Figure 1. Unemployment rate in Slovakia in the period July 2019–February 2021.

The unemployment rate reflects not only changes in the labor market but also changes in self-employment. The need to close or reduce operations (albeit with direct or indirect financial support from the state) has led to the closure of several trades. On the other hand, redundancies and reduced demand for labor (due to reduced or complete closure of operations and enterprises) may have influenced the growth of the individuals' interest in starting a trade business (self-employment).

4.3 New trades, extinct trades, and bankrupted trades

We analyze the development of self-employed persons under the COVID-19 pandemic by the means of the number of newly established trades, a number of extinct (terminated) trades, and the number of bankrupted trades. In the case of bankruptcies, we consider the date of the first registration related to the bankruptcy process. For this reason, the number of bankruptcies in each quarter may not realistically correspond to the corresponding part of the extinct trades in the same quarter. Therefore, we interpret the number of bankruptcies and the number of extinct trades separately.

The following figure (Figure 2) displays the development of trades in the period from 2Q 2017 till 1Q 2021.

From 2017 until 2019, the lowest number of new trades was established in the fourth quarter of each year. This may be related to the expectation of changes in the following fiscal year, but also to the fact that persons prefer to start a trade at the beginning of the year so that they do not have to process a tax return and pay tax for three or fewer months. On the other hand, this is related to the highest share of established trades in the first quarter of the year (which is confirmed by data for both 2018 and 2019). This situation changed under COVID-19, and, in 2020, the highest number of trades was established during the last quarter of the year (opposite situation than before the pandemic). It is linked with high uncertainty during the whole year 2020, as well as with growing redundancy of employees and growing unemployment rate. We suppose that part of the dismissed employees decided to focus on the entrepreneurial activities (the trade). The overall number of new trades increased in 2020 by 3% compared to 2019.

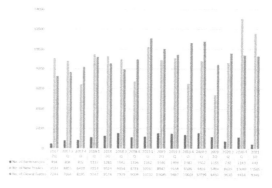

Figure 2. Development of trades (new trades, extinct trades, bankrupted trades) in Slovakia in 2Q 2017–1Q 2021.

An interesting finding, however, is that the number of extinct trades in 2020 decreased (compared to 2019, the decrease is 7%). Also, the number of forced extinctions (bankruptcies) was lower in 2020 than in 2019 (for almost 20%). It could be linked with the state measures, particularly with the direct financial aid in the case of closing operation or decrease of the sales, as well as with the possibility of postponement of the payment of compulsory social insurance levies (in 2020, the minimum value of compulsory levies to Social insurance was 167.89 euro monthly; considering the possibility to postpone the payment of the levies from March 2020, this value is multiplied by 10 months). The payment of compulsory levies was postponed until June 2021. It will be interesting and necessary to analyze the situation after June 2021, when the compulsory levies are due.

5 CONCLUSIONS

The aim of the paper was to examine the short-term effects of COVID-19 pandemic on self-employment (represented by trades as the most significant part of self-employment) in Slovakia. By using the data on the registered unemployment rate, number of newly established trades, number of extinct and bankrupted trades, as well as information on state measures to support self-employment, the author pointed out the relatively favorable situation in the development of trades in 2020. Growing number of newly established trades and, on the other side, a decrease of extinct trades and bankrupted trades is an interesting phenomenon under the COVID-19 pandemic. However, the author was analyzing only the short-term consequences of the pandemic, in the period of significant direct and indirect financial support to the self-employed persons based on the state measures. It is a reasonable limitation of the analysis because short-term effects could not reflect the real influence of COVID-19 pandemic on self-employment. In further research, it is necessary to analyze changes in self-employment in the medium and long term, also in combination with other variables (such as the structure of employment and unemployment, an increase of public debt due to the state measures to support self-employment, survival of newly established trades, etc.). It can be assumed that the situation will change after June 2021, and the number of extinct and bankrupt trades will increase (of course, provided that the state does not allow another postponement of the payment of compulsory insurance levies of self-employed persons). One can conclude that the higher number of newly established trades is related to the growth of unemployment and greater interest of individuals in their own business. The lower mortality of trades in 2020 compared to 2019 indicates the use of state support for self-employed persons. However, it is questionable how long this situation will be sustainable and whether the mid-term and long-term effects of COVID-19 pandemic will reflect into the growing trade mortality (including bankruptcies).

ACKNOWLEDGMENT

This paper is an output of the scientific project of Grant Agency VEGA No. 1/0366/21 "Dependent Entrepreneurship in Slovakia – Reflection, Measurement and Perspectives" at the "Faculty of Economics, Matej Bel University in Slovakia."

REFERENCES

Beland, L. P., Fakorede, O., & Mikola, D. 2020. Short-Term Effect of COVID-19 on Self-Employed Workers in Canada. *Canadian Public Policy* 46(S1): 66–81.

Blundell, J., & Machin, S. 2020. *Self-employment in the Covid-19 crisis*. Centre for Economic Performance, London School of Economics and Political Science.

Graeber, D., Kritikos, A. S., & Seebauer, J. 2021. COVID-19: a crisis of the female self-employed (No. 788). *GLO Discussion Paper*.

Kalenkoski, C. M., & Pabilonia, S. W. 2020. Initial impact of the COVID-19 pandemic on the employment and hours of self-employed coupled and single workers by gender and parental status. *IZA Discussion paper* no. 13443.

World Bank. 2020a. COVID-19 and the World of Work. Rapid Assessment of the Employment Impacts and Policy Responses. North Macedonia. *ILO and World Bank*, April 2020.

World Bank. 2020b. COVID-19 and the World of Work. Rapid Assessment of the Employment Impacts and Policy Responses. *Montenegro. ILO and World Bank*, June 2020.

World Bank. 2020c. COVID-19 and the World of Work: Rapid Assessment of the Employment Impacts and Policy Responses SERBIA. *ILO and World Bank*, 2020.

Yue, W., & Cowling, M. 2021. The Covid-19 lockdown in the United Kingdom and subjective well-being: Have the self-employed suffered more due to hours and income reductions?. *International Small Business Journal*, 0266242620986763.

Economic and Business Management – Huang & Zhang (Eds)
© 2022 Copyright the Author(s), ISBN: 978-1-032-06754-4

Research on the development of rural credit bank's e-commerce platform in China

Baolin Ma & Yihan Wang
Inner Mongolia University of Finance and Economics, Hohhot, China

Dongxue Zhao
Inner Mongolia University of Science & Technology, Baotou, China

Kexin Ma
Hohhot Vocational College, Hohhot, China

ABSTRACT: With the rapid development of internet finance, major commercial banks have adapted to market trends and started internet finance business. One of the representative businesses is to establish online e-commerce platforms. The rural credit banks that mainly serve "agriculture, rural areas, and farmers" and small enterprises have established WeChat banks, community banks, online banks, and e-commerce platforms. This article takes the e-commerce platform of rural credit banks in China as the research object, summarizes the current distribution characteristics, development status, and business models, and puts forward reasonable suggestions for the future development of the platforms

1 INTRODUCTION

After the emergence of e-commerce, it quickly penetrated all areas of social and economic life. It not only has had a huge impact on the traditional retail industry, but also on the financial industry. It has changed the financial format and pattern, and has deepened financial disintermediation (He 2015). With the continuous integration of e-commerce and the finance, Internet finance gradually took shape, and has profoundly affected all aspects of the financial industry. Especially the P2P lending, due to being pervasive, convenient, efficient, and low-cost, reduced difficulty for SMEs to access financing (Gang 2021; Wang 2020). In March 2012, "Jiaobohui" and "Shanrong Business" came into being. The e-commerce platforms of the two banks have adopted a combination of B2B and B2C (Wang 2013). It can be said that 2012 was the beginning of the banking e-commerce platform.

While most commercial banks have proposed countermeasures against Internet finance, the response of the Rural Credit Bank has been slightly slower and less impacted by Internet finance. This may be due to the relatively fixed business scope and customer groups. Due to its inherent characteristics, rural credit banks are faced with multiple difficulties in the development of Internet finance, such as weak risk supervision capabilities, lagging information construction, etc. They need to adopt strategic measures that focus on point and key breakthroughs (Wang 2018; Zhang 2019;. At present, bank-based e-commerce platforms

mainly have three models: credit card malls, integrated online malls and shopping guide platforms. Compared with traditional e-commerce platforms, bank-based e-commerce platforms have short establishment time, low website popularity, rely on bank resources, and focus on financial services (Liu 2015).

For most rural credit banks, the e-commerce platform is just a means of acquiring customers, not the main business. The purpose is to increase customer stickiness, maintain small business customer resources, and provide value-added transaction chains. Finally, a three-dimensional financial ecosystem will be built that includes functions such as clothing, food, housing, transportation, payment, medical shopping, and so on (Ma 2016).

2 DISTRIBUTION RESEARCH

2.1 *Distribution profile*

The rural credit banks in China are counted in this study, except for the banks in Hong Kong, Macao, and Taiwan. In Figure 1, 0 means there is no e-commerce platform in the local rural credit bank; 0.5 means there is one, but the webpage is abnormal or the content is missing, and normal transactions cannot be performed, or it is a simple point mall that cannot be used; 1 means there is one e-commerce platform; 2 means there are two; >2 means there are more than two e-commerce platforms.

It can be seen from Figure 1 that the provinces with more than two e-commerce platforms are Shandong, Jiangsu, Zhejiang, Henan, and Guangdong, which are all major economic and agricultural provinces, with a relatively high level of social and economic development. The e-commerce platforms in these five provinces are mainly established by provincial or city-county rural credit banks. Different cities and counties may have different e-commerce platforms, and the distribution is characterized by regional dispersion. The developed cities or counties and larger rural credit banks often establish e-commerce platforms.

Figure 1. Distribution map of different numbers of rural credit e-commerce platforms in China.

The number of e-commerce platforms is 1 in Beijing, Tianjin, Shanghai, Chongqing, Jiangxi, Anhui, and Fujian. In Beijing, Tianjin, Shanghai, Chongqing, the management structure of the Rural Credit Bank has changed from a multi-level legal person to single legal person. One bank corresponds to an e-commerce platform, so these provinces and cities have only one unified platform. Anhui, Fujian, and Jiangxi are in the upper-middle position in China in terms of economic and social development. The common feature is that these provinces are adjacent to the developed economic regions in southeast China, and are radiated by developed economic regions. The e-commerce platforms of Rural Credit Banks in Qinghai, Ningxia, and Yunnan are points malls, which can only be exchanged for points, not cash. This study defines the quantity as 0.5.

2.2 *Comparative analysis of distribution differentiation*

Analysis is carried out in terms of the relationship between the total assets of each rural credit bank and the number of e-commerce platforms. The three rural credit banks in Shandong, Jiangsu, and Zhejiang of which the total assets exceed one trillion yuan, operate their own e-commerce platforms, while the rural credit bank in Henan and Guangdong, of which the total assets also exceed trillions, do not operate e-commerce platforms themselves, but they are built and operated by municipal or county-level rural credit banks. Further analysis of the total assets of other provinces and municipalities of rural credit banks with 0 and 1 e-commerce platforms, it is not difficult to conclude that there is no obvious regular correspondence between the size of the total asset and the number of e-commerce platforms.

From the analysis of the two factors of region and total assets, it can be concluded that the number of e-commerce platforms of rural credit banks is closely related to the level of economic and social development and characteristics of the region, but little to the total assets of rural credit bank. It is worth noting that Henan Province ranks among the top five in terms of economic aggregates, and the total assets of Henan Rural Credit Bank are also among the best, but the provincial rural credit bank has not established an e-commerce platform. E-commerce platforms are established by rural credit banks at the city and county levels. This study believes that the agricultural economy occupies an important position in the cities and counties of Henan Province, and the establishment of e-commerce platforms has a great relationship with their economic development characteristics.

2.3 *Summary of distribution law*

After research, the basic conclusion is that the distribution of Rural Credit Bank's e-commerce platform has dual characteristics of economy and agriculture. Whether it is distributed in a certain area and how much is mainly determined by the local economic development level and the characteristics of agricultural development, and has little to do with the size of a specific rural credit bank. Areas with a high level of economic development and more important agricultural development often have an e-commerce platform. Analyzed from the micro level, the rural credit bank e-commerce platform mainly sells agricultural and sideline products, which also makes the platform have the dual attributes of finance and agriculture at the micro level, which is in line with its macroeconomic and agricultural characteristics. In addition, it is worth exploring that Hebei, which is close to the super city Beijing, has not established a rural credit e-commerce platform, which shows that the two factors of economy and agriculture cannot drive the establishment of e-commerce platforms. This reflects from another aspect that the economic development gap between Hebei and Beijing is large and the structural imbalance is serious.

3 RESEARCH ON THE CURRENT DEVELOPMENT AND STATUS

3.1 *Research on market status*

Since the rise of Internet finance, major banks have put forward countermeasures to integrate into Internet finance. Since 2012, large banks such as Industrial and Commercial Bank of China have successively established online e-commerce platforms. After 2015, rural credit banks have followed the market and established e-commerce platforms in order to respond to the impact of Internet finance and increase the bank's own technical and talent reserves; on the other hand, e-commerce platforms can increase the stickiness of original customers and develop new customers. From the statistics of this study, by the end of 2016, there were fewer than 100 e-commerce platforms of rural credit banks, most of which had been established for fewer than 2 years, small in scale and experience. By the end of 2019, the e-commerce platforms of rural credit banks in the provinces had not changed much, and there was no explosive growth trend. Looking at the development of bank e-commerce platforms in recent years, including CCB and ICBC, their market influence and share have not changed much. As a new thing, emerging due to Internet finance, the platforms' growth, sustainability, economic benefits, and social benefits are worthy of further study.

Rural credit bank's e-commerce platforms mainly sell agricultural products, and the scale of the mall, the number of products, and the back-end technology are relatively limited. Therefore, the benefit of the platform is very small for the entire bank, even to be ignored. The main role of rural credit bank's online e-commerce platform is to develop new card-holding customers and increase stickiness, including corporate customers and individuals. Restricted by the positioning and technical level, the e-commerce platforms' scale and market share are difficult to develop.

3.2 Research on the operation model

There are two main models for establishing rural credit e-commerce platforms. Most banks establish themselves, and a few cooperate with other e-commerce platforms. For example, in Beijing, Tianjin, Shanghai, Zhejiang, etc., Rural Credit Bank established its own e-commerce platform and operated independently; while the Shandong platform was established in cooperation with JD. As a local responsible party of JD.com, the platform not only sold its own products but also distributed the products of JD.com.

Relying on the advantages of community banks or branches, almost all platforms adopt online and offline operation methods for the aspects of merchants' entry, product promotion, and sales links. In logistics and distribution, they mainly rely on full-time employees and other logistics companies.

The current banks' e-commerce platforms mainly include three models: credit card malls, online malls, and shopping guide platforms. Credit card and online malls are common, and the shopping guide platforms are rarer. Rural credit banks' e-commerce platforms are mainly credit card malls and online malls, and there is no report on the shopping guide platform. It can be further divided into six models.

3.2.1 Independent establishment of comprehensive online shopping mall

Many rural credit e-commerce platforms adopt this model. Network maintenance, logistics and distribution, customer acquisition, and publicity are all done by the bank itself. This model requires banks to provide a large amount of manpower, material, and financial resources to support the operation. In the initial stage, many big banks did adopt this model, but after operating it, they found that the platform's revenue was too low and always required continuous investment. So some banks began to evaluate the sustainability of the model and made some adjustments.

3.2.2 Cooperating with other e-commerce platforms

Self-operated e-commerce platforms will involve merchant review, product quality control, logistics and distribution, warehousing, information processing, and other links. However, these links are not the traditional advantage of banks, so some rural credit banks establish online shopping malls together with other famous E-commerce platforms. Banks mainly offer payment, installment, channel promotion, and other aspects to achieve complementary advantages. The e-commerce platform of Shandong Rural Credit Bank was officially launched in September 2016, integrating a smart e-shopping mall, smart e-life community O2O services, and smart e-pay Internet payment. The platform was built by the bank and cooperated with JD.com to realize the deployment and sales of JD's products. The rural credit bank integrates customers and merchants through the platform, links finance and consumption, realizes localized, high-quality, and differentiated financial and non-financial services, and strives to create a platform that customers love, merchants rely on, and that integrates payment and financing.

3.2.3 Financial services added to the e-commerce platform to form a financial supermarket

Finance is an advantageous business of banks, and many banks use mall platforms to provide financial services. In particular, the provision of financing services for merchants and enterprises staying in the mall is a typical supply chain financial business. Customers can make credit and pledge loans online, and apply 24/7 hours online.

3.2.4 Jointly carry out e-commerce platform business and share customer resources

As a regional financial institution, rural credit banks' e-commerce platforms are often regionally restrictive and only serve the local area, so it is difficult to form a scale effect. Therefore, some large provincial-level rural credit banks took the lead in building a unified online platform, in which each city and county-level rural credit bank launched the same platform, unified services and management, and realized the province-wide coverage of shopping mall products, and unified management in logistics distribution, information processing, etc.. This saves on operating costs and achieve economies of scale. For example, Rural Credit Banks Funds Clearing Center has built "Linong Mall," an e-commerce financial service platform integrating e-commerce, finance, B2C, and B2B supply chains. There is also the Feng Acquisition platform built by Zhejiang Rural Credit Bank, of which all members use a unified Feng Acquisition Mall to form a flow advantage and achieve economies of scale.

In addition, the O2O models are focused on online and offline integrated services, using the bank's customer, channel, and financial business advantages, combined with offline physical stores, to obtain more customer resources for physical stores and bring customers more discounts.

4 COUNTERMEASURES AND SUGGESTIONS

4.1 Rural credit bank e-commerce platforms are often limited to local areas, which require full consideration of the local economic development level and characteristics when establishing online platforms, accurate selection of platform product types, and logistics and distribution methods.

4.2 Rural credit bank's e-commerce platforms are limited by the bank's own financial, material, and human resources. When establishing the platform, it is necessary to fully consider the limiting factors and establish a scale suitable for its own development and strategic positioning.

4.3 Most rural credit bank's e-commerce platforms mainly aim at assisting in customer acquisition, increasing customer stickiness, and providing supply chain financial services. Their profitability is very limited, and with small scale, small trading volume, and continuous loss. This requires making the best use of the advantages and bypassing the disadvantages in the daily operation, as well as minimum investment to achieve maximum customer acquisition and financial service value, so that the marginal value is at a high level, not seeking short-term profit, but intensive cultivation.

4.4 The operation of rural credit e-commerce platforms should fully integrate online and offline superior resources, rely on Internet thinking, activate rural markets and customers, facilitate payment methods, improve market experience, and innovate propaganda methods. Full consideration should be given to the decentralization of rural customers, and customer service capabilities in non-banking scenarios should

be strengthened, such as payment, medical care, daily necessities, housing, transportation, and all-in-one cards, in order to enhance customer stickiness and customer conversion rate.

4.5 Control risks and isolate the risk channels of banks and e-commerce platforms. Financial risks cannot spread to e-commerce platforms, nor can the risks of e-commerce platforms affect the reputation of banks. Improve the threshold standards for merchants to check in, and strictly control the quality of products. In particular, most of the products on the rural credit e-commerce platform are agricultural and sideline products, which are closely related to the daily diet, so the quality of products is more important.

ACKNOWLEDGMENTS

This research was supported by the Inner Mongolia Key Laboratory of Economic Data Analysis and Mining, (No.: SYSKT21006), and Research Base Special Project of Inner Mongolia Social Science Planning Office (No.:2020ZJD012).

REFERENCES

Gang, K.A. & Yong, X.A. & Yi, P.B. 2015. Bankruptcy prediction for SMEs using transactional data and two-stage multiobjective feature selection, *Decision Support Systems* 140:1–14.

He, G.W. & He, J. 2015. Development of e-commerce platform of ABC, *China finance* 20:64–66.

Liu, S.C. 2015. Development characteristics and SWOT analysis of China's banking e-commerce platform, *Southwest finance* 11:32–35.

Ma, L.J. 2016. Building a localized e-commerce platform, rural commercial bank is making waves in the Internet era, *China cooperation times*, September 9.

Wang, F.X. 2018. Impact of Internet Finance on rural credit cooperatives and countermeasures, *Economic & Trade* 22:136.

Wang, H. & Kou, G. & Peng, Y. 2020. Multi-class misclassification cost matrix for credit ratings in peer-to-peer lending, *Journal of the Operational Research Society* 2:1–12.

Wang, J.Y. & Wang, J.M. 2013. Research on the development of e-commerce platform of commercial banks, *Financial Perspectives Journal* 6:86–91.

Zhang, Y.J. & Chen, X.Y. 2019. Research on the Difficulties and Breakthrough Paths of Internet Finance in Rural Credit Cooperatives, *Science & Technology for Development* 01:89–95.

Economic and Business Management – Huang & Zhang (Eds)
© 2022 Copyright the Author(s), ISBN: 978-1-032-06754-4

The impact of consumer perceived value on purchase intention under Blockchain Technology

Dejuan Fu, Chong Wang & Yiwen Deng
School of Business and Tourism, Sichuan Agricultural University, Chengdu, People's Republic of China

ABSTRACT: This paper takes Sichuan consumers who have bought commodities in Tmall global after 2018 as the research object and takes Blockchain Technology and online shopping as the research background From the perspective of supply chain information integration, this paper analyzed the perceived value of consumers under Blockchain Technology and established a structural equation model to explore the relationship among perceived value, consumer trust and purchase intention.

1 INTRODUCTION

With the popularity of online shopping, consumers are not only enjoying convenience but also worried about fake and shoddy goods. Especially in recent years, consumers are gradually losing confidence in online shopping. The reason is that the information in the supply chain is distorted due to the lack of information integration Yan Yong (2017) pointed out that the emergence of Blockchain Technology can overcome information asymmetry to a large extent, effectively solve the problem of fake and shoddy goods and accountability [1], and then reduce consumers' concerns about online shopping. At present, Blockchain Technology is widely used in the field of overseas purchase. In early 2018, Tmall global announced that it would apply Blockchain Technology to commodity traceability. In collaboration with the government, China Inspection Group and China Institute of Standardization established a set of globally recognized traceability standards cooperation mechanism. Through effective information integration, it will realize information transparency and reduce the import of fake and shoddy commodities, to a certain extent and also it brings added value to consumers. However, whether this value is perceived by consumers and whether it can improve their purchase intention is rarely explored by academia. Therefore, this paper takes Tmall global as an example, and from the perspective of supply chain information integration, regards consumer perceived value as a comprehensive embodiment of the supply chain information integration and studies its impact on purchase intention; this paper also introduces the intermediary variable of consumer trust to explore the role of consumer trust between perceived value and purchase intention under the Blockchain Technology.

2 THEORETICAL ANALYSIS AND HYPOTHESIS

In academic circles, many scholars have done a lot of research on the relationship between perceived value and purchase intention. The dimension of perceived value is different because of the different research background. Kim byoungsoo (2020) divides perceived value into three dimensions: functional value, hedonic value and social value [2]; Li Jiamin (2020) and others divide the perceived value into functional value, symbolic value, experiential value, economic value, perceived risk and other dimensions when exploring the perceived value of consumers to the brand [3]. Few scholars divide the dimensions based on the background of online shopping under the Blockchain Technology. Therefore, based on this background, this paper divides consumer perceived value into service value, convenience value, knowledge value and security value. By building a theoretical model, as shown in Figure 1, this paper introduces the intermediary variable of consumer trust, and studies the influence of each dimension of consumer perceived value on purchase intention under Blockchain Technology, and then provides suggestions for enterprise marketing decision-making.

2.1 Consumer perceived value and purchase intention under Blockchain Technology

Usually, after purchasing goods or services, consumers will make an overall evaluation of the goods by weighing the benefits and costs, which is the perceived value. Ni Ziyin (2003) said that consumer perceived value is a subjective evaluation of products and services [4]. Based on the previous definition of perceived value,

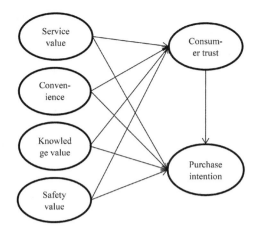

Figure 1. The model of this study.

this paper defines perceived value as the comprehensive evaluation of Tmall global under the information integration of Blockchain Technology supply chain. Purchase intention refers to consumers' willingness to pay for a product or service. Xu Zaiquan (2020) pointed out that when consumers have higher perceived value, they tend to increase their purchase intention [5]. Melly kurnia pratiwi et al (2020) pointed out that good perceived value of products will generate purchase intention [6]. Based on this, the research hypothesis is put forward as follows:

H1: Consumer perceived value has a significant positive impact on purchase intention under Blockchain Technology

Service value and purchase intention. Service value is the service experience that enterprises bring to consumers which use Blockchain Technology, including service quality, efficiency and so on. When the server can timely and enthusiastically answer consumers' questions, and the platform can timely launch high-quality products according to consumers' needs under Blockchain Technology, consumers will feel better service experience, and the possibility of purchase will increase.

Convenience value and purchase intention. Convenience value refers to the convenience for customers to purchase products or services, including logistics convenience, payment convenience, information convenience, and so on. When consumers have more channels to learn about commodity information and have more options on payment and logistics under Blockchain Technology, consumers will feel more convenient and their purchase intention will be enhanced.

Knowledge value and purchase intention under Blockchain Technology. Knowledge value refers to the new knowledge and education that customers learn in the process of purchasing products or services. Many consumers buy products or services and expect that the products bring them new experience, and they can contact new things and acquire new knowledge by purchasing the products.

Security value and purchase intention under Blockchain Technology. Safety value refers to the quality and security of products and services, transaction environment and transaction information under the online purchase environment. When consumers decide whether to purchase the product, they often consider the security value of the transaction. Only when the safety of products and services, the transaction environment and transaction information is ensured, consumers will be willing to purchase.

Therefore, the following specific research hypotheses are proposed:

H1a: The service value has a significant positive impact on purchase intention under Blockchain Technology.

H1b: The convenience value has a significant positive impact on purchase intention under Blockchain Technology.

H1c: The knowledge value has a significant positive impact on purchase intention under Blockchain Technology.

H1d: The security value has a significant positive impact on purchase intention under Blockchain Technology.

2.2 *The mediating role of consumer trust*

Zeng Hui (2014) and others pointed out that higher consumer's perception of commodity value is conducive to establishing corporate image and influencing consumers' continuous online trust in B2C businesses [7]; Sun Kai (2016) and others conducted research based on the perspective of value relationship, believing that customer perceived quality has a positive impact on consumer trust [8]; Yang Yang (2020) and others believe that consumer perceived value has a significant positive impact on consumer trust [9]. Based on the social exchange theory, whether consumers are willing to buy a product or service depends on the degree of trust. The higher the degree of trust, the stronger the willingness to buy. Li aixiong (2010) and others believe that consumer trust has a significant positive impact on purchase intention [10]. Varinder M. sharmaa et al (2020) studied consumers' online group purchase intention and found that there is a strong relationship between perceived value and consumer trust, and perceived trust has a significant relationship with their willingness to participate in online group buying [11]. Based on this, the following hypotheses are put forward:

H2: Consumer trust plays a mediating role between perceived value and purchase intention under Blockchain Technology.

H2a: Consumer trust plays a mediating role between service value and purchase intention under the Blockchain Technology.

H2b: Consumer trust plays a mediating role between convenience value and purchase intention under Blockchain Technology.

H2c: Consumer trust plays a mediating role between knowledge value and purchase intention under the Blockchain Technology.

H2d: Consumer trust plays a mediating role between security value and purchase intention under Blockchain Technology.

3 RESEARCH DESIGN AND DATA ANALYSIS

3.1 *Concept measurement and data collection*

This paper collects data through questionnaire survey, and the respondents are Sichuan consumers who purchase goods in Tmall global after 2018. Combined with the background of Internet shopping and Blockchain Technology, this paper regards perceived value as the comprehensive embodiment of information integration under Blockchain Technology, and measures it from four dimensions of service value, convenience value, knowledge value and security value. The measurement of the core concept mainly refers to the developed mature scale, which can be used after subtle adjustment. The measurement of service value and knowledge value refers to the research of Wang Lina (2019) [12], the measurement of convenience value refers to the research of Liu Rui (2019) [13], and the measurement of security value is a new dimension based on the background of real online shopping. The reliability and the validity of the measurement items have been tested; the measurement of consumer trust is based on the research results of Fu Anshu (2018) [14]; the measurement of purchase intention refers to the research of Zhou Hanliu (2019) [15]

This paper uses Likert-five scale to investigate consumers. First, the questionnaire was preinvestigated, the ambiguous sentences were modified, and the sentences with similar semantics were combined. After passing the reliability and validity test, the formal questionnaire was formed and implemented. The subjects of this survey are all consumers in Sichuan Province who have bought commodities in Tmall global, and the survey time is from September to December 2020. A total of 211 questionnaires have been collected and 139 valid ones have been used. The specific samples are described as follows

According to the statistical results, 69.06% of female consumers buy goods in Tmall global, more than twice as many as men; 87.77% of the consumers were between 20 and 29 years old, 9.35% were under 19 years old and 2.88% were over 30 years old; in Tmall global, most of the consumers are female college students and company employees, accounting for 56.12% and 17.26% The proportion of consumers in civil servants and other institutions is 8.63% and total proportion of other occupations is 17.99% Therefore, young women are the main consumers in Tmall global.

3.2 *Data analysis*

Firstly, this paper analyzes the reliability and validity of the questionnaire, so as to judge the reliability and validity of the sample data; then SPSSAU is used to test the fitting degree of the model; finally, this paper discusses the relationship among the perceived value dimension and consumer trust and purchase intention through path analysis and intermediary test.

Reliability test of questionnaire. First, according to Cronbach's α, the overall reliability of the questionnaire is 0.864, Cronbach's α of each latent variable coefficients is shown in Table 1. According to the results in Table 1, each Cronbach's α is greater than 0.8, so the questionnaire has good internal consistency.

Table 1. Reliability test of questionnaire.

Measurement variables	Item code	CITC	Cronbach's α
Service value	FWV1	0.630	0.836
	FWV2	0.725	
	FWV3	0.742	
Convenience value	BLV1	0.634	0.813
	BLV2	0.691	
	BLV3	0.692	
Knowledge value	ZSV1	0.701	0.868
	ZSV2	0.767	
	ZSV3	0.780	
Safety value	AQV1	0.655	0.854
	AQV2	0.753	
	AQV3	0.822	
Consumer trust	XR1	0.836	0.912
	XR2	0.832	
	XR3	0.804	
Purchase intention	YY1	0.762	0.873
	YY2	0.771	
	YY3	0.734	

Table 2. Validity test of the questionnaire.

Measurement variables	Item code	KMO	Bartlett	P
Service value	FWV1	0.705	169.342	0.000
	FWV2			
	FWV3			
Convenience value	BLV1	0.713	143.553	0.00
	BLV2			
	BLV3			
Knowledge value	ZSV1	0.727	204.791	0.000
	ZSV2			
	ZSV3			
Safety value	AQV1	0.680	235.632	0.000
	AQV2			
	AQV3			
Consumer trust	XR1	0.739	207.299	0.000
	XR2			
	XR3			
Purchase intention	YY1	0.756	281.894	0.000
	YY2			
	YY3			

Validity test of questionnaire. In this paper, the KMO and Bartlett are calculated by SPSSAU to determine whether the potential variables are suitable for factor analysis. The specific results are shown in Table 2. The KMO of each potential variable and the total KMO value of the questionnaire are all above 0.6, and Bartlett is relatively large. Therefore, it is suitable for factor analysis of each potential variable; then, the aggregation validity and differentiation validity of the questionnaire were tested by confirmatory factor analysis, and from the result shown in Tables 3 and 4, we can find that the AVE of each variable in the table is greater than 0.5, and the CR of each variable is greater than 0.7, which indicates that each variable has better aggregation validity; the square root of AVE of each variable is greater than the correlation coefficient with other variables, so it has better differentiation validity.

Structural equation model fitting analysis. The model fitting indicators are used to test the overall fitting validity of the model. Generally, it is difficult for all indicators to meet the standard. In the study, GFI, RMSEA, RMR, CFI and NFI are used to judge the overall fit of the model. The specific results are shown in Table 5. The index values in the table are in line with the commonly used research standards, indicating that the model as a whole has a good degree of fitting.

Table 5. Model fitting indexes.

Indicators	X^2/df	GFI	RMSEA	RMR	CFI	NNFI
Standard value	<3	>0.9	<0.1	<0.05	>0.9	>0.9
	2.282	0.92	0.96	0.43	0.929	0.910

Table 3. CR and AVE.

Variable name	AVE	CR
Service value	0.641	0.842
Convenience value	0.759	0.813
Knowledge value	0.685	0.867
Safety value	0.678	0.863
Consumer trust	0.776	0.912
Purchase intention	0.695	0.872

Table 4. Pearson correlation coefficient and square root of AVE.

	FWV	BLV	ZSV	AQV	XRV	YYV
Service value	0.811					
Convenience value	0.657	0.871				
Knowledge value	0.670	0.761	0.828			
Safety value	0.689	0.688	0.794	0.823		
Consumer trust	0.671	0.720	0.782	0.801	0.881	
Purchase intention	0.662	0.712	0.809	0.810	0.827	0.839

Path analysis. According to the model fitting results, the model can measure the sample data better, so the data is substituted into the model for further analysis, and the main path coefficient among the variables is obtained. The specific results are shown in Table 6. Service value, convenience value, knowledge value and safety value have significant positive effects on purchasing intention; at the same time, service value, knowledge value and security value have significant positive effects on consumer trust, but convenience value has no significant impact on consumer trust; there is also a significant positive relationship between consumer trust and purchase intention.

Mediating effect test. This paper uses SPSSAU to test the mediating effect. The results show that the mediating effect of consumer trust on the relationship between convenience value and purchase intention is not significant; it plays a partial mediating role in the relationship among service value, knowledge value, security value and purchase intention. The test results are shown in Table 7.

Table 6. Main path coefficient.

X	$\rightarrow$	Y	Coefficient	SE	z	p
Service value	$\rightarrow$	Consumer trust	0.62	0.17	3.564	0.00
Convenience value	$\rightarrow$	Consumer trust	0.086	0.54	1586	0.113
Knowledge value	$\rightarrow$	Consumer trust	0.181	0.54	3.348	0.001
Safety value	$\rightarrow$	Consumer trust	0.563	0.61	9.193	0.00
Service value	$\rightarrow$	Purchase intention	0.044	0.21	2.050	0.40
Convenience value	$\rightarrow$	Purchase intention	0.59	0.27	2.128	0.33
Knowledge value	$\rightarrow$	Purchase intention	0.189	0.055	3.457	0.01
Safety value	$\rightarrow$	Purchase intention	0.277	0.83	3.319	0.001
Consumer trust	$\rightarrow$	Purchase intention	0.361	0.067	5.365	0.00

Note: $\rightarrow$ indicates the path influence relationship

Table 7. Summary of mediating effect test results.

Model	Total effect	Mediating effect [95% BootC]	Direct effect	Test conclusion
①	0.66**	0.022** [−0.014 ~ 0.073]	0.044**	Some intermediaries
②	0.090**	0.031 [−0.004 ~ 0.141]	0.059**	The mediating effect is not significant
③	0.254**	0.065** [0.006 ~ 0.150]	0.189**	Some intermediaries
④	0.480**	0.203** [0.078 ~ 0.352]	0.277***	Some intermediaries

4 CONCLUSION AND ENLIGHTENMENT

Based on the perspective of supply chain information integration under Blockchain Technology, this paper makes an in-depth analysis of consumers' perceived value. By establishing structural equation model and introducing consumer trust as an intermediary variable, this paper studies the impact of various dimensions of perceived value on purchase intention. The results obtained are discussed in the following paragraphs.

The application of Blockchain Technology can promote enterprise information integration and improve consumer perceived value; Blockchain Technology can make information highly shared through decentralization, which provides a way for enterprises to efficiently integrate supply chain information.

Under the application of Blockchain Technology, there is a significant positive relationship between perceived value and purchase intention, security value has the greatest impact on purchase intention Hypothesis 1 is verified. In the information society, the problem of network security directly determines consumers' purchase intention. Only when the trading environment is safe and the information will not be leaked, consumers could buy at ease. In addition, in the context of the epidemic, consumers are also very worried about product safety, and the application of Blockchain Technology can enable consumers to trace the source and ensure product quality and safety.

Consumer trust has no significant mediating effect on the relationship between convenience value and purchase intention, the Hypothesis 2b is not verified. The reason is that when enterprises provide consumers with multiple payment methods and logistics methods under the Blockchain Technology, consumers will not trust the enterprise by enjoying the convenience, but directly affect their purchase intention by perceiving the value brought by the convenience.

Consumers' trust plays a partial mediating role in the relationship among service value, knowledge value, safety value and purchase intention, Hypotheses 2a, 2c, and 2d are verified. When consumers can perceive more security value, service value and knowledge value from the application of Blockchain Technology, consumers' trust will increase, so as to enhance their purchase intention.

To sum up, this paper puts forward the following suggestions: on the one hand, Blockchain Technology is used to maximize the integration of supply chain information, provide consumers with targeted services, deal in time with consumers' opinions and suggestions, provide customers with open and transparent information; in addition, we should also improve the traceability system, provide channels and guarantee for consumers to protect their rights and interests, and let consumers gain experience and knowledge through shopping. At the same time, we should use blockchain information encryption technology to build a safe and reliable trading environment to ensure consumers' information security, so as to improve consumers' perceived value and enhance consumers' trust. On the other hand, while applying new technologies and methods, enterprises should constantly improve the technologies and methods in practice, so as to maximize the value of new technologies and methods and better serve the enterprise management.

5 LIMITATIONS OF THE STUDY

Firstly, most of the respondents are college students and company employees in Chengdu, Sichuan Province, and the research conclusions may not be universal for consumers in other regions; secondly, gender is not taken as an influencing factor for differentiation analysis in the study of perceived value, so the conclusion may be too general

ACKNOWLEDGMENTS

First of all, I would like to thank the editorial team for their hard work in editing and typesetting my articles. Secondly, I would like to thank my tutor for his strong support for our research with the National Natural Science Foundation of China (71972136 and 71602134) and the youth fund for Humanities and Social Sciences Research of the Ministry of Education (17yjc630098 and 19yjc630063) I would also like to thank him for his careful guidance from the beginning of the thesis topic selection to the end of the thesis; thanks for his rigorous academic attitude and pragmatic work style, which set an excellent example for us. Finally, I would like to thank my friends for helping me a lot in the questionnaire stage!

REFERENCES

[1] Yan Yong, Zhao Junhua, Wen Fushuan, et al(2017) , Block chain in energy system: concept, application and prospect *E lectric power construction*, 38(02), 12–20

[2] Kim Byoungsoo, Lee Yoonjae (2020), Effects of Perceived Value and Value Congruence on Loyalty about Products or Services Provided by Social Enterprises: Focused on Commitment and Trust. *Journal of Digital Convergence*, 01(18), 83–92

[3] Li Jiamin, Zhang Xiaofei (2020), The impact of brand perceived value on customers' repurchase intention: the mediating role of customer emotion. *Business economics research*, (18), 63–66

[4] Niziyin (2003), Customer value evaluation and innovation. Economist, (03), 241–242

[5] Xu Zaiquan (2020), The interaction between horizontal trust and consumer decision making: mediated by perceived value. *Business economics research*, (18), 74–77

[6] Melly Kurnia Pratiwi, Handayani Riniastuti, Lalu M,et al (2020), The Effectiveness of Social Media as an Influence on Perceived Value and Consumer Purchase Intentions Y Generation of Women: A Case Study. *Journal of Innovation and Social Science Research*, 07(07), 22–31

[7] Zeng Hui, he Liao gang (2014), Empirical research on consumer's continuous online trust in B2C environment. *Management modernization*, 34(06), 34–36

[8] Sun Kai. Qiu Changbo (2016), Research on customer satisfaction driven model based on value relationship perspective. *Modern management science*, (06), 30–32

[9] Yang Yang, Zhenghua Zhao, Cong Liu, et al (2020), Improvement of Customer Perceived Value under O2O Model. *World Scientific Research Journal*, 10(06), 17–21

[10] Li aixiong, Jiang Wen (2016), The influence of trust on purchase intention in the e-commerce environment of agricultural products – Based on the mediating effect of perceived risk. *Business economics research*, (05), 150–152

[11] Varinder M. Sharmaa, Andreas Kleinb (2020), Consumer perceived value, involvement, trust, susceptibility to interpersonal influence, and intention to participate in online group buying. *Journal of Retailing and Consumer Services*, (52), 1–11

[12] Wang Lina (2019), Research on the influence of customer perceived value on behavior intention of picking leisure agricultural tourism. *M.S. thesis*, Northeast Normal University, Northeast, China

[13] Liu Rui (2019), Research on the relationship between perceived value and behavioral intention of B & B tourists from the perspective of place attachment. *M.S. thesis*, Shandong Normal University, Shandong, China

[14] Fu Anshu (2018), Research on the relationship among online negative comments, business feedback, perceived fairness and consumer trust. *M.S. thesis*, Jilin University, Jilin, China

[15] Zhou Hanliu (2019), Research on the influence of customer perceived value on purchase intention of innovative products. *M.S. thesis*, Hebei University, Hebei, China

Economic and Business Management – Huang & Zhang (Eds)
© *2022 Copyright the Author(s), ISBN: 978-1-032-06754-4*

The impact of policy risk perception in media information on stock markets during epidemic events

Tong Li, Hualong Yu & Guang Yu*
School of Management, Harbin Institute of Technology, Harbin, China

Yongtian Yu
Zhiwei Research Institute, Beijing, China

ABSTRACT: As an important channel for policy information transmission, policy risk perceptions in media information often influence investors through emotions and perceptions, which in turn bring about abnormal capital market movements. This paper investigates the relationship between policy risk perceptions in the media and abnormal stock returns. 25 policy introduction events during the COVID-19 emergency were selected as samples, and the impact of policy risk perceptions in media information on abnormal stock returns was empirically analyzed based on the event study method. It was found that the impact of policy risk perception in media information on the capital market was more significant compared to the number of media reports. Further analysis reveals that policy risk perception in media messages has a significant positive impact on abnormal stock returns on the last day of the event during the policy introduction event, while the impact on cumulative abnormal returns over the entire event period is not significant. The study reveals that the impact of policy risk perception in media messages on the capital market does not follow the development of the event, but is a gradual process of "getting into the hearts and minds"; it also shows that the active and effective use of media communication is important for the transmission and implementation of policies in the event of an epidemic outbreak.

1 INTRODUCTION

COVID-19 is a major public health emergency in China that has occurred with the fastest rate of spread he widest range of infection, and the greatest difficulty in prevention and control since the founding of the country. In order to avoid the further spread of the epidemic, relevant prevention and control measures were introduced one after another: such as strengthening isolation measures, reducing the mass movement and gathering of the population, etc. This also led to a significant drop in social demand, which brought a great impact on economic operation. At the same time, some enterprises and other market micro-entities have poor risk resistance and are vulnerable to secondary risks triggered by the epidemic (Jia Wenqin & Tang Shilei 2020), which in turn generate greater market dislocations. Under this complex and severe situation, governments at all levels have introduced a number of policy measures to combat the spread of the epidemic and ensure the orderly conduct of economic activities, including traffic control requirements, financial support policies, and livelihood protection policies.

It has been shown that policy risk perceptions accompany the release of policies to influence people's behavioral intentions (Li Chenguang et al. 2018). When there is a high degree of uncertainty in information transmission, following the herd becomes a relatively convenient and safe practice because the public is not completely rational, which in turn generates a "herding effect" that brings shocks to the economy. Research on the impact of policy risk perception on economic activities has received extensive attention from scholars since Baker et al. (2016), mostly drawing on or deepening Baker's economic policy uncertainty index based on the frequency of news coverage to explore the impact of the perceived degree of policy risk in media messages on capital markets (Brogaard & Detzel 2015), business operations (Liao et al. 2019), and so on. It has been pointed out that media information can often influence the rational judgment and decision-making of traders through investor sentiment, thus causing abnormal volatility in capital markets (Yu et al. 2013). Therefore, it can be seen that the perception of policy risk in media messages is an important factor in changing investors' beliefs and perceptions.

However, prior studies have mostly focused on the impact of media policy risk perceptions in normal situations, ignoring the differences in the impact of policy

---
*Corresponding Author

222

DOI 10.1201/9781003203704-41

risk perceptions in media messages during emergencies. In normal situations, the media reports policy information with a certain degree of caution, while the public will also be moderately deliberate in receiving relevant information and maintain certain rational characteristics. However, these prudential characteristics fade when emergencies break out. In the case of COVID-19, a large amount of media information has flooded into people's view in a short time, bringing a considerable impact on the cognitive level of the information audience.

In an information environment of high-intensity media engagement and public opinion discussions, any information about the introduction of policies attracts a massive influx of media. The ensuing weakening of the cautionary characteristics of the media and the increasing level of panic among the public in a state of high tension, which in turn leads to a lack of rational judgment among individual investors, complicate the perception of policy risk in media information and the impact it brings. Therefore, exploring policy risk uncertainty in the media and their impacts will be important for achieving the expected policy effects.

In this paper, we focus on the impact of policy risk perception in media information on investment behavior, and explore the relationship between policy transmission efficiency and capital market dislocation. We use 25 policy introduction events during the COVID-19 epidemic as a sample, and obtain 59,672 media messages related to these events through data crawlers; then we construct a measurement of policy risk perception in media messages based on text analysis techniques; at the same time, we will empirically test the impact of the degree of policy risk perception on abnormal stock returns during an event window based on the event study method. It is found that policy risk perception in media messages has a significant positive impact on abnormal stock returns on the last day of the event window during the policy introduction period, however, it does not have a significant impact on cumulative abnormal returns during the whole event window period, which to some extent indicates that policy risk perception in media messages affects the efficiency of policy delivery. Unlike existing studies, the effect of the number of articles reported in the media on abnormal stock returns during the event period is not significant; suggesting that the perception of policy risk in media content is more important for effective policy transmission in major unexpected events compared to the number of media reports.

With the continuous innovation of Internet technology, an in-depth analysis of policy risk perception based on media information in the rapidly developing media environment has certain theoretical and practical significance. The possible contributions of this paper are: first, theoretically, it makes up for the lack of research on policy risk perception derived from media information in major emergency situations, which complements the research in the field of policy risk perception, and also provides a new perspective for policy effect research. Secondly, in practice, it has a certain guiding reference value for how to construct a more effective policy delivery strategy in major emergencies, so as to enhance people's awareness of the policy and improve the efficiency of policy delivery. We explored the characteristics of media wording in the policy delivery process, and point out that more uncertainty in wording brings higher abnormal returns.

2 BACKGROUND AND RELATED WORK

2.1 *Media information and risk perception*

The media control the content of the information the audience receive, they disseminate the relevant events themselves and also convey the information with certain value tendencies to the audience, who are unconsciously influenced by the information from the media and transform it into their personal cognitive level in the process of internalization (Lang Jingsong & Hou Yuejuan 2004).

Risk perception can be regarded as a level of people's perception of risk. In emergencies, the dissemination process of Internet public opinion information is essentially a cognitive process in which people's perceptions and opinions about risk information are exchanged (Liu Jianzhun et al. 2019). The Internet medium is an important thrust for changes in public risk perception (Wang Zhiying et al. 2018). The media play an important role in the process of risk formation, and the media further influence potential risk perceptions by influencing people's irrational fears to some extent through the content they report. Gigerenzer (Gerd 2004) suggested that higher risk perceptions can lead to irrational decision-making behavior. It has been shown that gradually increasing negative emotions in an emergency situation will increase the irrational behavior of individuals, which will further escalate the emergency (Wang Zhiying et al. 2018).

2.2 *Policy risk perception in media messages*

In 2016, Baker constructed an index of economic policy uncertainty using the frequency of media coverage (Baker et al. 2016), which has received much attention. The connotation of economic policy uncertainty can be explained as the various types of unpredictable components contained in future economy-related policy changes, and the forms of uncertainty include the likelihood of future policy changes, the frequency of changes, the content of changes, and the changes in the manner of implementation and the effects of implementation. The creation of this index has made an outstanding contribution to the effective quantification of economic policy uncertainty, and the continuous quantification results obtained by searching the media content and counting the number of reports related to economic policy uncertainty among them have been widely used by academics.

Scholars have conducted numerous studies by citing an index of economic policy uncertainty constructed based on the frequency of media coverage, which has been shown to have an impact on macroeconomic trends (Gholipour 2019), stock market volatility (Brogaard and Detzel 2015), and enterprise risk management (Liao et al. 2019) all have some impact.

2.3 The impact of media information on stock market

Scholars have mostly approached the issue from two perspectives. First, the amount of media information: Fang and Peress (2009) examined the relationship between media coverage and stock prices using media coverage as the research objective, and the number of times a firm is mentioned as a proxy for the firm's level of media exposure, and the study found that highly exposed firms have lower stock returns than neglected firms, which in turn illustrates the need for stocks with low perception to provide a higher rate of return to compensate for the perceived market risk borne by their holders. Second, news content: Tetlock (2011) characterizes the information content of news by comparing text similarity to determine whether the news content is stale; the study found that stock prices reflect stale information relatively mildly, which the less value the information contains, the less impact the information has on the stock price. Barber and Odean (2008) revealed the function of media in terms of how investors allocate their attention, arguing that the media affects investors' access to information and ultimately influences their behavior by affecting their attention. Da et al. (2011) found that an increase in search volume, using search index as a proxy variable for internet user's attention, will cause an increase in future returns for this stock.

3 METHOD

3.1 Research framework

We proposed the research framework of this paper, and by collecting media information data as well as stock data, we measure policy uncertainty in media news and empirically analyze policy uncertainty and abnormal stock returns based on event study approach.

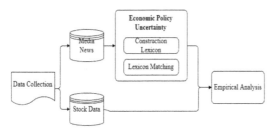

Figure 1. Research framework.

3.2 Data collection

In this paper, we collected 25 policy events about COVID-19 government initiatives, during the period of January 21, 2020 to March 3, 2020, and the media information data sources we obtained included online media, Weibo platforms, and WeChat public accounts, with a total of 59,672 data obtained. Among them, data from online media and WeChat public accounts are long text articles, and data from the Weibo platform re short articles. The sample distribution is shown in Table 1.

Table 1. Media information source distribution.

Data Source Platform	The number of articles	The number of words in articles
Online media	23,439	39,390,133
Weibo platform	18,772	3,207,149
WeChat public accounts	17,461	33,210,430
Total	59,672	75,807,712

This paper selected listed companies in the A-share market as object, and after excluding ST and *ST companies, a total of 2785 listed companies were selected as the sample. The stock trading data and market index data used in this paper were obtained from the CSMAR database.

3.3 Policy risk perception measurement

Media influences the degree of perception. The economic policy uncertainty index constructed by Baker et al. (2016) based on the frequency of media coverage seeks to capture the uncertainty embodied in media coverage, including who will make policy decisions, what policy actions will be taken and when they will be implemented, the economic impact resulting from the policy actions, and the uncertainty caused by the policy inaction, reflecting exactly the perceived policy risk in media information that this paper attempts to measure. Therefore, the measurement of policy risk perceptions in this paper will follow the measurement strategy of the Economic Policy Uncertainty Index.

The measurement of economic policy uncertainty method based on the frequency of media coverage effectively combines natural language processing techniques, thus enabling the processing of massive text information. Among the 59,672 data we obtained, the text word count reached 7.58 million, which can be applied to the measurement method of economic policy uncertainty indicators. We used text analysis techniques to identify whether the content of articles is related to policy uncertainty, so as to calculate the number of media articles discussing policy uncertainty and obtain the results of policy uncertainty with specified measurement dimensions (time period or event range).

First, we reconstructed the Chinese dictionary of policy uncertainty by referring to the keyword lists constructed by Baker et al. (2016) and Huang and Luk (2020). Among them, the category of "policy" mainly includes expressions related to national policy and fiscal policy; the category of "uncertainty" mainly includes Chinese expressions similar to the word "uncertainty/".

Next, we analyzed the full text of media information, and marked the article as policy uncertainty related if it contains both of the terms in the categories of "policy" and "uncertainty". Then, we calculated the policy uncertainty index of each event, i.e., the number of policy uncertainty-related articles measured is used as the numerator, and the total number of articles for each policy event is used as the denominator, so as to calculate the perceived policy risk of each policy event. The calculation formula is shown in equation (1).

$$EPU_{event\ i} = \frac{the\ number\ of\ EPU\ articles\ in\ Event\ i}{the\ number\ of\ total\ articles\ in\ Event\ i} \quad (1)$$

3.4 Empirical analysis methods

We used an event study approach to examine the short-term impact on stock returns due to policy risk perception during the epidemic.

First, we measured abnormal returns. We chose an estimation window of [0-60, 0], i.e., the 60 days prior to the event date as the period for estimating normal returns; the time of the obtained media information released was used as the event window, i.e., the period from the beginning to the end of the media coverage was used as the period for testing abnormal returns, the event window in our dataset is [0, n] if the event has been reported on media over n days. Next, the market model is used to forecast the normal return, which is the return that would be expected if the event did not occur. The formula is: $R_{it} = \alpha_i + \beta_i R_{mt} + \varepsilon$, where R_{it} is the normal return of stock i at moment t and R_{mt} is the market index return at the corresponding moment t. The coefficients $\hat{\alpha}_i$ and $\hat{\beta}_i$ are obtained by the least squares method for the stock transactions in the estimation period. Then, the abnormal return of each stock in event window is calculated: $AR_{it} = R_{it} - \hat{\alpha}_i - \hat{\beta}_i R_{mt}$, which is the difference between the actual return and the normal return of the stock for each day during the period. When the abnormal returns of stocks for each day in the event window were accumulated, the cumulative abnormal return of the sample can be obtained: $CAR_t = \sum_{t=1}^{n} AR_{it}$.

Finally, we tested the shocks of stock returns due to perceived policy risk in media information. We separately analyzed the abnormal returns and cumulative abnormal returns for the last day in event window and test the model as follow:

$$CAR_i = \alpha_i + \beta_i News\_num_i + \beta_i EPU_i + \beta_c Controls_i$$
$$+ \varepsilon_t \quad \text{(Model-1)}$$

$$AR_i = \alpha_i + \beta_i News\_num_i + \beta_i EPU_i + \beta_c Controls_i$$
$$+ \varepsilon_t \quad \text{(Model-2)}$$

In Model 1, we tested for the cumulative abnormal return in event window, where CAR_i denotes the cumulative abnormal return of event i in event window, $News\_num_i$ denotes the number of media coverage of event i, and EPU_i denotes the perceived policy risk of event i. In Model 2, we tested for the abnormal return on the last day of event window, where AR_i denotes the abnormal return of event i on the last day of event window. Meanwhile, we selected the number of stock trading, trading amount, and market capitalization outstanding as the control variables in the model. The key variables involved in this paper are shown in Table 2.

Table 2. Variables description.

Variable Name	Variable Type	Variable Definition
$News\_num_{eventi}$	Independent variable	The number of media coverage related to event i
EPU_{eventi}	Independent variable	Perceived policy risk of event i (percentage of media coverage that include the words "policy" and "uncertainty")
CAR_i	Dependent variable	Cumulative abnormal stock returns of event i in the event window
AR_i	Dependent variable	Abnormal stock returns of event i in the event window
$Trade\_num_t$	Control variable	Average of the number of individual shares traded at time t
$Trade\_price_t$	Control variable	Average value of individual stock trades at time t
$Market\_value_t$	Control variable	Average of the market capitalization of individual stocks outstanding at time t

4 EMPIRICAL RESULTS

4.1 Risk perception of policy release

We measured the policy risk perception of 25 events based on the measurement mentioned above, and obtained the policy uncertainty results for each event as shown in Figure 2. What can be seen is that media reflect different policy uncertainties in different types of policy events, such as: "Central Bank: China will not experience massive inflation", "Ministry of Transport activates Level II emergency response" and other related financial initiatives, policy events that have a significant impact on the development of economic activities reflect higher policy uncertainty; while the policy events related to livelihood policies and stable economic development, such as "the General Office of the State Council issued an urgent notice on the organization of arrangements for the resumption of work of key material production enterprises for epidemic prevention and control" and "Wuhan City set up a special inspection group to inspect the situation that patients 'should live as much as possible'," have a low perception of policy risk.

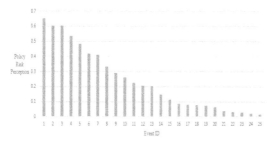

Figure 2. Measure results of policy risk perception.

4.2 Descriptive statistical analysis

Table 3 shows a descriptive analysis of variables. It can be seen that the average number of media coverage per event is 2386.88, among which the least number of media reports is 38 and the most is 23,745; in terms of sample distribution, most of the events have around 2000 coverages.

Table 3. Descriptive results.

Variable Name	Mean	Sd.	Min	Max
News_num$_{eventi}$	2386.88	4802.04	38	23745
EPU$_{event\ i}$	0.241	0.2088	0.0139	0.6549
R_{it}	0.0014	0.0186	−0.0898	0.0415
R_{mt}	0.0006	0.0161	−0.0788	0.0329
AR_i	0.0009	0.0114	−0.0342	0.02

4.3 Findings

This paper focuses on the effect of policy risk perception on investment behavior, and Table 4 shows the test results of the model. In Model 1, the cumulative abnormal returns during the event window were examined as the dependent variable, column (1) contains only control variables, column (2) added the number of media coverage to the former, and column (3) added the policy risk perception. The

Table 4. The impact of policy risk perception on investment behavior.

Variable	Model-1_CAR (1)	(2)	Model-2_AR (3)	(4)
EPU$_{event\ i}$			0.102 (1.03)	0.777** (2.58)
News_num$_{eventi}$		−0.019 (−0.36)	−0.006 (−0.10)	−0.235 (−1.41)
Trade_num	−4.945** (−3.23)	−5.119** (−3.00)	−5.091** (−3.00)	−10.669* (−2.08)
Trade_price	4.372** (3.19)	4.514** (2.97)	4.412** (2.91)	9.845* (2.15)
Market_value	0.438*** (5.14)	0.446*** (4.76)	0.483*** (4.83)	−0.026 (−0.09)
Cons	−0.602*** (−4.08)	−0.486 (−1.34)	−0.428 (−1.17)	0.827 (0.75)
r^2	0.873	0.876	0.898	0.792

* p < 0.1, ** p < 0.05, *** p < 0.01

results show that neither the number of media coverage generated with policy events nor the policy risk perception has a significant effect on the cumulative abnormal stock returns during the event period.

In Model 2, the abnormal stock return on the last day of the event window is used as the dependent variable, and column (4) tested for the inclusion of the number of media coverage and the perception of policy risk. The results show that the number of media coverage does not have an effect on the abnormal stock return on the last day of the event window, while the perception of policy risk during the event has an effect on the abnormal return on the last day of the event window and is significantly positive at the 5% level (0.777). It can be seen that even though there is a lot of media information about policies, it is the perception of policy risk in media messages, which have the content of expressions of policy uncertainty, that really has an impact on the stock market. From the analysis, it can be obtained that the higher frequency of the words of policy uncertainty expressed by the media leads to a stronger panic psychology among the recipients of the information, which has a certain impact on the cognitive ability and investment sentiment of the public; and further mapped to the investment behavior, the higher the abnormal return of the stock market, which in turn affects to some extent the effect of the policies related to stabilizing the economic order introduced during the epidemic period.

From the results above, it can be seen that, on the one hand, the quantity of media information does not have a significant effect on investment behavior, indicating that in the process of policy transmission, even if the number of articles is increased and the massive amount of media information is flooded into people's view, it does not bring about the effect of stock price fluctuations as a result; however, the policy uncertainty embodied in the media content has a significant effect on stock market fluctuations, indicating that in the process of policy transmission, the perception of policy risk has an impact on stabilizing the economic order. On the other hand, the perception of policy risk has a significant positive effect on abnormal returns on the last day of the event window, but not on cumulative abnormal returns during the event period; one possible explanation is that media messages require a dissemination process, and similarly, the perception of policy risk does not immediately affect the psychology and behavior of the public, and does not influence investment behavior throughout the media coverage period.

5 CONCLUSIONS

We analyzed the impact of policy risk perceptions on investment, and explored how policies are effectively delivered during the COVID-19 epidemic. 25 policy events during the epidemic were selected as samples, and the policy risk perception during different events was analyzed by measuring whether the media content contained words related to policy uncertainty; and the impact of policy risk perception on abnormal stock returns during the event window was further verified.

The study found that the perception of policy risk in media has a significant positive impact on the abnormal returns on the last day of the event window, and the higher the perception of policy risk, the greater the abnormal stock returns. However, the impact of policy risk perception on cumulative abnormal returns during the entire event window is not significant, reflecting the fact that media messages gradually penetrate to influence people's perceptions and behaviors during the transmission process.

Based on the above analysis, it can be seen that in emergencies, ensuring the timely and accurate transmission of policy content is important for effective policy implementation and will greatly reduce the negative impact caused by emergencies. Therefore, government departments should not ignore whether the process of information transmission and communication will bring about such "information gap" phenomenon as bias, suspicion, and distrust. In order to effectively ensure rapid adaptation in public emergencies, government departments must coordinate with the media and the public in order to better address the perception of negative risks and abnormal market fluctuations in the process of policy transmission.

It is worth noted that since media information transmission is an abstract process, how it is done for individual investors' trading behavior requires more in-depth research on mediating effect and moderating effect in the future. So as to better explore how media information affects investors' behavior.

ACKNOWLEDGMENT

This research was supported by the National Natural Science Foundation of China (71531013 and 71774041). We also thank Zhiwei Data for data support of this study.

REFERENCES

Baker S R, Bloom N, Davis S J. Measuring Economic Policy Uncertainty[J]. *Quarterly Journal of Economics*, 2016, 131(4): 1593–1636.

Barber B M, Odean T. All That Glitters: The Effect of Attention and News on the Buying Behavior of Individual and Institutional Investors[J]. *The Review of Financial Studies*, 2008, 21(2).

Brogaard J, Detzel A. The Asset-Pricing Implications of Government Economic Policy Uncertainty[J]. *Management Science*, 2015, 61(1): 3–18.

Da Z, Engelberg, Gao P. In search of attention [J]. *The journal of Finance*, 2011, 66(5): 1461–1499.

Dyck A, Zingales L. Private Benefits of Control: An International Comparison[J]. *The Journal of Finance*, 2004, 59(2).

Fang L, Peress J. Media Coverage and the Cross-section of Stock Returns[J]. *The Journal of Finance*, 2009, 64(5).

Gerd G. Dread risk, September 11, and fatal traffic accidents. [J]. *Psychological science*, 2004, 15(4).

Gholipour H F. The effects of economic policy and political uncertainties on economic activities[J]. *Research in International Business and Finance*, 2019, 48: 210–218.

Huang Y, Luk P. Measuring economic policy uncertainty in China[J]. *China Economic Review*, 2020, 59.

Jia Wenqin, Tang Shilei. Analysis of the Macroeconomic Impact of COVID-19 Epidemic and Policy Recommendations[J]. *China Development*. 2020, 20(01): 1–3.

Lang Jinsong, Hou Yuejuan. Modern political communication and press release system [J]. *Modern Communication(Journal of Communication University of China)*. 2004(03): 34–37.

Li Chenguang, Zhang Yongan, Wang Yanni. The Influence of Policy Perception and Decision-making Preferences on Intention of Innovation Policy Response[J]. *Science of Science and Management of S.& T.* 2018, 39(5): 3–15.

Liao F, Ji X, Wang Z. Firms' Sustainability: Does Economic Policy Uncertainty Affect Internal Control?[J]. *Sustainability*, 2019,11(7943).

Liu Jianzhun, Shi Mi, Liu Chunlei. Semantic Graph of Net Citizens' Information Perception on Network Group Emergencies[J]. *Information Studies: Theory & Application*. 2019, 42(02): 158–163.

Manela A, Moreira A. News implied volatility and disaster concerns[J]. *Journal of Financial Economics*, 2017, 123(1).

Tetlock. P C. All the News That's Fit to Reprint: Do Investors React to Stale Information?[J]. *The Review of Financial Studies*, 2011(24(5)): 1481–1512.

Wang Zhiying, Liang Jing, Liu Xiaodi. A Review of Risk Perception of Public in Emergencies[J]. *Journal of Intelligence*. 2018, 37(10): 161–166.

Yu Y, Duan W, Cao Q. The impact of social and conventional media on firm equity value: A sentiment analysis approach[J]. *Decision Support Systems*, 2013, 55(4):919–926.

Economic and Business Management – Huang & Zhang (Eds)
© 2022 Copyright the Author(s), ISBN: 978-1-032-06754-4

The offsetting role of diversification for negative impact of COVID-19 on firm performance: Evidence from China

Feiyang Guan & Tienan Wang
Harbin Institute of Technology, China

ABSTRACT: This paper selects Chinese listed companies as samples to examine how diversification moderates the impact of COVID-19 on firm performance according to firm size, firm nature, and slack resource. The present study finds diversification offsets the negative relationship between COVID-19 and firm performance and abundant slack resources can help firms offset the negative effects of COVID-19 through diversification. The diversification of non-state-owned firms offsets more obviously the negative relationship between COVID-19 and firm performance. Contrary to our hypothesis, the diversification of large firms in China cannot offset the COVID-19 crisis.

Keywords: COVID-19, diversification, firm size, firm nature, slack resource; China

1 INTRODUCTION

The sudden emergence of COVID-19 in 2020 has a long duration and a wide range of effects on the socio-economic and brings unprecedented impact to all industries. From the change of total retail sales of consumer goods released by the National Bureau of Statistics of China in 2020, it can be seen that both the total retail sales of consumer goods and the total retail sales of consumer goods of business above the designated size showed a sharp decline trend in March of 2020. COVID-19 has indeed caused a relatively large impact on the Chinese economy, but the above indicators have rebounded after a sharp decline. About 30 provinces in China launched a first-level response to deal with this sudden public health event, including extending the Chinese New Year holiday, putting off the start of school, and returning to work, therefore, COVID-19 in China is under control. As can be seen from Figure 3, the cumulative number of newly diagnosed patients in China has been controlled after the rapid increase, and the number of newly diagnosed patients has also been controlled after March, laying a foundation for work resumption.

According to the resource-based theory, diversification strategy can not only disperse operational risks but also establish an effective internal capital market, thus breaking through the financing constraints of the external capital market and realizing economies of scale. However, some studies believe that diversification will disperse the limited resources of a firm to different business units, which makes organizational management within the firm became very difficult. The establishment of the internal capital market to allocate the limited resources of the firm is likely to cause over-investment or under-investment, which reducing the

investment efficiency, increasing the business risks, and destroying firm value (Barry & Bateman 1996; He 2012). Therefore, there is still no fixed conclusion as to whether diversification is beneficial to firms. However, many firms have alleviated the pressure caused by the COVID-19 through diversification strategies. During the epidemic, in addition to passively adapting to changes in the environment, firms tried to reduce expenses, some firms actively engaged in open source activities through cross-industry operations. Due to the huge demand for face masks, SAIC-GM-Wuling Automobile turned its spare factory into a production workshop to make face masks and became the first automobile firm to make face masks all over the world. Foxconn, Sinopec, PetroChina, Country Garden, Midea, BYD, and other firms have followed suit. However, the expediency of these firms in a special period does not mean that the firm must implement a diversification strategy. In the era of rapid development of artificial intelligence, blockchain, cloud computing, and big data, diversification strategy without core competitiveness will bring greater risks to firms. Diversification is a double-edged coin. Therefore, whether a firm is suitable for the diversification strategy should be considered according to the external environment and the internal environment of the firm.

2 HYPOTHESES

The COVID-19 spreads rapidly and becomes a sudden force majeure event in the economic operation. With the economy facing tremendous downward pressure, the epidemic has brought many problems and challenges to business management. COVID-19 has led to declining orders, putting off work resumption, staffing shortages, overburdened fixed costs, supply chain disruptions, market supply, and demand declining, credit and debt risks, and then hurts the performance of most firms (Kano & Oh 2020; Mahajan & Tomar 2021). Restricting population movement and delaying to return to work hurt the supply side, resulting in the insufficient use of firm resources. Traffic control causes the rise of logistics costs, which leads to the decline of firm performance. Therefore, we propose the following hypothesis.

H1: COVID-19 has a negative effect on firm performance.

Compared with diversified firms, firms with the single and inflexible business model are more likely to fail under an emergency public health event. The diversification of products, services, and sales channels is the most powerful way to combat the epidemic (Andreou et al. 2016). In addition to the diversification of business models, cross-industry development is also a way for firms to help themselves during the epidemic period. We believe that diversification can offset the negative impact of COVID-19 on firms. Because not all industries are affected by COVID-19, a diversified product portfolio is advantageous. Different industries have shown varying degrees of resilience, and we find that diversified firms were less affected by the COVID-19 than concentrated ones. Therefore, we propose the following hypothesis.

H2: Diversification offsets the negative effect of COVID-19 on firm performance.

Since the founding of New China, state-owned firms gradually spread across all industries. State-owned firms have long grasped the lifeline of Chinese economy. Compared with non-state-owned firms, state-owned firms face more constraints and restrictions and have less discretion. Compared with non-state-owned firms, state-owned firms are often subject to government intervention, including the appointment of senior managers, leading the mergers and acquisitions between state-owned firms or between state-owned firms and non-state-owned firms, and taking on more social responsibility (Sanchez et al. 2017). Therefore, this has led to the following problems for state-owned firms. Firstly, low market competition will lead to low innovation ability and efficiency of state-owned firms (Lv et al. 2019; Zhou et al. 2017). Second, compared with non-state-owned firms, state-owned firms are not only for profit and efficiency but also for many social functions, such as people's livelihood, employment, and social responsibility, which are not beneficial to the effective accumulation of resources and thus to the implementation of diversification (Sanchez et al. 2017; Tang et al. 2020). Third, if the future demand of a firm's product market is too uncertain to predict accurately, the firm may look for other ways to spread the risk. Therefore, we propose the following hypothesis.

H3: Compared with state-owned firms, the diversification of non-state-owned firms has a more positive offsetting effect on the negative relationship between COVID-19 and firm performance.

Firm size is not only a result of diversification but also an important stimulus for diversification. The larger the firm size, the more unutilized resources it contains and the more kinds of resources it can use for other undertakings. For example, the State Grid of China, the third-largest company in China, has expanded to financial fields such as investment, insurance, trust, and securities, as well as related equipment manufacturing. Its subsidiary firms cover coal, transportation, hotel, real estate, and education, etc., forming a relatively diversified operation pattern. After years of production and operation, large firms of China, driven by the pressure of market competition, have a perfect system and a higher reputation. Therefore, large firms have diversified advantages compared with small firms.

H4: Compared with small firms, the diversification of large firms has a more positive offsetting effect on the negative relationship between COVID-19 and firm performance.

A necessary condition for firms to implement diversification strategies is the availability of slack resources (Hauschild & Knyphausen-Aufsess 2013; Nasiriyar et al. 2014; Sakhartov 2017). The slack resources include not only sufficient capital strength and talent reserve but also enough energy for decision-makers to engage in research, development and management of new industries. What type and how much of a firm's resources can be used to implement diversification strategies must be based on the products and market segments to be entered, as different products and market segments have different resource requirements (Nath et al. 2010; Wan et al. 2011). Therefore, we believe that no matter what type of slack resources will promote the diversification of firms. The more slack resources a firm has, the more likely it is to succeed in diversification. Therefore, we propose the following hypothesis.

H5: Compared with firms with insufficient slack resources, diversification of firms with abundant slack resources has a more positive offsetting effect on the negative relationship between COVID-19 and firm performance.

3 METHODOLOGY

This paper selects Chinese listed companies from 2016 to 2020 as the research samples. Listed financial companies and companies that were ST and PT for two consecutive years during the study years were excluded. After filtering, this paper finally obtained 3173 samples. Variables are defined as follows. Firstly, this paper counted the year when COVID-19 occurred as 1 and the year when it did not occur as 0. Secondly, according to the existing research, Tobin Q as dependent variables is used to measure firm performance. Thirdly, we mainly choose two indexes to represent diversification: the income entropy index and the number of industries accounting for more than 10% of the main business revenue, and the number of industries accounting for more than 10% of main revenue used for robustness testing. Fourthly, we measure firm size by the natural logarithm of its total assets (Munjal et al. 2019). And then, we use the liquidity ratio to measure the slack resources of a firm. Fifth, referencing the research of Zhu and Yoshikawa, this paper uses a dummy variable to measure state-owned companies (Zhu & Yoshikawa 2016). It is considered to be a non-state-owned company with a value of 0. Finally, growth, age asset-liability ratio, industry, and year are selected as the control variables according to the existing studies and the needs of our study. This paper uses STATA for data analysis.

4 RESULTS

Table 1 shows that regression coefficient of COVID-19 is negative, indicating that compared with the non-occurrence of COVID-19, firm performance declines after COVID-19 occurs (M1, $\beta = -0.319$, $p < .01$). Table 1 also shows that diversification has a negative moderating effect on the relationship between COVID-19 and firm performance (M2, $\beta = 0.073$, $p < .05$). Hypothesis 1 and 2 is supported. Table 2 shows the offsetting effect of state-owned firms' diversification on the negative impact of COVID-19 on firm performance. The interaction coefficient between COVID-19 and diversification is not significant (M3, $\beta = -0.001$, $p > .1$). Table 2 also shows the offsetting effect of non-state firms' diversification on the negative impact of COVID-19 on firm performance. The interaction coefficient between COVID-19 is significant (M4, $\beta = 0.1$, $p > .05$). Compared with state-owned firms, the diversification of non-state-owned firms has a stronger offsetting effect on COVID-19 and firm performance. Therefore, hypothesis 3 is supported.

Table 1. The moderating effect of diversification.

Variables	Tobin Q M1	Tobin Q M2
COVID-19	−0.319***	−0.278***
	(0.048)	(0.065)
Diversification		−0.112***
		(0.011)
COVID-19* Diversification		0.073*
		(0.042)
Age	−0.007	0.002
	(0.010)	(0.010)
Growth	0.014	0.013
	(0.010)	(0.009)
Lev	−0.139***	−0.129***
	(0.011)	(0.011)
Constants	0.385***	0.384***
	(0.022)	(0.022)
Industry	Control	Control
Year	Control	Control
R^2	0.154	0.164
Adj R^2	0.146	0.156
F	100.26***	91.09***

Note: Coefficients shown with p values reported in brackets, * $p < .1$, **$p < .05$, *** $p < .01$.

Table 2. Synergistic effect of nature on diversification.

Variables	Tobin Q State M3	Tobin Q Non-state M4
COVID-19	−0.236***	−0.291***
	(0.081)	(0.084)
Diversification	−0.053***	−0.123***
	(0.015)	(0.014)
COVID-19* Diversification	−0.001	0.100*
	(0.054)	(0.054)
Age	0.020	0.022*
	(0.017)	(0.013)
Growth	0.004	0.013
	(0.016)	(0.012)
Lev	−0.145***	−0.106***
	(0.016)	(0.013)
Constants	0.045***	0.537***
	(0.029)	(0.028)
Industry	Control	Control
Year	Control	Control
R^2	0.185	0.242
Adj R^2	0.160	0.232
F	23.98***	71.41***

Note: Coefficients shown with p values reported in brackets, * $p < .1$, **$p < .05$, *** $p < .01$.

Model 5 shows that large firms are less likely to use diversification to suppress the negative effects of COVID-19 on firm performance than small firms ($\beta = -0.102$, $p < .05$). Model 6 shows that diversification of firms with abundant slack resources has a stronger offsetting effect on the negative relationship between COVID-19 and firm performance ($\beta = 0.092$, $p < .1$). Therefore, hypothesis 4 and 5 is supported.

5 CONCLUSION

The empirical results show that COVID-19 negatively impacts firm performance, and diversification offsets the negative impact of COVID-19 on firm performance. Slack resources help firms offset the negative effects of COVID-19 through diversification. Compared with state-owned firms, the diversification of non-state-owned firms has a stronger offsetting effect on the negative relationship between COVID-19 and firm performance. To our surprise, the synergistic effect of firm size on diversification is contrary to the hypothesis. This may be because when the firm size is large enough in the Chinese market, the risks of diversification are not market risks and external risks, but more likely systemic risk caused by a firm's strategic mistakes. Driven by capital, the so-called diversification of many Chinese firms has become distorted and extensive. In particular, we find under the background of China's response to the COVID-19, two large firms in China, Founder Group and HNA Group, have been reorganized due to excessive diversification driven by capital leverage. Instead of effectively integrating to

Table 3. Synergistic effect of firm size and slack resources on diversification.

Variables	Tobin Q M5	Tobin Q M6
COVID-19	−0.238***	−0.284***
	(0.061)	(0.064)
Diversification	−0.230***	−0.110***
	(0.010)	(0.011)
Size	−0.414***	
	(0.011)	
Slack resources		0.095***
		(0.012)
COVID-19* Diversification	0.054	0.083*
	(0.041)	(0.042)
Diversification* Size	0.081***	
	(0.010)	
Diversification*Slack resources		−0.054***
		(0.011)
COVID-19*Size	0.207***	
	(0.056)	
COVID-19* Slack resources		0.080
		(0.072)
COVID-19* Diversification* Size	−0.102**	
	(0.040)	
COVID-19*Diversification* Slack resources		0.092*
		(0.056)
Age	0.010	0.001
	(0.010)	(0.010)
Growth	0.016*	0.015
	(0.009)	(0.010)
Lev	0.018*	−0.072***
	(0.011)	(0.012)
Constants	0.372***	0.376***
	(0.020)	(0.022)
Industry	Control	Control
Year	Control	Control
R^2	0.280	0.176
Adj R^2	0.273	0.170
F	184.88***	74.02***

Note: Coefficients shown with p values reported in brackets, $* p < .1$, $** p < .05$, $*** p < .01$.

form a synergy, the diversified acquired businesses are becoming increasingly fragmented.

ACKNOWLEDGMENT

This work was supported by National Natural Science Foundation of China [grant numbers N71972061].

REFERENCES

Andreou, P. C., Louca, C. , & Petrou, A. P. (2016). Organizational learning and corporate diversification performance. *Journal of Business Research*, 69, 3270–3284.

Barry, B. , & Bateman, T. S. (1996). A social trap analysis of the management of diversity. *Academy of Management Review*, 21, 757–790.

Hauschild, S. , & Knyphausen-Aufsess, D. Z. (2013). The resource-based view of diversification success: Conceptual issues, methodological flaws, and future directions. *Review of Managerial Science*, 7, 327–363.

He, X. (2012). Two sides of a coin: Endogenous and exogenous effects of corporate diversification on firm value. *International Review of Finance*, 12, 375–397.

Kano, L. , & Oh, C. H. (2020). Global value chains in the post-COVID world: Governance for reliability. *Journal of Management Studies*, 57, 1773–1777.

Lv, D. D., Chen, W. H., Zhu, H. , & Lan, H. L. (2019). How does inconsistent negative performance feedback affect the R&D investments of firms? A study of publicly listed firms. *Journal of Business Research*, 102, 151–162.

Mahajan, K. , & Tomar, S. (2021). Covid-19 and supply chain disruption: Evidence from food markets in india. *American Journal of Agricultural Economics*, 103, 35–52.

Munjal, S., Requejo, I. , & Kundu, S. K. (2019). Offshore outsourcing and firm performance: Moderating effects of size, growth and slack resources. *Journal of Business Research*, 103, 484–494.

Nasiriyar, M., Nesta, L. , & Dibiaggio, L. (2014). The moderating role of the complementary nature of technological resources in the diversification-performance relationship. *Industrial and Corporate Change*, 23, 1357–1380.

Nath, P., Nachiappan, S. , & Ramanathan, R. (2010). The impact of marketing capability, operations capability and diversification strategy on performance: A resource-based view. *Industrial Marketing Management*, 39, 317–329.

Sakhartov, A. V. (2017). Economies of scope, resource relatedness, andthedynamics of corporate diversification. *Strategic Management Journal*, 38, 2168–2188.

Sanchez, R. G., Bolivar, M. P. R. , & Hernandez, A. M. L. (2017). Corporate and managerial characteristics as drivers of social responsibility disclosure by state-owned enterprises. *Review of Managerial Science*, 11, 633–659.

Tang, P. C., Yang, S. X. , & Yang, S. W. (2020). How to design corporate governance structures to enhance corporate social responsibility in china's mining state-owned enterprises? *Resources Policy*, 66.

Wan, W. P., Hoskisson, R. E., Short, J. C. , & Yiu, D. W. (2011). Resource-based theory and corporate diversification: Accomplishments and opportunities. *Journal of Management*, 37, 1335–1368.

Zhou, K. Z., Gao, G. Y. , & Zhao, H. X. (2017). State ownership and firm innovation in china: An integrated view of institutional and efficiency logics. *Administrative Science Quarterly*, 62, 375–404.

Zhu, H. J. , & Yoshikawa, T. (2016). Contingent value of director identification: The role of government directors in monitoring and resource provision in an emerging economy. *Strategic Management Journal*, 37, 1787–1807.

Economic and Business Management – Huang & Zhang (Eds)
© 2022 Copyright the Author(s), ISBN: 978-1-032-06754-4

The influence of family on the development of family business

Wenglong Zhang & Baojun Feng

School of Economics and Management, Dalian University of Technology, Liaoning, China

ABSTRACT: The development of family business is significant in promoting China's economic transformation and the stability of national economy. Using listed family firms from 2010 to 2018 as a sample, we explored the different effects of family shareholding ratio on the development of family business and analyzed the internal mechanism. We found that family shareholding ratio promotes short-term development of the firm, social responsibility and R&D play an intermediary role in it. The conclusions of this paper reveal the impact of family business equity allocation, and the function of social responsibility and firm innovation, which can provide references for family businesses to develop in a better way, fulfill social responsibility performance, and improve corporate innovation.

Keywords: Family business; Family control; R&D; ROE

1 INTRODUCTION

China is in an important period of economic transformation, the development of family business is related to economic development and market economic stability. As the cornerstone of private enterprises, family businesses play an important role in R&D, employment, and social responsibilities. However, there are significant differences in current academic attitudes towards family businesses, it is still unclear how family holdings will affect the development of the family business [1]. The starting point of family holdings research is based on the control chain. But there are many indirect and mixed shareholding methods of listed family firms in China, and lack of analysis at the enterprise level. The controlling family's direct control and influence on the family business determine its right in key corporate decisions, and formulation of the direction of business development. Therefore, it is necessary to analyze the effect of family control and influence at the enterprise level on the development of family business.

The emergence of social emotional wealth (SEW) theory provides a reasonable explanation for the risky behavior of family business. Most scholars believe that the controlling family's emphasis on the non-economic demands of social emotional wealth is an important factor that distinguishes it from non-family businesses, because of the non-economic demands of the controlling family's sense of identity with the company, emotional dependence, and the desire to continue family control. Both need to be satisfied [2]. Therefore, when making decisions, the holding family tends to avoid the choice of social emotional wealth loss, rather than considering the development of the firm.

However, the dominant power of this choice is closely related to the control-ling family's control over the company's equity. The greater the influence of the family, the more it can lead the decision-making of the enterprise.

We explore the impact mechanism of family holdings at the corporate level on corporate development through the dual perspectives of social responsibility and R&D. Based on the data of listed family firms from 2010 to 2018, this article draws the following conclusions: (1) family holdings have a promoting effect on the short-term development of the company; (2) family holdings are positively affecting social responsibility and corporate R&D, but the impact on R&D is not significant; (3) corporate social responsibility and R&D have a significant mediating effect in the relationship between family holdings and business development. Family holdings will guide enterprises to assume more social responsibilities and thus affect development, but they will have a restraining effect on enterprise R&D and thus affect enterprise development.

2 RESEARCH HYPOTHESIZED

This part is the theoretical analysis and research hypothesis of this article. There are three hypotheses based on the social emotional wealth theory.

2.1 *The influence of family holding on enterprise development*

Existing research pays more attention to the largest shareholder, the premise is the largest shareholder that

232

DOI 10.1201/9781003203704-43

has no relationship with the other shareholders. But in the pyramid shareholding structure of listed companies, it is apparently unrealistic, especially in family businesses. The relationship between the top 10 shareholders should be considered when calculating family equity concentration. The higher the concentration of equity, the stronger the family's control over the firm. The closer the controlling family is to the firm, the more motivated it will be to promote the better development of the firm by treating the firm as the inseparable property of the family [3]. So, the family will give full support to the firm so as to guarantee the short-term development. On the other hand, with the increase of the shareholding ratio of the family, there will be a synergistic effect of interests. Major shareholders are in line with the interests of the firm and are more synergistic with the interests of minority shareholders [4], thus exerting a better influence on the firm. Furthermore, the increase in family holdings can effectively play the supervisory and supporting role of major shareholders, constrain the opportunistic behavior of the management [5], alleviate the first type of agency problem existing in the firm, and thus affect firm's performance. Moreover, the current changeful external environment leads to huge challenges for the development of family businesses; companies need to make timely adjustments to keep their development unaffected; the more shares when family control, the faster the decision-making speed to respond to changes in the external environment, ensure that the development of enterprise is not affected. So we have hypothesis H1.

H1: Family holding has a positive effect on the short-term performance of the family business.

2.2 The mediating role of social responsibility

Based on the theory of SEW, the higher the family holding, the stronger the emotional endowment to the company [6]. Family members have more sense of identity and emotional investment in the firm. The family will try its best to protect and enhance the reputation of the firm and maintain the pride and social identity of the family members as the owner of the firm. Social responsibility is an effective way to improve corporate reputation, so the family will fulfill more social responsibilities. Secondly, the fulfillment of social responsibility is an important way to enhance corporate legitimacy [7]. Family businesses face more serious financing constraints than ordinary enterprises, so they need to improve corporate legitimacy in order to obtain external resources. Therefore, the higher the family holding, the higher the social responsibility level of family enterprises will be. Finally, with the increase of the shareholding ratio of the family, the family has the ability to promote the enterprise to make more social responsibility behaviors.

Fulfillment of social responsibility can improve the corporate reputation, thus expanding consumer awareness and influencing consumer loyalty [8]. The reputation mechanism is an important factor affecting consumer purchase. When an enterprise has a high reputation and consumer recognition in the market, its performance will inevitably be improved. Secondly, the fulfillment of social responsibility can increase the legitimacy of family business, so that the enterprise can obtain market resources and policy support, to promote the better development of the enterprise. Therefore, we have hypothesis H2.

H2: Social responsibility plays a mediating role in the relationship between family holding and firm's short-term performance.

2.3 The mediating role of R&D

SEW theory points out that the decision-making point is the family's non-economic goal rather than the firm's economic goal. R&D requires continuous investment of resources and talents, but it is often difficult to meet the needs of continuous R&D with self-owned resources. Therefore, external resources need to be introduced, which will undoubtedly lead to the loss of family control, and control is the basis for the maintenance of family SEW [9]. The perception of threat to the loss of SEW will encourage the family to avoid too much R&D activities, which will have a inhibiting effect on R&D. Secondly, the higher the family holding, the more eager the family will be for the everlasting business, and the greater the willingness to inherit [9]. In order to make the wealth to be completely passed on to the next generation, the controlling family will take a conservative attitude in the face of the high-risk activities. R&D is highly uncertain and is likely to face the loss of failure, thereby damaging the integrity of family wealth. Risky activities do not conform to the family preference; thus, the higher the family stake, the more likely they are to restrain R&D of the enterprise.

R&D activities are the key for enterprises to gain competitive advantages [10]. Firstly, it is helpful to improve products to meet the changes in external consumer demand, maintain the stability and loyalty of consumers, and enable the company to have a good performance. Secondly, it is helpful to reduce the production cost, so as to have a bigger profit space. Moreover, the increase in R&D investment will inevitably bring the corresponding increase in R&D results, which will bring a solid competitive advantage for the enterprise and become the source power for development. Therefore, we have hypothesis H3.

H3: Enterprise innovation plays a mediating role in the relationship between family holding and firm's short-term performance.

3 RESEARCH DESIGN

This section gives the basis for the selection of samples and variables, as well as the statistical indicators of the main variables.

3.1 Sample selection

This paper selects listed family companies from 2010 to 2018 as samples. According to previous studies, family businesses are screened according to the following criteria [11]: (1) the actual controller of the firm is a natural person or family; (2) the actual controller is directly or indirectly the largest shareholder of the firm; (3) family control is not less than 10%. Excluding ST and *ST firms, financial firms, and enterprises with missing samples, we finally get the balance panel data of 3411 samples, and the continuous variables were reduced by 1% up and down.

3.2 Variable measurement

Explaining variable: Family holding (FI). In this paper, family holding refers to the sum of shares related to the controlling family among the top ten share-holders at the company level.

Explained variable: Firm Development (ROE). ROE is selected as a performance indicator to measure the short-term development of an enterprise. In the robustness test, use ROA instead of ROE.

Mediating variables: Corporate social responsibility (CSR) and corporate research and development (R&D). CSR is based on HeXun social responsibility score and R&D is measured by the natural logarithm of R&D investment of the family business.

Threshold variable: Financing Constraints (SA). Where the Size is the firm size in millions, and the Age is the establishment age of the firm. SA value calculated is taken as the absolute value. The larger the value, the smaller the financing constraint of the firm:

$$SA = |0.043\ size^2 - 0.737\ size - 0.04\ age| \qquad (1)$$

Control variable: Based on previous research, this paper uses debt paying ability (Debt), comprehensive risk (TL), degree of stock-right concentration (Crio), family ownership (Fo), enterprise scale (Size), firm's Age (Age), executive compensation (Wage), the board Size (D), the proportion of independent directors (DD), and chairman and general manager of situation (DZ). And, we also control the possible influence of Industry and Year on the development of the enterprise.

3.3 Descriptive statistics

The results in Table 1 show statistical indicators of core variables. The average of family-affected shares is 41.9%, and the maximum value reaches 81.5%. The mean value of ROE is 0.080, but the gap within the group is obvious. The average values of social responsibility and R&D are 24.258 and 17.225, respectively.

4 EMPIRICAL RESULTS AND ANALYSIS

In this part, we first test the correlation of the core variables, and use the fixed effects model and bootstrap test for hypothesis testing [12].

Table 1. Descriptive statistics of major variables.

Var	Min	Med	Max	Mean	SD
FI	0.156	0.401	0.815	0.419	0.151
ROE	−0.336	0.078	0.370	0.080	0.091
CSR	−2.62	21.25	73.46	24.258	15.030
R&D	12.121	17.465	20.789	17.225	1.528
SA	3.122	3.638	4.191	3.648	0.244

4.1 Correlation test

Table 2 shows the correlation between core variables. FI has a significant positive impact on ROE. In terms of CSR, the higher the FI, the higher the score of CSR, but the weaker the initiative of R&D, which is also in line with the view that the controlling family will take the preservation of social emotional wealth as the primary goal.

Table 2. Correlation test of major variables.

Var	FI	ROE	CSR	R&D
FI	1			
ROE	0.175***	1		
CSR	0.093***	0.438***	1	
R&D	−0.089***	0.092***	0.073***	1

Note: *** $P < 0.01$, ** $P < 0.05$,* $P < 0.1$, the same below.

4.2 Empirical result

We do Hausman test before regression to determine the model used for regression, and it was verified that the model was suitable for fixed-effect regression. The results are shown in Table 3.

From Table 3, the family holding has a significant positive effect on the firm's performance ($\alpha = 0.182$, $P < 0.01$), indicating that in family firms, the more shares controlled by the family, the stronger the promoting effect on firm's development. H1 is certified. In terms of CSR, the regression of family holding to corporate social responsibility is significantly positive ($\alpha = 21.526$, $P < 0.01$), indicating that with the increase of family holding, the corporate social responsibility will be better, and FI is conducive to the fulfillment of CSR. CSR plays an intermediary role between family holding and enterprise development, that is, family holding has an impact on enterprise development by influencing the fulfillment of CSR, H2 is certified. But there is no significant relationship between FI and R&D, we used the bootstrap method for verification. From Table 4, the confidence intervals of bootstrap test results don't contain 0, indicating that R&D plays a mediating role in the relationship between family holding and firm's development, and H3 is verified.

Table 3. The influence of FI on the enterprise.

Var	ROE	CSR	R&D	ROE	ROE
CSR				0.002***	
R&D					0.015***
FI	0.182***	21.526***	0.362	0.130***	0.177***
Debt	−0.049***	−10.181***	−0.138	−0.024*	−0.046***
TL	0.000	−0.212*	−0.003	0.001	0.000
Crio	0.078***	−2.326	0.263	0.083***	0.074***
Fo	−0.045	−11.825*	−0.502	−0.016	−0.037
Size	0.004	4.553***	0.627***	−0.007*	−0.005
Age	−0.000	−0.046	−0.003	0.000	−0.000
Wage	0.017***	1.093	0.133***	0.014***	0.015***
D	0.007***	0.236	0.029**	0.007***	0.007***
DD	0.139***	−1.375	−0.545	0.142***	0.147***
DZ	−0.003	0.073	−0.106***	−0.003	−0.001
Year	Control	Control	Control	Control	Control
Ind	Control	Control	Control	Control	Control
Con	−0.410***	−87.898***	1.511**	−0.196**	−0.432***
N	3411	3411	3411	3411	3411
F	19.36	16.55	106.07	34.52	19.97
R^2	0.176	0.154	0.539	0.281	0.185

Table 4. The mediating effect of R&D.

Indirect effects	B(boot SE)	LLCI[a]	ULCI[a]	P
$FI \rightarrow R\&D \rightarrow ROE$	−0.006***	−0.0107	−0.0003	0.038

Note: Mediating effect test is based on 1000 cycles, 95% confidence level; the absence of 0 within the interval indicates (LLCI and ULCI) that the mediating effect is established.

4.3 Robustness test

(1) *Replace variables.* Use ROA instead of ROE to measure family business development. And, the results show that the proposed results are still robust.
(2) *Replace the regression method.* In order to avoid the effect of endogeneity, GMM method was used and the conclusions in this paper were still robust.

5 CONCLUSION AND ENLIGHTENMENT

The healthy growth of the family business has always been an important measure to promote the development of a national economy. In the era of changing environment and coexistence of risks and opportunities, it is important to help the development of family business and realize the lasting prosperity of the foundation of the family business. Based on the data of listed family businesses from 2010 to 2018, this paper empirically analyzes the influence of family holding on the development of family business at the enterprise level. The results show that family ownership contributes to the improvement of firm's performance; the higher the family holdings, the stronger the promoting effect on the undertaking of CSR. But the

influence of family holdings on corporate R&D is not significant. CSR and R&D play an intermediary role in the relationship between family holding and enterprise development.

The conclusion of this paper provides some references for the development of family business: Firstly, it provides a reference for enterprise equity structure adjustment; the control family should control more shares for the short-term development of the company. Secondly, to provide a reference for the development of CSR and R&D, family companies have the motivation to fulfill social responsibility instinctively, and the fulfillment of social responsibility will eventually be transformed into the business results of the enterprise. Thirdly, R&D can promote short-term development of enterprises, the government should encourage and guide enterprises to conduct research and development.

ACKNOWLEDGMENTS

Financial support from Humanities and Social Science Planning Fund project of The Ministry of Education of China (18YJA630101).

REFERENCES

[1] Evert, R. E., Martin, J. A., McLeod, M. S. et al. 2016. Empirics in family business research: Progress, challenges, and the path ahead. *Family Business Review.* 29(1), 17–43.
[2] Gómez-Mejía, L. R., Haynes, K. T., Núñez-Nickel, et al. 2007. Socioemotional wealth and business risks in family-controlled firms: Evidence from Spanish olive oil mills. *Administrative science quarterly.* 52(1), 106–137.

[3] San Martin-Reyna, J. M., Duran-Encalada, J. A. 2012. The relationship among family business, corporate governance and firm performance: Evidence from the Mexican stock exchange. *Journal of Family Business Strategy*. 3(2), 106–117.

[4] Huacheng W, Feng C, Kangtao Y. 2015. Monitoring or Tunneling?: The Proportion Held by the Big Shareholders and the Risk of the Crash of the Stock Price. *Management World*. (02):45–57+187.

[5] Porta, R. L., Lopez-de-Silanes, F., Shleifer, A. et al. 1998. Law and finance. *Journal of political economy*. 106(6), 1113–1155.

[6] Gomez - Mejia, L. R., Makri, M., & Kintana, M. L. 2010. Diversification decisions in family – controlled firms. *Journal of management studies*. 47(2), 223–252.

[7] Meng, M., Tao, Q., Zhu, B. 2019. The effect of corporate social responsibility on the organizational legitimacy—moderating role of perceived institutional environment and legal efficiency. *Research on Economics and Management*. 40(03):118–129.

[8] LoisA. Mohr, DeborahJ. Webb. 2005. The effects of corporate social responsibility and price on consumer responses[J]. *Journal of Consumer Affairs*. 39(1): 121–147.

[9] Jing L, Ying Z. 2021. Research on the Ownership Structure,Slack and Family Business's Cooperation—Based on the Data of the Listed Family Business. *Journal of Soochow University*. 42(01): 117–133.

[10] Varma, A., Bhalotia, K., & Gambhir, K. 2020. Innovating for competitive advantage: managerial risk-taking ability counterbalances management controls. *Journal of Management and Governance*. 24(2), 389–409.

[11] Ellul, A., Pagano, M., & Panunzi, F. 2008. Inheritance law and investment in family firms. *CEPR Discussion Papers*. 100(5): 2414–2450.

[12] Lozano-Reina, G., Sánchez-Marín, G., & Baixauli-Soler, J. S. 2021. Say-on-Pay voting dispersion in listed family and non-family firms: A panel data analysis. *Journal of Family Business Strategy*, 100423.

Economic and Business Management – Huang & Zhang (Eds)
© 2022 Copyright the Author(s), ISBN: 978-1-032-06754-4

A two-stage model of tacit knowledge updating in family business

Yin Liu & Xiufeng Sun
School of Economics and Management, Dalian University of Technology, Liaoning, China

ABSTRACT: The rich yet homogeneous tacit knowledge is insufficient to adapt Chinese family firms to the environment of economic transformation and upgrading. Knowledge must be updated and then be integrated, where intergenerational entrepreneurship provides opportunity as multilevel interactions of family business increased. Adopting the knowledge-based view and conceptual pillars of the individual-family-firm interface, we develop a model composed of knowledge acquisition and knowledge transfer that is mediated by intergenerational entrepreneurship, we evidence a superior mechanism considering the unique structure of family business and idiosyncratic resources.

1 INTRODUCTION

Tacit knowledge is the strategic resource of a firm, it is mainly acquired from practical experience and be endowed with characteristics of scarcity, appropriateness, and difficulty in trading and imitating. The background of China's economic transformation and upgrading demands more knowledge for features of dynamism and evolution, which can hardly be met by the highly homogeneous family business tacit knowledge that attaches more importance to accumulation than expansion in terms of intergenerational transition. To be specific, hitherto, advancements are concentrated on the discerning of senior generation's tacit knowledge, and the methods and influential elements to transfer that knowledge. Recently, a small but increasingly vibrant body of literature underlines the knowledge of successor [1–2], implying a knowledge updating opportunity that starts from the individual level. Since the formation of tacit knowledge is closely related to entrepreneurial activities, and intergenerational entrepreneurship as an effective intermediary way to transfer Chinese family firms has reached a consensus gradually, we are enlightened to examine whether the vibrant intergenerational entrepreneurship propels successor to acquire tacit knowledge of heterogeneity, as well as how intergenerational entrepreneurship reshapes the knowledge transfer in family, and the effect on the firm's end.

Herein, adopting the knowledge-based view and the conceptual pillars of the individual-family-firm interface appropriate for intergenerational succession, we develop a two-stage model of tacit knowledge updating in a family business. The model we built is against the proposed intergenerational entrepreneurship context and is composed of two complementary yet interdependent stages of knowledge acquisition and knowledge transfer. With participants advancing from the basic level of individual to the family, then to the firm's end, we delineate how family firms can use their unique structure and idiosyncratic resources in the context of intergenerational entrepreneurship to maintain competitiveness in the knowledge-based view. We evidenced a mechanism of competitive edge over nonfamily firms that transcend the traditional advantages of resources, provide a reconciliatory approach for Chinese family business to overcome organizational inertia, and smoothen transgenerational succession.

2 LITERATURE REVIEW

2.1 *Knowledge-based view and the homogeneity of family business tacit knowledge*

To explain what makes difference in family business intergenerational succession and how to maintain competitiveness across generations, the knowledge-based view (KBV) provides a powerful theoretical framework. According to the traditional resource-based view, superior returns achieved by firms are attributed to the resources and capabilities which are valuable, rare, inimitable, and non-substitutable. Although the resource profile of the firm may be important to performance, the actions it should take to exploit these resources would not be self-evident. To constitute a competitive advantage, resources "must be managed appropriately to produce value" [3], and the management like integration, coordination, and mobilization, requires the tacit collective knowledge embedded in the firm's routine [4]. In the theory of KBV, knowledge is argued as the critical productional input, the primary source of value, and tacit knowledge is the organizational resource that most likely leads to enduring success [5]. In fast-moving business environments which open to global competition, knowledge should evolve with the times [1,6].

DOI 10.1201/9781003203704-44

Within the tacit knowledge framework identified by KBV, there are distinct ways of doing things, like technology or a commercial know-how, deep firm-specific managerial knowledge, industry-specific knowledge and information [3,5,6], etc. Against the Chinese traditional culture and regulation systems, entrepreneurial characteristics (e.g., hard work, perseverance), management values, and the social capital of entrepreneur are integrated into tacit knowledge category [7]. Nonetheless, while the unique and embedded exchange of relationships among family members creates idiosyncratic value, the closed network of members limits the variety of knowledge resources available and threatens the adaptiveness of the family firm in a high-velocity environment like China.

Contradictorily, learning about new knowledge before others increases the likelihood of discovering opportunities to make use of that new knowledge. It would be better for Chinese family firms to deliberately acquire heterogeneous knowledge, in particular, the experience-based tacit one; then by transferring knowledge internally, these enterprises are able to respond to challenges effectively and advance with the times, and also realize cross-generational value creation.

2.2 *Intergenerational entrepreneurship of family business*

To trigger innovative ideas and form experience-based tacit knowledge, the external environment is indispensable. Take routines that have strong tacit elements, for example, an established one can adapt to certain types of contextual change, but turns to be a source of inertia at other times of turbulence [8]. In avoiding obsolescence and realizing escalation, the external environment serves as both the supplier of diverse stimuli and substance for internal reflections on possible applications to improve existing routines, and a selection mechanism in the classic evolutionary sense as it provides the feedback on the value and viability of the organization's current behaviors [9]. In this respect, intergenerational entrepreneurship is the appropriate context. It is close enough to the external environment hence meets the basic requirement of triggering innovative ideas and tackling new challenges, and shapes tasks variously in aspects of frequency, homogeneity, and degree of causal ambiguity. By revising old knowledge, challenging traditional assumptions, changing perceptions, self-understanding, and behavior at a much deeper level, the successor can familiarize with the nature of the business and develop the specific capabilities needed for the business.

Besides, intergenerational entrepreneurship is related to family business succession in ways profound and extensive. Intergenerational succession is a family's continued commitment to entrepreneurship and pursuit of new business opportunities; the successor must assume the central entrepreneurial role that his or her predecessor occupied. If failed to inherit "entrepreneurial legacy," successor's motivation and ability to act entrepreneurially would be weakened, and the entrepreneurial orientation of family business tends to diminish gradually and gives way to family orientation. Thus, we select intergenerational entrepreneurship as the context to conduct our research, and define it as an innovative activity for successor to pursue intergenerational wealth accumulation through the establishment of new business independently, at the same time to inherit entrepreneurial spirit as the descendant of family [10].

3 THEORETICAL FRAMEWORK

Intergenerational entrepreneurship increases interactions and interdependency between the individual, the family, and the business, and affords family firms intergenerational succession with the opportunity for breaking the path dependence. Herein, taking the conceptual pillars of the individual-family-firm interface to the context of intergenerational entrepreneurship, we develop a knowledge updating model to describe how Chinese family business can use this special phase to better adjust the high-velocity environment, which is composed of knowledge acquisition and knowledge transfer.

Knowledge acquisition is an indispensable stage of solving knowledge deficiency in variety, often exemplified as incorporating new sources of knowledge— the human capital, in this work refers to successor. By drawing on tips from the resource management model of family business developed by Sirmon and Hitt [3], we elaborate the selective and legitimatized process of knowledge acquisition against intergenerational entrepreneurship context, since knowledge is a typical tacit resource, and when managed consciously can create competitive advantages, more in line with the adopted theory of KBV. The literature in framework of KBV also highlights the strategic significance of knowledge transfer, in which family firms yield uniqueness and superiority. Turning to the fields of knowledge transfer[11-12], and considering the enhanced family business idiosyncratic resources [13] by entrepreneurial activities, we explicate how effective and reliable transmission of tacit knowledge occurred bidirectionally in family, which will exert effects on the firm's end ultimately.

4 A MODEL OF FAMILY BUSINESS TACIT KNOWLEDGE UPDATING

4.1 *Knowledge acquisition of individual successor*

We selectively apply and modify the model of Sirmon and Hitt [3] to depict how an individual successor legitimizes heterogeneous knowledge through intergenerational entrepreneurship and then reaches the state of knowledge acquisition.

Firstly, as depicted in Figure 1, intergenerational entrepreneurship provides the successor diverse and substantial stimuli directly and comprehensively, while his or her reactions to challenges and opportunities that influence the knowledge formation depends on prior knowledge, which is derived from internal and external sources.

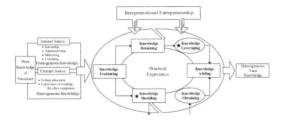

Figure 1. A knowledge acquisition model against the context of intergenerational entrepreneurship.

When the environment of high velocity erodes knowledge values and reduces its applicability over time, prior knowledge has to be evaluated and then decide if it is to be retained, shed, or added other than those reused recklessly. Intergenerational entrepreneurship shortens the distance between successor and the dynamic external environment; hence, making young entrepreneurs sense that similar things do not remain static or uniform and are changed by outside forces; then, revise their way of thinking, as well as confirming, amending, or rejecting attachments to prior beliefs, knowledge, and ideas that have served well previously. Accordingly, estimating the value of prior knowledge preliminarily is an efficient choice; then, based on the results of reusing past knowledge which is presumed as valuable for tackling new problems, the successor decides the later management of prior knowledge.

Knowledge that is sufficient to tackle problems or reach the desired effect could be retained, while for that has been validated as obsolete should be shed. Entrepreneurial setting that separates successor from the family business environment stuffed with strong emotional attachment to the old ways of doing things makes the shedding process easier. While gaps in knowledge bring a less desired result, successor can add knowledge resource either externally obtained from the open market like recruiting talents, purchasing patents, etc., or internally developed through leveraging. We argue that bundling and configuring the retained prior knowledge entrepreneurially can give rise to the knowledge leveraging. Analogical for intangible resources since they are most valuable when bundled with complementary resources, the prior knowledge acquired externally may have an idiosyncratic value when integrated with the inherited family tacit knowledge thereby creating additional value. Knowledge leveraging also brings extra strategic advantages in that some intuitive, subtle, and causal ambiguous configuration is difficult for competitors to replicate.

4.2 *The bidirectional knowledge transfer in family and to the firm's end*

Framework for knowledge transfer can be summarized as actors, context, content, and media. The characteristics of knowledge, context, knowledge source, and knowledge recipient, all together affect the validation of knowledge transfer. We sought to unveil how intergenerational entrepreneurship accelerates knowledge transfer bidirectionally in family context with the aid of family business idiosyncratic resources.

Family social system overlapping into the family business operation brings certain resources referred to as "familiness"—a unique concept emerged to describe how family firms are differentiated from other organizational forms [13]; the discussion of resource flows in family business is closely aligned with this concept. Although qualities as highly personal, context-related specific, hard to formalize and communicate lower the transferability of tacit knowledge, family business idiosyncratic resources can greatly enhance the efficiency and reliability of knowledge transfer. With "family language" allowing information exchange with more accuracy and efficiency, and family relationship creating strong ties among family members, and shaping characteristics of the source and the recipient of knowledge in the family as reliable, motivated, and trustworthy, with frequent informal family conversations, tacit knowledge transfer is promoted even if it cannot be encoded.

Following the theoretical framework of Albino et al. [11], we contend that intergenerational entrepreneurship of sufficient autonomy and without interference from the older generation is the media to carry out the knowledge transfer. Correspondingly, conversations linking to content of knowledge sharing mainly happen in the context of family other than the business environment. As entrepreneurial activities positively shaped the characters of influential factors of knowledge transference, the related actors served as both the source and recipient of knowledge. The intergenerational knowledge transfer presents a feature of two-way, as is depicted in Figure 2.

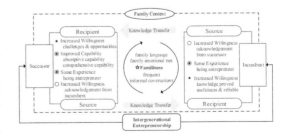

Figure 2. A bidirectional knowledge transfer model against the context of intergenerational entrepreneurship.

Entrepreneurial activities are saturated with challenges and opportunities. To tackle problems, successors' willingness of being knowledge recipient is significantly augmented, their absorptive and comprehensive capabilities are also improved through practices of variety, on the ground that the knowledge exchange is more fruitful. Being an entrepreneur also increases the successor's awareness of difficulties experienced by the old, and tends to be more respectful to the senior generation's capability, while acknowledgement of tacit knowledge motivates the senior generation to share more frankly in turn. The enhanced mutual understanding strengthens family emotional ties, along with the more frequent family communication. All facets above drive a more efficient and effective knowledge transfer from the elder generation to the later, and better prepare the successor to take the rein of family business.

On the other hand, heterogeneous knowledge built by successor is the reflection of creative improvement response to stimuli offered by the context of intergenerational entrepreneurship. Meanwhile, entrepreneurial context functions as the selection mechanism as it provides the feedback on the value and viability of the newly acquired knowledge. Therefore, the knowledge held by the successor is characterized by a proven record of past usefulness, hence being legitimated and allowing for more ready transfer. Specifically, the senior generation often relies on gut feeling and bypasses science and technology; since the necessity and validity of modern and standardized management is manifested by the repeated testation in successor's independent entrepreneurial activities, senior generation is better motivated of being the knowledge recipient. Still, knowledge transfers from successor to incumbent are affected by and positively influences the idiosyncratic resources of family business.

The bidirectional knowledge transfer between generations has a feature of circularity, and it is in this circular and bidirectional sharing process, the efficiency and reliability of knowledge transfer and familiness are mutually reinforced in comparison to the traditional unidirectional transfer. Moreover, the knowledge transferred from the successor could be applied to the family firm end and encourages a change in the actions and behaviors of the senior generation [2]. It is common that the incumbent implements drastic strategic reform for the successor's benefits in the preparation stage; the frequent and fruitful exchanging of ideas allows the incumbent to better understand the successor's business vision, then may reshape or set shared goals to reduce intergenerational strategy changes, and hence promise a steady transition.

5 CONCLUSION AND ENLIGHTENMENT

In this work, we adopt the theory of KBV, illustrate how intergenerational entrepreneurship can be the intermediary way to transfer family business smoothly, and update its tacit knowledge. Against intergenerational entrepreneurship, we develop a two-stage model composed of knowledge acquisition and knowledge transfer.

The knowledge acquisition model we proposed presents a circular manner that involves continuous feedback and kept being amended in the context of entrepreneurship. After repeated testing in the independent intergenerational entrepreneurship, tacit knowledge in successor could also be valued, and its transference from the younger to the older is equally, if not more, important. Besides, the process of shedding obsolete knowledge becomes easier as less fierce resistance is encountered than in family firm which has overarching emotional ties.

The bidirectional knowledge transfer model we built, which is mediated by the intergenerational entrepreneurship, extends the unidirectional knowledge sharing literature that extensively focuses on incumbents. In this two-way process, efficiency and reliability of knowledge transfer and family business idiosyncratic resources are mutually enhanced by virtue of entrepreneurial activities. Particularly, the qualified reverse tacit knowledge sharing increases the incumbent's understanding of the successor's views; hence, may modify the existing strategy to incorporate them, sacrifice the maximized immediate outcomes to pave way for later generation through strategic adjustment, and reduce the misalignments in strategies stemming from leadership transition.

While this model is not applicable to every potential family firm intergenerational succession, a mechanism advantage it reveals enriches the studies of family business heterogeneity, provides a reconciliatory approach for Chinese family firms to overcome organizational inertia, and smoothens transgenerational succession in practice.

ACKNOWLEDGMENTS

Financial support from Humanities and Social Science Planning Fund project of The Ministry of Education of China (18YJA630101).

REFERENCES

[1] Cabrera-Suárez, M. K., García-Almeida, D. J., & De Saá-Pérez, P. (2018). A Dynamic Network Model of the Successor's Knowledge Construction From the Resource- and Knowledge-Based View of the Family Firm. *Family Business Review*, 31(2), 178–197.

[2] Woodfield, P., & Husted, K. (2017). Intergenerational knowledge sharing in family firms: Case-based evidence from the New Zealand wine industry. *Journal of Family Business Strategy*, 8(1), 57–69.

[3] Sirmon, D. G., & Hitt, M. A. (2003). Managing resources: Linking unique resources, management, and wealth creation in family firms. *Entrepreneurship theory and practice*, 27(4), 339–358.

[4] Grant, R. M. (1991). The resource-based theory of competitive advantage: implications for strategy formulation. *California management review*, 33(3), 114–135.

[5] Grant, R. M. (1996). Toward a knowledge – based theory of the firm. *Strategic management journal*, 17(S2), 109–122.

[6] Teece, D. J. (2007). Explicating dynamic capabilities: the nature and microfoundations of (sustainable) enterprise performance. *Strategic management journal*, 28(13), 1319–1350.

[7] Sun, X. F., Song, Q. K., & Feng, H. T. (2017). Intergenerational Transfer of Family Business Entrpreneur Tacit Knowledge: A Multiple Case Study Based on Intergenerational Entrepreneurial Perspective. *Journal of Management Case Studies*, 10(01), 20–33.

[8] Turner, S. F., & Fern, M. J. (2012). Examining the stability and variability of routine performances: the effects of experience and context change. *Journal of Management Studies*, 49(8), 1407–1434.

[9] Zollo, M., & Winter, S. G. (2002). Deliberate learning and the evolution of dynamic capabilities. *Organization science*, 13(3), 339–351.

[10] Chen, W. T. (2012). The Research on Intergenerational Entrepreneurial Succession of Family Business on the Resource-based View. *Journal of Dongbei University of Finance and Economics*, (04), 3–9.

[11] Albino, V., Garavelli, A. C., & Schiuma, G. (1998). Knowledge transfer and inter-firm relationships in industrial districts: the role of the leader firm. *Technovation*, 19(1), 53–63.

[12] Szulanski, G. (1996). Exploring internal stickiness: Impediments to the transfer of best practice within the firm. *Strategic Management Journal*, 17(S2), 27–43.

[13] Habbershon, T. G., & Williams, M. L. (1999). A Resource-Based Framework for Assessing the Strategic Advantages of Family Firms. *Family Business Review*, 12(1), 1–25.

Economic and Business Management – Huang & Zhang (Eds)
© 2022 Copyright the Author(s), ISBN: 978-1-032-06754-4

A review on crisis management for small and medium-sized travel companies under COVID-19

Yan Feng
Macau University of Science and Technology, Macau, China

Xiaolian Chen
City University of Macau, Macau, China

Zhiyang Huang
Macau University of Science and Technology, Macau, China

ABSTRACT: This research aims at putting forward relevant strategies and suggestions for those small and medium-sized travel companies during the difficult time. The COVID-19 pandemic has had a significant impact on China's economy, especially the tourism economy. Small and medium-sized travel companies, as an important force to promote the development of China's tourism economy, suffered a very fatal blow in the COVID-19. More than 10,000 tourism companies closed down between March and May 2020 alone. A systematic review was conducted to analyze the results of research at the national level. 14 journal articles specializing in discussing the measures for travel companies in China to cope with the COVID-19 crisis were analyzed. This study has classified those measures into four different categories, including human resources, marketing, maintenance and government support.

1 INTRODUCTION

The literature on small and medium-sized travel companies (SMTCs) has increased during the past few years from various organizational and managerial research perspectives (Gang et al., 2021; Thukral, 2021). Likewise, crisis management has been well documented in recent literature especially under the COVID-19 pandemic (Kare et al., 2020; Ratten, 2020; Salem et al., 2021). However, given bundles of literature on COVID-19 and crisis management, little comprehensive knowledge is known about SMTCs' coping strategies under the COVID-19 (Alves et al., 2019; Kaufman et al., 2020; Klein & Todesco, 2021), especially in the context of China. Thus, this study aims to provide a systematic review on existing studies of SMTCs' crisis management under the COVID-19 conducted by researchers. As a systematic review, it helps identify research gaps and synthesizes the development of a research schema to guide SMTCs' crisis management and practices.

2 CONCEPTS

2.1 *Crisis management*

The definition of crisis can be traced back to the research of Hermann (1963). He believes that the crisis arises from an accident, and it threatens long-term goals and provides managers with little time to respond. At this time, crisis is a relatively general concept. Coombs (2007) synthesizes several definitions and views of the term of crisis and defines it as an unpredictable event that threatens the expectations of stakeholders, seriously affects organizational performance and produces negative results. Crises usually involve a large number of stakeholders (Acquier et al., 2008; Brunet & Houbaert, 2007). Therefore, crises cover a wide range, not just a single enterprise. The research on organizations and crises have accordingly derived the discipline of crisis management. Crisis management is defined as how organizations deal with crises (Hale et al., 2005). As an operational activity, crisis management includes plans and coordination that prepare for and respond to threats which may prevent or hinder operational activities.

2.2 *COVID-19 pandemic*

The first symptom of coronavirus disease 2019 was reported in December 2019 and then broke out in 2020. The spread of COVID-19 has led governments to take drastic measures, including the lockdown of epidemic area and social distancing (Thukral, 2021). It has significantly changed the global society (Parnell et al., 2020), as the individual behavior and personal interaction are no longer the same as before (pre-pandemic). Physical and social distancing becomes normal and this "new normal" way helps to stop the spread of the virus and to reduce its influence (Ratten, 2020). Due to the lockdown and social distance measures, this pandemic has disrupted many enterprises around the world, especially those in the field of tourism.

2.3 Small and Medium-sized Enterprises (SMEs)

The important role of SMEs in supporting economic growth and livelihoods through job creation has been recognized by most countries and is often referred to as the "backbone" and the "economic power". With a significant impact on the overall local economy, SMEs also dominate the tourism industry, and play a key role as the direct providers, agencies and distributors of products and services, (Garay & Font, 2012). However, there is no universal definition of SMEs in the existing literature due to the different understanding of the terms of large, medium and small enterprises (Platteau et al., 2017). Most existing definitions use some indicators to define SMEs, such as the number of employees, assets and turnover of enterprises, but these indicators also vary according to different countries, regions or industries (Dayour et al., 2020). In mainland China, the small enterprises are with 10–100 employees, while the medium-sized enterprises are with 100–300 employees.

3 METHODOLOGY

A systematic review was conducted to analyze the results of research at the national level. As the situation and influence of COVID-19 crisis diverse in different countries, this research only focuses on the local travel companies in China. Literature review was conducted through rigorous, explicit and reproducible procedures to answer relevant research questions (Green et al., 2006; Kitchenham & Charters, 2007; Klein & Todesco, 2021). Table 1 shows the details of the procedures. After being carefully checked, 14 journal articles were selected for the relevance. These 14 papers were distributed from 2020 to 2021.

4 RESULTS AND DISCUSSION

According to the previous paper, travel companies have carried out measures to tackle the existing problems caused by the COVID-19 crisis. In this paper, those measures are classified into four different categories, namely human resources, marketing, maintenance and government support, which is also consistent with Perl and Israeli (2011).

4.1 Marketing

A three-stage incremental marketing campaign was proposed by Li and Lu (2020). The first stage is before the epidemic, and travel companies use social media to carry out warm-up marketing to increase customers' expectations; The second stage is the restart stage, which is mainly to clarify the safety of public places to customers and actively plan various tourism activities to attract customers; The third stage is the revitalization stage, during which travel agencies should constantly develop their own brands and refine the market.

Table 1. Systematic review: Reproducible research protocol.

Parameter	Value
Research question	How are travel companies responding to COVID-19 crisis? What Strategies can those SMEs develop to survive under COVID-19?
Objective	To find response actions from travel companies under COVID-19 crisis; to obtain insights about opportunities for SMEs to survive
Combination of keywords (in title orabstract)	"COVID-19" (新冠); "epidemic situation" (疫情) "travel company" (旅遊公司); "travel agency (旅行社)"
Database	China National Knowledge Infrastructure (CNKI) database (http://www.cnki.com.cn/).
Type of materials	Academic Journal articles
Year of publication	Only 2020 & 2021
Selection criteria	1. Preference on peer-reviewed journals (refereed or scholarly), from management and tourism field of study 2. Search for keywords in title and abstract 3.The most related materials
Data extraction method	Text/content analyses: Focus on objectives and main results
Total Number of articles analyzed	Fourteen

Specifically, in this study, the marketing mix-4 Ps (product, price, promotion and places) was used to classify the marketing practices mentioned in previous literature. Firstly, in terms of product, new products have been introduced to fit into the current "new normal" situation. A lot of researchers suggested that travel companies should focus more on the Eco tour, road trip and short-distant weekend tour (Cui, 2020; Gao, 2020; Guo, 2021; Li & Lu, 2020; Ming & Zhao, 2020; You & Wang, 2020; Wu, 2021). Another popular type of tour product recommended is related to health. Guo (2021) proposed to combine the concept of health with tourism, developing special health tourism routes such as sunlight, spa, geothermal, seaside, forest and hot spring, and to carry out health recuperation and chronic disease recuperation. Additionally, the digital transformation also has influenced the future trend. With the development of the 5G and VR technology, virtual tour is gaining popularity (Gao, 2020). To conclude, diversification and individualization are the two main directions for the new product development (Cui, 2020; Deng, 2020; Guo, 2021; Ming & Zhao, 2020; Wang & Huang, 2021; Wu, 2021; Yin, 2020). Secondly, though Perl and Israeli (2011) put reducing prices on special offers and reducing list prices of office services as the marketing practices, Chinese researchers do not emphasize a lot on this aspect. Instead of reducing prices, they focus more on improving the quality of both product and service (Guo, 2021; Wang & Huang, 2021; Wu, 2021). Thirdly, it was recommended that advertising should be shown on different media channels, especially the new social medias (Guo, 2021; Li & Lu, 2020; You & Wang; Wei & Liu, 2021). Lastly, tour guides are also encouraged to use the live stream platform as the new channel to do the live commerce, so as to increase their income (Guo, 2021; Wu, 2021).

4.2 Human resources

As the financial situation is crucial for the survival of the SMEs, some researchers suggest to cut the budget by carrying out some practices, such as dismissing employees, using unpaid vacation, reducing number of office hours, management voluntary salary reduction, freezing or reducing pay rate, etc. (Perl & Israeli, 2011). In fact, some employees are not happy with those practices. Hence, it is important for the company to communicate effectively with the employees to reach a consensus and to work together during the difficult time (You & Wang, 2020). Training is also a key to cope with the crisis (Ming & Zhao, 2020; You & Wang, 2020; Wang & Huang, 2021). Different topics have been covered. Common topics are selling skills, customer relationship management (CRM) and data analysis in marketing (Wang & Huang, 2021). Gao (2020) empathized that now it is a good chance to turn the "threat" into the "opportunity" by offering online training. Besides, some researchers also encourage travel companies to develop smart tourism (Jiang & He, 2020) and hire talent from IT as the smart Tourism develops fast in recent years (Wei & Liu, 2021).

4.3 Maintenance

While some researchers pay attention to the quality management (Cui, 2020; Wu, 2021), some scholars emphasize the importance of cutting operation cost to survive (Ming & Zhao, 2020; Wu, Yang, & Guo, 2021). To be more specific, Wu, Yang, and Guo (2021) suggested that when the pandemic has not been fully controlled, measures related to operating cost such as reducing wages and benefits, reducing advertising, reducing inventory of low value consumables and working from home should be taken if necessary.

4.4 Government support

The COVID-19 has led a catastrophic damage on the tourism industry. Without the support of the government, it seems very difficult for small and medium-size travel companies to survive. Researchers suggest the government to provide financial supports mainly from the following four aspects. First, returning the deposit to travel companies has been supported and carried out by the government (You & Wang, 2020). It helps those companies with financial problems. Second, lowering the tax is also suggested by researchers (Gao, 2020; You & Wang, 2020; Yu, 2020; Wu, Yang, & Guo, 2021). Third, providing loan with a lower interest rate or to extend the time of the loan is another effective measure that can help travel companies to survive (Wu, Yang, & Guo, 2021). Fourth, cutting the rent was conducted by the government in some areas (Wu, Yang, & Guo, 2021). Besides the financial support, the government should take the leading role in recovering the tourism industry (Cui, 2020; Ming & Zhao, 2020).

5 CONCLUSIONS

During the past year, the number of papers published in the field of crisis management and COVID-19 has increased substantially which implies tourism scholars greater publishing opportunities. With this work, four types of measures were summarized to be mostly taken by China's SMTCs as coping strategies to the COVID-19: human resources, marketing, maintenance and government support. The details regarding the four types of measures were discussed in the results section of this study. The main contribution of this work is its synthesis of crisis management measures by SMTCs which were studied in existing research. This study has several limitations; First, it is bound by the time frame of the COVID-19. Second, only journal articles in Chinese language were collected. Third, the sample size is small, as only articles in the CNKI database were used. As a result, only the crisis management of SMTCs in China was addressed and summarized. Taking the limitations of this study into account, future studies might consider the crisis management of SMTCs related studies from other countries in other languages.

ACKNOWLEDGMENT

The research is supported by Education and Youth Development Bureau of Macao S.A.R. Government (TET-MUST-2020-04).

REFERENCES

Acquier, A., Gand, S. & Szpirglas, M. 2008. From stakeholder to stake s holder management in crisis episodes: A case study in a public transportation company. *Journal of Contingencies and Crisis Management* 16(2):101–114.

Alves, N., Lok, N., Luo, N. & Hao, N. 2020. Crisis challenges of small firms in Macao during the COVID-19 pandemic. *Frontiers of Business Research in China* 14(4):403–425.

Brunet, S. & Houbaert, P. 2007. Involving stakeholders: The Belgian fowl pest crisis. *Journal of Risk Research* 10(5): 643–660.

Coombs, W.T. 2007. Protecting organization reputations during a crisis: The development and application of situational crisis communication theory. *Corporate reputation review* 10(3):163–176.

Cui, F.J. 2020. Impact of Novel Coronavirus Pneumonia on Cultural Tourism Industry and Countermeasures—Sensitivity and Vulnerability of the Cultural Tourism Industry. *Journal of Taizhou University* 42(1):1–5.

Dayour, F., Adongo, C.A. & Kimbu, A.N. 2020. Insurance uptake among small and medium-sized tourism and hospitality enterprises in a resource-scarce environment. *Tourism Management Perspectives,* 34: 100674.

Deng, X.H. 2020. Research on challenges, opportunities and countermeasures of traditional travel agencies in the post-epidemic era. *Marketing Industry* 34:50–52.

Gang, K. A., Yong, X. A., Yi, P. B., Feng, S. C., Yang, C. A. & Kc, D. 2020. Bankruptcy prediction for smes using transactional data and two-stage multiobjective feature selection. *Decision Support Systems*, 140.

Gao, L.Y. 2020. Strengthening the support of tourism enterprises during the epidemic prevention and control period. *Fendou* 6:68–69.

Garay, L. & Font, X. 2012. Doing good to do well? Corporate social responsibility reasons, practices and impacts in small and medium accommodation enterprises. *International Journal of Hospitality Management* 31(2):329–337.

Green, B.N., Johnson, C.D. & Adams, A. 2006. Writing narrative literature reviews for peer-reviewed journals: secrets of the trade. *Journal of Chiropractic Medicine* 5(3): 101–117.

Guo H. 2021. On Problems Faced by Travel Agency and Pathways of Transformation and Upgrading in the Post-epidemic Period. *Journal of Huanggang Polytechnic* 23(2):89–93.

Hale, J.E., Dulek, R.E. & Hale, D.P. 2005. Crisis response communication challenges: Building theory from qualitative data. *The Journal of Business Communication (1973)* 42(2): 112–134.

Hermann, C.F. 1963. Some consequences of crisis which limit the viability of organizations. *Crisis Management* 8:210.

Jiang, L.Y. & He, Z. 2020. Research on the impact of tourism crisis on the tourism industry and countermeasures – taking COVID-19 as an example. *Rural Economy and Science-Technology* 19:107–108.

Jiang, Y., Ritchie, B.W. & Benckendorff, P. 2019. Bibliometric visualisation: An application in tourism crisis and disaster management research. *Current Issues in Tourism* 22(16):1925–1957.

Kare, M., Soriano, D.R. & Porada-Rochoń, M. 2020. Impact of COVID-19 on the travel and tourism industry. *Technological Forecasting and Social Change* 163:120469.

Kaufman, K. R., Petkova, E., Bhui, K. S. & Schulze, T. G. 2020. A global needs assessment in times of a global crisis: world psychiatry response to the COVID-19 pandemic. *BJPsych Open* 6(3):1–11.

Kitchenham, B.A. & Charters, S. 2007. Guidelines for performing Systematic Literature Reviews in Software Engineering. Retrieved from: http://www.robertfeldt. net/advice/kitchenham_2007_systematic_reviews_report_ updated.pdf

Klein, V.B. & Todesco, J. L. 2021. COVID – 19 crisis and SMEs responses: The role of digital transformation. *Knowledge and Process Management* 28(2):117–133.

Li, S.S. & Lu. J. 2020. Development and upgrading of travel agencies in the post-epidemic era. *New Silk Road Horizon* 10:72–73.

Ming, Q.Z. & Zhao, J.P. 2020. The impact of COVID-19 on the tourism industry and countermeasures. *Academic Exploration* 3:124-131.

Parnell, D., Widdop, P., Bond, A. & Wilson, R.2020. COVID-19, networks and sport. *Managing Sport and Leisure*:1–7.

Perl, Y. & Israeli, A.A. 2011. Crisis management in the travel agency sector: a case study. *Journal of Vacation Marketing* 17 (2):115–125.

Platteau, J. P., De Bock, O. & Gelade, W. 2017. The demand for microinsurance: A literature review. *World Development* 94:139–156.

Ratten, V. 2020. Coronavirus (COVID-19) and entrepreneurship: changing life and work landscape. *Journal of Small Business & Entrepreneurship* 32(5): 503–516.

Salem, I. E., Elkhwesky, Z. & Ramkissoon, H. 2021. A content analysis for government's and hotels' response to COVID-19 pandemic in Egypt. *Tourism and Hospitality Research,* 14673584211002614

Thukral, E. 2021. COVID-19: small and medium enterprises challenges and responses with creativity, innovation, and entrepreneurship. *Strategic Change*, 30(2):153–158.

Wang, G. 2020. Application of smart tourism in tourism enterprise management. *Times of Fortune* 1:211–212.

Wang, B.Q. & Huang, Y.W. 2021. Research on the Development of Online Travel Agencies in China under the impact of the Epidemic—A Case study of Ctrip. *Economic Research Guide* 8:38–41.

Wei, Y.R. & Liu, H.F. 2021. The impact of short video dividends on the revival of tourism after the epidemic. *Co-Operative Economy & Science* 6s:29–31.

Wu, Y. 2021. Analysis on the development countermeasures of travel agencies in the post-epidemic era. *Modern Business Trade Industry* 17:37–38.

Wu, K.J., Yang, Z. & Guo, Y.Y. 2021. The impact and countermeasures of COVID-19 on tourism industry in Guangdong, Hongkong and Macau. *Practice and Theory of SEZS* 3:87–93.

Yin, L. 2020. Research on how domestic travel agencies get out of trouble during the epidemic period. *Co-Operative Economy & Science* 18:108–110.

You, S.X. &Wang, S.S. 2020. The impact of tourism crisis on travel agencies and countermeasures. *Modern Communication* 9:245–246.

Yu, L.W. 2020. Suggestions on assistance policies for Hainan tourism enterprises under the epidemic crisis. *The New Orient* 2:15–18.

Construction and analysis of green logistics service supply chain operation model

Qimeng Ding
Engineering, Shanghai Polytechnic University, Shanghai, China

Hehua Li
Economics and Management, Shanghai Second Polytechnic University, Shanghai, China

ABSTRACT: 2021 is the beginning of the 14th Five-Year Plan period. During the 14th Five-Year Plan, it has repeatedly emphasized "green transformation of production and life style" and "green transformation in economic and social development". The concept of green and environmental protection puts forward higher requirements for enterprises and society, and it is imperative to improve the green level of the logistics service supply chain. With the logistics service integrator as the core, this paper analyzes the characteristics of the service supply chain based on the new definition of the concept of the green logistics service supply chain, and establishes the Green Logistics Service Supply Chain Operations Reference- model, GLSSCOR), the first, second, and third-tier operation models, and in-depth analysis of the service process of service companies.

1 INTRODUCTION

In recent years, the state has intensively issued a series of supporting policies and guidance, emphasizing the promotion of green supply chain. In 2017, the general office of the State Council issued the guiding opinions on actively promoting the innovation and application of supply chain, which included "actively advocating green supply chain" in the six tasks, which marked that China's supply chain began to enter the path of green development. When the problem of environmental pollution becomes more and more serious, the demand for environmental protection from all walks of life is increasing, and the concept of "green" is gradually extending from tangible products to intangible services, especially in the field of logistics, the public gradually need to pay attention to the improvement of the green level of the service supply chain. 2021 is the first year of the 14th five year plan. The key word "green" has been mentioned many times in the 14th five year plan, and "green transformation of production and life style" and "comprehensive green transformation of economic and social development" have been emphasized many times.

At present, the research on service supply chain is limited to the characteristics of individual service industries. Lianlian Qin constructs the performance evaluation index system of tourism service supply chain, and expounds the performance evaluation process of tourism service supply chain by using AHP-FCE method. Qiaobo Wang established the overall

Figure 1. Basic framework of green logistics service supply chain operation mode based on SCOR.

equilibrium model of aviation logistics service supply chain network management, which effectively improved the market supply and demand structure.

However, there are few studies on the impact of environment on service supply chain, and there is little analysis on the operation process of logistics service supply chain. Therefore, this paper will focus on the process operation of green logistics service supply chain, and use the tool of supply chain operation reference model (SCOR) to establish an operation reference model in line with the logic of green service supply chain according to the characteristics of green service supply chain, which has important practical and theoretical significance.

2 GREEN LOGISTICS SERVICE SUPPLY CHAIN OPERATION REFERENCE MODEL

2.1 Structure of green logistics service supply chain operation reference model

It has only been about 15 years since Lisa M. ellram first proposed the concept of service supply chain in 2004. Compared with the nearly 40 year history of physical product supply chain, the current research content of service supply chain is relatively scarce. The green logistics service supply chain studied in this paper refers to the logistics service supply chain composed of logistics service integrators as the core and various functional logistics service providers, including third-party logistics companies and customers. In the coordination process of the whole supply chain, it will fully advocate the green concept and emphasize environmental protection and corporate social responsibility. Including green procurement, green transportation, green packaging and other aspects.

The supply chain operation reference model (SCOR) was proposed by the Supply Chain Council (SCC) in 1996. It is the most influential, widely used and authoritative supply chain performance evaluation model at present. The model can be divided into process definition layer, process configuration layer and process decomposition layer. As a supply chain operation model, SCOR can study the operation process of service supply chain from a macro perspective.

With the development of social economy, new requirements are put forward for the supply chain. The original SCOR model for building service supply chain is no longer applicable. This paper will establish a green logistics service supply chain operations reference – model (GLSSCOR), including marketing & sales (M & S), service plan (P, plan), service procurement (s, sourcing), service integration (I, integration), service delivery (D, delivery), maintenance (m, maintenance) and enabling process (E, Enable) seven basic processes, which can be comprehensively measured from the perspectives of supply chain reliability, reactivity, flexibility, cost, assets and environmental protection, as shown in the figure. These seven basic processes define the scope and content of gsscor model and determine the basis for the competitive objectives of logistics service enterprises.

2.2 The first layer operation mode of GLSSCOR model

The first layer of GLSSCOR model proposed in this paper is the definition layer. According to the market demand and resource characteristics of logistics service supply chain, this paper defines its process as marketing, service planning, service procurement, service integration, service delivery, maintenance and enabling process. Each process is defined below.

(1) Marketing process. Marketing originally refers to the process in which enterprises discover or explore the needs of quasi consumers, let consumers understand the product and then buy the product. In this

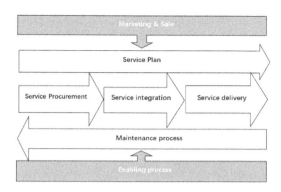

Figure 2. The first layer operation mode of GLSSCOR model.

paper, marketing is defined as the process that logistics service integrators must do in the face of fierce market competition. It requires all links in the service supply chain to establish, maintain and consolidate cooperative relations under common interests to achieve win-win or multi win. So that they can meet the needs of customers more profitably than their competitors and provide better services.

(2) Service plan. The original plan in SCOR refers to the process related to determining requirements and corrective actions to achieve supply chain objectives. This paper holds that service planning refers to establishing and developing a series of activities in a specific period of time, including receiving customer demand information and using these service supply chain resources in a planned way to meet the needs of customers in the service supply chain according to the ability of the service system. It includes the planning of the whole service supply chain and each service supply chain.

(3) Service procurement. SCOR's original plan refers to the process related to the ordering, delivery, receipt and transfer of raw materials, components, products and / or services. GLSSCOR refers to the evaluation and selection of various functional logistics service providers according to the service procurement plan after fully analyzing customer needs. The functional logistics service providers here include storage service providers, transportation service providers, customs declaration and inspection agencies and some third-party logistics companies.

(4) Service integration. In SCOR model, manufacturing link refers to the process of adding value to deliverables by manufacturing or creating products or deliverables; Or in the service industry, the process of adding value to deliverables by creating deliverables. This process is the most critical step in the whole logistics service supply chain. Logistics service integrators need to centrally integrate all resources purchased. This process needs to coordinate multi-party resources to ensure foolproof before service delivery.

(5) Service delivery. Processes related to the execution of customer-oriented order management and order fulfillment activities. This process refers to the process

of delivering service products to the final customers on the basis of integrating the service resources and service capabilities of the service system, and completing the service at the service place designated by the service integrator by the service provider, including service environment setting, customer positioning process, service acceptance to service execution and completion, and customer confirmation after service completion.

(6) Maintenance. The return process in SCOR refers to the process of transporting materials back from customers through the supply chain to solve defects in products, orders or manufacturing, or carry out maintenance activities. Considering that the service supply chain will not only have a service feedback process, but also have physical recovery in actual operation, such as the recycling of packaging materials such as pallets and cartons, which is in line with the initiative of green supply chain, this paper combines the two processes into a maintenance process, including information feedback and physical recovery.

(7) Enabling process refers to the process related to establishing, maintaining and monitoring the information, relationships, resources, assets, business rules, compliance and contracts required for supply chain operation, as well as monitoring and managing the overall performance of the supply chain. Enabling processes provide key inputs and guidance to support the implementation and governance of supply chain planning and execution processes. Enabling processes to interact, manage and coordinate with processes in other domains requires the support of enabling processes throughout the service supply chain.

2.3 The second layer is the configuration layer

The second layer of GLSSCOR proposed in this paper is the process configuration layer, which expands the first layer according to the classification of service supply chain objects. Organizations can choose their own process to configure the appropriate supply chain process according to the actual situation, that is, the process of the configuration layer is optional. For logistics integrators, they need to provide customers with professional and flexible services. Some customers' needs can be achieved with existing resources, and some special needs need the help of peers. Therefore, this paper divides the services of the improved supply chain operation reference model into two categories: one is the business that needs to be outsourced to peers, and the other is the business that directly faces supplier procurement. As shown in the figure.

Therefore, the implementation process can be divided into two categories. The marketing process can be divided into undertaking projects for internal peers and marketing for external markets. In the face of market competition, marketing is indispensable in any industry, especially as a logistics service integrator. According to statistics, only in Hongkou District, Shanghai, the number of relevant enterprises that can provide logistics service supply chain is up to 3000. In

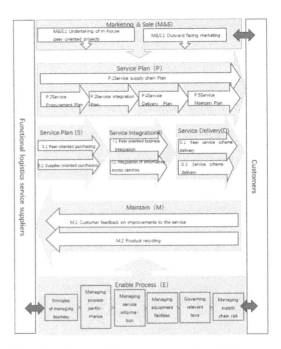

Figure 3. The second layer operation mode of GLSSCOR model.

the process of marketing, integrators should publicize the green concept and take green environmental protection as their advantageous selling point to attract customers.

(1) Service planning is the core process of the service supply chain and supports the operation coordination of the whole supply chain. There are five processes: planned service supply chain, planned service procurement, planned service integration, planned service delivery and planned service maintenance.

Service procurement, service integration and service delivery are also divided into two sub processes. Facing the market competition, logistics service integrators need to provide customers with the best supply chain scheme, screen functional logistics service providers in line with the green concept, and realize green procurement, green packaging and green transportation. Then integrate the resources of all suppliers, coordinate the service resource time and arrangement of each supplier, and finally deliver the complete service supply chain plan to customers. However, when the existing resources can not fully meet the requirements of customers, they can seek resources from peers, or outsource them all to peers. After peers complete the service supply chain integration in line with the green concept, the audit scheme will be delivered to customers.

(2) The maintenance process in GLSSCOR not only has feedback on customer service, but also has product recycling. On the one hand, after completing the customer's plan, investigate the customer's satisfaction, optimize the service plan according to the

customer's feedback and opinions, and prepare for the next service. On the other hand, there may be physical recycling during the operation of the whole plan, such as pallets, cartons and other packaging materials. The treatment methods of these materials also need to be discussed with the customer.

(3) In the process of green logistics service supply chain operation, an enabling process is required to ensure that each process can play a role. The enabling process plays a role in the service planning process, preparation, maintenance and management information and relationship in the implementation process. The enabling process mainly includes the following seven parts:

Management business system. The process of establishing, recording, communicating and publishing supply chain business rules for each main process. Business rules are statements or parameters that define or constrain some aspects of the business, which are usually used for decision-making. Business rules are designed to affect the results of service supply chain operations. Business rules can be applied to people, processes, corporate behavior and computing systems in the organization, and can help the organization achieve its goals while maintaining compliance with internal and external policies and laws.

Manage and evaluate performance. The process of defining performance objectives for supply chain indicators in line with the overall business strategy and objectives, which is used to report performance, identify performance gaps, analyze causes, and develop and initiate corrective actions to fill performance gaps. This process describes all levels and versions of managing service supply chain performance.

Manage service information collection. The process of collecting, maintaining and publishing data and information required to plan, operate, measure and manage the supply chain.

Manage equipment and facilities. It refers to the scheduling, maintenance and disposal process of supply chain assets developed for supply chain execution. This includes arranging, executing, optimizing, calibrating and maintaining other activities required for the implementation of the service supply chain. This is more like a scheduling process to ensure that all devices can be used normally at the right time.

Manage service supply chain contracts / agreements. Manage and communicate contractual and non contractual agreements to support business objectives and service supply chain objectives. This includes all agreements related to the operation of the service supply chain, including resource and service procurement, performance objectives, planning and decision-making, logistics transportation and delivery, data exchange and visibility.

Manage relevant laws and regulations. The process of identifying, collecting, evaluating and integrating regulatory requirements in service supply chain processes, policies and business rules. This process also includes managing voluntary compliance with standards and certification.

Manage service supply chain risk. The process of identifying and assessing potential disruptions or risks in the supply chain and formulating plans to mitigate these threats to supply chain operations. Logistics service supply chain risks include: demand interruption, such as customer closure; Supply interruption, such as route cancellation; Environmental damage, weather reasons, etc.

2.4 The third layer is the process decomposition layer

The third layer of GLSSCOR model is the process decomposition layer, which describes the process details of each ring in the second layer in detail. This paper will select the key operation links for analysis.

Service procurement process. The status and role of service procurement in the daily operation of logistics integrators are mainly reflected in ensuring the normal supply of service resources required by customers, that is, timely supply according to the service quality requirements, and ensuring the personalization and timeliness of services. Logistics service integrators can provide a variety of logistics schemes according to the specific requirements of the demander, but in the green logistics service supply chain, they need to consider the possible impact and consequences of each logistics scheme on the environment and social system, and design a green procurement service scheme to ensure that the whole logistics activities have the least impact on the environment and the highest resource utilization efficiency, Carry out green service procurement. Green procurement can not only help logistics service integrators reduce the total procurement cost, but also meet the public's demand for environmental protection. Therefore, green procurement can bring competitive advantages and economic benefits to logistics service integrators. Green procurement requires logistics service integrators to pay attention to the selection and management of suppliers, and can effectively screen suppliers. When selecting partners, in addition to conventional factors such as service quality, service price and service timeliness, we need to focus on environmental factors and give priority to suppliers with ios14001 certification. Through effective communication with suppliers, it can realize the information sharing of supply chain node enterprises, pay attention to saving resources and protecting the environment, and improve the value-added space of logistics services. Functional logistics service providers must ensure green supply when providing services for logistics service integrators, so as to realize the transformation from end-to-source governance.

Service integration process. Both peer-oriented business integration and supplier information integration need to be contacted and communicated in time to respond to changes in customer needs and ensure the green and environmental protection of service schemes at all times.

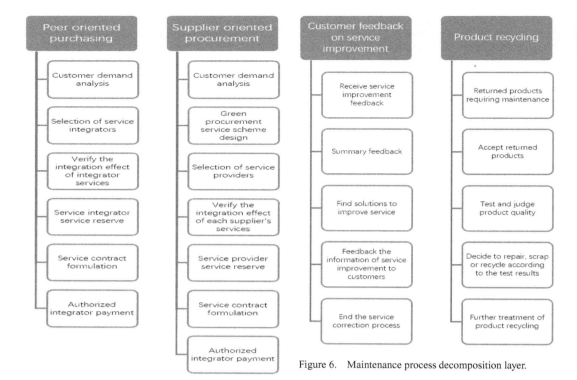

Figure 4. Service procurement process decomposition layer.

Figure 6. Maintenance process decomposition layer.

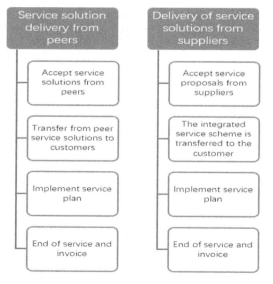

Figure 5. Service delivery module decomposition layer.

Service delivery process. In this process, the first is the delivery of service suppliers to integrators, and the second is not only the handover of service schemes, but also the implementation of schemes. Therefore, green packaging and green transportation are also reflected in this process. It is necessary to design green packaging scheme, reasonably plan transportation routes and use clean energy transportation tools to improve resource utilization efficiency to the greatest extent.

Maintenance process. Logistics service is inseparable from production and consumption. Through the analysis of the supply chain structure model of green logistics service, it can be seen that all node enterprises and end customers in the supply chain participate in the production process of logistics service, and may produce all kinds of waste products, waste materials The maintenance link of the green logistics service supply chain mainly includes the recycling, recycling and waste treatment of various waste materials. Each subject of green logistics service supply chain must participate in each recycling link in order to reduce the impact on the environment and improve resource utilization efficiency.

3 IMPLEMENTATION OF ENTERPRISE GREEN LOGISTICS SERVICE SUPPLY CHAIN OPERATION MODEL

3.1 *Customer thinking*

In the face of market competition, as a logistics service integrator, everyone needs to analyze customers' needs and take the initiative instead of waiting for customers to seek help. In the new media era, everyone has the right to produce and disseminate content. Everyone should be able to use the characteristics of this new media platform to carry out brand marketing, publicize the concept of sustainable development and green cycle, enhance the importance of greening the service supply chain, and take green environmental protection as the competitive advantage of our own service supply chain.

3.2 *Ultimate thinking*

Extreme thinking is to make the product to the extreme, beyond the imagination of customers, focus and simplicity. The ultimate thinking in the green service supply chain should first focus on green, and then provide customers with ultra-high cost-effective services beyond their imagination.

3.3 *Big data thinking*

Users generally generate data at three levels of information, behavior and relationship on the network. The precipitation of these data is helpful for enterprises to predict and analyze. Enterprises must build their own big data platform, and even small enterprises need the support of big data. The scale of enterprises in the logistics service chain is mainly small and medium-sized enterprises. It is more necessary to collect customers' information needs to help enterprises improve better.

3.4 *Platform thinking*

Platform thinking refers to an open, shared and win-win thinking to create a win-win ecosystem. At present, most members of the logistics service supply chain, including service providers, integrators and customers, have not formed an information network. As a result, the communication cost between enterprises is very high, and it also brings bad experience to customers. If company can build a platform to form an ecosystem, we can better reduce the cost of the supply chain and improve the operation efficiency of the service supply chain.

4 CONCLUSION

The proposal of green service supply chain operation reference model enriches the theoretical research on service supply chain and SCOR model by domestic and foreign scholars, and expands the application scope of SCOR model. Logistics enterprises should change from the traditional management mode of "internal supply chain" to the "whole process logistics service supply chain" management that focuses on the performance of the whole chain from customers to logistics service providers. Under the concept of green development, they also gradually begin to pay attention to the improvement of the green level of the service supply chain. GLSSCOR model can provide theoretical basis and operational tools for service enterprises to optimize and restructure business processes. Logistics service integrators can draw their own business process framework diagram according to their own business process status and by referring to GLSSCOR model, so as to provide basic data for continuous business process optimization. Therefore, GLSSCOR model provides a theoretical basis and operational tools for service enterprises to carry out business process greening and business process reengineering.

REFERENCES

Ertugrul Ayyildiz1 Alev Taskin Gumus1.Interval-valued Pythagorean fuzzy AHP method-based supply chain performance evaluation by a new extension of SCOR model: SCOR 4.0. *Complex & Intelligent Systems*. 56(2), 36–51.

Fu Qiu- fang, WANG Wen- bo. Study on the Operation Reference Model of Service Supply Chains. *Commercial Age-Supply chain management*. 2010, 8(5): 112–116.

Ilbahar E, Kara san A, Cebi S, Kahraman C (2018) A novel approach to risk assessment for occupational health and safety using Pythagorean fuzzy AHP & fuzzy inference system. *Saf Sci* 103:124–136.

Kechagias, E.P.; Gayialis, S.P.; Konstantakopoulos, G.D.; Papadopoulos, G.A. An Application of an Urban Freight Transportation System for Reduced Environmental Emissions. *Systems* 2020, 8, 49.

Miguel Nunez-Merino, Juan Manuel Maqueira-Marin. Information and digital technologies of Industry 4.0 and Lean supply chain management: a systematic literature review. *International Journal of Production Research*. 4(2), 159–176.

Zhang Qingzhen. Research on Service Supply Chain Operation Risk Management of Community Aged Care Based on SCOR Model. *A Systematic Review. Sustainability* 2021, 13, 7104.

Economic and Business Management – Huang & Zhang (Eds)
© 2022 Copyright the Author(s), ISBN: 978-1-032-06754-4

When is "free" a bad choice? An empirical approach of promotional effects on "free trials" reviews

Xue Sun, Yuhao Li & Yu Pan
School of Business and Management, Shanghai International Studies University, Shanghai, China

ABSTRACT: Free trials[1] have become an important way for business to increase popularity and raise user evaluation via review websites. However, how free trials review may affect business performance is still unclear. This paper investigates whether these free trial reviews affect the overall score positively or not and how much the merchants can benefit from "free trials". By analyzing 37,513 reviews from 79 restaurants located in China generated in dianping.com, the results indicated that the reviews posted by "free trials" users have higher score than those posted by paid users. In addition, the sales performance of these merchants who have used the "free trials" strategy is higher than those who have never used it in short term, but this effect may be reversed in the long term (e.g., 3 months). Our findings provide novel insights for scholars contributing online "free trials" review as well as for practitioners seeking to propagate online influence.

Keywords: Free trial; Review manipulation; difference-in-difference

1 INTRODUCTION

In order to improve online influence, merchants expect more positive reviews while avoiding negative reviews (Hu, Bose, Koh, & Liu, 2012). Hu (2012) found that 10.3% of the products are subject to online review manipulation. Although review manipulation is considered to hinder fair competition and generally not allowed on these platforms, free trials as one of the most feasible marketing campaign can harvest numerous customers and valuable reviews in a short period of time. The focus of this research is the review manipulation method based on free trials, which is allowed by the platform. In order to help some start-ups or merchants that need to increase popularity, the platform provides opportunities for consumers to experience services or products for free. These consumers are expected to write reviews for merchants after the trial.

However, it is unclear whether the benefits from implementing free trial are greater than the cost of free trial.

Based on the above discussion, this paper proposes the following research questions:

RQ1: Is the review rating after the free trial higher than that of the non-free trial in average?

RQ2: Do the sales of the merchants increase/decrease after the implementation of the free strategy compared with the sales when the free strategy is not implemented?

2 RELATED LITERATURE AND HYPOTHESIS DEVELOPMENT

2.1 Review manipulation

The free trials can be seen as a legal means of review manipulation. The existing research on online review manipulation can be divided into three categories according to its subject, namely, from the perspectives of the platform, consumers, and merchants.

From the platform perspective, the literature focuses on the recognition of review manipulation, which can be divided into two categories. The first category is to identify positive reviews which are ghostwritten by individuals. This type of research mainly judges from the content of reviews. Plotkina, Dariaand Munzel, Andreas (2020) found that false reviews are different in semantic linguistics. In addition, clues to distinguish false reviews can be found from writing style, construct, informativeness, etc. (Hu, Bose, Koh, & Liu, 2012; Huang, Yang, Lin, & Shih, 2012); the other type is positive reviews ghostwritten by programs. This type of research mainly identifies the reviews written in batch by computer programs and mainly judges from the published time and user ID of the review. The platform's purpose to identify manipulated reviews is to eliminate false reviews and maintain fair and legal competition among merchants. The existing literature from the consumer perspective

---

[1]The merchant provides free services or products to customers. After trying the service or product, customers are expected to write reviews for their trials in return. It is called '霸王餐' in dianping.com.

mainly focuses on consumers' perception of manipulated reviews, doubts and uncertainty (Ma & Lee, 2014; Song, Park, & Ryu, 2017), as well as the resulting perception of helpfulness of reviews, and impacts on perception of merchant reputation and purchase intention (Munzel, 2016). From the merchant perspective, existing literature mainly studies the motivation of merchants to manipulate reviews, the characteristics of merchants that may conduct review manipulation (Li, Du, Zheng, Xue, & Zhu, 2018), the review manipulation methods (Thakur, Hale, & Summey, 2018) and the results of review manipulation (Anderson & Simester, 2014; Zhuang, Cui, & Peng, 2018).

2.2 Hypothesis development

Most consumers who have tried services for free show gratitude to the merchants, which can be intuitively seen from the review content (Luca & Zervas, 2016). Out of gratitude to the merchants and as a reward for the merchants who provided the free services, consumers are more likely to give a rating higher than the normal level. Therefore, the following hypothesis is proposed:

H1: The review rating of a free trial is higher than that of the non-free trial.

On the one hand, with the addition of free trial user reviews, the number of reviews of the merchant will increase (Wang et al., 2018), reducing the perceived uncertainty of users, thereby facilitating consumer purchases. On the other hand, after using the free trial strategy, the merchant's own publicity will increase and users who have signed up for the free trial but do not get the free trial quotas in the lottery will be attracted. They may spend money to try the service. Therefore, the free trial strategy may increase the possibility of potential customers' consumption and also encourage consumers to make purchases. Based on the above analysis, the following hypothesis is proposed:

H2: After using the free trial review manipulation strategy, merchant sales will increase.

3 DATA

3.1 Data source

This paper takes the data from the dianping.com. The merchants who intent to use the free trial function show the information in the designated section of dianping.com, interested consumers can submit an application.

This kind of review manipulation method recognized by the platform is favored by many merchants. On the one hand, free experienced users are expected to write reviews in return for the merchants' free service, which would increase the number of reviews. On the other hand, although only several hundreds of free places are available, the actual number of applicants is far more than that, which can be up to 1:1000 in ratio.

The platform will issue an identification code to each selected user, who will use this code to verify the user's identity after arriving at the store and then try the service item for free. In dianping.com, the reviews of users who have verified the codes will be marked as 'Review after free trial' (Figure 1).

3.2 Data collection

We collected 37,513 reviews, in the time range from January 2018 to March 2020, from 79 merchants classified in the category of food in dianping.com randomly, including 65 merchants who have never used free trials and 14 merchants who have used free trial at least once. By using monthly sales as the basic unit of analysis, we define the first month, namely, January 2018 as t=1, and code the whole period successively.

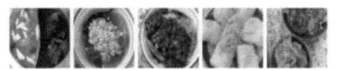

Figure 1. The marked review issued by free trial user.

4 DATA ANALYSIS

4.1 The rating comparison of free trial review and non-free trial review

We employ t-test by using SPSS22.0 to compare the free trial review ratings of non-free trial merchants with those who have used free trials. The t-test is appropriate, because by comparing the mean of the rating issued by free trial users and non-free trial users, the rating difference under these two conditions could be tested. In this paper, 575 free trial reviews and 8414 non-free trial reviews are collected for t-test. According to the results (Table 1), it can be seen that the rating difference between free trial and non-free trial is significant (p<0.001), and the mean of free trial review is 4.68 (S.D.=0.59), and the mean of non-free trial review is 4.54 (S.D.=0.73). Therefore, H1 is supported. The review rating of a free trial is indeed higher than that of the non-free trial.

Table 1. The comparison of review rating between free trial and non-free trial.

Trial	Sample	Mean	S.D.	t	p
Non-free	8414	4.54	0.73	−5.672	0.000***
Free	575	4.68	0.59		

* $p<0.05$; ** $p<0.01$; *** p<0.001

4.2 The impact of the implementation of free trial strategy

To justify H2, the DID is used for analysis. We aim to explore whether using the policy, namely, free trials will have an impact on the performance of the merchant. Some merchants did not use this policy, while others implemented it. This article compares the difference in sales between merchants who have implemented the policy and those who have not implemented the policy before and after the policy is implemented to examine the effect of the policy of free trials. Therefore, it is appropriate to choose DID for analysis. The treatment group is the merchants which carried out free trials at least once, and the control group is those which have never used free trials. Since merchant sales cannot be accurately obtained, we use the number of reviews of non-free trial to measure merchant sales. As the more the merchant sells, the more the reviews are issued. In addition, the number of reviews employed in previous studies to measure merchant sales has been proven to have a significant positive effect (Ye, Law, Gu, & Chen, 2011).

On a monthly basis, compared with those which have never used the free trial, whether those which have used the free trial have significantly higher monthly sales after using the free trial than when they have not used it. The empirical specification is as follows:

$$Yit = \beta0 + \beta1Afterit + \beta2Treatit + \beta3Afterit \times Treatit + Ctl + uit,$$

where t is the monthly basis, the first month of all data is recorded as t=1, and the subsequent months are t+1. i means merchants. After is a dummy variable, 1 indicates in time t, shop i has already received treatment, 0 means it has not received treatment. Treat is also a dummy variable, 1 indicates shop i ever receive treatment, 0 means reverse. Y is the monthly sales of shop i in time t. Ctl means control variables, including business overall rating to control the effect of merchants themselves.

Of all 14 merchants that have used free trial in our collection, 12 merchants used free trial between May and July 2019. Therefore, we only select these 12 merchants as treatment group. The period of May-July 2019 was regarded as the policy implementation period, and the data during this period were excluded. The 65 merchants that have never used free trial were used as control group to compare the difference in monthly sales changes between treatment group and control group before and after the policy (free trial) was implemented. We use Stata15 for DID analysis. Table 2 shows the result of difference-in-differences.

Table 2. The result of DID analysis.

	Model 1	Model 2
Treatment	−13.170* (0.025)	−11.440 (0.051)
After	20.610*** (0.000)	19.001*** (0.000)
Treatment* After	14.862* (0.031)	14.420* (0.035)
Average Score		−66.879** (0.005)
Merchant Control	No	Yes
F	20.74	15.62
P	0.000	0.000
N	736	736

Notes. Dependent variable is Sales which is measured by the number of reviews excluding free trial reviews.
*p<0.05; **p<0.01; ***p<0.001

Consistent with the hypothesis, the implementation of free trial has positive impact on the performance of the merchants ($\beta = 14.420$ p= 0.035).

In addition, we have also verified that before using the free trial (t < 17), the sales of free trial used merchants showed a roughly parallel trend compared with that of free trial unused merchants (Figure 2).

More information can be found from the graph given in Figure 2. Firstly, the sales will increase rapidly after free trial is employed, and the increased effect of

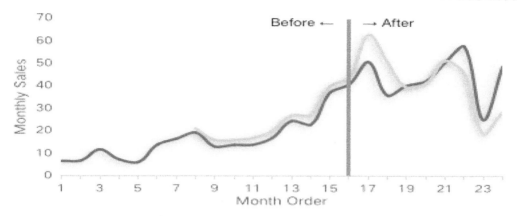

Figure 2. Monthly sales comparison (before free trial used vs. after free trial used).
*In the first 8 months, there are reviews issued only from the merchants which have never used free trials. At the time of t=16, the strategy of free trials was implemented with a period of 4 months, to compare the difference of before and after intuitively, we deleted the period of these 4 months in the graph. As we count the average sales of each month, so only the data on the coordinate axis points represents the current sales, and the curve of non-coordinate points has no meaning.

the free trial on sales mainly occurs in the following 2 months. Then, after that, the effect of free trial on sales seems to disappear. Surprisingly, in the fifth month after using free trial, there was even a relative decline in sales, although free trial has a statistically positive effect on sales in our data collection period.

5 CONCLUSIONS

Our finding proposes a new and allowable approach for the merchants to refine the online review score and sales performance. In the previous research relevant to manipulation review, it was necessary to judge whether it is a manipulated review first based on the review content, publisher's information, etc., and then perform the evaluation (Anderson & Magruder, 2012), which is destined to cause errors in the measurement results. In this research, whether it is a review written after a free trial can be seen directly from the review tag. Hence, the results are more accurate and reliable compared to previous study.

However, there are still some limitations in our research. Firstly, free trial reviews do bring positive effects, but this study does not measure the period of the free strategy timeliness, i.e., how long the implementation of the free strategy takes for the merchant to gain benefits. Secondly, delayed effect has not been examined, i.e., whether review manipulation in period t has an impact on sales in period t+1. Thirdly, whether the above results are different across various industries and regions. People have different ratings for experiential and practical products. Can the above strategy be extended to other industries is not clear. We will continue to explore these issues in future research.

ACKNOWLEDGMENTS

This work was supported by grants from the National Natural Science Foundation of China (Grant nos. 71942003 and 71802135).

REFERENCES

Anderson, E., & Simester, D. (2014). Reviews without a Purchase: Low Ratings. *Loyal Customers.*

Anderson, M., & Magruder, J. (2012). Learning from the crowd: Regression discontinuity estimates of the effects of an online review database. *The Economic Journal*, 122(563), 957–989.

Hu, N., Bose, I., Koh, N. S., & Liu, L. (2012). Manipulation of online reviews: An analysis of ratings, readability, and sentiments. *Decision Support Systems*, 52(3), 674–684.

Huang, Y. K., Yang, W. I., Lin, T. M., & Shih, T. Y. (2012). Judgment criteria for the authenticity of internet book reviews. *Library & Information Science Research*, 34(2), 150–156.

Li, N., Du, S., Zheng, H., Xue, M., & Zhu, H. (2018). Fake reviews tell no tales? dissecting click farming in content-generated social networks. *China Communications*, 15(4), 98–109.

Luca, M., & Zervas, G. (2016). Fake it till you make it: Reputation, competition, and Yelp review fraud. *Management science*, 62(12), 3412–3427.

Ma, Y. J., & Lee, H.-H. (2014). Consumer responses toward online review manipulation. *Journal of Research in Interactive Marketing.*

Munzel, A. (2016). Assisting consumers in detecting fake reviews: The role of identity information disclosure and consensus. *Journal of Retailing and Consumer Services*, 32, 96–108.

Plotkina, D., Munzel, A., & Pallud, J. (2020). Illusions of truth—Experimental insights into human and algorithmic detections of fake online reviews. *Journal of Business Research*, 109, 511–523.

Song, W., Park, S., & Ryu, D. (2017). Information quality of online reviews in the presence of potentially fake reviews. *Korean Economic Review*, 33, 5–34.

Thakur, R., Hale, D., & Summey, J. H. (2018). What motivates consumers to partake in cyber shilling? *Journal of Marketing Theory and Practice*, 26(1-2), 181–195.

Wang, C. C., Li, Y., Luo, X., Ma, Q. G., Fu, W. Z., & Fu, H. J. (2018). The Effects of Money on Fake Rating Behavior in E-Commerce: Electrophysiological Time Course Evidence From *Consumers. Frontiers in Neuroscience*, 12, 9. doi:10.3389/fnins.2018.00156

Ye, Q., Law, R., Gu, B., & Chen, W. (2011). The influence of user-generated content on traveler behavior: An empirical investigation on the effects of e-word-of-mouth to hotel online bookings. *Computers in Human Behavior*, 27(2), p.634–639.

Zhuang, M., Cui, G., & Peng, L. (2018). Manufactured opinions: The effect of manipulating online product reviews. *Journal of Business Research,* 87, 24–35.

Economic and Business Management – Huang & Zhang (Eds)
© 2022 Copyright the Author(s), ISBN: 978-1-032-06754-4

The empirical study of trust and behavioral intention to use the smart healthcare system based on structural equation modeling

Jinxuan Ling & Ni Sheng
Macau University of Science and Technology, Macau, China

Wenzhe Ling
People's Hospital of Ningxia Hui Autonomous Region, YinChuan, China

He Huang
NingXia Medical University, YinChuan China

ABSTRACT: In recent years, many cities across the country have gradually begun to popularize the smart healthcare system. It enables patients to pay medical expenses online with a shorter waiting time and can enjoy relatively convenient, high-quality, and safe diagnostic services. This paper is based on the technology acceptance model, exploring the factors that affect the intention of using smart healthcare system. A total of 315 valid questionnaires were collected in this study and analyzed using AMOS and SPSS statistical software. According to the result, the perceived ease of use and perceived privacy will significantly affect the patient's attitude to use, and the attitude of use will also significantly affect the intention of use. The image of a hospital is also one of the important factors for the intention of intelligent medical use. It will significantly affect trust, and trust will further affect attitude and intention of use. Hospitals should increase investment in the construction of smart healthcare system, pay attention to the security of patient diagnosis and treatment data, and system developers should pay attention to protecting the security of patient diagnosis and treatment data, including personal information, electronic medical records, and payment security. The smart healthcare system should design the interface should be more concise, easy to use, and simple to operate.

Keywords: Smart healthcare system, intention, perceived privacy

1 INTRODUCTION

In recent years, China has gradually improved its smart healthcare system. This system has various functions such as querying the location of the hospital, outpatient registration, queuing, online payment, and self-service medicine, which greatly improves the efficiency of medical treatment. The smart healthcare system can process, store and transmit patients' diagnosis and treatment information and health status based on big data, and now it has gradually become popular with electronic medical records. China has issued several policies to support the construction of a smart healthcare system. The "New Generation Artificial Intelligence Development Plan" officially issued by the State Council in 2017 has included relevant smart healthcare in the new generation of artificial intelligence plans. In December 2021, the State Council issued the "Opinions on Promoting the Healthy Development of the Internet + Medical Care". All localities and departments have achieved significant results in promoting the "Internet + Medical Care" development, especially during the epidemic prevention and control period, which played an important supporting service role. At present, Chinese Grade A tertiary hospitals have almost completely universalized smart medical care, which has greatly eased the medical pressure on hospitals and has achieved remarkable results.

2 THEORETICAL FRAMEWORK AND HYPOTHESES

2.1 Technical Acceptance Model (TAM)

The technology acceptance model (TAM) was first proposed by Davis [1] in 1989, and he emphasized that attitudes would be influence behavioral intention. Smart healthcare system is an information technology-based application that can discuss the technology acceptance model as a theoretical basis.

DOI 10.1201/9781003203704-48

2.2 Perceived ease of use (PEOU) and attitude (AT) toward using

Perceived ease of use is defined as the degree to which consumers think it is easy to use when using a smart healthcare system. The following factors are usually examined. One is whether the function, interface, and content that patients can observe are clear and easy to understand, and the other is the initial simplicity of using the website at the stage, and the third is the speed at which patients can find the content they need [2]. Davis [1] believes that perceived ease of use can improve the attitude of users to use a new system and new technology. Perceived ease of use will be influenced by web design and online transactions [3]. Therefore, hypothesis 1 is proposed:

H1: Patients' perceived ease of use (PEOU)will have a positive effect on their attitudes (AT) towards the use of smart healthcare system.

2.3 Perceived privacy (PP) and attitude (AT) toward using

Perceived privacy can be divided into physical privacy and information privacy [4]. Users often weigh the risks and benefits to decide whether to use online technology. If the benefits outweigh the risks, they will do so and start using the technology [5]. Applying this theory to our situation, if patients think that the smart healthcare system is beneficial to them when visiting a doctor, they will be more likely to use the smart healthcare system despite the potential privacy issues. There are researches using hotel robots to explore the impact of customer privacy perception on attitudes. Through interviews, customers often believe that online systems should be obliged to protect personal data and transaction information. Customers said that the information system actually has no facial expressions and no judgments, so when there is customers' personal information on the information system, they will not feel embarrassed [6]. Therefore, the following hypothesis is expected:

H2: Patients' perceived privacy (PP)will have a positive effect on their attitudes (AT)towards the smart care system.

2.4 Hospital image (HI) and trust (TRU)

Consumers' evaluation of corporate image positively affects their trust in the company [7]. If consumers have a better image of a company or a company, their perceived usefulness will be significantly affected and they trust the company's services more [8]. When consumers perceive that the hospital has attributes that are positive, reliable, or value the rights of consumers, the positive evaluation of the hospital will increase. Therefore, this study defines the image of the hospital as the user's perception of the positiveness of a hospital with a smart healthcare system Appraisal that is reliable or values the attributes of consumer rights. Therefore, we formulate our third hypothesis:

H3: Hospital image (HI) will have a positive effect on patients' trust (TRU) in the smart healthcare system.

2.5 Trust (TRU) and attitude (AT) toward using

Users' trust in the information system positively affects its use attitude, and also positively affects its purchase intention [9]. When making payment actions, trust has a positive impact on the user's current will [10]. Users' trust in the smart healthcare system should have the following characteristics, one is whether the hospital can fulfill the expectations entrusted by patients, and the other is whether the hospital has a good technical performance. Therefore, hypothesis 4 of this study is proposed:

H4: Patients' trust (TRU) in the smart healthcare system will have a positive effect on their use attitude (AT).

2.6 Attitude (AT) toward using and behavioral intention to use (BI)

Davis [1] believes that the behavioral intent was influenced by the use attitude. For online shopping, attitudes have an impact on its continuing intentions [11]. The users' attitude towards new information and new technology has a positive relationship to the intention to use behavior [12]. Therefore, hypothesis 5 of this study is proposed:

H5: The patient's attitude (AT) towards the use of the smart healthcare system will have a positive effect on their behavioral intention to use (BI).

3 RESEARCH METHODOLOGY

3.1 Questionnaire development

The variables of perceptual ease of use, attitude, and intention of patients using smart healthcare system are mainly from Davis [1]. Perceptual privacy is mainly from Korzaan [13]. The hospital image is mainly from Luis [2]. Trust mainly from Mayer [14]. We use SPSS22.0 analysis the descriptive statistical and reliability, and AMOS22.0 analysis the structural equations.

The questionnaires were distributed mainly through an online crowdsourcing platform. The participants in the survey were patients in the hospital. A total of 556 questionnaires were collected, and 315 were found to be valid. To ensure that the samples were representative, the participants were selected from Grade A tertiary hospitals, and the effective questionnaire recovery rate was 57.2%. The questionnaire was comprised of 5-point Likert scales, ranging from strongly disagree to strongly agree.

3.2 Sample size and data collection procedure

The samples were collected from Grade A tertiary hospitals in Guangdong and Ningxia provinces.

Among the 315 questionnaires obtained, the sample consisted of 147 males and 168 females. The functions of patients using the smart healthcare system are mainly for appointment registration and mobile payment. Most patients are between 20 and 40 years old, and the education level is mainly above college degree. (See Table 1.)

Use AMOS 22.0 statistical software to perform confirmatory factor analysis (CFA) and structural equation modeling (SEM) on the collected data, and use the maximum likelihood estimation method.

Table 1. Sample demographic.

Demographic data.	Category	Frequency	Percentage
Gender	Male	147	46.7
	Female	168	53.3
Age	Under 20 years	9	2.8
	21–40	263	83.5
	41–50	27	8.5
	Above 50	16	5.2
Qualification enrolled	Less than high school	9	2.8
	High school	50	15.8
	Undergraduate	259	81.4

4 RESULTS

4.1 Measurement model

Generally, the Kaiser-Mayer-Olkin (KMO) value and Bartlett's test are suitable for CFA before this. The KMO value of each variable is above the minimum of 0.70. The chi-square values of Bartlett's sphere test for each variable are significant, which means that the correlation between the variables is strong and independent, and it is suitable for factor analysis. It can be seen from the results of confirmatory factor analysis that the model fit indices value of perceived ease of use, perceived privacy, trust, and behavioral intention to use is much higher than the minimum recommended by other researchers [15]: ratio of chi-square and freedom of each item is less than 5, GFI, AGFI is greater than 0.85, RMSEA less than 0.08 and NFI, CFI greater than 0.80, so no modification is required. But the value of attitude, and hospital image chi-square is less than 5, so the model needs to be modified. When the model fit indices are not ideal and the errors are found to be correlated, the related items can be deleted. The SEM model requires at least three questions for one variable. After deleting the attitude and hospital image, the model fit indices were good, the Cronbach's Alpha values were all above 0.70 [16]. And the standardized factor loading of each item is over 0.70, and the SMC value is higher than 0.36, indicating good fit indices and good internal reliability. According to Bagozzi [17], the measurement error variation must reach a

significant level, and the other is that the error variation cannot be negative. The estimated value of error variation for each topic in this article is significant and positive, indicating that there is no unexplainable situation. (See Table 2.)

Table 2. Internal reliability and convergent validity of the measurement.

Construct	Item	Cronbach's α	SMC	Factor loading	Error Estimate
Peceived ease of use	PEOU1	0.838	.398	.642	.624
	PEOU2		.850	.891	.138
	PEOU3		.555	.755	.288
	PEOU4		.578	.784	.265
Perceive privacy	PP1	0.803	.774	.812	.262
	PP2		.512	.753	.317
	PP3		.471	.721	.340
Attitude	AT1	0.873	.646	.771	.218
	AT2		.870	.807	.220
	AT3		.480	.751	.319
Hospital image	HI1	0.832	0.700	.721	.273
	HI2		0.580	.722	.263
	HI3		0.360	.659	.353
Trust	TRU1	0.829	.589	.802	.216
	TRU2		.790	.835	.170
	TRU3		.503	.731	.289
Behavioral Intention	BI1	0.876	.695	.842	.021
	BI2		.613	.785	.015
	BI3		.624	.769	.027
	BI4		.653	.813	.022

4.2 Structural model

According to the evaluation fit indices of the structural model, the fit indices value of the structural model needs to meet the requirements of the recommended value to prove that the model fits well before hypothesis testing can be carried out, as shown in Table 3. The recommended according to Wu [18], the ratio of chi-square and freedom of each item is less than 5, GFI, AGFI is greater than 0.85, RMSEA less than 0.08, and NFI, CFI greater than 0.80, these values are within the recommended values, so the hypothesis can be tested.

Table 3. Fit indices of the model.

Fit index	$\chi2/df$	GFI	AGFI	RMSEA	NFI	CFI
Recomend value	<5	>0.85	>0.85	<0.08	>0.80	>0.80
Structural model	2.595	0.886	0.853	0.071	0.900	0.935

As depicted in Figure 1. and Table 4., the value of the Standardized coefficient is positive, indicating that the direct influence is positive, and the direct causal relationship between each variable can be obtained. The structural model revealed that the standardized coefficient of all proposed paths was significant. The five hypotheses are all supported.

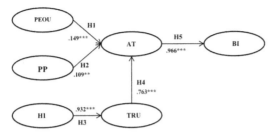

Figure 1. Result of the research model.

Table 4. Summary of hypothesis tests.

Hypothesis	Standardized coefficient	t-value	Status
H1:PEOU→AT	.149***	2.559	supported
H2:PP→AT	.109**	2.224	supported
H3: HI→TRU	.932***	10.596	supported
H4: TRU→AT	.763***	9.174	supported
H5: AT→BI	.966***	15.478	supported

Note: Significant at * * * : p<0.001

5 DISCUSSION AND CONCLUSION

5.1 Strengthening investment in the construction of smart healthcare system

This article discusses the intention of using a smart healthcare system. With the increasing popularity of the smart healthcare system, patients gradually adapt to the smart healthcare system from the traditional diagnosis and treatment process. However, smart healthcare system has not yet been fully popularized. The government should increase the capital investment to improve the pressure of the hospital's diagnosis and treatment process.

5.2 Pay attention to the safety of patient diagnosis and treatment data

In traditional diagnosis and treatment, the information of many patients is unavoidably leaked by medical workers in public. Cases of patients being leaked due to their personal medical history and diagnosis and treatment information also occur from time to time, resulting in tension between doctors and patients. The preservation of the case solves this problem. The smart healthcare system can call the patient's number, and the patient's examination and inspection report can also be directly obtained through the patient's mobile phone. There is no need to queue to the hospital to wait. The empirical analysis also confirms the perception of privacy. Attitude to use has a positive and significant impact. Therefore, system developers should pay more attention to protecting the security of patient diagnosis and treatment data, including personal information security, electronic medical record security, payment security, and protecting patients' privacy and security issues.

REFERENCES

[1] Davis,F.D.1989.Perceived usefulness, perceived ease of use, and user acceptance of information technology [J]. *MIS Quarterly* 13(3), 319–340.

[2] Casal, L. V., Flavin, C., & Guinalu, M. 2007. The role of security, privacy, usability and reputation in the development of online banking [J]. *Online Information Review* 31(5), 583–603.

[3] Flavian, C., Torres, E. &Guinaliu, M.2004.Corporate image measurement: a further problem for the tangibilization of internet banking services [J]. *International Journal of Bank Marketing* 22(5), 366–84.

[4] Jeff Smith, H., Dinev, T., & Xu, H. 2011. Information privacy research: an interdisciplinary review[J]. *MIS Quarterly* 35(4), 989–1015.

[5] Dinev, T., Hart, P.2006.An extended privacy calculus model for e-commerce transactions. *Information systems research* 17(1), 61–80.

[6] Lin, I. Y., & Mattila, A. S. 2021.The Value of Service Robots from the Hotel Guest's Perspective: A Mixed-Method Approach[J]. *International Journal of Hospitality Management* 94, 102–876.

[7] Doney, P. M., & Cannon, J. P. 1997.An Examination of the nature of trust in buyer-seller relationships [J]. *Journal of Marketing*, 61(2), 35–51.

[8] Featherman, M. S., Miyazaki, A. D., & Sprott, D. E. 2010.Reducing online privacy risk to facilitate e-service adoption: the influence of perceived ease of use and corporate credibility[J]. *Journal of Services Marketing* 24(3), 219–229.

[9] Linwu,W. The Influence of Electronic Commerce Personalized Recommendation System On Consumer Purchase Intention[M], *Tianjin: Tianjin University* 2017.

[10] McKnight, D. H., & Chervany, N. L. 2001. What Trust Means in E-Commerce Customer Relationships: An Interdisciplinary Conceptual Typology [J]. *International Journal of Electronic Commerce*, 6(2), 35–59.

[11] Lee, H. Y., Qu, H., & Kim, Y. S.2007. A study of the impact of personal innovativeness on online travel shopping behavior - A case study of korean travelers[J]. *Tourism Management*, 28(3), 886–897.

[12] Lee, H.J., & Lyu, J. 2016. Personal values as determinants of intentions to use self-service technology in retailing[J]. *Computers in Human Behavior* 60, 322–332.

[13] Korzaan, M. L., & Boswell, K. T. 2008. The Influence of Personality Traits and Information Privacy Concerns on Behavioral Intentions[J]. *The Journal of Computer Information Systems* 48(4), 15–24.

[14] Mayer, R., Davis, J., & Schoorman, F.1995.An Integrative model of organizational trust[J]. *Academy of Management Review* 20(3), 709–734.

[15] Bentler, P. M., & Bonett, D. G. 1980, "Significance tests and goodness-of-fit in the analysis of covariance structures" [J]. *Psychological Bulletin*, 88(3), 588–606.

[16] Hair, J. F., Ringle, C. M., & Sarstedt, M. (2011), "PLS–SEM: indeed a silver bullet", *Journal of Marketing Theory and Practice*, 19(2), 139–152.

[17] Bagozzi, R. P., & Yi, Y. 1988. On the evaluation of structural equation models[J]. *Journal of the Academy of Marketing Science* 16(1), 74–94.

[18] Minglong, W. Structural Equation Modeling: Operation and Application of AMOS[M]. *Beijing: Chongqing University Press* 2009

APPENDIX

List of Measurement Items

Perceived ease of use
1. I think it does not take a lot of time to learn to operate the functions in the smart medical system.
2. I think the interface of the smart medical system is easy to operate.
3. I can quickly find the information I need in the smart medical system.
4. Overall, the smart medical system is easy to use.

Perceived privacy
1. I believe that no one can use my personal cases and data in Smart Medical for any other purpose, unless authorized by me.
2. I think the smart medical system should take more measures to ensure that the personal consultation in the database is correct and correct, such as age, gender, ID number, etc.
3. I think the smart medical system should spend more time to prevent personal data from being accessed illegally.

Attitude
1. I like to use smart medical system.
2. I think using smart medical system is a good choice.
3. When I use the appointment registration and other functions provided by Smart Medical, these functions make me feel convenient and happy.

Hospital image
1. I think the overall image of the hospital is good.
2. I think the hospital is honest.
3. I think the hospital is innovative and forward-looking.

Trust
1. I have confidence in the smart medical system.
2. I think the smart medical system is trustworthy.
3. Pay and make an appointment on the smart medical system, so I can rest assured.

Behavioral Intention to Use
1. I have the will to use the smart medical system.
2. I am willing to use the smart medical system frequently.
3. If the smart medical system has new functions, I will try to use it.
4. I would recommend the smart medical system to others to use.

Demographics
1. What functions of the smart medical system have you used? (Multiple choice)
   ☐ Basic information of the hospital
   ☐ Intelligent diagnosis-guide you to the departments where you need to be registered according to your symptoms
   ☐ Appointment registration
   ☐ Inquiry about the doctor's profile
   ☐ Mobile payment fee
   ☐ Report query
   ☐ Satisfaction survey
2. What is your gender:
   ☐ male ☐ female
3. What is your age:
   ☐ Under 20 years (inclusive) ☐ 21–40 ☐ 41–50
   ☐ Above 50 (inclusive)
4. What is your education level:
   ☐ Less than high school ☐ High school
   ☐ Undergraduate

Economic and Business Management – Huang & Zhang (Eds)
© 2022 Copyright the Author(s), ISBN: 978-1-032-06754-4

Impacts of job insecurity on burnout: Examining the mediating role of job stress among Thai bank tellers

Bangxin Peng & Wisanupong Potipiroon
Prince of Songkla University, Songkhla, Thailand

ABSTRACT: The COVID-19 pandemic has promoted online banking services. There is tendency that jobs of bank tellers are going to be replaced by online banking service. This study draws attention to the effects of job insecurity on burnout for Thai bank tellers. Furthermore, we examine the mediating role of job stress between job insecurity and burnout. Based on survey data of 520 bank tellers in 53 bank branches located in the southern regions of Thailand, our structural equation modeling (SEM) based on the analysis result of SPSS PROCESS Macro 4.0. confirms job insecurity impacted burnout positively. Job stress can positively mediate the relations between job insecurity and burnout.

Keywords: Job insecurity, Burnout, Job Stress, Bank Tellers

1 INTRODUCTION

The COVID-19 pandemic does not only have a strong adverse influence on normal social lives, but also facilitates organizational change for enterprise worldwide (Kaushik & Gulerin, 2020). The most significant organizational change is organizational downsizing With the shrinking of commercial profit during the period of the COVID-19 pandemic, impacted business organizations seek to reduce operational cost by downsizing their organizational scale. Consequently, the company must lay off redundant employees. Thai bank industry is experiencing such scenarios. To protect individual health from infections of COVID-19, bank clients are asked to apply on-line banking service for their transactions rather than using counter service. With a dramatic decrease for counter service, Thai commercial banks have begun industry level downsizing. In 2020, around 256 bank branches terminated service (The Nation Thailand, 2020). Bank tellers may perceive uncertainty for their future career or job insecurity when experiencing the organizations' downsizing Meanwhile, changes in working environments may stimulate job stress, which would have negative effects on their physical and mental health (Devereux et al., 2004; Dollard, 2003). When job stress is not relieved adequately, it will spark more negative effects such as burnout (Dekker & Schaufeli, 1995). Several past studies have examined multiple stressors related with the job content of bank employees that can predict burnout including time pressure, continuous physical energy, and role conflict (Ashill, Rod & Gibbs, 2015; Brauchli et al., 2011; Li et al., 2015;

Kan & Yu, 2016) However, though an important job stressor for bank tellers in COVID-19 pandemic, job insecurity has been studied by limited previous works (Batool & Nawaz, 2021; Oginni et al., 2013). There is not any study to examine job insecurity and its impact on Thai bank tellers so far. Thus, our study can fill this gap to investigate the relationship between job insecurity, and burnout for Thai bank tellers in the period of the COVID-19 pandemic. We furthermore examine whether job stress has a mediating influence on the relationship between job insecurity and burnout.

2 LITERATURE REVIEW AND HYPOTHESIS

2.1 *Job insecurity and burnout*

According to psychological contract theory (Shruthi, 2012), job insecurity can increase burnout through the violation process of psychological contract. Job insecurity refers to perceived powerlessness and uncertainty to maintain desired continuity in a threatened job situation (De Witte, 2005; Shoss, 2017). Job insecurity discussed in our study is driven by the result of technological innovation within the banking industry rather than poor job performance and work attitude of individual. Burnout is a syndrome of emotional exhaustion, depersonalization, and low professional achievement, which occurs among individuals with service jobs (Maslach & Jackson, 1981). Based on psychological contracts, there is a psychological exchange agreement relationship between employers and employees. This relationship is based on trust for

262

DOI 10.1201/9781003203704-49

both parties (Rousseau, 1998; Shruthi, 2012). High performance can be expected from the employee if the employer respects the norms of employees underlying this theory. However, when the bank tellers are threatened by job insecurity, the psychological contract is violated because they may perceive his or her career life will be terminated soon by the current organization ruthlessly. Consequently, emotional exhaustion, personal distance and indifference, which are syndromes of burnout, could occur between themselves and the remaining organization. Low performance is a consequence of these negative psychological changes. Thus, we have the following hypothesis.

H1: Job insecurity has a positive impact on burnout.

2.2 The mediating role of Job stress

Job insecurity can stimulate job stress based on transactional stress theory (Lazarus & Folkman, 1984). Job stress is caused by "a process that occurs when environmental demands exceed the adaptive capacity of persons, this process results in both negative biological and psychological changes" (Cohen, Gianaros, & Manuck, 2016). When an individual perceives job insecurity that personal resources are insufficient to cope with, they would feel stress. With high job insecurity perceived, high job stress may be sensed by individuals. Meanwhile, the intrinsic energic resources are exploited when job stress cannot be coped with over a prolonged period. However, once the intrinsic energy resources such as emotional robustness, cognitive agility, and physical vigor are deprived, burnout would occur (Gorgievski & Hobfoll, 2008; Wu et al., 2020). Thus, with more job stress, higher burnout can be triggered for an individual. Thus we proposed:

H2: Job stress partially mediates the relationship between job insecurity and burnout positively (Figure 1).

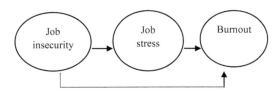

Figure 1. Conceptual framework.

3 METHODOLOGY

3.1 Sample and procedures

The sample in this study has been randomly drawn among a population of commercial banks which are operating in the 5 largest southern provinces of Thailand. A total of 520 bank tellers from ten commercial banks participated in the survey. The major instrument of this study is a questionnaire.

3.2 Measures

All original survey instruments in this study are developed in English. Thus, back translation is needed (Brislin, 1970), where the original English version has been translated to Thai first, then translated back into English.

The questionnaire includes four sections: job insecurity, job stress, burnout, and basic demographic information namely, gender, age, education, job position and tenure. Job insecurity was estimated using 4 items from the scale developed by De Witte (2000) The responses were assessed on the 5-Lickert scale ranging from "1 = strongly disagree" to "5 = strongly agree."

Burnout was estimated using 14 items from the scale development by Maslach et al. (2001), which uses a 7-point scale for responses ranging from "1-never" to 7-every day".

Job stress was measured using a 10-item form developed by Cohen and Williamson (1988), which used a 5-point scale for responses ranging from "1-never" to "5-very often".

There were 125 males and 395 females in the sample, and 79.6 percent of them had a bachelor's degree. About 34.2 percent of respondents were between the ages of 31 and 44, and 56.3 percent of respondents work as an operation officer. About 46.2 percent of respondents had worked for their present organization for 1–5 years in terms of organizational tenure.

3.3 Data analysis

Firstly, SPSS 24.0 was utilized by us to test common method bias (CMB) and analyze descriptive and inferential statistics. Then, we tested the model fit with Mplus Version 7.2 (Muthén & Muthén, 1998–2012). Finally, SPSS PROCESS macro (Hayes, 2013) was utilized for conducting the structural equation modeling (SEM) procedure to analyze the hypothesized connections.

3.4 Common method bias (CMB) test

In the study, all measurements of variables were evaluated by self-reports of individuals. This method may probably result in common method variance (CMV) (Podsakoff et al., 2003). Thus, we conducted Harman's single factor test for variables. The result shows 47.12% which is less than 50%. Thus such a result suggests CMB does not affect our data.

3.5 Measurement models

Confirmatory factor analysis (CFA) is conducted to examine the convergent and discriminant validity. A good model fit needs both CFI and TLI values which should be greater than .90, whereas both RMSEA and SRMR values should be less than .08; Normed Fit Chi-square ($\chi 2/df$) should be less than 3 (Hair et al., 2014; Hox et al., 2010). The results showed that the hypothesized model provided an acceptable fit to the data ($\chi2$ /df=2.94, P =.00, RMSEA =.05, TLI =.949, CFI =.957 SRMR=.036). To assess the convergent validity of the measurement items, this study examined Cronbach's alpha, factor loadings, average variance extracted (AVEs) and composite reliabilities (CRs). Cronbach's alpha should be larger than .70 (Fornell & Larcker, 1981) CRs also should be more than .60 (Bagozzi & Yi, 1988). The factor loading should be at least 0.7 (Hair Jr, Sarstedt, Hopkins, & Kuppelwieser, 2014). Thus, the discriminant validity of the constructs in this study was supported (see Table 1).

Table 1. Reliability and validity.

variables	Min loading	Alpha	CR	AVE
JI	0.759	0.882	0.919	0.740
BO	0.750	0.929	0.964	0.661
JS	0.779	0.877	0.937	0.681

Note: JI= Job insecurity, BO = burnout
JS= Job Stress

3.6 *Descriptive statistics and mean difference*

Table 2 illustrates that burnout is positively correlated with both job insecurity and job stress. Job insecurity also has positively correlations with job stress.

Table 2. Means, standard deviations, and correlations.

Variables	Mean	SD	JI	BO	JS
JI	2.772	1.063	1		
BO	2.836	1.419	0.506**	1	
JS	2.953	0.729	0.450**	0.654**	1

Note: JI= Job insecurity, BO = Burnout, JS= Job Stress
** $p > 0.01$

3.7 *Structural models*

To examine the indirect effects, a bootstrap procedure is applied which obtains a confidence interval based on 10,000 resampling. This method gives more accurate results than using standard techniques involving Sobel tests (Hayes & Preacher, 2010).

The findings in Table 3 show that the direct relationship between job insecurity and burnout was supported ($\beta = 0.355$, p < 0.001) R2=25.62%, which means 25.62% variance of burnout is explained by job insecurity. The indirect effects of job insecurity via job stress were significant on burnout ($\beta = .321$, p<0.05; SE = .044; 95% confidence interval [CI] = [.240, .409]). R2=22.78%, which means 22.78% variance of burnout is explained by job stress. Thus H1, H2 can be supported by such results.

Table 3. Structural model.

Effect	Point estimate	SE	BC 95% CI Lower	Upper
H1: JI→ BO	0.355***	0.047	0.262	0.448
H2: JI → JS → BO	0.321*	0.044	0.240	0.409

Note: JI= Job insecurity, BO = Burnout, JS= Job Stress
*** $p > 0.001$, * $p > 0.05$

4 DISCUSSION

4.1 *Theoretical implications*

In this study, we found that job insecurity has a positive influence on burnout among Thai bank tellers. This consequence is in line with past empirical studies (Batool & Nawaz, 2021; Oginni et al., 2013). Also, this finding responds to the result of psychological contract violation between bank tellers and their employers. High job insecurity can facilitate burnout via increasing job stress for the bank tellers. This finding corresponds with the conclusion of transactional stress theory (Lazarus & Folkman, 1984). In this study, job stress comes from a process when individuals appraise the stimuli of organizational downsizing as potential threats to their job security. Our findings manifest similar conclusions, which have been examined by past empirical studies which focused on the relationship between stress and burnout on the population of other industries (Dekker & Schaufeli, 1995; Gorgievski & Hobfoll, 2008; Leung, Chan, & Dongyu, 2011; Westman et al., 2001; William et al., 2010; Wu et al., 2020).

4.2 *Practical implications*

Burnout does not only harm personal well-being and health but also can impair organizational performance (Maslach, 2016). When involved with dramatic organization change driven by the technological innovation of the Thai bank industry, both the bankers and employers need to seek causes of burnout clearly in this specific period. Thus, it is possible to find right resources to cope with job burnout. This study has found job insecurity is one significant stressor to worsen job burnout for Thai bank employees when Thai banks experience rapid downsizing. To reduce burnout, we suggest individual bank employees need to think about how to control job insecurity with individual resources. Meanwhile, this study also advises bank employers to appraise job insecurity and the negative effects for the organization thoroughly, then apply organizational resources to help employees cope with burnout, which has a further negative impact on organizational performance.

5 LIMITATION AND FUTURE RESEARCH

This sample is drawn randomly from commercial banks in southern Thailand, and the sample size was large enough for the findings to be generalizable. But our sample mainly included females. Male populations may not have been well represented. Thus the generalizability of our findings may be limited. This study does not propose effective job resources or personal resources to alleviate negative effects job insecurity and job stress for the bank tellers. Thus a future study needs to find effective job resources for Thai bank tellers to cope with job insecurity and relevant job resources.

6 CONCLUSIONS

Though there are several limitations, this study has found that high job insecurity perceptions were associated with high levels of job stress and high levels of burnout. Thus the results imply that job insecurity must be controlled or coped with by both individuals and the organization.

REFERENCES

Ashill, N. J., Rod, M., & Gibbs, T. 2015. Coping with stress: A study of retail banking service workers in Russia. *Journal of Retailing and Consumer Services*, 23, 58–69.

Bagozzi, R. P., & Yi, Y. 1988. On the evaluation of structural equation models. *Journal of the Academy of Marketing Science*, 16(1), 74–94.

Batool, I., & Nawaz, S. 2021. The Effects of Job Insecurity on Job Performance among Banking Employees: The Mediating Role of Work Engagement. *South Asian Journal of Social Sciences and Humanities*, 2(4), 51–67.

Brislin, R. W. 1970. Back-translation for cross-cultural research. *Journal of Cross-Cultural Psychology*,1(3), 185–216.

Brauchli, R., Bauer, G. F., & Hämmig, O. 2011. Relationship between time-based work-life conflict and burnout: A cross-sectional study among employees in four large Swiss enterprises. *Swiss Journal of Psychology* / Schweizerische Zeitschrift für Psychologie / Revue Suisse de Psychologie, 70(3), 165–173.

Cohen, S., & Williamson, G. M. 1988. Perceived stress in a probability sample of the United States. In S. Spacapan & S. Oskamp (eds.), *The social psychology of health*: 31–67. Newbury Park, CA: Sage.

Cohen, S., Gianaros, P.J. & Manuck, S.B. 2016. A Stage Model of Stress and Disease. *HHS Public Access* 11(4): 456–463.

De Witte, H. 2000. Work ethic and job insecurity: assessment and consequences for well-being, satisfaction and performance at work. In Bowen R, De Witte K, De Witte H, Taillieu T (eds.), *From group to community*: 325–350. Garant: Leuven.

De Witte, H. 2005. Job insecurity: Review of the international literature on definitions, prevalence, antecedents and consequences. *SA Journal of Industrial Psychology*, 31, 1–6. http://dx.doi.org/10.4102/sajip.v31i4

Dekker, S.W. & Schaufeli, W.B. 1995. The effects of job insecurity on psychological health and withdrawal: a longitudinal study. *Australian Psychologis* 30(1): 57–63.

Devereux, J., Rydstedt, L., Kelly, V., Weston, P., & Buckle, P. 2004. The role of work stress and psychological factors in the development of musculoskeletal disorders. *Robens Centre for Health Ergonomics University of Surrey Guildford: Surrey*.

Dollard, M.F. 2003. Introduction: context, theories and intervention. In Dollard, M.F., Winefield, A.H., & Winefield, H.R. (eds.), *Occupational stress in the service professions*:1–42. New York: Taylor & Francis Inc.

Fornell, C., & Larcker, D. F. 1981. Evaluating structural equation models with unobservable variables and measurement error. *Journal of marketing Research* 18(1): 39–50.

Gerbing, D. W., & Anderson, J. C. 1988. An updated paradigm for scale development incorporating unidimensionality and its assessment. *Journal of marketing Research* 25(2): 186–192.

Gorgievski, M. J. & Hobfoll, S. E. 2008. Work can burn us out or fire us up: Conservation of resources in burnout and engagement. In J. R. B. Halbesleben (ed.), *Handbook of stress and burnout in health care*: 7 - 22. Huntington, NY: Nova Science Publishers, Inc.

Greenhalgh, L., & Rosenblatt, Z. 1984. Job insecurity: Toward conceptual clarity. *Academy of Management Review* 9(3):438–48.

Hair Jr, J. F., Sarstedt, M., Hopkins, L., & Kuppelwieser, V. G. 2014. Partial least squares structural equation modeling (PLS-SEM): An emerging tool in business research. *European business review* 26(2): 106–121.

Hayes, A. F., & Preacher, K. J. (2010). Quantifying and testing indirect effects in simple mediation models when the constituent paths are nonlinear. *Multivariate Behavioral Research*, 45(4), 627–660.

Hayes, A.F. 2013. Introduction to Mediation, Moderation, and Conditional Process Analysis: A Regression-Based Approach. *New York: Guilford Press*.

Hox, J. J., Maas, C. J., & Brinkhuis, M. J. 2010. The effect of estimation method and sample size in multilevel structural equation modeling. *Statistica Neerlandica*, 64(2), 157–170.

Gorgievski, M. J. & Hobfoll, S. E. 2008. Work can burn us out or fire us up: Conservation of resources in burnout and engagement. In J. R. B. Halbesleben (Ed.), Handbook of stress and burnout in health care (pp.7–22). *Huntington, NY: Nova Science Publishers, Inc.*

Kan, D. 2015. The mediating role of psychological capital onthe association between occupational stress and job burnout among bank employees in China. *Int. J. Environ. Res. Public Health* 2015, 12, 2984–300.

Kaushik1, M & Guleria, N. 2020. The Impact of Pandemic-COVID -19 in Workplace: *European Journal of Business and Management* 12(15): 9–18.

Lazarus, R. S., & Folkman, S. 1984. Stress, Appraisal, and Coping. *New York: Springer*.

Lee, S. Colditz, G.A., Berkman, L.F. & Kawachi, I. 2004. Perspective study of job insecurity and coronary heart disease in US women. *Annals of Epidemiology* 14(1): 24–30.

Leung, M., Chan, Y.S.I. & Dongyu, C. 2011. Structural linearrelationships between job stress, burnout, physiological stress, and performance of construction project managers. *Engineering, Construction and Architectural Management* 18(3): 312–328.

Li X, Kan D& Liu L, 2015 The mediating role of psychological capital on the association between occupational stress and job burnout among bank employees in China. *Int J Environ Res Public Health*. 201512(3): 2984–3001

Maslach C. 1993. Burnout: a multidimensional perspective. In W.B. Schaufeli, C. Maslach & T. Marek (eds.), *Professional Burnout: Recent Developments in Theory and Research*: 19–32. Washington, DC: Taylor & Francis.

Maslach, C., & Leiter, M. P. 2016. Understanding the burn out experience: recent research and its implications for psychiatry. *World psychiatry: official journal of the World Psychiatric Association (WPA)*, 15(2), 103–111.

Muthén, L., & Muthén, B. 1998–2012. Mplus user's guide. *The Nation Thailand*, (2020, May 7). Many more bank branches might close in the aftermath of Covid-19. https://www.nationthailand.com/in-focus/30387390

Maslach, C., Schaufeli, W.B. & Leiter, M.P. 2001. Job burnout. *Annual Review of Psychology* 52(1): 397–422.

Oginni, B., Afolabi, G., and Erigbe, P. (2013). The place of job stress in laborturnover of the banking sector in the nigerian economy. *Int. J. Bus. Manag. Invent.* 2, 93–99.

Podsakoff, P. M., MacKenzie, S. B., Lee, J.-Y., & Podsakoff, N. P. (2003). Common method biases in behavioral research: A critical review of the literature and recommended remedies. *Journal of Applied Psychology*, 88(5), 879–903. doi: 10.1037/0021-9010.88.5.879

Shoss, M. K. 2017. Job insecurity: An integrative review and agenda for future research. *Journal of Management*, 43, 1911–1939.

Westman, M., Etzion, D., & Danon, E. 2001. Job insecurity and crossover of burnout in married couples. *Journal of Organizational Behavior* 22(5): 467–481.

William, D. R., Tahira, M. P., Swee-Lim C., Cesar M. M., & Cornelius, J. K. 2010. The Effects of job insecurity on job satisfaction, organizational citizenship behavior, deviant behavior, and negative emotions of employees. *International Studies of Management & Organization* 40(1): 74–91.

Wu, F., Zheng, R., & Wang, Q., 2020.The relationship between job stress and job burnout: the mediating effects of perceived social support and job satisfaction. *Psychology, Health & Medicine*. 26. 1–8.

Economic and Business Management – Huang & Zhang (Eds)
© 2022 Copyright the Author(s), ISBN: 978-1-032-06754-4

Research on the impact of corporate social responsibility fulfillment on ambidextrous innovation performance of high-tech enterprises

Yuxin Hu & Jinzhi Huang
Harbin Engineering University, Harbin, China

ABSTRACT: Based on the patent data of 497 listed high-tech enterprises from 2016 to 2020 and the financial indicators reflecting their CSR performance, this paper discusses the impact of four dimensions of CSR performance of seven stakeholders on their ambidextrous innovation performance. The results show that CSR performance of human resource dimension has an inverted U-shaped impact on both exploitative and exploratory innovation performance. The CSR performance of shareholders at the capital source dimension promotes the development of exploitative innovation to a certain extent, while the CSR performance of creditors has a negative impact on exploratory innovation. At the social CSR dimension, there is a positive relationship between government CSR fulfillment and exploitative innovation and exploratory innovation. At the supply chain dimension, supplier CSR performance has a negative relationship with exploitative innovation, while customer CSR performance promotes the growth of exploitative innovation performance and has an inverted U-shaped impact on exploratory innovation performance.

1 INTRODUCTION

Until Clarkson (1995) introduced stakeholder theory to explain corporate social responsibility (CSR), the contradiction between internal economic interests and external social responsibilities had been resolved. As Porter and Kramer (2006) proposed the strategic view of CSR, CSR gradually embedded in the strategic framework, in order to ensure the win-win of corporate interests and social benefits. Gallego et al. (2011) find that innovative thinking will erupt when enterprises actively implement CSR to achieve strategic goals. There are also many researchers who have discussed the positive impact of CSR on enterprise innovation, such as Luo and Du (2015), Gong and Bi (2018), and Ko et al. (2020).

However, as competition intensifies and the pace of change accelerates, it is difficult for enterprises to obtain sustainable competitive advantages only by one single form of innovation (Yu 2015). Therefore, organizations should equip with a capacity for ambidextrous innovation (March 1991). Benner and Tushman (2003) argued that exploratory innovation pursues new knowledge and develops new products and services for emerging customers or markets, whereas exploitative innovation builds on existing knowledge and extends existing products. These two different innovations compete for limited resources. Therefore, it is important for enterprises to consider the rationality of resource allocation strategically (Ma et al. 2019).

Hughes (2021) finds that different strategic choices will have a differentiated impact on ambidextrous innovation performance. Correspondingly, CSR activity, which is embedded in strategic framework, needs to weigh the pros and cons among different demands of stakeholders, because they will result in different strategic choices and resource allocation bias. Will this difference have a differentiated impact on the ambidextrous innovation performance? There is rare discussion about that issue.

Therefore, this research seeks to figure out: at the strategic level, whether CSR activity that aims for different stakeholders will have differentiated impact on ambidextrous innovation or not. Drawing upon prior literature and stakeholder theory, we divided the CSR's target objects (seven stakeholders) into four dimensions and analyzed on a secondary data of 497 high-tech enterprises listed in Shanghai and Shenzhen from 2016 to 2020. The results show support for the hypothesized different linkages between four dimensions of CSR and ambidextrous innovation.

2 THEORY AND HYPOTHESES

2.1 *Dimensions division of CSR*

Nowadays, the definition of CSR as "the broad array of strategies and operating practices that a firm develops in its efforts to deal with and create relationships with its numerous stakeholders and the natural environment" (Waddock 2004) has been widely adopted

DOI 10.1201/9781003203704-50

by firms. As Clarkson (1995) introduced stakeholder theory to the CSR research, the study on the dimensions division of CSR has been broadened. Dividing CSR activities into different types by different target objects make the motivation of implementing CSR clearer. In organizational behavior studies, CSR is usually classified into two dimensions: internal and external CSR (Zhang & Lim 2018). Furthermore, Wang and Peng (2010) divided CSR into three dimensions: internal, external, and marginal stakeholders CSR; Zhao et al. (2012) classified the CSR practices of construction enterprises into seven stakeholder groups (employees, shareholders, creditors, government, community, customers, suppliers); Chen et al. (2017) divided CSR into three dimensions (currency layer; manpower layer; social layer). Based on the research of Zhao et al. (2012) and Chen et al. (2017), we also considered these conditions: (1) Gu and Zhai (2014) argued that because of financial constraints, there is heterogeneity between exploratory innovation and exploitative innovation in the investment they can get from funding source; (2) Jiang (2015) proposed that most enterprises need to utilize social capital from its suppliers and customers to promote knowledge exchanging and resource sharing, the impact of which on innovation is different from other stakeholders. Hence, this paper divides CSR performance into four dimensions: human resource CSR (employees), funding source CSR (creditors and shareholders), social CSR (government and community), and supply chain CSR (suppliers and customers), so as to explore the differences in the impact of four dimensions CSR fulfillment on exploratory innovation and exploitative innovation.

2.2 *Human resource CSR dimension and ambidextrous innovation*

For high-tech enterprises, talents are the most important core competitiveness. Li et al. (2017) proposed that among all the major stakeholders, the employees have the most significant impact on the innovation performance of the enterprise. R&D personnel are the key factors for their innovation survival. Only by actively implementing CSR to employees can they attract more high-quality talents. The research of Shao et al. (2020) indicated that equity incentives for executives can significantly promote exploratory innovation of high-tech enterprises, and there is an inverted U-shaped relationship between equity incentives and exploitative innovation. Performing good human resource CSR directly reflects on the high salaries and benefits devices for employees. But considering "the labor supply curve bending backwards", there is a certain point of salaries value that can bring about the most working time of employees, when salaries exceed the peak value, employees would not be stimulated by the marginal salaries because they have to balance the working time and leisure time, also there are fewer talents in labor market that can match such high salaries. Hence, we make the following assumptions:

H1a: There will be an inverted U-shaped relationship between the implementation of employees' CSR and exploitative innovation of high-tech enterprises.

H1b: There will be an inverted U-shaped relationship between the implementation of employees' CSR and exploratory innovation of high-tech enterprises.

2.3 *Funding sources CSR dimension and ambidextrous innovation*

The support of capital is vital for R&D activity. According to Pecking Order Theory of financing, enterprises prefer to adopt internal financing or low-risk debt financing (Gu & Zhai 2014). Performing CSR well can help enterprises to get the favor of investors and creditors, so as to get more funding to support innovation (Sun & Cui 2014). Debt financing requires that enterprises ensure stable and continuous cash flow in the future for debt service. Considering the exploratory innovation make the enterprise face higher uncertainty, the increase of its investment is likely to make it more difficult to get external support. On the contrary, exploitative innovation faces lower financing constraints, so it is relatively easy for enterprises to obtain external financial support. Therefore, the following assumptions are made:

H2a: Implementing shareholders' CSR positively impact the exploitative innovation performance.

H2b: Implementing shareholders' CSR positively impact exploratory innovation performance.

H3a: Implementing creditors' CSR positively impact the exploitative innovation performance.

H3b: Implementing creditors' CSR negatively impact the exploitative innovation performance.

2.4 *Social CSR dimension and ambidextrous innovation*

Government macro-control policy directly affects the future development direction of high-tech enterprises. Tellis et al. (2013) believed that political relations could help enterprises obtain policy support, such as R&D subsidies, tax relief, and intellectual property protection. Legal protection can improve the benefits of exploratory innovation. For performing CSR well to the government, enterprises should operate legally and pay taxes on time so as to obtain more political support. However, high-tech enterprises enjoy higher tax reduction policies than other enterprises, so using tax indicators to measure their CSR responsibilities may be opposite, because enterprises that respond to government policies well will get more tax incentives, thus paying less tax, but their innovation performance is improved. Therefore, the following assumptions are made:

H4a: Implementing government's CSR positively impacts the exploitative innovation performance.

H4b: Implementing government's CSR positively impacts the exploratory innovation performance.

On the other hand, CSR implementation at the social level is mainly reflected in the positive externalities, such as environmental protection and public welfare contributions, which enable the enterprise to establish a good brand image and reputation to achieve sustainable development. Waheed et al. (2020) believed that producing eco-friendly innovative products will satisfy the consumers' environmental protection requirements. It shows that the satisfaction of community citizens' demands for environmental protection will promote new exploratory innovation of high-tech enterprises. Therefore, the following assumptions are made:

H5a: Implementing community's CSR positively impacts the exploitative innovation performance.

H5b: Implementing community's CSR positively impacts the exploratory innovation performance.

2.5 Supply chain CSR dimension and ambidextrous innovation

From a strategic perspective, CSR is regarded as a tool to acquire social capital, to win business trust for mutual benefit, and to achieve win-win cooperation. Cousins and Spekman (2003) argued that as the requirements of product innovation and technical knowledge integration become stricter, enterprises need technical support from the supplier more than usual. Suppliers can provide upstream technical knowledge for enterprises to promote product improvement and obtain some fresh knowledge to promote their exploratory innovation. For exploitative innovation, the improvement of existing products will greatly sharpen the bargaining power of suppliers who provide the special equipment, so they won't accept the rapid change of existing products. Therefore, the following assumptions are made:

H6a: Implementing suppliers' CSR negatively affects the exploitative innovation performance.

H6b: Implementing suppliers' CSR positively affects the exploitative innovation performance.

On the other hand, customer demand is the most sensitive factor of innovation. Gallego-Alvarez et al. (2011) believed that customers' demand for innovation will motivate enterprises to implement CSR to achieve product differentiation. For those enterprises that are not so innovative, they need to add added value to their products through CSR. To achieve differentiation, customers' demands for enterprise are good propellants to exploratory innovation, but once the customer needs reach beyond affordable, existing technology could not catch up with the change of customer demand, and too much inventory and low rate of return will offset the benefits of exploratory innovation. Therefore, the following assumptions are made:

H7a: Implementing customers' CSR positively impacts exploitative innovation performance.

H7a: There will be an inverted U-shaped relationship between the implementation of customers' CSR and exploratory innovation performance.

To sum up, the conceptual model of this study is shown in Figure 1.

3 METHOD

3.1 Data collection

High-tech enterprises are knowledge-intensive and technology-intensive economic entities with huge development potential (Shao & Wu 2020). Therefore, we chose A-share companies listed in Shanghai and Shenzhen which meet the identification of high-tech enterprises, to be our research objects. Firstly, we searched in Juchao information website to collect the companies who got the high-tech identification from January 1, 2018 to the time this research began (because the validity of identification is 3 years). Seven hundred and thirty-two initial sample enterprises were obtained, and the following conditions were screened: (1) select companies that only issue A shares to avoid the difference between B shares and H shares; (2) remove ST and *ST companies in each year; (3) remove companies whose listing date is after 2018; (4) the companies with zero patents from 2016 to 2020 were excluded. The final research sample is 497 listed companies, and a total of 2335 sample observation values from 2016 to 2020 are obtained in this period. Due to the absence of some financial index data (not affecting the analysis results), we form an unbalanced panel. In order to eliminate the influence of extreme values, continuous variables are treated with 1% winsorize. The patent data (IPC classification number) of enterprises are from the Patsnap database, and the other data are from the CSMAR database and Hexun website.

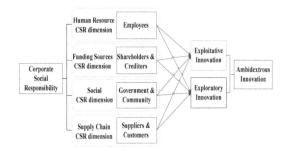

Figure 1. Conceptual model.

3.2 Variable index selection and model construction

Dependent variables. Drawing upon previous research (e.g., Shao & Wu 2020; Xu et al. 2017), this paper uses enterprise's patents' IPC number to calculate its innovation performance. The specific measurement is shown in Table 1.

Independent variables. This paper divides CSR into four dimensions according to different target objects. According to the research of Wang et al. (2011) and Yang et al. (2016), corresponding measurement indicators are set (see Table 1).

Control variables. Referring to the research of Chen (2020), enterprise size, listing years, proportion of

R&D investment, and proportion of R&D personnel are set as control variables, and the specific measurement method is shown in Table 1. Given that the measurement value of the dependent variable in this paper is a non-negative integer, which is a counting variable and generally follows the Poisson distribution, it can be seen from the descriptive statistics in Table 2 that the variance of the explained variable is not equal to the mean value (17.26,38.05; 3.627,5.771), so the negative binomial regression panel model was adopted in this paper.

To figure out the heterogeneity of the impact between exploratory innovation and exploitative innovation that the different four dimensions of CSR bring about, this paper established eight main models and two models (only contend control variables), to make regressions analysis; for the specific model see Table 3. At the same time, Hausman test was carried out on each model. Specific models have been reported in Table 3 of regression analysis results.

4 DATA ANALYSIS AND RESULTS

4.1 *Descriptive statistics and correlation analysis*

The mean value, standard deviation, correlation coefficient, and VIF value of the study variables are shown in Table 2. In terms of the mean value, the average performance of exploratory innovation is much lower than the average performance of exploitation innovation, indicating that in recent 5 years, high-tech industry pays more attention to the improvement and transformation of existing technologies and products, while the learning and utilization of new knowledge and technology needs to be improved. The average value of CSR performance indicators at the social level is slightly lower than that at other levels, indicating that high-tech enterprises are mainly profit-oriented and contribute less externality to society. If the VIF coefficient of variance inflation factor is lower than 5, it indicates that there is no collinearity between variables, which can be included in the regression equation for analysis.

Table 1. The dimensions and measurements of variables.

		DIMENSIONS	CODE	MEASUREMENT
Dependent Variable	Ambidextrous Innovation Performance	Exploitative Innovation Performance	INOI	The number of patent grants whose top four IPC classification is the first to appear compared with its previous 5 years' patent grants (per sample year, per company)
		Exploratory Innovation Performance	INOR	The number of patent grants whose top four IPC classification is a repeated number compared with its previous 5 years' patent grants (per sample year, per company)
Independent Variables	Corporate social responsibility	Human Resource CSR	ECSR	Wage-to-income ratio: cash paid to and for employees/operating income
		Funding Sources CSR-shareholders	DCSR	Earnings per share from CSMAR
		-creditors	LCSR	Asset-liability ratio from CSMAR
		Social CSR-government-community	GCSR	Tax contribution rate:(various taxes paid - tax refunds received)/ operating income
			PCSR	Social responsibility data obtained from Hexun database
		Supply Chain CSR-suppliers	SCSR	Accounts payable turnover from CSMAR
		-customers	CCSR	Operating cost ratio from CSMAR
Control Variables	The enterprise scale		SIZE	ln (Total assets at end)
	Listed years		AGE	(Sample period December 31 - company listing date)/365
	Proportion of R&D investment		RDSY	Proportion of R&D investment from CSMAR
	Ratio of R&D personnel		RDEP	Ratio of R&D personnel from CSMAR

4.2 Regression analysis

Based on the hypothesis, this study establishes 10 negative binomial regression models, which are two sets of models with exploitative innovation performance and exploratory innovation performance as dependent variables. Among them, models 1 and 6 only include control variables, and models 2 and 7 introduce variable ECSR to represent CSR implementation to employees. The results show that the CSR performance of employees has an inverted U-shaped impact on both exploitative innovation and exploratory innovation, and the impact is significant. H1a and H1b are supported.

Models 3 and 8, respectively, examine the effect of CSR of capital source layer on ambidextrous innovation performance, in which CSR fulfillment of shareholders (DCSR) has a significant positive impact on exploitative innovation performance ($\beta = 0.001$, $p<0.1$), and CSR performance of creditors (LCSR) has a significant negative effect on exploratory innovation performance ($\beta = -0.004$, $p<0.05$). H2a and H3b are supported.

Models 4 and 9, respectively, examine the effect of CSR implementation at the social level, and the impact of government CSR implementation (GCSR) on the two types of innovation performance is significantly negative ($\beta = -0.014$, $p<0.01$; $\beta = 0.014$, $p<0.05$), but the measurement index here is tax contribution rate. High-tech enterprises are already exempt from preferential tax policies, so it is assumed that H4a and H4b are supported, while the implementation of community CSR (PCSR) has no significant impact on them.

Models 5 and 10 explore the impact of CSR fulfillment on ambidextrous innovation performance at the supply chain level. The results show that CSR fulfillment of suppliers (SCSR) has a significant negative impact on exploitative innovation performance, which proves H2a and H6a, but has no significant impact on exploratory innovation performance. However, CSR performance of customers (CCSR) significantly positively promotes exploitative innovation performance and has a significant inverted U-shaped effect on exploratory innovation, supporting H7a and H7b.

The summary of hypotheses tests is shown in Table 4.

5 CONCLUSION AND DISCUSSION

5.1 Conclusion

This paper takes 497 listed high-tech enterprises as research samples, uses their patent IPC classification numbers from 2016 to 2020 to measure exploratory innovation performance and exploitative innovation performance, and uses financial index to represent CSR performance from four dimensions, to explore the heterogeneity of the impact that the different four dimensions of CSR bring about between exploratory innovation and exploitative innovation. This research makes several key contributions. First, we expand the

Table 2. Descriptive statistics and correlation analysis of variables.

	Mean	Sd	1.INOI	2.INOR	3.ECSR	4.DCSR	5.LCSR	6.GCSR	7.PCSR	8.SCSR	9.CCSR	10.SIZE	11.AGE	12.RDSY	13.RDEP
1.INOI	17.26	38.05	1												
2.INOR	3.627	5.771	0.523***	1											
3.ECSR	13.16	8.509	0.029	-0.049**	2.10										
4.DCSR	38.66	41.56	0.080***	0.019	-0.164***	1.65									
5.LCSR	29.97	15.8	0.121***	0.131***	-0.125***	-0.164***	1.59								
6.GCSR	4.151	5.096	-0.052**	-0.086***	0.126***	0.190***	-0.275***	1.53							
7.PCSR	3.434	3.24	0.056***	0.033	-0.044**	0.169***	-0.083***	0.131***	1.38						
8.SCSR	10.26	12.3	-0.085***	-0.053**	-0.161***	0.080***	-0.109***	-0.017	-0.060***	1.34					
9.CCSR	68.63	18.11	0.036*	0.080***	-0.306***	-0.288***	0.382***	-0.595***	-0.172***	0.090***	1.29				
10.SIZE	21.35	0.779	0.278***	0.249***	-0.209***	0.083***	0.306***	-0.097***	0.094***	-0.02	0.113***	1.12			
11.AGE	6.15	4.728	0.134***	0.127***	0.028	-0.264***	0.132***	0.037*	0.033	0.005	0.042**	0.456***	1.12		
12.RDSY	8.314	8.956	-0.008	-0.018	0.081***	0.057***	-0.083***	0.076***	0.105***	-0.077***	-0.144***	-0.190***	-0.222***	1.09	
13.RDEP	13.21	11.24	0.082***	0.108***	0.193***	-0.056***	0.007	-0.070***	-0.073***	-0.015	-0.112***	-0.004	0.074***	-0.153***	1.08

Notes: The diagonal of the independent variable is the value of VIF
*p<0.10,**p<0.05, ***p<0.01

Table 3. Regression analysis of four dimensions of CSR on INOI and INOR.

	INOI					INOR				
	Model 1	Model 2	Model 3	Model 4	Model 5	Model 6	Model 7	Model 8	Model 9	Model 10
Constant	−3.955*** (1.093)	−6.640*** (0.963)	−3.911*** (1.128)	−3.700*** (1.102)	−4.297*** (1.104)	−7.933*** (0.970)	−8.442*** (1.007)	−7.353*** (1.012)	−7.697*** (0.981)	−8.538*** (0.998)
SIZE	0.235*** (0.052)	0.357*** (0.045)	0.232*** (0.054)	0.226*** (0.052)	0.237*** (0.052)	0.371*** (0.046)	0.377*** (0.047)	0.336*** (0.049)	0.363*** (0.046)	0.363*** (0.046)
AGE	0.021** (0.010)	0.000 (0.008)	0.017 (0.010)	0.021** (0.010)	0.021** (0.010)	−0.002 (0.008)	−0.007 (0.008)	0.000 (0.008)	−0.000 (0.008)	0.001 (0.008)
RDSY	0.004 (0.003)	0.000 (0.003)	0.004 (0.003)	0.005 (0.003)	0.004 (0.003)	0.003 (0.003)	0.014*** (0.004)	0.003 (0.003)	0.004 (0.003)	0.004 (0.003)
RDEP	0.014*** (0.003)	0.012*** (0.002)	0.014*** (0.003)	0.014*** (0.003)	0.014*** (0.003)	0.014*** (0.003)	0.008*** (0.003)	0.014*** (0.002)	0.014*** (0.003)	0.015*** (0.002)
ECSR		0.033*** (0.008)					0.026** (0.010)			
ECSR^2		−0.001*** (0.000)					−0.001*** (0.000)			
DCSR			0.001* (0.001)					0.001 (0.001)		
LCSR			0.003 (0.002)					−0.004** (0.002)		
GCSR				−0.014*** (0.005)					−0.014** (0.006)	
PCSR				−0.005 (0.005)					−0.007 (0.007)	
SCSR					−0.006*** (0.002)					−0.002 (0.002)
CCSR					0.005** (0.002)					0.020** (0.009)
CCSR^2										−0.0001* (0.000)
Hausman_test	FE	RE	FE	FE	FE	RE	FE	RE	RE	RE
Year	yes		yes	yes	yes		yes			
Wald_chi2	141.273	190.169	146.869	149.826	157.664	128.160	169.739	133.281	134.852	140.738
N	2224	2279	2224	2223	2224	2279	2279	2279	2278	2279

Notes. Standard errors are in parentheses
*p<0.10,**p<0.05,***p<0.01

Table 4. The results of hypotheses test.

	Human Resource	Funding Source		Social dimension		Supply Chain	
	Employees (ECSR)	Shareholders (DCSR)	Creditors (LCSR)	Government (GCSR)	Community (PCSR)	Suppliers (SCSR)	Customers (CCSR)
Exploitative innovation performance (INOI)	H1a: √ (inverted U)	H2a: √ (positive)	H3a: ×	H4a: √ (positive)	H5a: ×	H6a: √ (negative)	H7a: √ (positive)
Exploratory innovation performance (INOR)	H1b: √ (inverted U)	H2b: ×	H3b: √ (negative)	H4b: √ (positive)	H5b: ×	H6b: ×	H7b: √ (inverted U)

Notes: "√" means the hypothesis is supported, whereas "×" means not be supported.

way of CSR dimensions' division, and broaden the research about CSR's innovative benefits. Second, we take different demands of stakeholders into account, revealing the differentiated impact of four dimensions of CSR on ambidextrous innovation, providing enterprises, especially high-tech enterprises, with practical references and suggestions.

5.2 Discussion

The implications are as follows:

(1) The impact of human resource CSR dimension performance on both exploitative innovation and exploratory innovation performance present an inverted U-shape, which is consistent with the study of Shao et al. (2020). As we know, most high-tech enterprises in our country are still in the growth stage, and the majority of their investments of R&D is allocated to equipment instead of labor payment, so human resource CSR performance has not reached the peak of the turning point, its effect on the innovation is still in the upside. Therefore, it is still significant for high-tech enterprises to attract external talents by performing CSR to employees well. In the meantime, for the existing internal staff, it is necessary to establish a perfect training system, so that they can better apply their learning to the innovation activities of the enterprise, and the corresponding talent performance appraisal, reward, and punishment system shall be clear and implemented, so as to allocate resources reasonably.

(2) The CSR performance of shareholders at the capital source level promotes the development of exploitative innovation to a certain extent, while the CSR performance of creditors has a negative impact on exploratory innovation. This result verifies Gu and Zhai's (2014) point of view and gives a clear reference for enterprises when choosing financing decisions for investment projects, that is, investing in long-term innovative projects requires more stable and lasting cash flow, so internal financing should be considered

at first. Also, the rights of shareholders should be given priority when fulfilling CSR, so as to obtain their support; for short-term exploitative innovation projects, enterprises should be good at using external financing to enlarge the role of financial leverage, so as to accelerate cash flow and better meet the needs of investment projects.

(3) At the social level, government CSR performance is positively correlated with exploitative innovation and exploratory innovation. This result suggests that the government's support can promote the innovation of enterprise as Tellis et al. (2013) proposed. Nowadays, the Chinese government has put forward the ambitious goal of becoming one of the top innovative countries in 2035 and becoming a world scientific and technological power by 2050. It is a bonus period for high-tech enterprises. Therefore, they should invest their full advantages in technological innovation, to promote their own core competitiveness as well as the country's overall competitiveness, and create more convenient and affordable new science and technology products for human beings.

(4) CSR performance of suppliers at the supply chain level has a negative relationship with exploitative innovation, while customer CSR performance promotes the growth of exploitative innovation performance, and has an inverted U-shaped impact on exploratory innovation performance. The results show that under the condition of resource constraints, enterprises shall give priority to meet requirements of customers. When companies focus on the innovation of the short-term benefit, a moderate increase in the occupation of accounts payable can be selected. Perhaps many suppliers will not provide corresponding technical support for fear that their core competitiveness will be weakened. Future studies should go further in this regard and explore how to stimulate the suppliers' willingness to offer technical support, so as to promote ambidextrous innovation performance of high-tech enterprises.

REFERENCES

Benner, M. J., & Tushman., M. L. 2003. Exploitation, exploration, and process management: The productivity dilemma revisited. *Academy of Management Review*, 2(28): 238–256.

Chen W, Sun R & Gui H. 2017. The Impact of GEM Corporate Social Responsibility (CSR) on Innovation Performance. *Science & Technology Progress and Policy*, 34(19): 28–35.

Chen Y, Jin B & Ren Y. 2020. Impact mechanism of corporate social responsibility on technological innovation performance: The mediating effect based on social capital. *Science Research Management*, 41(09): 87–98.

Clarkson, M. E. 1995. A stakeholder framework for analyzing and evaluating corporate social performance. *Academy of Management Review*.

Cousins, P. D., & Spekman, R. 2003. Strategic supply and the management of inter- and intra-organizational relationships. *Journal of Purchasing & Supply Management*, 9(1): 19–29.

Gallego-Alvarez, I., Prado-Lorenzo, J. M., & Garcia-Sanchez, I. M. 2011. Corporate social responsibility and innovation: a resource-based theory. *Management Decision*, 49(9–10): 1709–1727.

Gong C & Bi K. 2018. Research on the Relationship between Manufacturing Corporate Social Responsibility and Innovation Performance under Low-carbon Situation. *Forecasting*, 37(01): 43–48.

Gu Q & Zhai S. 2014. Financial Constraints, R&D Investment and Funding Sources: The Perspective of R&D Heterogeneity. *Science Of Science and Management of S.&T.*, 35(03): 15–22.

Hughes, M., Hughes, P., Morgan, R. E., Hodgkinson, I. R., & Lee, Y. 2021. Strategic entrepreneurship behaviour and the innovation ambidexterity of young technology-based firms in incubators. *International Small Business Journal-Researching Entrepreneurship*, 39(02662426209437763): 202–227.

Jiang Xu. 2015. A Social Network Perspective on Learning Orientation and External Knowledge Acquisition. *Management Review*, 27(08): 141–149.

Ko, K., Nie, J., Ran, R., & Gu, Y. 2020. Corporate social responsibility, social identity, and innovation performance in China. *Pacific-Basin Finance Journal*, 63(101415).

Li W & Liu Y. 2017. Technology Innovation, Corporate Social Responsibility and Corporate Competence: An Empirical Analysis Based on Data from Listed Companies. *Science of Science and Management of S.& T.*, 38(01): 154–165.

Luo, X., & Du, S. 2015. Exploring the relationship between corporate social responsibility and firm innovation. *Marketing Letters*, 26(4): 703–714.

March, J. G. 1991. Exploration and Exploitation in Organizational Learning. *Organization Science*.

Ma Lianfu, Gao Yuan, Qin He. 2019. Exploratory Innovation or Exploitative Innovation: Based on the Impact of Capital Allocation Efficiency. *Science Of Science and Management Of S.& T.*, 40(08): 18–32.

Porter, M. E., & Kramer, M. R. 2006. Strategy and society: the link between competitive advantage and corporate social responsibility. *Harvard business review*, 84(12).

Shao J & Wu S. 2020. Stock Incentives and Ambidextrous Innovation of High-Tech Enterprises. *R&D Management*, 32(04): 176–186.

Sun W, K Cui. 2014. Linking corporate social responsibility to firm default risk. *European Management Journal*, 32(2): 275–287.

Tellis, G. J., Prabhu, J. C., & Chandy, R. K. 2013. Radical Innovation Across Nations: The Preeminence of Corporate Culture. *Journal of Marketing*, 73(1): 3–23.

Waheed, A., Zhang, Q., Rashid, Y., Tahir, M. S., & Zafar, M. W. 2020. Impact of green manufacturing on consumer ecological behavior: Stakeholder engagement through green production and innovation. *Sustainable Development*, 28(5): 1395–1403.

Waddock, S. 2004. Parallel Universes: Companies, Academics, and the Progress of Corporate Citizenship. *Business and Society Review*, 109(1).

Wang Haihua & Peng Zhenglong. 2010. Research on the interactive relationship between corporate social responsibility performance and open innovation. *Science and Management research*. 28(01): 18–21.

Xu L, Zeng D & Li J. 2017. The Effects of Knowledge Network Centralization, Knowledge Variety on Firms' Dual-Innovation Performance. *Chinese Journal of Management*, 14(02): 221–228.

Yang W & Yang S. 2016. An Empirical Study on the Relationship between Corporate Social Responsibility and Financial Performance under the Chinese Context: Based on the Contrastive Analysis of Large, Small and Medium-size Listed Companies. *Chinese Journal of Management Science*, 24(01): 143–150.

Yu Renzhi. 2015. A Study on Cultural Adaptability and Mediating Effect of Enterprises' Ambidextrous Innovation. Unpublished Doctoral Dissertation. *University of Science and Technology of China*.

Zhao, Z., Zhao, X., Davidson, K., & Zuo, J. 2012. A corporate social responsibility indicator system for construction enterprises. *Journal Of Cleaner Production*, 29–30: 277–289.

Zhang, Q., Oo, B. L., & Lim, B. T. H. 2018. Drivers, motivations, and barriers to the implementation of corporate social responsibility practices by construction enterprises: A review. *Journal Of Cleaner Production*, 210: 563–584.

Economic and Business Management – Huang & Zhang (Eds)
© 2022 Copyright the Author(s), ISBN: 978-1-032-06754-4

The success of salesforce.com: From the perspective of social capital

Zongjie Dai & Wenhong Chiu
Asia University, Taiwan, China

ABSTRACT: The rapid development of customer relationship management (CRM) is an important topic today. It is of great theoretical and practical significance to study the factors behind the success of its leading enterprises in CRM industry. Based on the three-dimension of social capital, this article adopts the method of case study to try to understand how Salesforce, a famous CRM company in the United States, integrates internal and external resources, to maintain rapid development speed and gain competitive advantages in the fast-changing international economic environment.

Keywords: Salesforce, Social capital, CRM industry, Innovation, Case study

1 INTRODUCTION

Customer relationship management (CRM) is one of the most fast developing business sections in Internet technology industry. In the research of CRM, the first company worth mentioning is Salesforce, which is the leading company in the CRM industry. Salesforce.com, founded in 1999, has won a huge market penetration in the field of CRM by using two major weapons, including flexibility and customization to subvert innovative business models (Muller, 2016).

Economic success is the foundation of the company, so that it can ensure its existence (Birkel, Veile, Müller, Hartmann & Voigt, 2019; Dyllick & Hockerts, 2002; Markley & Davis, 2007; Schulz & Flanigan, 2016) Previous research has shown that there are many factors affecting the enterprise's strategy formulation, including the firm size, age, organizational structure, and development stage (Köseoglu, Altin, Chan & Aladag, 2020). However, in addition to these obvious factors, there existed some hidden reasons. One of them is social capital, which is defined as the composition of social networks and relevant norms that affect productivity, and these resources will have a positive impact on the development of the community (Chakrabarty, 2013; Putnam, 2001). The purpose of this case study is to find out the reason behind the success of Salesforce by adopting the framework of social capital.

Most of the previous research on social capital focused on economic and social phenomena. There are few research on corporate cases, especially the impact of social capital on CRM industry. The theoretical

construction of social capital can be mainly divided into two categories: one is the structural, cognitive, and relational dimensions proposed by Nahapiet and Ghoshal (1998); the other is the external, internal, and internal/external social capital proposed by Adler and Kwon (2002). This case study mainly adopts the first category as the analysis framework, which will be illustrated in detail in the following pages of the chapter.

This study adopts a single case study as the research method. Salesforce was founded in 1999 by Benioff, a former senior Vice President of Oracle, who is known as 'software terminator'. The main advantages of Salesforce over other competitors are the characteristics of flexibility and customization. The goal of the company is 'No software'. The company started the revolution of the software industry, which has changed the impression of complex software operation in the past, and the main research and development goal is to provide customers with simple and easy-to-use experience. It has successfully changed the way software is built, purchased, and deployed in the enterprise. Salesforce ranked 70th in the 2019 Interbrand rankings, proving that its brand influence has attracted worldwide attention.

In the next part of this study, after literature review, the research methods are introduced, including case analysis methods and secondary data analysis. By adopting time series analysis method, the development process of Salesforce company is analyzed in detail, and it can be divided into four different stages. There are altogether 64 events collected and categorized by using the three dimensions of social capital. To conclude, two findings have been summarized.

DOI 10.1201/9781003203704-51

2 LITERATURE REVIEW

2.1 Social capital

The term 'social capital' first appeared in community studies, emphasizing the central importance of strong and cross personal networks developed over time for the survival and operation of urban communities, which provide the basis for trust, cooperation, and collective action (Jacobs, 2016; Nahapiet & Ghoshal, 1998). As time goes by, the definitions of social capital have changed greatly. Coleman (1990) argued that the foundation of social capital lies in social relations. However, Portes (1998) holds a different view. He criticized that the definition above is too vague, and he gave a more systematic definition as there are four sources of social capital: value introjection, bounded solidarity, reciprocity exchanges and enforceable trust. There is a choice between bottom-up and top-down approaches (Adam & Rončević, 2003). In the bottom-up approach, it focuses on the networks as both a source and a form of social capital (Adam & Rončević, 2003; Putnam, 2000). Moreover, there is a more robust definition which introduced three dimensions of social capital including structural, relational, and cognitive (Nahapiet & Ghosal, 1998). The views of different authors believe that it depends on their academic background and the problems they solve with the concept of social capital (Adler & Kwon, 2000).

2.2 Three dimensions of social capital

As mentioned above, we take the three dimensions of Nahapiet and Ghosal (1998) as our theory construct in this article. The previous literatures proposed three dimensions of social capital, including structures, cognition, and relationships (Fang et al. 2010; Inkpen & Tsang 2005; Nahapiet & Ghoshal 1998; Simsek et al. 2003; Soetanto & van Geenhuizen 2015; Theodoraki, Messeghem & Rice, 2017; Tötterman & Sten 2005).

Structural dimension describes the impersonal relation between people which is the 'hardware' of social networks (Adam & Rončević, 2003). Structural dimension of social capital includes network ties, density, configuration, and appropriateness (Ganguly, Talukdar & Chatterjee, 2019). Structural dimensions are characterized by formally established relationships in the network, their configuration and stability (Inkpen & Tsang 2005; Theodoraki, Messeghem & Rice, 2017; Tötterman & Sten 2005). The basic proposition of social capital theory is that network ties provide a way to obtain resources (Nahapiet & Ghoshal 1998; Theodoraki, Messeghem & Rice, 2017; Tötterman & Sten 2005).

The cognitive dimension refers to common goals and shared culture, language, and code (Inkpen & Tsang 2005; Theodoraki, Messeghem & Rice, 2017; Tötterman & Sten 2005). Common goals, language and understanding determine the impact of what knowledge is collected and evaluated (Ganguly, Talukdar & Chatterjee, 2019; Kogut & Zander, 1996).

The relational dimension describes resources which can affect the performance of an organization. They can provide shared representations, interpretations, and systems of meaning (Adam & Rončević, 2003; Nahapiet & Ghosal, 1998;). Hughes et al.'s (2014) conceptualization of social capital's relationship dimensionality is 'resource interdependence', which provides a behavior choice for main participants to establish ties with other people that exhibit trust and generate value creation (Ganguly, Talukdar & Chatterjee, 2019).

2.3 Social capital and enterprise development

The narrowest concept of social capital is regarded as a set of 'horizontal connections' among people: social capital consists of social networks and related norms that affect community productivity (Chakrabarty, 2013; Putnam 1993). This concept was initially limited to groups that had a positive impact on development. Its main feature was that it helped to coordinate and cooperate for the common interests of members of the association (Putnam 1993). A much broader concept was proposed by Coleman (1988), who defined social capital as various entities with two common elements: they are all composed of a social structure and promote the same action of actors—whether individual actors or corporate actors which broadened the concept to include vertical and horizontal associations, as well as the behavior between other entities such as enterprises. However, previous literature on the relationship between enterprisesrelated social capital and firm performance in the periphery is mainly focused on production related social capital in the form of innovation or connect with customers and suppliers and these linkages (Habersetzer, Grèzes-Bürcher, Boschma & Mayer, 2019). Researchers emphasize that countries and global knowledge sources are essential for innovation, providing global competitiveness for the company's success (Flåten, Isaksen & Karlsen, 2015).

3 METHODOLOGY

3.1 Research design

In this study, the first criterion aims to answer the research issues on how Salesforce became a representative enterprise in CRM industry. It investigated the specific analysis significance of typical practical case of social capital theory from the three dimensions of social capital (structural, cognitive, and relational dimensions). So, it is 'the question of how'. In the second criterion, it is necessary to manipulate on the event of Salesforce development. The research focuses on the incident at the time, so it provides a suitable reason for adopting case study method (Scholz & Tietje, 2002; Yin, 2016). Since this research adopts the CRM industry as a research object, the qualitative research method of this study is a single industry case study based on the research strategy. In addition, time series analysis method is adopted to explain the development of

Salesforce and the integration of resources from 1999 to 2019. Data set of important historical events which affect the development of Salesforce are selected. By summarizing the data under each dimension, the reasons for the success of the Salesforce company are concluded.

3.2 *Data collection and coding process*

In terms of case data acquisition and analysis, it mainly relies on secondary data to collect the data of Salesforce operations, development strategies, and company big events. In the research method of case study, its main research object is usually in the historical interpretation and cause-effect relationship analysis (Yin, 1994), so this study has collected important historical incidents of Salesforce through the collection of information and evidence. The time range for this qualitative research is conducted from 1999 to 2019. In addition to reviewing the academic research on social capital, the data source is secondary data. Through searching the keywords (Salesforce, CRM, Salesforce Development, Salesforce Strategy, also included keywords from the definition of three dimensions as network ties, trust and trustworthiness, shared goals, etc.) in the following ways, it established a complete case database to increase the reliability of the research:

(1) 'NASDAQ/Market Watch' (annual report, financial statements): Understand the company's operating status/financial status.
(2) 'Salesforce official website' (the latest news), newspapers and magazines: Collect related newspapers and periodicals.
(3) Published journals
(4) 'Google Scholar website': Collect related research of Salesforce.
(5) 'Intelbrand': Collect company background and industry brand ranking.

Finally, altogether 64 cases are collected, including year of the event with a streamlined description. And the coding process is given in Table 1.

Table 1. Example of the open coding process.

Original Events	Dimension category
In 2003, business covers the United States, Australia, Japan, Ireland, England, France, Spain, and Germany.	Network ties (Structural dimension)
Successfully listed on the New York Stock Exchange	Network ties (Structural dimension)
The first Dreamforce event	Network ties and shared goals (Structural and cognitive dimensions)
Recruit Cindy Robbins, President and Chief People Officer	Trust and trustworthiness (Relational dimension)

3.3 *Timeline analysis*

Altogether 64 events from 1999 to 2019 are collected as the analysis data set. According to the time series analysis, the development stages of Salesforce enterprise are divided into four sections, including the start-up stage, the expanding and globalization stage, the platform cooperation stage, and the AI industrial ecology stage. In each section, the three dimensions of social capital are adopted to categorize the events happened during the enterprise development period.

3.3.1 *The start-up stage (1999–2002)*

Salesforce was founded in 1999 by Benioff who was the former senior Vice President of Oracle. In this start-up stage, the main dimensions of social capital are structural and cognitive as the companies are engaging and exploring the way to grow up in the competitive markets. In 2000, Salesforce started to launch the product and debut the 'no software' concept. At the same time, it established the Salesforce foundation to help those people in need and made contribution to the society. This kind of event belonged to the cognitive dimension which shared a common belief and faith in a relatively broader way. In the next two years, Salesforce company continuously reserved technical strength and launched CRM new products to make a good preparation for the subsequent rapid expansion. It is worth to mention that, in the HR discipline, Salesforce also started to recruit those talented people to expand management team such as Elizabeth Pinkham who joined Benioff team in 2000 as an Executive Vice President in global real estate. This kind of intangible capital belongs to the relational dimension of social capital.

3.3.2 *The expanding and globalizing stage (2003–2005)*

After emerging in the field of SaaS, from 2003 to 2005, Salesforce company began to expand and globalize its business. Salesforce service was extended to overseas with a strong marketing propaganda and the founder Benioff was named Forbes top ten entrepreneurs. In this stage, the dimension of social capital mainly belongs to the structural which is more tangible rather than intangible social capital. Salesforce company expanded its business outside the United States, including Australia, Japan, Ireland, England, France, Spain, and Germany. As mentioned previously, structural social capital concerned about mode, structure, and rules. During the expansion, Salesforce built its regional headquarters worldwide which need to build new and suitable structure and rules according to the cultural characteristics of each region. One milestone is that in 2004, Salesforce was successfully listed in the New York Stock Exchange. This step gained social capital and built potential foundations for the increase of the company's value and the subsequent platform cooperation stage of Salesforce. The first Dreamforce event was held in 2003, which provided a new way for people to share, learn the latest technologies and get inspired. In this article, the social capital dimension of the Dreamforce event is structural and cognitive.

3.3.3 *The platform cooperation stage (2006–2010)*

In the stage of platform cooperation, Salesforce was no longer satisfied with the online service, but aimed at the development of the SaaS vendor's infrastructure platform. By launching App Store of AppExchange, the first cloud computing platform Apex language, Force.com PaaS platform and a series of products, Salesforce created the PaaS platform to build up an ecosystem of applications platform. From 2006 to 2007, Salesforce has developed software web2.0 services, providing software developers to share resources which aimed at service expansion. ISV companies can sell applications through the App Exchange. In addition, enterprises can develop their own applications on the Form.com platform. In the following several years of this stage, Salesforce alliance with other Internet giants to increase brand exposure and software penetration and to make CRM applications can be used across multiple platforms. To build up the platform ecosystem, Salesforce completed a series of acquisitions and mergers projects. All these companies are part of Salesforce's strategic deployment. To better manage these companies, Salesforce has made corresponding strategic adjustments in structure and corporate culture. After 2009, the focus of acquisitions has shifted from adding features to existing services to diversifying into new related services, including the introduction of the Marketing Cloud. Therefore, the dimensions of social capital in this platform cooperation stage are mainly structural and cognitive.

During this platform cooperating stage, Salesforce gained many recognitions such as won the Wall Street Journal Technology Innovation Award and being selected by Forbes Magazine as the fastest growing technology company. All of these can be categorized to the cognitive dimension of social capital which is concerned about fame and trust in broad cognition on a generalized social background.

3.3.4 *The AI industrial ecology stage (2011–2019)*

In the ecological stage of the AI industry, the main performance is to provide corporate with internet services and provide customers with social enterprise upgrade services. In addition, by launching the mobile terminal product Salesforce1, Salesforce company seized the entrance of Enterprise Internet. Moreover, it focused on data and marketing intelligence through mergers and acquisitions and launched the artificial intelligence platform 'Einstein' to create a 'CRM+AI' ecosystem. This stage is characterized by many acquisitions and mergers. The same as the above stage, the social capital dimensions of M&A are related to structural and cognitive. Due to the strategic layout such as the AI ecosystem, Salesforce company has also adjusted in the deployment of company management personnel. In 2013, the company recruited Amy Weaver as President of Legal and General Counsel.

The reason behind it may come from two aspects. One aspect is that the combination of CRM and AI integration business will involve some legal issues. The other aspect is that a lot of mergers and acquisitions need to be more compliant. During this stage, the recruitment of core members of management team becomes more frequent. Relational social capital is a dimension of social capital, which is related to the characteristics and qualities of personal relations such as trust and obligations. Therefore, the event of recruiting perhaps belongs to the dimension of relational social capital. There are some events concerned about the cognitive dimension of social capital. For example, in 2014, Salesforce.com ranked no.1 on Forbes list of The Most Innovative Companies which is a cognitive dimension example. In addition, in 2017, Dreamforce conference advocated the concept of customer success and believed that the first concept of enterprise service is customer success, which is another example of cognitive dimension.

3.4 *Validity and reliability*

Finally, to improve the validity of construction, this study adopts various methods to collect evidence sources and establish evidence chain in the stage of data collection and compares many resources from many aspects to improve the internal validity. In terms of reliability, the research process will be recorded in detail, and a case study database will be established to provide evidence for future research, to obtain the same results

4 FINDINGS AND DISCUSSION

This article analyzes the 64 events in Salesforce's development process through the three-dimension of social capital and classifies each event to summarize the company's successful experience based on social capital theory. The conclusions and recommendations of the study include the findings, theoretical contributions, management implications and future research recommendations which are summarized in four parts to discuss and explain in accordance with the sequence. According to the time series analysis, Salesforce's development process is divided into four stages, in which the social capital of each development stage is different. Further, this article concluded with the following two findings.

4.1 *Finding 1. According to the Salesforce company's strategic development, the focus of the company's social capital is shifting at different development stages*

It will be illustrated in detail as follows. In the stage of start-up, the focus is on the structural dimension of social capital, as the company has just started to operate. Everything is from scratch, just as in accumulating of the structural dimension of social capital such as structure, rules etc. In the stage of expanding and globalizing, the focus of social capital is shifting from structural to cognitive, because the foundation of expanding is the good fame of the enterprise which belongs to the cognitive dimension of social capital. Moreover, in the stage of platform cooperation and the stage of AI industrial ecology, the focuses of social capital are structural and cognitive dimensions. The reason behind is that in these two stages, in order to achieve the strategic goal, Salesforce company needs to merge and acquire many companies from other industries or disciplines. After the merger and acquisition, the Salesforce company will carry out the adjustment of management structure and corporate culture for the target company to be better absorbed and integrated.

4.2 *Finding 2. In terms of relational dimension of social capital, the leadership layout of management team is different among development stages*

It will be illustrated in detail as follows. In the start-up stage, the core members of the management team include Benioff (Chairman & CEO), Harris (Co-Founder and oversees product strategy) and Pinkham (Executive Vice President, Global Real Estate). However, when it comes to the stage of AI industrial ecology, the number of core members of the management team increased significantly. With the strategy of building up the AI ecosystem, the layout of leadership changed correspondingly. With the joining of Taylor (Chief product officer), Hawkins (President and Chief financial officer), Buscemi (Chief marketing officer) and Weaver (Legal and general counsel), the AI ecological layout can be realized step by step successfully. The relational dimension of social capital is related to trust and honesty, duty and expectations which belongs to the HR management of enterprise. Therefore, in this article, the leadership of Salesforce is categorized in the relational dimension of social capital.

Most of the previous studies of social capital are focused on the economic and social phenomena. There are few research on corporate cases, especially the impact of social capital on CRM industry. Therefore, the theoretical contribution is to investigate in detail about the success story on how Salesforce becomes the industry leader in the perspective of social capital.

The management and practical implications of this study can be divided into two items. First, for Salesforce company, it will help to enhance the understanding of its own development process and advantages in-depth. This study uses time series analysis method to retrospectively describe Salesforce's development process. It can observe past events and changes in the social capital of Salesforce company and may predict the future development path. Second, it can provide a successful experience for other CRM companies to get inspired. The main purpose of this research is the systematic analysis of Salesforce company.

Therefore, it also has practical implications for other CRM companies all over the world.

Suggestions for future research include the following two aspects. Firstly, in the future research, according to previous research on social capital, there are different ways to divide the dimensions. Therefore, there could be a possible way to adopt another theory of social capital dimension in more detail and analyze the sample events. Secondly, more samples of events or more corporate cases can be collected for comparative research, in the future. Moreover, researchers can collect more events to test whether the above findings are making sense or not.

5 CONCLUSIONS

Social capital theory is a mature theory because it has undergone long-term development and exploration. At present, Salesforce has certain reality and high brand influence. CRM companies represented by Salesforce lead the development of the industry. According to changes in national policies and market environment, Salesforce has changed resource integration strategy and company positioning, which can be tested as a key and mature case. The theoretical and practical contributions are concluded as follows:

5.1 *Theoretical contributions*

In the theoretical contribution, this paper constructs a conceptual model of social capital based on the 'structure', 'cognitive', and 'relationship' Single case research method (Yin 2016) was adopted to analyze the development strategy of Salesforce. This research followed the procedure of research contribution (Pettigrew, Woodman, & Cameron, 2001), collected business history data, conducted time series analysis, and discussed Salesforce's strategy during its development process. In addition, this case study enriches the research of three dimensions of social capital in strategy development of enterprises. Moreover, this study conducted major events based on time series analysis analyzed the development strategy of the case and categorized the three dimensions of social capital into several important stages. It may supplement the gap of existing social capital literatures on the research of single enterprise case.

5.2 *Practical contributions*

This study adopts the three dimensions of social capital as the research framework to analyze the internal and external capital of the structural, cognitional, and relational of the case firm Salesforce. Managers can convert social capital issues according to company development stages and innovative opportunities to produce new markets. The practical contribution is described as follows. First, the company will transform in the development of social capital, and the focus will change in different development phases, which requires managers to make good preparation in advance. Second, managers can learn to integrate internal and external resources and relationships from social capital three-dimensional perspectives.

REFERENCES

Adam, F., & Rončević, B. (2003). Social capital: Recent debates and research. trends. *Social Science Information*, 42(2), 155–183.

Adler, P., & Kwon, S. (1999). Social Capital: The Good, the Bad, and the Ugly. *SSRN Electronic Journal*.

Bardhan, P. (1993). Economics of Development and the Development of Economics. *Journal of Economic Perspectives*, 7(2), 129–142.

Birkel, H., Veile, J., Müller, J., Hartmann, E., & Voigt, K.-I. (2019). Development of a Risk Framework for Industry 4.0 in the Context of Sustainability for Established Manufacturers. *Sustainability*, 11(2), 384.

Chakrabaty, A. (2013). Social Capital and Economic Growth: A study. International Journal of Business, *Management and Social Sciences*, 2(2249–7463), 23–25.

Coleman, J. (1988). Social Capital in the Creation of Human Capital. *American Journal of Sociology*, 94, 95–125.

Coleman, J. (1990). Foundations of social theory. Harvard University Press.

Dyllick, T., & Hockerts, K. (2002). Beyond the business case for corporate sustainability. *Business Strategy and The Environment*, 11(2), 130–141.

Fang, S.-C., Tsai, F.-S., & Lin, J. L. (2010). Leveraging tenant incubator social capital for organizational learning and performance in incubation programme. *International Small Business Journal*, 28(1), 90–113.

Flåten, B., Isaksen, A., & Karlsen, J. (2015). Competitive firms in thin regions in Norway: The importance of workplace learning. Norsk Geografisk Tidsskrift - *Norwegian Journal of Geography*, 69(2), 102–111.

Ganguly, A., Talukdar, A., & Chatterjee, D. (2019). Evaluating the role of social capital, tacit knowledge sharing, knowledge quality and reciprocity in determining innovation capability of an organization. *Journal of Knowledge Management* 23(6), 1105–1135.

Habersetzer, A., Grèzes-Bürcher, S., Boschma, R., & Mayer, H. (2019). Enterprise-related social capital as a driver of firm growth in the periphery? *Journal of Rural Studies*, 65, 143–151.

Hughes, M., Morgan, R.E., Ireland, R.D. & Hughes, P. (2014). Social Capital and learning advantages: a problem of absorptive capacity. *Strategic Entrepreneurship Journal*, 8(3) 214-233.

Inkpen, A. C., & Tsang, E. W. K. (2005). Social capital, networks, and knowledge transfer. *Academy of Management Review*, 30(1), 146–165.

Jacobs, J. (2016). The death and life of great American cities. *Vintage Books*.

Jap, S. D. (2001). The Strategic Role of the Salesforce in Developing Customer Satisfaction Across the Relationship Lifecycle. *The Journal of Personal Selling and Sales Management*, 21(2), 95–108.

J, Y. (2020). Enterprise Internet Report 2: From. Salesforce See Services Giant Cloud How to Make. *Orient Securities*.

Kogut, B. & Zander, U. (1996). What firms do? Coordination, identity, and learning. *Organization Science*, 7 (5), 502–518.

Köseoglu, M. A., Altin, M., Chan, E., & Aladag, O. F. (2020). What are the key success factors for strategy formulation and implementation? Perspectives of managers in the hotel industry. *International Journal of Hospitality Management* 89, 102574.

Lee, R., Tuselmann, H., Jayawarna, D., & Rouse, J. (2019). Effects of structural, relational, and cognitive social capital on resource acquisition: a study of entrepreneurs residing in multiply deprived areas. *Entrepreneurship & Regional Development* 31(5-6), 534–554.

Markley, M., & Davis, L. (2007). Exploring future competitive advantage through sustainable supply chains. *International Journal of Physical Distribution & Logistics Management* 37(9), 763–774.

Muller, DBA, W. (2016). An Analysis of Salesforce.Com, a Cloud Based Solutions Provider, Best Known for Its Customer Relationship Management (CRM) Products. *SSRN Electronic Journal*.

Nahapiet, J., & Ghoshal, S. (1998). Social Capital, Intellectual Capital, and the Organizational Advantage. *The Academy of Management Review* 23(2), 242.

Portes, A. (1998). Social Capital: Its Origins and Applications in Modern Sociology. *Annual Review of Sociology* 24(1), 1–24.

Putnam, R. (1993) The Prosperous Community: Social Capital and Public Life. *The American Prospect*, 4, 35–42.

Putnam, R. (2001) Social capital: Measurement and consequences. *Canadian Journal of Policy Research*, 2, 41–51.

Putnma, R. (2000). Bowling Alone: The Collapse and Revival of American Community. *Simon & Schuster*.

Scholz, R. W., & Tietje, O. (2002). Embedded Case Study Methods: Integrating Quantitative and Qualitative Knowledge. *Thousand Oaks, CA: Sage Publications*.

Schulz, S., & Flanigan, R. (2016). Developing competitive advantage using the triple bottom line: a conceptual framework. *Journal Of Business & Industrial Marketing*, 31(4), 449–458.

Soetanto, D., & van Geenhuizen, M. (2015). Getting the right balance: university networks' influence on spin-offs' attraction of funding for innovation. *Technovation*, 3637,2638.

Simsek, Z., Lubatkin, M. H., & Floyd, S. W. (2003). Inter-firm networks and entrepreneurial behavior: a structural embeddedness perspective. *Journal of Management*, 29(3), 427442.

Theodoraki, C., Messeghem, K., & Rice, M. (2017). A social capital approach to the development of sustainable entrepreneurial ecosystems: an explorative study. *Small Business Economics* 51(1), 153170.

Tötterman, H., & Sten, J. (2005). Start-ups. *International Small Business Journal*, 23(5), 487511.

Yin, R. (2016). Qualitative research from start to finish (2nd ed.). *The Guilford Press*.

Economic and Business Management – Huang & Zhang (Eds)
© 2022 Copyright the Editor(s), ISBN: 978-1-032-06754-4

Author index

Bai, X. 130
Bao, Y. 39
Benčiková, D. 17

Cai, J. 149
Chen, C. 138
Chen, F. 198
Chen, J. 25
Chen, X. 242
Chen, Y. 111
Cheng, V.T.P. 1
Chiu, W. 275

Dai, Z. 275
Dang, X. 82
Deng, C. 192
Deng, L. 153
Deng, Y. 216
Ding, Q. 246

Fan, Y. 192
Feng, B. 232
Feng, Y. 242
Fu, D. 216

Gong, K. 158
Guan, F. 228
Guo, K. 21

He, X. 198
Hong, F. 130
Hu, L. 172
Hu, X. 88
Hu, Y. 267
Huang, H. 257
Huang, J. 267
Huang, S. 158, 186

Huang, Y. 204
Huang, Z. 242

Jiang, F. 61
Jiang, X. 138
Jin, H. 192

Knapková, M. 208
Kordoš, M. 34
Kožiak, R. 17

Li, C. 165
Li, H. 77, 246
Li, J. 192
Li, T. 222
Li, X. 13
Li, Y. 252
Liang, H. 25
Ling, J. 257
Ling, W. 257
Liu, Y. 55, 61, 66, 73, 176, 237
Lu, W. 138
Lv, L. 158
Lyu, C. 21, 39, 204

Ma, B. 212
Ma, K. 212

Pan, Y. 252
Pei, S. 138
Peng, B. 262
Peng, C. 153
Potipiroon, W. 262

Salim, Z. 121
Sheng, N. 257

Song, J. 180
Song, Y. 180
Sun, K. 49
Sun, W. 165
Sun, X. 237, 252
Sun, Y. 198

Tang, G. 44
Tao, Y. 143

Wang, C. 216
Wang, F. 106
Wang, H. 21
Wang, S. 126
Wang, T. 228
Wang, Y. 212
Wong, J.W.C. 126

Xia, Y. 77

Yang, C. 176
Yang, Y. 93
Yang, Z. 204
Yu, G. 222
Yu, H. 222
Yu, Y. 222

Zeng, H. 44
Zhang, W. 232
Zhang, X. 9, 49, 73
Zhang, Y. 66, 134
Zhang, Z. 180
Zhao, D. 212
Zhao, Z. 1
Zhu, N. 158
Zhu, X. 111

CPSIA information can be obtained
at www.ICGtesting.com
Printed in the USA
BVHW010804230422
634676BV00015B/87